THE
INSIDERS'®
GUIDE
TO
North Carolina's
Mountains

# THE INSIDERS' GUIDE TO

## North Carolina's Mountains

*by*
*Sara Pacher*
*and*
*Constance Elizabeth Richards*

The Insiders' Guide®
An imprint of Falcon® Publishing Inc.
A Landmark Communications company
P.O. Box 1718
Helena, MT 59624
(800) 582-2665
www.insiders.com

Sales and Marketing: Falcon Publishing, Inc.
P.O. Box 1718
Helena, MT 59624
(800) 582-2665
www.falconguide.com

•

4th EDITION
First printing

•

©1999
by Falcon Publishing, Inc.

•

Printed in the United States
of America

•

Publications from *The Insiders' Guide*® series are available at special discounts for bulk purchases for sales promotions, premiums or fundraisings. Special editions, including personalized covers, can be created in large quantities for special needs.
For more information, please contact Falcon Publishing.

ISBN 1-57380-095-3

# Preface

We have traveled the world over and seen this country from one end to the other, and it's true — amazing places abound everywhere. We have had the good fortunes of living in exotic lands and grand cities, yet ultimately, we found our way to these mountains. They are not the highest nor the most rugged, but they are serene and ancient and envelope all who live here with comfort, beauty, and plenty of adventure.

Those of us who were lucky enough to be born here, or whose ancestors stem from these mountains, grew up hiking the trails hooded by flowering rhododendron, splashing around chilly mountain-stream-fed swimming holes, and catching lightning bugs in dewy green fields at twilight. The mountains always beckon to us as our childhood home. Others of us, who have serendipitously found our way here, speak of a magnetism of the Blue Ridge Mountains of North Carolina. Together we make a fascinating blend of old and new, city and country.

The past several years have seen an influx of new residents in these mountains. Newcomers live side-by-side with neighbors whose families have been here for generations.

Asheville, the largest city in western North Carolina, has evolved into a lively city of professionals, artists, writers, New Age movement followers, students, retirees, young adults, and everything in between. Walking the spirited streets day or night, you will observe skateboarders, bicyclists, people enjoying a drink or meal under colorful awnings at sidewalk cafes and shoppers scouring the antique shops and art galleries. On any given evening, the music clubs and auditoriums host concerts — classical, bluegrass, reggae, ska, funk, rock, folk, modern dance, guest ballet performances, and any number of other cultural events. Yet even with so much to do, the pace is still slower and more personal than in large American urban centers — just a few visits to a downtown eatery and the owner will know you by name. Many well-known writers, artists, sculptors, artisans, producers and playwrights have chosen this area as their home or second home, enjoying the benefits of the town's intellectual offerings close to the bounty of the wilderness. Thomas Wolfe, O. Henry and George Vanderbilt are but a few of the historical names we can add to the list. (See our Overviews and Arts and Culture chapters, as well as our chapter on Biltmore Estate and Winery.)

The wilds are of course another drawing point of the mountains. Pisgah Forest to the west formed the nucleus of what was to become America's first national forest; Mount Mitchell, the highest mountain on the Eastern seaboard is to the east of Pisgah. Numerous state parks thread through these mountains. Just a short drive from the city will take you to waterfalls, streams, rivers, gorges and any other number of outdoor wonders. Every season is a good one here: Mild winters mean sweater weather with a bit of rain, perhaps an occasional snow, and skiing in the higher elevations; spring is a glorious mix of sunshine and blooming azaleas and rhododendron; summers aren't too hot for hiking, but hot enough for dipping into a frigid mountain stream on the way; and autumn, well, that's when the mountains radiate their ancient magic. Stepping out into the late-October sunshine with a crisp, clear sky stretched overhead, you can lose yourself in wave after wave of colored splendor — reds, oranges, yellows and golds, set off against occasional splashes of evergreens. (Read more about this in our Recreation and Blue Ridge Parkway chapters.)

This is also the home of the Cherokee Indians. We are invited to observe the traditions of these Native Americans in Cherokee, North Carolina, to the south. The Ocanoluftee Indian Village, for example, tastefully re-creates an 18th-century community with traditional ornamentation, living quarters and working conditions. (You will read more about the Cherokees in our chapter on the Cherokee Indian Reservation).

Crafts are well-served in these mountains. Traditional mountain-craftmaking abounds, as do crafts and art with a contemporary twist. You might find a studio next to fields of flowering tobacco plants, still a mainstay in North Carolina farming. Visit the farmers' markets in our towns and go home with baskets of juicy tomatoes, sweet corn, yams, baby squash, strawberries, cherries, apples, not to mention jars of homemade jams, jellies, relishes, apple butter and honey. (Read more in our Mountain Crafts chapter).

Whether you are visiting, considering the mountains as a new home, or have just moved here, you'll be pleased with the balance that this area maintains. As for dining, an important part of traveling and enjoying a community, our Restaurants chapter discusses the best down-home cookin' to be found, as well as the plethora of fine gourmet and ethnic eating establishments that have opened their doors to accommodate every palate. Traditional Bed and Breakfasts and Inns are scattered throughout the mountains, and modern resorts, many with superb golfing opportunities and other outdoor activities, as well as simpler hotels and motels mean you can chose your dream accommodation while you are here. Perhaps you would prefer to stay in a log cabin deep in a cove . . . It won't be a problem. (You can find your heart's desire in our Bed and Breakfasts and Country Inns and Other Accommodations chapters.)

The mixture of outdoor activities and cultural attractions, town and country, tradition and influx of progressive ideas is what keep us here — and others coming.

# About the Authors

## Sara Pacher

. . . a south Georgia native, made her second trip to these mountains one August when she was 14 — and it was love at second sight. At a motel on Lake Chatuge, she awoke her parents and insisted, "I want to stay here." By September, she was enrolled in a private school in the Blue Ridge Mountains. She went on to colleges in Georgia, Colorado and Florida, and her career took her to Manhattan and Europe. Her son, Amadeus, was born in Geneva, Switzerland.

Back in the United States, she helped start *ATLANTA* magazine, worked in publishing in New York and moved to San Francisco to become assistant editor for *Western Skier* and Western travel editor for *Better Homes and Gardens.* To satisfy her gypsy heart, she lived for extended periods in Mexico and also became a certified tour director. Then, in 1978, she saw an ad for a writer/editor position at *The Mother Earth News* magazine in Hendersonville, and her old love for these mountains came back into focus. She was senior editor of the magazine for 12 years and also organized and led the magazine's "Tours that Teach" all over the world. Sara has biked China, trekked and rafted in both the Himalayas and Alaska, camped in Tanzania's Serengeti, played with Rwanda's mountain gorillas and toured health spas all over the former Soviet Union. She's also studied wild plants in the Alps, reef fishes in the South Seas, horticulture in Japan, arts and crafts in Scandinavia and Nepal, alcohol-fuel production in Brazil and solar power in Israel. She now freelances from her home 8 miles outside Brevard on a small lake with a waterfall below her study's deck. Her articles have appeared in *Utne Reader, Green Prints, New Realities* and *BackHome* magazines. Reflecting her love of gardening, she has serves as contributing writer to Rodale Press' *All New Encyclopedia of Organic Gardening, The Experts Book of Garden Hints* and *Garden Answers.* An article based on an interview with President Jimmy Carter and his wife, Rosalynn, appears in *The Engaging Reader,* a Macmillan Publishing Co. college textbook on writing. A few years ago, Sara wrote a series called "Cream of the Country" about great places to live all over the United States — but when it came to Western North Carolina's Mountains, her philosophy was, "Never tell."

Now, with four successful editions of this book under her belt, her silence on the subject has truly been broken.

## Constance Elizabeth Richards

. . . is a writer, journalist and interpreter currently based in Asheville, North Carolina. She was born in Landstuhl, Germany, where she began cultivating her taste for travel at the age of five months with a trip to Spain (in the arms of her doting parents). Many travels ensued, becoming as much a part of her life as breathing, and almost as vital.

Frequent summers were spent in her mother's birthplace of Dillingham, North Carolina among cousins, aunts, uncles, and Granny. These were North Carolina's Mountains. Her family left Europe and moved to the then-sleepy city of Asheville. Richards graduated from Georgetown University with degrees in Russian and German, and a minor in Russian Area Studies. She also studied at Bochum University in Germany and Plekhanov Institute of Economics and Social Sciences in Moscow.

Richards lived in Berlin, then moved further east to Russia, where she was a production assistant for the Moscow bureau of ABC News. Richards moved on to print media as Moscow correspondent for *LIFE* magazine and reported for *Time* magazine in Russia, where she eventually spent six years. Her work has also appeared in *People* magazine, *Moscow Magazine*, *The Moscow Times*, *Conde Nast Traveler*, and the British *Daily Telegraph* newspaper. She has also reported on occasion for *Sports Illustrated* and *Fortune*.

Living in Russia gave her the opportunity to witness the demise of the Soviet Union and travel in the republics of the former USSR, including far-flung regions like Turkmenistan, Uzbekhistan, Bashkiria, Tatarstan, Siberia, and places in between. Subsequent trips took her to Poland, Slovenia, the Czech Republic, Hungary, and other parts of Eastern Europe. Her favorite travel experiences are sharing a meal of dried milk curds, goat yogurt, and fermented mare's milk with a Mongolian family in their yurt outside Ulan Bator and swimming in an emerald green underground lake in the desert of Turkmenistan, 6 miles from the Iranian border.

North Carolina's mountains are a well-earned respite, never to be taken for granted again, and just as adventurous when you know where to look.

# Acknowledgments

## Constance . . .

Thank you to the Chambers of Commerce of Alleghany County, Ashe County, Avery County, Banner Elk, Beech Mountain, Blowing Rock, Madison County, Mitchell County, Yancey County; the Boone Area Chamber of Commerce; High Country Host in Boone; Asheville Chamber of Commerce; Ina Parr, Blue Ridge Parkway, Asheville; Iris Photographics in Asheville, and to all of the kind participants in this book who have kindly provided information and great experiences.

A very special Thank You and much love to my parents Irene Dillingham Richards and Ken Richards for instilling in me a love of travel at a very young age, as well as an understanding that all places can be delightful and interesting if you just look. I also thank them for their patience as I yet again turned the home/office upside down in a whirlwind of letters, papers, brochures, books, folders, and notes during the months of research for this book. Thank you to my godparents Lib and Gene Green for the delightful meals of fortification and good chats at the halfway point of many trips.

Thank you to many friends scattered throughout the world now (you know who you are), for their encouragement in trying out this still-new American adventure and for remaining close even though you are thousands of miles away. I still miss you! Thank you to bon vivant Tom Szypulski for his encouraging e-mails; he's now enabling me to vicariously travel to exotic places. Thanks to fashion king Walter Denning whom I was glad to reacquaint with these mountains, now that he's a Londoner! Thanks to other old friends for introducing me to the American Road Trip. Thanks to photographer Steve Mann for his contribution of exceptional photos for our Nightlife chapter. Thanks to Sveta and her mother for visiting these mountains and thank you to Gulnara Medeubekova for making the mountains a jollier place with her presence here.

Last, but not least, a big thank you to my new North Carolina-based friends. You've made me feel right at home.

## Sara . . .

...offers deep thanks to the staff and volunteers of chambers of commerce and visitors centers in the cities and counties of Clay, Cherokee, Graham, Haywood, Henderson, Jackson, Macon, Polk, Swain and Transylvania, as well as the Cherokee Indian Reservation. As always, she is especially grateful to the cheerful, helpful residents, both old and new, of these lovely mountains, who make living and traveling here such a delight.

A special thanks and love are due to Carolyn Smoot, her super-wise big sister, who "retired" here just in time to provide her with support, companionship, research, great food, a sharp proofreader's eye and the world's greatest cups of coffee throughout this project. Finally, thanks to Stanley, the almost-perfect parrot, whose brilliant conversational skills banish the loneliness of a writer's life.

Black bears roam the peaks and valleys, balds and hollows of our enchanted mountains.

# Table of Contents

How to Use this Book ........................................................................................... 1
Area Overviews ................................................................................................... 5
Getting Around .................................................................................................. 31
Climate: The Pretty Place ................................................................................. 37
Restaurants ....................................................................................................... 43
Nightlife ............................................................................................................. 73
Resorts .............................................................................................................. 83
Bed and Breakfasts and Country Inns ............................................................ 101
Other Accommodations ................................................................................... 149
Shopping Destinations .................................................................................... 173
Outdoor Safety ................................................................................................ 215
Recreation ....................................................................................................... 223
Skiing ............................................................................................................... 267
Golf .................................................................................................................. 273
Forests and Parks ........................................................................................... 285
Attractions ....................................................................................................... 309
Kidstuff ............................................................................................................ 325
The Biltmore Estate and Winery ..................................................................... 333
The Cherokee Indian Reservation .................................................................. 339
Waterfalls ........................................................................................................ 347
The Blue Ridge Parkway ................................................................................. 361
Rock Hounding ................................................................................................ 375
Annual Festivals and Events ........................................................................... 383
Arts and Culture .............................................................................................. 411
Mountain Crafts ............................................................................................... 461
Summer Camps ............................................................................................... 475
Real Estate ...................................................................................................... 485
Retirement ....................................................................................................... 507
Healthcare ....................................................................................................... 525
Education ......................................................................................................... 545
Index of Advertisers ........................................................................................ 562
Index ................................................................................................................ 565

# Directory of Maps

North Carolina's Mountains (Showing Counties) ............................................. xii
Northern Mountains .......................................................................................... xiii
Central Mountains ........................................................................................... xiv
Southern Mountains .......................................................................................... xv

# North Carolina's Mountains
## (Showing Counties)

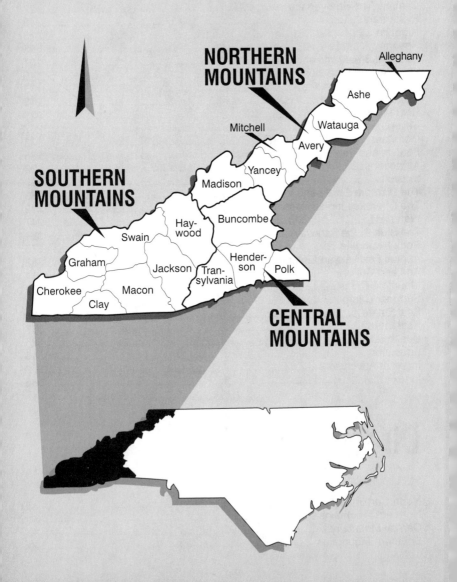

NORTHERN MOUNTAINS

Alleghany

Ashe

Watauga

Mitchell

Avery

Yancey

Madison

Buncombe

SOUTHERN MOUNTAINS

Hay-wood

Swain

Graham

Jackson

Hender-son

Polk

Cherokee

Macon

Tran-sylvania

Clay

CENTRAL MOUNTAINS

# Northern Mountains

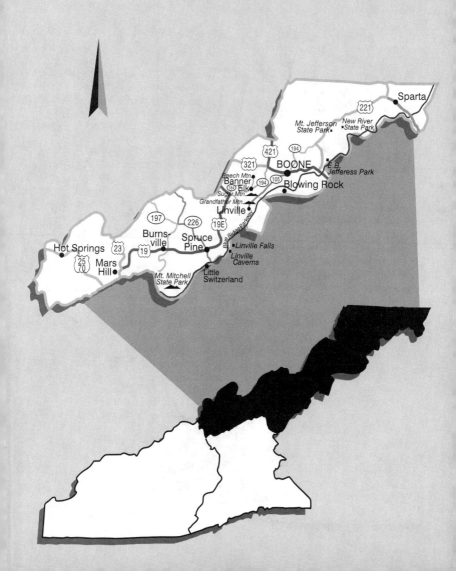

Sparta

(221)

Mt. Jefferson
State Park

New River
State Park

(421) (194)

(321)

BOONE

E.B.
Jefferess Park

Beech Mtn.

Banner
Elk

(184)

(194) (105)

Blowing Rock

Sugar Mtn.

Grandfather Mtn.

Linville

(197) (226) (19E)

Blue Ridge Parkway

Burns-
ville

Spruce
Pine

Linville Falls

Linville
Caverns

Hot Springs (23)

(19)

Mars
Hill

(25)
(70)

Mt. Mitchell
State Park

Little
Switzerland

# Central
# Mountains

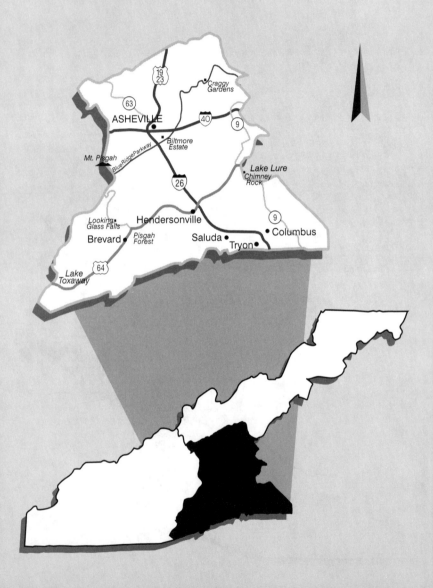

19 23
Craggy Gardens
63
ASHEVILLE
40
9
Biltmore Estate
Mt. Pisgah
Blue Ridge Parkway
Lake Lure
Chimney Rock
26
Looking Glass Falls
Hendersonville
9
Brevard
Pisgah Forest
Saluda
Columbus
Tryon
64
Lake Toxaway

# Southern
# Mountains

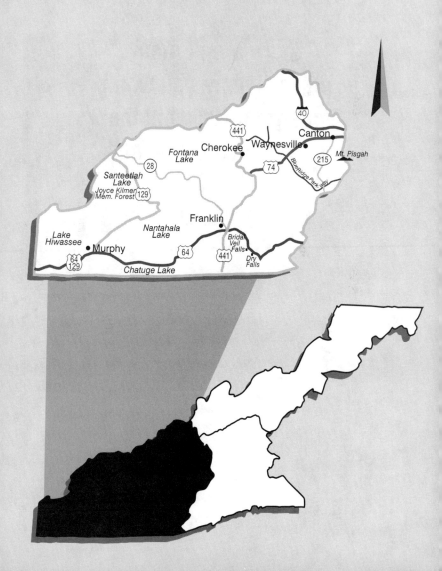

There aren't many places where you won't get great view, but the ones we've mentioned are some of the classics.

# How to Use This Book

For years now, we have wandered Western North Carolina's beautiful peaks and valleys, its towns and forests, seeking out the new and revisiting the old in an effort to bring you just a glimpse of all that's wonderful here. But even a glimpse — when it includes 18 dynamic counties, plus the mountainous sections of Polk and Rutherford counties — can be a bit overwhelming. Here then is a short explanation of how to find your way around in this, our fourth edition.

To begin with, we've divided the whole region into the Northern Mountains, the Central Mountains and the Southern Mountains. Then, within those northern, central and southern sections, we've listed the counties they contain in alphabetical — not geographical — order. Under those headings, we've again tried to put most listings in alphabetical order. For example, if you're interested in a particular county, you can just flip through and read all those entries under each subject. But county lines, like most man-made things, are sometimes a little arbitrary. For example, though Highlands is in Macon County, and Cashiers, 10 miles away, is in Jackson County, people around here refer to the Highlands-Cashiers area as if it were a single unit, which — geographically and socially speaking — it pretty much is.

We only move away from this region/county format on a few occasions, such as when listing back-country outfitters or other recreational specialists who serve the whole region, but we list the names of the towns where their main headquarters are located.

In our Shopping chapter, too, we have listed "Shopping Destinations" rather than running county-by-county and city-by-city classifications. But you will still find them under their northern, central and southern mountain headings with the shops listed in alphabetical order under those headings. There are, of course, some great shops in almost any town you happen to find yourself, and you might discover just what you're looking for tucked into a little establishment by a roadside. But we feel that the places we've listed are worth a special trip, because they're filled with great stores or fantastic little shops.

We have also included a chapter on our vast and wonderful Forests and Parks. These public lands stretch over a large majority of our counties, making our usual format impossible, though in our County Overviews we have tried to note, where it's significant, what and how much public land a particular county includes. You should also be aware that, while part of the Blue Ridge Parkway runs through the Pisgah and the Nantahala National Forests, the road is still under the authority of the National Park Service. Camping in these areas is listed in our Recreation chapter.

And, while you don't need to read this whole book for it to be very useful to you, reading the County Overviews chapter will give you a good idea of what is where. We've also included maps, which you should look over carefully to orient yourself to the region. It's easy to be confused, for example, about the town of Cherokee that is on the Cherokee Indian Reservation (the Qualla Boundary) in the northwestern part of the state and the county of Cherokee, which is some miles away

Photo: Cherokee Tribal Promotion Office

The Great Smoky Mountains dominate the scenery in western North Carolina with peaks rising over 6,000 feet. Ninety percent of the Smokies are in this area of North Carolina, and America's most scenic drive, the Blue Ridge Parkway, has its southern entrance less than one mile from Cherokee.

in the far reaches of southwest North Carolina. (Its county seat is Murphy.) They are two entirely separate entities. Likewise, you will see the same name applied to wholly different locations. For example, down around Clay County, the name Tusquitee is given to a bald, a creek, a community and a chain of mountains. There are also two Hiwassees. The one we write about is the name of a large lake in Cherokee County, but there is also the nearby Georgia town of Hiwassee on Lake Chatuge, a body of water that covers part of Clay County in North Carolina and Towns County just over the border in Georgia. Native American names can also present a problem: on some maps, you'll find a river in Jackson County spelled Tuckasegee; on other maps it is spelled Tuckaseigee. We've chosen the former version. Likewise, some maps list a Jackson County lake as Lake Glenville; others call it

Lake Thorpe (see "Lakes" in our Recreation chapter).

And speaking of Native Americans, scattered throughout this book are just a few of the legends and other lore of the mountains, much from the Cherokees, who still contribute so richly to our culture here. We could write (and books have been written) a volume or two on this subject. We've also listed some places you can go for spectacular views in our special "Great Views" boxes. We have to grin a little bit about that: There aren't many places where you won't get great view, but the ones we've mentioned are some of the classics.

We've aimed to make this an easy and enjoyable guide to use. We'd be pleased if you'll let us know where we've missed something that absolutely, without-a-doubt should be included. The whole area is changing and growing right before our eyes. Nothing but the great and rugged peaks appears to stay the same. That's another reason we'll be updating this guide yet-again in the near future, and we welcome your suggestions. Please send your comments to:

Editor, *The Insiders' Guide to
North Carolina's Mountains*
Falcon Publishing, Inc.
P.O. Box 1718
Helena, MT 59624

Or visit our website at www.insiders.com and let us know what you think via our comments box.

Some of the state's
most scenic rivers —
the Nantahala,
Oconaluftee and
Tuckasegee — add their
beauty and recreational
possibilities to all the
other attractions.

# Area Overviews

Welcome to the North Carolina Mountains. They are as rich in history, folklore, indigenous culture and natural wonder as you have been led to believe. Come join us on a journey through mossy coves and hollows, over wildflower-studded pasture lands and dewy forest trails, past gurgling mountain streams and mellifluous waterfalls, into the green valleys and onto the misty blue ridges that comprise this glorious mountain range. Leave the cement jungles to their urban decay for a moment and revel in the rejuvenating air, water and earth of North Carolina's mountains.

Each county in western North Carolina bears its own individual geographical features, history and lifestyle, too abundant to capture in one book. We could write volumes about each one. Certainly each major town deserves a chapter, from cultural, educational and medical centers like Asheville and Boone, to the smaller pastoral settlements of Blowing Rock and Lake Lure. Many of these smaller mountain settlements and villages are made distinct by becoming "incorporated," indicating that they are legal townships unto themselves with their own tax bases and may not be swallowed up by the next larger town which might be growing beyond its boundaries.

Each county and township and the natural land connecting them are worth the exploration we hope you will undertake. In the following chapters, we offer you only "thumbnail sketches." After you read more about each of our counties under their headings in the chapters that follow, we trust you will be sufficiently inspired to come out here and do your own exploring of our mountain enclaves.

## Northern Mountains

### Alleghany County

Tucked up against the border of Virginia is rural Alleghany County, the northernmost of North Carolina's mountain counties. Only 230 square miles, Alleghany is one of the smallest counties in the state. It was once known as "the lost province," and for good reason, since it can only be reached by winding two-lane roads. Alleghany County has a moderate climate, with distinct seasonal changes. Snow is not uncommon here, but the elevation, which ranges from 2,500 to 4,000 feet, does not sustain the winter sports of its neighboring counties.

Indian hunters roamed this land thousands of years ago, but it was the ruggedly independent Scotch-Irish, English and German pioneers who settled these hills and valleys in the late 1700s. The county was officially established in 1859 from parts of the surrounding counties of Ashe, Surry and Wilkes. The name Alleghany is derived from the Indian word for "fine stream," which is fitting for an area nourished by the New River, one of the oldest rivers in the world. According to historians, this ancient river was named by surveyor Peter Jefferson, Thomas's father, who was surprised to find another "new" river behind the mountains.

The geographic remoteness of this county is more a blessing than a hindrance, for Alleghany County's natural isolation has preserved the rural America of 30 years ago. The pace is gentler here in this small county of just 11,550 people. It's a friendly place where everyone knows everyone, where children can grow up never knowing a stranger and where trust is an unspoken certainty. Many in Alleghany County still live on family land that has been handed down for generations. And in tiny Sparta, the county seat with a population of only 2,000, Main Street is not just a location but an atmosphere.

Seven percent of the county's labor force of 5,000 works in agriculture-related businesses, such as tobacco, beef cattle, corn and hay. Christmas tree production is the fastest growing farm industry in the county, and outside manufacturing is being established by Hanes/Sara Lee Knit Products; Bristol Compressors; Sparta Industries, makers of Dr. Grabow's presmoked pipes; New River Artisans, manufacturers of custom-designed rugs; and NAPCO, makers of Trivial Pursuit game boards. Economic development is expected to continue in Alleghany County, especially with the improvement of more direct roads.

www.insiders.com
See this and many other **Insiders' Guide®** destinations online.
Visit us today!

But it is still a joy to ride the winding two-lanes of Alleghany County up and down its spectacular rolling hills and along its far-reaching pastures. In an era of shrinking rural farmland, the expanse of unspoiled beauty is striking. Just a few minutes to the east is the Blue Ridge Parkway, which had its historical beginning in 1935 at nearby Cumberland Knob and forms some 30 miles of the eastern boundary of the county. Then drive a little farther south on the Parkway to Doughton Park with its network of hiking trails and camping facilities. The easily accessible New River, well known among canoeing enthusiasts, provides easy and inexpensive opportunities for outdoor recreation.

For more information, contact the Alleghany County Chamber of Commerce, (336) 372-5473, (800) 372-5473, P.O. Box 1237, Sparta, North Carolina 28675.

# Ashe County

Ashe County, the extreme northwestern mountain county bordered by Tennessee and Virginia, is marked by the curling length of the New River, one of this country's few north-flowing rivers. The New River's pervasive presence in Ashe is responsible for much of the unique character of this remote North Carolina county. Like its eastern neighbor Alleghany, Ashe County has enjoyed its isolation, allowing it to retain the more relaxed flavor of yesteryear.

Shawnee, Creek and Cherokee Indian hunters preceded the European settlers who arrived here in the 1750s. The first permanent settlement was erected in 1771 along Helton Creek. Ashe County's early settlers were part of the famous contingent of "overmountain men" who fought the decisive battle of Kings Mountain during the Revolutionary War. By 1799, these lands were formally organized as a county and named for the Revolutionary patriot and North Carolina governor Samuel Ashe. It was not until the mid-1800s that sizable Ashe County lost part of its original 977 square miles to the formation of Watauga and Alleghany counties, leaving it with its present 427 square miles.

The county seat was established at Jeffersonton in 1803. The town, named for Thomas Jefferson, is known today as Jefferson and lies a mile east from West Jefferson. The separately incorporated town of West Jefferson began as a lumber-industry village when the railroad made its way here in 1914. Other villages sprang up along the path of the growing rail service. But the decline of the railroad in the decades since World War II had a detrimental effect on rural counties such as Ashe, and the ultimate termination of the county's rail service in 1927 served to isolate the area economically as well as physically.

The 1990s, however, are proving to be a time of growth. Rather than lumber, it is a combination of Christmas tree farms, golf and tourism that has begun its revitalization. Ashe's pristine landscape and less complicated lifestyle also attract new blood, particularly retirees. The county is actively seeking industrial growth, beckoning business with vastly improved and widened county roads.

The prominence of the New River in Ashe County and New River State Park make canoeing and camping popular activities in the area. Mount Jefferson, at an altitude of 4,683 feet, rises majestically out of a 474-acre state park filled with easy-to-moderate hiking trails abundant with wildflowers. A cave near the top of the mountain is said to have sheltered runaway slaves during the Civil War. The Churches of the Frescoes in West Jefferson and Glendale Springs (see our Arts and Culture chapter) have gained national attention and brought surprising numbers of visitors to the remote hilltops of Ashe County.

With only 10 percent of the county population of 23,000 living in the towns of Jefferson and West Jefferson, Ashe County is still largely rural. Villages cluster at crossroads and individual farms crown the hillsides. There is no roadside clutter here—the scenic hillsides are dotted with grazing cows and the ubiquitous fragrant stands of Christmas trees. Its proximity to bustling Boone, just 30 minutes away, makes Ashe County an appealing destination for the city person with a country heart.

For more information, contact the Ashe County Chamber of Commerce, (336) 246-9550, P.O. Box 31, West Jefferson, North Carolina 28694.

## Avery County

Avery County, with a population of roughly 15,000 today, is a curious mix of peaceful rural life and sophisticated tourism. Settlement came slowly to this rugged place. Indians and mountain men alike hunted the land, yet few pioneers chose to make these peaks their home. One who did was the locally well-known settler William Linville, who came with his sons in 1766 only to be slain by hostile Indians near the spectacular waterfall and gorge that now bears his name.

This high mountain land is harsh in winter, but its clear air and cool summer temperatures attracted tourists as early as the 1870s. Boarding houses opened in Banner Elk to serve the seasonal visitors, and in 1891 the town of Linville was founded as a summer community for the wealthy. Roads continued to develop around the advancing railroad spurs that pushed through the area, opening remote ridges and valleys. Even so, the twists and turns of the topography left pockets of rural settlement untouched. It was not until 1911 that Avery County, named for Revolutionary patriot Waightstill Avery, was officially formed, making it the newest and one of the smallest counties in North Carolina (only 247 square miles). Newland is the county seat.

Today, Avery County boasts the South's highest ski slopes, nine major golf resorts (public and private), and a number of natural landmarks.

Many visitors, now lowland residents, have returned for generations and maintain beautiful second homes in the exclusive areas of Grandfather Mountain, Elk River and Linville Ridge. Banner Elk, home of Lees-McRae College and the famous Woolly Worm Festival, is also a popular skiing and golf resort community. Beech Mountain, the mile-high winter sport community, straddles Avery and neighboring Watauga counties. These two communities are the more populated, tourism-driven parts of Avery County, while outlying areas of rural farmland continue much as they were early in the century.

Tiny Crossnore, in southern Avery County, was settled in 1833 and incorporated in 1925. Known for the Crossnore School established in 1911 to educate mountain children, this community is a pleasant reminder of early Western North Carolina town life. The county has a strong tradition in crafts, ranging from pottery and quilts to jewelry and furniture.

## INSIDERS' TIP

You can see three states from Mount Jefferson in Ashe County. This vantage point is especially breathtaking at sunset. Take U.S. 221 from Jefferson, turning onto S.R. 1152, and drive all the way to the top to the parking area. The Summit Trail is just a fraction of a mile from the highest point on Mount Jefferson.

The only notable changes in the rural landscape of Avery County are the geometric patterns of green that cover the hills around Linville, a sign of Avery County's successful Christmas tree industry, in which over 900 families are active.

For more information, contact the Avery County Chamber of Commerce, 733-4737, P.O. Box 700, Newland, North Carolina 28657. Or call the Banner Elk chamber, (800) 972-2183, or the Beech Mountain chamber, (800) 468-5506.

# Madison County

The rugged terrain of this western county, bisected by the powerful French Broad River, reflects the self-reliant spirit of the local folk and their industrious predecessors.

Madison County lies northwest of Buncombe County, bounded by Haywood and Yancey counties and the state of Tennessee. Formed in 1851 from parts of Buncombe and Yancey counties, Madison County is named for America's fourth president. The county is largely rural and has a population of only 17,200 with 48 percent of that population living on farms (the highest percentage in the state). The remainder live in family homes with acreage or in the towns of Mars Hill, Marshall or Hot Springs, the county seat.

Agriculture — wheat, cattle, corn and tobacco farming — is still the primary source of income here, but some small manufacturing has also moved into the county. In the last 20 years, an increasing number of artisans and craftspeople have made Madison County home, finding the solitude of the county's heavily wooded mountains conducive to their work.

Mars Hill, the county's largest town, lies 20 minutes northwest of Asheville. As the home of Baptist-affiliated Mars Hill College, it is defined both by its scholastic roots and by the rugged individualism of Madison County's heritage. Attractive old brick storefronts face Main Street, a two-lane artery so narrow you could almost jump over it. While the town remains pretty much as it was 40 or 50 years ago, the infusion of newcomers is increasing. Main Street, for example, now has two stop lights, and growth is creeping up the hill from the interstate. Being a college-town, the ubiquitous coffeehouse has also made an appearance. Mars Hill is home to the Rural Life Museum and the Southern Appalachian Repertory Theater, and skiing is always nearby at Wolf Laurel. Still, this remains a charming old-fashioned hamlet that is kept dynamic by the presence of Mars Hill College.

Marshall, about 15 minutes west of Mars Hill, straddles the narrow hillsides cut by the French Broad River. Established around 1851, this town is much as it was at the turn of the century. The river has seen to that. Its ebb and flow, and frequent overflows, seem to have suspended the city in time — this is Marshall's charm. Homes hug the hillsides surrounding the town. The cupola-topped courthouse, designed by Richard Sharp Smith of Biltmore Estate fame, commands a position at a crossroads within walking distance of the river. The town's self-appointed philosophers still convene on the courthouse benches along Main Street. Another prominent town landmark is the elementary school on the island in the middle of the river. Needless to say, students here have long looked forward to flood holidays as much as snow days.

As early as the 1830s, Hot Springs was host to wealthy visitors in search of the healing powers of its springs. A number of hotels, taverns and boarding houses sprang up, only to fade away in later years. Today the town is experiencing a revival as travelers, day-trippers, retirees and summer residents converge on the hills and settle into old hotels that are now quaint bed and breakfast inns. The Hot Springs Spa has also been reborn (see our Attractions chapter). Easy access to the French Broad River makes whitewater rafting an important part of the town's tourist economy. And with the Appalachian Trail winding through town, Hot Springs is a popular respite for weary hikers.

In the county's northwest corner near Tennessee, you can still find remote hamlets where families have lived for generations. Madison County natives take pride in their rugged, independent Scotch-Irish heritage.

For more information, contact the Madison County Chamber of Commerce, (828) 689-9351, P.O. Box 1527, Mars Hill, North Carolina 28754, (877) 262-3476.

# Mitchell County

Mitchell County was formed in 1861 from portions of five counties: Yancey, Burke, Caldwell, McDowell and Watauga. With a population of 14,500 today, this county of only 220 square miles was named in honor of Dr. Elisha Mitchell, explorer of famed Mount Mitchell, the highest peak east of the Mississippi. The county is bordered by Tennessee and Avery, Yancey and McDowell counties. Mining of quartz, feldspar and mica are major industries here. In fact, the Spruce Pine Mining District is recognized the world over for its ultra-pure quartz which is vital to the computer industry. Agricultural products such as tobacco, corn, apples and more recently Christmas trees are also important in the county.

Spruce Pine is the largest town in the county with a population close to 3,000. Bakersville, the county seat, is surrounded by the long-established communities of Rock Creek, Cane Creek, Mine Creek and Toe Cane. These tiny towns nestled in the twisting mountain coves of Mitchell County are home to generations of families. The origin of other delightfully named hamlets such as Loafer's Glory, Relief, Ledger, Bandana and Altapass are worthy of note. Loafer's Glory, about 3 miles north of Bakersville on N.C. Highway 226, was christened by the wives of the community after they observed the unabashed loitering of their men on the front porch of the community store. Relief is named for a once-popular cure-all tonic, Dr. Hart's Relief, which was sold in the community at Squire Peterson's Store around 1870. No doubt the popularity of the tonic came from the large volume of alcohol it contained. The community of Ledger was named for the ledger book sent to Washington, D.C. by community residents who were trying to establish the amount of mail passing through the area and their need for a local post office. The railroad played a part in naming two Mitchell County hamlets. Bandana got its name from the bandanna a railroad brakeman used to locate a proper site for a railroad station. The Clinchfield Railroad, passing over these mountains from Tennessee, reached its highest point at the aptly named community of Altapass before heading down the mountain.

The proliferation of gem mines in Mitchell County has long made this county popular with rock hounds. The North Carolina Museum of Minerals is just off the Blue Ridge Parkway (see our chapter on Rock Hound-

Photo: Mitchell County Chamber of Commerce

Golden ragwart blooming on top of Roan Mountain is a wonderful springtime sight.

ing). Mitchell County is also home to the PenlandSchool of Crafts. Sitting atop a mountain ridge, this internationally acclaimed school of the arts draws talented craftspeople and artists from all over the world (see Mountain Crafts).

For more information, contact the Mitchell County Chamber of Commerce, 765-9483 or (800) 227-3912, Route 1, Box 796, Spruce Pine, North Carolina 28777.

# Watauga County

This county of 39,360 lies at the heart of North Carolina's high country. Formed in 1849, Watauga's 320 square miles are bounded by Tennessee and the counties of Avery, Ashe, Wilkes and Caldwell. It was named for the Watauga River, which rises near Grandfather Mountain and flows north into Tennessee, where it converges with the Holston River. Watauga is an Indian word for "beautiful water."

Early emphasis on education led to the development of Watauga County as a center of higher education. The county was largely rural until 1899 when the Dougherty brothers founded the Watauga Academy in Boone, the forerunner of Appalachian State University. Part of the University of North Carolina system, ASU plays an important role in the growth of the area, with thriving Boone, the county seat, at its heart. Boone's permanent resident population of 13,550 doubles with the addition of the students and swells even more with the arrival of tourists throughout the year.

The cultural base of the university and the town's tourist-geared entertainment offer something for everyone.

Boone has become a magnet for tourism and related industries. Its many restaurants, for example, have turned the city into a dining destination. The climate is suited for both winter and summer sport, with golf and skiing the prime diversions in the county. Resorts such as Hound Ears, Hawksnest, Seven Devils and Beech Mountain (partially in Avery County) offer a multitude of recreation options. And potters, weavers, painters, storytellers, traditional mountain musicians, actors and artisans fill the area with creative energy.

Blowing Rock, 15 minutes south of Boone, is a picturesque mountain town perched on a ridge overlooking the John's River Gorge. The town takes it name from the rock formation over the gorge that creates an unusual current of air spiraling up from the valley below. The view from the Blowing Rock is breathtaking, as is the scenery from nearly every vantage point in town. Charming specialty stores and fine restaurants line Main Street, and excellent bed and breakfast inns are scattered along Blowing Rock's side streets, just a few steps from downtown. You can walk to almost everything here, including the town square, which is the scene of concerts and art shows in summer. Tourism is important to Blowing Rock, so the town leadership is working to retain its village-like character.

Foscoe, on N.C. Highway 105 leading into Boone, has become known for its selection of craft and antique shops. The community is

Photo: Constance E. Richards

The Flat Iron Building is so named because when seen from the air it looks like an iron.
This is one example of Asheville's unique architecture.

blessed with a glorious view of Grandfather Mountain in nearby Avery County.

Valle Crucis, in central Watauga County, is also off N.C. 105 at the junction of Dutch Creek and the Watauga River. Established as an Episcopal mission in 1842, it retains a largely rural character and has become a popular site for summer homes, unique restaurants, renowned inns and unusual shopping.

Despite the busy pace of the tourist meccas, Watauga County offers plenty of quiet countryside. Heading toward Tennessee you can see some of the most scenic farmland in Western North Carolina. U.S. Highway 321 winds up, down and around hillsides studded with craggy rocks and threaded with lazy, meandering creeks.

For more information, contact the Boone Area Chamber of Commerce and Convention & Visitors Bureau, (828) 264-2225 or (800) 852-9506, 208 Howard Street, Boone, North Carolina 28607; High Country Host, (828) 264-1299 or (800) 438-7500, 1700 Blowing Rock Road, Boone, North Carolina 28607; Blowing Rock Chamber of Commerce, (828) 295-7851, P.O. Box 406, Blowing Rock, North Carolina 28605.

# Yancey County

Indians and mountaineers played vital parts in the development of Yancey County. The area was a thoroughfare for Cherokee Indians who roamed these rich hunting grounds. But the path of the Scots-Irish settlers seeking a new country also led to these mountains and the fertile valleys fed by Yancey's Cane and South Toe rivers. Land grants for former Cherokee lands were awarded to hardy pioneers as early as 1777. In 1797, John Gray Blount was awarded a blanket charter for land that eventually became Yancey County. Traders, entrepreneurs and new settlers began to arrive. The new county, formed in 1833, soon became one of the busiest and most prosperous in the region. Burnsville, also established in 1833, had long been a stage stop.

Prosperity blossomed until the Civil War left its mark both emotionally and economically. The Scots-Irish settlers who dominated the area had no use for a war they viewed as based on slavery, a practice that was little heard of in the hard existence of most mountain families. And the heavy taxes and conscription imposed by the government to finance the war were burdens for Yancey's citizenry. The discord and hard times resulted in the formation of new counties. Madison, Mitchell and the area that later became Avery County were separated by the war's end, leaving Yancey County with 311 square miles.

The pioneer heritage of Yancey County has been preserved in Burnsville, a charming town that is a fine illustration of a bygone era. The county's largest community and county seat, Burnsville is anchored by a classic town square with a statue in honor of its namesake, Captain Otway Burns, a privateer during the War of 1812 and also a member of the North Carolina General Assembly. Life in the town still revolves around the square, and homes are nestled on the mountains rising on one side.

The county, with a population of 17,000, was economically distressed during the 1980s by crippling unemployment of 23 percent. But with the resilience of their ancestors, Yancey County citizens banded together to revitalize their homeland and as a result gained national attention and new industries. In 1980, when the comeback plan was launched, Yancey County placed an advertisement in *The Wall Street Journal* that included a group photograph of the unemployed workers of Yancey County with the caption, "We want to work for you." The bold move attracted Fortune 500 industries that are now part of Yancey County's growing industrial base.

Agriculture — tobacco, corn, dairy products and cultivated berries — still plays a vital part in the county's economy, as it did in pioneer times. Ornamental shrubs and Christmas tree production have also gained a hold. Mining has always been important here: the excavation of mica, feldspar and sand and gravel operations are found in the northern part of the Yancey County, near Mitchell County.

The proximity of Asheville, just 35 minutes away, is a plus for Yancey County. Increasing numbers of retirees are settling here, and premier golf communities are springing up. The rich traditional local arts heritage has always drawn creative people, nurtured by the support of the dynamic Toe River Arts Council.

Yancey County is blessed with seasonal changes and a topography that lends itself to outdoor recreation. The presence of the South Toe and Cane rivers makes camping, tubing, canoeing and kayaking easily accessible. The nearby Nolichucky River, flowing into Tennessee, is extremely popular with whitewater enthusiasts. Hiking is favored due to the county's network of some 100 miles of trails of varying degrees of difficulty. The Black Mountain Range in Yancey County features Mount Mitchell, at 6,684 feet the highest peak east of the Mississippi. You can see this majestic peak from the Blue Ridge Parkway, which runs the length of Western North Carolina's mountains.

For more information, contact the Yancey County Chamber of Commerce at 106 West Main, Burnsville, North Carolina 28714, (828) 682-7413 or (800) 948-1632.

# Central Mountains

## Buncombe County

Sitting high on a plateau surrounded by mountains, Buncombe County, population 190,200, has enjoyed a history of good fortune due to its position as a geographical crossroads. Development historically follows the path of primary water sources, and so it did along the mighty French Broad River.

Trade with the Cherokee Indians was established as early as 1673 along the well-worn Indian paths that crossed at the site of present-day Asheville. The natural riches of the region and the flow of commerce soon drew large numbers of settlers. Samuel W. Davidson and his family were the first to settle in the region in 1784, along Christian Creek in the Swannanoa Valley. Trade continued to boom, and the county was officially formed in 1791. The business of government brought in scores

Photo: Grove Park Inn Resort

The Grove Park Inn Resort in Asheville is one of the most storied and historic hotels in the country.

of new settlers, traders, speculators and adventurers. With this influx of new citizens, the well-traveled Indian paths soon became thoroughfares for traders and stock drovers from Kentucky and Tennessee moving through the French Broad Valley on their way to the open markets in South Carolina. The construction of the Buncombe Turnpike from 1824 to 1828 further secured this steady stream of trade.

From the early 1800s to 1880, Buncombe County settled into a period of bucolic bliss. Recovery from the Civil War was slow, and it was not until completion of the railroad in 1880 that the county came into its own. The railroads brought the moneyed class, which was attracted by the healthful climate, crisp mountain air and sparkling social atmosphere. One young visitor, George Vanderbilt, vowed to return, and when he did he changed the county forever. After purchasing 125,000 acres, he set about building a castle. The construction of his Biltmore Estate in 1895 brought a legion of artists and craftsmen whose legacy remains as an influence on the area's architecture.

The 1920s were Buncombe County's boom time. The architectural character of Asheville, the county seat, was formed during these glory days, giving it the unique cosmopolitan flavor that continues to attract visitors and newcomers alike. An exciting buzz has been developing about this city over the past few years. A magnet for professionals, artists, artisans, retirees, students, New Agers and alternative-lifestyle seekers, Asheville was named All-American City in 1997. This city of roughly 66,700 retains a small-town mountain charm wrapped in big-city sophistication. The noted American novelist Thomas Wolfe was born here, bringing his native city unwelcome notoriety when he wrote of it in his coming-of-age novel, *Look Homeward, Angel*.

The city's geographic growth has always been limited by the mantle of mountains that surrounds it, but modern transportation links the county with nearby cities like Atlanta, Knoxville and Charlotte that comprise the fastest growing region in the United States. Downtown Asheville boasts the finest collection of art deco buildings this side of Miami Beach, and restoration of these old gems is booming. Pack Square, historically central to the city, and Haywood Street form the cultural and commercial heart of downtown.

The county is framed at all points of the compass with interesting communities. Just 15 minutes north of Asheville lies Weaverville, a town of roughly 2,390 with a charming Main Street. Many retirees choose to live in Weaverville, along with a growing number of young professionals seeking the slower pace of country life (they reside in Weaverville or its outlying farmland and make the short commute to Asheville). The completion of the Interstate 19/23 connector to Tennessee will open this area even more in the next five to 10 years.

Ten more minutes north on the interstate will lead you to the area of Big Ivy, a pastoral mixture of bald hillsides, meadows, tobacco farmlands and barns that connect the communities of Barnardsville and Dillingham. The pioneer Absolom Dillingham settled at the foot of the Great Craggies in the early 1800s, and his descendants continue to make it their home today. Several excellent examples of pre-Civil War and Civil War-time cabins remain in the area, with the Carson Cabin and schoolhouse restored to its former self. Carson Cabin, which is on Dillingham Road, is open on certain holidays for viewing.

Twenty miles east of Asheville, Black Mountain was established in 1893 as a quaint summer-resort town known as Grey Eagle, attracting visitors looking for relief from the heat of the low country. Today much of its turn-of-the-century charm is still intact. It is known for its wealth of antique shops and diverse cultural events. Avant-garde Black Mountain College operated nearby from 1933 to 1956, and a museum capturing the school's glory years is in the planning stage.

The French Broad River divides West Asheville from Asheville, giving West Asheville its distinct personality. Before being incorporated into the city of Asheville, West Asheville was very much its own town. Haywood Road, the main thoroughfare in West Asheville, is reminiscent of America in the 1950s or '60s. Old coffee shops, green grocers, dusty secondhand shops, a pharmacy and gas stations mingle with storefront offices. West Buncombe County still retains much rural farmland, old homesteads and pastures dotted

The city of Asheville takes pride in its architecture — so much so that even the parking garages are designed with aesthetics in mind.

by grazing cattle. The Arden/Skyland area to the south is Buncombe County's fastest growing section, populated by many young families attracted by the quality of life in the county. Buncombe County benefits from its closeness to the French Broad River, Pisgah National Forest and the Blue Ridge Parkway, which form the northern and eastern edges of the county and offer outstanding recreational opportunities.

City and county economic development groups are working together to develop a plan for sustained industrial growth for the area without compromising the unique flavor of this central mountain county.

For more information, contact the Asheville Area Chamber of Commerce, (828) 258-6101 or (800) 257-1300, 151 Haywood Street, Asheville, North Carolina 28801. Or call the Black Mountain Chamber of Commerce, (828) 669-2300, (800) 669-2301.

# Henderson County

From almost any place you happen to be in Henderson County you can see mountains, yet much of the land consists of rolling hills. There are also marshes here similar to those in the lowlands, and some of the rich river valleys are surprisingly flat. That's because the county rests on a high plateau between the Blue Ridge and the Great Smoky Mountains. Elevations here range from 5,000 feet on Little Pisgah Mountain down to 1,400 feet at Bat Cave.

Hendersonville, the prosperous county seat, sits at an altitude of 2,200 feet, almost smack-dab in the middle of the county. This bustling and ever-growing little city, with its pretty and very-much-alive downtown area, is just off Interstate 26 and is actually closer to the Asheville Airport than Asheville is. It's long been one of Western North Carolina's most popular retirement areas. In 1838, when the 378-square-mile county was established out of a former section of Buncombe County, the Flat Rock community, just a few miles south of Hendersonville, was already a very grand summer retreat for the wealthy citizens of Charleston, South Carolina.

Before the Revolutionary War, the land that makes up Henderson County was under the control of the Cherokees, who used it not for settlements but as hunting grounds.

In 1787, William Mills received one of the first land grants west of the Blue Ridge and left his mark in many of the names he gave to the area: Mills River, Mills Gap, Sugar Loaf Mountain and Bald Top, to list a few. Mills was a Loyalist who was wounded and left for dead during the Revolutionary War's Battle of King's Mountain in 1781. The night after the battle, he made his escape in the darkness back to his home on the Green River in what was then Rutherford County. But Tories were frequently hanged during those volatile days (see Polk County information later), so he continued on up into the high country and hid in a cave in Sugar Loaf Mountain, which overlooked this rich plateau. He must have liked the land he saw stretched out below him, because he and his wife Eleanor eventually became the first white settlers in the area, and others soon followed.

More than 60 years later, in 1841, a vote was taken on whether to put Henderson County's seat of government in the little community of Horse Shoe (still a small and friendly place) or to situate it some 8 miles away near the Buncombe Turnpike close to the foot of Stoney Mountain. The voters chose the more centrally located Turnpike site at what became Hendersonville. Charleston's Judge Mitchell King, who had a summer home in Flat Rock, gave the county a 50-acre tract on Mud Creek, known as Chinquapin Hill. Two other men donated an adjoining 29 acres. Streets were quickly laid out, and a courthouse was finished in 1842.

In 1847, Hendersonville, which already had several hundred residents, was granted its charter and grew slowly but steadily, with agriculture as its economic base. In 1879, the long, dusty trip up the Turnpike was shortened considerably when the railroad came to town, bringing with it new growth and prosperity. The first train's arrival, it's said, prompted the greatest celebration to date held in North Carolina's mountains. In this century, a number of well-known personalities have visited or established homes in Henderson County, including F. Scott

Fitzgerald and Carl Sandburg. The Sandburg home in Flat Rock is now a National Historic Site open to the public.

In the 1920s, Florida's real estate boom reached up into Western North Carolina, as Sunshine State developers saw the potential for tourist dollars in all sorts of locales. Large hotels and resorts, some of them highly speculative, blossomed on ridges with grand mountain views. Many still dot the Western North Carolina mountains, but not all were so lasting. Nevertheless, many Floridians were introduced to Henderson County during this era, and the migration of residents from that state still occurs each spring, as they, like the Charlestonians more than 150 years ago, seek to escape lowlands' heat and humidity.

Such part-time residents almost double the population of this and other Western North Carolina counties each summer. Today, Henderson County has 79,148 full-time residents. Hendersonville proper has a population of nearly 10,000, with approximately 30,000 in the Greater Hendersonville area, reflecting a slow but steady growth. There are many reasons for this besides the area's climate, beauty and recreational possibilities. The very fact that the county has been "a summer place" for so long allows visitors and new residents to feel welcome and to be quickly absorbed into community life. It's reputation for tolerance led a *New York Times* writer to describe Henderson County residents as "polished yet fleshy and down-to-earth," just like their famous apples. They certainly make good use of any talents newcomers want to share, which has resulted in a rich cultural environment. In the county, for example, you'll find the Flat Rock Playhouse (North Carolina's State Theater), a number of amateur and semi-professional theater groups, a symphony orchestra and scores of talented writers, artists, musicians and craftspeople.

Henderson County's economy is a diverse mix of light manufacturing, tourism, agriculture and retirement (in descending order of economic importance). The county goes out of its way to fulfill the needs of its many senior citizens and anticipates future requirements as that population grows.

If there is a problem looming on the horizon, it's the rapid disappearance of good agricultural and undeveloped land. Subdivisions are eating up the land, as more and more visitors and summer residents decide to make the county their year-round home. Unlike many of the other areas of Western North Carolina, Henderson County doesn't have, relatively speaking, a whole lot of public land. A number of small towns, such as Mountain Home and Fletcher, are beginning to merge into a nearly unbroken strip of businesses. Many of the small farms that stretched along U.S. Highway 64 W. going toward Brevard are now broken up into large suburban plots or housing developments.

In the opposite direction, once U.S. 64 E. passes under Interstate 26, the county still remains "apple country," where approximately a million trees—a sight to behold during spring bloom—make the county the largest apple producer in the state and seventh in the nation. This glorious harvest is celebrated each September with a three-day Apple Festival, the largest and most popular of the many annual events held in Henderson County.

The drive through apple country is dramatic for reasons other than spring apple blossoms and the fall harvest. Just down the road from the center of fruit production at Edneyville (about 8 miles from Hendersonville), you'll cross the crest of the Blue Ridge. Then, for the next 5 miles or so, the highway takes a precipitous dive through perpendicular peaks to Bat Cave and Hickory Nut Gorge. It's a quick reminder that Henderson is, indeed, very much in the mountains.

For more information, contact the

## INSIDERS' TIP

**Mount Mitchell in Yancey County is the highest peak in the eastern United States, and it's a pretty sight, even though it is frequently foggy. Take N.C. Highway 128, off the Blue Ridge Parkway at Milepost 355.4. On a clear day, the stone observation tower at the top of the mountain affords a 70-mile view.**

The Blue Ridge Mountains showcase Asheville's distinctive skyline.

Photo: Asheville Convention and Visitors Bureau

Hendersonville Visitors and Tourists Travel Information Center, (828) 693-9708 or (800) 828-4244, 201 S. Main Street or P.O. Box 721, Hendersonville, North Carolina 28793.

## Polk County

Most of Polk County's 234 square miles lie within the Blue Ridge foothills, but the western edge, the area that's covered in this book, is quite mountainous. In this section we'll present an overview of the county's three municipalities: Saluda, Columbus and Tryon.

Saluda, with a population of approximately 680, is on the county's western border at an elevation of 2,095 feet. It sits at the top of the steepest standard-gauge railroad grade in the eastern United States, known as the Saluda Grade. It's a small and winsome village that has long been a vacation and retirement spot and is home to quite a few artists and craftspeople. As in Henderson County, apples are the main source of farm income here.

Columbus and Tryon are "twin-towns," separated by I-26 that goes north to Hendersonville and Asheville and south to Spartanburg and Charleston. It also connects at this point to U.S. Highway 74, which is a four-lane shortcut to Charlotte. Columbus, sit-

ting at an elevation of 1,131 feet, is the smaller of the two towns. Its population is only 948, but it's the county seat and the site of much of the area's economic growth with a township population of 3,992. It was named for Dr. Columbus Mills of Mills Spring, a small community that still retains its pristine character. Dr. Mills' ancestor, Colonel Ambrose Mills, had been a Loyalist like his son William Mills, the man who first settled Henderson County. Unfortunately, Ambrose was not as lucky as William. After the British lost the Battle of King's Mountain, William was left for dead and escaped, Ambrose was captured by Patriots and hanged.

The county was established in 1854, and in 1855 the North Carolina Legislature appointed a committee to locate a county seat within 2 miles of the center of the county. That done, a 100-acre tract of land was purchased for $1. By 1857, Columbus's imposing courthouse of handmade bricks was finished. The town is now a mix of late-19th-century homes, buildings and churches combined with condominiums, a modern hospital and high school and a college campus. The county population is now approaching 17,000.

Neighboring Tryon has a population of 1,776 full-time residents, more than half of whom moved here from some other part of the country. These transplants are mostly writers, artists, educators, professional people and industrial executives who have helped to magically transform the area into a cultural center that attracts even more of the same types of people. Tryon's original attraction was its climate, and for years the sick came here to improve their health. There's a well-publicized weather phenomenon in this area of the mountains known as the isothermal belt, or thermal belt, which provides a more equitable climate than other areas in the region. Caused by inversions of warm air, particularly in the spring and fall, this mini-climate enables apple growers in the region to produce abundant crops, and grapes and peaches thrive in the botanically rich Tryon area.

It's understandable that the area's longtime landholders, the Cherokees, wouldn't give up this fine property without a fight, but for a couple of decades the relationship between the British and the Cherokees prospered. A peace treaty in 1730 resulted in a steady stream of British and American-born traders traveling up the old Blackstock Road from Charleston to exchange cooking utensils, cloth and other items for furs and hides. Before too long, a sprinkling of trading posts and white families dotted the area.

But the French and Indian War ended this "perpetual peace," and by 1756, forts were constructed in the face of the conflicts between the two cultures. The Block House, a fort near Tryon, still stands. Though it became a private home many years ago, the annual Block House Steeplechase was held here until the event became so popular that it was moved to the Foothills Equestrian Nature Center. (See our Recreation and Attraction chapters for more information on the event.)

The bloodshed was so heavy that finally, in 1767, the Royal Governor William Tryon came in person to parley with the Cherokees. They established a boundary line that ran from a point near Greenville, South Carolina, to the highest point on White Oak Mountain, which was renamed Tryon Peak by the grateful settlers. The peak towers over the area and is particularly dominant when seen from I-26 and as you travel north toward Columbus and Tryon: The mountain comes into view dead ahead right at the North Carolina-South Carolina state line. The boundary, however, meant little to land-grabbing settlers, and it wasn't until the Battle of Round Mountain in the spring of 1776, which the Cherokees lost due to the defection of an Indian named Skyuka, that the Indians gave up their claim to this attractive territory.

By 1839, a post office, also named for Governor Tryon, stood at the foot of Tryon Peak. The community that grew up around it became a favorite resting place for drovers transporting livestock from Kentucky, Tennessee and the higher mountains of North Carolina to ports on the coast. Though Tryon is now Polk County's largest town, it wasn't incorporated until 1885, primarily to accommodate the rail line that runs through the center of town.

Today the Tryon area is well known to horse lovers all over the nation for its large equestrian estates, steeplechases, fox hunts and miles of bridle trails. In this storybook-like town, you'll find a number of charming antique and gift shops and other family-owned businesses. The Tryon Theater on Trade Street was originally a 1920s vaudeville theater that now shows first-run movies and occasionally hosts theatrical performances.

Poet Sidney Lanier, who penned "Song of the Chattahoochee" and "The Marshes of Glynn," came to this area to try to cure the tuberculosis he contracted during five months in a Union prison camp during the Civil War. He had planned to stay in the Mimosa Inn in the little community of Lynn, but it was full, so he was given an upstairs room in the Lemuel Willcox house across the road, where he died on September 8, 1881. The Mimosa Inn is still in business (see our Bed and Breakfasts chapter). The Willcox house too still stands and is known as the Lanier House. Though the poet's stay in the area was brief, he has become a part of local lore. Nearby Lake Lanier was named for him, and Tryon's architecturally interesting and active public library is known as the Lanier Library.

For more information, contact The Polk County Chamber of Commerce, (828) 859-6236, 401 N. Trade Street, Tryon, North Carolina 28782; or Polk County Travel and Tourism, (800) 440-7848.

# Transylvania County

This county, with a population of 27,500, has the distinction of being the only one in America called Transylvania. The name naturally leaves the residents open to some teasing about vampires and makes for wonderful T-shirts slogans and Halloween festivals. However, the name, which means "across the woods," is more than appropriate, because 80 percent of this fair county's 378 square miles are covered by forests, almost half of which are managed by the U.S. Forest Service. Elevations in the county range from 1,020 feet at Horsepasture to 6,025 feet on Chestnut Ridge.

One of the most popular entrances to Pisgah Forest, with all its beauty and recreational possibilities, is just outside Brevard, the county seat. From this entrance, U.S. Highway 276 climbs 16 miles to the Blue Ridge Parkway. Along that route, you'll pass such alluring attractions as Looking Glass Falls, the Fish Hatchery, Sliding Rock (a natural water slide) and the Cradle of Forestry. (See our chapters on Waterfalls, Arts and Culture, and Forests and Parks.)

The county has more than 150 large waterfalls, hence its nickname, "The Land of Waterfalls." It could also be called "The Land of Music," because, in addition to the music of falling waters, rivers and more than 200 miles of streams, it's the home of the international Brevard Music Festival. (See our Arts and Culture chapter.) In addition, Brevard College, a liberal arts institution within the town limits, is known for its fine music department, and the college hosts numerous events in all the arts. This creativity is contagious: Performing groups, artists, writers and talented craftspeople contribute to the area's cultural milieu of art and music festivals, craft shows and other events that are an accepted part of daily life here. Most recently, an international film festival was added to the city's cultural scene.

For the Eastatoes, a band of the Cherokees that claimed this land until 1787, this area was mostly hunting grounds, where the Eastern buffalo was quite prevalent. At one time, the Eastatoes had a small settlement near the present town of Rosman, where a hunting path crossed the headwaters of the French Broad River. Another well-used Indian trail came up from South Carolina near what is now Ceasar's Head State Park in South Carolina. It was this path, which came to be known as Douthit's Pass, that many settlers used when they migrated into the areas of Transylvania and Henderson counties. As the whites pushed into the area, the peaceful Eastatoes retreated farther up into the mountains.

(John Douthit Jr., the great-great-great-grandfather of this book's co-author Sara Pacher, nee Douthit, grew up near the Moravian settlement of Old Salem and, in 1790, bought 1,000 acres of land at Table Rock Mountain in South Carolina near the beginning of this path. His sister, Jose Douthit, married Robert Orr Jr. and lived in Brevard. We assumed they must have visited each other a lot for the trail to have been named after them, but we were recently told that this same John Douthit cut or improved many other trails through this rugged territory.)

Civil War battles came no closer to Transylvania than Asheville, though a number of its citizens fought and died for the Confederate cause. Others, loyal to the Union, helped smuggle Union sympathizers through an "underground" from Georgia to Tennessee and on to the north.

There were, however, a couple of battles called the Walton War that took place here between Georgians and North Carolinians in 1802, when both states laid claim to this area. The federal government, which had gotten the land through a treaty with the Cherokees, gave the property to Georgia, and its legislature named it Walton County in honor of George Walton, a signer of the Declaration of Independence. North Carolina claimed that the disputed area was a part of what was then Buncombe County. Hostilities arose, and in 1804, the North Carolina militia was sent in to throw the Georgians out. Skirmishes took place 2 miles southeast of Brevard and also at the site where the Ecusta Division of the P. H. Glatfelter Company Plant now stands, not far from the entrance to Pisgah Forest. A few lives were lost, and a few prisoners were taken in the Walton War, but the two states finally agreed that the 35-degree line of latitude was the official boundary—only because each one believed they would end up with the territory. The issue was finally settled when surveyors proved in 1813 that the land belonged to North Carolina.

Transylvania County itself wasn't established until May 20, 1861 — the same day North Carolina seceded from the Union — when it was carved out of an eastern section of Henderson County and a western part of Jackson County. Brevard, Transylvania's county seat, was incorporated in 1868 with only 70 residents and seven registered voters. The town was named after Dr. Ephraim Brevard, a physician and the author of the Mecklenburg Declaration of Independence, which preceded the national Declaration of Independence by a year. (The Mecklenburg Declaration, which was drafted at the Mecklenburg Council of Safety in 1775, was sent to the Continental Congress in Philadelphia, but it never arrived.) Dr. Brevard died in 1780 at the age of 37 while in a British prison in Charleston, South Carolina; his statue now stands on Transylvania's courthouse lawn.

Brevard's first post office was in The Red House, which is now a bed and breakfast inn. From those humble beginnings, Brevard, with a population of nearly 6,000 full-time residents, has blossomed into a lovely flower of a town with an attractiveness that is still growing. Several years ago, the *Rand-McNally Places Rated Retirement Guide* chose Brevard as the best of 107 locations in the nation to retire. It scored high in climate, terrain, leisure activities and safety from crime. It was above average in housing, cost of living and health care, and the town's friendliness and nearness to attractions was particularly noted. Brevard has continued to rate at or near the top of similar lists. A five-lane connector to I-26 and the Asheville Airport, less than 20 miles away, is bringing new life to Brevard and to Transylvania's other small municipalities of Rosman and Lake Toxaway, the latter having some of the highest-priced real estate in the mountains. In fact, this already outstanding county is in the middle of a renaissance.

For more information, contact the Brevard Chamber of Commerce, (828) 883-3700 or (800) 648-4523, 35 W. Main Street or P.O. Box 589, Brevard, North Carolina 28712.

# Southern Mountains

## Cherokee County

Cherokee County, the westernmost county in this region, is bordered by both Georgia and Tennessee, with Murphy, its county seat, only 20 minutes from either state and just two-hour drives from either Chattanooga or Atlanta. (The 1996 Olympic whitewater canoe event was held at the Ocoee Venue just 31 miles from the Town of Murphy.) It's a rural county of fertile river valleys lined with glorious mountain ridges. One of the most beautiful is the 10-mile-long, 2-mile-wide Valley River Valley, with the Snowbird Mountains soaring on one side and the Valley River Mountains on the other. Cherokee's other small municipality, Andrews, lies near the head of this valley. Both it and Murphy are surrounded by the Nantahala National Forest, which takes up 92,363 acres of the county's 300,100 acres, offering facilities for all kinds of outdoor recreation, including off-road vehicle trails. (See our Forest and Parks and Recreation chapters for more on the Nantahala.) Another 37,000 acres is under the control of the Tennessee Valley Authority. This includes the 22-mile-long Lake Hiwassee and its connecting and much smaller Appalachia Lake, which together cut diagonally across the center of the county. They were created when the Hiwassee River was dammed in 1936 for both electricity and flood control, providing the county with a source of water-based recreation.

In 1549, Hernando DeSoto and his men, who were in search of gold, were the first Europeans to pass through the area. They stopped for a time at the Cherokee town of Guasili near present-day Murphy. Later Spanish adventurers mined here, as evidenced by old tunnels, shafts, coin molds and Spanish cannon balls found in the region. However, it wasn't until the early 1700s that the first English-speaking explorers ventured into this corner of North Carolina. They described it as

Cherokee basket weavers demonstrate their craft at the Oconaluftee Indian Village.

a "hilly land where the soil is deep and rich and rivers promise an easy route to the heart of the continent — or even beyond." Nearly another half-century passed before the Baptist Church established a mission school and church at the Old Natchez town on the Hiwassee River in 1820. The French had thrown the Natchez Indians out of Mississippi, and some ended up in this area, merging with the Cherokees. Ten years later, Colonel A.R.S. Hunter built an Indian trading post at the present site of Murphy and called it Huntersville; in 1835, when a post office was established, he changed the name to Huntington and made himself the first postmaster.

In 1838, Fort Butler was built here as headquarters for the removal of the Cherokees, who were to be relocated in Oklahoma. Once that tragic task was accomplished, settlers flooded into the area. In 1839, Cherokee County was formed out of a portion of Macon County, and a year later, it had a population of 3,427 residents. In 1851, Murphy was incorporated as its county seat. A decade later, when the county had little more than 9,000 citizens, it was asked to send 1,100 men to fight for the Confederate cause. The last battle of the Civil War took place at Hanging Dog Creek, about 4 miles northwest of Murphy near the site of the Nantahala National Forest's popular Hanging Dog Recreation Area, which offers camping and access to Lake Hiwassee (see the Close-up on Hanging Dog in the Recreation chapter). Today, Murphy's population is estimated at 1,650; Andrews has 1,550 residents, and the county as a whole tops out at around 22,000.

The first of Cherokee County's four ill-fated courthouses, a brick structure built in Murphy in 1844, was burned in a raid near the end of the Civil War. A second was torn down and replaced, and two more burned. Understandably, concerned citizens, and especially the local lawyers, urged that the next courthouse be "as totally fireproof as possible." So the fifth and very beautiful structure was built in 1927 of a regal blue marble found only in the Valley River Valley. You can visit the town of Marble (home of the blue marble) on N.C. Highway 141. The town prospered in the early part of the century but is now a ghost of its former self.

In 1891, the Southern Railroad reached Murphy from Asheville, and a logging boom began. Not much remains from the pioneer and antebellum days of 1838 to 1870, but Cherokee County has a substantial number of buildings and homes dating from the prosperous era that began in the 1880s. You can see examples of Greek Revival, Federal, Neoclassical, Victorian and Queen Anne architecture here, and the residents have taken great pains to preserve this heritage. You'll also find an even larger slice of history preserved in the interesting Cherokee County Museum next to the courthouse. And the cultural preservation and influence of the John C. Campbell Folk School at Brasstown on the line between Cherokee and Clay counties can't be overestimated (see the Clay County listing next). Many festivals and fairs also take place in the region, including an old wagon train tradition, which is a highlight of the July 4th celebration in Andrews.

We think you'll love this rural and remote, but far from isolated, county that its residents refer to simply as "God's Country." For more information, contact the Cherokee County Chamber of Commerce, (828) 837-2242, 805 Highway 64 W., Murphy, North Carolina 28906.

# Clay County

If you tend to look back with nostalgia to a simpler place and time, you'll want to travel to Clay County, western North Carolina's smallest county in the southwestern-most corner of the state. When trying to come up with adjectives to describe the 213-square-mile area, "quaint" always come to mind, along with "time-warp" and "Mayberry," that mythical North Carolina town featured on television's The Andy Griffith Show. The rolling farmlands and mountain-ringed valleys dotted with cattle and picturesque barnyards full of foraging chickens look more like paintings than a real landscape, but Clay County is real all right, and down-to-earth, too.

The county is as uncluttered and unpolluted a place as can exist on this planet today while being two hours, more or less, from Atlanta, Chattanooga and Asheville. Stretched along its southern border you'll find beautiful, mountain-encircled Lake Chatuge and its 132-mile shoreline. It's called the crown jewel of the Tennessee Valley Authority's (TVA's) many lakes because of its lovely setting. The lake, which North Carolina shares with Georgia, is not only pretty to look at; it's also prime area for fishing and other water sports. The county, with a population of 7,155, also has 65,650 acres of Federal Land, 43,400 of which make up part of the Nantahala National Forest, including the Fires Creek Bear Sanctuary in the high mountains of the northeastern corner of the county.

Much of Clay County is at an altitude of 1,900 feet, but peaks here can soar as high as 5,400 feet. In 1830, eight years before the Cherokees were forced out of the area, a single white settler, John C. Moore, moved here from Macon County with his wife and son. He grooved together a cabin of poplar logs in the Tusquitee section and cleared land for planting. After the Cherokee removal, people began to settle around Fort Hembree, a mile west of the present-day county seat of Hayesville, which had been built to enforce that removal. But even up into this century, Clay was an isolated area. It didn't become a county until 1861, when it was separated from Cherokee County. Its first industry, in fact, was a tanning company that sold its tanned deer hides at 12.5¢ per pound. Local folk used the hides to make shoes since there was no market where they could buy footwear.

Once the site of the county seat was chosen, W.H. Hancock donated 20 acres, and chestnut logs were split into rails to fence the town, with gates at different points to let the traffic in and out. The town was named after a state representative, George Hayes, who had helped establish the new county. Within a few years, Hayesville had a courthouse and a log jail that stood where the old brick jail (now the Clay County Historical Museum) now stands. The present redbrick courthouse at the center of town was built in 1888 and is on the National Register of Historic Places. The Licklog Players, a regional theatrical group, makes its home at Hayesville's state-of-the-art Peacock Playhouse.

Unlike so much of the rest of area, the population of Hayesville continues to shrink. Some 20 years ago, the town had a population of 385; today 279 live here. This lack of crowds and too-fast development is one of the county's main attractions. Despite its laid-back lifestyle, or perhaps because it, Clay County's schools have continuously ranked among the top four districts in the state. The students exceed state expectations in all area of achievement and performance, and Clay County posts one of North Carolina's lowest dropout rates, although the county spends only about 60 percent of the state's average local expenditure per student. According the Child Advocacy Institute in North Carolina, Clay County has ranked as the best place in the state to raise a child and has been first on the Children's Index (used to rate such factors as prenatal care, child abuse rates, family violence, education and income).

No place reflects the spirit of Clay County's magical preservation of some of the best aspects of the past better than the John C. Campbell Folk School at Brasstown. (Both the school and Brasstown straddle the Cherokee/Clay county line and both counties claim it, but since its just a bit closer to Hayesville than is it to Murphy, we are including it in this overview.) The school, established in 1925, is not only one of the best craft schools in the nation, it also teaches music, dance, fly-tying and gardening. The public is invited to traditional music concerts, dances, gospel sings, craft demonstrations and other events. (See our chapter on Mountain Crafts.)

This homegrown, do-it-yourself spirit is obvious in other areas of life here, such as the Mountain Valley Farmers Market, which takes place every Saturday of the growing season from 7 AM to 11 AM on the square in Hayesville. Everything sold at this market is guaranteed to be homegrown or handmade, including vegetables, flowers, eggs, herbs, honey, ornamentals, baked goods and crafts. It's also alive in the many festivals held on the town square. (See our chapter on Festivals and Annual Events.)

For more information, contact the Clay County Chamber of Commerce, (828) 389-3704, P.O. Box 88, Hayesville, North Carolina 28904.

# Graham County

There are sections of any county in Western North Carolina that can be called "rugged," but in 1872, when this area became a county, it was described by early explorers as "the most rugged, isolated, inaccessible land in all Eastern America." This 274-square-mile county is literally walled-off by the Snowbird Mountains, the Cheoah Range, the Yellow Creek Mountains and the western range of the Great Smoky Mountains called the Unicoi. Elevations in the county range from 1,777 feet to approximately 5,560 feet at the western end of the county, which adjoins eastern Tennessee.

Graham County, with a population of 8,000, is at the southwestern boundary of the Great Smoky Mountains National Park. Approximately 60 percent of the county is in the Nantahala National Forest, including the 3,800-acre Joyce Kilmer Memorial Forest of virgin timber. Here you'll find trees that are hundreds of years old and grow 150 feet tall. Some are 20 feet in circumference at their bases. This memorial forest is a part of the 14,000-acre Joyce Kilmer-Slickrock Wilderness Area, which offers more than 60 miles of wilderness hiking trails. A 27-mile portion of the Appalachian Trail also crosses Graham County.

In addition to other wildlife, the woods here are famous for their "Rooshians," German wild boars that were mistakenly thought to be from Russia. An English company that planned to establish a high-priced hunting preserve in the mountains shipped them, along with other exotic game, to America. The preserve was a failure, but the boars escaped, multiplied and are still hunted here and in other sections of the mountains where they are notorious for rooting up the native habitat. Graham also contains more than 100 miles of clear mountain streams and 14,000 acres of lakes, including the fjord-like Calderwood and Cheoah lakes, 2,800-acre Lake Santeetlah and 30-mile-long Lake Fontana. On the latter you'll find Fontana Village, a former town for the workers who built Fontana Dam in the early 1940s, now a large and lovely resort. (See our chapter on Resorts.)

Graham County was once the home of Chief Junaluska, the Cherokee leader who saved General Andrew Jackson's life in the Battle of Horseshoe Bend in 1814. Ironically, the same Andrew Jackson, while President of the United States, issued the order to round up and send the Cherokees to Oklahoma. Junaluska walked all the way back to North Carolina from that state and was ultimately successfully in his struggle to keep the remaining Cherokee people in the mountains. He was more than 100 years old when he died. His grave is in Robbinsville (population 777), Graham's quaint county seat. The first road into Graham County was built in 1838 for the specific purpose of removing the Cherokees from their native land. Now, a number of excellent highways enter the area from south, east and north. Graham County's borders are 79 miles from Knoxville, Tennessee, and 88 miles from Asheville.

For more information, contact Graham County Travel and Tourism Authority, (800) 479-3790, 427 Rodney Orr Bypass, P.O. Box 1206, Robbinsville, North Carolina 28771.

# Haywood County

No one knows exactly when the first white settlers moved into the area that now makes up Haywood County, but some came more than 200 years ago, lending their names to many of the geographic points of interest here, such as Mary Gray Mountain. Others whose names stuck to the areas that they settled— Allens Creek, Francis Cove, Stamey Cove and Ratcliffe Cove—have descendants whose names help fill the Haywood County phone book today.

Actually, back then, all the land that is now in Buncombe and Haywood counties, plus all the territory west to the Tennessee line—including the present-day counties of Macon, Jackson, Swain, Graham, Clay and Cherokee—were a part of Burke County. In 1792, Buncombe County was broken off from Burke, and in 1809 Haywood County was formed from a section of Buncombe and named for John Haywood, North Carolina's state treasurer from 1787 to 1827. Since local Cherokees moved west of the Tuckasegee River after the Revolutionary War, the new county was made up of 2,500 white residents.

Land grants were given to numerous English, Scotch-Irish, German and Dutch settlers.

Today, Haywood County has approximately 50,000 residents and consists of 546 square miles of craggy mountains, rolling foothills and deep valleys. The county is surrounded by the Great Smokies on the north, the Newfound Mountain Range on the east, the Pisgah Ridge on the south and the Balsam Mountain Range on the west. Elevations range from 1,400 feet at Waterville on the Pigeon River to 6,621 feet on top of Mount Guyot. In fact, 19 peaks in the county are higher than 6,000 feet, but currently, it's most famous peak is 6,030-foot Cold Mountain, the star of Charles Frazier's best-selling novel, *Cold Mountain*. Almost 40 percent of land is under the protection of the National Forest Service (Pisgah National Forest) and the National Park Service (24 miles of the Blue Ridge Parkway runs through the county).

Interstate 40 and a number of other highways, including U.S. Highway 19, U.S. Highway 23 and U.S. Highway 276 serve the county seat of Waynesville, 27 miles from Asheville. Haywood has three other incorporated towns: Canton, Clyde and Maggie Valley. Waynesville is one of the county's oldest towns, established in 1809 as a voting precinct in an area that had been called Mount Prospect. When the county courthouse and jail were built here in 1810, the town's name was changed to Waynesville. A charming, arty town with its pretty Main Street, Waynesville is perched on top of a small plateau with striking views in all directions. It has a population of 9,424 full-time residents.

Canton is the next largest town, with a population of 3,783. In 1861, there were only two houses where Canton now stands at the ford of the Pigeon River. After the Civil War, the hamlet known as Pigeon Ford grew to village size, and in 1881, the railroad track crept up into the Blue Ridge Mountain and stopped here, and the name was changed to Buford in honor of the railroad's president. In 1891, Buford was renamed Pigeon Ford, and in 1893, it was given the name it goes by today.

Canton's major industry, the Champion Paper Company, turned the place into a boomtown for a while. Still one of the area's major employers, Champion, under the threat of various lawsuits, is in the process of cleaning up the air and water pollution it created, and the town is starting to show signs of new life.

Of the other two municipalities, Clyde, the home of the excellent Haywood Community College, has a population of 1,189; and Maggie Valley, named for the young daughter of its first postmaster, has just 354 people. However, don't let Maggie Valley's small size fool you. This popular resort town 7 miles west of Waynesville draws thousands of visitors with its many attractions, including Ghost Town in the Sky, the music and dancing at The Stompin' Ground and the Cataloochee Ski Area, North Carolina's oldest ski resort.

With its easy access to Asheville, the Blue Ridge Parkway, and the Great Smoky Mountains National Park, more and more people are noticing how nearly perfect Haywood County is.

For more information, contact the Haywood County Chamber of Commerce, (828) 456-3021, 107 Woodland Drive or P.O. Box 600, Waynesville, North Carolina 28786, and the Maggie Valley Chamber of Commerce, (828) 926-1686, 623 Soco Road or P.O. Box 87, Maggie Valley, North Carolina 28751.

# Jackson County

Jackson County has a growing population of more than 28,000. Here, the Blue Ridge Mountains, with their dramatically shattered and steep rock faces, roll in long, forested ridges toward the southwest. Elevations in the county range from 1,850 to 6,450 feet, with many 5,000-foot summits, and cool, high valleys that sit at 3,000 to 4,000 feet. Rainfall and waterfalls are abundant in the region and lend, along with the 28,000 acres of national forests, a lush beauty to the landscape.

The prehistoric hieroglyphics made by ancient Native Americans who long predate the Cherokees on Judaculla Rock, between Cashiers and Cullowhee, give mute evidence that the area has attracted humans throughout the ages. (See our Attractions chapter.) However, it wasn't until 1828 that the first white settlers moved into the area. Yet, by 1850 there were enough people in this broad depression between two mountain ranges drained by the Tuckasegee River to warrant a new county. Both Haywood and Macon counties consented to part with some territory to form one.

The county stretches between the Balsam and Cowee Mountains and runs from the top of the Blue Ridge on the south to the Great Smoky Mountains in the north. The new county was named for Andrew Jackson, seventh President of the United States, and its first seat of government, Webster, for Daniel Webster, the American statesman and orator. Its settlements, strung along picturesque Tuckasegee River, grew into rustic towns. Three of them — Sylva, Dillsboro and Webster — are incorporated and three others — Cashiers, Cullowhee and Whittier — are not.

Sylva, at 2,039 feet in the northwestern section of the county, has more than 2,000 full-time residents. Most of the area's businesses and industries are here. The courthouse, which is reached by climbing 107 steps, was built in 1914 when the county seat was moved to Sylva. From its hilltop vantage point, the courthouse overlooks the river and the bustling town that stretches down two long streets.

A mile away, Dillsboro, founded in 1884, has a population of only 150, but its 50 or more shops have become home to the works of hundreds of artists and craftspeople. Thousands of visitors come here to ride the Great Smoky Mountain Railroad's excursion trains and to shop and spend time in this pretty and creative place. The famous old Jarrett House inn is also here. (See our chapter on Bed and Breakfasts and Country Inns.)

Webster, the former county seat and the site of a number of historic homes, has a growing population of 452. The town was built on an Indian mound, and the surrounding area offers sweeping views of the Tuckasegee River.

Cullowhee, situated in the scenic Tuckasegee River basin and surrounded by mountains, forests and streams, is the home of Western Carolina University. It has a student body of 6,700, has a faculty of some 325 professors and is the center of arts and culture in the county. The university also has the Mountain Heritage Center, with its museum and programs that preserve and promote this region's unique heritage. The annual Mountain Heritage Day, a festival of traditional music, crafts, food and fun that attracts thousands, is also held in Cullowhee.

Whittier lies at Jackson County's lowest elevation, 1,839 feet, in farming country on the border of Swain County. Dr. Clark Whittier of California, a relative of the Quaker poet John Greenleaf Whittier, established it. Nearby is the site of the Cherokee town of Stikohi or Stecoee, destroyed in 1776 in a preemptive strike after the Cherokees sided with the British at the beginning of the Revolutionary War. Later, Colonel William H. Thomas, white chief and friend of the Cherokees, established his home here and used treaty funds to buy land that became the Qualla Boundary, the home of the Eastern Band of Cherokees. (See our chapter on The Cherokee Indian Reservation.)

The deceptively small town of Cashiers actually has 1,250 residents with several thousand more in the area surrounding it. The town sits high up in a mountain valley at an elevation of 3,478 feet, not far from spectacular Whiteside Mountain, whose sheer rock faces are the highest vertical drops in the east. Right outside town, you'll find the historic High Hampton Inn, which maintains its old traditions and a fine golf course. In the early 1900s, several other inns were established in the area to serve Southern gentry escaping lowland heat and humidity. Many of these visitors ended up building summer homes, and the area has continued to attract vacationers and those who serve them. Nearby, for example, is Sapphire Valley, a huge community resort with all the amenities. Lake Glenville, right on the highway between Cashier and Cullowhee — along with other small lakes in the Cashiers area — offers fishing, boating, canoeing and other watersports.

A promotional writer once remarked that this area "is not only beautiful [to see]; it's a beautiful feeling, too." That's not hype.

For more information, contact the Jackson County Chamber of Commerce, (800) 962-1911 or (828) 586-2155, 116 Central Street, Sylva, North Carolina 28779 and the Cashiers Area Chamber of Commerce, (828) 743-5191, N.C. 107 S. or P.O. Box 238, Cashiers, North Carolina 28717.

# Macon County

Somewhere back in time, American Indians built a mound known as Nik-wa-si along the banks of the Little Tennessee River. A town council house was built on its top, and the lodges of the city were spread up and down the valley. This site formed the government and spiritual center of the Middle Cherokee tribe. A marker at the mound is now on E. Main Street in Franklin, Macon's county seat.

It was here that Hernando DeSoto came in search of gold in 1540; ironically, his expedition totally overlooked the wealth of gemstones for which this area is now so famous. DeSoto's visit, however, was relatively peaceful compared to what came later. In 1760, war broke out between the Cherokees and encroaching settlers, and the ancient town of Nik-wa-si was attacked by the British on several occasions and eventually destroyed. Finally, in the Treaty of 1815, the Cherokees gave up the land east of the Nantahala Mountains. (The Indians called the area Nantahala, meaning "land of the noonday sun," because only at midday did sunshine reach the bottom of the deep Nantahala Gorge).

This newly conquered territory became a part of Haywood County, and in 1817, Jacob Siler and William Britton journeyed from Buncombe County to set up a trading post, thus becoming the first white settlers in the area. They were not, however, the first to get to know it well. Botanist William Bartram had been hospitably received by the Cherokees during his stay at Nik-wa-si in 1777, and today's Bartram Trail, second in popularity only to the Appalachian Trail, actually passes through the city limits of Franklin. (See our chapter on Forests and Parks.)

Macon County was formed in 1828 and named after Nathaniel Macon, who served in the U.S. Congress for 36 years. The large territory that made up the original county was later reduced to eventually form all or parts of Cherokee, Jackson, Clay, Swain and Graham counties. Macon now covers 517 square miles and has a full-time population of about 26,000, though vacationers and second-home owners more than double that number every summer.

The town of Franklin, with a permanent population of around 3,000, was named after Jesse Franklin, one of the men who surveyed the town in 1820 and became governor of North Carolina within the year. The town was not incorporated until 1855. During the Civil War, Franklin was staunchly for states' rights and sent 1,000 of its 3,000 adult males to join the Confederate Army. More than 50 percent of these men became casualties. As the war drew to a close, Colonel George W. Kirk's Union regiment rode into Franklin and burned and looted the town.

Today, Franklin sits at the convergence of three major highways — U.S. Highway 441, U.S. Highway 64 and N.C. Highway 28 — at an elevation of 2,800 feet. Elevations in Macon County overall range from 1,900 feet in the Little Tennessee River basin to 5,500 feet at Standing Indian Mountain.

Macon County's other town is Highlands, which sits atop a mountain plateau at 4,118 feet, making it the highest incorporated town east of the Mississippi. Driving the narrow, curving stretch of U.S. 64 along the Cullasaja Gorge that connects the two towns is an adventure in itself and offers some of the most most-photographed waterfalls in the mountains, including Lower Cullasaja Falls, Bridal Veil Falls and Dry Falls. Highlands was purposely created in 1875 by Samuel T. Kelsy and Clinton C. Hutchenson, who bought the land from the Dobson family of Horse Cove, a small community south of Highlands. A year later, the two men sent flyers all over the country advertising the climate and altitude of the new "town," and by 1883, Highlands had 300 residents and was incorporated. Now its winter population hovers around 1,000, but that grows to 20,000 to 25,000 during the summer, not counting all the visitors who arrive to shop and take in the attractions of the surrounding area.

Where Franklin is rich in gemstones, Highlands is rich in botanical treasures. Macon County as a whole gets 50 inches of rain a year, but Highlands averages 70. This contributes to its unique plant life and led to the establishment of one of the oldest research centers in the country, the Highlands Biological Station, where scientists from all over the world study the area's flora and fauna. Highlands also has some of the most expensive real estate in the mountains. Summer residents support its fine shops, restaurants and cultural events.

Macon County loves its visitors, and tourism is its leading industry, but the county is not solely dependent on it. Forestry products, farming and ranching are still a large part of the local economy, and managers of new, nonpolluting industries are finding that this is an area where business and outdoor pleasure can be easily combined.

For more information, contact the Franklin Area Chamber of Commerce, (828) 524-3161, 180 Porter Street, Franklin, North Carolina 28734 and the Highlands Area Chamber of Commerce, (828) 526-2112, Fourth Street or P.O. Box 404, Highlands, North Carolina 28741.

## Swain County

Swain County was created in 1871 out of parts of Jackson and Macon counties and was named for David L. Swain, a former governor and president of the state university. Eighty-five percent of the county's 553 square miles is federal land, which means it's mostly mountains, forests, streams, rivers and wilderness. Yet this unspoiled, unhurried, unpolluted piece of paradise is just 60 miles from Asheville and 85 miles from Knoxville, Tennessee. The southern part of the Great Smoky Mountain National park comprises 216,662 acres of the county; the Nantahala National Forest manages another 21,000 acres. And the Blue Ridge Parkway finally comes to an end — or originates, depending on which way you're traveling — in Swain County and takes up 709 acres of county land. In addition, 29,000 acres of the Cherokee In-

dian Reservation, including the town of Cherokee with its many diversions, is also within the county. The elevation at Bryson City, the county seat, is only about 1,800 feet, while just a dozen miles away, as the crow flies, the mountains soar to 6,643 feet at Clingman's Dome.

Some of the state's most scenic rivers — the Nantahala, Oconaluftee and Tuckasegee — add their beauty and recreational possibilities to all the other attractions. The Nantahala River alone draws thousands of rafters and kayakers, and many whitewater outfitters, including the well-known Nantahala Outdoor Center, are in or near Bryson City. Some great mountain biking trails in the area attract such events as Knobscorcher, one of the state's most popular series of mountain bike races. Fontana Lake stretches into the county just a few minutes west of Bryson City.

Bryson City, population 1,250, is a lively, attractive town on the banks of the Tuckasegee River, with parks both along the river and on its islands. It's a popular stop for passengers on the Great Smoky Mountain Railroad, which offers train excursions through the area. As if that weren't enough, annual riverfests, high-school band competitions, chili cook-offs and other celebrations are held throughout the year. Needless to say, if you like the outdoors, you're going to love it here, because the 11,800 full-time Swain County residents have quick access to some of the largest expanses of wilderness areas in the eastern United States.

For more information, contact the Swain County Chamber of Commerce, (828) 488-3681, 16 Everett Street or P.O. Box 509, Bryson City, North Carolina 28713.

The North Carolina
Scenic Byways project
covers 1,500 miles of
picturesque North
Carolina back roads,
free of man-made
eyesores.

# Getting Around

Just a few decades ago, many parts of the western North Carolina mountains were considered wild and remote. A few rail lines reached the region, along with fewer paved, curvy two-lane roads. There's still a wealth of "wildness" to be found, but access to nature preserves and the area's other attractions is easy — so easy that literally millions of visitors travel here each year.

Numerous national and state highways now crisscross this ancient land of the Cherokees. The beautiful Blue Ridge Parkway winds its way southwest at an average elevation of 3,000 feet through the northern and central mountains, finally turning northwest in the southern mountains. It ends at Cherokee and the southern entrance to the Great Smoky Mountains National Park (see our Blue Ridge Parkway, The Cherokee Indian Reservation and National and State Forests and Parks chapters). Two busy interstate highways — Interstate 40 and Interstate 26 — intersect in Asheville, and just an hour or so south, I-26 crosses Interstate 85 at Spartanburg, South Carolina, on that interstate's busy leg between Atlanta and Charlotte.

Getting to many of the best hiking trails, the prettiest waterfalls and some of the most beautiful areas of the woods can involve taking Forest Service (F.S.) or unpaved Secondary Roads (S.R.). Many of these are steep, curvy, narrow, graveled and often one-lane with only small pullouts to get around oncoming traffic. Passing is mostly impossible and certainly inadvisable. But, if your vehicle is in decent shape and full of gas, we encourage you to explore these adventuresome byways. Don't, however, be in a hurry, and watch out for logging trucks. It's also a good idea to stop by the closest ranger station (the numbers are listed in the Forests and Parks chapter) and ask about road conditions. Bad weather sometimes washes out whole sections of these roads or creates landslides.

The Asheville Regional Airport, adjacent to I-26 and strategically located between Asheville and Hendersonville, is connected to Brevard by a five-lane highway. This more metropolitan central mountain area is also served by the ever-growing Greenville-Spartanburg International Jetport. The Charlotte-Douglas International Airport, one of the nation's busiest air hubs, is just two hours southeast. Some of the southern mountains residents, however, find that it's just as convenient (and closer) to fly out of the Atlanta-Hartsfield International Airport or from Chattanooga or Knoxville, Tennessee. The mountains also have several general-aviation airports.

A number of railroads provide freight service to the mountains, and Amtrak serves nearby Greenville and Clemson South Carolina, but rail passenger service in western North Carolina is limited to the delightful and popular railroad excursion company, the Great Smoky Mountains Railway. Based in Dillsboro, it makes March-through-New Year's Eve runs through the southern mountains (see our Attractions chapter).

## Driving in the Mountains

While airports and interstate highways make arriving in the western North Carolina mountains extremely easy, you'll be taking other highways and byways in order to enjoy all the scenery and attractions this region offers. And that brings up the subject of patience. Driving in the mountains can require abundant patience, but it's usually not the kind demanded by bumper-to-bumper traffic jams. In many areas you'll have the roads mostly to yourself, yet you may need to allow double the time it would normally take to drive a set distance. There are a number of reasons for this. The very nature of these steep-graded, twisting roads demands slower speeds. The top speed allowed on the Blue Ridge Parkway, for example, is 45 miles per hour, and some hairpin curves, even on major routes, require that you slow down to 15 miles per hour. (All milepost indications that are given in this book refer to the Blue Ridge Parkway.) In addition, sudden weather changes can bring blinding fogs or downpours. In winter, unexpected ice, snow and freezing rain can bring travel to a dangerous crawl.

Another thing that can — and probably should — cut into your traveling time is the incredible scenery you'll encounter along the way. Smoky mist curling out of a deep valley, a sunset turning a lake to rosy pink, a waterfall cascading down a mountainside, a highway pull-off offering a green-dappled vista that stretches for miles will tempt you to stop for a look. For those who enjoy the journey as well as the destination North Carolina Scenic Byways project covers 1,600 miles of picturesque North Carolina back roads, free of man-made eyesores. Each route was chosen for its particular attractions, based on historic significance or natural beauty, such as waterfalls, rivers or land formations.

Here in the mountains of western North Carolina, we are fortunate to have nine of these scenic byways, which cover 410 miles. You can identify the road you're traveling as a scenic byway from the distinctive white sign decorated with green mountains and blue waterways and the title "NC Scenic Byway" emblazoned at the bottom. The signs have been in place along North Carolina's mountain roads since fall of 1994.

The North Carolina Department of Transportation has issued a helpful, 91-page guide booklet for the entire state system of scenic byways. You can get a copy at most North Carolina welcome centers and DOT offices, or you can write to Scenic Byway Program, NC DOT, P.O. Box 25201, Raleigh, North Carolina 27611-5201. The publication is free, but in it, you'll find an envelope that allows you to make a much-appreciated donation.

Even if your schedule forces you to pass by all this beauty, other motorists may have traveled great distances just to enjoy the sights, and passing them safely may be impossible for several miles — another time when patience can be a lifesaver. In case you're the sightseer, remember to pull over, when you can do so safely, to let those who must hurry pass you by.

Pay attention and be ready to maneuver when driving through an area with "falling rocks" or "rock-slide area" signs. (Interstate 40 north of Asheville was closed for months in 1998 due to a huge landslide.) It's possible to come around a curve and find a fair-size boulder in your path. Likewise, be prepared to share the roads with pedestrians, bicyclists, horseback riders and a variety of wildlife. The latter is particularly prevalent at night.

At lower elevations, flash floods are common. These sometimes send rivers and creeks flooding across bridges and low-lying roadways. Never try to cross such stretches. The water can be deceptively swift and deep.

There are a few other rules you should be aware of.

• A new resident must apply for a driver's license within 30 days after moving here. Bring your out-of-state license, proof of insurance and proof of residency to a driver's license office of the North Carolina Department of Motor Vehicles; you'll have to pass a written and eye exam. Each county has a DMV office. Most offices are open from 8 AM to 5 PM but close for lunch from noon to 1 PM.

• New residents also must register their vehicles and purchase license tags within 30 days. The title of the car or name of the lien holder, proof of insurance and the odometer reading are required. Vehicles must also be inspected within 10 days of the registration date.

• The North Carolina Safe Roads Act forbids drivers to drink alcohol or to have an open container of an alcoholic beverage in the passenger area. All front seat passengers are required to wear seat belts. Children younger than 4 must ride in child safety seats. All children younger than 12 must wear seat belts in both the front and back seats. There is no longer an exemption for vehicles registered outside the state. Children younger than 12 may not ride in the open beds of pickup trucks except when an adult is present to supervise the child or the child is secured or restrained by an approved seat belt. Other exceptions are if an emergency situation exists, if the vehicle is operated in a parade with a valid permit or in an agricultural enterprise, or if the vehicle is being operated in a county that has no incorporated area with a popula-

tion greater than 3,500. The state requires that headlights be on whenever windshield wipers are on. Motorcyclists are required to wear helmets and use their headlights at all times.

# Commercial Airports

## Central Mountains

### Asheville Regional Airport
**708 New Airport Rd., Fletcher**
• **(828) 684-2226**

Western North Carolina's only commercial air service is centrally located on N.C. 280, just 15 miles south of Asheville, and is easily accessed from I-26. The airport is tourist-friendly and not far from all the most popular vacation destinations in the Land of the Sky. Hendersonville is 8 miles from the Asheville airport; Brevard only 20; Waynesville, 36; Sylva, 57; Cashiers, 58; and Highlands,

Photo: William Russ

The Linn Cove Viaduct at Grandfather Mountain seems suspended in midair. The S-shaped bridge, which was completed in 1983, joins the 7.5-mile Blue Ridge Parkway stretch between Blowing Rock and Linville.

69. This airport, the fourth-largest in the state, sees about 27 flights a day, 16 of which are jets. Four carriers — Comair, USAirways, Atlantic Southeast Airlines (ASA), and USAirways Express — carry passengers to hubs in Raleigh, Charlotte, Atlanta, Pittsburgh and Cincinnati. ASA is a Delta connection carrier and USAirways Express does the same for USAirways.

The 900-acre airport has a wide primary runway, 8,001 feet long and 150 feet wide, capable of serving large aircraft. A full-service fixed-base operator caters to all corporate, private and charter needs, offering fueling, tie-down and hangar storage, instruction and maintenance. Shuttle service is provided by Ground Transportation, which is available for long or short distances. Also on hand are four auto rental services: Hertz, Avis, Budget and National.

A special visual feature of the expanded 80,000-square-foot terminal is the new 40-foot-high atrium running the width of the terminal, which opens up the existing space with welcome daylight. Four boarding gates on two levels, increased parking (including 190 short-term and 590 long-term spaces), a new cafeteria and a lounge provide a pleasant seating area for those seeking sustenance. A welcome center, a gift and periodicals shop, a full-service travel agency, an ATM machine, lockers, and the U.S.S. *Asheville* display round out the goods and services available on-site at the Asheville Regional Airport.

# General Aviation

## Northern Mountains

### Ashe County Airport
639 Airport Rd., Jefferson
• (336) 982-3713; (336) 982-3899 after hours

This public airport, which is off U.S. Highway 221, has a 4,300-foot paved and lighted runway. Tie-downs, fueling, flight instruction and light aircraft maintenance are available. Rental cars are available from Ford and Chevrolet, (336) 246-8806, dealers in West Jefferson, 5 miles from the airport. The facility is open daily from 9 AM to 5 PM.

### Avery County Airport
U.S. 19E., Spruce Pine • (336) 765-4564

The elevation of this public airport is 2,750 feet. It has a 3,000-foot runway; fuel, flight instruction and aircraft maintenance are provided. Its hours are 8 AM to 5 PM Monday through Saturday and 1 to 5 PM Sunday.

### Elk River Airport
N.C. 194, Banner Elk • (336) 898-9791

Use of this private airport, which is in Avery County and has a 4,600-foot paved runway, is restricted to members and guests of the Elk River Club. No fuel is available, and the runway is not maintained (snow clearing, etc.).

### Boone Airport
346 Bamboo Rd., Boone
• (336) 265-3598

This airfield, though privately owned, is open to all visitors to the Boone area in Watauga County. The field contains a 2,670-foot paved runway. Use is restricted to daylight hours only. Rental cars or taxis service the airport. Also available are maintenance, fuel, air tours and flight instruction.

## Central Mountains

### Hendersonville Airport
1232 Shepard St., Hendersonville
• (828) 693-1897

This private airport, which began in a pasture in 1936, is open for public use. It has a 3,000-foot paved and lighted runway that can handle a wide range of aircraft. The facility also has hangar space, rents aircraft, provides fuel and maintenance, conducts flight training and offers scenic flights, including rides in vintage aircraft provided by the nearby Western North Carolina Air Museum.

## Southern Mountains

### Andrews-Murphy Airport
Airport Rd., Andrews • (828) 321-5114

Constructed in 1947 2 miles from Andrews on U.S. Highway 19/129, this Cherokee County facility has a 5,000-foot lighted, asphalt runway and provides fuel and opera-tional-level maintenance. It also offers hangars, tie-downs, plane rentals, charter flights throughout the country, air ambulance service, flight instruction and sightseeing flights, along with a pilot lounge.

### Jackson County Airport
**Gribble Gap Rd., Cullowhee**
• **(828) 586-2960**

The Jackson County Airport sits just above Western Carolina University at Cullowhee on Berry Ridge about 2 miles northwest of town. The original plan for a 3,200-foot runway was altered when a few hundred feet fell off the mountain during construction. Even so, twin-engine aircraft are accommodated on the present 2,900-foot asphalt runway. You can also obtain fuel, flight instruction, sightseeing flights, car rentals and on-call mechanic service.

### Macon County Airport
**201 Airport Rd., Franklin**
• **(828) 524-5529, (800) 435-9686**

The lighted runway of the Macon County Airport, called "the biggest little airport in North Carolina," has been extended from 3,800 feet to 4,400 feet. The facility, which is about 3 miles northwest of town off N.C. 28, provides both 100LL-octane gas and jet-A fuel. On-site car rentals, flight instruction, sightseeing tours

and hangar space are other services. The airport can do maintenance work on most general aviation aircraft.

# Bus Lines

## Central Mountains

### Greyhound Bus Line
**2 Tunnel Rd., Asheville** • **(828) 253-5353**
**350 Seventh Ave. E., Hendersonville**
• **(828) 693-1201**
**1880 Dellwood Rd. W., Waynesville**
• **(828) 926-2327**

The Greyhound Bus Line is the only bus company servicing the mountains at this writing. The Buncombe county terminal is located east of the tunnel that connects downtown Asheville to Tunnel Road. The Waynesville terminal is located at The Red Barn convenient store, and the Hendersonville office is easily located in downtown Hendersonville.

These Greyhound facilities provide passengers and package service to all major U.S. destinations. The terminals open at 8 AM but closing times vary so call ahead. The toll-free number for Greyhound central reservations is (800) 231-2222.

You seldom have to travel far, if at all, for a mountain-high view of brilliant star- and moon-studded nights scarcely dimmed by man-made lights.

# Climate:
# The Pretty Place

"It's just so darn pretty!" a newly arrived resident exclaims as she gazes toward ridge after ascending mountain ridge fading into lighter and lighter shades of blue.

"Oh, how pretty!" a local child sighs as she picks some wild yellow violets tucked beneath a granite outcropping draped in emerald-green moss.

"Now, I call that pretty!" a tourist remarks as he watches a crystal-clear river throw itself over a precipitous cliff and dissolve into a roaring, rainbow-filled mist.

"It doesn't get prettier than that!" a convention guest announces as shafts of sunlight break through gray winter clouds to spotlight the Asheville skyline and the snow-draped mountains beyond.

Though grand expressions such as "rugged," "spectacular" and "majestic" would be just as appropriate, "pretty" seems to be the word that is most often used by those experiencing these 18-plus small counties nestled near the bottom of the great Appalachian chain in the far-western corner of North Carolina. There are, in fact, several magnificent beauty spots scattered around the area, each of which is known to locals as simply "the pretty place."

The effort to capture the essence of these ancient, garden-like mountains in a word or phrase has been going on for centuries. The Cherokees, who managed to push the previous tribes out of the area before the Europeans came, referred to their home as Sa-koh-na-gas, which means "blue." It referred to the mountains' blue haze, which is created when sunshine and warm, humid air combine with the hydrocarbons produced by the region's thick forests. This single word was later elaborated into "the great blue hills of God" and "land of the blue mists."

The Great Smoky Mountains, on the other hand, were named for the fog that forms from temperature differences between the air and the mountains' many water sources. This cloud-like mist curls up from valleys and mountain peaks like smoke from a fire, particularly in the early morning, around sunset and after rains.

This blue mist and curling "smoke" are integral parts of the landscape of both the Great Smokies and the Blue Ridge Mountains as well as all the lesser-known cross ridges, such as the Graham, Nantahala, Snowbird, Balsam and New Found mountains.

The Land of the Sky, a more recent de-

## INSIDERS' TIP

During the past decade, Asheville and its surrounding mountains have become a "spiritual center" rivaling that in Sedona, Arizona. You can find centers for spiritual healing, worship and research in the area, as well as seminars or discussions hosted in downtown coffee shops. Check the *Asheville Citizen-Times* as well as the weekly *Spirit* (found in coffee shops and stores) for more information.

scription, was culled from the title of an 1876 romantic novel set in this tranquil region. The phrase has remained popular ever since, perhaps because our eyes, indeed, our very beings, are forever tempted skyward by the many mile-high peaks found here. And what a sky it is! Washed year round by frequent showers, its intense daytime hue, bracketed by rosy dawns and riveting, multicolored sunsets, has been given its own name: Carolina blue. And you seldom have to travel far, if at all, for a mountain-high view of brilliant star- and moon-studded nights scarcely dimmed by man-made lights.

## A Place for All Seasons

Others herald the region as the Land of the Four Seasons, for it is the long-lasting springs and autumns, plus mild winters and summers, that have attracted tourists and new residents to the area for nearly two centuries.

Crocuses and daffodils start pushing up through the earth in late February, and the false spring that usually occurs around this time of the year can have you hiking or playing golf in your shirt sleeves. In March, tulip magnolias, yellow forsythia and other early-spring flowers bravely brighten the landscape despite the real possibility of a late snowfall. By the end of April, dogwoods and silverbell trees are blooming everywhere, while in May, mountainsides are afire with flame azaleas, and the dense thickets of several species of native rhododendrons begin their bloom bursts, a show that lasts right into July. May is

also the time when a large portion of the mountains' spring wildflowers reaches its peak, including pink and white mountain laurels that coat the slopes and overhang roadways, rivers and boulder-strewn creeks.

By June, summer greens up the region with all the lush, ferny beauty of a rain forest. Daytime temperatures are mostly in the 70s and 80s, but as summer plays out, a week now and then can be hot and humid enough for air conditioners and electric fans, at least until a cooling thunderstorm comes along. Even then, by early evening, the thermometer drops into the 60s, cooler still at higher elevations, and it's an extremely rare night when it could be considered too hot to sleep.

At any time, you can find vast temperature differences by a quick change in elevation. For example, you can stretch the spring by several weeks if you follow the bloom from the valleys to the tops of the mountains, and in the fall, the color changes begin at the top and slowly work their way downward. The first hints of the colorful autumn to come are seen tinting some of the leaves at higher elevations as early as late August. In October, visitors by the thousands arrive to enjoy the brilliant red, yellow and gold foliage display (see our sidebar on autumn leaves in the Blue Ridge Parkway chapter).

By mid-November, the barren branches of deciduous trees give mountain ridges a crew-cut look, and previously unknown lodgings peer from their wooded perches enjoying "winter views." But, while nights may bring freezing temperatures, days can be pleasantly

---

**INSIDERS' TIP**

The sourwood tree is the only tree member of the big botanical Heath (Ericaceae) family, which includes mountain laurels and rhododendrons. Like those shrubs, the trees' gray or brown trunks, fissured into narrow scaly ridges, often grow in curvy and bent shapes. In July, when the sourwood produces its thick clusters of flowers, which are reminiscent of lily-of-the-valley, honeybees will pass up other blooms for the tree's sweet nectar. The result is sourwood honey. You'll see this prized sweet in stores and at roadside stands. It's a luscious souvenir of any trip to this region. The sourwood is also one of the first trees to light up the autumn mountainsides with its wine-dark to bright-red leaves.

Photo: Asheville, NC, Convention and Visitors Bureau

Breathtaking views inspire contemplation in the North Carolina mountains.

warm. It's usually not until Christmas that the first frigid Alberta Clipper roars south out of Canada. On those occasions, temperatures can plummet to zero or below for a short period of time, and from then until well into spring, short spurts of bitterly cold weather, along with occasional snow or ice storms, alternate with surprisingly pleasant winter days. In most places, the average snowfall in a typical year is around one foot, and even heavy snows usually disappear in a matter of days.

Rain, on the other hand, is a year-round event. Slightly more falls in the summer than the winter. (Winter wet fronts, rising up from the Gulf of Mexico, actually warm things up.) In summer, rain often takes the form of sudden crashing, late-afternoon and evening thunderstorms, sometimes with damaging winds and lightning. While such storms can spoil picnics and other outdoor activities, most residents enjoy these natural light-and-sounds shows, knowing the mountains offer protection from destructive tornadoes and hurricanes found elsewhere.

On the average, rainfall totals from 40 to

## INSIDERS' TIP

Temperature changes are drastic in the mountains. Always take a sweater or jacket when driving from low altitudes to higher ones. We experienced a sunny warm day in town, which turned into a windy, icy hailstorm only 2,000 feet higher at a picnic area on the Parkway.

55 inches per year, depending on the location. But in the rain belt, which includes a large part of Transylvania County and the southern sections of Jackson and Macon counties, 80 inches or more can fall in a typical year. All that water has to go somewhere, and much of it tumbles off cliffs and down mountainsides. Transylvania, which dubs itself the Land of Waterfalls, has more than 150 of these splendid water shows. Even so, the county hasn't cornered the waterfall market. Cascades and waterfalls, some of which plunge hundreds of feet, can be found in abundance throughout the region. (See our Waterfalls chapter.) So can seeps, springs, creeks, rivers, ponds and lakes. In fact, homes with such water sources are almost more the rule than the exception, and real-estate ads touting "bold streams" are common, even inside the city limits of some towns.

## A People for All Seasons

All in all, nature has done things beautifully right in this small corner of the world, and the people here are not far behind in their own accomplishments. While the stamp of the Cherokee and the original Scotch-Irish settlers have made a deep mark on the area, later arrivals brought — and keep bringing —

Photo: Hugh Morton

Azaleas in bloom on the majestic Grandfather Mountain.

a wonderful array of cultural diversity and talent to the region. The hills still resound with the sounds of dulcimers and bagpipes, but you can hear rock 'n' roll and classic symphonies too. Here in the mountains, star-studded concerts and homegrown festivals are likely to attract the same enthusiastic crowds, while high-tech industries and nationally known New Age spiritual centers thrive beside handmade crafts and old-time religion. The mix of Old World and contemporary lifestyles, played out against the dramatic backdrop of the mountains, make this region irresistible to visitors and transplants alike.

Western Carolina, indeed, seems to have much of the best of the modern world and has managed to hold on to a great deal that is wonderful from its past. As a part of their old mountain heritage, neighbors tend to respect your privacy yet always seem to be there when you need them. And, despite the influx of new residents from all over the country, the area maintains a thick overlay of old-fashioned Southern hospitality and friendly service. Menus range from Old South standards such as biscuits and gravy, grits, fried catfish and presweetened iced tea to the finest of continental cuisine and the best imported and domestic wines as well as local vintages. (See our Biltmore Estates and Winery chapter.)

Best of all, it's still a place where fear is far from being a part of daily life. In most places, you don't have to worry if you forget to lock up your house or car. So far, the cost of living is within reason too.

So there you have it: a mild climate, inexpensive, friendly, laid back, safe and — oh, yes — it's very, very pretty.

Native mountain cooking is still the finest representation of the flavor and heritage of the mountains.

# Restaurants

Mountain cooking brings to mind visions of fluffy biscuits, thick gravy, corn bread, soup beans, buttery grits, soft-cooked vegetables like okra and squash, fried chicken, molasses-based barbecue and, of course, deep-dish pies of all assortments. Certainly, that has been the history of mountain cooking from the early settlers onward: canning your own garden vegetables, wild berries and fruits and making any dough from scratch. You will find plenty of family-style restaurants specializing in this type of down-home cookin' throughout the region, but you also might be surprised to find quite a number of fine international restaurants as well as those serving contemporary American cuisine.

Over the past 10 years, North Carolina has experienced an upsurge in fine dining locales, largely attributed to those who have fled the urban sprawl in other parts of the nation in favor of the more tranquil surroundings of our mountains. Arriving with creative energy and widely diverse cultural backgrounds, these newcomers seem to soak up the sensory pleasure of their new landscape, many transforming this experience into culinary expression. The result: a regional microcosm of international fine dining that rivals many metropolitan areas of the Southeast.

Asheville and Blowing Rock are enjoying this restaurant boom in particular and have become dining destinations in their own right. You could easily plan a vacation around the culinary options in each of these cities and the smaller towns on their perimeters. Towns such as Banner Elk, Weaverville, Black Mountain, Hendersonville, Brevard, Waynesville, Bryson City and Dillsboro have also established quite a reputation for delicacies which makes the drive quite worthwhile.

Much of the delight of taking to the North Carolina mountain back roads is stumbling across a marvelous old inn or hotel. Back when travel to the big city was not as easy and eating out was a rare treat, many people in the rural countryside made their way to these establishments that regularly set a table for a Sunday crowd. Today these old inns and hotels are great gathering places, open to local residents and travelers alike, for sumptuous dining every day. Many renovated beauties are home to world-class chefs whose elegant fare seems quite at home amid the burnished patina of antique surroundings. And there are other innkeepers who take pride in maintaining the family-style atmosphere and good, basic cooking of their ancestors.

We have scoured the cities, small towns and countryside in an effort to provide you with a variety of quality-rich epicurean experiences, unique to our area. Our selections may vary greatly in style, from the smallest coffee shop with the best biscuits, burgers and chocolate malt in the area to the most elegant in haute cuisine from a French master chef. Variety is the spice of life, after all. Because of the scope of this book, we have undoubtedly missed some locales that would be worth

## INSIDERS' TIP

Dining-in can be a real treat when ingredients are made up of fresh, homegrown produce. During the growing season, most small towns here have farmers' markets once or twice a week, where local gardeners and farmers come to sell what they've harvested that morning. You can often find such things as homemade jams, jellies, relishes and the like here, too. Just ask around.

mentioning. There are also plenty of fast-food and franchise restaurants throughout the mountains, but since their menus don't vary from one place to another, we don't cover them in this chapter. As you make your way through North Carolina's mountains, we welcome your recommendations of your personal dining favorites. If they're not included here, tell us about them for next year. The restaurants are featured by region.

# Northern Mountains

## Alleghany County

### Marion's Old Homeplace
**$-$$ • Off N.C. Hwy. 21 S., Glade Valley • (336) 372-4676**

Just 10 minutes outside Sparta you'll see the signs to Marion's Old Homeplace in Glade Valley, one of those pastoral crossroads that once had a country store, a community school, farmhouses with wide front porches and a country doctor. The picturesque ghosts of the store and the school remain, and the old farmhouses grow lovelier with time.

Marion's Old Homeplace restaurant was built in 1921 as the 12-room home and clinic of Glade Valley's country doctor, G.F. Duncan. In 1927, as Dr. Duncan's health failed, the lovely old home passed to Glade Valley's Presbyterian minister, the Rev. Wayne Thompson. After his death in 1956, the house was purchased by Mr. and Mrs. J. Coke Marion. A longtime restaurateur, Mr. Marion parlayed his culinary expertise into the smoked-ham business, which he established next door. Marion hams were enjoyed in this northwest North Carolina and southwest Virginia region for decades. After J. Coke Marion's death in 1972, his son, Bud Marion, transformed the residence into an elegant country restaurant that offers hearty, family-style dining. Recently Yolanda and Rodolfo Prito bought the restaurant, keeping the same menu and theme of good country food.

Marion's Old Homeplace has become a mecca for loyal diners within a 100-mile radius of Glade Valley and Sparta. Folks from Winston-Salem, Boone, Charlotte and towns as far into Virginia as Pulaski regularly make the pilgrimage to the Old Homeplace for a favorite table in any number of rooms: the Sitting Room, the Sun Porch, the Bedroom and other dining rooms that have been named for their original use.

Servers present you with a basket of homemade breads and a plate heaped with your selection of the all-you-can-eat choice of tender country ham or old-fashioned fried chicken, homemade biscuits and genuine redeye or chicken gravy. Fresh vegetable selections change daily and include such old-time favorite side dishes as green beans, mashed potatoes and pinto beans with relish. Baked apples, buttered corn and homemade slaw round out the list. For dessert, you'll want to loosen that belt and order heavenly, freshbaked blackberry or apple cobbler served with a scoop of ice cream.

Marion's is open from the last weekend in April through the last weekend in October. Dinner is served on Friday and Saturday, and lunch and dinner are served on Sunday.

### Jubalo's
**$-$$ • Sparta Square, Sparta • (336) 372-5000**

Jubalo's, a popular, fun-filled neighborhood grill and pizza place, is down at the east end of Main Street in the town's newest shopping center. The Marions, of Marion's Old Homeplace restaurant, have done it again with their second Sparta restaurant, which is named for Bud Marion's father, Jubal Coke Marion. This great family restaurant is not only Sparta's source of great pizza, subs and other Italian American dishes, it's also a weekend stage for local bluegrass musicians who strut their stuff and bring on the "jubilation" evoked by the restaurant's moniker.

The pleasant, playful decor is an eclectic combination of modern styles. The wallcovering serves as a backdrop for old movie stars' photos, and the dining room is filled with wooden tables and chairs and green plants. Order your pizza with the usual toppings, or get a vegetarian pie. The most expensive one on the menu — a 16-inch supreme pizza with four toppings — costs a reasonable $12.50. You can also get Italian dishes such as lasagna and spaghetti or American-style steaks and subs. Jubalo's Reuben sandwich, corned beef on rye, old-fashioned quarter-pound hamburgers, rib eye steak sandwiches and French dips are other favorites. While you're waiting for the main meal and tapping your toe to the bluegrass, you can munch on appetizers, such as potato skins, chips and salsa, Buffalo wings, cheese sticks and fried mushrooms. Jubalo's serves imported and domestic beer, wine and wine coolers and serves lunch and dinner. The restaurant is closed Mondays.

## Ashe County

### Don's Mountain Aire
### Seafood & Steak House
$-$$$ • Intersection of N.C. Hwys. 16 and 163, Glendale Springs • (336) 982-3060

This friendly restaurant is a welcome sight after working up an appetite traveling the winding two-lanes of Ashe County. Don's is just minutes from Holy Trinity Church, up the road in Glendale Springs, where you can see the exquisite Ben Long fresco of the Last Supper. Don's Mountain Aire Seafood and Steak House is noted for its extensive selection of fresh seafood, delivered several times a week from the coast. Fresh stuffed flounder, salt-and-pepper catfish and stir-fried shrimp are customer favorites. You can also order a substantial filet mignon, chicken strips (grilled or fried) and even delicacies such as frogs legs. Don't forget to try out the generous-size, homemade hush puppies — they're delicious.

Well-prepared, ample portions and excellent service, overseen by the manager, Curtis Jarvis, have created a loyal clientele at Don's. The restaurant is open daily for dinner year round (hours change with the season), and there's a Sunday lunch too.

### Glendale Springs
### Inn and Restaurant
$-$$$ • 7414 N.C. Hwy. 16,
Glendale Springs
• (336) 982-2103, (800) 287-1206

Artist Amanda Smith is innkeeper and owner of this newly restored inn and restau-

Photo: Lavidge & Associates

Fontana Village Resort dining room offers delicious meals and an appealing mountain resort atmosphere.

rant in the 1892 structure of what once was first a general merchandise store, a circuit courthouse, a post office, a chapel, a community center, a boarding house and also an inn. (Read more about the Inn in our Bed & Breakfast and Country Inns chapter). Two wood-paneled dining rooms and one white and peach room offer guests plenty of seating, while side porch dining by the garden is also available. Lazy fans spin overhead in the main dining hall where creaking wooden floors and an old piano evoke visions of Saturday night country jamborees. Smith brings in a pianist or a country fiddler or two at times, but don't let the sounds of down-home music mislead you: The ambiance and cuisine are quite sophisticated.

Tables are covered in crisp linens, and the menu offers delicacies whipped up by Chef Christopher Magee, a graduate of the famed Culinary Institute of America. A former chef at Morton's in Chicago, Magee worked with Smith to create a varied and seasonally changing menu, offering sautéed blue point oysters, mushroom ravioli, bronzed spice-encrusted rib pork chops with goat cheese, mashed sweet potatoes and green apple and leek ragout, to name only a few of the dishes and their complements on the menu when we were there.

For our summer luncheon we tried the marinated grilled chicken club sandwich — fresh, tender and filling, and the fried salmon cake salad, with ratatouille, slim green beans and napa cabbage served with crisp Vidalia onion rings and roasted red pepper remoulade, all served with bread fresh out of the oven. A summer brunch offers everything from breakfast fare such as poppy seed pancakes and poached eggs with chicken confit potato croquettes to salads and hot entrees such as free-range chicken and dumplings, coriander-encrusted salmon and petite filet mignon with barbecued shrimp. Do call for

evening reservations, but feel free to walk in for lunch.

## Louisiana Purchase

**$$-$$$$ • N.C. 184, Banner Elk • (828) 963-5087, 898-5656**

If your heart belongs to the moss-draped avenues of New Orleans and the sultry tones of Bourbon Street, and your palate enjoys Cajun, Creole or classic French cuisine, you'll want to try Louisiana Purchase in Banner Elk. Owner and chef Mark Rosse has created a classy restaurant with the flavor of old New Orleans here in the High Country, with a special emphasis on classic French. Murals of the Big Easy lend atmosphere to this casually elegant restaurant, and live jazz on weekends adds to the New Orleans ambiance of Louisiana Purchase. The restaurant has an extensive wine list, too. Louisiana Purchase serves dinner Sunday through Saturday and stays open late on Fridays and Saturdays. Reservations are suggested.

## River House

**$$-$$$$ • 1896 Old Field Creek Rd., off N.C. Hwy. 16 N., Grassy Creek • (336) 982-2109**

The River House restaurant, part of a lovely 1870 farmhouse bed and breakfast inn, is a destination for diners from across the country and abroad. The rustic, antiques-filled restaurant boasts the culinary talents of Chef Billy Klein of Hickory, North Carolina. The fare at River House is an unusual mix of European haute cuisine and down-home American style. Unlike the petite-sized servings you get in some restaurants, where presentation is the primary goal, generous portions are guaranteed at River House — and the presentation is impressive too. Chef Klein combines the artistry of Europe with the flavors and substance of American food.

At River House, start with a popular appe-

---

**INSIDERS' TIP**

After dinner in Blowing Rock, head over to Kilwin's Chocolates and Ice Cream in the middle Main Street. It stays open until 10 PM and offers sundaes, malts and a wonderful assortment of ice cream on cones or in dishes. During the daytime, candy cooks stir and cook the fudge on marble slabs right before your eyes.

tizer known as gyoza, a spicy, scallop-shaped Japanese-style dumpling served with a lemon dipping sauce. Another tasty lead-in is roasted red peppers served with a mild, vinegar-based sauce. Homemade soups such as curried vegetable are always popular. There is a wide choice of River House specialties, medallion of beef tenderloin, baked tortellini and rotini, Southwestern vegetable lasagna and rainbow trout, as well as luscious desserts such as coeur a la creme, chocolate mousse cake and chocolate bourbon cake. The River house is only open for dinner.

# Avery County

## Bear Trail Lunch Counter

**$, no credit cards • 3 Main St., Newland • (828) 733-4050**

This little burger joint will give you a malt and a burger like you've never had! More than that, it's a fully functioning soda fountain, and the building itself was a former pharmacy. Sit at the black-top counter on a blue vinyl stool or at one of the wooden chairs and tables in the black-and-white-tiled locale. The young owner was working the grill like a Labor Day cookout as we sipped our thick chocolate malt, so rich it almost sufficed as lunch. Homemade soups and chili complement the fresh salads. Deli sandwiches are piled high with a quarter-pound of deli meats, lettuce, tomato and your choice of cheese. The Charbroiler provides various sizes of juicy burgers, while the chef on the grill can concoct a patty melt, Reuben, grilled ham and cheese and even a Western omelet. It's too good to pass by such quality, simple food.

For dessert, you have your choice of banana splits, ice-cream sundaes, giant cookie sandwiches, shakes, malts and apple pie. Wander to the back with your root beer float and check out the old *Life* magazines, antique pharmaceutical equipment and medicine bottles saved from the old drugstore.

## Black Diamond Bistro and Grill

**$$-$$$ • N.C. Hwys. 184 and 194, Banner Elk • (828) 898-7555**

The herbs growing outside the front door aren't just decoration. This upscale restau-

rant serves nothing but fresh food made from scratch. Executive Chef Mitchell Mack has created an ever-changing menu that draws on the best from American, European and Middle Eastern cuisine. Lunch includes a selection of soups and sandwiches, pastas and burgers and fresh seafood entrees. Start dinner with one of his inventive appetizers such as sautéed black tiger shrimp, spiced oysters with onion brulee or a saffron free-range chicken soup. From the open wood-fired grill emerge specialties such as rack of American lamb, Atlantic salmon and tenderloin of Angus beef. For those watching their weight (or saving calories for the fabulous desserts), Mack offers a spa entree nightly. The atmosphere in the main dining areas is contemporary chic, with a more casual atmosphere in the grill area. Lunch is served Wednesday through Sunday. Dinner is served nightly. Dinner reservations on weekends are recommended.

## The Corner Palate

**$-$$ • N.C. Hwy. 184, Banner Elk • (828) 898-8668**

This is one of those delightful places that seems to have it all. The shake roof and cottage-like construction make it feel like home. Window boxes and lace curtains add that individual touch. Blue-plate specials appeal to those who burn calories for a living, and pasta and stir-fries give it a contemporary flair. Add soups, salads, quiches, omelets, quesadillas, jambalaya, steak, chicken and fish entrees, and, well, what more could you want? A children's menu is also available. Lunch and dinner are served every day except Tuesdays.

## The Daily Grind

**$ • One block off N.C. Hwy. 184 at The Village, Banner Elk • (828) 898-8686**

Banner Elk's own fashionable coffeehouse is the Daily Grind. You can purchase fresh-roasted, organically grown gourmet coffees in bulk or, on a smaller scale, try an espresso, cafe latte, cappuccino and a host of other tantalizing beverages at this popular gathering place. Stop in early for a fresh bagel or muffin and stay late on Saturday night. Quiches, foccacia and other homemade breads, soups and chili are on the menu.

# Avery County: Beech Mountain

You'd expect a mile-high mountain to offer spectacular views, and Beech Mountain won't disappoint you. Take U.S. Highway 184, which turns into Beech Mountain Parkway and look for Pinnacle Ridge Road, which you follow until you come to Sunset Park. There are several overlooks going up the mountain beyond the park as you pass through residential areas. Small turnouts with decks allow you to stop and take a look. If you go at night, you can see the glow of Boone's city lights behind the mountains.

There are homemade candies and preserves for sale too. The cafe is open for breakfast and lunch through early evening Monday through Friday; it stays open until 10 PM Saturdays. Sunday hours catch the pre-church crowd, then the shop opens again from 1 to 5 PM.

## Famous Louise's
## Rock House Restaurant
**$-$$ no credit cards • U.S. Hwy. 221, Linville Falls • (828) 765-2702**

You can dine in three counties and never step outside the door of Famous Louise's Rock House Restaurant, which is just 3 miles north of Linville Caverns. This quaint family-owned restaurant has the distinction of sitting directly on the spot where Burke, McDowell and Avery counties meet. Signs point the way to your dining location — and favorite county — or you can sit near the fireplace, the spot where all three counties come together! Your food will be cooked in Avery County, picked up by your waitress in Burke County and very often served just over the line in McDowell County.

Famous Louise's serves bountiful lunch and dinner specials seven day a week: pork loin, country-style steak, roast beef, turkey with all the fixin's, fried chicken and a full complement of side dishes that includes pinto beans, snap beans and creamed corn. For seafood lovers, the Rock House receives deliveries from the coast three times a week. Leading the list of desserts is Famous Louise's spectacular strawberry rhubarb pie. Top this with a scoop of vanilla ice cream, and you're in dessert heaven.

This rock building has a somewhat checkered past that dates from the early part of the century when it was a Prohibition-era roadhouse followed by numerous incarnations as mediocre restaurants. Famous Louise's was the restaurant magic that finally "took," due chiefly to owner, Louise Henson, the original "Famous Louise," and her devoted family and loyal patrons. You can see Louise's personal photo gallery upstairs in the banquet room — that's her in one glossy framed photo from the 1950s, as a high school basketball star for Linville Falls! Take note of the set of unusual diamond, circle, square and heart-shaped rocks built into the outside wall at the restaurant's entrance. As you leave, you can pay your check in Avery County. Now where'd you leave that car? Was it in Burke or McDowell?

## Stonewalls
**$$-$$$ • N.C. Hwy. 184, Banner Elk • (828) 963-6161**

This rustic stone building is home to a marvelous family restaurant that specializes in American cuisine, specifically well-turned steaks, luscious prime rib and popular seafood dishes (the lobster is melt-in-your-mouth luscious). Stonewalls also has a superb salad bar. Stonewalls serves dinner only, seven days a week.

## Tartan Restaurant
**$-$$ • Hemingway St., Linville • (828) 733-0779**

Here's a cozy, unassuming restaurant near Grandfather Mountain that serves a pleasing array of mountain favorites with Scottish flair.

The menu offers breakfast, lunch and dinner specialties, but the unique lunch sandwiches seem to be the place's calling card. The Cameron is a hearty construction of cold roast beef slices topped with Swiss cheese, grilled mushrooms, onions and green peppers. You can make a meal of the Shad's Scottish Spud, a baked Idaho potato stuffed with ham, green peppers, mushrooms, onions and American and Swiss cheeses topped with sour cream and bacon bits. And since you're in Linville and in a Scottish mood, try the Loch Ness. In this dish, Nessie is disguised as a filet of flounder served with slaw and the Tartan's own tartar sauce. For dinner you can order steak, seafood and barbecued ribs.

Tartan's is open everyday for breakfast and lunch and in the spring and summer for dinner too.

## Madison County

### Cafe Nostalgia
**$ • Main St., Mars Hill • (828) 689-9556**
This cafe is rich in memories. Practically every inch of this diner is covered by mementos of the '30s, '40s, '50s and '60s. Matchbooks, posters, license plates, sheet music, autographs, post cards, glassware, old radios, theater photos, college memorabilia — you name it, you'll find it displayed at Cafe Nostalgia.

The lunch menu is a throwback to a simpler time also. Those beloved "Blue Plate Specials" of the Eisenhower era are daily fare here. You can also sample other standards of American pop-food culture: hamburgers, taco salads, pot roast, pork roast, chicken, chef salads and lasagna. Rounding out the menu are homemade desserts such as coconut pie, blackberry cobbler and the house specialty, Tar Heel Pie, a sinfully rich chocolate fudge extravaganza topped with walnuts.

Cafe Nostalgia also serves a late breakfast. Don't miss the spontaneous piano interludes of owner Harley Mays (sing-alongs are not uncommon). The establishment keeps a schedule compatible with neighboring Mars Hill College. Hours are 8:30 AM to 2 PM Monday through Friday, and the restaurant is closed during school breaks and holidays.

### Papa Nick's
**$-$$ • U.S. Hwy. 23 N., Mars Hill • (828) 689-9774**
Ten minutes north of town, tucked away high on a hill above the highway, is Papa Nick's, a superb Italian-American restaurant. Despite this hermit tendency, Papa Nick's has a loyal following that knows just where to go. The steep parking lot is full during the season, mid-April through October.

Don't expect an elegant atmosphere here. At Papa Nick's you feel like you are in the family dining room. Solid wood tables and chairs, a stone hearth, piled high with souvenirs and a hodgepodge of antiques as well as the daily-special boards only add to the festive environment of Nick's. Everything here is fresh and homemade. The garlic bread is served in the shape of small croissants, and the hearty soups are swimming with chunks of fresh vegetables. Sauces are also made fresh, as is the creamy garlic salad dressing. Linguine, shrimp scampi and a lusty seafood platter provide ample sustenance at Papa Nick's and are served in enormous bowls. No one leaves here without a doggie bag for tomorrow's lunch. Hours vary by the season.

## Mitchell County

### Cedar Crest
**$-$$ • 311 Locust St., Spruce Pine • (828) 765-6124**
On Locust Street, one of the two main thoroughfares of tiny Spruce Pine, you'll notice numbers of people making their way into an obscure doorway. Follow them. They're heading for the Cedar Crest, a popular local restaurant in an old storefront with a rustic interior. The ceiling still boasts the old pressed tin found in so many turn-of-the-century mercantiles. Cedar Crest has a menu of hearty selections. You may order a beef specialty — prime rib, filet mignon, rib eye or New York Strip — cut fresh to order. Also popular are Cedar Crest's rainbow trout and the house specialty, trout amaretto, pan-fried boneless trout topped with sautéed almonds and amaretto. The tender baby-back ribs, smoked on the premises, are a local favorite. The Friday night buffet features all-you-can-eat cat-

# Watauga County: Howard's Knob Park

This is one of the best views in Boone, since it's at the highest elevation in the city. The 5.7-acre park has picnic tables that are often used by business people for a peaceful lunchtime getaway from May through October. To find the park, turn at the Daniel Boone Inn on King Street and then immediately turn right, following that road to the top of the hill.

fish and popcorn shrimp. Summer and winter hours vary slightly, but breakfast, lunch and dinner are served year round. The restaurant is closed Sunday and Monday.

## Watauga County

### Daniel Boone Inn Restaurant
**$-$$ • 130 Hardin St., Boone**
**• (828) 264-8657**

Since 1959, this old-fashioned, family-style restaurant has been drawing locals and visitors for hearty dining in a historic structure that was Boone's first hospital. For a fixed price, big serving bowls and platters of food are brought to your table, including fried chicken, country-style steak, biscuits, mashed potatoes, green beans, slaw, corn, fresh-stewed apples, dessert and beverage.

In the summer, lunch and dinner are served each day. In the winter, dinner is served at 5 PM. Lunch and dinner are served on Saturday and Sunday starting at 11 AM. A large family-style breakfast is served 8 AM to 11 AM every Saturday and Sunday throughout the year. Children ages 4 to 11 receive discount meals, and meals are free for children 3 and younger. Reservations may be made for groups of 15 or more.

### The Gamekeeper Restaurant
**$$$-$$$$ • Shull's Mill Rd., Boone**
**• (828) 963-7400**

The Gamekeeper is in a rustic lodge-style converted house built in 1926 near Yonahlossee Resort on Shull's Mill Road between Boone and Blowing Rock. This elegant restaurant, with starched linens, impeccable service and unforgettable fare, accommodates guests in cozy private nooks warmed by a fireplace.

Dining here is a culinary experience: The menu is composed entirely of wild game — and not just venison either. Selections often include boar, antelope, venison and duck. The restaurant has a selection of fine wines to complement these exotic dishes.

From January through March, the restaurant serves dinner Friday and Saturday only. It's open every day except Tuesday through the summer. Reservations are required.

### Howard Street Grille & Cottonwood Brewery
**$-$$ • 161 Howard St., Boone**
**• (828) 262-1221**

Owner Bart Conway brings authentic Mexican and Southwestern cuisine to the mountains at this great restaurant, at its new roomier location on King Street.

This is food with substance and style. The lunch menu lists such classics as black beans and rice, a chipotle-shrimp Caesar salad and huevos rancheros (corn tortillas layered with jack and cheddar cheeses and topped with two fried eggs and red chili sauce). You can also add mesquite sausage to your huevos rancheros. Select dinner from either the Mexican or Southwestern menu. On the Southwestern side are such choices as the Cottonwood Cazuela, a Santa Fe-style casserole prepared fresh daily with changing ingredients; and Anasazi chicken, a sautéed chicken breast with ancho chilis and goat cheese finished off with a Madeira wine sauce and tobacco onions. From the Mexican menu comes taco al carbon, which is your choice of steak, white-meat chicken or shrimp grilled over mesquite wood, folded into a flour tortilla with lettuce, tomatoes, cheese and sour cream. For health conscious Mexican food lovers, Cottonwood prepares vegetarian and tofu burritos.

Have you ever tasted a chocolate enchilada or an ice cream frito? Cottonwood's chocolate enchilada crepe is filled with chocolate mousse and topped with a heavenly Kahlua sauce and whipped cream. And yes, you can make an ice cream frito. Cottonwood's version is ice cream rolled in a crunchy coating, deep fried (quickly!) and served smothered in chocolate Kahlua.

You can slake your thirst from Cottonwood's own award-winning brewery, which produces pure, all natural ales. Wines, imported beers, espresso, herb tea, sangria and the classic Margarita are also available.

Cottonwood Grille & Brewery is open daily for lunch and dinner and into the late evening.

## Jackalope's View
**$$-$$$ • Beech Mountain Pkwy., Banner Elk • (828) 898-9004**

Jackalope's View, located in Archer's Inn on Beech Mountain, may indeed have the best view on the mountain, aside from the ski lifts that is. (See our Bed & Breakfast and Country Inns chapter for more on Archer's Inn.)

Surrounded by lush flora, the restaurant faces the Grandfather Mountain ridge directly opposite. Open for dinner year-round, the restaurant and bar retain a familiar feel thanks to the individual attention of the proprietors. The hosts have created an eclectic menu of exquisitely crafted dishes, which changes seasonally. Wild game, including antelope steak, makes an appearance several times a year. Fresh herbs from the garden add bursts of flavor to the fresh brochette, thinly sliced toasted French bread with diced garlic, tomatoes and fresh basil sprinkled over the top. Each entree, be it filet mignon, shrimp ziti, or tender crab cakes, shares the attractively presented dinner plate with fresh vegetables hand-picked from the local farmer's market by the chef. Do not miss the pommerey mustard vinaigrette on the garden salad served with the entree.

Ceiling fans turn slowly overhead as the lights begin to twinkle in the valleys below and the time for dessert and coffee pulls nigh. The fresh homemade desserts are impossible to resist, complemented with several different coffees and espressos made in the beautiful brass machine looming over the bar. We were treated to an exhilarating strawberry sorbet, so pungent it literally burst into flavor in our mouths. A terrace provides for outdoor dining on warm summer evenings.

## Murphy's Restaurant & Pub
**$-$$ • 747 W. King St., Boone • (828) 264-5117**

Murphy's has been a landmark in Boone for the last nine years. In downtown Boone, the drawing card at this busy place is its imaginative menu, which attracts a lively crowd to its four dining venues. The traditional dining room is furnished with comfortable booths. The sunny deck out back is an option until the end of October, when temperatures start to dip in the High Country. The bar area is a friendly place for a quick bite to eat, a little liquid refreshment and a gander at a favorite sports channel on wide-screen TV, and an attached game room.

Appetizers at Murphy's are advertised as "munchies," but you could make a meal on some of them. Try the Monterey jack cheese sticks, which are dipped in beer batter and fried until they're crunchy with a soft middle. There's also white pie quesadilla, a tortilla topped with Gruyere and feta cheeses, basil and garlic and served with guacamole, salsa and sour cream. Murphy's smoked mountain trout comes halved, served chilled with sliced onion, egg wedges, a cucumber dill sauce and crackers. Remember, these are just appetizers! On to lunch.

Burgers, barbecue and subs all have that special Murphy's touch. They do serve traditional grilled or smoked burgers. A vegetarian nut burger is topped with a nest of sprouts, bread crumbs, spices, almonds and sunflower seeds topped with Monterey jack cheese, tomato and onion. Murphy's specializes in combination salads ranging from grilled chicken to seafood, fajita, spinach and chef salads.

For dinner, there are Murphy's hand-cut

rib-eye steaks, baby-back ribs, pasta dishes and much more. All are served with fresh salad, sourdough rolls, rice pilaf or baked potato. Desserts include corporate lawsuit ice-cream pie, fudge brownie with Kahlua and homemade carrot cake. A particular favorite at Murphy's is Sunday brunch, which features classic items including eggs Benedict, Belgian waffles and specialty omelets. Murphy's is open for lunch and dinner with the bar open until 1 AM seven days a week.

## Our Daily Bread
**$ • 627 W. King St., Boone**
**• (828) 264-0173**

Our Daily Bread may become part of your daily routine after you try one of their sandwiches, homemade soups and chilis and homemade pumpkin bread. The sandwiches are imaginative combinations, such as the Jamaican, a generous portion of turkey topped with pepper cheese and sweet relish on a roll; and the South of the Border, roast

Photo: Constance E. Richards

Boone is a college town, so many coffee houses offer a wide variety
of interesting reading material.

beef with pepper cheese and a spicy picante sauce. If you want a hot dog with a twist, you can order Our Daily Bread's not dog, a tofu-based vegetarian hot dog. But the most engaging items on the menu have to be the chilis (vegetarian chili is one choice) and homemade soups ladled into an edible bowl of scooped-out sourdough bread! Blue and white checkered tablecloths add a bit of color to this otherwise pleasantly plain locale. The simple good food and selection of imported beer and wines are calling card enough for the cafe.

Try the teas, juices and those trendy flavored waters; you can also take home your own custom-ground gourmet coffees. The restaurant is closed Sundays.

## The Red Onion Cafe
**$$ • 227 Hardin St., Boone**
**• (828) 264-5470**

Walk into this chic establishment and you'll think you've found an art gallery until the tempting aromas and solicitous waitstaff confirm that, indeed, you've found The Red Onion Cafe. Sitting in the heart of the university district, the restaurant serves creative soups, salads, sandwiches, quiche, pasta and specialty items.

Prints, paintings and sculpture by local and regional artists surround diners, and all of it is for sale. The plant-draped piazza outdoors is also a popular dining spot, weather permitting.

Culinary styles include Southwestern, Italian and American. The Southwestern Wrap, a new twist on the traditional burrito, has sautéed vegetables blended with a black-bean sauce and cheddar cheese wrapped in a flour tortilla and served with tortilla chips and a spicy salsa. On the Italian side, fettuccine verde with shrimp is a mix of spinach fettuccine, fresh mushrooms and diced tomatoes tossed with a creamy parmesan sauce and served with six tasty tiger shrimp. The Red Onion Cafe's grilled steak Caesar salad is a combination of spicy, marinated grilled slices of New York strip served on a bed of mixed greens and tomatoes with croutons, parmesan and Caesar dressing, served with a whole wheat roll. The cafe is known locally for its bountiful salad bar and ample desserts,

including the house specialty, the Horace cookie — a butterscotch brownie with pecans, warmed and served with vanilla ice cream. Wines, imported and domestic beers, herb teas and flavored waters head the beverage list.

The Red Onion is open daily for lunch and dinner.

## The Village Cafe
**$$-$$$ • Main St., Blowing Rock**
**• (828) 295-3769**

It is a rare experience when a restaurant can transfer you to distant shores, evoke forgotten memories, or fulfill long-sought after daydreams. Step off Main Street in Blowing Rock and down the path beside Kilwin's. At its end you'll find a tree-shaded bower and The Village Cafe. It could be an English garden in Britain's Lake District, it could be a flowered courtyard in the Provence, but we only have to travel within our own mountains to find this jewel. The restaurant is tucked into the Randall Memorial Building, a quaint, white frame cottage on the National Register of Historic Places that housed a mountain crafts co-op in 1907. Later the building served as the Blowing Rock Village Library.

Today, with her culinary expertise and style, chef Annie Esposito has transformed this site into one of the premier dining destinations in the High Country. A constant stream of guests makes the pilgrimage down the path to the cafe for exquisite breakfasts and lunches and deliciously crafted desserts. The thoughtfully chosen menu makes use of the best in flavors and fresh ingredients. Imagine the soft sweetness of Belgian waffles made to order, garnished with plump, fresh raspberries, blueberries and strawberries and an unbelievably light honey syrup.

A casual lunch of Greek chicken salad serves up tender, poached chicken breast on a bed of fresh greens blended with herbs, feta cheese, sliced cucumbers, black olives and scallions. Other entrees include garlic and parsley linguine, orzo pasta and wild mushrooms with Marsala and hazelnut cream sauce, and Pawley's Island crab cakes with a Dijon sauce and fresh vegetables. Plenty of hot and cold sandwiches are other lunch selections (the smoked turkey and cheddar or the substantial Ploughman, a grilled marinated beef served medium rare with lettuce, tomato and spicy horseradish Dijon sauce, are good choices). Most memorable are the variety of fresh soups daily — mushroom and hazelnut, sweet corn and green-pepper sauce, tomato and smoked gouda. A Cafe specialty is the marvelous homemade Argentine fugasa bread, which you may also pick up to take home. Desserts were flowing out of the kitchen the sunny afternoon we spent there. Diners were not being shy with the bananas Foster and a warm pear-and-hazelnut crisp . . . à la mode. For refreshment, choose a Mimosa, a delightful combination of freshly squeezed orange juice and champagne. Sangria, fresh fruit juices, cappuccino, espresso and hot chocolate are also available. The delightful staff even picked fresh flowers out of the garden for a birthday bouquet gracing our table.

You may dine in the courtyard under the trees in fair weather. The Village Cafe is open seasonally, from late April to late October. Breakfast and lunch are served from 8 AM to 3 PM daily, except Wednesdays.

### Woodlands Barbecue and Pickin' Parlor
$ • U.S. Hwy. 321 Bypass, Blowing Rock
• (828) 295-3651

Woodlands has been a favorite High Country dining landmark for several decades. The menu features chopped and sliced pork and beef, ribs, chicken and home-style Mexican food. Woodlands caters too. It's open for lunch and dinner seven days a week. There's also live acoustic entertainment with no cover charge.

# Yancey County

### Garden Deli
$-$$ • Town Square, Burnsville
• (828) 682-3946

Ed Yuziuk is a transplanted mountaineer from New York City. This former owner and editor of *The Yancey Journal* couldn't find a real New York-style deli like the ones he remembered as a boy, so he opened his own. Satisfaction at last! All deli-lovers who happen upon this great little spot couldn't be more satisfied. During the summer season many customers prefer to eat on the spacious outside deck shaded by wisteria vines and willow trees.

Ed and wife Carolyn prepare menu favorites the way they like to eat them, sending to New York for such authentic deli ingredients as Grossinger's Rye or real New York cheesecake. They meticulously slow-smoke their own meat for barbecue, removing all visible fat and hand-chopping the meat that is then blended with the Yuziuks' own barbecue sauce. Carolyn's three-bean chili, pastrami sandwiches, super-thick subs and unique Reubens are popular items. The Garden Deli Reuben is a New York-style blend of fresh corned beef topped with Ed's family-secret, Ukrainian-style Kapusta kraut and then covered with melted Swiss on that famous Grossinger's rye bread.

The deli is open for lunch Monday through Friday all year and is open Saturday during the summer.

### Mountain Breeze Restaurant
$-$$ • Banks Shopping Center, Burnsville
• (828) 682-3002

Steaks, seafood and real pit-cooked barbecue are the main attractions at this popular spot. The menu also includes sandwiches, breads, salads and desserts. It's where the locals eat, which is always a good recommendation. Mountain Breeze is open seven days a week for breakfast, lunch and dinner.

### Nu-Wray Inn
$-$$ • Town Square, Burnsville
• (828) 682-2329

As long as anyone in these parts can remember, this legendary inn, c. 1833, has been serving up family-style meals. The native mountain heritage of good, basic food is in capable hands at the Nu-Wray Inn, an establishment that perpetuates tradition.

The Nu-Wray serves breakfast and dinner, offering an old-fashioned bounty that strains the tables of the communal dining hall. Food is served on platters and in large bowls, and all guests help themselves. Breakfast (complimentary for inn guests) includes country ham, grits, scrambled eggs and sausage or bacon. Or you can sample the inn's famous flaky homemade biscuits smothered in local honey and old-fashioned apple butter. Supper is another culinary accomplishment: fried chicken, turkey, ham, homemade whipped potatoes, corn on the cob, salads and fresh seasonal vegetables straight from the garden. In our opinion, no mountain supper is complete without cornbread and biscuits, especially at the Nu-Wray Inn, so take a crusty piece of cornbread to put alongside your homemade biscuit. Finish off this hearty repast with desserts like Grandma used to make: shortcake, steaming fruit cobblers and flaky-crusted fruit pies.

The Nu-Wray Inn celebrates Thanksgiving with a harvest bounty, but you must make reservations well ahead of time. Some guests have booked this meal a year in advance!

Breakfast is served every day year round; supper includes breakfast and lunch items, served from 1 PM onward on Sundays. (There is no evening meal on that day.) Dinner seatings vary with the season: June through October, dinner is served Monday through Saturday; November through April, dinner is served Friday and Saturday only. Reservations are always suggested.

# Central Mountains

## Buncombe County

### Cafe on the Square
$-$$$ • 1 Biltmore Ave., Asheville
• (828) 251-5565

This elegant cafe that opened in 1990 set the tone for the resurgence of Pack Square. And not only the Square, but its neighboring thoroughfare, Biltmore Avenue, have emerged in the last five years as the corridor for culinary and artistic expression in Asheville. At Cafe on the Square, at the corner of Biltmore Avenue and Pack Square, conversation sparkles at tables framed in the tall windows of this elegant turn-of-the-century building. With this light and airy cafe, the transplanted restaurateurs/owners have brought a West Coast flavor blended with a sophisticated continental style to the mountains.

Angel hair pasta, a vegetarian quesadilla and a marvelous spinach and feta torte are highlights of the luncheon menu. For dinner, you can choose from grilled ginger lime chicken with a coconut curry sauce, hickory smoked pork loin chops with roasted shallots and pecan butter or the Szechuan linguine with vegetables in a spicy peanut sauce. In the warm season, the cafe sprawls out onto the cobblestone sidewalk with tables and chairs shaded by red umbrellas.

The cafe is closed Sunday but serves lunch and dinner the rest of the week.

### Blue Moon Bakery and Cafe
$ • 60 Biltmore Ave., Asheville
• (828) 252-6063

Blue Moon is essentially a gourmet bakery that offers great stone-ground, organic grain breads and the lovely imported cheeses, olive oil, vinegars, jams and pastas that accompany these heavenly loaves so well. But it is also a trendy lunch spot.

The aroma of fresh bread greets you at the door of the shop that's housed in one of those grand old renovated storefronts on the revived Biltmore Avenue. You can pick up your daily loaf quota and dawdle for a casual lunch with friends at intimate little tables, sampling Blue Moon's savory homemade soups and sandwiches. Round out your midday meal with pastries or maybe focaccia, the crisp and chewy Italian flat bread topped with rosemary. Cappuccino, espresso and juices are in abundant supply. Do allow ample time for the ordering and serving process, as creative confusion reins behind the counter.

Blue Moon is open Monday through Saturday for breakfast and lunch, Sunday for brunch, and newly in the evenings for light dinners. Call, as the times are not yet set in stone.

### La Caterina Trattoria
$$-$$$ • 5 Pack Square, Asheville
• (828) 254-1148

Robbin and Victor Giancola arrived in Asheville several years ago. Like many, they were looking for that perfect place to get away from their former, hectic existence in California. When Victor, an experienced chef at a top-rated restaurant in San Francisco, decided to put the brakes on the fast pace, he couldn't leave his first love, the restaurant business. The result was the Giancola version of a neighborhood Italian trattoria as he remembered it from his youth in the Bronx. He christened his restaurant La Caterina in honor of his mother, whose picture, a lovely sepia wedding photo of decades ago, hangs in the restaurant.

The flavorful menu is devoid of the usual heavy sauces most people expect with Italian cooking. These are true Southern Italian dishes, just like Victor's mother used to make.

"No spaghetti and meatballs here," says Victor. Instead, try dishes like roast chicken with rosemary, light pastas (the pasta is made fresh daily right in the front window), Italian greens such as arugula and light desserts such as zabaglione, an Italian egg custard with fresh fruit topping. Preparation is the key here, light and spontaneous, just like the atmosphere. A cafe with an overhead awning sprawls out onto the town center. These are the prize tables — diners stake them out all evening, sipping wine and people watching. Be sure to peruse the extensive wine list, more than 100 to choose from at quite economical prices.

La Caterina serves Sunday brunch. Dinner is served seven days a week. Lunch is Tuesday through Saturday.

## Salsa
$ • 6 Patton Ave., Asheville
• (828) 252-9805

This relatively sassy little downtown restaurant is short on space but big on taste and innovative cuisine. Salsa is the creation of Hector Diaz, who brought the wonderful culinary heritage of his native Puerto Rico to this popular eatery.

This is not the usual quickie Tex-Mex joint. It's gourmet Mexican and Caribbean fare with pizzazz.

The menu includes herb chicken quesadillas and tacos made salsa-style (fire-roasted pepper tacos and black bean and goat cheese tacos, both served with pico de gallo salsa, are two favorites). The Caribbean menu sparkles with unique ingredients, such as plantains with gazpacho salsa. Exotic root vegetables, unique to the Caribbean, as well

as sweet potato and pumpkin are regular ingredients in the gigantic burritos and enchiladas. Pinonos, plantains stuffed with a variety of fresh herbs, meats, and vegetables, are always on the specials.

Whatever you chose, it's guaranteed to be an explosion of flavor. The hearty servings usually mean you have something for lunch tomorrow as well. Salsa is a staple with locals, and since showing up in *The New York Times* and *Southern Living* recently, Salsa has gained a following with folks just visiting or passing through. Be prepared for a wait in the high season. Waiting diners mill around on the sidewalk in front talking about what they'll try *this* time.

Salsa is open Monday through Saturday for lunch and dinner.

## Sycamores
**The Blake House Inn**
**150 Royal Pines Dr., Arden**
• (828) 681-0420

Sycamores is located on the first floor of the Blake House Inn. Chef Kevin Rice and Chef Andrew Loesch have created an exciting menu of contemporary southern cuisine for lunch, dinner, and Sunday brunch. There are two formal dining rooms with 14-foot ceilings and original ornamental plaster moldings from England. Both have gas-log-equipped fireplaces with original mantles, antique buffets and original antique pieces of art. Each dining room seats 30 to 35. A large patio and covered porch allow guests to enjoy the fresh mountain air and beautiful landscaping with their meals. (See our Bed and Breakfast and Country Inns Chapter for more information on The Blake House Inn.)

## 23 Page Restaurant at Haywood Park
$$-$$$ • 1 Battery Park Ave., Asheville
• (828) 252-3685

This elegant restaurant is a highlight of the Haywood Park Hotel and of downtown Asheville. Over ten years ago this establishment set the standard for fine dining in the downtown district and continues to feature the finest American cuisine, including such specialties as rack of lamb and succulent sea-

food filets. The menu changes every few weeks. 23 Page serves dinner only, seven days a week, and reservations are suggested.

## The New French Bar
**$-$$ • 1 Battery Park Ave., Asheville**
**• (828) 252-3685**

This classy little bistro in an intimate space adjacent to the lobby of the Haywood Park Hotel in downtown Asheville.

At the New French Bar soups are always excellent, from mushroom and green pepper to tomato bisque. Bread made fresh daily at the restaurant complements each meal. Try a baguette filled with menu offerings, such as Italian arugula greens, brie, peppers and other tasty tidbits. Elaborate salads with seafood and fresh greens garnished with fresh and unusual fruits are popular with the outdoor lunch crowd.

Make your dessert a thick rich brownie, or a glass of sweet aged port. Coffee drinks heat you up after the theater. NFB also has excellent outdoor dining. Dinner reflects the same concern for freshness and unique tastes. The cafe is closed Sundays.

## Uptown Café
**$-$$ • 22 Battery Park Ave., Asheville**
**• (828) 253-2158**

In the heart of downtown, the Uptown is a local favorite. Whatever you order will be fresh and hearty, filled with flavor and worth every penny. Their fresh fish specialties are some of the best around, seasoned just right, cooked to perfection and served with a healthy helping of savory rice and zesty vegetables. The Uptown's chef also whips up lovely pasta dishes, tender steaks, chicken dishes and vegetarian entrees.

Every day there is a fresh selection of homemade soups, sandwiches and quiches, and on Sundays the bar turns into a smorgasbord of breads and muffins, fresh fruit and yogurt to complement the regular menu and specials. Uptown Café is open for lunch Monday through Saturday and for dinner on Friday and Saturday. The key lime pie and pecan pie are our favorite desserts, and somehow we can always manage them even after a big Uptown lunch. Sunday brunch is a local favorite here, with a fresh-fruit, muffin, bread, and granola buffet bar, which you can order by itself. Or order any of the scrumptious omelets, pancake plates, breakfasts burritos and more, and receive a complementary trip to the breakfast bar.

## The Laughing Seed Café
**$-$$ • 40 Wall St., Asheville**
**• (828) 252-3445**

Tucked into one of the bends of twisting Wall Street is The Laughing Seed Cafe, which specializes in international vegetarian cuisine.

If you're not accustomed to an entirely vegetarian menu, you will be pleasantly surprised. Owners Joan and Joe Eckert are dedicated folks who strive to educate the dining public to the delicacies and flavors, not to mention the outright good health, that can be achieved with vegetarian cooking.

And this is not just rice and beans. We're talking about exotic and delicious dishes from Morocco to Thailand sharing the extensive menu with old favorites closer to home. Try the Moroccan sweet and sour carrots, Tanzanian eggplant, *channa dal* from India (garbanzos stewed in fruit juice and spiced with curry, garam and Marsala) or Mushroom Madness (a scrumptious pizza-like concoction). Order a combination of baked avocados, garden burritos and black bean chili, or make a meal with one dish. If you choose to limit yourself to one dish, we recommend the Laughing Seed's Harmony Bowl: layers of brown rice, beans, steamed vegetables, plain tofu and sesame ginger sauce mingle in one harmonious dish. The moss green spirulina refresher is a delightful sweet fruit smoothie packed with vitamins.

Sunday brunch at the Laughing Seed is a real treat too. Dishes such as poached eggs atop vegetable pancakes and whole wheat French toast complement the regular menu.

## The Market Place
**$$-$$$$ • 20 Wall St., Asheville**
**• (828) 252-4162**

Open since 1979 in downtown Asheville, breaking bread is a celebratory ritual here. Over the last two decades, The Market Place has become a world-class restaurant acclaimed by publications ranging from *The New York Times* and *Food & Wine* to *Bon Appetit, Southern Living* and *Wine Spectator.* In the heart of Asheville's renovated downtown, a sophisticated, urban look provides a backdrop for classic culinary traditions infused with imaginative, contemporary twists. The freshest fruits, vegetables, meats and seafoods of the season guide the ever-evolving menu. Featured are over 150 wines with more than 20 served by the glass. The Market Place Wine Bar offers a lighter fare, designed to blend perfectly with the selected wines of the week.

Reservations are suggested. Serving dinner Monday through Saturday, The Market Place is also open Sundays in October.

## Possum Trot Grill
**$-$$$ • 8 Wall St., Asheville**
**• (828) 253-0062**

Here's a cozy eatery on a quaint little street where you can sit down to a feast of New Orleans-style dishes created by Swiss chef Roland Schaerer, who, with wife Sybil, owns the Possum Trot. Cajun music plays in the background for added ambiance. The menu is weighted with spicy gumbo, red beans and rice, blackened seafoods, chubby po'boy sandwiches, shrimp creole, sturdy salads and a smooth bread pudding — the soul food of Deep South kitchens. A wide variety of daily specials are available at both lunch and dinner. Lunch and dinner are served Tuesday through Saturday. Take-out is available, but most folks prefer to eat in the sunny dining room, which you enter by passing the kitchen. Vegetarian meals are also served, and beer and wine are available.

## Flying Frog Café
**$$-$$$$ • 76 Haywood St., Asheville**
**• (828) 254-9411**

This exciting restaurant features creative interpretations of classical dishes by chef Vijay Shastri. This child prodigy had his own restaurant in this very spot six years ago when he was only 17 years old. Today he and his father, Jay Shastri, who also owns The Windmill restaurant, have pooled the family's expertise to make this one of Asheville's most unusual — and delicious — restaurants. Vijay lends his special flair to the French Cajun, Indian and Caribbean specialties.

For an appetizer, try a Crawfish Cocktail or Dahl, a traditional Indian lentil soup with ginger, herbs and spices. Entrees range from Rasta Pasta, strips of spicy jerked chicken sautéed in fruity olive oil with garlic, bell peppers, onions, mushrooms, green olives, Parmesan cheese and pasta; to bouillabaisse, crab cakes and, of course, frog legs. A whole page of Indian specialities features curry and spices in palette-pleasing combinations.

The restaurant serves lunch Wednesday through Friday and dinner Tuesday through Sunday.

Photo: Constance E. Richards

Take advantage of the outdoors — pack a picnic lunch
or sit outside in one of our sidewalk cafes.

## La Paz Restaurante — Cantina
**$-$$ • 10 Biltmore Plaza, Asheville**
**• (828) 277-8779**

La Paz owners constructed their distinctive cantina in Biltmore Village from the ground up. With its wraparound dining porch and patio, La Paz dominates the north corner near the old Asheville train station. The interior features brick walls and lovely hardwoods. The atmosphere is lively, and the upscale food an authentic blend of Mexican and Southwestern flavors prepared by an all-Hispanic staff led by master chef Juan Quiroz. The ample bar features Mexican drink specialties.

La Paz is open for lunch and dinner seven days a week.

## Hathaway's Cafe and Market
**$ • 3 Boston Way, Biltmore Village,**
**Asheville • (828) 274-1298**

In a quaint century-old cottage in Biltmore Village, Hathaway's is part shop, part cafe and all charm. Lunch here has an intimate, casual atmosphere, and you can order from a variety of quiches, crusty chicken pot pies, light sandwiches, delicate homemade soups, bagels and croissants. Hathaway's has North

Carolina wines and imported and domestic beers. The shop also features its own in-house roasted coffee.

Breakfast and lunch are served daily.

## The Windmill, European Grill/ Il Pescatore
**$$-$$$ • 85 Tunnel Rd., Asheville**
**• (828) 253-5285**

Owner Jay Shastri is understandably proud of his culinary success. In business since 1985, The Windmill has become one of the prime dining attractions in the region, touted for its ambitious international menu.

You can find a miniature United Nations of culinary delights at The Windmill: grilled Polish kielbasa, Jager schnitzel, veal Marsala, Kassler rippchen, filet Tuscany, roast duckling Hamburg, chicken Parmesan.

Dinner only is served Tuesday through Saturday.

## Boston Pizza
**$ • 501 Merrimon Ave., Asheville**
**• (828) 252-9474**

Do you ever have one of those nights when you'd rather have a root canal than cook, or

The Old Europe Café brings a bit of Old Europe to Asheville
with delightful Hungarian pastries and tortes.

maybe you forgot to thaw out that hamburger for dinner? Well, we've got just the place for you. Boston Pizza, in North Asheville, is a laid-back family-kind-of-place where you can come in your jeans, sweats and sneakers and feel perfectly at home, while someone else waits on you.

This lively, popular little neighborhood restaurant has a large menu that features steak subs of every description and hot-oven subs of turkey, pastrami, chicken, roast beef or ham dripping with cheeses. We have often taken home the seafood pizza, replete with shrimp, scallops, and other fruits of the sea. Boston Pizza is open Monday through Saturday.

### The Greenery Restaurant & Lounge
**$$-$$$ • 148 Tunnel Rd., Asheville**
**• (828) 253-2809**

James Gaddy, chef/owner of this charming restaurant, combines classic cuisine with a fresh, original approach. The menu features fresh seafood in season, including salmon, mountain trout, crab (the crab cakes are a popular item), duck, lamb and beef dishes. The ambiance is intimate and unhurried, enhanced by candlelight, fine art, fresh flowers and delicate hand-crocheted placemats on antique tables. You can select a fine wine with confidence here; The Greenery has received *Wine Spectator* magazine's Award of Excellence several times.

The Greenery is open for dinner every evening.

### Rio Burrito
**$ • 11 Broadway, Asheville**
**• (828) 253-2422**

Tom and Andrea, transplanted San Franciscans, were driving on the Blue Ridge Parkway when they dipped into Asheville and decided to stay. They saw the need for big burritos in this town and made Rio Burrito Asheville's busiest lunch locale. The restaurant is fairly small — and you can watch the cooking going on right in front of you — and many downtown office workers take out the giant roll-ups and eat them on the run. Even so, you get your suits, your hippies, your young mothers and kids, your high schoolers, and pretty much anyone else lining up for made-to-order burritos stuffed with succulent

chicken, steak, seafood, vegetables, beans, and many combinations.

Rio Burrito closes early, so if you desire a burrito dinner, get there by 7 PM . Rio Burrito is open for lunch and early dinner every day except Saturday and Sunday.

### Weaverville Milling Company
**$$ • Reems Creek Rd., off Old U.S. 19, Weaverville • (828) 645-4700**

Set in a century-old mill, tzhis charming restaurant is big on homey atmosphere and fine dining served with down-home style. The French onion soup is a cheesy, savory favorite, and the menu has hearty entrees that include fresh rainbow trout, substantial beef stroganoff and luscious prime rib. This is rib-sticking fare, and you'll be entertained just gazing around the lofty environs of the rustic Weaverville Milling Company interior and the antique mill structure, much of it still in place.

The restaurant has seasonal closings and hours that vary throughout the year. Call if you wish to make specific plans or for directions from Asheville. It's a short and scenic 15-minute drive.

## Henderson County

### Echo Mountain Inn
**$$$ • 2849 Laurel Park Hwy., Hendersonville • (828) 693-9626**

Dining here, with the lights of Hendersonville twinkling below, is as pretty as a picture, and the food is definitely gourmet. The menu changes seasonally although signature dishes such as the pecan-crusted mountain trout with an orange herb sauce will be found year-round. A well-known appetizer at the inn is the goat cheese-stuffed Portobello mushroom with grilled vine-ripened tomatoes in sautéed spinach. All entrees are served with a house salad, chef's choice of starch, vegetable du jour, and bread and butter.

For dessert you can choose from such items as orange-cinnamon crème brulee and a flourless chocolate cake with homemade vanilla ice cream and a raspberry sauce.

Echo Mountain Inn also has an outstanding wine list. Dinner is served from Tuesday through Saturday. The inn is open year round and most holidays. Reservations are recommended.

## Expressions
### $$$ • 114 N. Main St., Hendersonville
### • (828) 693-8516

Expressions has been a well-loved fixture of simple elegance on Main Street for more than a decade, and award-winning chef Tom Young still takes as much care with the quality of his food as when he first won our hearts and palates.

This is upscale cuisine beautifully and innovatively presented. To tell you that you can get seafood, beef, duck, quail, pork and chicken here doesn't begin to tell the story of the subtle flavors that imbue the dishes. To accompany one of these splendid meals, you can choose from a list of more than 200 fine domestic and French wines. Reservations are recommended. Expressions also has a comfortable upstairs lounge that's perfect for unwinding after a busy day or for quiet conversations with old friends.

## Highland Lake Inn
### $$$ • Highland Lake Rd., Flat Rock
### • (828) 693-6812

With much of the food grown right on the premises in organic gardens and greenhouses, which you're welcome to tour, you can be assured that the food here is some of the freshest you'll find anywhere. It's also some of the tastiest. While there's always the popular prime rib, you can also have seared grouper in almond crust with fresh chive and green herb butter, cheese tortellini with roasted red pepper cream and Dijon hen stuffed with prosciutto ham, Dijon mustard and fresh herbs.

At Sunday brunch you can select such dishes as poached whole blue trout over aspic with dill mayo dressing and cucumber and Alpine wheat crepes with Swiss cheese, ham and asparagus (these brunches change themes frequently so that you can have Brunch Santa Fe one day and Brunch Orleans another).

The once-a-month Wednesday buffet also has theme menus. The Caribbean buffet, for example, includes among its 15 items banana chicken with peanut sauce, shrimp kabobs in coconut sauce, stir-fry white cabbage with pumpkins and cashews, and conch fritters with Key-lime mustard.

Dinner is served Tuesday through Saturday. Attire is casual but nice. Spirits are served at all dinners and after noon on Sunday. Reservations are recommended. For more information on Highland Lake Inn, see our Resorts chapter.

## Hubert's
### $$ • Laurel Park Shopping Village, U.S. Hwy. 64 W., Hendersonville
### • (828) 693-0856

Austrian Hubert Boeck, owner and chef, learned his skills in his home country and Switzerland, Italy, Germany and France. He then brought his international cuisine to the mountains, tantalizing us with such dishes as shrimp Provencale (a stir-fry of jumbo shrimp, asparagus, tomatoes, mushrooms, garlic and sherry) and veal scallopini Florentine (veal turned in eggs and parmesan cheese and served on butter-leaf spinach). Your entree includes selections from the Accents Gazebo, which includes a splendid array of breads, cheeses, salads and desserts. Or you can just skip the entree and head for the Gazebo.

Hubert's is open for lunch Monday through Friday and dinner Monday through Saturday. A family diner is served from noon to 3 PM Sunday and a complete dinner from 3 to 8 PM. Reservations are suggested.

## Majdi's Tent
### $ • 502 N. Main St., Hendersonville
### • (828) 696-8804

The founder of Sinbad's, listed below, sold that restaurant to his brother and opened this tasty stop on Main Street. The atmosphere here is cozy, but it's not fancy. Yet the food served is an exotic delight and a real bargain. For breakfast, for example, you can have French toast with sausage or honey-smoked ham and Mediterranean-style syrup with rose water. Or try out one of the Middle Eastern breakfasts like fava and chick peas with garlic, lemon, olive oil, chopped onions and tomato, served with freshly made hot pita bread. Lunches are equally wonderful. There are hot sandwiches on pita buns, roasted leg of lamb, vegetarian dishes and pizzas with a difference: perhaps spread with herbs, fresh spinach, mozzarella cheese, mushroom and roasted peppers or decked out with feta cheese, olives, onions, peppers and tomatoes on herbed flat pita. Pies — meat, spinach or herb — are baked daily.

You can also buy wonderful breads and homemade pastries here as well as a large selection of herbs and spices and gourmet groceries imported from Greece, Turkey and the Middle East. You can also get cooking advice. In addition, there are gourmet dinner takeouts for very low prices. Majdi's Tent is closed on Tuesdays.

### Park Deli Cafe
$ • 437 N. Main St., Hendersonville
• (828) 696-3663

A family fleeing the Michigan cold opened this cafe over a decade ago and quickly established it as a favorite dining spot. Its decor features more than 60 feet of murals that give it a parklike atmosphere.

The Park Deli Cafe has an eclectic menu, and all the soups, dressing and sauces are prepared from scratch. You'll get great service and huge helpings of food here. And — watch out! — it has the broadest selection of desserts in the area.

The cafe is open for breakfast and lunch from Monday through Saturday.

### The Samovar Cafe
$ • Heritage Square Mall, Hendersonville
• (828) 692-5981

For over 20 years, this enduring and endearing little luncheon establishment has served its customers a wide selection of homemade foods. You can choose from 24 hot and cold sandwiches, soups, quiches, crepes, 10 different salad platters, hamburgers, desserts and frozen yogurt, all priced between $3 and $5. Daily specials, beer and wine are also available.

If you aren't familiar with Hendersonville, you might pass the place right by. Keep an eye out; it's at the corner of Church and Barnwell streets. The Samovar is open for lunch seven days a week.

### Sinbad Restaurant
$$ • 133 Fourth Ave., Hendersonville
• (828) 696-2039

If you like well-prepared Middle Eastern cuisine and seafood — or even if you don't — you should try the dishes here. They are superb and served amid authentic Lebanese ambiance. You can order Middle Eastern classics such as kabobs, curry, grape leaves, kebbeh, tabouleh, hummus, baba and falafel or select from delicately prepared seafood, Sinbad's own creation, daily specials or vegetarian dishes.

For those of you who are less adventurous, local dishes are prepared with a European influence. The bread alone would be worth coming for. Downstairs, a bar with a fireplace is an ideal place for small, private parties.

Sinbad's is open for lunch and dinner Tuesday through Saturday. The restaurant also serves beer, wine and cocktails. Note, however, than, due to its success, Sinbad may be moving to large quarters in the late summer of 1999. If they aren't at the above address, call for the new one.

### Woodfield Inn
$$ • U.S. Hwy. 25, Flat Rock
• (828) 693-6016

Three dining rooms await you in this historic 1850 inn, where you can have dinner or Sunday brunch surrounded by antebellum charm. Porch and patio seating is also available. Specialties include Morgan Mill trout, fresh seafood, including lobster dishes and filet mignon. All dinners include a fresh garden salad, garden vegetables and hot, home-

### INSIDERS' TIP
Are you hungry and want to know a great place to eat wherever you are? Strike up a conversation with a few of the local residents. Ask their favorite places to dine. The result will probably be some excellent down-home cookin' at a great price.

made bread. Much of the produce comes from the inn's own gardens. Special items are on the menu for the health-conscious individual. For more information on the Woodfield Inn, see our Bed and Breakfast and Country Inns chapter.

During the summer, Woodfield is open for dinner from Wednesday through Sunday and for a memorable brunch on Sundays. Winter hours are modified. Call for information during that season.

# Polk County

## The Orchard Inn
**$$$$ • U.S. Hwy. 176, Saluda**
**• (828) 749-5471, (800) 581-3800**

This lovely, plantation-type inn with its beautiful view of the Warrior Mountains has an elegant glassed-in dining area that stretches across the back and around one corner of its main building. The chef will carefully prepare your four-course dinner according to the seasonal food available.

"Freshness," she says, "dictates the menu." The day we dropped in she was preparing a curried carrot soup and a fresh tossed garden salad with classic bleu cheese dressing. Diners would also have their choice of a meat (perhaps rack of lamb or beef tenderloin), fish (mountain trout or maybe salmon) or poultry (which could be duck breast, Cornish hen or quail), with vegetarian dishes on request.

Dessert the day we were there was a low-fat, chocolate-decadence cake. Prior to dinner the inn serves complimentary hors d'oeuvres. (Since this is a dry county, you are welcome to bring your own favorite alcoholic beverage). The Orchard Inn is open year round. Dinner is served Tuesday through Saturday and is open to the public by reservation.

## Pine Crest Inn
**$$$$ • 200 Pine Crest Ln., Tryon**
**• (828) 633-3001**

The dining room at Pine Crest, with its hunter green, burgundy and deep blue decor, is reminiscent of an elegant English tavern. Both breakfast and dinner are served to the public here by reservation only, and the menu changes every day. If you're lucky, they might be serving cornmeal crusted catfish with citrus-horseradish reduction. All entrees are perfectly matched with fresh vegetable and various starches, such as chive mashed potatoes or creamed barley on mushroom risotto. The Pine Crest Inn's dining room is open Monday through Saturday.

## Stone Hedge Inn
**$$$ • 300 Howard Gap Rd., Tryon**
**• (828) 859-9114**

A meal at this stately stone manor is an equally stately pleasure. Big picture windows cover one wall, so no matter where you sit in the dining room you have a stunning mountain view. After sunset, tables are illuminated with candles in crystal globes, and the ambiance is romantic. Chef Thomas Dinsmore has designed an eclectic menu that offers contemporary cuisine as evening specials and traditional favorites such as broiled North Carolina mountain trout, Black Angus beef filet, veal piccata and shrimp scampi. Entrees include homemade soup or salad; rice or potato or pasta and rolls. A delectable selection of homemade desserts include the Chocolate Amaretto Passion Cake, rum cake, seasonal pies, cheesecake and locally made ice cream.

The restaurant is open for dinner by reservation Wednesday through Saturday and for Sunday brunch.

# Rutherford County

## Lake Lure Inn
**$-$$$ • U.S. 64/74, Lake Lure**
**• (828) 625-2525, (800) 277-5873**

This stately inn overlooking beautiful Lake Lure has been a tradition in Hickory Nut Gorge since 1927. The dining room is an elegant setting for its gourmet offerings such as roasted vegetable and herb cheese terrine, lobster ravioli with lobster sauce, Rendang shrimp and scallops or veal medallion au poivre vert. For the little ones who might have trouble pronouncing these fancy dishes, Lake Lure Inn offers chicken finger and hamburger platters (and cheese tortellini in tomato sauce for discriminating pint-sized palates).

Dinner is served April through October, and the restaurant offers a Sunday brunch. Hours vary during the off-season, so call ahead.

# Transylvania County

## Cardinal Drive-In
**$, no credit cards • 328 S. Broad St., Brevard • (828) 884-7085**

Here's a flash from the past: an honest-to-goodness, old-fashioned drive-in right out of the '50s. Of course, you can eat in the air-conditioned dining room, but who would want to when you can get service without getting out of your car? You can also get a Cardinal Burger that's cooked fresh when you order it; foot-long hot dogs; fresh, homemade onion rings; and fried chicken and shrimp dinners. If you'd like something a bit more health conscious, Cardinal can oblige with grilled skinless chicken breast in a sandwich or on a platter. But whatever you order, don't miss out on the fresh strawberry, pineapple or banana shakes. To use an old '50s Campbell Soup slogan, they're mmm-mmm good! The place is open daily.

## Chianti's Italian Restaurant
**$$ • U.S. Hwy. 64 and 280, Pisgah Forest • (828) 862-5683**

Right across the street from the entrance to Pisgah Forest, this restaurant can fulfill your yen for almost any Italian cuisine you might care to eat. Two favorite entrees: a seafood medley with shrimp, scallops, mussels, clams and calamari in a basil sauce over pasta; and veal medallions with mozzarella in a cognac cream sauce. There's also a patio for outside dining in good weather. Chianti's has a fully stocked bar serving cocktails and various beers. The restaurant also has a superb wine list. It is open for dinner daily.

## The Corner Bistro
**$ • 1 E. Main St., Brevard • (828) 862-4746**

This is the place to stop for a healthful, prettily prepared, inexpensive lunch or light dinner. There are more than a dozen "meatwiches" and even hot dogs served here (we particularly liked the smoked salmon with horseradish mayo, capers, onions, tomato and spinach on cracked wheat bread). There's an even finer array of salads and "vegiwiches," such as a veggie tortilla made with spinach, sprouts, avocado, tomatoes, mushrooms, onions, carrots and shredded cheddar topped with balsamic vinaigrette and wrapped in the flour tortilla. All sandwiches are served with a choice of tortellini salad, rice and bean salad or chips. And there are daily delicious dessert selections. The Corner Bistro is open Monday through Saturday. The hours vary from day to day so be sure to call ahead of time to make sure it's open at the time you want to eat.

## Earthshine Mountain Lodge
**$$$ • Golden Rd., Lake Toxaway • (828) 862-4207**

This unusual resort takes pride in offering healthful, delicious foods prepared from scratch — "or pretty darn close" — and has opened its almost-red-meat-free, buffet-style lunches and dinners to the public. Though each meal is limited to a one-menu entree, these change frequently. You might, for example, be served a lunch consisting of everything you ever wanted for building your own Mexican creation: flour tortillas, refried beans, seasoned taco meat, sauteed chicken strips with onions and peppers and Spanish rice — and that's just the hot stuff! Or you could be served chicken Cordon Bleu, Earthshine-style. You can be sure that lunch will include homemade bread and a fresh salad bar. Now you can go there for breakfast too.

For dinner, you might get marinated swordfish chunks skewered with a variety of peppers and onions; Cornish game hens prepared with a lovely orange glaze; or lemon and ginger pork loin. All dinners include homemade bread, a fresh salad bar, a vegetable, potato, pasta or rice and a dessert, such as fresh apples baked with brown sugar and oat topping plus fresh whipped cream or vanilla ice cream. Or how about chocolate pecan pie?

To get to Earthshine, go west out of Brevard on U.S. Highway 64 and follow the signs, or see our chapter on Resorts for more specific directions and information. Earthshine opens its dinner to the public on Friday and Saturday.

## Essence of Thyme Coffee Cafe and Gourmet

**$, no credit cards • 37 E. Main St., Brevard • (828) 884-7171**

Here's another fine place to relax after wandering in and out of Brevard's interesting shops. Essence of Thyme opened in December 1994 and was welcomed by Brevard's coffee lovers. Shoppers will get an energy boost after relaxing over a cup of cappuccino. Or how about a cafe latte, that great mix of espresso and steamed milk topped with foamed milk? To go along with these and other special coffees, you can treat yourself to a variety of freshly baked New York bagels, yummy cakes and an array of fresh pastries. Luncheon specials, such as soups, sandwiches and salads, are also available. If you're lucky, you may find a really comfortable spot in one of the limited number of upholstered chairs in the back of the cafe. And more and more, there is some good live music at Essence of Thyme, which is open daily.

## The Falls Landing Restaurant

**$$ • 23 E. Main St., Brevard • (828) 884-2835**

When it comes to fresh seafood with a Caribbean touch, the owners of The Falls Landing, former longtime residents of the Virgin Islands, know how to do it right! Their Cajun mahi-mahi is done to a turn too. When you come here, it's essential that you try the famous conch fritters (we bet you can't eat just one!).

Fresh nightly specials include lots of fresh seafood, steaks, pasta and chicken. Friday night is lobster night. If you're lucky, you might be there when superb cheese soup is on the menu. The bar in The Falls Landing also mixes some excellent drinks. Lunch is served at The Falls Landing, located just across from the Courthouse on Main Street, every day; it's open for dinner from Tuesday through Sunday.

## Jordan Street Café

**$$ • 30 W. Jordan St., Brevard • (828) 883-2558**

This small, elegant, non-smoking restaurant serving truly fine American cuisine has only been open for slightly more than a year, but it's already a favorite with locals with discriminating taste. For that reason, reservations are recommended, particularly for Sunday brunch. When the weather permits, you can dine in Jordan Street's outdoor patio. Brunch is served on Sunday from 10 AM until 2 PM. The restaurant is open for dinner every evening except Tuesday.

## October's End

**$$ • 115 U.S. Hwy. 64 W., Lake Toxaway • (828) 966-9226**

Even if the food here wasn't delicious — and it is — it would be worthwhile to stop in for a meal just to be able to enjoy a leisurely view of Toxaway Falls as it pours over its great granite dome into the valley below.

Here at October's End you can sit out on a wide, enclosed deck that overlooks the falls while you enjoy either American or Italian dishes. If the weather isn't conducive to outdoor dining, you'll find the dining room, with its gas-log fireplace, cozy and friendly. For lunch, the restaurant offers Italian subs, gourmet pizza-for-one and hot dishes, such as eggplant parmigiana and fried mozzarella served with a marinara sauce. You can also get such standards as hamburger platters and barbecue and other sandwiches.

For dinner, we did an informal survey that seemed to break down by gender: The women preferred Chicken Piccata sautéed with white wine, lemon and capers and the men went for Veal October stuffed with cheese, spinach and prosciutto and topped with fresh tomatoes, basil and olives. You'll also find great seafood and a full service bar and lounge.

October's End is open from May until the end of October — thus, the name. Hours vary, so call for a specific time.

## Rocky's Soda Shop & Grill

**$ • 36 S. Broad St., Brevard • (828) 877-5375**

Like the Cardinal Drive-In listed earlier, Rocky's offers another trip into "the old days" with its ice-cream concoctions, great shakes, real old-time hamburgers and other treats hot off the grill. It's a nice complement to D.D.

Bullwinkel's general store right next door. You can get breakfast, lunch and dinner at Rocky's Monday through Saturday. It's also open on Sundays for lunch.

### Twin Dragons Chinese Restaurant
$ • U.S. Hwy. 64, Chestnut Square Plaza, Brevard • (828) 883-3197

When you're really hungry, this is the place for you. Of course, there are Chinese buffets all over the place, but we particularly like this one, both for the excellent flavor of the food and for the large selection of dishes. The choices overflow two large hot-tables, so there's no way to even take a tiny taste of each one on a single plate, but you don't have to feel embarrassed about going back as many times as necessary to sample them all or for a second helping of a particularly tasty dish. In fact, the luncheon buffet proved so popular that, after being open a year or so, Twin Dragons decided to have an evening buffet too, though you can still order single dishes from the menu at both lunch and dinner. There is also a nice selection of seasonal fruits to finish off the meal — if you're still hungry. Chestnut Square Plaza is better known (and easier to spot) as the Food Lion Plaza. It's open daily.

## Cherokee County

### The Oak Barrel Restaurant
$$$ • 163 County Home Rd., Murphy • (828) 837-7803

You won't find a finer place to eat in this section of the country than this restaurant, housed in what was once an old home. In this lodge-like atmosphere, you'll find smoking and nonsmoking dining rooms, private dining rooms and a covered porch where you can eat during spring, summer and fall. You'll also find an extensive menu of gourmet continental cuisine, along with five or six specials, including the chef's choice of hors d'oeuvres. Occasionally, the chef will prepare a "game table" laden with such treats as venison, duck and the like. Another great favorite is The Oak Barrel's Chateaubriand, but you can also order most any kind of steak you desire. There's

also the catch of the day, and Cajun dishes are nice variations. The pub is available for private bookings. Reservations are recommended.

## Clay County

### Broadax Inn Restaurant
$$ • Elf Rd., Hayesville • (828) 389-6987

This is a truly unique restaurant housed in the old Elf Schoolhouse (see our Bed and Breakfast and Country Inns chapter). The two former large classrooms, separated by an archway, can seat as many as 96 people, and the place is often filled because it's a popular spot for parties and banquets. Owners Roger and Ruth Young had thought that of all their menu items the excellent prime rib would be most in demand, but of late, they say the hit of the restaurant is crab-stuffed shrimp. We can recommend it, and the friendly Broadax too (it's closed in January and February).

The restaurant is open for dinner Wednesday through Sunday in the summer and Thursdays through Sunday in the winter.

## Haywood County

### Cataloochee Ranch
$$ • 119 Ranch Rd., Maggie Valley • (828) 926-1401, (800) 868-1401

Cataloochee Ranch has endured and prospered in the same family for more than a half-century for many reasons, including its lovely location high on a mountain overlooking Maggie Valley. The food it serves has also played a big part in its popularity. These are family-style meals to which the public is invited by reservations only. And what feasts they are! Here's a sample menu, though they change regularly: potato and wild leek soup, smoked turkey breast served with cornbread dressing and giblet gravy, stuffed pork loin with spinach and black walnuts, cranberry chutney, sweet potato pie, sauteed sugar snap peas, freshly baked breads with homemade preserves, Chef Patsy's homemade desserts and assorted beverages. The price is all inclusive.

The Cataloochee Ranch is open year round, but meals are only served in the winter by special arrangements (for more information, see our Resorts chapter).

## Grandview Lodge
$$$ • 466 Lickstone Rd.,
Waynesville • (828) 456-5212

Hearty fare awaits guests in the dining room at Grandview Lodge, which is open to the public by advance reservation only. All meals are served family style with guests seated around tables in groups from two to 10.

Breakfasts consists of juice, fruit, hot and cold cereals, biscuits, eggs, bacon or locally made sausage, homemade jams and jellies and a beverage of choice. Pancakes, waffles, French toast or a cheese strata provide alternate fare.

The dinner menu changes daily and consists of an appetizer, salad, entree, five vegetables (most locally grown) or sides dishes and homebaked bread beverage and desserts. Typical entrees are marinated pork roast, barbecued brisket of beef, beef burgundy and chicken roasted in wine and orange juice. (For more information on Grandview Lodge, see our Bed and Breakfast and Country Inns chapter.)

## Lomo Grill
$$$$ • 121 Church St., Waynesville
• (828) 452-5222

Brick walls, hardwood floors, a quiet elegance and the sweet smell of the wood-burning Argentine grill enfold you when you enter the Lomo Grill. This is the place to come when you're in the mood for a relaxed, leisurely dinner.

In the true Italian and Mediterranean tradition, each selection is cooked to order with the finest natural ingredients available. You could, for example, start with an appetizer of Lomo Involtini de Melanzane, which is grilled eggplant, French goat cheese, sun-dried tomatoes, parmesan cheese shavings, fresh basil, tomato sauce and cumin yogurt sauce. Follow that with a Lomo Ceasar salad and then choose from an extensive menu of entrees that include pastas, fish, poultry, veal or beef. (Though the restaurant has only been open for around three years, it's beef has al-

ready won awards.) To end this fine repast, we'd suggest the homemade flan with caramel spread and fresh whipped cream or homemade crepes stuffed with bananas and caramel. Lomo Grill is open for dinner daily except in the winter.

## The Old Stone Inn
$$ • 900 Dolan Rd., Waynesville
• (828) 456-3333, (800) 432-8499

The rich warmth of wood envelopes you in The Old Stone Inn's guest lounge and dining room, and dinner here is a hearty affair. Entrees include such choices as beef tenderloin in puff pastry, Muscovy duck with apricot glas and cedar planked salmon trout fillet. Your entree is accompanied by several vegetables, including fantastic vegetable casseroles, and freshly baked bread. Desserts include Grand Marnier Crème Caramel, and such ice cream delights as the Smoky Mountain Brown Bear Ice Cream Coupe for Two.

Dinner is available here by reservation (for more information, see our Bed and Breakfast and Country Inns chapter).

## The Swag
$$$$ • Hemphill Rd., Waynesville
• (828) 926-0430, (800) 789-7672

The Swag, an exclusive inn 5,000 feet up in the Smoky Mountains with 50-mile views, takes a limited number of outside guests by reservation only for its lunches Monday through Saturday, its sensational dinners seven days a week and its unforgettable Sunday brunches. The chef-chosen dinners feature four-course meals of such favorites such as tomato-basil soup, fresh salads, grilled rainbow trout or beef tenderloin and desserts that might include lime mousse or Derby Pie.

The Swag is open from mid-May through October (see our Bed and Breakfast and Country Inns chapter for more information).

# Jackson County

## Balsam Mountain Inn
$$$ • Off U.S. Hwy. 74/23, Balsam
• (828) 456-9498

Many people come to dine at the Balsam Mountain Inn for the older-era atmosphere captured by this turn-of-the-century inn, only to come back again and again for the great food. Both lunch and dinner are offered to guests as well as to the public in its huge dining room. Lunches are light, consisting of sandwiches and salads, except on Sundays, when a full dinner menu is served. Dinners, from rotating menus, offer such entrees as trout, prime rib, ham with brown sugar-citrus glaze or chicken in an artichoke, mushroom and white wine sauce. These are accompanied by a variety of fresh fruits, vegetables and breads with a choice of too-tempting desserts and an eclectic selection of beer and wine. (For more information on Balsam Mountain Inn, see our Bed and Breakfast and Country Inns chapter.)

Balsam Mountain Inn's dining room is open to the public Tuesday through Sunday by reservation.

## The Market Basket
**$$ • U.S. Hwy. 107 S., Cashiers**
**• (828) 743-2216**

This is a highly unusual restaurant. During the day, The Market Basket is a delicatessen, a caterer and a gourmet grocery store with a full line of health food, fresh produce, meat and seafood — all set in an atmosphere that includes a grand piano. At night, it becomes a fondue restaurant without the oil, where you can saute your own food on a 500- or 600-degree granite slab. But that doesn't begin to tell the story of this place.

Basically, it serves health-conscious cuisine, but that doesn't mean it's not exciting. For lunch, there's an array of soups, hot foods, sandwiches and salads. At night, tables are put into the store's aisles (you might find yourself sitting next to the artichokes or the flour), and it becomes a super-popular cafe. In fact, people are turned away all the time, even in winter, so we highly recommend you make reservations. You can start your dinner with an appetizer, such as baked garlic, smoked salmon, baked brie or baby-back ribs and move on to entrees that include lamb chops, filet mignon, fresh seasonal seafood dishes, an array of marvelous vegetarian dishes and huge salads. Or you can try something from the hot-rock menu, which also includes vegetarian, chicken, beef, seafood or a combina-

tion of them all. If you're the least bit Southern — or want to be — we suggest you try shrimp and grits, a mouthwatering, New Orleans-style dish.

The Market Basket is open for lunch Monday through Saturday. It's open for dinner Thursday through Monday; it's closed Tuesday and Wednesday. Guitarist/singer Cy Timmons usually entertains in the evenings, and there's live piano music for lunch on Friday and Saturday.

## High Hampton Inn
**$$ • U.S. Hwy. 107, Cashiers**
**• (828) 743-2411, (800) 334-2551**

The High Hampton Inn believes in tradition, right down to the food it serves. Many dishes you'll eat in the inn's buffet-style meals are the same favorites you'd have found here 50 years ago: fried chicken, fresh local trout and prime rib; a memorable cream of peanut soup; a cranberry Waldorf salad; Southern-style vegetables such as stewed corn; homemade bread, including sausage cornbread; and peppermint ice cream with chocolate syrup.

The High Hampton Inn is open April through November, and breakfast, lunch and dinner are available to the public (for more information, see our Resorts chapter).

## Lulu's Cafe
**$$ • 612 W. Main St., Sylva**
**• (828) 586-8989**

Dining at Lulu's is a lovely adventure in eating. You can choose from a menu that includes really good vegetarian, Greek, Italian, Caribbean, Indonesian and American food. For example, you can have a melt of provolone and feta cheese, Greek olives, tomatoes, onions and pepperoncini (a spicy pepper) in a Greek pita bread, or perhaps Island Jerk chicken served with Caribbean black beans, jicama, saffron basmati rice and grilled plantain. We were impressed with a delicious vegetarian black-bean chili accompanied by a glass of beer (wines are served here too). You can then follow your full-course dinner with an old-fashioned dessert. Lulu's always-unusual decor has a fresh new look. It consist of mulberry walls, moss green chairs and floral tablecloths; black accents and burgundy ceiling fans set off colorfully matted black and white photos. Lulu's is open year round for lunch and dinner Monday through Saturday.

## The Jarrett House
**$$, no credit cards • U.S. Hwy. 441, Dillsboro • (828) 586-0265, (800) 972-5623**

When R. Frank Jarrett owned this inn from 1894 until his death in 1950, he let his wife, "Miss Sallie," run the place (see our Bed and Breakfast and Country Inns chapter). However, he cured the hams that were served here, and the great platters of fried ham, red-eye gravy, hot buttermilk biscuits and North Carolina's famous sourwood honey were said to make strong men weep because they were too full to eat as much as they wanted.

Great platters of food, which still include ham, gravy and biscuits, load down the tables in The Jarrett House, and people still line up as they've done for more than a century to eat in the large dining room that seats as many as 125. You'll also still find other longtime favorites such as fried chicken and mountain trout, along with all the fixin's.

From November 1 through May 1, The Jarrett House serves lunch Tuesday through Thursday and dinner on weekends. The rest of the year, breakfast is served on weekends, lunch Monday through Saturday and dinner seven days a week. No reservations are required except for groups of 10 or more (for more information on The Jarrett House, see our Bed and Breakfast and Country Inns chapter).

# Macon County

## The Gazebo Creekside Cafe
**$, no credit cards • 44 Heritage Hollow Dr., Franklin • (828) 524-8783**

This award-winning cafe is the perfect place to relax and unwind. Built around an old gazebo, the beautiful outdoor setting allows for creekside seating while enjoying the abundant North Carolina bird life. Open for lunch only, the homemade fare includes soups, salads, deli sandwiches, desserts, gourmet coffees and ice-cream delights. The Gazebo is open from April through October.

## On The Verandah
**$$$ • Lake Sequoyah, Highlands • (828) 526-2338**

The scenic dining setting overlooking Lake Sequoyah sets the tone for the exquisite menu at this restaurant, to which *Wine Spectator* magazine has given its Award of Excellence yearly since 1987. The food is prepared with fresh ingredients and is cooked to order.

For starters, you can order roasted eggplant with fresh tomatoes, herbs and goat cheese or flame-roasted shrimp with citrus soy dressing, followed by a Thai roasted-peanut salad with romaine lettuce, scallions, shredded carrots and alfalfa sprouts. For an entree, you could have, among other things, stir-fried scallops on angel-hair pasta with a peppered ginger-scallion sauce or sautéed lamb chops with a honey-roasted pecan and ancho chili crust, mint aioli and lemon walnut couscous. Daily fresh fish and seafood specials are paired with complementary wines.

In addition to dinner, On the Verandah offers a Sunday champagne brunch with soup, a salad bar, Mimosa cocktails or Kir Royale and such entrees as poached eggs on crab cakes topped with fresh lime Hollandaise sauce. Piano entertainment is featured nightly at the wine bar as well as more than a dozen wines by the glass. On The Verandah is open daily for dinner from Easter through New Year's. A champagne brunch is served on Sunday.

## Wolfgang's On Main
**$$$ • Main St., Highlands • (828) 526-3807**

Wolfgang's is located in one of the oldest houses in Highlands, built in 1880. Whether dining inside by a fireplace on a handmade rhododendron table, outside on the awning-covered deck or in the garden pavilion, you're in for a dining treat.

Chef Wolfgang, a former Executive Chef for the Brennan's Family Commander's Palace in New Orleans, is internationally acclaimed, having won numerous awards, including Chef of the Year in both Jamaica and Texas. His background brings a freshness and variety to a menu that's so attractive, it's really difficult to decide what to order.

New Orleans specialties include Wolfgang's Signature Soup, a shrimp and lobster bisque, Crawfish Etouffee, Maryland blue crab cakes served on a lobster cream sauce with pecan-crusted shrimp. Veal Medallions Wolfgang on a cabernet sauce topped with crawfish and bearnaise sauce, as well as many other selections.

Some favorites with locals are Chef Wolfgang's fresh mountain trout with pine nuts, Trout Cote D'Azur and Trout Admiral. For unforgettable Bavarian fare try the Wiener Schnitzel or rostbraten — a trimmed sirloin steak, pan-fried and topped with thinly sliced fried onions. For that special romantic evening in the mountains, try the Chateaubriand for Two, presented on a silver platter with an assortment of fresh vegetables.

The extensive wine list includes a variety of wines to complement each meal as well as over two dozen daily selections available by the glass. And to complete your meal, try Wolfgang's apply strudel made from a family recipe, Black Forest Torte, Strawberries Romanoff, the famous Bananas Foster or one of the daily special desserts. Espresso, cappuccino or one of a wide variety of ports and a cigar from the restaurant's humidor are delightful ways to finish a wonderful dining experience.

Wolfgang's is open for lunch and dinner all year every day except Wednesday.

# Swain County

## Hemlock Inn
**$, no credit cards • Off U.S. Hwy. 19, Bryson City • (828) 488-2885**

The food at the Hemlock Inn, set on 65 wooded acres 3 miles from the Great Smoky Mountains National Park, is so good that, at their guests' insistence, the inn put many of its recipes into a cookbook called *Recipes From Our Front Porch*. If you are not a guest here (see our Bed and Breakfast and Country Inns chapter), you can still make a reservation for dinner Monday through Saturday. You'll be seated at a lazy-Susan table laden with native foods, including fruits and vegetables provided by the Hemlocks' neighbors' gardens (in the summer, you may be offered corn-on-the-cob picked just a few minutes before it's cooked and served). Entrees might include country ham and fried chicken accompanied by homemade yeast rolls and biscuits with mountain honey. The delicious desserts are all made from scratch too.

The Hemlock Inn is open May to November. While you're here, make time to sit in a rocking chair out front and enjoy the view.

## Relia's Garden Restaurant
**$$ • U.S. Hwy. 19/74 W., Bryson City • (828) 488-2176**

This attractive restaurant is 20 minutes out of Bryson City at the Nantahala Outdoor Center across a steel bridge over the Nantahala River, one of the most popular whitewater rivers in the mountains (see our Recreation chapter). Here you can be served, weather permitting, on the open-air porch that overlooks the restaurant's herb and vegetable garden, the harvest of which makes up the fresh salads and other great dishes. Entrees include mountain trout, shish kebobs, the freshest of vegetarian dishes and nightly specials. Along with the entrees, there are homemade breads, soups and fabulous desserts.

Relia's Garden is open April through October; during April and May, breakfast and lunch are served only on weekends, but dinner is served daily. Lunch and dinner are served daily from Memorial Day through October; breakfast is served weekends only.

The first-rate musical entertainment in the area ranges from piano mood music to mellow acoustic guitar, honky-tonk country to hot jazz, and pulse-blasting rock to the rhythms of reggae.

# Nightlife

Admittedly, most people visiting the mountains don't come for a rousing club scene. The appeal of life in the mountains is the love of the land, the fascinating variety of the people who live here and the opportunity to control the pace of our lives.

The past few years have seen an exciting growth in night spots and locales which lend themselves to socializing after the theater or concert, especially in the more dense population centers of the area. Asheville, for one, has become a beacon for sophisticated diners, theatergoers and art aficionados. It is now quite unlike any American town of its size, with a living, thriving downtown, day and night. The people who live downtown, in the vast lofts with wooden floors and beamed garrets, grab their morning coffee and newspaper at the corner coffee shop, walk to Sunday brunch at several cafes with such offerings, and spend their summer evenings chatting over a glass of wine at the outdoor Italian trattoria.

Join them in sampling nightlife into the wee hours dancing at a disco, or listening to jazz in the intimate atmosphere of a New Orleans-type jazz bar. A downtown cinema features first-run foreign films and award-winning American movies. A space for poetry slams and original plays, evening exhibition openings at art galleries, and several excellent venues for daily live music and dance propel this area into the forefront of local entertainment. Asheville and a number of the smaller cities in the North Carolina mountains maintain brewpubs, manufacturing their own special flavors and types of beer and housing a dartboard or two, and possibly even a pool table.

Mainstream nightlife here is generally found in the restaurant/bars in most larger mountain cities (see our Restaurants chapter). Not only can you enjoy a night out with friends over a great meal, you can also find first-rate musical entertainment. This ranges from piano mood music to mellow acoustic guitar, honky-tonk country to hot jazz, and pulse-blasting rock to the rhythms of reggae. The fine restaurants and cafes in Blowing Rock, Hendersonville, Boone, and other communities often offer such live music, be it a jazz pianist, folk singer, string quartet, or local bluegrass music.

Colleges and universities in the region contribute much to mountain nightlife (see our Arts and Culture chapter). We've got your typical raucous college pubs and bars found in any campus town, if that's what you crave. On the flip side, however, you can also find mellow, laid-back coffeehouses featuring singer/songwriters, poetry evenings, author's readings, or even individual games of checkers and backgammon.

A smattering of dance clubs also serves the club scene. Other types of clubs accommodate the still-popular country line dancing.

Major concert arenas are still out of our region, as far away as Atlanta and Charlotte, but Asheville's own Civic Center is undergoing changes and working to book the big-league names in entertainment. Local colleges and universities sporadically bring big-name groups to the area. And a number of intimate little clubs, especially in Black Mountain in the central mountains, have become springboards for local talent moving on to the big time. Be Here Now, a smoke-free bar and concert club in Asheville, is a unique space —and fast becoming the premier music club in the region. And a number of other alternative clubs catering to the avant-garde, the bizarre or performance art, maintain a bit of Bohemia.

An average night out for the younger set often includes plowing through the popcorn-

and-nachos crowd at the local moviehouse. Megaplex cinemas are a-plenty in the mountains. They are social gathering places for families, couples, seniors and movie critics. Don't try to get into a sneak preview 30 minutes before show time. We also have film societies, film discussion groups and film festivals.

But nightlife here can also be as basic as a Friday night high school football game, a Saturday night dance at the town hall or listening to the chorus of crickets and tree frogs on a hot summer night.

Here we have a number of representative nighttime entertainment listings in the mountains, including some of the restaurants that offer exceptional entertainment as part of the dining experience (see our Restaurants chapter for more on these places). Because of the trendy nature of nightlife, nightspots lend themselves to frequent openings and closings and changing of hands. Therefore we have noted the more established and highly recommended locales, and urge you to check local newspapers for up-to-the-minute entertainment listings. Unless otherwise noted, don't expect a cover charge for the following locales.

# Northern Mountains

## Alleghany County

### Alleghany Jubilee
Main St., Sparta • (336) 372-4591

Start stompin' your foot and tappin' your toes — this is old-time music. Housed in the old 1930s-era movie theater on Main Street in Sparta, the Alleghany Jubilee provides a weekly stage for local country talent, old-time music and lively square dancing. Other than high school football, the Alleghany Jubilee is Sparta's main attraction on the weekend.

The Jubilee square dance is held every Friday night from 8 to 11. The Jublilee old-time music livens up Saturdays again at 8 to 11 or whenever the music stops. This is family entertainment, folks.

Admission is usually around $4 for adults and children get in free.

### Mountain Music Jamboree
Burgiss Barn, 294 Elk Knob Rd., Laurel Springs • (828) 233-5105, (800) 233-1505

The old barn at the Burgiss Farm Bed and Breakfast in southern Alleghany County has found new life as a rollicking, good-time music hall with a worldwide reputation. Tom and Nancy Burgiss are the genial hosts of this rousing, regular weekend party dedicated to the preservation of traditional mountain music and dance, generally held on Saturday nights.

The barn, smartly dressed in an upscale Nashville Barn Dance decor, with feed sack banners and a polished wooden dance floor, swells with good feeling to the sounds of 64 different local family bands. Two different bands play each week, spotlighting the creative talents of mommies and daddies, aunts and uncles. The Burgisses also serve up a delicious meal and enough tasty fixins to require at least one round off the dance floor.

Elk Knob Road is off N.C. Highway 18. Admission is $5 for adults, and children are admitted free. No smoking or alcohol are permitted in the barn.

## Ashe County

### Glendale Springs Inn & Restaurant
7414 N.C. Hwy. 16, Glendale Springs •(336) 982-2103, (800) 287-1206

This restaurant and inn (covered in both our Bed & Breakfast and Country Inns and Restaurant chapters) also often provides live music on weekend evenings and on holidays. Usually local bluegrass and country music strummers, or even a single pianist will play for the dinner and dessert crowd in the wood-paneled dining room of the Inn.

As Ashe County is a "dry" county, the restaurant is not allowed to sell alcohol, but brown-bagging is permitted. Call ahead for a schedule of performers and restaurant hours, as they change by season.

# Avery County

## Beech Mountain Street Dances
**Beech Mountain Hwy. • (800) 468-5506**

In summer, check out these lively monthly street dances in mile-high Beech Mountain. This unique recreational community offers fun every season of the year. Dates and times vary, so call ahead of time.

## Louisiana Purchase
**391 N.C. Hwy. 184, Banner Elk**
**• (828) 963-5087,(828) 898-5656**

Jazz is a popular weekend feature of this upscale restaurant inspired by the saucy energy of New Orleans (see our Restaurants chapter).

# Watauga County

## beansTalk
**352 W. King St., Boone • (828) 262-0999**

This is one of the new wave '90s coffeehouses that thrives on mellow music and New Age individuality. This great little place is on Boone's main thoroughfare downtown. The aroma of gourmet coffees and fresh pastries will make you want to linger.

## Chetola Resort
**N. Main St., Blowing Rock**
**• (828) 295-5505**

The mellow piano of Charles Ellis is a tradition at the Hearthside Cafe at Chetola. While you wait for your table, sit by the fire with your significant other and dream on. (See our Resorts chapter.)

## Contra Dancing and Traditional American Folk Dancing
**165 Morris St., Blowing Rock**
**N.C. Hwy. 194, Apple Barn, Valle Crucis**
**• (828) 297-1393**

Enjoy the resurgence of these art forms of traditional folk dances. In winter, dancers gather from 7 to 10 PM the second Saturday of the month at Blowing Rock Elementary. The summer schedule is the same, but the groups meets at The Apple Barn at Valle Crucis. Newcomers are welcome!

## (Shag Club at) Geno's
**949 Blowing Rock Rd., Boone**
**• (828) 262-0020**

The Boone area's Shag Club hosts this series of weekly shag dances at Geno's in the Quality Inn/Appalachian Conference Center in Boone. Talk about bringing back memories — you'll want to head to the beach. Call for changing dates and times. There's a nominal admission fee.

## Howard Street Grille and Cottonwood Brewery
**179 Howard St., Boone • (828) 266-1004**

The Howard Street Grille and Cottonwood Brewery serves up authentic Southwestern and mountain regional cuisine. This popular upscale cantina is a hot spot in Boone by night and day. The atmosphere is noisy and lively, the food is fresh and artfully prepared, and you can cool off with a beer from Cottonwood's own microbrewery.

A Sunday brunch with omelet bar provides a hearty beginning for the day after your late night out! The Grill and Brewery are open for lunch and dinner, and the bar does stay open late. Reservations are suggested, especially on weekends (see our Restaurants chapter).

## Klondike Cafe
**441 Blowing Rock Rd., Boone**
**• (828) 262-5065**

The Klondike Cafe is a diamond in the rough. This gutsy bar serves deli sandwiches, gourmet burgers, Mexican dishes and imported and premium domestic beers. But the grub is not the attraction. Outside, the patrons claim spots at the long tables running the length of the building. Sitting like birds on a wire, Klondike's clientele, mostly college students but also locals and hardy tourists, hang out and watch Boone go by on U.S. Highway 321, the Blowing Rock Road. Inside, live entertainment keeps the place rockin', and sports on wide-screen TVs and weekly dart tournaments add to the mix. The place opens at 11 AM and closes when everyone goes home. You kind of figured that, didn't you?

## Murphy's Restaurant & Pub
**747 King St., Boone • (828) 264-5117**

Murphy's has been a landmark in Boone

# Henderson County: Jump Off Rock

The view from here stretches across the high plateau of Henderson and Transylvania counties to the ascending peaks of Pisgah Forest. Jump Off Rock got its name more than 300 years ago when a young Cherokee chieftain and the woman he loved used to meet here. When he was called away to tribal wars, she would climb to this overlook to watch for his return, often singing an Indian love call — but there was never an answer. Finally, returning warriors brought news of her lover's death in battle.

At twilight, it's said, she climbed to the rock, sang a few notes and jumped off. Lore has it that on some moonlit nights you can still hear her song. To reach the rock from Hendersonville, drive out Fifth Avenue W., which turns into Laurel Park Drive, and follow the road until it ends at Jump Off Rock.

for seven years. The drawing card at this busy place is its imaginative menu that attracts a lively crowd to its four dining areas. Two bars offer a friendly place for a quick bite to eat, a little liquid refreshment and a gander at a favorite sports channel on one of three widescreen TVs. See our Restaurant chapter for more information on Murphy's.

## Regal's Litchfield Cinemas
### 210 New Market Center, Boone • (828) 262-3800

This modern multiplex cinema on Boone's east side offers first-run features in seven theaters. The box office opens at 4 PM weekdays (1 PM Saturday and Sunday). If you go before 6, you'll catch the cheaper matinee rate.

# Central Mountains

## Buncombe County

### Alibi's
### 2310 Hendersonville Rd., Arden
### • (828) 684-2646

This is your regular pool and food club. Karaoke three nights a week brings in a fun-loving clientele and the club features sports watching on Monday; line dancing and live music also figure into the club's repertoire. The club is open from 5 PM until 2 AM.

### Barley's Taproom
### 42 Biltmore Ave., Asheville
### • (828) 255-0504

Barley's Taproom is part of the growing renaissance of turn-of-the-century storefronts on Biltmore Avenue, just off Pack Square in downtown Asheville. Drawing on a grand mixture of the young professional crowd, visitors, good ol' boys, couples, rugby players, alternative types, and just about everyone else who lives in Asheville, Barley's offers 40 beers on tap. On certain nights, jazz, acoustic guitar and blues resonate over the convivial din. There is no cover charge.

Regional micro-brewed beers are on tap from Highland Brewing Company, Asheville's first microbrewery which is downstairs at Barley's. The pub's Universal Pizza Company offers innovative, healthful, create-it-yourself pizzas with ingredients you won't find at your typical Italian place. (Read more about the menu in our Restaurants Chapter).

The friendly staff, a combination of students, artists, actors and jolly bartenders, will make you feel like a regular your first time there. This is the place where everyone comes for and after barhopping! But upstairs, Barley's has created its own new bar. This loft, where smoking is allowed, contains red pool tables, dartboards and lots of young vivacious people. No food may be taken to this upstairs bar, so eat downstairs first before you go up to play.

Barley's is open from 11 AM to 2 AM daily.

Lunch and dinner are served weekdays until midnight and Fridays and Saturdays until 1 AM.

## Be Here Now
### 5 Biltmore Ave., Asheville
### • (828) 258-2071

This unusual smoke-free pub and dance hall began very quietly several years ago near the Square in the heart of downtown Asheville. Today this innovative music hall has emerged as the premier music club in the region, drawing some of the biggest names in recent popular music history and lines of interested local listeners. Leon Russell, J.J. Cale, Doc Watson, and the Squirrel Nut Zippers are just a few of the notables who have stepped onto the intimate stage at Be Here Now.

The club also focuses on rising talent, such as Black Mountain's own David Wilcox, who has appeared on *The Tonight Show with Jay Leno* and continues to honor his roots in Buncombe County. International acts like Congolese Samba Ngo and Latin bands are extremely popular events, as are reggae and funk. The club's varied clientele — young professionals, hippie-types, Generation Xers and aging baby boomers — flocks to the blues, jazz, acoustic guitar, soul-pop and boogie-woogie playing the stage. Other regular and popular features are Tuesday night Celtic music and occasional contra dancing.

## Beanstreets
### 3 Broadway, Asheville • (828) 255-8180

Beanstreets is Asheville's preeminent coffeehouse. In addition to flavored coffees, cappuccino, lattes, and giant soup-bowl-sized hot chocolates, pastries, breads and light sandwiches, the main thrust of Beanstreets is the atmosphere. The bizarre, eclectic clutter only enhances the acoustic guitar, Celtic sounds and alternative poetry performances that accompany the gentle clank of coffee mugs. Local art and a hodgepodge of sofas, easy chairs, and whimsically painted tables and chairs seem to be popular with all walks of life: This corner coffeehouse is unlike anything in downtown Asheville.

Sit on a barstool at the large picture windows and watch the world go by, or sit in the sunken "living room" for conversation or a game of chess, backgammon, or a board game or two. Watch local gurus plot astrological charts, students hunched over homework papers, couples discussing their romantic futures, business men and women pouring over data, and the downtown dwellers grabbing their morning cup-a-joe.

In the summer, outdoor tables attract a collection of dog owners and sun-worshippers. The staff and owners always have a kind word. Twirl the Magic Eight Ball at the cash register for the chance at a free cup of coffee.

## Fine Arts Theater
### 36 Biltmore Ave., Asheville,
### • (828) 232-1536

Asheville's only downtown cinema is an ode to resplendent movie houses of the past. The Fine Arts Theater maintains a grand hall with art deco sconces, mauve stucco walls, and plush seats in the high-ceilinged main theater. Upstairs, another more intimate theater runs an alternate film offering. Fine foreign films, independent and less commercial American films are featured here.

Besides the usual sweets and popcorn, beer and hard ciders, coffee and biscotti are also sold. This cinema, a drama theater at its inception, and later an X-rated movie theater during a period of downtown Asheville decay, has been fully reconstructed and restored to lavish splendor. Go for the quality films, go for the atmosphere, go for the history!

## Green Door
### 49 Broadway, Broadway Arts Building, Asheville • (828) 258-9206

The Green Door . . . eclectic might describe it, but then again . . . it is but one facet

---

**INSIDERS' TIP**

**Everything tends to slow down in the winter months when the tourists and summer residents return home. During the cold season, therefore, it's always wise to call ahead to make sure the entertainment in this chapter is still happening.**

of the versatile Broadway Arts Building dedicated to the visual and performing arts. This popular stop in downtown Asheville is known for exhibiting contemporary fine arts and handmade crafts and presenting avant-garde theater, dance, music and Poetry Slams.

The Green Door is an intimate space on the lower level of the building, which was one of the first to be restored in an ongoing revitalization of historic downtown Asheville. With local art on the walls, tables with snapshots of people and events pressed under the glass tabletops, and little white lights strung throughout the low-ceilinged hall, this is an Asheville favorite. Too bad it's only open for special events! The Green Door posts its schedule on the door, but do call to see when a performance, play, exhibitions, or poetry slam is happening.

The nominal admission to most performances usually ranges from $5 to $15. Some wines and beers, juices and coffee are also available.

## Hollywood Cinemas
**1640 Hendersonville Rd., Asheville**
• **(828) 274-9500**

Hollywood Cinemas is a biggie. This monster megaplex on a hill in south Asheville near Skyland houses 14 big screens under one roof and is the largest movie house in the state. The design is well-thought out and patron-friendly. Not long ago Hollywood Cinemas added two additional larger theaters to accommodate growing crowds and offer first-run art films as well as popular box office hits.

One of the best bargains in town is the twilight showing at the Hollywood. For just $2.75, patrons can take in the first-run feature at twilight, usually between 4 and 6 PM. Matinees are $3.50, and senior citizens and children 2 to 11 are always admitted for $3.50. A number of enterprising fast-food restaurateurs have set up shop just down the hill from the theater for your convenience.

## Lone Dove Saloon
**886 Patton Ave., Asheville**
• **(828) 285-0789**

Lone Dove Saloon, west Asheville's country music nightspot, is housed in a renovated 1970s steakhouse (and appropriately, 16-ounce ribeye steaks are the specialty). Country line dancing, traditional bluegrass and popular karaoke are featured at Lone Dove in an Old West atmosphere complete with roaring fireplace and wide-screen TV. In addition to the steaks, the Saloon menu includes barbecue, ribs, hamburgers and chicken. The club is open Wednesdays through Sundays.

## McGuffey's Bar and Grille
**1853 Hendersonville Rd., Asheville**
• **(828) 277-0440**

This popular restaurant nightspot in L.A. (that's lower Asheville, or south Asheville to the uninitiated) is part of the successful local McGuffey's restaurant chain. Food is featured, but the real attraction is the total experience. It's a popular weekend dinner/date spot for young couples. But this is also a lively family place, despite the presence of the bar. A large-screen TV plays sports events, and arcade games keep quarter-toting kids busy while mom and dad get to know each other again.

Musical entertainment, mainly on weekends, changes frequently — from Top 40 rock to new country and karaoke. Kids and grownups alike take advantage of the white butcher paper tablecloth and free crayons to express themselves.

## O'Sullivan's of Asheville
**711 Biltmore Ave., Asheville**
• **(828) 252-5225**

This DJ-hosted dance club in the Biltmore

area of Asheville, (directly behind Gold's Gym) draws large crowds of energetic singles. Techno lighting and industrial-strength sound provide the atmosphere in this nightclub.

Thursday is College Nite starting at 9 PM with live bands, Friday is Ladies Nite starting at 9 PM, and Saturdays are devoted to the Allnite Dance Party from 9 PM to 3 AM. Expect to pay up to a $10 cover charge.

### The Town Pump
**135 Cherry St., Black Mountain**
**• (828) 669-9151**

Black Mountain, a picturesque resort town east of Asheville, has long been a creative source for artists in all media, including music. The Town Pump has been a proving ground for aspiring musicians, both native and transplants, for almost 15 years. This pub, in the heart of the Cherry Street historic district in town, draws locals and visitors from a wide regional radius. Stop in; you may see a star in the making. It opens daily at 4 PM.

### Tressa's Downtown Jazz & Blues
**28 Broadway, Asheville • (828) 254-7072**

The New Orleans-style jazz bar, a private club which welcomes guests for a nominal fee, has all the ambiance, musical variety, and spectacular patrons of a major cosmopolitan center. Nut brown walls, a long oak bar, original pressed-tin ceiling, and linen-covered individual tables, including two window tables, make up the foundation of Tressa's, which is in a building dating back to 1913. The fully-stocked bar, mirrored and framed with columns, offers exquisite martinis, spicy Bloody Marys, wines, champagnes, and many other cocktails. Candles flicker, vases of fresh flowers decorate the antique furnishings in the entrance, conversation heightens . . . everything is awaiting the culmination of the evening — jazz and more jazz.

Photo: Steve Mann

Sarah Sutton sings the blues
at an Asheville club.

A red-lipped torch-singer, bow-tied pianist, and jazz quartet are the musicians you might encounter every night at Tressa's. A pianist from New Orleans moved to Asheville to be Tressa's house player. Tressa and Terry, co-owners, stir up liquid concoctions while dressed in elegant evening garb. The partrons often follow suit. Call ahead for the music schedule, and for information concerning membership if you'll be around for a while. This is one place you will want to toss on a silk scarf, a bevy of beads, a dress shirt — all without pretension but with fun. Monday nights are reserved for amateurs, of which there have been quite a few talents found behind the open-mike. Every few Sundays, Tressa's hosts a magnificent Gospel Brunch, with catered

### INSIDERS' TIP

**Need we say Don't Drink and Drive? Especially with the curving mountain roads, you won't want to be behind the wheel with a couple of beers in you. Ask the manager of the bar or restaurant to call a cab for you, or to contact your hotel, which can dispatch a car to pick you up.**

delicacies some of the most incredible, foot-stomping, hand-clapping gospel singing in all the Carolinas.

# Transylvania County

### Earthshine Mountain Lodge
**Golden Rd., Lake Toxaway**
**• (828) 862-4207**

When you have dinner at this unusual resort, you get entertainment that alternates between folk sing-along and folk dance to interactive Cherokee programs and campfire tales (see our Resorts chapter). Reservations are required.

### Essence of Thyme
**37 E. Main St., Brevard • (828) 884-7171**

Entertainment at Essence of Thyme, a coffeehouse on Main Street, is very eclectic and often very fine. The musicians and other entertainers who perform here do so for no charge (there's a tip jar), so they tend to practice their arts here when they have a Friday or Saturday night free of a paying gig. Therefore, the establishment often doesn't know who will be performing until the actual week of the event.

Things usually get underway around 7 or 7:30 PM and go on until about 9 PM in winter and until 10 PM in summer. When the entertainment is firmed up, it's posted in the front window.

### The Greens
**102 N. Broad, Brevard • (828) 883-8584**

Just a block from the center of town, The Greens — in addition to billiards, darts, video games and a snack bar — has entertainment one or two nights a week. Saturday night offers a live band or karaoke. On Saturdays, there's a $2 cover charge. Beer and wine coolers are sold here.

### Two-Step Junction
**Henderson Hwy. (U.S. Hwy. 64),**
**Pisgah Forest • (828) 862-4051**

This is the place for dancing of all kinds: swing, two-step, line dancing, round dance, waltz and cha-cha. Lessons are offered Tuesday through Thursday from 7 to 9 PM. Friday and Saturday nights a disc jockey plays the music for open dancing until around midnight. If you don't dance but would like to learn — or just want to improve your style, the Junction offers lessons. Call for more information.

# Southern Mountains

## Cherokee County/ Clay County

### John C. Campbell Folk School Dance Events
**1 Folk School Rd., Brasstown**
**• (828)-2775, (800) FOLK SCH**

Square and contra dances, clogging and circle dances with live musicians and callers are held here both on weekends and during the week. You also can learn English country dances, Balkan and other folk dances. A free introduction to contra, square and circle dances with recorded music is held every Tuesday night from 7 to 8 PM for folk school students and interested local residents. Community contra and square dances with live music are held twice a month, usually on the first and third Saturdays from 8 to 11 PM. Beginners, couples and singles are welcome.

---

**INSIDERS' TIP**

Make an evening stroll through town one of your activities in a new place. Seeing the town at night, lit up with old street lamps, the sights and sounds of cafe and restaurant interiors spilling onto the street, couples dressed up for dates, high school kids skateboarding on the empty roads, will make you feel more like an Insider. Discover the towns by night, window shop, and drink in the sounds of the communities getting ready to slumber.

Admission is $4 for adults, $2 for ages 12 to 18 and $1 for children under 12. Call the above number for details.

# Cherokee Indian Reservation

### Harrah's Cherokee Casino
777 Casino Dr., Cherokee
• (800) HARRAHS

Open seven days a week, 24 hours a day, this new and popular casino, three-football-fields big, has 2,300 video gaming machines, three restaurants, a gift shop, a child-care facility, and a 1,500-seat theater with big-name, live entertainment. Tribal Bingo is also available in Cherokee. (See our Attractions chapter for details.)

# Haywood County

### Bogart's Restaurant and Tavern
222 S. Main St., Waynesville
• (828) 452-1313

No matter what type of music you like, you'll eventually hear it if you drop into Bogart's for a couple of Friday or Saturday nights. A little bit of everything — folk, country, rock and blues — is played here. The music starts about 8:30 PM and goes until sometime around midnight.

### Carolina Nights
3732 Soco Rd., Maggie Valley
• (828) 926-8822

Full-scale productions of country music, gospel and pop, along with magicians and comedians can be enjoyed here every night from spring until fall and on weekends in the winter.

### Diamond K. Dance Ranch
Soco Rd., Maggie Valley
• (828) 926-7735

The Diamond K. took over the nightspot

formerly known as Country Roads. But you will still enjoy country music and dancing here on the fabulous 2,000-square-foot dance floor.

### Maggie Valley Opry House
3605 Soco Rd., Maggie
Valley • (828) 926-9336, (828) 684-7941

From May through October, bluegrass, mountain music and dancing take place beginning at 8 PM nightly. Maggie Valley is the home of Raymond Fairchild, four-time world champion banjo picker. He and his special guest performers are always dropping in to keep everyone's toes tapping.

### Saratoga's Café
2723 Soco Rd., Maggie Valley
• (828) 926-1448

You can enjoy great food and live music in the pub-like atmosphere of Saratoga's Café on Friday and Saturday nights. Wednesday is jazz night. There is no cover charge.

### The Stompin' Ground
3113 Soco Rd. (U.S. Hwy. 19), Maggie
Valley • (828) 926-1288

From spring through fall, The Stompin' Ground offers nightly music and dancing in "the mountain clogging capital of the world." No alcohol is served at this 2,000-seat music hall, so it's fun for the whole family. Just come in and stomp!

### Shephard's Thunder Ridge
2701 Soco Rd., Maggie Valley
• (828) 926-9470

Thunder Ridge, next door to Saratoga's Café, is Maggie Valley's newest nightspot presenting world-class country and rock concerts. If you like this type of music, you'll enjoy it even more due to the club's spacious dance floor and excellent sound system. Special guest bands frequently appear here.

The unique allures of western North Carolina's mountains as a resort area are the same as they have been for more than a century.

# Resorts

Resorts have been a part of this region for as long as some of the towns have been here. They weren't quite as fancy as some of the vacation spots we have now, but, just like today's, they drew flocks of visitors seeking the relaxing and restorative beauty of the mountains.

As early as 1827, when this area was still known simply as "The Wilderness," wealthy planters from Charleston were building large summer homes in Flat Rock, which would become Henderson County. They realized (though they didn't know why) that malaria, which plagued the coast, was not a problem here. Twenty years later, in 1847, a number of these folks built the Flat Rock Hotel, later called the Farmer Hotel, after its new owner, Squire Henry T. Farmer. Today, it is known as the Woodfield Inn, an elegant place where people still relax in their rocking chairs on its wide verandah (see our Bed and Breakfast and Country Inns chapter).

Similarly, two entrepreneurs purchased 839 acres in 1876 in Macon County for the sole purpose of establishing a town in what they thought would become the major population center of the mountains. In a brochure published that same year, these men claimed that there was "no better climate for health, comfort and enjoyment" than in what would become the upscale resort town we fondly know as "Heavenly Highlands." By 1879, they had opened the Smith Hotel to tourists here. It's still in business today, although it's now named Highlands Inn. Similar stories of countless old inns and resorts prevail throughout these mountains.

Amenities have changed with the times. Golf courses, swimming pools, Jacuzzis and the like have been added, but such attractions can be found almost anywhere in the country. The unique allures of Western North Carolina's mountains as a resort area are the same as they have been for more than a century: a mild, healthful climate with four distinct and equally lovely seasons; botanical diversity unmatched in America; rock-strewn rivers and streams that'll sing you to sleep; mountains older than time stretching out to forever; more unspoiled wild areas than you could ever explore; and people who take the time to be polite.

In selecting the resorts for this book, we focused on those that could be "destinations." In other words, there is enough to do in these places that, if you so choose, you can arrive and not feel it necessary to seek diversions outside the resort for quite a while. With all the attractions in the surrounding areas, you might be cutting yourself short, but that was our criteria. We think you'll like these selections, but, as usual, there are others just as interesting around the bend. Let us know what you discover.

## Price Code

Most of the accommodations in these chapters will accept major credit cards; we have noted those that accept none. Rates are based on double occupancy.

| | |
|---|---:|
| $ | $50 to $70 |
| $$ | $71 to $90 |
| $$$ | $91 to $110 |
| $$$$ | $111 and more |

# Northern Mountains

## Madison County

**Wolf Laurel Resort**
$$$$ • Rt. 3, off U.S. 23 N., Marshall
• (828) 689-9670, (800) 221-0409
   Spread below 5,600-foot Big Bald Mountain, Wolf Laurel Resort is a 5,000-acre private resort community about 15 minutes north of Mars Hill. The resort is also open to mountain vacationers. Play 18 holes of golf on a challenging mountaintop course full of ridges, hills and winding curves. The ski slopes of Ski the Wolf are just next door. (See our Golf chapter.) Two tennis courts provide sport and recreation, as does hiking in the surrounding areas. A portion of the Appalachian Trail passes just a mile away. Fish in a mountain stream, swim or picnic in a wooded glade — this resort uses the surrounding environment to its great benefit.
   If you'd like to visit Wolf Laurel, there's a variety of vacation lodging available, from privately owned rental units ranging from one- or two-bedroom condominium suites with kitchenettes to private homes with one to five bedrooms. A clubhouse restaurant is also available.
   From Asheville, take U.S. Highway 23 N. and follow Wolf Laurel signs which you begin seeing after the Mars Hill exit.

## Watauga County

**Chetola Resort**
$$$$ • N. Main St., off U.S. Hwy. 221, Blowing Rock
• (828) 295-5500, (800) 243-8652
   Chetola is the Cherokee word for "haven of rest." And as you approach the resort lodge down the country lane that winds around serene Chetola Lake, you will understand the inspiration for the name.
   This fine resort just outside Blowing Rock (off of N.C. Highway 321 bypass) has a long history. The estate was first purchased by Lot Estes back in 1846 for a mere $5. He called it Silver Lake. The property changed hands and served the next 50 years primarily as a way station for coach traffic. Then at the turn of the century, as roads improved, the inn became a fashionable accommodation for lowlanders escaping the oppressive heat of the Deep South. One such lowlander, Alabama lumberman W.W. Stringfellow, fell in love with the High Country, purchased the Silver Lake property, renamed it "Chetola" and built the fine manor house that remains today. The property was sold once again, in 1924, to J. Luther Snyder, known as the "Coca-Cola King of the Carolinas." Snyder bought additional adjoining property and continued to improve the estate. He built houses on the property for his children and their families and added a swimming pool and bowling alley.
   The estate found new life in 1982 as Chetola Resort. Local business people envisioned bringing the splendor of Chetola to the public. Developers of the present resort have been mindful of the tradition and history of Chetola, incorporating this legacy whenever possible. The marvelous manor house is now home to the Manor House Restaurant, its ambiance enhanced by the rich architectural character of the structure. Snyder's Soda Shoppe opened just two summers ago, featuring sandwiches, burgers and ice cream specialties. It is located in the recreation center. Try the newest addition to the resort — the Manor House Pub. In 1988, construction of the adjacent 42-room Chetola Lodge and Conference Center was completed. The facility includes spacious suites and professional meeting and conference space.
   The resort offers a wide variety of diversions: boating on 7-acre Chetola Lake, hiking on the trails of Moses Cone Memorial Park just over the hill, cross-country skiing on the nearby Blue Ridge Parkway and tennis on Chetola's five courts. Highlands Sports & Recreation Center at Chetola houses an indoor pool, a fitness center, whirlpool, sauna, massage therapy, body wraps, and regulation racquetball courts. Premier golf and skiing re-

**www.insiders.com**
See this and many other **Insiders' Guide®** destinations online.
**Visit us today!**

sorts are just minutes away in nearby Blowing Rock, Boone and the Banner Elk area. You can fill your days and nights entirely with the luxury of Chetola. (See our Golf and Skiing chapters for more information.)

If you become enamored of your surroundings, you can make Chetola home: Condominiums are also available for purchase.

## Green Park Inn & Resort
**$$-$$$$ • U.S. 321, Blowing Rock • (828) 295-3141**

Green Park is one of the South's oldest luxury resorts. Established in 1882 and listed in the National Register of Historic Places, it's situated 4,300 feet above sea level in the Blue Ridge Mountains, affording guests an atmosphere of breathtaking splendor and relaxation. The inn has 85 guest rooms and offers numerous amenities. The furnishings and spaciousness reflect a time when heads of state, noted actors, playwrights and business leaders were guests of the Green Park. Franklin Roosevelt, Calvin Coolidge and J.D. Rockefeller, and more recently Newt Gingrich, have brought their entourages to the Green Park for lavish galas.

Green Park's restaurant, Lafayette's, serves European cuisine (see our Restaurants chapter). The Divide Pub, which features an extensive wine list, has the ambiance of a classic English pub, complete with billiards and a sporting throw of darts. It's is a popular spot for relaxing after a round of golf or tennis at the adjacent Blowing Rock Country Club, a private club where Green Park guests have privileges.

Only 2 miles from Blowing Rock, the Green Park Inn offers easy access to all the area's attractions: Hiking on the Blue Ridge Parkway or taking in a view from the town's namesake Blowing Rock are two options. You can reach the Inn by heading south on U.S. Highway 321 out of downtown Blowing Rock; it's just less than 2 miles on the left.

Suites and single guest rooms are available in several combinations.

## Westglow Spa
**$$$$ • U.S. 221 S.,Blowing Rock • (828) 295-4463, (800) 562-0807**

This is a year-round European-style spa set in an elegant, historic plantation-style mansion that looms over the highway on its green hill. The object here is to pamper, rejuvenate, and reenergize yourself. The spa's program includes a variety of treatments including body sloughing, aromatherapy, herbal body wraps, Parisian body polish, facials, foot Reflexology and body massage. Fitness programs are also a large part of the schedule. Weekly weight management programs that include nutrition and diet assessment are also offered.

A poolside buffet lunch is open to the public, but be sure and make a reservation beforehand.

Choose from a day sampler to all-inclusive overnight stays. Rates vary according to the kind of treatment and length of stay.

## Hound Ears Club
**$$$$ • N.C. Hwy. 105, between Boone and Blowing Rock, • (828) 963-4321**

Cradled in a splendid valley of the magnificent northern Mountains south of Boone off N.C. Highway 105 S. is Hound Ears Club, which takes its curious name from a prominent rock formation on the ridge high above the club. You can reach the club on N.C. Highway 105, 6 miles from Boone. (A large sign will alert you.)

A scenic, 18-hole golf course, complete with waterfalls, lakes and streams, makes an interesting challenge for avid golfers. Tennis players can take to one of the six clay or two hard-surface courts here. Tennis instruction is available for all ages, or you can just enjoy a leisurely game with friends.

The swimming pool at Hound Ears is unique and secluded, tucked back into the mountain. The huge rock grotto surrounding the pool and pavilion area creates a natural swimming spot with an important man-made comfort: The pool is heated to a constant 85 degrees.

If you like horseback riding, stables and bridle trails are just a few miles away at Moses Cone Memorial Park.

The long-range panoramic view from the balcony guest rooms in the Hound Ears lodge is incredible. The tastefully decorated double bedrooms provide all the amenities, including maid service. Modified American Plan rates and special golf and tennis pack-

# Transylvania County: The Pretty Place

This is one of those spots known more by locals than by tourists. Well-attended Easter sunrise services are held here, as are many weddings. The waves-of-mountains vista is framed by an open-sided chapel, called Symmes Chapel, with steeply sloping tiers of seats fitted to the side of the mountain. The view is — we aren't exaggerating — truly breathtaking.

To find The Pretty Place, which is part of the facilities of Camp Greenville, a summer camp, take U.S. 276 out of Brevard toward Greenville, South Carolina. Drive 12 miles until you see the turnoff at the YMCA Camp Greenville sign on the left. Follow the signs for about 4.5 miles, enter the camp and drive to the chapel. It's a side trip well worth taking. However, no picnicking is allowed in the area.

age rates are available at various times of the year.

If you decide that a weekend is too short a stay, other long-term accommodations are available at Hound Ears. You can choose from Clubhouse suites, privately owned condominiums and chalets on the lovely wooded hillside near the golf course. You can also purchase property and make engaging Hound Ears your home year round.

## Yonahlossee Resort & Club
**$$$$ • Shulls Mill Rd., Blowing Rock**
**• (828) 963-6400, (800) 962-1986**

The emphasis at Yonahlossee is on horseback riding and tennis. Both recreations are taken seriously here, and this former girls' camp with its spectacularly lush, secluded 300 acres is the perfect setting for both. The tennis and equestrian community of Yonahlossee, Cherokee for "trail of the bear," is protected on three sides by Moses Cone Memorial Park. Property developers have taken great care to preserve the pristine quality of the land.

As a guest of the resort, you can indulge in a variety of pleasurable pursuits. The award-winning Racquet Club at Yonahlossee won the tennis industry's prestigious Court of the Year award in 1989. Six outdoor clay courts are surrounded by large viewing decks. Bad weather doesn't stall tennis enthusiasts here: Three indoor Deco-Turf courts with large climate-controlled viewing areas assure tennis play summer or winter, rain or shine.

Yonahlossee's Saddle Club continues a 60-year tradition and accommodates the serious rider as well as the novice. A large 28-stall barn, spacious tack rooms, generously sized stalls, a lounge and wash stalls provide all the necessary convenience any horse person (or horse!) could want. There are also miles of trails, an outdoor arena and a cross-country jumping course. If you vacation with your horse, you can board him here while you visit. Year-round boarding is also available.

You can also take advantage of the outdoors at Yonahlossee's small lake, an ideal place for canoeing, fishing and swimming. Or swim inside in the lovely 75-foot indoor swimming pool. Other golf and ski areas are about 20 minutes in either direction.

Accommodations include fully equipped, beautifully appointed cottage suites nestled in the woods of Yonahlossee. These casually elegant, rustic cabins have fireplaces and private decks. The resort also has two- and three-bedroom townhomes in contemporary designs of wood and glass, many with long-range views of the surrounding mountains.

The Gamekeeper Restaurant is on the resort grounds and has a tempting menu studded with exotic wild game dishes and other fine cuisine (see our Restaurants chapter for more about the restaurant).

To find the resort, take N.C. 105 S. to Foscoe, turn off onto Old Shull's Mill Road, then drive 2 miles. Or, from Blowing Rock, take U.S. 221 to Shull's Mill Road, then drive 2.5 miles.

# Yancey County

## Clear Creek Guest Ranch
$$$$ • 100 Clear Creek Dr., Burnsville
• (828) 675-4510, (800) 651-4510

Ever had a hankering to spend some time at a dude ranch? Well here's your chance, right here in the mountains. The Clear Creek Guest Ranch is truly a resort for the entire family. Don't expect to be lounging around the pool with cocktails at this resort. Owners Rex and Aileen Frederick have created so many fun-filled diversions that you probably won't even get to the heated pool until well after twilight.

Able to accommodate up to 50 people at a time in one- to three-bedroom units, the Ranch welcomes families, couples and groups, as well as individuals, since you won't be on your own here for long. You will have plenty of opportunities to join in group activities such as horseback riding, tubing, white water rafting, hiking, barbecues, and other fun. The family-style seating in the dining room of the main lodge, a grand hall with a rustic adjacent living room area, ensures that you will get to know your neighbors over breakfast and other meals.

The atmosphere of Clear Creek is casual. Rex and Aileen stroll the grounds in jeans and make a concerted effort to make everyone feel at home. They are hands-on hosts and enjoy spending time with guests, be it at mealtimes helping plan guests' itineraries with them, over a game of checkers, or simply sitting out on one of the spacious front porches for a chat among the rocking chairs.

At an elevation of 3,000 feet, the Ranch perches at the foot of a mountain range and offers a splendid view of Mount Mitchell and the Pisgah National Forest environs. The guest units, built of rough-hewn log siding, are spacious and modern, with porches and rocking chairs outside each door. Air conditioning and ceiling fans in each room are perfect for sultry summer nights, and large pine beds, covered with fluffy pillows and patchwork-quilt comforters keep you toasty warm on cooler evenings. The Fredericks like to keep life simple, so you will only find one television and a telephone in the main lodge. There is cable, though, and a fax for those who need to do a bit of business anyway.

Most of your day will be spent on the trails, either riding (Western saddle) on the morning ride, afternoon ride, or all-day ride, led by experienced Wranglers (also students, many from a college specializing in equestrian studies); tubing down the South Toe River; whitewater rafting with one of the local outfitters; golfing at the nearby Mount Mitchell Golf Course; hiking some of the many trails of the Pisgah National Forest; or sightseeing.

The Fredericks arrange trips to local artisan studios, including nationally known glass-blower Billy Bernstein's, and into the larger communities of Asheville, Spruce Pine and beyond. If you plan on staying for several days, you will experience at least one, if not more, barbecues at the Toe River where the Fredericks set up a large picnic dinner, replete with table cloths and dishes under a cozy wooded shelter at the South Toe River swimming hole. "Brunch on the Mountain" and grilling by the pool are also weekly features.

Counselors offer special activities for children between the ages of 5 and 12 during the summer. Ping-Pong, volleyball, pool, and video games are provided in a special building "just for kids."

The live-in chef and his helpers, usually college students from all over the country,

INSIDERS' TIP

When our long-lasting, colorful autumn season finally ends, and the leaves float from the trees, the best views of the mountains suddenly appear. Clean, picture-perfect streams sparkle along roadsides; waterfalls tumble over icicle-covered rocks and with summer haze a thing of the past, Blue Ridge Parkway views, unhampered by foliage, stretch forever. Come and see!

whip up three hearty meals a day for guests, including homemade soups, breads, pastries and main dishes. Apple-cinnamon pancakes slathered with maple syrup are on the breakfast menu, and there is plenty more to choose from — bacon, eggs, biscuits — the menu changes daily. Blackberry cobbler with a flaky, buttery crust and vanilla ice-cream melting over the top, was an incredible end to a wholesome dinner of porkchops, salad, green beans, yeast rolls, and spicy rice — this is comfort food at its best! The chef will pack picnic lunches for guests to take with them on their outings, and after several hours of trail riding, tubing, or hiking, you'll be ready for lemonade, ice tea, fruit, and cookies provided in the dining room in the afternoon.

A constant supply of fresh coffee, hot chocolate, and juice in the main lodge came in handy after our evening swim under the stars. It gave us just enough energy to climb into the hot tub for a steaming soak, amidst vapor mixed with moonlight.

# Central Mountains

## Buncombe County

### Grove Park Inn Resort
**$$$-$$$$ • 290 Macon Ave., Asheville • (828) 252-2711**

The Grove Park Inn is one of the premier landmarks of the city of Asheville. Kings, U.S. presidents, inventors, golf legends, famous actors and writers (Eleanor Roosevelt, Franklin Roosevelt, Harry Houdini, George Bush, Henry Ford, Thomas Edison and Mikhail Baryshnikov to mention a few) have all passed through the massive stone portico of the Grove Park Inn.

The Inn, built in 1913 from tremendous boulders blasted out of nearby Sunset Mountain, was an engineering marvel and the personal vision of dynamic entrepreneur E.W. Grove, who invented Grove's Chill Tonic, a drink claiming to have "medicinal" value for many aches and pains. He came to Asheville during the city's turn-of-the-century boom period, attracted by the natural beauty of the area and the city's possibilities. With the Grove

Park Inn, E.W. Grove not only left an architectural legacy to the city of Asheville, but, by example, a spirit of business foresight and daring that continues to define the unique character of our small mountain city.

The Inn has had continuous success through the years. The Sammons Corporation acquired the Grove Park Inn in the 1950s, and the resulting growth and innovation spearheaded by this ownership continues a tradition of more than 80 years. Two new wings, designed to maintain the architectural integrity of the original structure, have been added. The 202-room Sammons Wing, built in 1984, also houses a gallery of specialty shops. In 1988, the Vanderbilt Wing was completed. It has 166 rooms, 28 of which comprise the private guest rooms and suites of the Club Floor. The original stone edifice is composed of 142 rooms.

The inn is furnished with antique pieces in the rich oak texture and artistic line of the Arts and Crafts style, so popular in the early 1900s. The Inn's Great Hall is dominated by fireplaces at either end. Measuring six-feet deep, six-feet high and 12-feet wide, these hearths are truly room-size in proportion. This majestic old inn with its distinctive red-shingled roof that sits commandingly on Sunset Mountain with the lush golf lawn spread before it makes a stunning visual impression on the approach from Kimberly Avenue.

Open year-round, the inn is alive with activity. Golf has always played a major role in the history of the Grove Park Inn. The 18-hole course, designed in the 1920s by renowned golf architect Donald Ross, has hosted many of golf's greats: Bobby Jones, Arnold Palmer, Jack Nicklaus, Ben Hogan, Sam Snead, Fuzzy Zoeller and Doug Sanders, to name a few. A comprehensive golf program is administered by the inn's golf professional. There is also a well-stocked sports shop for your convenience.

Other recreation at the inn includes both an indoor and an outdoor pool, racquetball and squash courts and three indoor and six outdoor tennis courts, two of them clay. A tennis pro is on staff to give instruction and lessons. The inn also has a health club for aerobics, weight training, sauna and whirlpool treatments and massage.

Forty-two meeting and conference rooms and 50,000 square feet of meeting space are available at the Grove Park Inn. Professional coordination and technical support serve numerous business, convention and reunion groups. Other guest services include child care (with a children's activity program), laundry, valet, shoe-shine and room service.

Dining is an experience at the Grove Park Inn. The Blue Ridge Dining Room, near the Great Hall, is a family place. Good, basic American cooking, prime rib, chicken and pasta, wonderful soups and other traditional entrees are available in a casual atmosphere. A scrumptious breakfast buffet is offered here seven days a week.

The Sunset Terrace, the inn's casually elegant outdoor restaurant, needs no decor, only the colors of the evening sky. The full menu for breakfast, lunch and dinner is light, classic cuisine. Evening entertainment of jazz, pop and classical music fills the air in the casually elegant atmosphere of the Terrace. For other fine dining, try Horizon at the Grove Park Inn. A pianist plays classical selections and light jazz for your pleasure. Reservations are required for Horizon and The Sunset Terrace.

There are a variety of accommodation packages at the Grove Park Inn, and any choice is an indulgence in this marvelous his-toric hotel. In addition to golf and tennis packages, Adventure Weekends offer planned events ranging from stand-up comedy to big band and jazz celebrations. Christmas is a 40-day Grove Park Inn celebration that starts the day after Thanksgiving and runs through a rousing celebration of the New Year.

# Henderson County

### Highland Lake Inn and Conference Center
**$$$ • Highland Lake Rd., Flat Rock**
**• (828) 693-6812**

More than 15 years ago, when one of us lived on Highland Lake Road in Flat Rock, a rather rundown summer camp backed up the property. The changes that have taken place on that land in the years since then have been nothing short of miraculous. That rather shabby camp and its marvelous old buildings have been transformed into a glorious retreat that has taken its place among the best in the area. The expansive grounds — 180 acres — and small guest list makes this a place of both sociability and solitude.

You can have your choice of accommodations. There are 20 rooms with private baths in the lodge that has a spacious lobby with a large fireplace and an atmosphere that is

Golf is just one of the attractions at the spectacular Grove Park Inn Resort.

# The White Owl of High Hampton

As we mentioned in the listing for High Hampton Inn in this chapter, Dr. and Mrs. Halsted, the second owners of the High Hampton property, gradually increased their holdings by buying out adjoining farms. In the process, Dr. Halsted made an offer for a 50-acre homestead owned by Mr. Hannibal Heaton and his wife. He wanted to sell, but Mrs. Heaton adamantly refused.

"I'll kill myself if you sell our home," she supposedly told her husband.

But Dr. Halsted must have made an offer that Hannibal felt he shouldn't refuse, so off he went to close the deal. But when he returned home with the bill of sale, he found his wife hanging from an oak tree, and the story goes that there was a white owl flying around her head screeching like a crying woman. Some said it was the spirit of the woman herself.

Shortly after that, Hannibal Heaton disappeared from the Cashiers area and was never heard from again. Mrs. Heaton, a woman of her word, was buried in the Upper Zachary Cemetery, now just a short distance from where the High Hampton Inn stands today. And it's still said by some that the owls heard at night around High Hampton are Mrs. Heaton, still crying over the home she loved and lost.

modern and rustic at the same time. Each cabin duplex has one large room with a fireplace and one small room; each unit has its own entrance and private bath. The "Inn" at Highland Lake has romantic rooms with fireplaces and whirlpools. There are also five cottages that range in size from two bedrooms and two baths to four bedrooms and two baths. They have lovely names: Waterlily, Honeysuckle, Periwinkle, Dogwood and Azalea. And, yes, you'll find all these wonderful plants in profusion here, for Highland Lake is known for its gardens. Not only are they pleasing to see, but the organic plots, which include berries and herbs, also provide much of the food, including delicious salads and grilled vegetables, that has made the inn's healthful, gourmet meals some of the most popular in Henderson County (see our Restaurants chapter).

There is a Spa, and of course there are the barns, where all kinds of amiable country critters are at home. They'll soon become some of a child visitor's best friends, followed closely by members of the Inn's attentive staff. For recreation, you can choose from tennis, swimming in an Olympic-size pool or in a lake, canoeing, fishing or playing volleyball, bas-

ketball, horseshoes or beach-ball games. A hundred acres of walking trails will take you through wildflower meadows and under venerable oaks. Just across the way, there's a nine-hole golf course and — remember this is "Historic Flat Rock," — The Carl Sandburg Home, St. John in the Wilderness Church and The Flat Rock Playhouse are also just minutes away (see our Attractions and Arts and Culture chapters).

To get to the Highland Lake Inn — a perfect place for business conferences, group retreats and family reunions as well as family or personal vacations — take U.S. Highway 25 S. out of Hendersonville for about 5 miles and turn left onto Highlands Lake Road at the Pinecrest Presbyterian Church. The entrance to the inn is at the waterfall.

# Rutherford County

### Colony Lake Lure Resort at Fairfield Mountains
$$-$$$$ • 201 Boulevard of the Mountains, Lake Lure • (828) 625-3000

Scenic Lake Lure and historic Hickory Nut Gorge are the backdrop for this spectacular mountain resort that's off U.S. Highway 64/74. This 2,500-acre golf community offers championship play on two challenging courses, one of which was designed by Dan Maples. Tennis courts, indoor and outdoor swimming pools, a fitness center and health club and boating facilities are also available for visitors and homeowners. Full-service dining is available 365 days a year in the Lakeview Restaurant.

One-, two- and three-bedroom townhomes on the fairways are available for summer rental. This popular Hickory Nut Gorge area has Chimney Rock Park, with miles of spectacularly scenic hiking trails, boating on lovely Lake Lure and charming restaurants and tourist shopping in the nearby hamlet of Chimney Rock.

# Transylvania County

### The Greystone Inn
**$$$$ • Off U.S. Hwy. 64, Lake Toxaway • (828) 966-4700, (800) 824-5766**

When you really want to reward yourself or celebrate something simply wonderful, spend a weekend or a week or two at The Greystone Inn.

First, a little history: A hundred years ago, a group called the Lake Toxaway Company built a 640-acre lake in the high mountains between Brevard and Cashiers that they called "America's Switzerland." There they created a five-story, 500-room hotel out of the finest woods and with the most modern conveniences, such as electric lights, bathrooms, elevators, steam heat, refrigeration and long-distance telephone and telegraph service. They offered European cuisine, full orchestras for dancing and lavish balls and all those outdoor sports we enjoy today: tennis, horseback riding, sailing, fishing and more.

Such a grand place attracted the likes of Henry Ford, Thomas Edison, John D. Rockefeller, Harvey Firestone, the Wannamakers and the Dukes. It also attracted Savannah-native Lucy Armstrong Moltz. In 1915, she moved into her "small summer place" on the lake — a magnificent six-level 16,000-square-foot Swiss chalet that was indeed small compared to her 30,000-square-foot marble mansion in Savannah that would

one day become a home for Armstrong College. But only a year later, in July 1917, a devastating flood weakened Lake Toxaway's dam. The following August, it gave way, wreaking havoc below the resort's lake all the way into South Carolina and exposing the huge dome of rock at Toxaway Falls (see our Waterfalls chapter). Faced with devastating settlements, the Lake Toxaway Company abandoned the property. The hotel was finally torn down in 1948. But despite the lost of the lake, Lucy Moltz loved the area and stayed.

"I have been around the world twice," she said, "and I've found there's no place more beautiful or special," she noted.

She lived to see a new dam constructed in 1960 and the area more than revived. Today, homes in the Lake Toxaway development are valued up to $1 million or more, and land here, along with that in Highlands, ranks as some of the richest real estate in the North Carolina Mountains. In 1985, the Moltz home, which is now on the National Register of Historic Places, was elegantly renovated and opened as The Greystone Inn.

Each of the 19 antique and period-reproduction bedrooms in The Mansion, as it's called, has its own unique character. There are canopied beds, brass beds, fireplaces, private patios and other charming touches that vary from room to room, but all come equipped with Jacuzzis. The Mansion's public rooms, which include a library, are the epitome of grace and elegance, yet are cozily comfortable and welcoming. The Lakeside Cottage, which was built in 1995, has two luxurious private suites with an adjoining door for families or couples traveling together.

Next door, the Hillmont Building (where 12 spacious, luxurious rooms have private balconies overlooking the lake) was built in 1988 in a manner that blends with the architectural style and furnishings of The Mansion. All these rooms have Jacuzzis, wet bars, sitting areas and gas fireplaces.

The rates, which are reasonable considering what you get, are on a Modified American Plan that includes your room, an incredible High Country breakfast menu from which you can order anything you desire and a six-course gourmet dinner with a varied menu.

# The Mystery of the Pink Lady

It's been said that there is a sad but gentle ghost residing within the gray granite walls of Asheville's historic Grove Park Inn, known as the Pink Lady. She has been seen, felt and experienced by hotel employees and guests for more than a half-century. The mystery centers around Room 545 in the Main Inn, where employees, guests, and repair workers have seen or heard ghostly phenomena, including unexplained chills and rushes of cold air and the feeling of a presence of some type, prompting the hotel's Engineering Facilities Manager in 1995 to write: "I was on my way back to check a recent bathtub resurfacing in Room 545. As I approached the room, my hair suddenly lifted from my scalp and stood on end on my arms. Simultaneously I felt a very uncomfortable cold rush across my whole body." His words echoed those of a painter who had worked in the hotel in the 1950s. Neither of these employees knew of each other's experiences.

Other employees as well as guests have mentioned that they have seen the luminous form of a lady dressed in pink party clothes, whisking around corners of the grand hotel. The legend dates back to senior employee's recollections of a young woman, dressed in pink who fell to her death in the Palm Court atrium around 1920, several stories below Room 545. The manager of Elaine's, the Grove Park Inn nightclub, who has seen the Pink Lady several times over the past five years explains: "It's like a real dense smoke — a pinkish pastel that just flows. It's a real gentle spirit, whatever it is." And still, to this day, it remains an unexplained presence at the Grove Park Inn Resort.

---

Complete bar service, not included in the rates, is available in the Library Lounge, and a fine wine list is available in the dining room. The rates include soft drinks and complimentary hors d'oeuvres; mid-afternoon tea, coffee and cake served on a wicker-filled sun porch; a daily newspaper; water skiing, hydro-sliding and tubing with the boat, equipment and driver provided; a daily champagne cruise on a canopied electric boat; use of a bass boat and fishing equipment; tennis court time; croquet, volleyball and other outdoor sports; swimming in the pool or off the dock at the lake; and evening turndown service.

At The Spa, you can drop in for a sauna (terry robe and slippers provided) or, for an extra charge, choose from massages, body treatments and skin and nail care.

Maps are available to spectacular waterfalls and hiking trails on the Lake Toxaway property, and the inn has six mountain bikes for guests' use. On Wednesdays, weather permitting, there's a mountaintop cheese and wine outing. Arrangements can be made for shopping excursions to Highlands, Cashiers, Brevard and Asheville. The Greystone also owns memberships in the Lake Toxaway Country Club so that all their guests can make use of those facilities, including its 18-hole, par 71 championship golf course. During certain periods, both green fees and golf carts are complimentary.

Though not included in the package rate, you can eat lunch at the Country Club from May 1 to October 31 or get a box lunch or picnic basket with advance notice. Many guests find, however, that after a generous late breakfast and a reasonably early dinner, lunch is easy to skip. But all the above is not the best part of staying at The Greystone Inn. The best part is feeling like you're truly welcomed. Innkeeper and owner Tim Lovelace told us, "We want you to feel like a guest in your own home."

The Greystone Inn is a little over an hour from Asheville off U.S. 64 W. in Lake Toxaway. You'll see the sign. Ask for directions at the gate.

## Earthshine Mountain Lodge
**\$\$\$\$ • Golden Rd., Lake Toxaway**
**• (828) 862-4207**

Think of a high ridge covered with flowering mountain meadows with even higher mountains soaring skyward around you. Better yet, remember the sense of wonder and adventure that gave childhood its magic, and you'll get a little of the feel of Earthshine. Its environmentally friendly simplicity makes it a wholly different kind of resort but one that has gained national fame. Accounts of visits and articles on this unique destination frequently appear in the national media, and the L.L. Bean company has used Earthshine more than once as the setting for the photos in its famous catalog.

The cedar-log lodge, with its eight guest rooms and massive rock fireplace, was built by hand in 1988 by owners Marion Boatwright and Kim Mauer (with a little help from their friends) on the site of a 100-year-old homestead bordering Pisgah Forest. Each room has a nice private bath and a "little house on the prairie loft" that makes it large enough for a family. Sunrise Cottage, a classic chalet, is also available for guests.

But as fine and old-fashioned-comfortable as the place is, the real attraction seems to be getting back to a simpler time and relating differently to the world and yourself. Earthshine's 70 acres adjoins Pisgah National Forest, and you can spend your time here hiking and horseback riding through forests and meadows. Or try challenging yourself on their High Ropes Course and then take on some real rock climbing. You can also learn homesteading skills, such as animal care and organic gardening. If you come in May, you can help shear sheep. Children

Photo: The Greystone Inn, T.L. Schermer Horn

The Presidential Suite at The Greystone Inn must surely rank as one of the most elegant in the country.

Photo: Judi Scharns, Courtesy of Boone Convention and Visitors Bureau

The North Carolina mountains are full of picturesque creeks, bridges and barns.

can travel back through time a 150 years when they spend their time working and playing at Earthshine's pioneer homestead or its secret Cherokee hideout, where they'll learn ancient games, dances, work skills and forest ways. They can also take a real wilderness trek with bushwacking and creek hiking and learn firebuilding. On most Sunday nights, kids can learn what it's like to camp out in a barn loft. On Tuesday, Thursday and Saturday morning and Wednesday, Friday and Sunday afternoons, Earthshine provides free babysitting for those under six at the Rabbit Hole playroom. Cowpokes that aren't

quite ready for the trail can hone their skills during ring rides.

In the evenings, you can join in rousing sing-alongs, mountain dances, Cherokee ceremonies, games and other entertainment. Or you can choose to simply relax in a hammock or rocking chair. Earthshine is also available for family reunions, weddings, training retreats and seminars, and it operates a year-round outdoor-education program for students from grade 4 and higher.

Rates include lodging and three mighty meals a day, prepared mostly from scratch (see our Restaurants chapter). There's an extra charge for horseback riding and the High Ropes Course.

"When you look at a crescent moon and see the rest of its sphere lightly lit, that's Earthshine," its owners have written. "It's the light that shines from us all. Come and see things in a different light at Earthshine."

To find Earthshine, take U.S. 64 W. out of Brevard for about 11 miles. Turn right at Thorpe's Convenient Store (Earthshine signs will mark the way). Go almost a mile and turn left onto a gravel road for 1.6 miles. Turn right at Earthshine's drive and go up the hill.

# Southern Mountains

## Graham County

### Fontana Village Resort
**$-$$$$ • N.C. Hwy. 28, Fontana Dam**
**• (828) 498-2211, (800) 849-2258**

If you want solitude without boredom, this is the place to come. Fontana is more than a resort. It's actually a small, secluded, self-contained town that's a fascinating part of our nation's history. In December 1941, the Japanese bombed Pearl Harbor, and the nation knew right away that it was going to need new sources of electrical energy to power the war effort. Twenty-four days later, on New Year's Day 1942, the Tennessee Valley Authority (TVA) got the assignment to build a 480-foot-tall dam, the highest in the eastern United States, across the Little Tennessee River. Overnight, a village for workers and their families sprang up; the village included a school, a 50-bed hospital, churches and space to play. Work on the dam went on around the clock, seven days a week. On November 7, 1944, the project was complete, Fontana Lake's 10,600 acres filled with water, and electricity began to zip through the wires to Oak Ridge not far away over the mountains.

After the war there was power to spare for rural electrification, and the dam proved itself in flood control. Not long after that, the village was transformed into a year-round resort that has been improving ever since. On the southern border of the Great Smoky Mountains

National Park, Fontana Village offers guided hikes, arts and crafts shops, three swimming pools (one indoor), a giant waterslide, an exercise spa, horseback and bike riding, miniature golf, volleyball, basketball, softball, tennis, a playground, a trout pond, a church, a post office, a village store, an ice-cream parlor, the Village Grill for hamburgers and pizza, the Peppermill Buffet House, a small museum and a host of activities, including traditional Smoky Mountain Dances and other entertainment. It also operates the Fontana Marina on Fontana Lake where you can take a lake cruise or rent all kinds of boats. The fishing is great in both the lake and nearby trout streams (see our Recreation chapter).

As for accommodations, you're almost sure to find something to fit your budget and group size. There are rooms at the inn (some with fireplaces), cottages with kitchenettes (some as large as three bedrooms and three baths with a fireplace and whirlpool) and campground sites. (Camping costs $8 without hookup and $20 with.)

In addition to the previously mentioned eating establishments, the Village also has a fine restaurant at the Inn, and the village store has provisions for meals in your cottage and for cookouts and picnics. Special weekend getaways are available in winter, including a Holiday "Christmas at Fontana Village" package. Nearby residents can get season passes to use all the amenities, from the swim club and waterslide to mini-golf. The resort is approximately 95 miles from Asheville and 22 miles from Robbinsville on N.C. 28.

## Haywood County

### Maggie Valley Resort
**$$$ • 1819 Country Club Dr., Maggie Valley**
**• (828) 926-1616, (800) 438-3861**

The mountains, as is typical in this particular area, soar almost straight up around the valley where this resort is nestled. They also shelter it from extremes in temperature. In summer, the greenness of its forested slopes and well-cared-for grounds and gardens is totally soothing to the soul. One of this resort's main attractions is its golf course. It has been the site of four North Carolina

Open golf tournaments, and *Golfweek* rates it as one of America's best. There is also a driving range and practice area, a pro shop, locker room and a professional staff that offers clinic and private instruction (see our Golf chapter for more information). Two hard-surface tennis courts are adjacent to the golf course. There's also an oversize swimming pool surrounded by trees, flower and herb gardens and relaxing scenery.

The Valley Room, the resort's restaurant, serves breakfast, lunch and dinner, including popular theme buffets. On some evenings there's live entertainment and dancing, including a clogging show on Thursday nights. A full-service lounge called The Pin High Club overlooks the golf course. Rates are reasonable here, and the resort also offers money-saving golf packages that include greens fees, use of the tennis courts and pool, full country breakfasts, and dinner at The Valley Room. In the winter, you can get ski packages that include lift tickets at the nearby Cataloochee Ski Area and a full country breakfast.

Rooms in the guest lodges are spacious, and each has its own balcony, cable TV and coffeemaker. Guest villas are on the golf course's back nine. Each villa has a living room, dining area and furnished kitchen, and both one-bedroom-one-bath and two-bedrooms-two-baths are available. Ask about special vacation and golf packages.

The Maggie Valley Resort is 35 miles west of Asheville. Take Exit 20 off of Interstate 40 onto U.S. 276. The resort is a half-mile from the intersection of U.S. Highway 276 and U.S. Highway 19.

## Cataloochee Ranch
**$$$$ • 119 Ranch Dr., Maggie Valley**
**• (828) 926-1401, (800) 868-1401**

For 64 years, Cataloochee Ranch has welcomed guests to its 1,000-acre resort that's a mile high in the Great Smoky Mountains. In 1934, when the area was still a pristine wilderness, Tom and "Miss Judy" Alexander acquired what had been a rugged sheep and cattle farm and turned it into this mountain legend. Family members still run the ranch today, which borders the Great Smoky Mountains National Park.

The name Cataloochee comes from the Cherokee ga-da-lu-sti, which has been translated as "standing up in a row" or "wave upon wave," a reference, no doubt, to the range upon range of mountains — both the Blue Ridge and the Smokies — that are visible here. The ranch itself has three major peaks: Fie Top, Moody Top and Hemphill Bald, with elevations from 4,700 to 5,680 feet. There are accommodations for 70 guests. You can stay in one of 16 cabins that sleep two to eight people (two of the cabins were originally pioneer log homes). Laurel and Wintergreen each have a living room, two bedrooms, two baths and a fireplace. Azalea, Rhododendron, Sourwood, Chestnut and Crabapple — one-bedroom-one-bath cabins — all have fireplaces. Four new cabins – Pond House, Willow, Dogwood and Sassfras — each have fireplaces and Jacuzzi tubs. They are great for couples. In four of the six rooms in the Silverbell Lodge, a fairly new and luxurious facility, or you can opt for one of the two two-bedroom suites, all with fireplaces. Here, also, is the Balsam room, a gathering place with a double fireplace that can be converted into a well-appointed conference room.

The historic main Ranch House, once a large barn, has six guestrooms, two dining rooms, the Big Room, a card room and offices. One of its six guestrooms, the Galax, is equipped with a Jacuzzi, and the Trillium, a corner room, has a wet bar and a private entrance. The furnishings throughout the resort feature colorful quilts and primitive or classic antiques that reflect the ranch's pioneer heritage. At this altitude, air conditioning is not needed. In early-morning and during the evening, even in summer, a fire in the fireplace is usually more desirable.

Daily rates include breakfast and dinner. These are family-style feasts you'll never forget (see our Restaurants chapter). There are also frequent outdoor cookouts and a beer and wine service. Other amenities include a trout pond, a 20-foot heated swim-spa, horseshoe pits, Ping-Pong tables, a croquet court and hiking paths.

But the real star here is horseback riding. These guided rides usually last two to three hours. Twice a year, longer trips for experienced riders are offered. Call the ranch for more information.

Photo: Cherokee Tribal Promotion Office

Long before the arrival of Spanish explorer Hernando de Soto in 1540, the Cherokee Nation's territory included the Great Smoky Mountains and parts of what are now eight states. To the Cherokee these ancient mountains were known as "The Land of the Blue Mist."

Cataloochee Ranch is also the closest facility to the Cataloochee Ski Resort, just a mile over the hill, which has winter ski packages. Though no meals are served at the ranch at this time, stays here are very reasonably priced. Restaurant services are available at the ski lodge (see our Skiing chapter).

When you stay at the ranch, entertainment is offered, and entertainment options are many in bustling Maggie Valley just down the road. But in our opinion, here, high in the mountains, you can't beat the star-studded show provided by a night sky with no city lights to dim the brilliance. As the ranch states in its brochure, "It's a show for everyone, and it's just outside your door."

To get to the ranch, take Exit 20 or 27 off I-40. Follow U.S. 19 S. through Maggie Valley to the west end and follow the directional sign. The ranch is 3 miles up paved Fie Top Road.

## Waynesville Country Club Inn
$$$ • 176 Country Club Dr., Waynesville
• (828) 452-2258, (800) 627-6250

This may be a contemporary resort, but it's kept one very old tradition of mountain inns: rocking-chair hospitality. French doors

lead from the modern lodge to the 270-foot-long main terrace that overlooks the manicured acres of its golf course. As in the old days, it's lined with rocking chairs — just one hint of the Southern hospitality you'll find here.

Nestled between the Blue Ridge and the western ridges of the Great Smokies, this resort offers 27 picturesque holes of golf with fairways winding like ribbons through the mountain valley (see our Golf chapter). Accommodations are gracious and varied. Rooms in the main lodge or its Woodcrest wing offer panoramic views of the first tee. The Brookside or the Fairway lodges have porches or balconies within putting distance of the golf course. For a more private setting, you can stay in the Senator or Governor cottages, or the two-bedroom Country Villa, which features a kitchen and dining area. All accommodations have cable TV and air conditioning. There is also a swimming pool and two tennis courts near the main lodge.

For meals, you have your choice of the main dining room or a light to lavish lunch at The Tap Room. (The Tap Room is also open at night.) Golfers can also grab a bite at the Creekside Pavilion. "Good food," the manag-

# Graham County:
# Maple Spring Observation Point

This 900-foot loop trail, designed for wheelchair use, includes a deck that opens to a sweeping view of mountain peaks and valleys. It is on Wagon Train Road (S.R. 1127) approximately 4.5 miles beyond the entrance road to the Joyce Kilmer Recreation Trail.

ers say, "is as important as good golf." In testament to this, all the bread is freshly baked on the premises.

The Tower Lounge is the place to go to quench your thirst. The resort's nine meeting rooms will seat from 10 to 300 people. Numerous golf, holiday getaway and special winter packages are available. Contact the inn for more information.

To get here, take Exit 27 off I-40, follow U.S. Highway 23/74 to the West Waynesville exit and follow the signs.

## Jackson County

### The High Hampton Inn and Country Club
$$$ • N.C. Hwy. 107 S., Cashiers
• (828) 743-2411, (800) 334-2551

In the early 1800s, Wade Hampton II, a South Carolina upcountry planter and owner of Millwood, a Columbia, South Carolina, plantation that was the social center of Southern aristocracy, bought 450 acres in Cashiers. The property served as a farm and hunting preserve and provided escape from heat, humidity and malaria. Hampton's son, Wade Hampton III, spent a lot of time here before he went on to become a general in the Confederate Army and, later, South Carolina's governor and U.S. senator.

In the 1880s, the Hampton Place in the mountains, which by now had a seven-bedroom "cottage," a kitchen building, servants quarters and outbuildings, was sold to Dr. and Mrs. Halsted's (she was Wade Hampton III's niece). Her husband had been the first professor of surgery at John Hopkins Hospital, and she had briefly served as head of nursing. They called the place High Hampton, from the title of his ancestral estate in England that was known as High Halsted. The couple gradually increased the property to 2,200 acres (see "The White Owl of High Hampton" Legend in this chapter). They are responsible for many of the lovely trees and shrubs that are still seen on High Hampton's current 1,400 acres.

After the Halsteds' deaths in 1922, E. Lyndon McKee of Sylva, the father of the present owner, William D. McKee, purchased the estate. A small inn was constructed on the site of the present building, but a fire in 1932 destroyed it and all the other buildings on the property. The present High Hampton Inn was completed in 1933, and to the pleasure of those who come year after year, time seems to stand still at this resort. "Nothing much changes here but the seasons," it's said. There are no televisions or telephones in the 120 rooms in the lodge and its cluster of cabins. And the accommodations are rustic rather than plush. You can also rent two-, three- and four-bedroom homes with fireplaces, kitchens, daily maid service and resort privileges.

On its many hiking trails, on its lake, in its rocking chairs and in its gardens, you can find all the peace of mind you might have been missing. Yet, there are nearly as many activities happening here as you'd find on a cruise ship. Very popular, but only one aspect of this venerable resort, is the 18-hole, par 71 golf course that offers a scenic vista with every swing of the club (see our Golf chapter). The late George W. Cobb, who designed the course, said, "I've yet to see a course designed by me or others with greater natural beauty or one more enjoyable to play." There are also five fast-dry clay tennis courts, a red-clay court and a complete tennis shop with regularly scheduled clinics and private lessons.

There are many hiking trails, guided walks and a fitness trail. The 35-acre Hampton Lake is the center of swimming, sunbathing, sailing, canoeing, rowing and pedal boating, and you can fish here year round without a license. A playgroup is conducted for children ages 2 to 4 and a kids' club entertains children ages 5 to 12. There are teen activities, croquet, archery and workshops, including seminars on golf, tennis, quilting, basket making, watercolor painting, bridge playing, fly fishing, native wildflowers, trees, birds, garden flora and many other subjects. More than 150 kinds of birds have been spotted in the vicinity, making High Hampton a great area for bird watching.

One of the most cherished traditions is afternoon tea served between 4 and 5 PM. It's also traditional for the guests to gather before and after dinner in the Rock Mountain Tavern to meet other guests. After-dinner entertainment is offered each night. These events (movies, games or other activities) are posted daily on the bulletin board. There are also special occasions, such as a Scottish Heritage Houseparty, a July 4th Picnic, a Teddy Bear Picnic for children and — the most traditional of all — the Thanksgiving Houseparty that closes down the Inn for the season (High Hampton is open from mid-April through November).

Daily rates are on a Full American Plan, which includes three buffet-style meals a day.

No gratuity or service charge will be added to your bill, and you are not expected to tip. There are extra but very reasonable charges for greens fees, golf carts, boats and the kids' club and playgroup.

To reach High Hampton Inn, take U.S. 64 to Cashiers and turn south on N.C. 107. The resort will be on your left a short distance out of town.

### Fairfield Sapphire Valley
**$$-$$$$ • 70 Sapphire Valley Rd., Sapphire • (828) 743-3441, (800) 533-8268**

It all began back in 1896 with the opening of Fairfield Inn on Fairfield Lake. Although the inn is gone, the pristine scenery and a distinctive way of life remain. Nestled in the south Blue Ridge Mountains, Fairfield Sapphire Valley has become a 5,700-acre, four-season resort community.

A wide variety of on-site amenities will please every member of the family. Sapphire Mountain Golf Club, a par 70 championship course, is highlighted by its signature waterfall hole. The tennis center features eight Har-Tru courts, two all-weather courts and a complete pro shop with instruction. The newly renovated recreation center features one indoor pool, two outdoor pools, miniature golf, an exercise room, Jacuzzi and sauna facilities, and a game room. Scenic trail rides are the pride of the equestrian center. Leisurely canoe and paddleboat rides are available in season. Fishing is abundant in the streams and lakes on the property. The recreation department also offers daily excursion to area attractions, a nature program and hiking. Kids Kamp makes summer an adventure for children ages 3 to 14. Winter sports include skiing and snowboarding.

Accommodations range from hotel rooms to three-bedroom condominiums. Three- and four-bedroom homes are also available.

There are two on-site restaurants that feature fine dining in a casual atmosphere. Mica's Restaurant and the Library Club are open for lunch and dinner to resort guests. O'Connell's Pub and the Library Lounge are available to members.

Fairfield Sapphire Valley is approximately 60 miles southwest of Asheville between Cashiers and Lake Toxaway on U. S. Hwy. 64 West.

**North Carolina's mountains are blessed not only with natural beauty but by scores of charming and graceful inns.**

# Bed and Breakfasts and Country Inns

Everyone needs to get away from time to time to recharge and renew the spirit. Leave behind all the encumbrances of real life and get back to ourselves. Some of us like the anonymity of an obscure roadside motel, or the pure convenience of it, but then there are those times when a bit of real creature comfort and coddling wouldn't be too bad at all. In fact, for many, it's the only way to travel.

North Carolina's mountains are blessed not only with natural beauty but with scores of charming and graceful inns. These jewels can be found scattered all across the area and offer you pampering you probably don't even get at home. The opportunity for making new acquaintances, enjoying stimulating conversations and experiencing gorgeous sights, sounds and tastes will last long after the key has turned in your door back home.

Country inns abound in the Southeastern United States, but bed and breakfasts are a newer breed of accommodation in this country, harking back to the old English style of housing a traveler and fortifying him with a hot breakfast before the long ride onward. The establishments we recommend to you in this chapter are some of the finest examples of the bed and breakfast inns and country inns North Carolina's mountains have to offer. Some have lavish surroundings and interiors worthy of a museum estate, and some sport the more simple comforts of home. All are devoted to making your stay as pleasing as possible. We've given you the choice of large or small, elegant or rustic, in the heart of town or secluded in the countryside. Undoubtedly there are other wonderful places we've

not included. But we continue to sample them all and will work to include them in future editions. You might find your own favorite country inn or bed and breakfast place tucked just around the bend. Let us know.

These establishments have varying policies concerning children, pets, and cancelation; please inquire about these when you call to make reservations.

## Price Code

The average nightly rate for two adults at the facilities in this chapter is indicated by a dollar-sign ($) ranking in the following chart. Most businesses accept major credit cards for payment, but where no credit cards are accepted, we've noted that information.

| | |
|---|---:|
| $ | $50 to $70 |
| $$ | $71 to $90 |
| $$$ | $91 to $110 |
| $$$$ | $111 and more |

# Northern Mountains

## Alleghany County

### Bed and Breakfast at Turbyvilla
$$ • N.C. Hwy. 18, Sparta • (336) 372-8490

This contemporary, two-story brick home sits in the midst of a wonderful rolling landscape on 20 acres of manicured lawns in the hills just outside rural Sparta. Visiting Turbyvilla is like going home to mom's. Mimi Turbiville will make you feel welcome and has added so many personal touches to the spacious accommodations that you're sure she prepared the room just for you.

Turbyvilla has three guest rooms, each with a private bath. The full breakfast, highlighted by homemade jams and jellies, is served on a glass-enclosed porch furnished in white wicker. You'll awaken to Turbyvilla's beautiful long-range view of the mountains and the rolling pastures of Alleghany County. This stylish, comfortable bed and breakfast is open year round.

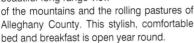

www.insiders.com
See this and many other **Insiders' Guide**® destinations online.
Visit us today!

## Burgiss Farm Bed and Breakfast
**$$$ • Elk Knob Rd. off N.C. Hwy. 18, Laurel Springs • (800) 233-1505**

The Burgiss Farm Bed and Breakfast offers a rollicking good-time atmosphere and country hospitality, thanks to its genial innkeepers Tom and Nancy Burgiss.

A substantial addition to this 1897 farmhouse has created a house-within-a-house. The addition, furnished with lodge-style comfort, has two guest rooms a private bath, a massive great room with a stone fireplace rising the full height of the vaulted ceiling, a large Jacuzzi room and even a mountain stream running through it. The complete privacy of these separate guest accommodations is very popular with honeymooners and families. Reservations are required and should be made as soon as you know your travel plans, as dates close out quickly. Also, an added goodie you might find in your room is complementary wine from the small winery on the premises.

Room prices include your choice of breakfasts — you'll have six from which to choose — served at the time you desire. Select items from Nancy's creative breakfast menu of such delights as Hawaiian pancakes, eggs Benedict, Canadian bacon, home fries, homemade breads and baked fruit. A real favorite is Nan's Cream Cheese Eggs, two baked eggs in cream cheese sauce served on an English muffin, with a special double-baked fruit dish

on the side — delicious! Kona coffee is the house specialty.

For lively entertainment, check out the Burgiss Farm's Mountain Jamboree (see our Nightlife chapter). This Bluegrass and old-timey mountain music community bash, which gets going every Saturday night in the restyled barn, provides great fun. The Burgisses also keep mountain bikes around at no extra charge, for those who like to take a spin down the country roads. Tom and Nancy will recommend a good trail for guests, according to one's abilities.

## Doughton Hall Bed & Breakfast
**$$$ • N.C. Hwy. 18, Laurel Springs • (336) 359-2341**

Less than a mile from the Blue Ridge Parkway's exit to rural Laurel Springs is Doughton Hall. Open year round, this lovely Queen Anne-style home, built in the 1890s, was once home to former Congressman Robert L. Doughton, an influential figure in Congress during the 1940s. Doughton Hall, listed on the National Register of Historic Places, has been newly refurbished by innkeepers Pam and Ed Hall. We felt like part of the family the minute we stepped into the wonderful old entrance hall. The inn has marvelous woodwork, high ceilings and old-fashioned sitting rooms. The Halls have furnished the home with antiques, some of them original to the house. Photos of Congressman Doughton during his term in Washington decorate the sitting room walls.

You have a choice of three guest rooms, two with private baths that include Jacuzzis. One room has a splendid queen-size brass bed. The buffet breakfast is generous enough to serve a crowd — eggs cooked to order, several kinds of fresh bread, country ham, sausage, bacon, croissants and more — even if the house isn't full of guests. Pam's mother, who frequently is responsible for preparing this bounty, explains that it's no trouble at all, because she's always cooked for a houseful at home.

You can fish from the creek at the end of the lawn, rock on the front porch or have a cool drink in the gazebo.

# Ashe County

## Glendale Springs Inn & Restaurant
$$$-$$$$ • 7414 N.C. Hwy. 16, Glendale Springs • (336) 982-2103, (800) 287-1206

This splendid inn is composed of two buildings: the original historic structure, whose foundations were built c. 1892 and completed between 1902 and 1905; and the guest house across the country road. The main house has been used over the century as a general merchandise store; a circuit courthouse; post office and chapel; a community center; a boarding house; and a private home. It now houses three dining rooms, five guest rooms with private baths and two parlors for relaxing. The guest parlors are peppered with owner Amanda Smith's family antiques, as well as those acquired later, including a Duncan Phyfe sofa upon which she remembers being courted and an old English sewing cabinet, a marble chess set and a slender "lady's desk" made of burlwood. Pine and oak broad-beamed wood floors creaked underneath our steps as we peeked into the cheerfully painted pastel bedrooms. Crisp sheets and comforters cover the one king- and four queen-size beds in the main house. Battenburg lace curtains surround the deep claw-foot tubs, and each bedroom has a television and air conditioning.

Our favorite accommodation here is the cottage, with four large bedrooms with fireplaces and Jacuzzis. Country quilts cover these cherry high-poster king- and queen-size beds, and one room is furnished with an extra bed for a child. We especially like the butler pantry in the guest cottage, featuring makings for tea, coffee and hot chocolate at any time of day or evening.

Rocking chairs on the front porch of the cottage and porch swings and white wicker furniture on the main house's front porch are perfect for watching the twilight curtain descend over Glendale Springs and the fireflies light up the evening. A full breakfast is pro-

vided for inn guests in the dining room (see our Restaurants chapter), and lest you not stray too far from the office, fax and a photocopier are available for your use.

The inn is just a walk down the road to one of the Ashe County Frescoes. The Blue Ridge Parkway is also close-by.

## River House
$$$$ • 1896 Old Field Creek Rd., off N.C. Hwy. 16 N., Grassy Creek • (336) 982-2109

Remember as a child when you and your parents would take a Sunday drive? You marked the time by counting the cows in the pastures and the bridges over creeks and rivers. As the sun began to mellow, you'd round a hill and there would be the comforting sight of your aunt and uncle's farmhouse. A wonderful aroma would drift from inside, and you'd hurry upstairs to find your favorite room just as you remembered it. Recapture that feeling in remote northern Ashe County, at River House.

Innkeepers Gayle Winston and John Stewart have taken pains to re-create and maintain the gentler pace of a time past. No televisions or room phones disturb the tranquility of River House, an elegant 1870 farmhouse that was once home to a local physician. The home has been meticulously restored and tastefully furnished with period antiques. River House sits near the Virginia border on 125 beautifully rolling acres, a mile of which hugs the New River. The inn, open year round, offers two guest rooms upstairs in the main house, each with a private bath and a choice of queen- or king-size beds. These two front bedrooms have views of the lazy New River, one of the oldest in the world, and to the mountains beyond.

You also have your choice of two cottages, one a former doctor's office, behind the main house. These offer guests a wonderful sense of privacy. Each of the four cottage rooms includes a sitting area and a whirlpool bath. Two rooms have private porches with views of the river or mountains or both!

River House is also home to an exceptional restaurant with a unique menu prepared by chef Bill Klein of Hickory, North Carolina. Guests who discover River House return frequently, say its innkeepers, not only for the gracious service of this old-style country inn, but also for the magnificent fare of the River House restaurant. Regulars come from across the country and abroad. (See our Restaurant chapter.)

# Avery County

## Archer's Mountain Inn
**$$-$$$$ • 2489 Beech Mountain Pkwy. (N.C. Hwy. 184), Beech Mountain • (828) 898-9004**

Archer's Mountain Inn, nearly 5,000 feet above sea level, offers views of Sugar and Grandfather mountains and acres of fresh mountain air, lush foliage and surrounding flower and herb gardens. With new owners, a new restaurant (Jackalope's View; see our Restaurants chapter) and new decor, the inn has captivated a youthful, inspired audience. Guests enjoy the wood-paneled rooms, with high cross-beamed ceilings, the personal fireplaces, the views of the opposing mountain ridge, the private porches with rocking chairs — somehow you just don't want to leave your room.

Three buildings compose the inn. Two are for guest housing — one has eight guest rooms with knotty pine panelling and exposed beams. Each room has a queen-size bed, a stone fireplace and small kitchenette, as well as private porches. The main building has six guest rooms, one with an outdoor hot tub on the broad balcony. All rooms have fireplaces, private baths, real down comforters and coffee and tea makers.

We love the Presidential Suite, a grand affair with 14-foot-high ceilings, a king-size four-poster bed, a large fireplace, our own balcony and a glassed-in bathroom with a Jacuzzi. We sipped from the complimentary decanter of port until late in the evening, watching the lights twinkle in the valley below. When we opted for company, we sidled up to the bar in the inn's dining room where locals, the innkeepers, guests and friends were watching the basketball playoffs. You won't be a stranger for long here.

The Hawk's View is another building offering spacious rooms decorated with struc-tural cedar beams, a fieldstone fireplace in each room, kitchen efficiencies and a broad porch for the unparalleled views.

Owners Candi and Tony have built walking trails around the inn, which is perched on the edge of Beech Mountain, and a small waterfall flowing into the garden below the terrace, open for dining in the warm months. Candi prepares a breakfast for overnight guests, who select from a menu of omelets, fluffy pancakes, French toast, fresh fruit, ham, sausage, bacon and other offerings. Personal service, excellent food and a homey but pampered atmosphere make it hard to leave Archer's Mountain Inn. Decor, which is simple, yet crisp and neat — like twig wreaths, dried flowers, neat floral trim on the painted walls, warm wood paneling in other rooms, soft antique bedspreads and mountains of fluffy pillows — will keep us coming back.

## The Azalea Inn
**$$$$ • Azalea Cir., Banner Elk • (828) 898-8195**

Originally owned by members of one of Banner Elk's founding families, the house had fallen into disrepair in the not so distant past. No longer! Extensive renovations have restored the house — including Banner Elk's first claw-footed bathtub — to its original charm. From its elegantly furnished rooms to cozy porches, this is a pleasing and restful escape.

In the heart of town, the inn is within walking distance of the village shops and many fine restaurants.

## Banner Elk Inn Bed & Breakfast
**$$$-$$$$ • 407 Main St. E., Banner Elk • (828) 898-6223**

This small, charming inn is convenient to Boone and the ski resorts of the northern mountains. The tasteful decor here has the flavor of both the Victorian era and Old World Europe. All five guest rooms have private baths. Ask about the third-floor Garrett Suite, which is perfect for honeymooners. It has a full bath with a tub for two, a view of the stone fountain in the English garden below, cable television and a king-size bed.

Breakfasts include banana nut muffins, Parmesan omelet souffle with cheddar cheese sauce, pumpkin bread might be on the weekend menu. Weekday breakfasts are full-service but a bit simpler.

## Eseeola Lodge
$$$$ • U.S. Hwy. 221, Linville
• (828) 733-4311, (800) 742-6717

This wonderful old inn is central to the history of Linville as well as to the development of the High Country as a tourist destination. The original Eseeola Lodge, destroyed by fire in 1936, had its beginnings at the turn of the century with the advent of the railroad in these long-remote mountains. As a result, Eseeola Lodge and Linville soon became a fashionable watering place for the wealthy of the Southeast. Golf became a passion at the lodge, and a premier 18-hole course designed by renowned golf architect Donald Ross was added in the 1920s. In those early years, Eseeola Lodge was the center of community activity and lively entertainment for the village of Linville.

Today's lodge, with its distinctive chestnut bark siding, continues the tradition of that early Eseeola Lodge. There are 29 small, tastefully furnished guest rooms, most with private porches. They surround the warm, richly furnished, wood-paneled main gathering room. The fireplace at one end draws people to its comfortably stuffed armchairs and perhaps a lazy nod by the fire. Adjoining the main gathering room is the lodge dining room where breakfast and dinner are served; the price of meals is included in accommodations. The elegant dinner menu includes specialties such as crab mousse with red and yellow pepper sauce, poached Carolina flounder stuffed with spinach and grilled loin of veal. Gentlemen are asked to wear a jacket and tie for dinner.

The manicured grounds offer a number of diversions: tennis on clay courts, a heated swimming pool, golf and croquet. The clubhouse serves lunch. Eseeola Lodge is surrounded by 2,000 acres for hiking and fishing. The lodge provides a special children's recreation program.

Eseeola Lodge is open from mid-May to mid-October.

## Linville Cottage
$-$$$ • Box 508, Linville
• (828) 733-6551

A whitewashed picket fence surrounds this restored, turn of the century Victorian farmhouse, with its English cottage perennial and herb gardens. The rooms are filled with antiques and collectibles. The charm of the cottage is accented by the eight-gable tin roof, plank floors, and featherbeds. A breakfast room overlooks Grandfather Mountain and the Blue Ridge Parkway. The accommodations allow comfortable lodging with enchanting rooms filled with simple country antiques and collectibles, but very, very casual. Delightful English country cottage perennial and herb gardens surround the inn. The innkeepers serve a deluxe full continental breakfast of homemade breads and baked goods served with jellies and jams preserved from the gardens. The Inn also houses a small shop out back filled with antiques and collectibles.

## Tufts House Bed & Breakfast
$$$ • Edgar Tufts Rd., Banner Elk
• (828) 898-7944

What a delight — this is old country estate sits on a mountainside overlooking Elk River Valley with views of both Beech and Sugar Mountains. The stone and wood home, run by innkeepers Nancy and Dean Barnett, features cozy rooms decorated with a blend of original furnishings, antique pieces, and modern bedding. Provided robes and slippers give you real reason to curl up in your room, and the added gift of fresh fruit and flowers is a pleasant welcome gift. You won't find televisions or phones in these rooms. Look out the window — that's entertainment enough! A den with fireplace and soft sofas beckon you to sit and warm up to the convivial atmosphere. The fresh aroma of coffee and cinnamon rolls will awaken you, and this is only a hint of the gourmet breakfast to come.

According to season and weather, Nancy and Dean will serve breakfast in either the dining room, terrace, or in front of the warm fire. If you prefer, they will even prepare you a picnic basket for a private breakfast in your room. With such pampering, it's almost hard to tear yourself away into the beautiful outdoors that surround Tufts House.

# Madison County

## Baird House
**$$-$$$ • 41 S. Main St., Mars Hill**
**• (828) 689-5722**

This fine old house was once the home of Dr. John Hannibal Baird, a medical doctor of the late 1800s, who served the people living in the mountains around Mars Hill. In appreciation for his dedicated service, local residents built this home in the 1890s for Baird, his wife and their nine children. It was considered one of the grandest homes in the area. Dr. Baird continued his medical practice until his death in the 1920s.

The home then passed to Dr. Baird's son, John W. Baird, also a physician. At his untimely death, his grieving widow, Lexine, left the area for rural Harlan County, Kentucky. There, carrying on the family medical tradition, she became a nurse-on-horseback to the folks of that remote area. She did return to Baird House, however, many years later, renting rooms to students of Mars Hill College. They knew her kindly as "Ma Baird" or "Aunt Lex."

Today, Yvette Wessel, a transplant from Connecticut, carries on the hospitality begun by the Baird family. She has furnished the home in 18th-century French, English and American antiques, all chosen with a particular nod to history and many with stories of their own, such as the Wellington chests used by British Naval officers or the wood-framed fanlight Yvette rescued from a building demolition in New York City.

Baird House contains five guest rooms, two with private baths. Two rooms have fireplaces. A full breakfast is served. Baird House is open year round except December.

## The Duckett House Inn & Farm
**$$-$$$ • N.C. Hwy. 209, Hot Springs**
**• (828) 622-7621**

Hot Springs, once a fashionable destination for Victorians seeking the curative waters for which the town was named, continues to evoke that earlier charm. Always a popular stopover for hikers of the Appalachian Trail that passes through town, Hot Springs is currently enjoying a renaissance of sorts, and The Duckett House Inn & Farm is part of that rebirth. With the inn as your base, you can enjoy whitewater rafting, the Hot Springs Spa mineral baths and hiking.

Room rates include a full vegetarian breakfast. Gourmet vegetarian dinners are available on weekends for an additional charge.

## Marshall House
## Bed & Breakfast Inn
**$-$$$ • 100 Hill St., Marshall**
**• (828) 649-9205**

Marshall House is nestled in the hillside above the town of Marshall, about 30 minutes northwest of Asheville. Noted society architect Richard Sharp Smith built this home in 1903 as the private residence of James H. White, a prominent Madison County community leader and political figure. The distinctive pebble-dash exterior is typical of the homes Smith built in the Asheville area and the cottages of Biltmore Village, commissioned by George Vanderbilt.

Marshall House fosters the serenity of that simpler time characterized by the town of Marshall itself, just below on the banks of the French Broad River. Innkeepers Ruth and Jim Boylan offer nine guest rooms at Marshall House. Choice antiques decorate the house. Two rooms have private baths, the others have shared baths. A sumptuous breakfast of pancakes, French toast or waffles, eggs and homemade breads or bagels is served to guests in the formal dining room. From the veranda you can see the spectacular French Broad River and the village that hugs its banks. A resident cat and dog share the house with you.

# Mitchell County

## Castle Inn on English Knob

**$$$$ • Castle Way, Spruce Pine
• (828) 765-0000, (800) 925-2645**

And just when you thought fairy tales were only for children . . .

Winding your way around the long gravel-and-dirt drive you will encounter a pristine white castle rising out of the top of the mountain. Two of the turrets were once part of a stately home begun in the 1970s, but water-treatment and the once-treacherous road were problems too difficult to surmount for the original owners. Bob and Norma Jean Schabilion took over construction, purchasing 130 acres surrounding the Castle as well. What they have created is an opulent and grand vision of splendor, the perfect place for weddings, over-the-top celebrations and honeymoons and for those desiring a little something different.

With only five suites, the Castle is not designed for crowds, but then, it is the individual attention the owners like to bestow on their guests that is key. The marble entrance leads to twin fireplaces flanking the stairs, crystal chandeliers and lamps lighting our way. The Great Room is dominated by a two-story native-stone fireplace and seating alcove at one end, a unique heirloom rectangular grand piano at the other. Period and many reproduction furnishings mark this hall and the various rooms. Look up and you will see skylights beyond the 5-foot-high chandelier and a wrap-around interior balcony leading off to each suite.

Before venturing upstairs, stroll out onto the terrace where a fountain provides the rhythmic sound of splashing water and the view continues over several ridges. A library with a fireplace, a massive table-size chess set and a coffee table of fossils and stone lend this room its rich, dark atmosphere. Upstairs, the Royal Tower and Lady-in-Waiting Suites boasts Jacuzzis off their private balconies, with a small tower observatory above. Each suite has its distinctive color scheme and style. We especially liked the gold gros-grain wallpaper of the large Tower Suite bath. The Royal Princess Suite afforded us a 180-degree view of the mountains beyond through our sliding shuttered windows. The all white-and-cream room, complete with strategically placed mirrors and skylight, was the smallest of the five, but didn't skimp on indulgent ornamentation, including a mirrored coffee table, crystal chandelier under the satin sweeping drape above the bed's headboard, and a white television in keeping with the color scheme. Each room has its own private bath.

Three dining rooms, including one under a starlit ceiling and one under a ceiling of decoupaged Old Master's works, brass and gilt, also serve as the breakfast area for guests. We were offered a cup of fresh sliced mango and strawberries, coffee, juice, and a plate of sausage, a poached egg and heart-shaped cocoa waffles with a delightful honey-cinnamon butter. The Castle's own limousine may be arranged for transportation and airport pickups.

## Chinquapin Inn

**$-$$, no credit cards • Penland
School Rd., off U.S. 19 E., Penland
• (828) 765-0064**

Chinquapin Inn sits in the woods within walking distance of Penland School of Crafts (see our Mountain Crafts chapter). This charming gray-shingled cottage was built in 1937 by Bill Ford's father, then an instructor at the Penland School. This former family residence has been maintained as an inn since 1986 by Bill and Sue Ford. They have filled Chinquapin with treasures from their travels to the Middle East, Africa and Asia. Family antiques also grace the guest areas on the first two floors. Bill and Sue's quarters are on the inn's third story, in effect leaving the remainder of the house to the use of guests. You'll enjoy the sunny rooms, stone fireplaces, pine floors and inviting old-fashioned, enclosed sun porches.

Sue Ford is the chef and serves up a fine breakfast featuring pancakes, waffles, home-made breads and muffins, fresh fruit and fancy, home-ground coffees. Four rooms are available, connected by two shared baths. These large rooms with sitting areas can be rented as two suites. Hiking trails and crafts studios are nearby.

## The Switzerland Inn
### $$$-$$$$ • Mi. 334, off the Blue Ridge Pkwy., Little Switzerland
### • (828) 765-2153, (800) 654-4026

The Switzerland Inn is a landmark in the northern Mountains. Perched high on a ridge, it straddles Mitchell and McDowell counties and commands one of the most spectacular views in the region. In fact, the view is so spectacular that the area derived its name from its resemblance to the equally beautiful mountain views of Switzerland, its European cousin. North Carolina State Supreme Court Judge Herriot Clarkson was the first to be inspired by the Swiss-like atmosphere of this knob, and he determined to make it his own, buying 1,100 acres in 1910. The charm of the place is its unchanging personality, remaining pretty much as it was 80 or so years ago.

It's no wonder that the Blue Ridge Parkway planners chose to guide the scenic highway along this route at its beginning in 1935. The exit at Little Switzerland is the only one on the Parkway that leads to private land. The Jensen family, longtime seasonal residents who are now permanent mountaineers, purchased the inn in the 1980s. They have maintained the 55-room lodge and its surrounding grounds with the same devotion Judge Clarkson brought to Little Switzerland so long ago.

The Switzerland Inn is a veritable kingdom unto itself. Quaint lodging, fine dining and unusual specialty shopping are all available here. The ambiance is wonderful in this rustic, Swiss chalet-style lodge, and in particular in its great hall. Guests mingle here, playing a friendly game of checkers, relaxing by the fire, listening to the charming strains of a Victorian-era music box or just burrowing into the comfortable armchairs to watch the mists roll in over the mountain ridge. For summer fun, the Switzerland Inn has an outdoor swimming pool, a tennis court and the pleasures of the magnificent Blue Ridge Parkway at your doorstep.

The restaurant at the Switzerland Inn is popular with area residents as well as with inn guests. The setting is elegant yet rustic, with interesting murals of actual mountain locations throughout the restaurant. The fare consists of chicken, steak and seafood combinations artfully prepared. The chicken pie, for instance, is a blend of meat and fresh vegetables in a hearty broth topped by a homemade biscuit crust — very satisfying on a fall afternoon.

Shopping along the little avenue of specialty stores adjacent to the Switzerland Inn is a bit like visiting Santa's Main Street. You can find anything from sinfully rich fudge and homemade candies to mountain crafts, unusual toys, ladies fine accessories and one-of-a-kind gift items. One of our favorite stores at the Switzerland Inn complex is Busy B's. This elegant shop has beautiful hand-painted Russian matryoshka dolls (nesting dolls) imported straight from a Russian village. Exquisite handmade jewelry, lovely white china decorated with a grape leaf motif, Depression-era glassware, hand-embroidered sweaters and other fine ladies clothing fill this charming shop. What caught our eye from the entry were unusual collectible gift items — shadow boxes highlighting hand-sewn miniature replicas of period ladies clothing (Victorian-era, 1920s, etc.), with every delicate detail in place.

If you stay a night at the Switzerland Inn, you'll want to stay a week. Book early for visits during mid-October, which is the peak of the leaf season in the North Carolina mountains. The inn is open May through October.

# Watauga County

## Gideon Ridge Inn
### $$$-$$$$ • 202 Gideon Ridge Inn Rd., Blowing Rock • (828) 295-3644

What is it about this Inn we like so much? Could it be the understated elegance of tasteful decor and magnificent family antiques throughout the house that enveloped us immediately into its fold? Was it the views from the rooms, porches and gardens that spread over countless mountain ridges? Or was it the gardens themselves — paths running through graduated banks dotted with rich yellow black-eyed Susans, rhododendrons of pink and white and ivy and a pergola under which to sit with our first cup of steaming coffee to gaze over the mountains? Perhaps it was just the small touches that captured our hearts. Afternoon tea was spread before us on the dining room island as we arrived. A pot of Earl Gray, which the innkeepers import from England, sat beside plates of light home-made shortbread and finger sandwiches.

Made of cedar and the red stone of Grandfather Mountain, the building itself hugs the ridge. The nephew of Moses Cone, a textile magnate who built textile mills in Greensboro, North Carolina, with the money from his Cone Export & Commission Company in New York City, constructed the home as a mountain cottage in 1939. In front of the fireplace in the living room is a soft leather sofa, perfect for sinking into and reading the magazines and newspapers provided, and a wide leather hassock. The carpet was designed by William Morris. Several carpets and Central Asian kilims lend the hall and dining room their natural earthen warmth. The walnut dining table, a fourth-generation family heirloom, is surrounded by high-back chairs. Four Russian impressionist paintings in muted hues decorate the walls. The artist was a friend of innkeeper Cobb Milner and his wife who they met when they spent nine months in Minsk, Belarus in 1993.

A 19th-century Bailey, Banks & Biddle grandfather clock ticks away the hours in the hallway. The butler's pantry is stocked for guests with cold juices and sodas, a kettle and plenty of tea, coffee and hot chocolate-making items. The 10 guest rooms are each unique — adorned with table and chair settings, a large bed and decorative knickknacks — they seem almost like small apartments. Seven of them have fireplaces. Think mahogany four-poster beds, marble sinks and antique furniture in every room. Our favorite is the Sunrise View, set apart from the others with its own private entrance. The king-size bed, piled high with thick pillows and quilts, offers a view out the picture window of the sun rising over 90 miles of mountain peaks. Under the beamed cathedral ceiling is a Franklin iron stove, an open whirlpool tub surrounded by a stone wall and a bathroom designed with an exposed stone wall in the shower. Each room has a private bath.

Breakfast, set at individual wooden tables in a glass-enclosed terrace above the gardens, is prepared by Jane, the younger Cobb Milner' mother. (His father is also named Cobb.) Once in textile restoration at New York's Metropolitan Museum of Art, Jane now whips up stuffed French toast, cornmeal pancakes, muffins, waffles, sausage and numerous other edibles, all attractively presented with fresh fruit. On our visit we were served genuine Vermont maple syrup and loved the added touch of apricots stewed with cinnamon sticks.

### The Inn at the Taylor House
$$$$ • N.C. Hwy. 194, Valle Crucis
• (828) 963-5581

This lovely, two-story farmhouse with double chimneys and a wraparound porch, was built in 1911 for the family of C.D. Taylor. Today, it has been transformed into a sophisticated European-style inn with farmhouse flair. Innkeeper Carol "Chip" Schwab runs her inn as an extension of her home, offering much more than an overnight stay. Guests also enjoy the inn's mountain escape for family reunions, wedding and anniversary celebrations, special luncheons or dinner parties, art shows, cooking classes and flower shows.

The Inn at the Taylor House is decorated with a mix of European and American country antiques, Oriental rugs and original art work. There are ten spacious rooms in the inn, all offering private baths and goose-down comforters. Three of the rooms are suites, complemented by comfortable sitting rooms. A gourmet breakfast is included and usually includes seasonal fruit, pancakes, fresh vegetables and specially prepared egg dishes.

The inn's old milkhouse has been converted into a charming gift shop that offers unusual items, garden accessories and specialty foods. A private massage parlor is located on the property, and a masseuse is on call for massages, manicures, and pedicures.

### Lindridge House Bed & Breakfast
$$$-$$$$ • U.S. 221 S., Blowing Rock
• (828) 295-7343, (800) 295-7343

This two-story home is nestled on top of a mountain 5 miles from Blowing Rock. Its park-like setting creates the atmosphere of a retreat. The home's large parlor has a warm stone fireplace, and an adjoining room has a pool table to wile away your time. Places of interest nearby will keep you busy too, including Calloway Gap, Grandfather Mountain, Tweetsie Railroad, Linville Caverns and the many ski areas.

Each of the three guest rooms here has a commanding view of the mountains. Miss Hannah's Room is decorated with antiques and is large on personality. The Colonel's Room has a king-size bed and an elegant ambiance. And the Rose Suite is charmingly decorated and features two rooms overlooking the Globe Valley and mountain ranges.

Each room has cable TV and a private bath. Breakfast is included, and off-season rates are available.

## Lovill House Inn
$$$$ • 404 Old Bristol Rd., Boone
• (828) 264-4204, (800) 849-9466

This historic home, built in 1875, was the residence of Capt. Edward Francis Lovill, a decorated Confederate officer, North Carolina state senator and a founding trustee of the Appalachian Training School, later Appalachian State University. In fact, it was in the front parlor of Lovill House, the Captain's occasional law office, where he and B.B. Daugherty drafted the papers establishing the university. The home continued as a Lovill family residence well into the 1970s.

Innkeepers Tim and Lori Shahen discovered Lovill House just five years ago and transformed this elegant residence and its 11 wooded acres on the edge of Boone into one of the premier bed and breakfast inns in the High Country. Personal service and attention to detail are the secrets of their success. Guests are pampered and often become friends.

You'll wake to the rich aroma of home-baked muffins and coffee outside your door. The Shahens prepare a full gourmet breakfast, including seasonal fruit, home-baked breads, Belgian waffles, eggs Benedict, garden vegetable strata and omelets, accompanied by country ham, sausage or bacon. The informal evening social hour is popular with guests of Lovill House. Groups gather outside by the stream, in the rockers on the front porch or around the cozy front parlor fireplace.

You can hike the trails on the lovely grounds, or Tim will map out scenic back-road auto trips. Tim and Lori have become immersed in activities in the Boone area and can recommend the best local restaurants. (They'll even make reservations for you.) Restoration of the grounds and outbuildings continues, with plans for additional accommodations in the future.

Lori has furnished the inn in a casually elegant country style, with a mix of antiques and quality reproductions. The wormy chestnut paneling was discovered during restoration and supplemented by matching refinished wood recovered from old, abandoned barns. The inn offers five guest rooms, each with a private bath, television (discreetly tucked away in a wooden cabinet) and telephone. Beds at the Lovill House are spread with down comforters. Lori and Tim encourage you to let them know if you have special dietary requirements, if you'll be celebrating a special occasion or if you require any other service to make your visit more enjoyable.

## Maple Lodge
$$$-$$$$ • 152 Sunset Dr., Blowing Rock
• (828) 295-3331

This charming inn reflects the simplicity and grace of the 1930s and '40s. Named for the maple tree in the front yard, this pleasant two-story frame home was built as a boarding house for tourists. Staying at Maple Lodge reminds us of visiting the elegant, treasure-filled home of a favorite aunt, one who greets you warmly at the door, offers delectable goodies served on fine china, hot cider from her sunny kitchen out back and ushers you to a more-than-perfect guest room. In short, you feel at home.

Maple Lodge has 11 guest rooms, each named for a garden flower. These rooms, with twin-, full-, queen- and king-size beds, all have private baths. Some beds have lovely crocheted canopies.

A hearty buffet breakfast that includes homemade muffins, breads, a variety of egg dishes and fresh fruit is served every day from 8:30 to 10 AM in the pleasant sun room overlooking the flower garden. The meticulous attention to detail of innkeeper Marilyn Bateman contributes to a memorable stay here.

Main Street Blowing Rock is just a stone's throw from Maple Lodge, convenient to restaurants and shopping. Blowing Rock Stage Company performs just down the street in summer.

### The Mast Farm Inn
**$$$$ • S.R. 1112, off N.C. Hwy. 105,
Valle Crucis • (828) 963-5857**

The Mast Farm Inn has been a landmark and vital part of the history of the High Country since 1885. It was operated as an inn by Finley Mast and his wife, Josephine, in the early 1900s. The Masts were known far and wide for their mountain hospitality, not to mention the bounty of their table. And it's still possible to find someone, as we did, with personal memories of that early Mast Farm. The gracious lady we encountered, who was visiting from Pulaski, Virginia, recalled the pleasure of her visit to the Loom House of Mast Farm more than 60 years earlier as a student from Appalachian State University in Boone.

In 1972 the Mast Farm Inn was included on the National Register of Historic Places. It remains one of the best examples of a self-contained mountain homestead in the state. The rambling 18-room Victorian farmhouse is the center of the inn and is open year round. The main house has nine guest rooms all with private baths. All rooms have queen- and king-size beds. Original outbuildings — the Blacksmith Shop, the Woodwork Shop and the Loom House — have been converted to additional, comfortably furnished guest quarters.

The Raspberry Hill Cabin is the newest accommodation here. Built from white pine logs and featuring a cathedral ceiling, it is both rustic and spacious. Sit on the porch and rock for a while — you'll feel as though you own the valley. The cabin features two full bedrooms (one king, one queen), two bathrooms (one with a whirlpool tub), a loft with a double futon, a great room and a fully equipped kitchen.

The Loom House, the log cabin originally built by David Mast in 1812, was Finley and Josephine Mast's first home. Here Josephine gloried in her weaving, of which she was expert. Some of her work has been featured in exhibits at the Smithsonian Institution. Today the Loom House is a special guest cottage with a kitchen, sleeping loft and fireplace. The combination of period farmhouse antiques and modern conveniences at The Mast Farm Inn allows guests to easily enjoy the charm of turn-of-the-century mountain life in North Carolina.

Rates include a bountiful breakfast. Breakfast offers something different on the menu every day, but it always features scrumptious homemade breads, fresh fruit and jams, jellies and preserves.

Wanda Hinshaw and her sister Kay Himshaw Philip took over the Inn 3 years ago and have made many changes since then. Changing the dining from family-style country cooking to fine dining a la carte is perhaps the most noticeable.

Dinner is served six nights a week from May through October, and on weekends the rest of the year.

## The Inn at Ragged Gardens
### $$$-$$$$ • 203 Sunset Dr., Blowing Rock • (828) 295-9703

This grand old inn surrounded by a stone wall and lovely English cottage-style flower gardens is covered by the rustic chestnut bark siding frequently found on fine older homes in the High Country. Owners Jama and Lee Hyett have refurbished and reconstructed the inn to reflect an architecturally and decoratively succinct masterpiece. Built as a seasonal summer "cottage," the estate has been remodeled to accept guests all year long in its twelve distinctive rooms, all designed and decorated by a Charlotte interior decorator working in conjunction with the Hyetts. These include five new suites designed in the Arts and Crafts period. Each of these five suites has separate sitting areas, whirlpool baths for two, fireplaces, and balconies or patios looking into the formal rock-walled garden.

Our personal favorites are the Rock Garden Garret and the Evergreen Garret — soothing bedrooms under the eves of the skylit roof. The Rock Garden is a suite with a king-size bed, a window seat, a whirlpool bath and a giggling fountain in the reading nook. The Evergreen is resplendent with a unique handcrafted king-size bed, a corner fireplace and a whirlpool bath with an old-fashioned dressing area — a lady's dream.

Another favorite is the Camelot Suite, a jewel-toned suite with soft ochre walls, a rock fireplace, wrought iron furnishings and a Middle Eastern wall tapestry. The queen-size bed is adorned with a fantasia-like coat of arms, with arcs of richly draped fabric emanating from its center. The sitting room contains a twin bed and a love seat, separated from the bedroom by a pair of antique French doors. Other rooms — Monet's Garden, Moss and Lace, Blue Wisteria and English Lavender — evoke floral garden visions as well. A very popular room has proved to be the new Lee & Ann's Treehouse, situated privately on the third floor of the new wing and fashioned after a treehouse lover's fantasy.

The central focus of the Ragged Garden Inn is its magnificent stone staircase in the grand hall. It leads down into the common room with a fireplace, a central television and a coffee table stacked with magazines, daily newspapers, albums of the Hyett's renovation of the inn and the ubiquitous bottle of port. Another excellent touch is the butler's pantry on the second floor, always furnished with sodas, juices, coffee, tea, mints, hot chocolate and rich home-baked cookies always present under a glass dome. If the cookies haven't spoiled your breakfast appetite, pull close to the lace-covered table and Jama and Lee will cook up eggs to order, fresh fruit cups, omelets, pancakes, waffles and sausage, only after you have helped yourself to the buffet of muffins, bagels and breads. Candles glow on the mantel on misty cool mornings, while summer days allow for breakfast out on the porch overlooking the brilliant variety of flowers of the Ragged Gardens.

## Rustic Barn Bed & Breakfast
### $$$$ 2171 Broadstone Rd., Valle Crucis • (828) 963-7339

Come enjoy the spectacular view of the valley with a thoroghbred horse farm and mountain as backdrop. Arrive via the private B & B entrance to Rustic Barn in Valle. This hillside log home maintains two rooms furnished in a blend of rustic antiques and family heirlooms. A bath and a sitting room are shared. The sitting room features a big-screen TV, a large selection of video movies, games and books. A continental breakfast featuring local homemade muffins, steaming coffee, fresh brewed tea and juices is served in the sitting room. The Rustic Room features a lodge pole style queen bed. The Antique Room features twin beds. With two roll-away beds, the B&B can comfortably accommodate six people.

# Yancey County

## Nu-Wray Inn

$$$-$$$$ • Town Square, Burnsville
• (828) 682-2329, (800) 368-9729

It seems as if the town of Burnsville grew up around the Nu-Wray Inn. The recorded heritage of this venerable accommodation dates back to 1833. It was long known as a stagecoach stop for weary travelers making their way through the rough country of North Carolina's mountains. From the wide, covered front porch to the second-floor balcony or topmost third floor aerie, the Nu-Wray Inn is a special place. One of the distinct pleasures of the inn is wandering its wonderfully creaky floors and twisting stairways. Everywhere you look, you discover another treasure: an antique lamp, an ornately carved Black Forest clock, quaint Victorian bric-a-brac, an old oak public telephone booth in the lobby and graceful Southern antiques on every floor.

The inn is a cumulative family history, a visible scrapbook of the union of Yancey County's prominent Ray and Wray families. The inn passed from the Wray family after the death in the mid-1980s of family scion Rush Wray. Now Doug and Barb Brown have shouldered the historic mantle of the Nu-Wray Inn and continue the guardianship of this grand old mountain landmark.

Noted writers Thomas Wolfe of Asheville and O. Henry, master of the classic short story, stayed here. It was here at the inn, an hour's distance from Asheville, that Thomas Wolfe retreated in 1937 to avoid a dubious welcome after the publication of *Look Homeward, Angel*, the thinly-disguised portrayal of Wolfe's boyhood home and its less-than-pleased citizenry. Faithful fans often request the room that housed a celebrity of a more recent era, the King himself, rock 'n' roll legend Elvis Presley.

With customary mountain hospitality, the Browns have maintained the gracious atmosphere that has always been identified with the Nu-Wray Inn. They've also added their own touches, including special events such as Mystery Weekend, holiday celebrations and craft workshops. Another tradition that continues is family-style meals, where local residents have long joined with guests for hearty country breakfasts and mouthwatering mountain suppers of generous proportions. A Victorian Reginaphone music box announces every meal. Special holiday meals are always well received, but remember to reserve your place early!

The Nu-Wray Inn has 25 guest rooms. Antique-filled sitting areas grace each of the three floors.

Breakfast is complimentary for guests. Meal prices for the public are $5.95 for breakfast, $11.95 for dinner and $11.95 for Sunday supper (served at 1 PM).

## Terrell House Bed and Breakfast

$$-$$$ • 109 Robertson St., Burnsville
• (828) 682-4505

A little off the beaten path in the friendly township of Burnsville, historic Terrell House is surrounded by mountains, offering its guests vistas of the Blue Ridge Mountains, the Bald and Unakas ranges and Seven Mile Ridge. The nearby Black Mountains are capped by the majestic Mount Mitchell. The inn is about 30 minutes from Asheville.

The 1900 Colonial-style home was built as a girls dormitory for the Stanley McCormick School. You can choose from six lovely guest accommodations, each with its own personality and furnished with a queen- or full-size bed. Each room has a private bath with shower.

Make yourself at home in the parlor, where the company of other guests adds to the pleasant stay here. Or seek out the tranquility of the garden swing or the wicker-furnished back patio.

## INSIDERS' TIP

If you don't feel like making conversation with strangers over early morning breakfast, tell your hosts beforehand. They may be able to seat you more privately if you prefer.

You will awake to the aroma of freshly brewed coffee, and a sumptuous breakfast is served in the dining room.

# Central Mountains

## Buncombe County

### A Bed of Roses
**$$$-$$$$ • 135 Cumberland Ave., Asheville • (828) 258-8700**

Styled after an English country cottage, this Queen Ann Victorian was built in 1897 and is on the Register of Historic Homes. A full Gourmet Breakfast is served in the formal dining room on fine china and includes a variety of homemade coffeecakes, fresh biscuits and jam, fresh fruit in season, and homemade granola. Gourmet coffee, fine English teas, and homemade cakes & cookies are served in the afternoon. Relax and smell the fresh flowers from the front porch rockers. Air-conditioned guest rooms are uniquely furnished with unusual antique pieces, handmade quilts, and fresh flowers. All rooms have private baths, some with Jacuzzi tubs and antique clawfoot tubs. There is also a private balcony with one room. You will find a charming Victorian honeymoon cottage behind the main house. The hosts now offer horseback riding excursions from the inn.

### The Black Walnut Bed and Breakfast Inn
**$$-$$$ • 288 Montford Ave., Asheville • (828) 254-3878**

Randy and Sandra Glasgow, innkeepers-extraordinaire, have traveled down from Canada to run this delightful bed and breakfast in Asheville's historic district of Montford. The Black Walnut Inn stands out significantly from its surroundings as a Shingle-style house built in 1899 by architect Richard Sharp Smith. It was restored as a Bed and Breakfast in 1992.

Only a short walk from downtown, the inn is surrounded by a lushly landscaped garden of flowers, black walnut trees, conifers, ivy, and perfectly trimmed shrubbery. Four guest rooms in the main house and two separate rooms in a garden cottage echo this perfec-

tion with an airy decor of pastels that blend antiques and fine-hewn traditional furniture.

The Walnut Room, a highlight of the inn, envelopes you in the comfortable luxury of a century-old armoire, dresser and queen size bed. A fireplace and clawfoot tub add to the historic ambiance of this suite. The Azalea Room next door can be opened to adjoin the two chambers or can be rented separately; it contains a queen-size sleigh bed, fireplace and bath with a whirlpool tub. This sunny room is decorated with a cabbage rose designer fabric and crisp white eyelet lace. The Holly Room, also airy and filled with the light of the sun, contains a special queen-size antique mahogany "rooster" bed. The carvings tell all. As for our favorites, we find it hard to choose between the Dogwood Room and the Magnolia Suite and Cottage Loft. The former, a turret-shaped room with a cloud-painted ceiling, brass antique double bed and clawfoot tub denotes romance and sweet dreams; but we also like the cottage with its spacious private living room and fireplace, lit by four unique art modern chandeliers, and a step-up bedroom. The Magnolia Suite also has a modern kitchenette for early morning coffee or midnight snacking. If you want to feel like an artist living in a cozy garret, we recommend the Cottage Loft; it also has a kitchenette and delightfully warm atmosphere, perfect for fall and winter lodging especially.

Come back to the main house for a sumptuous breakfast of Belgian waffles, fruit salads, banana breads, coffeecake, muffins, eggs Benedict, omelets, and many other concoctions that Randy whips up in the kitchen every morning. Looking like the foods on the covers of gourmet magazines, the breakfast "courses" often include fresh raspberry syrups, fresh berry garnishes, and other fruits. No dish is simple; there is always that cleverly added, distinguishing touch. We loved the flaky pear turnover with dustings of powdered sugar. The innkeepers also provide flavored and regular coffees, roasted and ground especially for the inn.

We enjoy cozying up to the fireplace in the graceful living room. A large front porch with rockers allows you to enjoy the garden. A phone and fax are available for guest use upstairs.

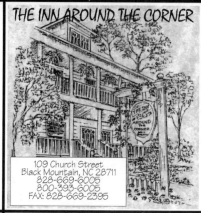

## Blake House Inn

**$$-$$$$ • 150 Royal Pines Dr. Arden • (828) 681-5227, (888) 353-5227**

Blake House Inn, originally "Newington," was built c.1847. Surrounded by 150 year old pine and sycamore trees, this fine example of Italianate architecture with Gothic Revival influence will bring you back in time to the more relaxed atmosphere of the 1800s. Conveniently located in the historic royal pines area, Blake House Inn was one of the beautiful summer homes built by wealthy low-landers to take advantage of the cool summer breezes in the mountains of North Carolina.

The Inn boasts 22-inch granite walls, 12-foot ceilings, and five spacious guest rooms, all with private baths. The newly remodeled Carriage House has a lovely king suite.

On the first floor there is a large center hall, a large parlor, Labrador Landing Pub, and a private dining room also used for breakfast. There are two large handicapped-accessible bathrooms. In addition, a large patio and covered porch allows guests to enjoy the fresh mountain air and beautiful landscaping with their meals, weather permitting.

Labrador Landing Pub is a congregating place for both Inn and dining guests. This room also has a fireplace, tables and chairs, a bar with stools, and cable TV for those all important sports events. This room is decorated with many lovely Labrador prints, portraits and other wildlife scenes. Sycamores Restaurant is located on the first floor and quite popular in its own right. (Read more about it in our Restaurants Chapter).

Guests awaken to the aroma of freshly baked breads and muffins, which will accompany their artistically presented fruit plates. This is just the beginning of a 2-course breakfasts prepared by the chefs. Afternoon hors d' oeuvres await your return from the day's activities.

## The Black Mountain Inn

**$$$-$$$$ • 718 Old Hwy. 70, Black Mountain • (828) 669-6528, (800) 735-6128**

Hidden away from the passage of time and nestled within the forest, the Black Mountain Inn embraces its guests with long-forgotten romance and charm. The house was built originally as a stagecoach stop approximately 160 years ago. At the turn of the century, the home was owned by Martha Mallory, who operated the inn as a TB Sanitorium until her untimely death. She was killed on the railroad tracks on her way home from town. The house fell into ruin and became a squatter's camp complete with cows stabled in the dining room! The property was purchased by Mary Aleshire and Daisey Erb in 1940. Mrs. Aleshire was the Manager of the Norton Art Gallery in Palm Beach, Florida. She restored and updated the historic property and two years later opened the house as The Oak Knoll Art Studio, which served primarily as a summer retreat for Mrs. Aleshire and her many famous guests. Ernest Hemingway, John Steinbeck, Norman Rockwell and Helen Keller were among the guests attending the garden parties that were common events all summer long. In 1989 the house, badly in need of further restoration and update, began its new life as the Black Mountain Inn.

The hosts of the Black Mountain Inn, June and Godfrey Bergeron, welcome you to our inn perfectly situated on a knoll in the Swannanoa Valley. With three acres of wooded property, it's an ideal location for guests who travel with pets. Seven comfortable guest rooms and one suite — the Artist Loft — are decorated in casual old fashioned furnishings. Each room has its own private bath.

The Artist Loft is a restored art studio with over 1,000 square feet of private sanctuary with wonderful views. Peter's room rests among the trees. Throw open the seven windows and wake up with the birds. Fern's room is one of the pet-friendly rooms. This large, first floor room is capable of sleeping four and is perfect for families with young children. Emily's room features a seven-foot claw foot tub.

Breakfast at the Black Mountain Inn is a sumptuous buffet featuring June's famous homemade granola. Fresh fruits, homemade breads or biscuits and a main egg course, along with special blend coffee or tea, greet you each morning.

The dining room is decked for the holidays with all white linens, lights and flowers.

## The Hawk & Ivy
**$$$ • 133 N. Fork Rd., Barnardsville**
**• (828) 626-3486, (888) 395-725X**

Wake up gazing over a country meadow, take a morning walk to the fish pond or an afternoon stroll through the wildflowers, or even pick a bowl of berries for your breakfast with innkeeper Eve Davis at this country bed and breakfast retreat. Eve and her husband James, an ordained minister and licensed contractor, wear many hats at The Hawk & Ivy. To give you an idea of the inn's many fine touches, let us mention that Eve's gardens and floral designs in Atlanta were featured in national magazines, books, and television. Eve's organic garden here grows a bounty of berries, produce, and cut flowers, all of which find their way into your sojourn at the inn. She also maintains a tiny craft gallery on the grounds, with small crafts from friends and local artisans, as well as her own crafts and dried flowers.

Set in 24 acres of wildflower fields, this farmhouse built in 1910 is only 20 minutes from Asheville but is completely in the country. You can choose between the main house bedroom or three bedrooms in the cottage across the way. The former has its own private bath and an heirloom four-poster bed covered in fine linens and down comforter. Two bedrooms, (one has a double bed, the other two twins), a large shared-bath, full kitchen, and living room with fireplace, sofa, television and phone composes the first floor of the guest cottage. Of course, Eve's flower arrangements embellish these charming quarters, as do the fine watercolors on the walls. A second floor suite completes the cottage, taking up the entire light-filled loft space, including a full kitchen, bathroom, extra-long double bed, single, and queen-size pull-out sofa. The private deck overlooks a valley, mountain ridges, and the small lake. In case the view is not enough entertainment, there is also a television. Both kitchens are supplied with fresh-ground coffee and tea, creamers and condiments.

Both Eve and James cook up incredibly innovative and fresh breakfasts, usually beginning with a bowl of fresh raspberries or other seasonal fruit from the garden. Guests dine at the long family table in the dining room surrounded by early American Impressionist paintings. If weather permits, breakfast is served on the verandah. Breakfast might include a combination of several of the following: fresh baked goods, asparagus omelet, melons with strawberry puree, coffeecakes, baked vanilla French toast or cheese grits casserole with jalapeños, all served on delicate family heirloom china.

The Davises encourage guests to stroll around the property, and will recommend hikes close by. In the field above the farmhouse, a large festival "barn" is the setting for many a wedding, wedding reception and family reunion. Two knolls have served as locations for nuptials, with live music and buffet tables elegantly arrayed in the rustic wooden structure. On occasion Eve teaches flower arranging and drying and herb preparation workshops out of the barn or in her art studio.

## Cedar Crest
**$$$$ • 674 Biltmore Ave., Asheville**
**• (828) 252-1389**

Less than a mile north of the entrance to Biltmore Estate sits another Victorian beauty. Rising from a flower-bedecked hill on lower Biltmore Avenue, Cedar Crest commands the ascent from Biltmore Village. The traffic scurries uphill toward downtown Asheville, but this exquisite bed and breakfast seems forever poised in the Gilded Age.

The opulent Queen Anne-style home was built in 1891 for prominent Asheville businessman William E. Breese. Breese played host to Asheville society, but as the century passed and the prosperous 1920s waned, Cedar Crest fell into disrepair. Through the years the home took on the guise of a sanatorium and, much later, a boarding house. Then Jack and Barbara McEwan answered an ad in Preservation News and came all the way from Wisconsin to rescue this lovely, faded lady. Careful restoration followed, much of it just removing decades of grime and ill-conceived decoration. What emerged was the amazing beauty of rich oak woodwork, intricately carved mantels and solid Victorian construction. The McEwans have lavished the inn with period antiques: claw-foot tubs, delicate lace, brass beds and Victorian collectibles.

Ten guest rooms are available at Cedar

## The Monte Vista Hotel

There was a time when every town
had an inn like The Monte Vista.
Step back in time as you
experience The Monte Vista Hotel.
"Murder Mystery" weekends
and golf packages available.

*Family owned for three generations*
308 West State Street
Black Mountain, NC 28711
828-669-2119
800-441-5400

Crest, described by its innkeepers as "a passage to 1890." All rooms are air-conditioned and have telephones and private baths; some rooms have working fireplaces. The upper two floors also feature a sitting area, and guests can sit on the wide veranda. A separate guest cottage, built in 1915, adjoins the main house and is wonderful for vacationing families. The inn is open year round, and its 4 acres are planted so that something is in bloom every season. (There is even a croquet court.)

### The Inn Around the Corner
**$$-$$$ • 109 Church St., Black Mountain
• (828) 669-2395, (800) 393-6005**

The Inn Around the Corner features five lovely guest rooms in a restored 1915 Four Square Victorian House. The upstairs porch, with porch swings and rockers, slows time to a standstill. All rooms are sold with private baths on a first-come, first-served basis. Adjoining rooms may be available as suites — just ask and the innkeepers will gladly accommodate you. Four of the rooms are on the second floor, and one room is on the first floor with a private bath. Quilts on the beds, soft colors, hand-stitched samplers and floral arrangements mark Grandma's Room, while Beau's is decorated in muted country colors with a patriotic theme. Available only as a suite with Beau's room, Ashley's is a lovely old fashioned room, located on the second

floor with full-size canopied bed. The Spring Garden bears soft yellows, greens and mauves, which carry out the botanical theme in this wicker-filled room with a full size bed and single bed. A full-size bed is also available on the porch. A lovely view of the mountains awaits outside the private entrance to the second story porch. A bountiful breakfast is served to guests in the dining room or on one of the porches, weather permitting. The innkeepers are amenable to special dietary requirements or requests, but be sure to tell them ahead of time.

The Inn is close to Black Mountain's quaint downtown shopping area, with a variety of dining possibilities. The Inn is also a short distance from a walking trail around Lake Tomahawk.

Hiking, kayaking, rafting, and fishing trips will gladly be arranged by the innkeepers for your enjoyment.

### The-Inn-on-Mill-Creek
**1407 Mill Creek Road , Ridgecrest
• (828) 668-1115, (877)-RELAX-NG**

The Inn-On-Mill-Creek provides guests a relaxing mountain bed and breakfast just 20 miles east of Asheville. Secluded among mountain laurel near the top of the Ridgecrest Pass, seven scenic acres are hidden in the Pisgah National Forest between the historic villages of Black Mountain and Old Fort. The

Carillons (Jim, Aline, Jeffrey and Kate) are your nurturing hosts.

The Inn features four newly appointed guest rooms or suites, each with private baths and many unique amenities. Also enjoy a two-story great room with a piano corner, a soapstone wood stove and cozy river-bed stone hearth. A library nook in the upstairs balcony for quiet reading is lit by an historic cathedral chandelier. The innkeepers provide two choices for your breakfast seating: a warm and open dining room with its own wood stove hearth and great view of the lake, or the south-facing solarium overlooking the dam and waterfall. The solarium also provides a hot tub for evening stargazing or relaxing. Be sure to check out the creek-side deck for sunning yourself as you listen to the waterfall or for enjoying a family cookout.

Enjoy the family fish lake, waterfall and dam which powers Andrews Geyser in the valley. A sunny deck overlooks the lake and the Long Branch of Mill Creek. The plentiful breakfasts are made with seasonal fruits and berries from the Carillon's own orchard.

## The Lion and the Rose
$$$$ • 276 Montford Ave., Asheville
• (828) 255-ROSE

The Montford Historic District is home to some fine examples of Victorian architecture. The Lion and the Rose, one of these homes, is listed on the National Register of Historic Places. This handsome bed and breakfast inn is a simplified Queen Anne/Georgian-style residence, built in 1898, that celebrates the English style. And this stately mansion certainly seems "to the manor born."

Innkeepers Rice and Lisa Yordy have furnished all five faithfully restored guest rooms with period antiques and Oriental rugs. High embossed ceilings, oak woodwork and leaded and stained-glass windows are just a few of the architectural details that give distinction to The Lion and the Rose. Each room has a private bath.

A delicious breakfast and traditional afternoon English tea are served on fine china in the dining room. However, guests can also savor their tea in the inviting parlor or the open air of the veranda.

## Monte Vista Hotel
$$ • 308 W. State St., Black Mountain
• (828) 669-2119, (800) 441-5400

The Monte Vista is one of those fine, old boardinghouse inns that used to dot the landscape of the South, particularly areas like Black Mountain, which grew up as a tourist retreat. Today the Monte Vista sits like an elegant dowager queen, still beautiful and still most interesting. The minute you enter the spacious lobby with its roaring fireplace, lofty ceiling, ornately carved Victorian settees and overstuffed armchairs, with an army of family photographs and vintage prints decorating every available space, you know you've passed the threshold of time.

This is America in the early '20s and '30s, when gasoline cost pennies a gallon and motoring was an adventure. You can just imagine an excited vacation party arriving at the Monte Vista, children bounding up the grand old staircase to a pleasantly appointed room, then back downstairs for a buffet meal in the cheery dining room.

Today, visitors come from all over the country, perhaps remembering this lovely old hotel from childhoods long ago. The distinct character of the Monte Vista has long drawn creative types — writers and artists — seeking the inspirational seclusion of the inn.

Monte Vista Hotel has been owned and operated by the same family for generations. Third-generation innkeeper Rosalie Johnston works to make your visit a memory you'll share with your own children. The 55 guest rooms are furnished in a comfy collection of 19th-century antiques and Depression-era pieces. Rooms have quaint private baths, no telephones and no televisions — they've pulled the plug on the hectic pace of the 1990s.

## Renee Allen House
$$-$$$$ • 303 Montreat Road,
Black Mountain
• (828) 669-1124, (888) 393-7829

Relax with a good book in the gazebo overlooking the gardens or rock away on the front porch and watch the world go by. Walk to town and browse the many antique and craft shops. Choose from these rooms: The

Carolina Room with two twin beds and private bath; the Rose Room with Queen bed and bath, the Garden Room with a private bath and private entrance, as well as an efficiency style kitchen and Queen canopy bed. The Captain Tyler Room houses a Queen sleigh bed, and has a private bath. And just recently opened is the Tree House, a two-story deluxe suite adjacent to the Renee Allen House. The bedroom has a queen Adirondack bed located under a skylight to view the stars. A two- way gas fireplace can be enjoyed from both the bedroom and the sitting room. The private bath has a six-foot roman tub for leisurely soaking. There is also a full size sleeper sofa in the sitting room for extra guests. In addition, you have a fully equipped kitchen, TV, phone and private deck. Rates include a full breakfast in the dining room of the Renee Allen House.

## Red Rocker Inn
$$$-$$$$ • 136 N. Dougherty St., Black Mountain • (828) 669-5991

The measured pace of the red rockers on the enormous porch overlooking the lovely gardens of this elegant inn gives you a feel for its relaxing atmosphere. Tucked away in a quiet residential neighborhood in the quaint village of Black Mountain, just 14 miles east of Asheville, The Red Rocker Inn is determinedly slow-paced. Innkeepers Craig and Margie Lindberg have elevated this calm to an art form.

The Inn was a boarding house known as Dougherty Heights back in 1927. It became The Red Rocker Inn in 1964. The tranquility of the place is its hallmark, and the 17 exquisite guest rooms (each with private bath) reflect this search for inner peace. The warm fireplace and lovers' window seat in Elizabeth's Attic, the inspired stained glass of the Preacher's Room and the white lace canopy bed in the romantic Anniversary Room are just a few of the Lindberg's thoughtful efforts to give visitors an island of calm. The Inn is centrally heated and air-conditioned.

The dining room is a celebrated spot for guests as well as the community. With the generous bounty provided by the innkeepers, the dining room seems to be the only place where guests might exhibit a lack of self-restraint in this peaceful domain. The family-style meals, served on lace-clothed candlelit tables, are robust and hearty Southern selections heaped on in generous proportions. The desserts are decadently delicious confections, such as "Heath Bar" pie or X-rated triple layer chocolate cake. Where's that rocker when you need it?

Photo: Constance E. Richards

Most bed and breakfasts have spots where you can absorb the beauty of the mountains.

The Red Rocker Inn is open almost year-round (February through December). Spectacular seasonal specials are offered during the winter, spring, and early fall.

## Richmond Hill Inn

**$$$$ • 87 Richmond Hill Dr., Asheville • (828) 252-7313**

Sitting on a promontory overlooking the French Broad River a short distance from downtown Asheville is the sparkling jewel known as Richmond Hill Inn. This magnificently renovated 12-room mansion, built in 1889, was the private residence of former congressman and international diplomat Col. Richmond Pearson and his wife, Gabrielle.

This elegant home faced the wrecking ball in the 1970s when it was propitiously rescued by the Preservation Society of Asheville and Buncombe County, which worked to have the mansion placed on the National Register of Historic Places. This designation was achieved in 1972, and by 1981 the society had purchased seven acres of adjacent land on which to move the mansion, should the need arise. Circumstances favored the society, which purchased Richmond Hill for $1 from North Carolina Baptist Homes Inc. with the provision that the home be moved from the original site. By 1984, with funds secured, the Preservation Society moved this grand old Queen Anne structure 600 feet to the east.

Richmond Hill had its rebirth in 1987, when the Preservation Society sold the mansion to Albert Michel, a Greensboro-based businessman and president of The Education Center. Michel and his wife, Margaret, were preservation advocates and took to the Richmond Hill project with gusto. The Michels began a mammoth, three-year renovation that necessitated the purchase of 40 additional acres from the original estate: the completion of a 900-square-foot, octagonal ballroom for meetings; the design of a glass-enclosed porch to complement dining; and the renovation of five third-floor guest rooms.

The richly paneled grand entrance hall features a portrait of the beautiful Gabrielle Pearson. The 12-foot ceiling rises to 23 feet as you ascend the wide staircase with its hand-turned spooled balusters. The 12 original guest rooms of the main house are dressed in Victorian splendor and richly furnished with Oriental rugs, period antiques and private baths as well as modern amenities. Second-floor rooms are all named for Pearson family members, and the recently renovated third floor honors noted authors from Asheville or those having Asheville connections. Downstairs, the library has more than 200 books, many of them first editions, from Mr. Pearson's personal collection. The world-class restaurant at Richmond Hill is named in honor of Gabrielle Pearson, who was a gracious hostess here and abroad during her husband's diplomatic career.

The Croquet Cottages, designed to complement the mansion's Queen Ann-style architecture, were built in 1991. Each of the nine cottages is individually decorated in a style reminiscent of a Victorian country estate with pencil-post beds, fireplaces, spacious baths and a porch with rocking chairs. Modern amenities such as televisions, telephones and refrigerators have been added. The Garden Pavilion, added in 1996, is a lovely U-shaped structure overlooking a Parterre Garden and waterfall. It houses 15 additional guest rooms, a banquet dining room, and a gift shop.

The improvements at Richmond Hill are like a string of pearls added to a natural beauty. As the Michel's reclaim the mountain around the mansion, they also reclaim the glory that once crowned this lovely Asheville landmark.

Richmond Hill Inn is open year round.

## Sourwood Inn

**$$$$ • 810 Elk Mountain Scenic Highway, Asheville • (828) 255-0690, 253-2785**

Located just off the Blue Ridge Parkway on 100 acres, this is what a country inn is all about. Walking trails crisscross the forested land, but even just sitting in your room looking out over the mountain through the dense foliage below, you will know you have truly "gotten away from it all." Sourwood Inn is finely constructed of cedar trimmed with stone. The entire structure sits on hilly terrain at an elevation of 3200 feet. Easily accessible to downtown Asheville, it is nonetheless in the countryside and can feel like wilderness, with densely growing trees and birdsong all around.

Each of the Inn's twelve guest rooms has a private balcony overlooking the Reems Creek Valley, a wood-burning fireplace, and a tub with a view! When you turn on your faucet to draw a bath, you will be amazed with the ensuing waterfall, thanks to Scandinavian faucetry. The French doors which open onto the guest room balconies let mountain breezes drift in at night. Decorated in muted forest and meadow colors, the rooms are as peaceful within as the idyllic countryside outside.

The Inn also maintains numerous public areas — porches with rocking chairs, a lobby with plush chairs in front of a crackling fireplace, and a library stocked with books for your leisure time. There's also a game room downstairs with a billiard table. Susan and Jeff Curtis who live on the premises are innkeepers with Susan's parents Nat and Anne Burkhardt. Susan cooks up delightful full breakfasts and stocks a table with juice and light snacks in the afternoon for guests who are coming back from their days' outings. Another treat which Susan (a professional chef) enjoys preparing with advance notice is a three-course dinner. You will have to make your summer reservations, and be assured that your salad will be crisp and sprinkled with pumpkin seeds, walnuts, feta cheese or some other tasty touch. You may have shrimp jambalaya with spinach and a side of sweet baby carrots sautéed in butter and fresh orange juice. Or you may be privy to steak and mashed potatoes, a fish dish, or whatever Susan chooses for that evening — ranging from comfort food with that extra elegant twist to a fabulous nouveau invention.

Sassafras Cabin is nestled in the woods 100 yards from the main inn. Complete with a screened-in porch, the cabin has two full baths, a fully-equipped kitchen, a living/dining area, and a bedroom loft. There's a wonderful variety from which to choose at Sourwood Inn. You may never want to leave. Sink back into those chairs, admire the perfectly designed and built carpentry work and decorative touches, grab a good book from the

library of Nat's favorites, kick up your feet in front of the fire, and plan a walk in the crisp fresh mountain air after dinner.

## Tree Haven
**$$-$$$ • 1114 Montreat Road, Black Mountain**
**• (828) 669-3841, (888) 448-3841**

A gracious welcome brings you back to a more relaxed, timeless serenity in this 1908 restored home, surrounded by mature oaks, hickory, pine, hemlock and chestnut trees. Centrally located just outside the gates of Montreat, only a mile from downtown Black Mountain, Treehaven is ideally situated for both the casual stroller and the serious hiker. Return home to sit on the porch and watch the fireflies light up the night skies, or stroll the acre grounds bordered by a gently flowing creek. Innkeeper Carol Redmond has traveled the world as a delegate for the sport of synchronized swimming after being honored as a member of the Helms Swimming Hall of Fame. Previously from the West Coast, she has found Black Mountain to be a perfect place for rest and relaxation amidst nature's wonderland. International guests, especially, will find a helpful, if not bilingual, resource for local travel. Carol, an avid hiker herself, will help you find those hidden mountain trails when you can tear yourself away from the homey surroundings of the inn. Private baths, a whirlpool tub, air conditioning and a smoke free environment ensure your comfort at Treehaven. You can chose from rooms with King or Queen beds. Vegetarian breakfasts are also available.

# Henderson County

## Apple Inn
**$$-$$$$ • 1005 White Pine Dr., Hendersonville**
**• (828) 693-0107, (800) 615-6611**

Situated on three acres just 2 miles from downtown Hendersonville, this lovely home with its large wrap-around porch was once the summer residence of a South Carolina lawyer and his family. Surrounded by dogwoods, azaleas and hundred-year-old oaks, poplars and maples, it provides a quiet retreat conveniently close to all the many attractions of this popular area. Two fine restaurants and a number of interesting shops are within walking distance at the Laurel Park Shopping Center.

The inn, in one of the nation's largest apple-producing counties, offers five bright and comfortable rooms with private modern baths, each named after a different apple. Innkeepers Pam and Bob Hedstrom have furnished them charmingly with antiques and keep them adorned with fresh flowers. In addition, there is the "Apple Branch," a two-bedroom, two-bath cottage that sleeps six. It has a full kitchen, dining area, and living room area, front porch, color cable TV, a private phone and a private driveway. It's available by the week, month or with a two-night minimum.

Each morning, a delightful, home-cooked breakfast of fresh fruits, a quiche, strudel or French toast and tasty breads or muffins awaits you on the patio, accompanied by gourmet coffees and teas. Though relaxation is a favorite occupation at the inn, you can also choose a game of billiards, badminton, croquet or numerous board games. It also has a corporate membership at Oak Hills Racquet Club where you can swim or play tennis.

To reach Apple Inn, take the U. S. Hwy. 64 exit off of I-26. Go 4 miles until you see a Hardee's on the right and an Exxon station on the left. Turn left here onto Daniel Drive and take the first right at a four-way-stop onto White Pine Drive. The inn's driveway is the first on the left.

### The Claddagh Inn
$$$ • 755 N. Main St., Hendersonville • (828) 697-7778, (800) 225-4700

The regal old Claddagh Inn was Hendersonville's first bed and breakfast establishment. Built around the turn of the century by an ex-mayor of Hendersonville, W.A. Smith, it was sold in 1906 and became The Charleston Boarding House, since it largely served Charlestonians escaping the heat of the coast for mountain coolness. In 1985, it was renamed The Claddagh (pronounced

CLAW-da), a Gaelic symbol that represents love and friendship. The hospitality of its owners, Gerri and Augie Emanuele, lives up to the name.

Here you'll have a choice of 14 uniquely decorated, air-conditioned rooms, all with private baths, telephones and televisions. Each has its own individual, old-fashioned and charming flavor. The inn also offers a very large parlor and a cozy library with books, games and a piano. Full — indeed, gigantic — breakfasts in the attractive dining room are included in the rates. The facilities are also available for small catered parties or meetings.

### The Echo Mountain Inn
$$$ • 2849 Laurel Park Hwy., Hendersonville • (828) 693-9626

This massive stone-and-frame inn 3 miles from Hendersonville was built in 1896 on a mountainside that overlooks the whole area — a spectacular view that's visible from many of the guest rooms and the dining room, which is open to the public for dinner. (See our Restaurants chapter.) The view is particularly pretty at night with the city lights twinkling below. The inn's 23 rooms, many with fireplaces, are decorated with antiques and reproductions. There is also one cottage and an annex with 10 suites, some with kitchenettes. All accommodations have cable television, telephones and some have air conditioning, although with an elevation of 3,100 feet, the latter is seldom needed.

On the grounds you'll find shuffleboard courts and a swimming pool. While the atmosphere at Echo Mountain is casual and leisurely in keeping with the nature of an authentic country inn, dinners here are quite exquisite and definitely gourmet. The inn, which is open all year, goes all out for a grand event, such as a wedding or banquet.

To reach Echo Mountain Inn, drive west on Fifth Avenue in Hendersonville; this street will turn into the Laurel Park Highway.

### Flat Rock Inn
$$$ • 2810 Greenville Hwy., Flat Rock • (828) 696-3273, (800) 266-3996

The Flat Rock Inn is across U.S. Highway

# Historic Hendersonville & Flat Rock Area

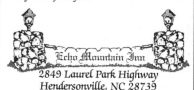

25 from the Woodfield Inn (see the listing below) and just as convenient to all local attractions. This elegant but homelike bed and breakfast was built in 1888 as a summer retreat by Charleston's R. Withers Memminger, a son of C.G. Memminger, the first Secretary of the Treasury for the Confederate States. Known locally as Five Oaks, the home was skillfully renovated in 1992, and its new owners, Dennis and Sandi Page (in their own words, "corporate dropouts from Dallas"), opened its doors to the public in 1993.

Currently, the Flat Rock Inn offers four rooms with private baths, each elegantly Victorian but with beautifully different atmospheres. Two of the rooms have private, second-floor porches; a third offers a six-foot tub in an alcove behind lace curtains. Flat Rock Inn also offers splendid, family-style, Texas-size breakfasts with such gourmet items as eggs Benedict or cherry blintzes as well as those country favorites: buttermilk biscuits topped with local jams and jellies.

Flat Rock Inn is open year-round, closing only during the first two weeks in January.

## Melange Bed & Breakfast
**$$-$$$$ • 1230 Fifth Ave. W., Hendersonville**
**• (828) 697-5253, (800) 303-5253**

Luxuriously cosmopolitan best describes this B&B just a 15-minute walk from downtown Hendersonville. The mansion, complete with a pony barn and a dollhouse with six-foot ceilings, was designed and built by North Carolina's famous architect, Erle G. Stillwell, in 1920. In the 1960s, a later owner added marble mantles from Paris, crystal chandeliers from Vienna and hand-painted porcelain accessories from Italy. In 1994, its new owners, Lale and Mehmet Ozelsel from Turkey, lovingly restored the bedrooms, the attic, the study and the kitchens, adding Mediterranean-style porches, splashing fountains and a rose garden. The name Melange was chosen to represent a blend of styles and cultures found here.

The old grandeur is still represented by the 11-foot, ornamented ceilings, the ornate mirrors and marble fireplaces, now graced by contemporary comfort, fine tiles, Turkish rugs, books, candles and flowers. Four guestrooms occupy the second floor and a full-floor suite with two bedrooms is on the third. Each is named after its predominant color scheme: Rose, Pearl, Cinnamon, Green and Red. And each has a private bath or Jacuzzi, hardwood floors, air-conditioning, a TV and VCR and a private telephone. A large collection of video films and books are available for guests.

Depending on the season, a gourmet breakfast is served on the rose-garden patio, a Mediterranean porch or in the formal dining room. It includes fresh fruits, an egg entrée, coffeecakes and thick, crusted bread served with self-prepared, compound butters and delicious preserves. The yogurt here is homemade.

Special services are offered at an additional fee, such as fruit plates, champagne or special chocolates in your room, an elegant high tea or a five-course candlelight dinner. You can also order a relaxation spa, a therapeutic massage or a reflexology session from a certified therapist.

Hendersonville's Fifth Avenue is just one block over from U. S. Hwy. 64 W. Drive .8 miles from Main Street to Blythe Street. Turn left. On Fifth Avenue, Melange is on the left behind a hemlock hedge. The driveway is after the Melange sign.

## Mountain Home Inn
**$$-$$$$ • 10 Courtland Blvd., Mountain Home**
**• (828) 697-9090, (800) 397-0066**

Built in 1915 as a cool haven for Floridians and extensively remodeled in 1986, the Mountain Home Inn, with its porch of Tennesee marble, is on the National Historic Register. Each of its seven elegantly furnished guestrooms has a private bath, cable television and a telephone, but each is unique. You can, for example, choose a romantic, canopied four-poster bed and a Jacuzzi, a sleigh bed with a fireplace, or perhaps you'd prefer a cozy suite with skylights. A large, gourmet, candle-lit breakfast, served in the inn's dining room, is included in the room rate. Each evening, Innkeepers Mike and Joni Hockspiel, invite guests to a social hour in the parlor.

Mountain Home Inn is located 5 miles north of Hendersonville, 15 miles from the

Biltmore Estate and Asheville, and 12 miles from the Blue Ridge Parkway. It is also very convenient to the Asheville Airport. To get there from I-26, take the Mountain Home exit (Exit 13). Follow U. S. Hwy. 25 south for 2 miles. Turn right onto Courtland Boulevard, and the inn is a quarter-mile ahead on the right. The inn is open all year.

## Old Teneriffe Inn
**$$$$ • 2531 Little River Rd., Flat Rock**
**• (828) 698-8178, (800) 617-6427**

A grand old Flat Rock estate opened in 1996 as an exclusive bed and breakfast. Built around the 1850s by a seafarer, Dr. J.G. Schoolbread, and named for one of the Canary Islands, it sits on 23 acres and is surrounded by venerable old trees, miles of walking trails and big stone verandas. The inn offers four large, lovely guest rooms, three with private baths and one with a bath off the hallway. You'll also find a huge great room with an unusual terra-cotta fireplace. Outside are a perfect croquet court and the old-but-renovated tennis courts where liveried servants once served "tennis teas."

The Old Teneriffe Inn specializes in gourmet breakfasts. Perhaps you'll be lucky enough to be there on when she's whipped up her fantastic salmon and egg pie and cornlaced biscuits served with our locally famous sourwood honey.

The inn, whose ambiance is not suited for children, is exactly 2 miles down Little River Road from the Flat Rock Playhouse.

## The Waverly Inn
**$$$ • 783 N. Main St., Hendersonville**
**• (828) 693-9193, (800) 537-8195**

For a stay in pretty Historic Downtown Hendersonville, you can't find more handy accommodations than at the three-story Waverly, the oldest surviving inn in town, which is listed on the National Register of Historic Places. It's a two-block walk from the Waverly to Hendersonville's dynamic downtown with its wonderful shops and restaurants and frequent art shows and festivals. Open year round, the Waverly is a large and gracious inn, even though it now faces a street whose steady stream of traffic reflects the popularity of the town.

You'll get a good view of all this activity from the inn's long, wide veranda, which holds about 20 rocking chairs; there's almost that many on the upstairs porch too. Polished wood, four-posters and turn-of-the-century fittings fill the 14 guest rooms and one suite, all of which come with private baths, cable TV and telephones. There are sitting rooms on all three floors.

In their rates, innkeepers John and Diane Sheiry and Diane's sister Darla Olmstead include a hearty breakfast cooked to order — and that means all you can eat. There's also a social hour between 5 and 6 PM. If hunger hits you anytime, we were told to just raid the cookie jar for one of Darla's famous delectables. That's a special delight for children, who are welcome at the inn. To find the Waverly, turn north on Hendersonville's Main Street.

## The Woodfield Inn
**$$$$ • U.S. 25 S., Flat Rock**
**• (828) 693-6016, (800) 533-6016**

Every time we drive up to the Woodfield Inn, we feel we should be in a carriage rather than a car. This impression has something to do with the elegant way this old establishment sits proudly back on its spacious grounds, immediately setting the tone of a more leisurely lifestyle.

The Woodfield Inn was built in 1847 by a group of prominent men who wanted to create "a good, commodious tavern on or near the Main Saluda Road." Their Flat Rock Hotel, as it became known, was a great success. Eventually Henry T. Farmer, a relative and ward of Charleston's Charles and Susan Baring, the original "founders" and social leaders of fashionable Flat Rock, bought it. One of Squire Farmers' most outstanding contributions to the inn was the creation of a style of black walnut rocking chair that didn't creep annoyingly across the floor when rocked. These Flat Rock Rockers were so well liked that Farmer opened a furniture factory to produce them. The factory closed down, however, during the Civil War, and although the inn's present rockers are still favorites with the guests, Squire Farmer's rocking chairs have never been duplicated.

Fortunately, the Southern congeniality for

# Transylvania County: Mount Pisgah

Mount Pisgah sits right at the point where Henderson, Transylvania, Haywood and Buncombe counties meet. You'll find a 1.5-mile trail leading to the top at milepost 407.4 on the Blue Ridge Parkway, .75 mile north of the Pisgah Inn. The trail begins at the far end of the parking lot. On clear days this path is very popular because it leads to a 360-degree view of the French Broad River Valley, Asheville, Waynesville and most points on the Pisgah District. Though it's a short hike, it's a very strenuous one, since you will gain nearly 1,000 feet in elevation from the Parkway to the summit. However, there are switchbacks and rock steps to help make the climb more manageable and benches along the way where you can sit and catch your breath. The viewing platform at the top was built by the Youth Conservation Corps in 1979. Aside from the WLOS-TV tower, the view is completely unobstructed.

which the inn was so famous has been handed down. Full of history and antiques, the Woodfield's 18 guestrooms have been redecorated by the inn's new owners, Rhonda and Michael Horton. Likewise, they have restored the outside of the inn to its historic colors of white and Charleston green.

The Woodfield is a popular place anytime, but it's particularly busy during the Flat Rock Playhouse's season late May through early September (the theater, which is the official state theater of North Carolina, is practically next door). So is the Carl Sandburg Historic Site (see our Arts and Culture chapter). The inn is also a favorite spot for weddings and other special events.

The Woodfield is open all year and serves dinner and Sunday brunch to the public. It's 2.5 miles from Hendersonville on the U.S. Highway 25 S. (Greenville Highway). If you're coming from town, the inn will be on your right.

## Polk County

### The Foxtrot Inn
**$$$, no credit cards • 800 Lynn Rd., Tryon • (828) 859-9706, (888) 676-8050**

Though Foxtrot is in Tryon's city limits, this 1915 home set high on 6 wooded acres is a quiet and elegant escape. It was purchased several years ago by Wim Woody, a Tryon native who grew up in the house next door. Graciously proportioned and tradition-

ally furnished, the inn has four air-conditioned guest rooms (two are suites with sitting rooms). Each room has a private bath. You can also stay in the two-bedroom guesthouse, which has a fully equipped kitchen, 1½ baths, a deck, air conditioning, cable TV and mountain views.

Wim and his wife, Tiffany, begin each day with a beautifully presented gourmet breakfast after which you can go for a walk in the woods or lounge by the pool. Evenings often find guests playing games in the card room or sitting by a roaring fire in the living room. The inn is in Tryon just off N.C. Highway 108, which leads to I-26.

### The Mimosa Inn
**$$ • 1 Mimosa Ln., Tryon • (828) 859-7688, (877) MIMOSAINN**

This pretty, rambling bed and breakfast inn with its column-lined veranda has 200 years of history behind it. In the 1700s, King George granted John Mills 90,000 acres of land in this area. He and his son operated Mill's Inn here along the trading trail that would become Howard Gap Road. After the Civil War, a Pennsylvania Presbyterian minister named Dr. Leland McAboy bought the inn, named it the McAboy House and, like the Millses, became known as a hospitable host. In 1903 Aaron French and David Sterns bought and modernized the property with innovations such as gaslight and hot-and-cold running water, added a casino/bowling alley and renamed it The Mimosa Inn. Fire destroyed most of the building in 1916, sparing only the casino/bowling alley, which was remodeled into the current Mimosa Inn. Here, innkeepers Jim and Stephanie Ott continue to uphold the inn's reputation for hospitality (see our Polk County write-up in County Overviews).

The Mimosa Inn has 10 guestrooms, many with mountain views, and serves a hearty breakfast on the veranda or in the dining room. From I-26 take the Tryon/Columbus Exit 36 and follow N.C. Highway 108 W. for 2 miles. The marked entrance drive is on the left beyond the mansion.

## The Oaks
**$$$ • Greenville St., Saluda**
**• (828) 749-9613, (800) 893-6091**

Built by a local banker as a private residence in 1894, this interesting, turreted house was a boarding home from 1905 until the 1940s. It's currently the home and business of Terry and Crowley Murphy. Tall trees set off the exterior, which features a wraparound porch with seasonal hanging baskets, wicker furniture and a swing. Inside you'll discover an inviting library with a fireplace and a large, airy living room. The center of the house is the gracious dining room where delicious gourmet breakfasts are served family style.

Each of the inn's four distinctively decorated guestrooms has a private bath and cable TV. You have your choice of the Blue, Gold, Green or Red Room, each of which contains a four-poster queen-size, an extra-long full-size bed or three single beds.

The property also has a separate and self-contained guesthouse, The Acorn, which boasts a nice view of the ivy-filled woods below.

The Oaks, which is open year round, is just a short walk from the antiques, arts, crafts and old-time stores of Saluda. To find this comfortable bed and breakfast, go to Saluda and take Greenville Street in the center of town. Drive a half-mile; The Oaks will be on your right.

## The Orchard Inn
**$$$$ • N.C. Hwy. 176, Saluda**
**• (828) 749-5471, (800) 581-3800**

Simply ascending the winding drive to the Orchard Inn will make you feel that you're arriving somewhere special — and you are. The inn, sprawled with plantation-like elegance on a ridge, was built by the International Brotherhood of Railway Clerks and Engineers as a mountain getaway in the early 1900s near the terminus of the steepest railway grade east of the Rockies. That engineering feat is a marvel even today, and a stay in this tranquil place is just as marvelous.

In addition to the nine guestrooms in the imposing main building, there are three remodeled cottages with fireplaces, whirlpool baths and private decks. Each room and cottage has a personality of its own, from the delicate patterns on the wallpaper to its paintings, prints, stenciling and quilts. The entire guest quarters are furnished with period pieces and antiques. Wide porches and a shaded deck hold swings, rockers, ferns and blooming plants. You can relax on swings out on the grounds too.

The Orchard Inn is a place of leisure, where a naturalist guides morning walks on nearby nature trails. The dining area is an airy, glassed-in porch that runs the length and along one end of the inn. From here, a stunning view of the mountains stretches all the way into South Carolina. Full breakfasts and French Provincial dinners "with a country flair," say the hosts, are served, and dinner is open to the public by reservation. Complimentary hors d'oeuvres are offered prior to dinner. The chef will also prepare an insulated strap-bag hiker's picnic, a romantic picnic basket or a box lunch for your journey home. You do need to keep in mind that Saluda is a "dry" town as far as alcoholic beverages go, but you may bring your own spirits. There's ice in the rooms.

The Orchard Inn, which is open year round, is a short distance outside of Saluda on the way to Tryon.

## The Pine Crest Inn
**$$$$ • 200 Pine Crest Ln., Tryon**
**• (828) 859-9135, (800) 633-3001**

In 1918, a hotel owner from Michigan, Carter P. Brown, created the charmingly rustic Pine Crest Inn. Later, in the 1920s, Brown played a leading role in establishing the Tryon Riding and Hunt Club that helped make Tryon the equestrian center it is today.

Pine Crest Inn is still thriving. It's full of fireplaces, wide porches, tranquil gardens, bright lawns and wooded grounds. The inn has 35 air-conditioned rooms, most with fireplaces and all with telephones, televisions and nice robes for guests. Rates include a full continental breakfast and complimentary sherry or port in the rooms. Both suites and cottages are available, along with a gourmet restaurant and The Fox and Hounds Bar. (See our Restaurants chapter.)

The complex also has a lovely conference center available for retreats, seminars or other gatherings. The innkeepers are Jennifer and Jeremy Wainwright. To meet them, turn off of Trade Street onto Market Street and follow the signs to the inn's entrance at the top of the hill.

## Stone Hedge Inn
**$$$ • 300 Howard Gap Rd., Tryon**
**• (828) 859-9114, (800) 859-1974**

The Stone Hedge Inn is on a 28-acre estate just 3 miles from Tryon town center. The Inn property includes the main house, a guest house and a poolside cottage all surrounded by gardens, wooded walks and rolling meadows. Each building is a unique fieldstone structure exhibiting the character of its 1930s vintage architecture. All six rooms are large with private baths, air conditioning, cable television and a telephone. Two rooms possess rich pine-paneled walls and ceilings with a fireplace for a rustic feel, while those in the main house have highly decorative sculptured ceilings and antiques for a more formal ambiance.

A full breakfast is served in the dining room, where large picture windows offer mountain views. The dining room, open to public, serves dinner with an eclectic mix of contemporary specials and traditional favorites. Owners Thomas and Shaula Dinsmore bring a fresh lightheartedness to the inn's peaceful atmosphere.

Stone Hedge is open all year. To get to the inn, which is about 2.5 miles from Tryon, take N.C. Highway 108 to Howard Gap Road.

# Rutherford County

## Dogwood Inn
**$$$ • U.S. Hwy. 64/74, Chimney Rock**
**• (828) 625-4403, (800) 992-5557**

This beautiful 1890s bed and breakfast inn originally served as a stagecoach stop between Asheville and Charlotte. Located on the rocky Broad River in scenic Hickory Nut Gorge just below Chimney Rock Park, the Dogwood Inn offers 11 guest rooms including two with Jacuzzis and one with a fireplace. Right on Chimney Rock's main road, the sprawling white mansion also houses a small gift shop and espresso bar that extends onto the stone verandah in warm weather.

Owner Marsha Reynolds has decorated the bedrooms with bright floral-patterned wallpaper and old-fashioned quilts on the large beds. Rooms have private baths. A central telephone and television for guest use are located in the living room that is also filled with antique wooden tables and plush chairs. Plenty of reading materials — magazines and newspapers — are provided for guests in the main lounge area.

Guests enjoy a hearty gourmet breakfast, including a choice of egg dish and waffles, pancakes, or other heavenly starch. Continental breakfast items are also included. Weather permitting, breakfast is served on the side porch, surrounded by lush foliage and the gurgling sounds of the river below.

## Lake Lure Inn
**$$$$ • U.S. Hwy. 64/74, Lake Lure**
**• (828) 625-2525, (800) 277-5873**

This stately inn overlooking beautiful Lake Lure has been a tradition in Hickory Nut

## INSIDERS' TIP
**Faced with choosing a restaurant in an unfamiliar place? Ask your innkeepers and specify what type of cuisine you prefer. They are a wealth of information and see this as part of the fun of innkeeping.**

Gorge since 1927. In its early days, F. Scott Fitzgerald, President Franklin D. Roosevelt and Emily Post came to Lake Lure Inn. Today the inn, with 50 guest rooms, has been renovated and attracts scores of vacationers.

Guests may choose from a variety of chambers — standard rooms with two double beds or one queen; deluxe rooms with a king; or rooms with king- or queen-size bed and a pullout sofa in a large sitting area. There are also two suites, and all rooms are furnished with antique historic inn furniture. All rooms have color cable TV, phone and a private bath. Playing on the old-world hunter green color scheme, hardwood tables and chairs, poster beds and clothes cupboards compose a sedately elegant atmosphere in each room. Come down to the lobby and dining area, however, and you are enveloped in cheery spring peaches and whites. The spacious lobby runs the width of hotel and is furnished with sofas, soft chairs and plenty of area literature and newspapers to help plan your local sightseeing. Fresh flowers and old photographs of famous former guests complement the decor. Cozy up to the fireplace in the main dining room for the complimentary continental breakfast, which includes cereal, breads, bagels, muffins fresh from the inn's kitchen, juices, coffee and tea.

If you are lucky enough to be staying over for Sunday, a champagne brunch, served mid-March until mid-November, can be your meal of the day. This lavish buffet features a cutting station with prime rib and ham, omelet bar, waffle station and a table of hot dishes and side dishes, including chicken, fish and vegetables. A salad bar and pasta varieties round out the main course, but don't forgo the dessert selection, which often features homemade cobblers and pies. The dining room also serves dinner Wednesday through Saturday year round; Tuesday dinner is added in peak season. Check with the front desk about the varying lunch schedule.

The inn's outdoor pool has a sundeck, and a shaded veranda with benches and chairs allows you to look out over Lake Lure at the front of the inn. Tennis courts are available next door. Chimney Rock Park and the Bottomless Pools are nearby.

Lake Lure Inn is open year round, and seasonal rates are available.

# Transylvania County

### The Inn at Brevard
**$$$ • 410 E. Main St., Brevard**
**• (828) 884-2105**
This elegant, columned inn, listed on the National Register of Historic Places, is within easy walking distance of all the great shops and restaurants in downtown Brevard, and the Silvermont Mansion (see our Arts and Culture chapter) is just down the street. The inn has a distinguished history. It was built in 1885 as the private home of Mrs. Woodbridge, a wealthy widow from Virginia who entertained the nobility of the Victorian era here, including her good friend, Lady Astor. Woodbridge bequeathed the house to her only daughter, Rebecca, who married William E. Breese, a prominent attorney and mayor of Brevard. In 1911 Breese hosted a reunion of the troops who served under Stonewall Jackson (Jackson's widow attended).

The house was sold in the 1940s and operated as the Colonial Inn for many years. There are five nonsmoking rooms in the main house, three with private baths. Ten cabin-style rooms with private baths are in the adjacent lodge. A full breakfast is included in the tariff.

When entering Brevard on U.S. Highway 64, turn east onto U.S. Highway 276 at the courthouse in the center of town. The inn is just a few blocks away on the left.

### Key Falls Inn
**$$ • 151 Everett Rd., Brevard**
**• (828) 884-7559**
A quiet and restful stay can be yours in this large Victorian farmhouse built between 1868 and 1869. Formerly know as the Patton House after its original owner, John Patton, this bed and breakfast has four guest bedrooms and a two-room suite furnished with antiques. All have private baths. The house's porches are popular for reading, relaxing and enjoying the view. A sumptuous breakfast is included in the price, and complimentary refreshments are served in the afternoon.

On the inn's grounds, you'll find a tennis

# The White Squirrels of Brevard

In 1986, the Brevard City Council declared the city a squirrel sanctuary because some of the squirrels around here are super-special — they're white! We enjoy our gray squirrels too, but the white variety, which you can  see darting throughout the town, have become a symbol of Brevard. These squirrels are not albinos, as they have normal dark eyes and a dark stripe down their backs. In the last few years, probably because of Brevard's increased urbanization, they are migrating to the countryside around the town.

White squirrels symbolize the city of Brevard.

court with a view of Pisgah Ridge Mountains and a cookout and picnic area, where you may want to fry up some of the bass or bream you've caught from the inn's pond. Key Falls Trail begins on the grounds and climbs up to Key Falls, one of the many waterfalls in Transylvania County. The French Broad River borders one side of the property, which is just 2½ miles from Brevard. Children 12 and older are welcome.

## The Red House Inn
## and Bed and Breakfast
$-$$ • 412 W. Probart St., Brevard
• (828) 884-9349

Four blocks from the center of town and on the road next to the Music Center, you'll find Brevard's oldest house. It was built as a trading post in 1851 after the first house, which was built in 1848, burned. The house survived years of neglect and several attempts to destroy it during the Civil War. It even managed to remain in the same family until some 20 years ago, when it was finally sold. The trading post closed in 1861, and the structure then became the W.P. Poor Tavern, which had four rooms for boarders. The street at that time was also called Poor Street, but the residents understandably didn't cotton to that! Hence, the name was changed to Probart Street, after Poor's middle name, and so it remains today.

Since its days as a tavern, the building has been used as a residence, a railway station, the county's first courthouse, Brevard's first post office, a boarding house, a hotel and briefly as a school. It's been added to and altered over the years, but the original foundation is still firm, and it's four corner chimneys are still functioning. Owner and operator Marilyn Ong has lovingly restored and charmingly furnished the home with turn-of-the-century antiques. The inn still has four guest rooms with private or shared baths, plus a small efficiency cottage with a queen-size bed. Stay for a week and your seventh night is free.

And, yes, the house is painted red — the trim on its wide upstairs and downstairs porches is a bright contrast in white. The story goes that in the days when the streets had no numbers, the houses all had names. As the New England branch of the family had several homes, each called Red House, the family in Brevard decided to use that name too.

The Red House is open all year. To reach it, turn off Caldwell onto Probart Street; the inn will be on your right.

## The Sassy Goose
**$$, no credit cards • Reasonover Rd., Cedar Mountain • (828) 966-9493**

The Sassy Goose, owned and operated by Bette and Bob Vande Weghe (pronounced "Vanda way") and daughter Linda, is really a miniature resort. The country-style lodge on a 50-acre site 10 miles from Brevard has three sunny guest rooms, each with a private bath and TV. Common space includes a library with a fireplace, a breakfast room and a deck overlooking the lake. Two new log-cabin suites with queen-size beds are tucked back in the woods. Each suite has a sitting room, a kitchenette and a screened porch or a deck. There is a two-bedroom, two-bath cottage, complete with living room, kitchen, dining room and sun porch, available as a weekly rental.

There are also a 6-acre lake for swimming, fishing and boating and a small par 2 golf course where you can practice your chip shot. Several regular golf courses are nearby. Bocce, croquet, horseshoes and hiking are also available on site. The continental-plus breakfast consists of melon and berries, cereal and a bread basket of good things to put in the toaster oven.

The Sassy Goose is open May through October. There is a two-night minimum on weekends, and reservations are required.

From Brevard, take U.S. Highway 276 south to Cedar Mountain. Turn left on Cascade Lake Road and immediately turn right on Reasonover Road It's another 2 miles to Sassy Goose.

## Twin Streams Bed & Breakfast
**$$$ • Twin Ponds Ln., Lake Toxaway • (828) 883-3007**

If you aren't from around here — and maybe even if you are — you may not know about this quiet, charming bed and breakfast inn with 11 lovely acres to explore. It's hidden away off U.S. Highway 64 and offers only three guest rooms — but they are something worth seeking out. Each room in this pretty, contemporary structure is on a different level. French doors lead out to covered decks that overlook a cascading stream. The Woodlands Room is furnished in elegant period antiques and features scenes from the surrounding mountains. The Falls Room has antique country furnishings and artwork depicting some of the many waterfalls in the surrounding area. The light and airy Wicker Room, as the name implies, has Southern wicker furnishings, which lend the charm of a bygone era. King-, queen- and twin-size beds are available.

Twin Streams' large main deck overlooks a pond stocked with rainbow and golden trout, and owners Paul and Celeste Thorington will provide food for you to feed them. Rates include a full gourmet breakfast and afternoon tea. The inn is open year round. To reach it, take U.S. Highway 64 to Lake Toxaway, turn onto N.C. Highway 281 N. and drive 2 miles. Turn right on Twin Ponds Lane. Twin Streams is the second driveway on the right.

## The Womble Inn
**$$ • 301 W. Main St., Brevard • (828) 884-4770**

At the opposite end of Main Street from The Inn at Brevard is the Womble Inn, which has been under the friendly care of Steve and Beth Womble since 1974. This well-kept, large structure with wrought-iron-railed upper and lower porches has six guest rooms furnished with antiques. A continental breakfast can be enjoyed the meal in the dining room or on the porch. At an additional cost, you can order a full American breakfast.

The gathering room is the place for watching television, listening to music and having conversation in front of a crackling fire on cool days. The inn will also prepare generous picnic baskets from varied menu suggestions. Since it's only a half-mile from here to the

Brevard Music Center, you might want to order one of these for a Music Festival dinner-on-the-lawn (orders should be placed 24 hours in advance). In addition, Beth Womble, who has long provided a catering service for many of Brevard's special occasions, has now started serving exquisite lunches to the public.

# Southern Mountains

## Cherokee

### The Hawkesdene House
**$$$ • Phillips Creek Rd., Andrews • (828) 321-6027, (800) 447-9549**

Nestled on 20 acres in a mountain cove adjoining the Nantahala National Forest, Hawkesdene House combines the simple elegance of an English country house with the rustic beauty of the mountains. Innkeepers Roy and Daphne Sargent offer five bedrooms in the main house, all with private baths and one with a full kitchen. There are also three cottages that will each sleep six, where children are welcome.

The Sargents have even built a special patio right beside the creek that meanders through the property, so parents can keep a relaxed eye on their offspring playing there. (It's rumored that there's gold to be found in the stream, and gold pans are available to borrow.) Children also love playing with the two resident dogs, Gigi and Tigger, and Smoky, the cat. In addition, there are four llamas you can come to know because your hosts will arrange a llama trek that includes lunch or supper if reserved a week in advance. The cost is $35 a person, with a maximum of eight or a minimum of four people per trek. Or they'll be happy to direct you to a hiking trail relevant to your fitness level.

### The Walker Inn
**$$ • 385 Junaluska Rd., Andrews • (828) 321-5019**

A lot of history comes along with a visit to this old inn, which more than deserves its place on the National Register of Historic Places. The Cherokee Indians had barely been forced into Oklahoma when, in 1839,

William Walker and his partner, Col. Waugh, received a 295-acre tract in an area called Old Valleytown. It's said they took down Chief Junaluska's home (see our Attractions chapter) and used the logs to construct a store that, in 1846, became the area's post office. Since those logs were burned for fuel in 1926, we don't know if they really were from Junaluska's house. At any rate, after Walker married Margaret Scott in 1844, he built a two-story log home that he eventually expanded into an impressive, 11-room Colonial-style classic known as the Walker Inn.

The Walker Inn became a vital stopover on the Asheville-to-Murphy turnpike. During the Civil War, however, drunken bushwhackers wrecked the house and forced an ailing William Walker away with them. He was never seen again, leaving a grieving Margaret to raise their five sons, which she did by becoming one of the finest innkeepers in the mountains.

Today, much still remains from Margaret's time: hinges, latches, beams, bubble-glass window panes, a grand piano, a stagecoach stepping stone, heirlooms and other memorabilia. The long, outside kitchen is now a dining room, and there's still a slave cabin on the grounds. Many of the inn's trees are at least 200 years old — one oak may be twice that old. There are five guest rooms, three with private baths. But despite modern conveniences, it's the past that's the attraction here. Just to the east of Andrews on U.S. Highway 19 Business, turn right onto Junaluska Road. The Walker Inn is about a half-mile down the road.

This wonderfully historic inn is open April to November, and the super-reasonable rates include breakfast.

## Clay County

### Broadax Inn Bed and Breakfast
**$$ • Elf Rd., Hayesville • (828) 389-6987**

Roger and Ruth Young run this unique inn, which is in the old Elf Schoolhouse outside town. The red brick building on 5 acres was built in 1928 and was used as a public school until 1968; the Youngs bought it in 1991. The Broadax is not only a bed and breakfast inn with the Broadax Restaurant on the premises, it practically operates as the town's community center because the Youngs have turned the old auditorium with its stage into a much-in-demand place for parties and other social events. The local high school, for example, holds its proms and Christmas dances here. In the past, such country greats as Minnie Pearl, Roy Acuff, Mac Wiseman, Lester Flatt, Earl Scruggs and the like performed on its stage.

The inn has five distinctive guestrooms, four furnished with queen-size beds and one with twin beds. There is also a two-bedroom, 1½-bath cottage. Breakfast is practically cooked to order, though Ruth says her standard offerings of oven-French toast, breakfast pizza and hot cakes are most in demand. There are also such items as eggs, potatoes, grits, sausage, bacon, ham and homemade muffins.

The Broadax Restaurant, open to the public, is housed in two former classrooms separated by an archway. The restaurant can serve 96 people; a bar with an adjoining porch (with rockers!) can hold 20 to 30 more.

The inn is closed from January 1 until April 1. It's on Elf Road, which dead-ends off of N.C. Highway 175. There is no sign to direct you to the inn, because this is a scenic highway where new signs haven't been allowed. And no one, by the way, knows why the school was called "Elf" — not even a man in his late 90s who used to own the property.

## Graham Country

### Snowbird Mountain Lodge
**$$$$ • 276 Santeetlah Rd., Robbinsville • (828) 479-3433**

Back in the 1940s, brothers Arthur and Edwin Wolfe of Chicago built this fine lodge high on a mountain near the Joyce Kilmer Memorial Forest (see our Forests and Parks chapter). In 1993, the lodge was added to the National Register of Historic Places in recognition of its distinctive characteristics of type, period and method of construction. The lodge is built of native stone and chestnut logs — that wonderful tree that a foreign blight took from our forests. A massive stone fireplace

dominates the main lodge room, which is paneled in butternut, and another warms up the dining room, paneled in cherry.

Twenty-five rooms — the lodge has a capacity for 50 guests — are paneled in a variety of native woods with furniture to match. Handmade quilts, many in-room amenities and private baths complete the comfort. None of the rooms have televisions or telephones.

From its spacious flagstone terrace, the inn offers a panoramic view of the Snowbird Mountain Range, and in the valley below are glimpses of Lake Santeetlah and the homes and fields of the Snowbird Indians. The lodge has an interesting 2,500-volume library and 2.5 miles of hiking trails on the property. You can swim in a mountain pool fed by a cool stream or spend the day fishing in any number of blue-ribbon trout streams nearby. Canoes and kayaks are available for rent at the Lodge and are a great way to explore nearby Lake Santeetlah.

Innkeepers Karen and Robert Rankin are always cooking up unique entertainment. Evenings sometime include bluegrass music entertainment on the front porch or a slide presentation given by a resident botanist, herbologist or wildflower expert.

The rates at Snowbird are on the full American plan, which includes an fine buffet-style breakfast, a hearty picnic lunch and an exquisite full-menu dinner prepared by Chef Karen Rankin and her staff with fresh, seasonal ingredients. There is a three-night minimum on holiday weekends and all stays during October. The lodge is open from April through November. Snowbird is 10 miles northwest of Robbinsville.

## Haywood County

### Grandview Lodge
**$$$ • 466 Lickstone Rd., Waynesville • (828) 456-5212, (800) 255-7826**

Stan and Linda Arnold are the innkeepers at this year-round lodge with loads of country charm. Grandview has nine year-round guestrooms and two two-room apartments available in the spring, summer and fall. The rooms look out on 2-plus rolling acres of landscaped grounds graced by apple orchards, grape arbors and a rhubarb patch. Comfortable rockers line the porch.

All guestrooms have a king- or queen-size bed and a second bed, a private bath, color cable TV and daily maid service. The three lodge rooms also have gas-burning fireplaces. A common room with a piano and other amenities will make you feel at home.

Full breakfast and dinner are included in the rates, and both are sumptuous meals planned around seasonal harvests of locally grown fruits, vegetables and herbs. Linda, the lodge's chef and a graduate home economist, prepares all dinner breads, breakfast muffins and biscuits; the jellies, jams and relishes are homemade too. Meals are served family style, and Linda can accommodate special dietary needs if she is notified in advance. The public may dine here by making advance reservations.

Stan, the other innkeeper, speaks Polish, Russian and German, so Grandview Lodge is ready for international travelers. When you're ready to explore the area, there's plenty to see. The lodge is a short drive to whitewater rafting, area golf courses, tennis clubs, outlet shopping and attractions at Maggie Valley, the Cherokee Indian Reservation and the Biltmore House and Gardens. The Blue Ridge Parkway and the Smoky Mountains National Par6k are readily accessible.

## Herren House
**$$-$$$$ • 94 East St., Waynesville • (828) 452-7837, (800) 284-1932**

Many B&Bs are converted from private homes, but Herren House has been known for its hospitality since 1897, when it was a boarding house named "Savannah." (It takes its present name from its second owner, Mollie Herren, who owned the house early in this century.) Innkeepers Frank and Jackie Blevins take great pride in continuing this long tradition of hospitality and in maintaining such distinctive elements as the original Victorian woodwork, fireplace fronts and mantelpieces that grace its rooms, along with other restored or replicated details. Added to these are Frank's skillful woodworking and Janet's art works. Six spacious guestrooms, one equipped for wheelchair accommodations, are full of vintage furnishings, complimented

by modern amenities, such as central air-conditioning. Each room has its own sitting area and private bath. There's even an octagon-shaped bedroom with a turn-of-the-century, 48-pane window.

As far as Frank and Jackie are concerned, you can't have a great B&B without a great breakfast. With seasonal fruit topped with orange-maple sauce, herb-baked eggs, gingery pancakes, apricot scones and pineapple muffins, along with homemade chicken sausage, the Herren House qualifies. (You'll be asking for the recipes.) Afternoon refreshments include chocolate delectables, homemade teacakes, nut breads, cookies, a variety of teas and freshly ground coffee.

Best of all, all this home comfort sits below soaring mountains on a quiet residential street just one block from Waynesville's captivating Main Street, full of irresistible shops and great places to eat. When you've worn yourself out enjoyng Waynesville and all its nearby attractions, you can relax on Herren House's sprawling porches or in its fragrant garden. It open all year, except for two weeks after New Year's Day.

To get to the Herren House, take U.S. Hwy. 276 to Main Street. Turn right on Main, then turn left at the second traffic light (East Street). Go one block on East Street to Welch Street. Turn right on Welch and left into the rear parking area.

## Mountain Creek Bed & Breakfast
**$$ • 146 Chestnut Walk Dr., Waynesville • (828) 456-5509, (800) 557-9766**

In 1995, Hylah and Guy Smalley were tandem-cycling through the Smokies and came upon a former corporate retreat cantilevered off the top of a hillside, 100 feet above a couple of creeks, a large trout pond and an old mill wheel. Three months later they moved in with their two dogs, Spuds and Booger, and welcomed their first guests to the Mountain Creek Bed & Breakfast.

Set on six acres at 3,500 feet just 5 miles from the Blue Ridge Parkway and from downtown Waynesville and 15 minutes from Cataloochee's ski slopes, this year-round establishment offers four rooms and two suites. All four bedrooms in the main house have a private bath with a shower and two have a

soaking tub. The interior walls are knotty pine and the closets are cedar-lined. The two upstairs rooms have their own private balconies overlooking a spectacular mountain view. Two suites located in the original carriage house just next door. Each has its own private porch, queen-size bed and Jacuzzi tub. The large common area features a huge fireplace along with 40 feet of floor-to-ceiling windows.

A full breakfast is served every morning, and guests can dine in or out on the 1,600-square-foot deck that wraps around the west side of the house with a view of the creek, trout pond and mountains. Menus include such items as egg truffles, banana- or strawberry-stuffed French toast or ham-and-cheese strudel. During winter holidays, Hylah and Guy will cook dinner for you. And since the two are avid tandem and mountain cyclists, they'll be happy to share their local cycling knowledge with you or arrange guided tours.

To get here from I-40, take Exit 27 onto U.S. Hwy.23/74. Turn right on Allens Creek Road, go 1 mile and turn left on Lickstone Road. Continue .8 miles up the road and turn left at Chestnut Walk. Go under the archway and turn right at the first driveway.

### The Old Stone Inn
$$$$ • 109 Dolan Rd., Waynesville
• (828) 456-3333, (800) 432-8499

If you're looking for a fine place to stay — or dine — near the wonderful shopping in downtown Waynesville, you can't beat The Old Stone Inn, formerly known as Heath Lodge. Built in 1946 out of stone and poplar logs, the inn consists of a number of buildings. The main lodge houses two guestrooms and the cozy guest lounge and restaurant centered around a large stone fireplace. Wendell's Attic, with its woodburning stove, is a more intimate room for drinks and conversation on the second floor of the building. Several other structures surrounding the main lodge house the balance of the inn's 22 rooms. Most of these neat, clean and rustic-feeling quarters have been recently restored and updated and have private baths, ceiling fans, cable TV and porches with rockers.

This in-town, country lodge sits on a heavily wooded hillside thick with large rhododendrons and mountain laurels. Both the

lodge's grounds and the menus reflect innkeepers Cindy and Bob Zinser's past (he was a university landscape architect whose job took him all over this country and several others). The couple collected recipes of their favorite dishes wherever they went.

A full gourmet breakfast is included in your room rate. Dinner and light appetizers are available to both inn and outside guests. Hours vary by season. The Old Stone Inn is open from April through December. To get here from N.C. Highway 23, exit onto U.S. Highway 276 S. and continue to Dellwood Road (the second stoplight). Turn right and proceed less than a half-mile to Love Lane. Turn right and drive up the hill to Dolan Road. Turn left, and you'll find The Old Stone Inn on your left.

### The Swag
$$$$ • 2300 Swag Rd., Waynesville
• (828) 926-0430, (800) 789-7672

When the innkeepers at The Swag, which refers to a dip in a ridge, call theirs a mountaintop inn, they mean it! This inn sits on 250 acres at 5,000 feet on a private mountain with 50-mile views. After negotiating the rather narrow gravel road and the 2.5-mile private drive, you might be tempted to think, "I'm obviously driving up to the end of the world, and what then?"

"What then" is a nationally known first-class inn with the types of amenities you expect of a fine hotel. Yet, when you ask many longtime residents if they've ever been to The Swag, they might respond, "The what?" Somehow, this place has mostly remained a secret except to those who travel hundreds, if not thousands, of miles to stay here. Certainly it seems better known outside the region than it is here. Dan and Deener Matthews built what was to be a private family retreat using native stone and hand-hewn logs from old buildings, including a century-old church. They ended up turning the retreat into this highly praised inn.

The Swag's handmade quilts, woven rugs and unique pieces of North Carolina art create an atmosphere of rustic elegance. Sixteen guestrooms all have private baths (some with whirlpools or steam showers, all with terry robes) and many feature balconies to bring that 50-mile view right indoors. Some rooms have fireplaces, but not small ones you might expect — these are impressive to say the least! There are also three cabins with separate sitting rooms and private porches and an extensive library to satisfy most literary tastes. One cabin has a billiard room and a hot tub. Outside, a split-rail fence marks the boundary of the Great Smoky Mountains National Park with its many hiking trails, reached by The Swag's own private entrance. At the inn itself, hammocks are handy places for a snooze, but for the more active, you can play racquetball on the indoor court, badminton and croquet outdoors or swim in the secluded spring-fed pond.

A two-night minimum stay is required. The rates include three meals a day for two people, prepared by gourmet cooks and served atop 12-foot-long, handmade walnut tables (many of the inn's beds are also handmade and oversize). There are a several private tables available, and a few outside reservations are accepted. Just remember that the inn is in a dry county, so bring your own spirits if desired.

Well, The Swag may have been a secret in this region once, but not any longer!

## Ten Oaks Bed & Breakfast
**$$-$$$$ • 224 Love Lane, Waynesville • (828) 452-9433, (800) 563-2925**

No expense was spared in restoring this beautiful colonial Queen Anne Revival house to its former grandeur. Built in 1898 on a hill for the Mayor of Waynesville it offers some of the loveliest views of the mountains you'll find anywhere. Containing over 8,000 square feet, Ten Oaks spacious rooms and porches, original mantels and oak floors reflect the ambience of the days when it was one of the centers of social activity in the area, and notables, such as Mrs.Woodrow Wilson, dined here.

Each of the establishments three rooms and two suites has a private bath, fireplace, sitting area and phone. From the Rose Room you can wake up in a queen-size, four-poster bed and watch the sun rise of the mountains. From the green-and-white Ivy Room there are mountain views to the east and west of the house. The sun-drenched sitting room of the Magnolia Room offers cable TV and a full-size sofa bed. The Daffodil Room overlooks the gazebo and Waynesvillle plus mountains

to the east and west. The bath in the romantic Oak Suite has a double whirlpool tub and shower. Guest robes are funished in all rooms.

Breakfast is another treat here, particularly when the weather permits enjoying it on the porch. A typical menu includes warm cinnamon grapefruit, sausage and strawberry-garnished lost bread, which is similar to, but much tastier than, French toast. Sunday brings a special breakfast buffet served in the formal dining room. Guests celebrating special occasions can receive breakfast in their rooms.

From Asheville, take I-40 west to Exit 27. Follow U. S. Hwy. 23/74 to Waynesville Exit 102; exit and turn right. Once in Waynesville turn right at the third traffic light (right past KFC) onto Dellwood Road. Turn right again just past the Stonegate Office Center onto Love Lane. Ten Oaks is the fourth driveway on the right.

## Windsong: A Mountain Inn
**$$$$ • 459 Rockcliff Lane, Clyde • (828) 627-6111**

Windsong is a romantic, contemporary log B&B with a special flair, romance and seclusion. Located on 24 acres at 3,000 feet with fabulous views, where the gentle mountain breezes flowing down the mountain and through the many wind chimes inspired its name. Once can be lazy here, sitting in the hot tub watching the hawks circling or perhaps lounging beside the swimming pool gazing at the flower and herb gardens. For the more active, there's tennis and hiking or visiting in the pastures with the llamas and pygmy goats. For the ink-black, starry nights there's a telescope for stargazing. In the morning you feast on an ever-changing gourmet breakfast served on fine English china. Innkeepers Russ and Barbara Mancini settler here after living many years in Bavaria, London, Berlin and Budapest. They have put together a unique blend of European antiques and art, as well as African, Southwestern and Alaskan art. You may find a Sioux Indian picture next to a 200-year-old English Clock.

Guestrooms feature queen-size bed, wood-burning fireplaces and private baths with tubs for two. Each has unique décor. Rooms are equipped with a TV/VCR, and there's a large collection of videotapes available.

In addition to the Main Inn, there's the Pond Lodge with two-bedroom suites, great for families or those desiring privacy. Each suite has a living/dining room with a pot-bellied stove, a fully equipped kitchen and a bath with a tub for two. Here you can sit on the deck and barbecue on the grill while watching the animals in the pasture. An extensive continental breakfast is provided for Pond Lodge guests.

To reach Windsong from Asheville, take Exit 24 off I-40, and go 2.5 miles north on N.C. Highway 209. Turn left onto Riverside Drive. Go 2.5 miles to Ferguson Cove Loop/ Rockcliffe Lane. Turn right and follow the Windsong signs 1 mile up to the inn.

### The Yellow House
**$$$$ • 89 Oakview Dr., Waynesville**
**(828) 452-0991, (800) 563-1236**

The Yellow House sits at 3,000 feet on top of a hill looking out to the ever-changing colors of the Blue Ridge Mountains. Located just a mile from Waynesville, it has been likened to a grand old Duchess on a throne. It has also been called Western North Carolina's most romantic inn. One thing is for sure, when you arrive at this 100-year-old home, surrounded by three acres of lawn, garden and ancient pines, prepare to be pampered. There are no televisions or other distractions in this quiet rural setting. Innkeeper Ron and Sharon Smith, have created a European flavor of casual elegance with a décor favoring the French Impressionists, even to a lily pond with a footbridge and deck.

There are three rooms and a two-room suite in the main house. All are charming and each has a fireplace, but our favorite is the E'staing suite with both rooms opening on a private upstairs porch. From here, there's a pine-framed view of the mountains and town, particularly fine at night when lights twinkle below and stars twinkle above. An adjacent cottage contains a French country kitchen. It offers two bedrooms, two baths, two fireplaces and a view of the pond from every room.

The rates include your choice of a breakfast served in your quarters, in the dining room

or on the front veranda. Other amenities include appetizers and conversation in the evening and a refrigerator stocked with soft drinks. All rooms have coffee service, terry robes and controlled music. For an extra charge, a licensed massage therapist is available on request, and you can also order a French Country-, Mediterranean- or American-style picnic hamper. Also ask about The Yellow House's Special Packages that include fly fishing, guided nature hikes, mountain memory photo tours, golf and trips to the Biltmore Estate.

To reach The Yellow House, from the south take Exit 100 off U. S. Hwy. 23/74. Proceed to the left for ½ mile on Plott Creek Road. From the north, take Exit 100 from U. S. Hwy. 23/ 74, turn right on Eagles Nest Road, left on Will Hyatt, and right on Plott Creek Road.

# Jackson County

### Applegate Inn Bed & Breakfast
**$$ • 163 Hemlock St., Dillsboro**
**• (828) 586-2397**

There are lots of sights to see in the beautiful countryside around the Applegate Inn, but you might just want to stay put in this quaint country home and enjoy the peace and quiet. With the village of Dillsboro as its backdrop and Scott's Creek just across the way, you don't have to go far to see the scenery that brings people to these mountains.

But if you do decide to wander, The Great Smoky Mountains Railway Depot and the town's 50 unique shops and restaurants are just a footbridge away. The inn is also within a few miles' drive of The Great Smoky Mountains National Park, Maggie Valley, Nantahala Gorge and other sights.

This one-story inn has five large guestrooms and three mini-suites. Each room has a queen-size bed and private bath with charming decor to make you feel at home. Air conditioning and cable TV are other amenities.

A full country breakfast served on old-fashioned Currier and Ives china includes apple pancakes, one of the inn's many specialties.

Room rates include breakfast. The inn offers special weekly rates too.

# Jackson County: Wet Camp Gap

This 3-mile, round-trip hike to a lovely mile-high meadow with superb views of the Pisgah National Forest is not difficult. For part of the walk, you will be on sections of the Mountains-to-the-Sea Trail. Be sure to take a sharp left at the trail junction about 15 minutes from the start of your walk. To reach the trail, drive to the Bear Pen Gap parking overlook at milepost 427.6 on the Blue Ridge Parkway in Jackson County. The trail begins at the lower end of the parking lot.

## Balsam Mountain Inn
$$$ • Off U. S. Hwy. 73/23, Balsam
• (828) 456-9498

This magnificent 1908, neoclassical Victorian inn owes its life to its delightful innkeeper, Merrily Teasley. Gracing 26-acres, the three-story structure with its two-tier, 100-foot-long porches sits at 3,500 feet and is surrounded by 6,000-foot peaks. It was once the popular destination of passengers on the old Southern Railway, but in recent years, the 50-room beauty had fallen into disrepair until Merrily bought it in 1990 and lovingly and authentically restored it. She also sets the happy, relaxed tone of her entire staff.

Today, you'll have a choice of large rooms with private baths (including a few suites and bed/sitting rooms) graced with flowery prints, 10-foot wide hallways, a wicker- and plant-filled lobby, a fine library, a gift shop, a nature trail on the property and easy access to Pisgah Forest hiking and the Blue Ridge Parkway. You'll also be very pleased with the inn's restaurant. Wonderful breakfasts are included in the rates, but you'll also want to enjoy the exceptional lunches and dinners offered to guests and by reservation to the public.

Balsam Mountain Inn is open all year. It's easily accessible from the Blue Ridge Parkway close to milepost 443; take the exit for U.S. Highway 74/23 and turn south toward Sylva. About a quarter-mile south of the parkway overpass over 74/23 coming from Waynesville, turn left at a small green sign marking the village of Balsam. Then make an almost immediate right up a hill, cross the railroad tracks and continue straight for another one-third mile. Drive across the tracks again before turning into the inn's driveway.

## Innisfree Victorian Inn
$$$$ • N.C. Hwy. 107, Glenville
• (828) 743-2946

As the name implies, this is a gabled Victorian. Wide porches run around two floors of this superb building overlooking Lake Glenville.

There are nine guest rooms named in keeping with its era, such as the Prince Albert Suite with French doors leading to a private veranda; the sensuous Cambridge Room, which has a parking place next to its private entrance; the cheerful Canterbury Room, with a bay-windowed love seat that affords a view of flower gardens and mountains; and the Windsor Room, which looks out on a fountain and has a roomy shower with a built-in seat, plus an Italian lavatory with gilded dolphins for faucets. Then there's Victoria's Grand Suite, which may be the most luxuriously romantic suite in the mountains. From its bay window you have a view of the lake and mountains that stretches for miles, and its elegant furnishings and art were gathered from around the world. A Jacuzzi is in the bathing chamber that also comes with a splendid view.

The Garden House, which follows the style of the main house, has two feminine boudoirs — the Elizabeth Barrett and Emily Bronte suites — each with a four-poster bed made up in French lace, a private veranda and two fireplaces, one in the bathroom. The Charles Dickens Suite is opulent with jade green walls and dark wicker, and its fireplace faces the two-person garden tub that actually has a view of the gardens. The secluded Robert Browning Room has its own entrance, fireplace and private garden. All the accommodations in the Garden House have wet bars, TVs and private phones.

Rates include the candle-lit breakfast in the Tower, a 5:30 hospitality hour with hors d'oeuvres served on the sweeping upper veranda and Irish coffee and hot chocolate by the parlor fire each evening. The Innisfree has gift certificates.

## The Jarrett House

**$, no credit cards**
- **U.S. Highway 19/23 Bus., Dillsboro**
- **(8280 586-0265, (800) 972-5623**

Not only is The Jarrett House one of the oldest inns in Western North Carolina, it's practically a tradition. William Allen Dills, founder of the town of Dillsboro, built it in 1882, just two years after the railroad came through. Because the train from Asheville stopped here at noon, the Mount Beulah Hotel, as The Jarrett House was called then, became the place for passengers and railroad employees to eat lunch. By 1894, the hotel was serving "comers and stayers" from great distances away, including two women from Edenton, North Carolina, who were the first females to be seen smoking cigarettes in these parts. As Mrs. Minnie Dills Gray, one of William Dill's daughters, recalls in her *History of Dillsboro*, the two smokers "set the countryside agog and gave zest to the neighborhood gossip."

Dill sold the hotel to R. Frank Jarrett of Franklin in 1894. Jarrett, capitalizing on a sulfur spring that bubbled up into a soapstone basin at the rear of the hotel, renamed the place the Jarrett Springs Hotel. However, the busy owner left the running of the hotel mostly to his wife, Miss Sally. After his death in 1950, a hotel operator from Gainesville, Georgia, bought the hotel and renamed it The Jarrett House. It has changed hands a number of times since then but has never changed its policy of serving copious and delicious country cooking.

The hotel, which is on the National Register of Historic Places, has 18 guest rooms with private baths and four with shared baths. While they're nothing fancy, they are loaded with atmosphere because the whole place is like a step back to the turn of the century — something right out of a Robert Redford/Paul Newman movie. The Jarrett is open year round. To find it, just go to Dillsboro — you can't miss it.

# Macon County

## Blaine House

**$$ • 661 Harrison Ave., Franklin**
- **(828) 349-4230, (888) 349-4230**

Though this beautifully restored and professionally decorated 1910 home has just four rooms and a cottage for guests, Innkeepers Suzy Chandler and Karin Gorboff like it that way. By being small and intimate, they feel they can pamper their guests. Here you'll find an elegant spacious room, Mildred's Suite, that offers a king-size bed, sitting area and private bath/shower. Annie Mae's Suite is more romantic with a queen-size bed and a spacious adjoining bath inviting you to relax in a 1925 pedestal foot tub. Minnie's room offer a cozy county French motif with a gabled ceiling and pickled knotty pine walls, a king-bed (or twins), dressing room and private bath/shower. Charles' Room is a delightfully decorated provincial room with original knotty pine walls and offers a queen-size oak bed with an adjacent cozy reading room enticing you to relax and read a book after an adventurous day. This room has a private bath/shower. All rooms have cable TV and air-conditioning. Finally, there's the two-story Blaine House Cottage, a fully furnished, one-bedroom with a living/dining area, full kitchen, daily linen service, TV, air-conditioning and a small balcony.

You'll enjoy the touch of elegance and warm hospitality Blaine House provides. To find it, follow U. S. Highway 441 Business to N.C. Highway 28 N. The Blaine House is ½ mile north of Franklin's Main Street on the right-hand side. There is a private off-street parking area.

## The Chalet Inn

**$$$ • 285 Lone Oak Dr., Whittier**
- **(828) 586-0251, (800) 789-8024**

In 1979, George Ware came through the North Carolina Mountains on his way to Fort Bragg and fell in love with the area. In 1985, while stationed in the Netherlands, he met and fell in love with his future wife, Holland-born Hanneke. When they decided to open a bed and breakfast inn, George wanted it to be in our mountains. After working in restau-

Photo: Judy Scharns, Courtesy of Boone Convention and Visitors Bureau

Skiers go cross-country at Bass Lake.

rant management and for a season at High Hampton Inn and Country Club, they started building The Chalet in an authentic Swiss/German design in the fall of 1990. The heavy posts and beams and large overhanging roof allowed the Wares to create a touch of Europe in North Carolina.

Nestled on 22 acres in a mountain cove, The Chalet provides gracious lodging and combines the traditions and congeniality of an Alpine gasthaus with rustic surroundings. A spring-fed brook curls around the inn on its way to the valley floor. The guestrooms have private balconies with carved wood railings festooned with flowers. European furnishings and German-Swiss windows continue the theme. The Wares even commissioned an award-winning German artist-blacksmith to make a traditional wrought-iron sign. From The Chalet's great room, you can view Doubletop Mountain, which dominates 19 miles of forested ridges. The inn is 20 minutes from the Great Smoky Mountains National Park and the beginning of the Blue Ridge Parkway.

The Chalet's four lovely rooms, one romantic suite and one family suite offer comfortable lodging for couples looking to spend some time alone and for families with older children exploring the mountains. All rooms and suites have private baths and air conditioning. The Romantic Suite has a sitting room with a fireplace and whirlpool tub, a private entrance and a private patio. Honeymooners and couples alike enjoy the ambiance and relish the seclusion of the inn's cove. Guests at The Chalet Inn can enjoy its hiking rails, lawn games and picnic area with a grill. A candlelit breakfast is served in the dining room or on the covered patio along the brook. It's a breakfast that satisfies all tastes: For the health conscious there's always plenty of fresh fruit, juices and low-fat yogurt; for the world traveler with a hearty appetite longing for memories of the Alps, the German-style meats are fresh and German whole-grain breads and Swiss mueslix are imported. Also included are a variety of cheeses, fresh-baked brotchen (rolls), soft-boiled eggs or an egg casserole. The less adventurous can opt for cereal, home-baked pastries and fruit compotes.

The Chalet is open from late March through New Year's Day and Valentine's Week. To find the inn from U.S. Highway 74/441 going toward Whittier, look for an old steel-girder bridge, turn left on Barkers Creek Road, drive less than a mile, bear right at the fork and drive another 1.1 miles to Nation's Creek Road. It's less than a mile to The Chalet's driveway.

## 4½ Street Inn
**$$$ • 22A 4½ St., Highlands**
**• (828) 526-4464**

We don't know what it is about the ambiance of a bed and breakfast, tucked away on large lot on a quiet street in Highlands, but when we visited one afternoon in early October, walking through the doorway felt like coming home at Christmas time. A fire crackled in the fireplace, music played softly and great smells wafted from the kitchen at the back of the house. It's a place where we think you will feel at home just enjoying the sun and shade in the side yard or in a rocking chair on the large wraparound porch. A wide deck extends off the back of the house, where there's a hot tub for soaking. The 10 guestrooms, each with a private bath, are retreats for watching TV or reading a good book. Most rooms have king- or queen-size beds.

The inn is about a half-mile stroll from Main Street through a pretty residential area where the houses are hidden behind giant rhododendrons. In addition to the gourmet breakfast, the rates include afternoon refreshments in the parlor and the use of the hot tub. There's a two-night minimum on weekends and a 10 percent reduction for stays of five nights or longer excluding holidays and October. The 4½ Street Inn is open March through December. To find the inn from Main Street, take U.S. Highway 64 E. toward Cashiers, turn right on Chestnut Street and then left on 4½ Street.

## Heritage Inn
## Bed and Breakfast
**$$ • 43 Heritage Hollow Dr., Franklin**
**• (828) 524-4150, (888) 524-4150**

This B&B is in the Heritage Hollow, a private village within the town of Franklin, with restaurants, antiques and mountain-craft shops within walking distance. Each of its five

immaculate bedrooms (two are available with kitchenettes) is decorated with antiques, collectibles and quilts in a country-comfortable theme. For added privacy, each room has its own entrance, porch and shower bathroom. There is a Gathering Room with fireplace, cable TV and phone, as well as a good selection of reading materials and videos. Most guests, though, end up in a rocking chair on the verandah enjoying the mountain scenery and serenity. Breakfast is hearty and homemade; early risers can have coffee on the verandah. Snack and some refreshments are available throughout the day.

There is also a fully furnished, self-contained one-bedroom apartment with a fireplace at the inn available for rent with a three-night minimum. (Breakfast is not provided with this rental.)

The inn is open year round.

### Hummingbird Lodge
**$$ • 1101 Hickory Knoll Ridge Rd.,
Franklin • (828) 369-0430**

The Hummingbird Lodge is a lovely log cabin on a mountaintop just 6 miles south of Franklin. Because woodlands surround it, hiking trails abound, including the Appalachian Trail. With advance notice the lodge will provide a picnic lunch for hikers or those out enjoying the scenery. Hummingbird has a large living room with a stone fireplace, a great

porch with a hammock, a swing and rocking chairs. There are three guestrooms, each with its own bathroom and each decorated with a different theme. The Garden Room is lined with a white picket fence, has a king-sized bed and a garden tub looking with a view of the mountains. The Appalachian Room has a king-sized bed and also has a mountain view and is decorated in local arts and crafts. The third room is adorned with Native American art from the Cherokee Reservation. The bed her is queen-sized, and the bathroom has a garden tub as well as a shower.

A full gourmet breakfast is included in the price and is served in the dining room or on the porch, weather permitting. Evening wine and hors d'ouevres are a wonderful way to end the day in this beautiful part of the world.

To get to this mountain top retreat, take U.S. 441 to Riverside Road. Turn left onto Hickory Knoll Road and bear right onto E. Hickory Knoll. Upon reaching the gravel road continue approximately 1 mile to Hickory Knoll Ridge Road; bear left, and it's 1 mile from there to the lodge.

### The Main Street Inn
**$$$-$$$$ • 270 Main St., Highlands
• (828) 526-2590, (800) 213-9142**

The Main Street Inn, built in the Federal Farmhouse style in 1885, has welcomed guests with Southern hospitality for more than a century. Formerly known as The Phelps House, it was restored to its original luster in 1998. The original hand-hewn beams in its adjacent Guest House were exposed through the addition of cathedral ceilings, and many of the original sand-forged windows were saved and reinstalled in the rooms as interior windows for the enjoyment of guests.

The inn, which is next door to all that wonderful Main Street shopping, features 20 cozy rooms, all with private baths, individual heating and air-conditioning, direct-dial telephones and cable TV. Some rooms have sitting areas or balconies. Room rates include a hot country breakfast and afternoon tea. The inn is open from April through December, and advance reservations are preferred.

### The Old Edwards Inn
$$$ • U.S. 64 E., Highlands
• (828) 526-5036
### The Highlands Inn
$$$ • E. Main St., Highlands
• (828) 526-5036

These two sister hotels sitting across from each other are almost as old as the town of Highlands itself, which was established in 1876. The Old Edwards Inn opened in 1878 and The Highlands Inn in 1880. Both are on the National Register of Historic Places and are owned by Rip and Pat Benton, who began renovating the Old Edwards Inn in 1981. With the opening of the Central House Restaurant in 1983, the renovation was complete. The couple purchased The Highlands Inn in 1989, and it has been undergoing renovation since.

The decor throughout both inns has been carefully researched and restored in the "county manner" with Colonial wall colors, wall coverings and stenciling by master artist Donna Feltman. Outstanding pieces of antique furniture and other decor add charm to every room. Both inns offer numerous non-smoking rooms, and for golfing guests, special arrangements can be made to play at several challenging nearby courses.

The Old Edwards Inn can't accommodate cribs or cots nor meet the special needs of the handicapped, so it's suitable only for ambulatory adults. The Highland Inn, however, will accept children in a limited number of rooms at an additional charge. All the rooms have private baths, and the rates include a continental breakfast. Weekly and monthly rates are also available. If you drive into Highlands on U.S. Highway 64, you can't help noticing these two inns — they occupy both corners on the east end of Main Street.

### Snow Hill Inn
$$ • 531 Snow Hill Rd., Franklin
• (828) 369-2100

Snow Hill Inn perches on 14 acres high above the gem-rich Cowee Valley on a mountaintop. It's the place to come if you want to get away from city sounds and stress. The two-story home no longer looks like the old schoolhouse that it was in 1914, but in one of the rooms, the traces of students' names carved in the wall can still be seen. Each of the eight guest rooms has its own private bath, air-conditioning and in-room phone. The 12-foot ceilings give an added dimension of spaciousness to all of the large guest rooms. There are two or more big windows in each room offering spectacular mountain views.

If you want to relax, this Bed and Breakfast on 14 acres is the place to do it. Sit on the covered front porch, sip your coffee and enjoy the panorama of 11 different mountain peaks floating above the morning mist. If the afternoon is more to your liking, enjoy the incredible views from the sun deck of different mountain peaks. If you feel more active, you can play croquet or badminton on the lawn.

Snow Hill provides a sumptuous hot breakfast from 8:20 to 10 AM in the glass-enclosed dining room. Owners and Innkeepers George and Rita Sivess's Southern hospitality is sure to make your stay here memorable.

# Swain County

### Fryemont Inn
$-$$ • Fryemont St., Bryson City
• (828) 488-2159, (800) 845-4879

Two generations of Browns have served as innkeepers at this comfortable 37-room inn that sits on a mountain shelf overlooking the Great Smoky Mountains National Park.

Everything about the inn, a tradition in hospitality here since 1923, is "woodsy": it's rustic exterior, its lusterous hardwood floors; its chestnut-paneled bedrooms, the mountainous view from its tree-top, rocking-chair porch; its lovely 80-degree swimming pool nestled in a grove of hemlock, dogwood and poplar. The large lobby is more than matched by a giant stone fireplace that can hold logs eight feet long. There is also a full-service lounge and a library.

All the rooms have private baths, but no two are alike, except for their many-paned, pocket windows that slide back to let in the mountain air and nature's night sounds. Adjacent to the main lodge are cottage suites, each with a living room, a bedroom with a king-size bed, a wet bar and a working fireplace. Some of the suites have loft bedrooms; others have private decks.

We think Fremont Inn is one of the best bargains in the mountains. It rates unbelievably reasonable and include both a hearty breakfast and dinner. The public is also invited to enjoy these wonderful meals by reservation. Fryemont Inn is open from April through November, but the cottage suites are open year-round.

## Hemlock Inn
**$$$$ • Off U.S. 19, Bryson City**
**• (828) 488-2885**
This is an unpretentious place, but there's nothing unpretentious about the view. Hemlock Inn is built on a small mountain that overlooks three valleys backed up by big mountains. Sitting on the front porch with a steaming cup of coffee in hand and watching the sunrise over this scene is something worth getting up early for! The inn opened in 1952 with nine rooms; its popularity grew over the next decade, and the owners added 12 rooms and four cottages to meet the demand. The growth stopped there, because owner/innkeepers Jo and John Shell and Elaine and Morris White and their guests like the informality and personal attention a small inn can provide.

The rooms and cottages (one very secluded and popular with honeymooners) are furnished in antiques and pieces made by mountain craftspeople. The rates include family-style breakfasts and dinners and all gratuities. Meals for the public are by reservation only. And, since the innkeepers always feature fresh foods native to the area, what good meals they are!

Hemlock Inn sits on 45 wooded acres 3 miles from the Deep Creek area of the Great Smoky Mountains National Park, between Cherokee and Bryson City. Take Hwy. 74 to Hyatt Creek Road (Exit 69). Turn right on Hyatt Creek and drive 1.5 miles, then turn left of Hwy.19. Drive 1.5 miles to the Hemlock Inn sign and turn right at the sign. The inn is 1 mile on the left.

# Other Accommodations

In the preceding chapter, we listed a whole lot of inns and bed and breakfast establishments, and even at that, we barely scratched the surface of the area's many intimate and often historic establishments that have thrown open their doors to travelers. But such places are not for everyone — or not for everyone all the time. They certainly don't reflect all the accommodations we have in the mountains. There are dozens of reasonably priced, family-owned motels and cabins in and around our towns, and all the big chain hotels are represented throughout the region at locations very convenient to our attractions. Even in a small city like Hendersonville, there are more than 60 places to stay, with more opening all the time. Cherokee, a popular resort, has 45 motels and 110 cabins from which to choose plus 27 campgrounds with more than 2,200 sites.

For this chapter, we have chosen just a few of the larger, better-known establishments, plus some special smaller places you'll want to know about. But keep in mind that this is a guide, not a directory. For every listing we have here, there are many more similar types of accommodations in the same area. In short — except perhaps during the fall foliage season when the region is jam-packed with leaf-lookers — finding a great place to spend the night or an extended vacation is never a problem. The average nightly rate for two adults at the facilities in this chapter is indicated by a dollar sign ($) ranking in the chart below. Most businesses accept major credit cards for payment, but we note those establishments that don't accept credit cards.

## Price Code

| | |
|---|---|
| $ | $50 to $70 |
| $$ | $71 to $90 |
| $$$ | $91 to $110 |
| $$$$ | $111 and more |

## Northern Mountains

### Alleghany County

**Alleghany Inn**
**$-$$ • 541 N. Main St., Sparta**
**• (336) 372-2501, (888) 372-2501**

If you get off the Blue Ridge Parkway at milepost 217 at its junction with N.C. Highway 18 and drive about 15 minutes west to Sparta, you'll find the Alleghany Inn, a nice, reasonably priced family stopover. This 64-room pleasantly furnished modern motel is open year round. The Inn offers cable TV, queen- and full-size beds and king-size waterbeds. One efficiency is also available. A conference center is a recent addition to the inn. Smoking is permitted.

**Bluffs Lodge**
**$$$ • Mi. 234.8, Doughton Park**
**• (336) 372-4499**

Bluffs Lodge sits on a broad hilltop on the Blue Ridge Parkway with expansive, long-range mountain views. Here, rangers provide interpretive talks around an outdoor fireplace in the patio area. The accommodations are comfortable, with lots of amenities like private baths and large closets in each room. Just across the road is the Bluffs Lodge Coffee Shop.

# Ashe County

## Best Western Eldreth Inn
**$$-$$$$ • 829 E. Main St., Jefferson • (336) 246-8845, (800) 221-8802**

Some people consider rocking chairs a way of getting fit. Others want something a little more heart pumping. This 48-room inn features both — rooms with a view of Mt. Jefferson, complete with rocking chairs on the balconies, and a well-equipped fitness center. It also offers a range of room sizes with double-, queen- and king-size beds. Non-smoking rooms are available. The inn's restaurant serves home-style meals for breakfast, lunch and dinner (except Sunday night). Should you want to sample something different, Eldreth Inn is within walking distance of six restaurants. It is also next door to a shopping center and is only a short drive from the Ashe Country Frescoes (see our Arts and Culture chapter), canoeing on the New River and local golfing.

## Greenfield Resort
**$-$$ • 1795 Mount Jefferson Rd., off U.S. Hwy. 221, West Jefferson • (336) 246-9106, 246-9671**

Greenfield Resort is spread over approximately 100 rolling acres of pasture, originally part of the Rufus McNeil farm, c. 1847, at the foot of Mount Jefferson. The McNeil homestead has been converted into a lively family-style restaurant. Greenfield also has a banquet room that seats 300, a convenience store with crafts, ice, and produce, 8 rustic rental cabins, camping facilities, three fishing ponds stocked with bass and blue gill and miles of hiking trails that wind around Mount Jefferson. The cabins sit on a ridge opposite Greenfield restaurant at the base of spectacular Mount Jefferson (see our Restaurants chapter). These units offer either one bedroom with a loft and shower or a two-bedroom efficiency

with shower. There is also a large recreation room with cooking facilities. A bunkhouse-type cabin holding up to 22 people is also available.

The campground has 125 sites and can accommodate both RVs and primitive tent camping. Tent sites are $14 per night; RV sites a full hookup costs $17.

Greenfield features buggy rides, Civil War reenactments and two rodeos a year, making the resort more than a tourist stop — it's a community gathering spot.

## Jefferson Landing Lodge
**$$$-$$$$ • N.C. Hwy. 88 and 16, Jefferson • (800) 292-6274**

Jefferson Landing Lodge is a superb addition to this premier golf community. The tastefully decorated facility has 17 units and numerous amenities, including a full-service lounge. The lobby has a vaulted ceiling and large windows that offer a breathtaking view of the golf course. Jefferson Landing Lodge is open year round, and townhome rentals and golf packages are also available.

## Nation's Inn
**$$ • 107 Beaver Creek School Rd., West Jefferson • (336) 246-2080, (800) 801-3441**

This 50-room, two-story hotel near N.C. Highway 221 opened in November 1994. The rooms, all with outside entrances, feature king-size or double beds. Complimentary continental breakfast is served from 6:30 to 10:30 AM. Nation's Inn also has a meeting room that accommodates 25.

# Avery County

## Beech Alpen Inn
**$$-$$$$ • Beech Mountain Pkwy., Beech Mountain • (828) 387-2252**

Beech Alpen Inn is a country inn under the same management as its neighbor, Top of the Beech, just down the road. The Beech Alpen Inn is open year round offering a cool retreat in the summer and ski opportunities in the winter. Some of the rooms in this rustic, European-style inn have fireplaces and balconies, and all rooms have exposed-beam ceilings as well as great views of the mountains and ski slopes at nearby Ski Beech. King- and queen-size beds are available. The Beech Alpen restaurant offers a menu of fine dining, featuring New York strip, filet mignon, superb crab cakes and mountain trout prepared by an award-winning chef.

### Holiday Inn of Banner Elk
**$$-$$$ • 1615 Tynecastle Hwy., Banner Elk • (828) 898-4571, (800) HOLIDAY**

This classic Holiday Inn is less than a mile from the entrance to Sugar Mountain Ski Resort and only 6 miles from Ski Beech. The motel has 102 rooms (some nonsmoking), king-size beds and cable TV with free HBO. Summer visitors can use the outdoor pool,

volleyball court, horseshoe pits and Ping-Pong tables. You can dine at Butler's, the inn's full-service restaurant. Meeting and banquet facilities are also available.

### Humpback Hollow
**$$$$ • U.S. Hwy. 221, Linville Falls • (828) 766-6555, (888) 263-3632**

Each of these unique cabins has a fully equipped kitchen including microwave and charcoal grill. If you'd like to relax indoors after all-day hiking, there's a VCR and great selection of videos. All the cabins are decorated with antiques and country charm. Hosts Tom and Karen Acheson provide all linens, complimentary wood for the woodburning fireplace and morning coffee. There are three cottages in all — the 200 year old historic log cabin Sunalee, with all the modern conveniences. It has a deck and covered porch, two full baths, a large bedroom and loft. The Conner Cottage

Photo: Constance E. Richards

Some of the area's accommodations re-create the grandeur of past decades.

has been built entirely of wormy chestnut, and contains a gas log fireplace and porch, also two bedrooms and one bath. Fiddlesticks is the newest log cabin with a gas log fireplace and air conditioning. With one bedroom and one bath, it's an ideal romantic getaway for couples. The large covered porch serves as a wonderful lounging area.

## Parkview Lodge
**$$-$$$ • U.S. Hwy. 221, off Blue Ridge Pkwy. at mi. 317, Linville Falls**
**• (828) 765-4787, (800) 849-4452**

This attractive lodge right off the Linville Falls Exit of the Blue Ridge Parkway is a pleasant place with a friendly atmosphere. In addition to the 16 rooms, the complex has two cottages with kitchenettes and a suite on the picturesque grounds that back up to the Parkway. You'll find plenty of wooded privacy and a swimming pool banked by cultivated wildflower beds. Parkview is popular with the Parkway's hikers and campers, who occasionally stop in for a dose of civilization, especially hot showers. Parkview Lodge is open year round and serves a complimentary continental breakfast. A craft shop and wine and beer shop are also on the premises. Satellite television includes HBO and Disney channels in addition to network programs.

## Pineola Inn and Pineola Motel
**$-$$ • U.S. Hwy. 221, Pineola**
**• (828) 733-4979**

Just at the head of the North Cove area on U.S. Highway 221 going up the mountain to Linville and Boone is the tiny crossroads of Pineola. The Pineola Inn and the Pineola Motel, both owned by the same family, are simple accommodations with reasonable rates. They're just a few minutes south of the major ski areas of Sugar Mountain, Ski Beech and Hawksnest. The High Country Ski Shop and Pineola Country Store, also part of the complex, offer gifts, souvenirs and ski gear. Ski equipment rentals and cross-country ski instruction are also available at the ski shop. You can ski cross-country on the nearby Blue Ridge Parkway. Ask the proprietor of the High Country Ski Shop about cross-country instruction and the best access to locations for this winter sport. Don't miss the Indian artifact museum at the rear of the Country Store. This amazing lifetime collection of Avery County's Dellinger family is one of the largest private collections of Native Indian artifacts in the area.

## Sugar Top
**$$$-$$$$ • 303 Sugar Top Dr., Banner Elk**
**• (828) 898-6211, (800) 764-2786**

If brilliant views, every modern amenity, and sleek contemporary decor top your list of must-haves at a vacation spot, then perhaps you should be staying at Sugar Tap. Perched atop Sugar Mountain, this ten story condominium resort offers arresting views from an elevation of 5,140 feet. The east side has a view of Grandfather mountain, while the west side overlooks the Sugar Mountain ski slopes. All suites are approximately 1,100 square feet, with two bedrooms, two baths, dining area, living room with fireplace, private covered balcony, refrigerator, dishwasher and wet bar. Amenities include an indoor pool, sauna, steam room, whirlpool, fitness center, twenty-four hour security and front desk service.

## Top of the Beech
**$$-$$$$ • Beech Mountain Pkwy., Beech Mountain • (828) 387-2252**

This Swiss-style ski lodge caters especially to — who else? — ski enthusiasts. The lobby, with a beamed cathedral ceiling, is dominated by a huge stone fireplace. The rooms, with two full-size beds, have wonderful views of the slopes of Ski Beech, just a half-mile away. You can get a "supersaver" discount rate Sunday through Thursday, and a complimentary continental breakfast is served each morning. An on-site conference room seats 50.

# Mitchell County

## Big Lynn Lodge
**$$$-$$$$ • N.C. Hwy., 226A, Little Switzerland • (828) 765-4257**

Just off the Blue Ridge Parkway milepost 332.5 is delightful Big Lynn Lodge, a welcome sight after a long drive. This rustic inn is a combination of individual rooms and cottages in a woodland setting. Some rooms offer a spectacular view of the valley below. An exceptionally nice feature here is the complimentary inclusion of breakfast and dinner with all accommodations. There's an early-bird discount if you make reservations prior to the busy fall season.

### Pinebridge Inn
$$-$$$$ • 101 Pinebridge Ave., Spruce Pine • (828) 765-5543, (800) 356-5059

The Pinbridge Inn has a history of hospitality. This school property, constructed in the early 1920s, was converted the area's premiere hotel and conference facility in 1985. The sturdy brick hotel houses 44 spacious rooms, a delux apartment with Jacuzzi bath, assembly and banquet space, for both small and large groups. Another accommodation on the grounds is a three bedroom cottage with fireplace. The high ceilings and tall windows in these former classrooms provide a view of the beautifully landscaped courtyard. An extensive continental breakfast is served each morning. Pinebridge Inn is open year round and offers group specials and discounts for area attractions.

Guests can also take advantage of the Pinebridge Center, located just across the parking lot. This recreational and fitness center offers numerous recreational diversions including seasonal ice-skating in one of the South's largest rinks. A lighted 410 feet long footbridge spans the Riverside Park and connects the facilities to downtown Spruce Pine.

## Watauga County

### The Alpine Village Inn
$$-$$$ • 297 Sunset Dr., Blowing Rock • (828) 295-7206

The Alpine Village Inn is in the heart of Blowing Rock, within walking distance of Main Street and all the shops and restaurants. This attractive motel offers many of the detailed amenities of a bed and breakfast inn: 100 percent cotton towels, percale sheets, magazines and flowers in the rooms, individual heat and air conditioning controls, cable TV and complimentary newspapers and morning coffee. Antique furnishings and collectibles complement the homespun decor. Room refrigerators are available. The rocking chairs

# Alpine Village

## VISTAS:
Yes, high elevation lookouts with postcard type views that go on and on; bring camera.

## TRAILS:
Yes, attractive Blue Ridge hiking trails through natural wooded scenery and waterfalls.

## GOLF:
Yes, 18 hole championship club in N.C.'s most beautiful setting; special rates for our guests.

## TENNIS:
Yes, carefully maintained mountain-top regulation court for tenants.

## SWIMMING:
Yes, sparkling heated pool with furnished pool-side deck during summer months.

RCI RESORT OF INTERNATIONAL DISTINCTION

State Road 80-S, just 3 miles W. of Blue Ridge Parkway. One hour NE of Asheville, NC (2 night min. - no pets)

**CALL 828-675-4103**

in the gazebo on the grounds are an invitation to take it easy.

## Brookside Inn
**$$ • 7876 Valley Blvd., Blowing Rock • (828) 295-3380, (800) 441-5691**

Brookside Inn is a small inn with 19 guest rooms and three villas situated on two landscaped acres of land, with a brook, lake, gardens, and orchard. Guest rooms and villas are furnished in a Victorian cottage motif, with quilts, comforters, wicker chairs, and painted furniture. In the center of the inn is Brookside Gallery, which exhibits and sells the works of regional artists. It is in the bright, gallery with high ceilings where the owners serve a complimentary continental breakfast of homemade bread, coffee, tea, and juice each morning. Rooms, most with two double beds, each have a private bath, telephone, and cable television.

The real drawing point of Brookside Inn is the park surrounding the establishment; only a short walk from downtown shopping and restaurants, you have a lush gardens with 50 year old apple trees, a rock Meditation Garden, resident ducks on the pond, and scads of flowers and plants. All guest rooms face the quarter-acre lake. Three villas contained in one building behind the inn each have kitchen facilities, and two have gas-log fireplaces.

## The Broyhill Inn & Conference Center
**$$$-$$$$ • 775 Bodenheimer Dr., Boone • (828) 262-2204, (800) 489-6049**

This inn on the campus of Appalachian State University features seven suites and 76 guest rooms. There are 15 rooms for small- to medium-size meetings and the Trillium Ball-

room for as many as 600 guests. Support services for conferences and meetings include a full catering service for meals and receptions, audiovisual equipment and the services of professional technicians. The Inn's dining room serves up a spectacular mountain view with every breakfast, lunch and dinner. Duggins Lounge, a quiet and relaxing getaway, is open in the evenings.

## The Castle Hotel
**$$-$$$$ • 205 Sampson Rd., Boone • (828) 264-4002, (888) 264-4003**

Yes, that is a castle rising out of the North Carolina Mountains, or rather one man's personal dream of one. Transplanted Virginian Doug Koger came to the mountains, became king of his own castle and then opened his kingdom to an appreciative public. This fantasy hotel, which is built to resemble a medieval castle, is fun for everyone. Each of the 29 one- and two-bedroom suites is decorated with elegant Queen Anne cherry furnishings and has a kitchens and sitting area; several have fireplaces. Compact studio rooms are also available.

The little lookout towers on each end of the castle buildings are not just places to watch for intruders — you can enjoy a leisurely game of chess or quiet reading time here. Biking and hiking are popular on the Blue Ridge Parkway, just minutes from The Castle. And Boone's restaurants and shops are nearby, should royal guests choose to leave their domain.

This place is perfect for groups, honeymooners and anyone who relishes the fun and fantasy of medieval romance. The Castle Hotel is open year round.

---

## INSIDERS' TIP

With the dominance of skiing and golf at Beech Mountain and in the Banner Elk area, tiny Avery County is very much a tourist-oriented rental area. You can find a variety of condo vacation rental packages for extended stays during winter and summer. For the latest price information — it changes frequently — contact the Banner Elk Area Chamber of Commerce, (800) 972-2183, or the Beech Mountain Area Chamber of Commerce, (800) 486-5506. These friendly folks will be glad to connect you with local real estate rental agencies.

## The Cottages of Glowing Hearth

$$$$ • 171 Glowing Hearth Ln., Valle
Crucis • (828) 963-8800

The term "cottage" is a great misnomer
here, since we are speaking of five 1,500-
square-foot houses with 18-foot white pine
tongue-and-groove ceilings, 100-gallon
double spas, king-size four-poster beds, imported Mexican terra cotta tile flooring, a private driveway and a parking area for each
domicile and 25 windows per "cottage" so as
not to miss any of the spectacular views.

A fully equipped kitchen, a 30-foot-long
front porch and a stone fireplace and hearth
enable you to feel quite at home on your vacation. Of course, it's not only the professionally designed interiors that make the Cottages
of Glowing Hearth a dream vacation home
but also the small touches as well. Hand-
painted ceramic tiles decorate the dining island, a video library with 500 titles can easily
distract you, and a full concierge service for
reservations, tee time and other needs provides a near-perfect vacation experience. All
you have to do is sit back and enjoy.

The proprietors live on the property and
maintain a fax, a copier and a computer in the
office if you must keep in contact with the
outside world. The property is a nonsmoking
environment and is open year-round. Weekly
rental rates are discounted.

## Days Inn — Blowing Rock

$$-$$$ • U.S. Hwy. 321 Bypass,
Blowing Rock
• (828) 295-4422, (800) 329-7466

Here's a good bargain for families. Deluxe king and oversize rooms are among the
118 guest rooms available. An enclosed
atrium has a heated swimming pool and hot
tub. The coffee shop serves a full breakfast
only. Days Inn has ski packages and discounts for senior citizens and tour groups.

## Fall Creek Cabins

$$$-$$$$• off Hwy. 421, Fleetwood
• (336) 887- 3131

Surrounded by miles of lush forest on all
sides, a gurgling creek and small waterfall,
Fall Creek Cabins seem far removed from civi-
lization. But open the front door to your two-
story cabin and you will soon realize that all

your creature comforts have been taken care
of. The cabins, built from a fragrant western
red cedar, house two bedrooms, two baths, a
living room, loft and kitchen. The full kitchen,
with dishes, blender, corkscrew, silverware,
washer and dryer, enables you to be com-
pletely self-sufficient once you've done your
initial grocery shopping.

Proprietors Tim and Beverly Thompson
have truly thought of everything—including
adjustable dimmer-lighting and thermostats in
every room, to create just that perfect individu-
alized atmosphere for whatever the occasion.
Stacks of newspaper for getting a good blaze
started have thoughtfully been placed in a bas-
ket by the stone fireplace. An enormous stack
of firewood sits just outside the cabin, and a
gas grill on the front porch means grilling those
steaks and sausages will be a snap, leaving
more time for outdoor activities or a longer
soak in the hot tub on the covered porch,
whichever your inclination may be. You can
find a VCR, videos and board games for the
whole family in each cabin. During the day, be
sure to explore the extensive hiking trails,
streams, waterfalls, and a trout stream stocked
by the state. You'll have to purchase a fishing
license for about $10, which you can find at
any hardware store, fishing and bate shop, or
even large superstores.

The Thompsons have built six cabins with
their own personal preferences in mind. Hav-
ing traveled the country and spent many a
vacation wishing for the perfect mixture of rus-
tic comfort, they have finally realized their
dream, and now wish to share it with you.
The lofty cathedral ceilings in each cabin con-
vey a sense of light and breeze. Light streams
into the dining room windows as well as
through the sliding glass doors into the living
room. Each cabin is decorated in a different
unobtrusive style, with country flavor and clean
lines. Cabins are far from one another, so you
will have no problem imagining you are the
only ones on the mountain, but with all pos-
sible amenities at your fingertips.

## Graystone Lodge

$$-$$$ • 2419 Hwy. 105, Boone
• (828) 264-4133

The gray stone exterior of this four-story
inn links it to the Scottish influence of Linville,

just south on the same highway. Built against the hillside, the inn's first two floors offer parking lot entrances.

The 100 rooms of the Graystone Lodge have a number of comfortable variations that include luxury suites with king-size beds, parlors and vaulted ceilings. Continental breakfast is free and served from 6:45 to 10 AM. All rooms have cable TV, and you can rent a VCR. The inn also features an indoor heated pool. Special discounts are available.

## Hemlock Inn
**$$ • Morris St., Blowing Rock**
**• (828) 295-7987**

For those of you who don't like to fool with the intimacy of a bed and breakfast, who prefer to be left to your own devices or who prefer to spend your money on sightseeing, gifts and food rather than your accommodations, then the Hemlock Inn is for you. This motel-style inn is just off Blowing Rock's main street. It offers tidy rooms with double, queen- or king-size beds, air-conditioning, private baths and the added plus of a kitchenette in every room. A microwave, coffee pot and refrigerator enable you to be quite independent in your travels here. Or if you plan on heavy-duty cooking, suites are available with fully equipped kitchens. You also have the choice of nonsmoking and non-allergenic rooms. Newly expanded and remodeled, Hemlock Inn will also feature handicapped-specialized rooms in 1998.

A hot tub shaded by a gazebo in the central courtyard, a picnic table and a grill are some of the amenities that make Hemlock Inn feel more like a vacation cottage than just another hotel or motel.

## High Country Inn
**$$-$$$ • 1785 N.C. Hwy. 105 S., Boone**
**• (828) 264-1000, (800) 334-5605**

Built against the side of the mountain, High Country Inn takes advantage of its scenic wooded surroundings. This inn of native stone provides a variety of comfortable to luxurious accommodations.

All 120 rooms have been recently refurbished. You can indulge yourself in a suite such as the deluxe Appalachian Room with a king-size bed, a whirlpool tub and a cozy fireplace. This is a popular honeymoon destination, but it also draws skiers, golfers and other

Photo: Constance E. Richards

While away the afternoon on the porch of one of our rural resorts.

groups interested in the High Country Inn's numerous discount packages. The inn also has several meeting rooms available.

Geno's is the popular sports bar at High Country, and The Waterwheel is the inn's own restaurant, specializing in authentic German cuisine prepared by its German chef. You might want to wander the grounds and the enjoy the duck and fish ponds and the rabbits who live in the serene natural habitat developed at High Country Inn.

### Hillwinds Inn
**$$-$$ • 315 Sunset Dr., Blowing Rock • (828) 295-7660**

This delightful little motel-style inn offers a relaxing respite from a day of shopping and dining. Choose from a variety of rooms with two double beds, or queen or king size bed, private bath and telephone and TV. No pretensions here — it's relaxed and close to shopping and restaurants in downtown Blowing Rock, the inn is the choice for business travelers, as well as those who don't like a lot of fuss, but do like privacy. Hillwinds' upstairs suite is favorite with honeymooners, but we like it too — a comfortable bedroom with four-poster bed, plus a living room with television, wet bar, stereo-entertainment system, and fireplace.

Just beyond the Inn's gazebo, filled with rockers for late evening chats, is a small guest house with mirror-image rooms; if two families or several friends are traveling together, you can share the cottage and still have thorough privacy. Containing a bath, bedroom and lounge area, the guest house also has a full kitchen in each suite which may be used for a slight surcharge. Flowers and benches decorate the exterior of the Inn, and the lobby maintains a cozy seating area for sorting through the vast informational material provided by the owners on the area.

### Holiday Inn Express
**$$-$$$$ • 1855 Blowing Rock Rd. (U.S. Hwy. 321 E.), Boone • (828) 264-2451**

The location is convenient — between Boone and Blowing Rock — and amenities are plentiful at this Holiday Inn Express, one of the national chain's new streamlined facilities. Recently renovated, this motel features comfortable rooms plus free daily breakfast bar, free local calls, a fitness center and an outdoor pool.

### The Meadowbrook Inn
**$$-$$$ • U.S. Hwy. 321 Bypass, Blowing Rock • (828) 295-9341, (800) 456-5456**

This gracious inn offers numerous amenities in elegant surroundings. Rooms and suites are furnished in a traditional decor, and deluxe accommodations include fireplaces and oversize whirlpool baths. A serene pond is bordered by landscaped grounds. The Meadowbrook Inn has an indoor, heated pool and whirlpool and a fitness center. A glass-enclosed room adjacent to the pool area is used for meetings, conferences and private dining. The Garden Restaurant overlooks the garden and pond. A seasonal menu features fine wine and American cuisine. The light and airy Dux Lounge is a pleasant stop before or after a meal.

### Quality Inn Appalachian Conference Center
$$-$$$$ • 949 Blowing Rock Rd., Boone • (828) 262-0020

Only minutes away from Appalachian State's campus, area businesses and recreation, this modern hotel offers big-city conveniences and amenities. Guests enjoy spacious suites, king and connecting rooms, an indoor/outdoor pool, a fitness center, a restaurant and lounge and cable television. Full-service banquet facilities include catering, several meeting rooms and a 3,750-square-foot ballroom. A complimentary morning paper is a nice touch. Smoke-free and handicapped-accessible rooms are also available.

### Smoketree Lodge
$$-$$$$ • N.C. Hwy. 105 S., Foscoe • (828) 963-6505, (800) 422-1880 in N.C., (800) 843-5581 outside N.C.

The Smoketree Lodge is tucked away off N.C. Highway 105 leading directly into Boone, just a few minutes away. This hidden delight is sheltered by a canopy of trees that do much to give Smoketree its sense of privacy so near to bustling Boone. The lobby is graced by a massive fireplace that rises to the full height of the vaulted ceiling.

The comfortable rooms at Smoketree each have kitchenettes, and laundry facilities are available on several floors. The complex also includes a game room, an indoor pool, a hot tub, a sauna exercise room and gas and charcoal grills out back for picnic fun on the hill behind the lodge.

### Swiss Mountain Village
$$-$$$$ • 2324 Flat Top Rd., Blowing Rock • (828) 295-3373

The mountain cabins and chalets of Swiss Mountain Village offer the homey charm of a bed and breakfast with the privacy of your own

home away from home. Set on lovely landscaped grounds surrounded by a forest filled with native rhododendron and mountain laurel, Swiss Mountain Village has log cabins built from rough-hewn timbers. Each authentic Swiss-style chalet has a loft and stairway over a native-stone fireplace, and each comes furnished with everything you'll need to feel at home, right down to the towels, linens, stoneware, pots and utensils. A washer and dryer are also included in each unit, so you could stay for days and only bring one suitcase. Hiking trails and a fishing pond are on the property for your outdoor recreation.

The variety of accommodations at Swiss Mountain Village is a plus, especially if you have a big family or a large group of vacation-minded friends. Studio and one-, two- and three-bedroom units are available, each with queen-size beds and queen-size sleeper sofas. Some have extra twin beds or bunks, so bring a crowd. Off-season discount rates are available March through May and again in November through December 20.

## Yancey County

### Alpine Village
$$-$$$$ • 200 Overlook Dr., Burnsville • (828) 675-4103

Alpine Village is a unique place to stay. It has the individuality of a bed and breakfast, the serenity of a retreat and the variety of a small resort. Yet it is highly affordable and a splendid alternative for large families or groups on the road for summer fun.

Set high back in the mountains in the shadow of spectacular Mount Mitchell, Alpine Village is a cluster of private one- and two-bedroom chalet-style condominiums with all the amenities of home, each accommodating from four to six people. Each cabin is equipped with a kitchen, a dishwasher, a washer/dryer, a telephone, a whirlpool bath, linens, private decks, cable TV and gas grills. A heated pool and a tennis court are on the grounds, and golf is available at a special discount to guests at nearby Mount Mitchell Golf Club. You can rent these cabins by the night, week or month. A two-night minimum stay is usually required.

A PLACE FOR ALL SEASONS...
FOR ALL OCCASIONS...FOR ALL AGES

**ENJOY NATURAL BEAUTY?**
The Blue Ridge Mountains are spectacular all seasons.

**PLANNING A PARTY OR MEETING?**
Small intimate reception or a corporate conference, we can accommodate your group (up to 800).

**HOOKED ON SPORTS?**
Play our 18-hole, par 70 golf course; swim laps in one of the two pools; or try your hand at tennis on one of our clay courts.

**BRINGING THE KIDS?**
Ask about our fun-filled programs.

SunSpree Resort®
Great Smokies • Asheville, NC

I-240 Exit 3B, One Holiday Inn Drive, Asheville, NC 28806
828-254-3211 or 1-800-733-3211 www.sunspree.com

## Blue Ridge Motel
**$-$$ • 204 West Blvd., Burnsville • (828) 682-9100**

The unusual interior wood paneling of the rooms at the Blue Ridge Motel is one of the attractions of this small family-owned motel, situated just a few minutes west of Town Square and U.S. Highway 19 E. This pleasant two-story, red-brick motel, built in the 1950s when wood paneling was not the life savings' investment it is today, boasts a distinctive variety of wood interiors, from apple wood to pine, walnut and oak. Some of the furniture was also handmade during that early period. You can sleep on a bed with a delightful handmade ash, oak, walnut or maple headboard. All rooms have private outside entrances, and the motel is within easy walking distance of shopping and a number of local restaurants.

This motel is popular with skiers, since Wolf Laurel is about 40 minutes away. Group rates and senior citizen discounts are available.

# Central Mountains

## Buncombe County

### Best Western Central
**$$-$$$ • 22 Woodfin St., Asheville • (828) 253-1851**

Just off I-240, which loops around the city,

Best Western Central is convenient to attractions at all points of the compass. This hotel has 150 guest rooms, a swimming pool, meeting rooms and Ashley's restaurant and lounge.

### Comfort Inn — Asheville
**$$ • 800 Fairview Rd., Asheville • (828) 298-9141, • (800) 228-5150**

This hotel is in the eastern part of Asheville, off I-240 at the River Ridge Outlet Mall. Accommodations are moderately priced, and the hotel has 178 guest rooms, including a number of luxurious two-room suites with large whirlpool garden tubs, king-size beds, a living room, kitchen and dinette areas and private balconies. A fax and a copier are in the lobby, and a continental breakfast is served by the fireplace in the large sitting area adjacent to the lobby. The Comfort Inn also has a pool, a playground and volleyball and basketball courts. You can walk down the hill to the Outlet Mall from Comfort Inn.

### Comfort Suites
**$$-$$$$ • 890 Brevard Rd., Asheville • (828) 665-4000, (800) 228-5150**

Comfort Suites caters to the corporate business traveler. The hotel contains 125 spacious one-room suites, each with a full- or queen-size bed, sleeper sofa, coffee pot and refrigerator. Two thousand square feet is devoted to meeting space that can accommodate gatherings of up to 100 people. Complimentary deluxe continental breakfast, free airport shuttle, an exercise and hot-tub room and an outdoor heated pool are some of the amenities provided by Comfort Suites. The hotel is next to the Biltmore Square Mall.

## Forest Manor Inn
**$$-$$$$ • 866 Hendersonville Rd., Asheville • (828) 274-3531**

South of Biltmore Village toward Arden is Forest Manor Inn, an oasis on four wooded, beautifully landscaped acres that at one time were considered out in the country. The lovely stone structure that now serves as the office was once a private residence, built in 1926. It has a curiously colorful history: During Prohibition, the sons who inherited this lovely home turned it into a rowdy roadhouse. As years went by, it became a somewhat subdued restaurant. Then it caught the eye of a nefarious local character who turned it into a gambling operation during the 1940s and '50s. Eventually, this checkered existence subsided, and the elegant old home took on respectable status as the pleasant motor lodge it is today.

Five cheerful, canary-yellow buildings surround the stone lodge. The inn's 21 guest rooms are either delicately papered or panelled in knotty pine. Parking is just outside your door. King-size beds, smoke-free rooms and continental breakfast are other amenities. A private, landscaped pool area is open during the summer season.

## Great Smokies Holiday Inn SunSpree Resort
**$$-$$$$ • 1 Holiday Inn Dr., Asheville • (828) 254-3211, (800) 733-3211**

This 120-acre resort caters to corporate and tourist groups. The individual traveler, however, may also find this an enjoyable resort conveniently located three minutes from downtown Asheville. An 18-hole golf course sprawls over rolling green hills and a fully stocked pro shop supplies all your sports needs. The resort's 10,000 square feet of meeting space accommodates a wide variety of functions, including ballroom banquets, sunset receptions and boardroom meetings. All rooms feature balconies or patios and, of course, some fairly incredible views. Recreational amenities include tennis, a jogging trail, several swimming pools, an on-site exercise room or a nearby full-service health club. Also available are children's programs and a game room.

This homeowner converted a grist mill into a vacation cottage. It's typical of places to stay in the Cashiers area.

Photo: Cashiers Chamber of Commerce

## Hampton Inn — Asheville
**$$-$$$$ • 1 Rocky Ridge Rd. off I-26, Asheville**
**• (828) 667-2022, (800) HAMPTON**

Southwest of the city, the Hampton Inn of Asheville has 121 nicely appointed guest rooms, a fully equipped fitness center, an indoor heated pool, a sauna and a hot tub. Free airport transportation, nonsmoking rooms and meeting facilities are also available. The Biltmore Square Mall, the Movies at Biltmore Square and several fast-food restaurants are nearby. You can also ask them about their new Tunnel Road Facility, which is close to Asheville Mall.

## Haywood Park Hotel
**$$$$ • 1 Battery Park Ave., Asheville**
**• (828) 252-2522, (800) 228-2522**

The Haywood Park Hotel was a prominent flagship in the resurgence of downtown Asheville. A full-service hotel in the heart of downtown was a risky business a decade ago, but the renovation of the historic Ivey's Department Store at the corner of Battery Park Avenue and Haywood Street into the sleek Haywood Park Hotel was backed by strong business commitment. The success of this undertaking brought a level of sophistication to the inner city that set the tone for the upscale mood and cultural renaissance enjoyed by downtown Asheville today.

The hotel renovation is an interesting use of space, opening up and reshaping the former boxy retail building. The adjoining atrium space, which houses shops, restaurants and offices, brings the sky inside the heart of this city block with its vaulted ceiling, skylights and gleaming glass elevator.

The Haywood Park Hotel has 33 exquisitely appointed guest rooms, some with great views of the architectural richness of downtown Asheville. Meeting rooms are also available, and the two superb restaurants, 23 Page for fine dining and The New French Bar, a chic cafe, make the Haywood Park Hotel a popular dining spot for downtown business professionals and visitors alike. This fine hotel has also hosted a number of celebrities, whose photos line the lobby walls.

## Holiday Inn — Tunnel Road
**$$-$$$ • 201 Tunnel Rd., Asheville**
**• (828) 252-4000, (800) HOLIDAY**

This Holiday Inn has been a fixture on Tunnel Road for a good while, undergoing major renovations in recent years. It is a popular site for corporate groups, reunions and senior citizen groups. It's an easy walk from here to the Asheville Mall and numerous restaurants along Tunnel Road. The 131 guest rooms feature double- and king-size beds, cable TV with free HBO and ESPN and room service. The inn has an outdoor pool, and you can purchase tickets to Biltmore Estate here.

## Mountain Springs Cabins & Chalets
$$$ • N.C. Hwy. 151, Asheville
• (828) 665-1004

Tucked back in the mountains as cabins and chalets are wont to do, Mountain Springs Cabins & Chalets are off of U.S. Hwy. 19/23; turn onto N.C. 151 and follow signs for five mils to Mountain Springs. You will find them almost adjacent to the Blue Ridge Parkway. A mountain stream meanders past the cabins.

All are furnished in fine country antiques, modern baths, fireplaces, cable TV, swings and rockers on the porches. Flowers decorate the window boxes and grapes dangle from arbors. Fragrant herbs grow outside in the herb gardens-all the better to use in your cooking in the charming kitchens. The cabins range in size from one-bedroom to two-bedrooms with loft. There are lots of places to stroll, swim, birdwatch and hike in the most enchanting acreage that surrounds the cabins and chalets. Or you can just while away the time in a hammock under the trees. A true retreat for lovers of nature and seclusion, Mountain Springs can be rented on a daily or weekly basis. Children are welcome.

## The Quality Inn — Biltmore
$$$-$$$$ • 115 Hendersonville Rd., Asheville
• (828) 274-1800, (800) 221-2222

This hotel in Biltmore Village has the distinction of the being the Quality Inn of the Year for 1994. Since its construction several years ago it has become one of the prime fixtures in the southern end of town. The hotel's brick-and-stone exterior is a modern blend of the angles and lines and stately presence of the turn-of-the-century architectural opulence characterized by its neighbor, Biltmore Estate. The light wood-paneled interior and dramatic lighting of the hotel lobby complement the elegance of the lush furnishings.

The hotel has 160 guest rooms, including 20 suites. All rooms have cable TV with HBO, valet and room service and electronic door locks. A gift shop and fax machine are in the lobby. This Quality Inn also caters to corporate business through several flexible meeting rooms and on-site advance coordination of catering, audiovisual equipment and entertainment.

The superb Criterion Grill for fine dining and the Biltmore Dairy Bar for lighter fare are both in the hotel.

## Radisson Hotel — Asheville
$$$-$$$$ • 1 Thomas Wolfe Plaza, Asheville • (828) 252-8211

The 12-story Radisson Hotel, a prominent feature on the skyline of downtown Asheville, provides guests with a breathtaking view of the city and the mountains beyond. This modern award-winning hotel has 278 guest rooms and seven suites, all decorated in an elegant Queen Anne style with all the amenities. Concierge service and health club privileges are available to guests, and there are nonsmoking floors.

The lobby contains a gift shop and Isadora's Sports Bar, and Burt & Harry's Deli at the Radisson serves up light sandwiches and side orders. The premier restaurant, Top of the Plaza, is truly at the top, on the 12th floor, with an incredible view. The hotel also has 14 flexible meeting rooms with state-of-the-art conference planning and support. An 8,100-square-foot ballroom is also at your disposal.

---

### INSIDERS' TIP

The Blowing Rock area has an array of small, clean and cozy motels too numerous to mention here. If you prefer the independence of the motel to a bed and breakfast and the price to larger resorts and inns, then take a drive through Main Street and the streets branching off this thoroughfare. Most of these smaller motels are happy to take walk-ins if you are not quite sure of your travel plans beforehand.

The Radisson is within walking distance of Pack Square, fine restaurants, shopping and downtown galleries.

## Ramada Plaza

$$-$$$$ • 435 Smoky Park Hwy., at I-40 and U.S. Hwy. 19/23, Asheville
• (828) 665-2161, (800) 228-2828

The six-story lobby atrium with a cozy fireplace is the focal point of the 166-room Ramada Inn West. The hotel has Lisa's Restaurant and the Eagle's Nest Lounge, and local crafts are highlighted at Ann's Gifts. Guests may use the hotel's health club, sauna, hot tub and indoor-outdoor pool.

## Sleep Inn — Biltmore

$$-$$$ • 117 Hendersonville Rd., Asheville
• (828) 277-1800, (800) 62-SLEEP

This Sleep Inn in Biltmore Village opened in the fall of 1994. It offers upscale quality accommodations for a reasonable price. Attractively furnished, this hotel offers a number of pleasing amenities: queen-size beds, both smoking and nonsmoking rooms, connecting rooms, free continental breakfast and free local calls. A fax and copier are also available for busy working travelers. Two restaurants, The Criterion Grill and Biltmore Dairy Bar, are next door in the Quality Inn. The Biltmore Estate entrance is just a few blocks away.

## Willow Winds

$$$ • 39 Stockwood Rd., Asheville
• (828) 277-3948

Only minutes from Biltmore Estate, this collection of seven individual homes on 40 acres of land gives you the full luxury experience of staying in a fully furnished domicile, including washers, driers, equipped kitchen, televisions, VCRs, and your own phone line. From one-bedroom homes, to three-bedroom homes with two stories, these beautifully furnished homes also contain Jacuzzi tubs inside and hot tubs outdoors.

If you haven't bought your groceries yet, not to worry, you'll be supplied with a gift basket containing fresh fruit, cookies, coffee, and wine. A stocked pond on the property enables you to fish for your own dinner if you care to. Houses may be rented for as little as two nights in the off season, and a minimum of five nights during high season.

# Henderson County

## Hampton Inn

$$ • 155 Sugarloaf Rd., Hendersonville
• (828) 697-2333, (800) HAMPTON

Hampton Inn, right off the junction of I-26 and U.S. Highway 64 (take Exit 18A going to Batcave), has 117 rooms and two suites. Amenities include cable television with HBO, free local phone calls, an outdoor swimming pool, health-club privileges, senior discounts and a free deluxe continental breakfast. Nonsmoking rooms are available, and third and fourth guests stay free of charge. From here, it's just a hop, skip and a jump to Wal-Mart, the Blue Ridge Mall and a number of familiar chain restaurants. A bit farther on is Hendersonville's historic Main Street, with its abundance of shops, restaurants and galleries.

### The Quality Inn and Suites
**$$ • 201 Sugarloaf Rd., Hendersonville • (828) 692-7231, (800) 4-CHOICE**

This large facility is also at the junction of I-26 and U.S. Highway 64 (Exit 18A). In addition to air-conditioned corporate, spa and two-room suites, the inn has an excellent restaurant court and lounge overlooking an indoor, Olympic-size, heated swimming pool. The motel offers a full range of amenities, including a fitness room, sauna, free newspaper and local phone calls, banquet facilities, room service, a hot tub and meeting rooms. All the sites of Main Street Hendersonville are nearby.

## Rutherford County

### Fairfield Mountain Resort
**$$$-$$$$ • 747 Buffalo Creek Rd., Lake Lure • (828) 625-9111, (800) 829-3149**

This resort offers efficiencies, condominiums, rentals and time shares for travelers wishing to enjoy the scenery of Lake Lure and Chimney Rock and the recreation of two golf courses on the 2400-acre Fairfield Mountain Resort property. Several of Fairfield's 100 units sit on the banks of the lake, opposite the town of Lake Lure. Others offer views of mountain ridges and foliage. Efficiencies include efficiency kitchens, telephones, TV and air conditioning. Larger two and three-bedroom units also contain these amenities, but with a full kitchen.

Because many of units are actually second homes that are rented out by the resort, you will find the interiors decorated with the individual tastes of the owners. This lends a delightfully homey and distinct atmosphere to each rental. Some homes maintain a two-

day rental policy, but many allow for anywhere from a one-night's stay to several weeks or months.

If you don't feel like cooking, two restaurants located at the resort can provide pleasant dining. Legends Bar and Grill serves breakfast, lunch and dinner, and Lakeview Restaurant serves dinner.

## Polk County

### Days Inn
**$ • I-26 at Exit 36, Columbus • (828) 894-3303, (800) 329-7466**

Situated between the twin towns of Tryon and Columbus, this facility offers many extras, such as an outdoor pool, suites with whirlpool baths, cable television with HBO, nonsmoking rooms, free continental breakfast, AARP discounts, mountain views and 24-hour desk and wake-up services.

## Transylvania County

### Brevard Motor Lodge
**$ • U.S. Hwy. 64 and Caldwell St., Brevard • (828) 884-3456**

While staying here, you'll be right across the street from Brevard College's picturesque campus, within walking distance of downtown Brevard and just minutes away from the Brevard Music Center. This small motel — all its rooms are on the ground floor — offers individual heating and air conditioning, a small refrigerator in each room, a heated pool and fax and copier service.

### Hampton Inn
**$$ • 800 Forest Gate Center, Brevard • (828) 883-4800, (800) HAMPTON**

In 1995, this 81-room Hampton Inn opened just off the main entrance to Pisgah Forest outside Brevard near the intersection of N.C. Highway 280 and U.S. Highway 64. The facility offers two conference rooms and continental breakfasts. There is no restaurant on the premises, but you'll be within walking of quite a few places to eat. Shopping, too, is at your front door in the Forest Gate Shopping Center, which contains a Belk and a Wal-Mart.

## Imperial Motor Lodge
$$ • U.S. Hwy. 64 and U.S. Hwy. 276 N.
(Asheville Hwy.) Brevard
• (828) 884-2887, (800) 869-3335

Situated between downtown Brevard and the entrance to Pisgah Forest, Imperial Motor Lodge is Transylvania County's largest motel. Each of its 92 rooms has individual heating, air conditioning and cable TV with HBO. Every room has a refrigerator. There is also a large sun deck and pool. Smoking and non-smoking rooms are available, and a continental breakfast is served in season.

## Pisgah Inn
$$ • Mi. 408.6, Blue Ridge Pkwy
• (828) 235-8228

The Pisgah Inn is a landmark on the Blue Ridge Parkway. From late April until early November, this inn's location at 5,000 feet and just a hike down a trail from Mount Pisgah itself offers the opportunity to explore nature's unspoiled mountain seasons — and you barely have to step outside to do it. In addition to two double beds, a private bath and color television, each room at Pisgah Inn has its own private porch or balcony directly overlooking Pisgah Ledge and the ever-changing play of lights and shadows on the mountain peaks below. A restaurant serves excellent food at very reasonable prices, and the view from the dining room is spectacular.

If you want to get out in all this beauty, you can hike on a number of trails — interconnecting with many other Pisgah Forest trails — that begin practically at the inn's door. This is a popular place so advance planning is important. You might be able to simply drop in and get a room, but it's wiser to make reservations. During fall-foliage days, early reservations are essential.

## Rainbow Lake Resort
$$$ • East Fork Rd., Brevard
• (828) 862-5354

This serene mountain valley just across the road from the trout-filled headwaters of the French Broad River is perfect for those who want a quiet stay in the mountains. The 12 rustic cottages have front porches with porch swings and rockers. They are sprinkled throughout the woods overlooking a 3-acre lake. Their simple board-and-batten exteriors belie the elegance within. The tastefully decorated interiors include original works of art, hardwood floors, fine furnishings and fully equipped kitchens. Each has a private phone, cable TV and air conditioning. Some have fireplaces. You can chose from one-, two and three bedrooms. Here you'll find trails, boating, fishing, badminton, horseshoes, volleyball, streams, waterfalls, hammocks, quiet reading nooks, tranquillity and a summer symphony of crickets and frogs to sing you to sleep. Rainbow Lake is the perfect place for holding seminars and family reunions. Well-behaved, fleasless pets are accepted with prior arrangements. Rainbow Lake Resort is located 8 miles from Brevard. Take either U.S. 64 W. or U.S. 276 S. out of Brevard for about 3 miles. Signs will tell you where to turn.

# Southern Mountains

## Cherokee County

## Cherokee Hills Golf and Country Club
$$ • Harshaw Rd., Murphy
• (828) 837-5853, (800) 334-3905

If you like to golf, this is the place to stay in Murphy (see our Golf chapter). The complex has 12 units available in the club's lodge that feature fully equipped efficiencies, including two queen-size beds, a bath with a tub and shower, kitchens, cable television, daily maid service and air conditioning. Spacious two-story townhouses are available for rent at little more per night than you would pay at a fine hotel. Golf packages bring down the price even more. Rentals also include access to the pool, tennis courts, a restaurant, a golf course, a driving range and a putting green.

## Comfort Inn
$ • 114 U.S. Hwy. 64 W., Murphy
• (828) 837-8030

Murphy's Comfort Inn, which is open all year, has 55 rooms, 10 of which come with whirlpools and refrigerators. One really nice attraction here is the heated indoor pool with a sun roof. Other amenities include a confer-

Photo: Constance E. Richards

Falls Creek Cabins allow you to vacation at your leisure.
All the amenities are there, you just bring the food.

ence room, cable television and movie rentals and free continental breakfasts.

one efficiency unit. All rooms have air-conditioning, cable television and telephones.

## Clay County

### Chatuge Cove Complex II
$$ • N.C. Hwy. 175, Hayesville
• (828) 389-6155

This complex on lovely Lake Chatuge (see our Recreation chapter) offers two-bedroom houses for rent at weekly and monthly rates. The complex also has a lakefront primitive campground, and you can rent dock space, houseboats, pontoon boats and fishing boats. Other facilities on Lake Chatuge are available in the Hiwassee area.

### Chatuge Mountain Inn
$ • U.S. Hwy. 64, Hayesville
• (828) 389-3873, (800) 948-2755

This facility is east of Hayesville on U.S. Highway 64 going toward Hiwassee, Georgia. It has 14 clean, comfortable rooms, including

## Graham County

### Thunderbird Mountain Resort
$-$$ • U.S. Hwy. 129 N., Santeetlah
• (828) 479-6442

Built on one of the many little peninsulas that poke out into Lake Santeetlah, Thunderbird Mountain Resort, about 6 miles from Robbinsville, has 32 rooms with lake views, plus cottages, lake swimming and a good restaurant. The seclusion of this comfortable resort is synonymous with a relaxing vacation. Right next door is the Santeetlah Marina with 70 slips and all kinds of boats for rent, including a giant water tricycle. You can buy fuel, bait, tackle, hunting/fishing licenses, boat registrations, ice and snack food here too. The marina also has a water ski shop and a ski instructor for private lessons.

# Haywood County

## Best Western

**$$ • 3811 Soco Rd. (U.S. Hwy. 19),
Maggie Valley
• (828) 926-3962, (800) 528-1234**

Best Western, formerly The Mountainbrook Inn, on the busy highway that cuts though the center of this highly developed resort town, is within walking distance of many Maggie Valley attractions. Even so, you can relax on the rocking chairs here while you view mountains right from the front porch of your room. Or, during the summer season, you can unwind in a heated pool and large whirlpool spa. The grounds include a picnic area with grills. The large motel-type rooms contain two queen-size beds. There are full baths and showers, a couple of upholstered chairs with a small table, cable television with free HBO and — probably best of all for the budget-conscious — a microwave, a refrigerator and in-room coffee. There is no charge for children 17 and younger staying in the same room with a parent. Cribs are available at no cost; rollaways are $8 night. A continental breakfast is served each morning.

## Best Western Smoky Mountain Inn

**330 Hyatt Creek Rd., Waynesville
• (828) 456-4402, (800) 218-2121**

At the Best Western Smoky Mountain Inn, you're within an hour's driving distance of some of our most famous attractions, including the Biltmore Estate, the Great Smoky Mountain Railroad, the Blue Ridge Parkway, the Cherokee Indian Reservation and Ghost Town in Maggie Valley to name a few. The Inn's 58 modern, spacious and comfortable rooms feature large picture windows revealing gorgeous mountain views. King-size, handicapped-accessible and nonsmoking rooms are available on request. Microwave, mini-refrigerators and color TVs are standard. Complimentary continental breakfast is served each day. Daily newspaper, magazine and reference books are available in the lobby. This inn is 5 miles north of the Blue Ridge Parkway on U.S. Highway 23/74. Take the West Waynesville Exit 95.

## Chalet Motel and Apartments

**$$ • Soco Rd. (U.S. Hwy. 19),
Maggie Valley • (828) 926-2811**

Nestled up and off U.S. Highway 19 in a secluded and quiet spot, Chalet Motel rents apartments, efficiencies and rooms. These vary in the types of accommodations offered. One efficiency, for example, has a king-size bed and a kitchenette; another has a queen-size bed and a full kitchen. The average apartment has a living/dining room combination, a bedroom with two double beds and a separate full kitchen. They have heat and air conditioning, cable television with HBO, AM/FM and private patios with pretty mountain views. The lawn is flat and expansive and has shade trees, picnic tables and grills; there are trails and trout streams close by.

## Days Inn

**$$ • 3325 Dellwood Rd., Maggie Valley
• (828) 926-0201, (800) 325-2525**

The 102 rooms at Days Inn have cable with HBO and ESPN and telephones; non-smoking and handicapped-accessible rooms are available. But there's much more here, including a restaurant, meeting facilities, a heated swimming pool, a game room, a playground, an outdoor hot tub and a train ride for children right on the property.

## Twinbrook Resort

**$$ • 230 Twinbrook Ln., Maggie Valley
• (828) 926-1388, (800) 305-8946**

Set on 20 acres, this four-season facility features 14 one-, two-, three- and four-bedroom, individually crafted cottages with fireplaces, phones and cable TV. The cottages are scattered among tall hemlocks. On site are an indoor pool, a hot tub, a game area, horseshoe pits, a volleyball court and a playground.

# Jackson County

## Comfort Inn

**$$ • U.S. Hwy. 23/74, Sylva
• (828) 586-3315, (800) 654-3315**

All 70 air-conditioned rooms at Sylva's Comfort Inn have phones and cable television. The inn also has a swimming pool, serves a complimentary continental breakfast and has other services and discounts you'd expect from a motel chain such as Comfort Inn. This one is near Sylva and Dillsboro on the highway to Waynesville.

### Cottage Inn
**$$$$ • Off U.S. Hwy. 64, Cashiers**
**• (828) 743-3033**

Since 1932, the year-round Cottage Inn has been a mountain hideaway for quiet, lovely vacations. Each of the 14 air-conditioned cottages has a fireplaces, a kitchens, a color TV, a full bath and a deck and porch. In addition to the cottages is the new Knolltop Lodge Bed and Breakfast with four guest rooms with private baths, air-conditioning, a common parlor with a TV and a fireplace and a full breakfast daily.

The 9-acre complex also has an enclosed heated pool, a tennis court with a basketball goal, a nature trail, a picnic pavilion, swings and hammocks, laundry facilities and the Heathstone room for meetings.

### Mountain Brook Cottages
**$$$ • 208 Mountain Brook Rd., Sylva**
**• (828) 586-4329**

Midway between Sylva/Dillsboro and Franklin, these 12 brookside cottages offer fireplaces and equipped kitchens. Some have bubble tubs/saunas and king-size beds. There is also a spa/sauna bungalow. In addition, Mountain Brook offers a game room, a stocked trout pond and a nature trail. Wedding and honeymoon packages are available.

### Mountain Creek Cottages
**$ • 2672 Dicks Creek Rd., Dillsboro**
**• (828) 586-6042**

The sounds of rushing water will lull you to sleep at this beautiful creekside setting. Accommodations for two to six people have full kitchens, DSS TV with HBO and private cookout areas. There's a lot to do in this area of the mountains, but you might just opt for hanging out in a hammock by the cascading stream.

# Macon County

### Heritage Cottages and Villas
**$$ • U.S. Hwy. 441 Business, Franklin**
**• (828) 369-2028**

Because it sits on 7 acres filled with rhododendrons, dogwoods and towering pines, this complex right in the heart of Old Town Franklin can offer amazingly quiet lodgings. You have your choice of villas or cottages. The villas, which can sleep from two to six people, have one or two queen-size beds, a bath with a separate dressing room, a full kitchen and a living/dining area with a fireplace. Each of the cottages, which are for two to three people, has a queen- or king-size bed, a sofa, eating areas and efficiency kitchens. All units have air conditioning, cable TV, an electric toaster and a coffeemaker. Even the dishes, cooking utensils and linens are furnished. You will be within walking distance of downtown Franklin with its shops, museums and restaurants. A bakery and a creekside cafe are practically on the premises.

### Highland Suite Hotel
**$$$$ • 200 Main St., Highlands**
**• (828) 526-4502, (800) 221-5078**

Just where the shopping stops on Main Street you'll find the Highlands Suite Hotel, where all rooms are suites, each with individual climate control, a whirlpool spa, two telephones, two cable TVs, a VCR, a microwave oven, a wet bar and A refrigerator. In addition, each living room has a queen-size convertible sofa bed, and each bedroom offers a choice of either one king-size or two extra-large twin beds. Many suites have gas-log fireplaces.

There are also complimentary continental breakfasts and evening wine and cheese, free parking in a covered garage and free local phone calls. Nonsmoking rooms and walk-in closets are available options.

### Skyline Lodge
**$$$ • Flat Mountain Rd., Highlands**
**• (828) 526-2121, (800) 5-SKYLINE**

At an altitude of more than 4,000 feet, Sky-

Photo: Judi Scharns, Courtesy of Boone Convention and Visitors Bureau

Snow, skis and sky — what more could one ask for?

Grab a sled. Find a friend. See the mountains from top to bottom.

line is housed in a Frank Lloyd Wright-designed, tastefully furnished building with 50 acres of grounds that have streams, lakes, waterfalls and nature walks. Other attractions include a swimming pool, tennis courts, a gourmet restaurant and a spa with a sauna, a steam room and a whirlpool. The facility also offers facials, full-body massages and foot- and hand-care sessions, along with guided fitness walks, aerobics, yoga and seminars on healthful living (seminars are offered only to guests participating in the lodge's "Holiday Health" specials). Skyline Lodge is open year round.

## Swain County

### Best Western Great Smokies Inn
$$ • U.S. Hwy. 441 at Acquoni Rd., Cherokee
• (828) 497-2020, (800) 258-1234

Right across the street from the 8,000-square-foot Great Smokies Convention Center, this Best Western has 152 extra-large rooms with cable TV with a free movie channel; it also has a swimming pool. Myrtle's

Table Restaurant at the facility serves breakfast, lunch and dinner.

### Hampton Inn of Cherokee
$$ • U.S. Hwy. 19 S., Cherokee
• (828) 497-3115, (800) HAMPTON

The 67 rooms here each have an inside entrance, temperature controls and cable TV with free movie channels. Half the rooms are designated nonsmoking. Children younger than 18 stay free in a parent's room. A free continental breakfast is available from 6 AM until 10 PM, and a full-service restaurant is right next door.

### Holiday Inn Cherokee
$$ • U.S. Hwy. 19 S., Cherokee
• (828) 497-9181, (800) HOLIDAY

Facilities here include 154 rooms with cable TV with a free movie channel, banquet facilities to accommodate up to 200, both indoor and outdoor pools, a whirlpool and a sauna. The Chestnut Tree Restaurant serves breakfast and dinner. This Holiday Inn received the Top Ten Customer Service Award and has earned a superior rating for seven consecutive years.

## Mountain View Log Cabin Rentals
**$$$$ • Off U.S. Hwy. 441, Cherokee**
**• (828) 497-9552, (800) 392-1003**

Here you'll find peace and quiet within minutes of bustling downtown Cherokee and the recreational opportunities of the Great Smoky Mountains National Park. These newly built cabins feature microwave-equipped kitchens, mountain-stone fireplaces, color cable TV, private indoor hot tubs, king-size beds, phones, all linens and porches with rocking chairs and swings. The Mountain View Log Cabin office is at the Discount Souvenirs gift shop on U.S. Highway 441 N. about a mile from the entrance to the Great Smoky Mountains National Park.

## Pioneer Motel and Cottages
**$$ • U.S. Hwy. 19 S., Cherokee**
**• (828) 497-2435**

Situated on 16 waterfront acres a half-mile from downtown Cherokee, Pioneer offers one-, two- or three-bedroom cabins with full modern facilities overlooking the Oconaluftee River, or you can choose a spacious room in the motel. All rooms are air-conditioned and have cable TV. Other recreational amenities are fishing (with a tribal permit), basketball, horseshoes, a pool and a picnic area on the premises.

Don't miss the buys
waiting for you out in
the countryside, where
a turn down a back road
can put you at the door
of a charming
country store

# Shopping Destinations

Besides memories and photographs, often the best memento of a certain place is that hand-woven scarf, a vase from the little antique shop on Main Street, the earrings from the gem mine, the humidor from the wood carvers. Let's face it, Americans are big shoppers; no tour is planned without the "shopping day" figured in. Thankfully, we can travel at our own pace in the mountains, and stop off for any little shopping expedition we please.

Each of the three geographical regions identified in this book is anchored by a major shopping location or group of locations: Boone in the Northern Mountains; Asheville, Hendersonville and Brevard in the Central Mountains; and Waynesville, Highlands and Dillsboro in the Southern Mountains. Fanning out from these cities are towns and country crossroads that add to your shopping options. The shops in our larger cities sell just about anything you could want: museum-quality mountain crafts, English antiques, international imports, fine art and upscale decorative items for your home, for starters. Furniture reproduction showrooms, factory-direct stores and upscale outlets are good places to stretch your dollars. And then there are the malls, where America's retail giants do business side-by-side local shopkeepers.

If you prefer a gentler pace, and want to really "know" a town, take a stroll down the "Main Street USA" of North Carolina's small mountain towns during midday lunch. The well-ordered rows of storefronts with their enticing shop windows are also often carefully preserved examples of early 20th-century architecture. And don't miss the buys waiting for you out in the countryside, where a turn down a back road can put you at the door of a charming country store. Once the backbone of our rural economy, these simple shops are often treasure troves of Americana. If you are an antique aficionado, you may be amazed at the great buys you can find in the middle of nowhere — a country community may have Saturday yard sales, for example. What looks like an old farmhouse with junk out on the front porch, may actually be an "antique barn," where you can find fascinating old farm tools, cupboards, tables, dishes, and scads more.

## Northern Mountains

### Ashe County

#### Glendale Springs

Up in the beautiful and remote countryside of Glendale Springs in Ashe County, you won't find scads of shops and malls: There's not a chain store in sight, but you will hit upon a few choice gift shops.

#### Greenhouse Crafts
**248 J.W. Luke Road, Glendale Springs • (336) 982-2618**

The place is booming despite its remote location, apparently proving the old saw, "if you build it, they will come," or rather, "if you paint it, they will come." And paint they do. Greenhouse Crafts sits across the road from the Holy Trinity Episcopal Church, where noted North Carolina artist Ben Long completed his fresco of The Last Supper in the early 1980s. (The other of the two Churches of the Frescoes is St. Mary's Episcopal, about 12 miles away near West Jefferson, off U.S. Highway 221.)

Greenhouse Crafts has tastefully complemented the frescos' religious theme with angel statuary, inspirational art, literature and an array of music. The shop also has traditional mountain crafts, collectible figurines and unusual functional and whimsical pottery, such as a playful set that depicts Noah's Ark. Handmade jewelry, including silver rings and bracelets made in the area, can be found here, along with stained glass lamps, gorgeous wooden dulcimers and other smaller gift items. The owner might even play a tune or two for you on the delightfully seraphic-sounding dulcimer. We can't begin to encompass all the items in the shop in a few words, so make it a definite stop and see for yourself when you're in the area.

## Jefferson

Jefferson and West Jefferson, only a few miles apart, are towns so small and ubiquitously 1950s America, that they could well be part of a Hollywood movie set. Instead, they are real places, which we are privy to stop in and stroll down the eerily quiet main streets. But quiet doesn't mean lifeless — in both of these towns you will find "five and dimes," secondhand shops, and even a gallery or two. Don't expect much in terms of quantity of shops, but do look into the few shops you will find. The shopkeeper will always be a wealth of local information.

### Country Charm & City Elegance
**314 E. Main Street, Jefferson**
**• (336) 246-4846**

This gift shop features handpainted birdhouses, traditional teddy bears, and other small items.

### Sugar 'n Spice
**205 Long Street, Jefferson**
**• (336) 246-4279**

This little shop will whip you up a giftbasket in no time, taking from the candy-by-

the-pound, boxed chocolates, bars, and many other sweets available. You can also make your own, choosing from the variety of little stuffed animals and other gifts to accompany your tasty selections, or just buy a handful of jaw breakers and taffy.

## Todd

### Todd General Store
**N.C. Hwy. 194, Todd • (336) 877-1067**

As you wend your way along scenic N.C. Highway 194 in Ashe County, you'll come upon the charming crossroads community of Todd, originally named Elkland, that's halfway between Boone and West Jefferson. Sixty years ago, this was a thriving lumber town where the railroad was king, but once the region was lumbered out, the community seemed to heave a great sigh and disappear. Where once there were two hotels, a bank, a post office, a buzzing mill, nine stores and doctor and dentist offices that served mill workers and railroad men, there is now only tough little Todd General Store, on the banks of the New River. The store is the heart of the tiny community and a reminder of its glory days.

Its interior has been restored, but in a leisurely way. The collectibles and genuine antiques that cover the 2½ stories seem like they've always been there. Folks still gather on stools and straight-back chairs around the potbellied stove, which is fired up in cold weather. Simple wooden shelves hold groceries, staples for a community that would rather come here to shop than drive north to Jefferson or south to Boone. And you can still buy home-baked goods here, prepared by the women of the valley. Penny candies (well, close to a penny) are crammed beneath vintage glass-front store cases.

A lunch counter is also open at the General Store, where you can get a hearty barbecue sandwich and monstrous pickles — no skimping on portions either. The store sells gift items, antiques, collectibles and souvenirs of your ramble here.

# Avery County

## Banner Elk

The Shoppes of Tynecastle is an attractive grouping of specialty shops at the junction of N.C. Highways 105 and 184. Sports shops, galleries, home furnishings shops and others are anchored by a distinctive stone tower that makes this destination easy to spot.

Head north on N.C. 184 to the town of Banner Elk and its attractive new upscale shopping complex called The Village at Banner Elk. This cluster of shops features the following.

### Almost Rodeo Drive
**Suite 101, N.C. Hwy. 184, Banner Elk • (828) 898-4553**

This is a boutique for ladies and children's clothing (the other location is on Main Street in Blowing Rock). The pieces are fairly unique and of natural fabrics.

### Eve's Leaves / J.W. Tweed's
**Main St., Banner Elk • (828) 898-6166**

This shop sells elegant ladies' clothing, men's apparel and shows.

### The Village Grocery
**101 Main St., Banner Elk • (828) 898-4889**

The Village Grocery is a local landmark in Banner Elk. For 50-plus years this old-timey grocery store has been located on the main street, making it the oldest continuing business in Banner Elk. You can get just about anything here, but not in bulk.

## Beech Mountain

Beech Mountain is primarily a ski resort community, but there is a hardy contingent that lives here year round. We've included a few of the places where year-rounders shop.

### Fred's General Mercantile Company
**501 Beech Mountain Pkwy., Beech Mountain • (828) 387-4838**

This store has stepped in to fill the void for these brave few as well as for the legion of tourists who continually make the pilgrimage to mile-high Beech Mountain. Fred Pfohl and his colorful, old-fashioned store anchor the community. Among Fred's inventory are groceries, ski accessories, warm clothing, crafts, toys, even hardware and toothbrushes.

Stay and have lunch at — yep, you guessed it —Fred's Backside Deli, (828) 387-9331, at the rear of the store. And you can't miss, nor would you want to, Wildbird Supply, (828) 389-4838, also inside Fred's General Mercantile Company. The company's motto is "Wildbird's supplies everything but the birds," and that includes seed, feeders, books and nature guides. In back of this store you can watch birds, squirrels and chipmunks romp and munch on the feed left in the landscaped forest-garden plot.

### The Wizard's Toy Shop
**503 Beech Mountain Pkwy., Beech Mountain • (828) 387-4848**

Next door to Fred's is a great shop for the kids which specializes in educational and creative toys, including Playmobil, Sanrio and Brio toys, erector sets, puzzles, games and electric trains.

# Watauga County

## Blowing Rock

This quaint mountain village about 15 minutes from Boone is a shopper's paradise. Its short, very walkable Main Street is an easy stroll from almost every accommodation in town, so you don't have to worry about parking. Irresistible specialty and antiques shops line this main thoroughfare. We've described some of the most interesting ones here.

### Appalachian Rustic Furnishings
**1085 N. Main St. Blowing Rock • (828) 295-9554**

Owned by Bill Fitch, this shop displays incredible handmade furnishings and objects for home, lodge, camp and cabins. We fell in love with the birch bark lamps and picture frames. Mirrors made of wood and moss brought out our primal instincts for house and home, and who wouldn't want a handmade rocking chair or table from the finest wood in the Blue Ridge?

Fitch's workshop is a few miles down the road in the countryside, so you won't get to see any on-site working, but he does maintain photographs around the shop of various pieces being hand crafted.

## Bless Your Heart
### 1009 Main St., Blowing Rock
### • (828) 295-9133

This cottage-style gift shop caters to "the romantic at heart." Garden items, freeze-dried flower arrangements and specialty gift baskets are among the gifts at the charming shop.

## Cabin Fever
### 915 Main Street, Blowing Rock
### • (828) 295-0520

Cabin Fever offers a complete collection of log cabin and vacation home furnishings. Choose from unique and distinctive furniture, lighting, kitchen items, bed and bath decor, hardware, gifts and more. Cabin Fever is a family owned business with its largest store located in downtown Blowing Rock.

## Crestwood Galleries
### 946 Main St., Blowing Rock
### • (828) 295-0008

On the corner of Main Street and U.S. 221, with another shop in Tynecastle, Crestwood Galleries carries a collection of popular furniture lines, hard-to-find items and original artwork. Under new management this year, the shop now includes new reproductions of antiques, as well as period pieces. Mirrors, lamps, oil paintings, kilims, and woven kilim pillows, as well as Russian lacquer boxes and Russian porcelain from the pre-Revolutionary Gzhel factory make this shop a decorator's dream.

Artist showings and seminars on restoring furniture are part of the fun here too.

## Hanna's Oriental Rugs & Gifts
### Main St., Blowing Rock • (828) 295-7073

Another fine shop on Main Street, Hanna's sells imported items of exceptional quality, including Oriental and Central Asian rugs, exquisite Austrian Swarovski crystal, Lladro porcelain figurines and cloisonné, jade, and ivory pieces from around the world.

## Martin House
### Main St., Blowing Rock

The Shoppes of Martin House is an assortment of shops all in one place. This former residence, built on Main Street in the late 1800s, and adjoining cottages showcase all kinds of pretty and practical things: clothing, candy, toys, gourmet coffees, gems, candles, vintage reproduction photographs and Victorian floral arrangements.

Some of the fine shops in the area include: The Chicory Suite Martin House, (828) 295-4231, a quaint cottage off the Martin House courtyard in back that sells gourmet coffees and kitchen items. It smells wonderful too! G. Whiliker's & Co. Martin House, (828) 295-9549, with a jumble of whimsical toys, games, puzzles and books to tickle any child's fancy. Sweet Rosie's Martin House, (828) 295-9318. Follow your sweet tooth to the Rosie's, where you can fill a brown bag with old-fashioned candies and nuts (you can also buy gourmet pet treats here).

## Olde World Galleries
### 1053 N. Main St., Blowing Rock
### • (828) 295-7508 , (800) 736-1269

Located in the old Blowing Rock Auction House, the Galleries specialize in fine jewelry, particularly estate pieces from the 1920s. But they also have unique antique items, such as chandeliers, music boxes, art (both prints and oils) and hand-knotted Oriental rugs in traditional patterns. Fine jewelry in classical platinum and gold settings with precious diamonds, emeralds, sapphires, and rubies are some of the exquisite investments one can make here. Also, antiques from the Ancient Far East and other objects d'art grace this gallery's showroom. The gallery's 20th anniversary this year means special discounts on fine jewelry.

## Pleasant Papers
### #105 Village Shoppes, S. Main St.,
### Blowing Rock • (828) 295-7236

One of our favorite shops tucked back into an alcove on S. Main Street is Pleasant Papers Inc. Here you can find any number of beautifully embossed notecards, cards with elegant floral and gold borders, or even with

# Art in ASHEVILLE

# THE VILLAGE OF
# *Blowing Rock*

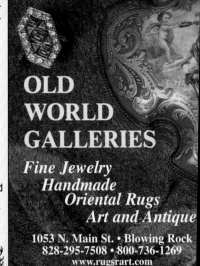

# THE VILLAGE OF
# *Blowing Rock*

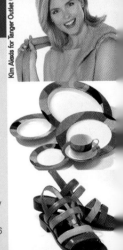

**The Blowing Rock Chamber of Commerce**
P.O. Box 406 • Blowing Rock, NC • (828) 295-7851 or (800) 295-7851
Visit us on the World Wide Web: http://www.blowingrock.com/northcarolina

# THE VILLAGE OF
# *Blowing Rock*

## Come for a vacation, stay for a lifetime.

YONAHLOSSEE
RESORT & CLUB

*Y*onahlossee Resort & Club combines superb accommodations with the grandest of amenities in an exceptional setting.

Cozy secluded cottages, spacious inn rooms and award winning recreational amenities that include the finest in tennis, horseback riding and swimming.

Incredible views accompanied by a unique cuisine at Yonahlossee in the Gamekeeper Restaurant.

If you want recreation, relaxation, and elegance, visit Yonahlossee Resort & Club. Come for a vacation, stay for a lifetime.

**FOR RESERVATIONS AND INFORMATION:**
**226 OAKLEY GREEN, BOONE, NC 28607**
**(828) 963-6400   800-962-1986**
www.yonahlossee.com

# THE VILLAGE OF
# *Blowing Rock*

$\mathcal{O}$nce upon a time,

there stood an enchanting

mansion where weary souls journeyed to find comfort.

$\mathcal{A}$t Westglow Spa, we've renovated our spectacular mansion to provide the perfect venue for revitalizing your body and soul. This European-style facility offers a vast array of luxuriating services such as massage therapy and herbal body wraps. Guests also delight in scenic mountain biking, recreational activities and delectable cuisine.

Make your reservation for a rejuvenating experience at Westglow today, so you can rediscover your self and live happily ever after.

WESTGLOW SPA
A place of leisure, recreation and rejuvenation

800-562-0807 • Blowing Rock, NC • www.westglow.com

# THE VILLAGE OF
# *Blowing Rock*

Visit our 54 acre private log cabin mountain retreat. Ideal for honeymoons, romantic get-a-ways, family vacations and reunions.

# Rocksberry Inn
## BED AND BREAKFAST

Formerly Known as Rocking Horse Inn

*Come to the Rocksberry Inn and enjoy the North Carolina mountains in quiet, country surroundings.*

*Antique-filled bedrooms, afternoon or evening refreshments, porch rockers and yard hammocks are all part of the ambience of the Rocksberry Inn.*

*Located a short distance from Blowing Rock, the inn is easily accessible to the Parkway.*

*In the morning, a country-style breakfast awaits you in the dining room or on the deck. Choose from a variety of rooms in the inn, all with private baths. Also available is a two bedroom cottage.*

**Carol Marton and Family**
*INNKEEPERS*
**P.O. Box 1417**
**Blowing Rock, NC 28605**
## (828) 295-3311

❧ Secluded, private wooded settings
❧ Two bedroom / two bath (2-8 people)
❧ Stone fireplaces (wood included)
❧ Full size hot tubs (seating for 5)
❧ Equipped kitchens / All linens included
❧ Covered porches, swing, rocking chairs, gas grill and wooded mountain views
❧ Trout stream, hiking trails, picnic areas, waterfalls and wildlife

Centrally located 5 miles from the scenic Blue Ridge Parkway, near the towns of Boone, Blowing Rock, W. Jefferson and Wilkesboro.

**For Reservations & Information:**
## 336-877-3131
www.fall-creek-cabins.com

**The Blowing Rock Chamber of Commerce**
P.O. Box 406 • Blowing Rock, NC • (828) 295-7851 or (800) 295-7851
Visit us on the World Wide Web: http://www.blowingrock.com/northcarolina

# THE VILLAGE OF
# *Blowing Rock*

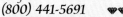

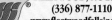

# THE VILLAGE OF
# *Blowing Rock*

The Blowing Rock Chamber of Commerce
P.O. Box 406 • Blowing Rock, NC • (828) 295-7851 or (800) 295-7851
Visit us on the World Wide Web: http://www.blowingrock.com/northcarolina

Photo: Constance E. Richards

Don't miss the many captivating bookstores in our mountains.

Southwestern and Impressionist motives — anything for wedding invitations, baby showers, New Year's party invites, and the list goes on. You can also order specially engraved writing paper, with your own logo or initials, and certainly you will find the perfect pen here for your correspondences. Writing the folks back home has never been so thrilling!

## Serves You Right!
**Southmark on Main Street,
Blowing Rock • (828) 295-GIFT**

Serves You Right! was conceived eight years ago by Karyn Kennedy Herterich, a Blowing Rock seasonal resident from Florida dedicated to offering unique gifts and essentials for the kitchen, dining room, and bar with particular emphasis on tableware, party, and entertaining accessories. Key vendors in this 1,000 square foot store are Bernardaud/ Limoges, Faberge, Battersea enamel collectibles, Herend Porcelains, Lynn Chase Designs, Mariposa, Penzo of Africa, Royal Worcester, Vietri and other quality lines. The shop also maintains a variety of whimsical gifts, such as Extendible Forks, which allow

you to eat off others' plates and other fun gift items. Styles and designs for trays, placemats, serving accessories and paper goods number in the hundreds in this charming store. Serves You Right! also has another store in Biltmore Village in Asheville, North Carolina.

## SouthMark
**Main St., Blowing Rock • (828) 295-3700**

SouthMark was the first new shopping development on Main Street in over 50 years, when the landscaped shopping center opened in 1992. Inspired by Blowing Rock's turn of the century thriving resorts, their distinctive Victorian influenced structures of towers and gables serve as a gateway into the South entrance of town. English gardens display summer topiaries of swans, lions, and rabbits, making SouthMark a unique place to shop. Eight of the area's most upscale shops are located here, with an additional six all-weather seasonal pavilions which open in May. Shoppers may find Herend and Faberge china here, or even paint their own pottery next door. Ladies' and children's apparel have a home in two shops here, as do high-end crafts, a sports collectibles shop, and a book store. The seasonal pavilions offer additional merchandise from wellness products, flowering baskets, and plants to pizzas and salads.

## Windwood Antiques
**1152 S. Main St., Blowing Rock • (828) 295-9260**

For English country pine and the cottage look, visit this shop across from Blowing Rock Realty. You can also find reproduction pieces, such as those popular antique armoires that have been converted into entertainment centers.

## Boone

Boone and the nearby towns of Blowing Rock, Foscoe, Banner Elk and Valle Crucis create a beehive of tourist shopping activity. Specialty shops, outlet sites, crafts and fine art galleries and antiques shops abound here.

## Downtown Boone

Shopping in downtown Boone gives you a chance to see the town's revived main thoroughfare, King Street. To find this historic street from N.C. Highway 105 as you enter the city, turn left at the intersection of U.S. Highway 321 and wind your way through the university district. The shops on W. King Street sell quality clothing, jewelry, gifts, fine art and pottery — a bit of everything in one place.

If you're looking for an unusual card or book, need a pen or sketch book, have a sweet tooth, want to find a special toy or game to keep your young back-seat driver busy, or would like to buy a CD with music as inspiring as the mountains, Boone's downtown shops can accommodate you.

## Ad-Lib
**611 W. King Street, Boone • (828) 264-0010**

Ad-Lib (also in downtown Asheville on Biltmore Avenue) is a women's clothing store that emphasizes natural fabrics and a casual but very elegant style — definitely the fashion trend for any time of year. Here, you will find fabulous richly hued cotton sweaters, silk skirts, linen shirts, and racks of scarves. Unique jewelry, beads, choice candle-holders and picture frames make this an emporium for fine gifts as well as fine additions to your own closet.

## Blue Planet Map Company
**487 W. King St., Boone • (828) 264-5400**

You can travel around the globe and never leave Boone, or so it will seem, when you walk into Blue Planet Map Company. If you love maps, you must visit this shop. They sell raised relief maps, travel guide books, world and state atlases, reproductions of antique maps, USGS topographical maps, geographic games, children's books, globes, calendars and even jewelry, clothing and gifts on the map theme. Oh, and they have lots of compasses too. You'll never get lost again.

## The Boone Antique Mall
**631 W. King St., Boone • (828) 262-0521**

This is a storehouse of American and European antiques spread over three floors and 27,000 square feet. Here you'll find antique jewelry, furniture, linens, decorative items, prints and family china from more than 75 dealers. Take your time browsing since each vendor has set up almost an entire store within the allotted space.

## Candy Barrel
**624 W. King Street, Boone • (828) 268-0666**

You'll be sorry if you pass up the decadently rich fudge and handmade candies in this 19th-century-style sweet shop. It carries more than 500 varieties of candy.

## Dancing Moon Earthway Bookstore
**553 W. King Street, Boone • (828) 264-7242**

This tiny shop offers those unique books, cards, and posters you can't find at a chain store. It also carries incense, candles and other items. (See our section on Bookstores at the end of this chapter.)

## Farmers Hardware
**661 W. King St., Boone • (828) 264-8801**

This is an old-fashioned, authentic full-service hardware store, started as Boone Hardware Company in 1924. Patrons step back in

time as they walk the aisles along creaky wooden floors.

Service is friendly and prompt, and you can buy nearly any kind of tool or supply you need for electrical, construction, painting, yard and garden and outdoor work, plus birdfeeders and more. The company also operates Farmers Lawn and Power Equipment Store, (828) 264-6044, 678 N.C. 105 Extension, for sales, repair and rentals.

### Farmers Hardware Ski Shop
**140 S. Depot St., Boone**
**• (828) 264-4565**

One of the area's premier ski shops, behind Farmers Hardware, this store has served the Southern skier since 1969. The year-round shop sells high-quality ski equipment, clothing, accessories and outdoor gear, such as hiking boots and backpacking equipment. The full-service snowboarding and skate shop with snowboard equipment, in-line skates and ice skates is a newer addition to the shop.

Top quality merchandise for the skier includes skis by Rossignol and Dynastar; boots by Nordica, Lange and Tecnica; and clothing by Columbia, The North Face, Helly, Hansen, Nils and Solstice. The shop is in Boone's oldest commercial building, constructed in 1911 to house the Ford dealership. Note the rustic, timbered interior that

which was renovated in 1976 but retains its yesteryear elegance.

### Footsloggers
**139 S. Depot Street, Boone**
**• (828) 262-5111**

Footsloggers carries all the stylishly rugged, top-quality clothing and footwear for those who like the outdoors or just the outdoorsy look. This is also the place to go in Boone for all kinds of camping, hiking and outdoor gear (see the "Outfitters" section of our Recreation chapter for more information).

### Grapevine Music
**641 W. King Street, Boone**
**• (828) 264-7168**

Celtic tunes and New Age music seem to be appropriate anthems for the mountains, and Grapevine Music has sounds that soothe the spirit. You can find mountain bluegrass on the rack too.

### Mast General Store
**630 King St., Boone • (828) 262-0000**

If you're looking for wool socks, flannel, down-filled and general mountain attire, this is the place. Just like its sister stores in Valle Crucis and other spots in this area, Mast General Store in Boone stocks quality leisure clothing, hats, belts, and other leather accessories.

We like the seasonal sale bins! The Boone store is a two-story, turn-of-the-century-style department store in the restored 1913 Boone Mercantile at the corner of King and Depot streets. Boone's Mast Store also carries shoes, housewares and gifts and has departments for children and maternity needs (see the Mast entry under Valle Crucis).

The candy shop adjacent to the clothing section is one step over the threshold in sugar heaven. Sold by the pound, the candy is stocked in barrels. Just carry your little basket around and start filling it up with old-fashioned horehound candy, peppermints, taffy and imported hard coffee candies, mints, and other tooth-rotting goodness!

### Purveyors of Art and Design Materials
**499 W. King St., Boone • (828) 265-0209**

This is where you can stock up on art materials, instruction books and frames — the expert staff will dole out free advice.

### The Stonehinge
**535 King St., Boone • (828) 262-1950**

This is the place for distinctive jewelry, treasures of nature and unique gifts.

### Varsity Men's Wear
**549 W. King Street, Boone • (828) 264-3520**

This shop carries fine men's clothing for business or casual occasions.

### Wilcox Warehouse Emporium
**161 Howard St., Boone • (828) 262-1221, 265-3973**

Enjoy shopping and dining under one roof in historic downtown Boone at the Emporium. The renovated building still smells of the herbs that once were brought here by the mountain people.

In 1944, Charles Wilcox built the warehouse for Wilcox Natural Products, a botanical company that gathered and sold herbs worldwide. Now, with its original hardwood

Photo: Constance E. Richards

The U.S. Post Office in the Mast General Store harkens back to the days when everything was found under one county roof.

floors and open-beam ceilings, the building houses shops, galleries, offices, a food court and a microbrewery. Visitor parking is off Rivers and Howard streets.

## From Boone to Blowing Rock, U.S. Highway 321

This busy highway serves as the primary link between Boone and Blowing Rock — and it is here where you might fulfill a great deal of your shopping needs if you take the time to stop.

### Blowing Rock Antique Center
**U.S. 321 Bypass, Blowing Rock**
**• (828) 295-4950**

This is one of those fun warehouse-style antiques centers that's stocked by independent dealers. Here you can observe the history of popular culture in America. "Eclectic" is the word for this place, where you can find a 19th-century trunk next to a 1920s dining table set with '50s Fiestaware and handmade linens. You might find an old Beatles album mixed in with turn-of-the-century sheet music or even a Brady Bunch lunch box like the one you had in the 5th grade. Browsing is half the fun! A second location is open in downtown Boone, (828) 264-5757.

### Country Farmhouse
**U.S. 321, Blowing Rock • (828) 295-9914**

This gift shop across from Chetola Resort (there's a second shop in Valle Crucis, (828) 963-4748, across from The Mast General Store) stocks gift items that include baskets, twig furniture, folk art, face jugs, quilts, birdhouses, afghans and even duck decoys.

### The Goodwin Weavers Showroom
**U.S. 321 Bypass, Blowing Rock**
**• (828) 295-3394, (800) 445-4437**

This long-established company still turns out Afghans woven in traditional mountain style. In their new retail showroom you can also find items from the Bob Timberlake Home Furnishings Collection as well as bedding accessories.

### The Incredible Toy Company
**3411 U.S. Hwy. 321 S., Boone**
**• (828) 264-1422**

Toys, toys, toys! The kids will see this one before you do, so you might as well be prepared to stop and enjoy this fun place between Boone and Tweetsie Railroad. It offers a large selection of educational toys, games, books, puzzles, science kits and the well-known Brio and Playmobil sets.

### The Mustard Seed Market
**U.S. 321, Blowing Rock • (828) 295-4585**

You might miss this little stand if you blink. This unassuming roadside market on U.S. 321 at Aho Road, 2 miles north of Blowing Rock, is open daily and is much more than a produce stand. English garden statuary, unusual perennial flowers, honey, herb vinegars, handpainted gifts and custom-made flags share the space with the fresh fruits and vegetables.

### Tanger Shoppes on the Parkway
**U.S. 321, Blowing Rock**
**• (828) 295-4444, (800) 720-6728**

This well-landscaped outlet center provides a delightful shopping experience while people are visiting the area. The center features 32 name brand outlets—some the best known in the industry— such as Gap, Nautica, Polo Ralph Lauren, Coach, Bass, Izod, Royal Doulton, Jones New York, Kaspar, Jockey, Big Dog, and Geoffrey Beene. Cooks will especially enjoy Corning Revere and Kitchen Collection, which feature every gadget a cook needs. The center also features a full-service restaurant, Parkway Café, and well-known Kilwins, serving locally made gourmet ice

## INSIDERS' TIP

As in many other parts of the country, you can usually find any item you're looking for at about one-tenth the retail price by traveling around to garage sales. There are hundreds happening here every week. Pick up a local paper to find out where they are.

Some of the area's bookstores have cafes where you can read, rest, and sip coffee or tea.

cream, candy, and fudge. Relax in the courtyard and enjoy a meal or a treat. Since being purchased by the national outlet industry giant Tanger Factory Outlets, the center has added amenities such as wheelchairs and strollers, as well as a centrally located office that sells gift certificates and disperses information about Tanger's 31 centers.

### Tanner Factory Store
**U.S. 321 Bypass, Blowing Rock**
**• (828) 295-7031**

This shop sells quality Doncaster fashions at attractive outlet prices. A second store is located near the entrance to Sugar Mountain in Avery County, (828) 898-6734.

### Foscoe

Where N.C. 105 passes through Foscoe, south of Boone, you'll find a corridor known for antiques shops. Classic English, French and American 18th- and 19th-century pieces are displayed by the community's many professional antiques dealers. The Foscoe area is a hot destination for western North Carolina innkeepers and bed and breakfast proprietors.

Going hand in hand with the sale of antiques in Foscoe are galleries of fine art, traditional crafts and unique specialty shops along N.C. 105.

### DeWoolfson Down
**9452 N.C. Hwy. 105, Foscoe**
**• 963-4144,(800) 833-3696**

Did you ever wonder where innkeepers get those sumptuous down comforters for your nightly lodging at some of the Boone area's best bed and breakfast inns? Well, the secret's out . . . it's DeWoolfson Down, 9 miles south of Boone on N.C. 105.

But there is so much more here: down pillows hand-stuffed to your order, silk comforters from China, Egyptian cotton sheets designed in France, crisp damasks from Germany and silky Jacquard sheets from Italy — up to 590 threads per inch. Clear out the trunk of your car before you come because you won't go home empty-handed.

### The English Shopper
**N.C. 105, Foscoe • (828) 963-6446**

Across from Mill Ridge, The English Shopper imports an abundance of goods from the United Kingdom, including handmade gifts, English foods, collectibles and even pub paraphernalia.

## Green Mansions Village
**N.C. 105, Foscoe**

Across from the entrance to Seven Devils on N.C. 105 (there's a large sign indicating the turn for Seven Devils), is a complex of antique, specialty and women's clothing shops. Finder's Keepers Green Mansions Village, (828) 963-7000, displays substantial antique English furniture — 18th-century chests, baronial tables and estate artifacts are among the treasures. Dreamfields Green Mansions Village, (828) 963-8333, has an eclectic selection of modern international decorative items and European antiques, as well as international fine art and unusual sculpture. The Country Gourmet, Ltd., (828) 963-5269, is a shop that reminds us of a cook's home — one where the cook loves to try every recipe that comes along. You can find scores of specialty kitchen tools, attractive functional stoneware, unusual cookbooks and items for the family hearth.

## Moss & Lace
**8970 N.C. 105, Foscoe • (828) 963-6914**

If you're looking for Victorian pretties, you can make several stops along N.C. 105. Across from Foscoe Family Health Center, Moss & Lace brings the Gilded Age home to you through antiques, reproduction books, greeting cards, floral arrangements, handcrafted jewelry and decorator baskets.

## Staffordshire Antiques
**8599 N.C. 105, Foscoe • (828) 963-4274**

Anglophiles, take note! This is one of two shops on N.C. 105 that imports directly from the British Isles. Eight miles south of Boone, this shop concentrates on 18th- and 19th-century antique furniture imports. Two red English phone booths stand outside of the shop. You can't miss them.

# Valle Crucis

## The Ham Shoppe
**N.C. Hwy. 105, Valle Crucis**
**• (828) 963-6310**

Up N.C. 105, just as you turn toward scenic Valle Crucis, is The Ham Shoppe. This is a store for jams, jellies, homemade breads, pies, dry pasta, and other staples for your kitchen. Even better though, are its made-to-order take-outs. Touted as "Ham Sweet Hams," the mouthwatering honey-glazed, spiral-cut baked hams are the obvious house specialty. But there is so much more to feast on here: strawberry-rhubarb pie, ham spread, cinnamon buns, preserves and fresh-baked sourdough bread. Use The Ham Shoppe as your special corner grocer, or as a deli — it serves this dual purpose well.

## Mast General Store
**N.C. Hwy. 194, Valle Crucis**
**• (828) 963-6511**

The ultimate shopping destination once you reach Valle Crucis is the historic Mast General Store on N.C. 194. Built in 1882 by Henry Taylor, the store was sold around the turn of the century to W.W. Mast. Over the next 70 years, the Mast family business established a tradition in the region for offering "everything from cradles to caskets." The interior of the store remains very much the same as it was a century ago. The old post office, still in service, is at one end, and the store's classic potbellied stove, an asset in these snow-prone hills, is still a central element.

You'll delight in a ramble around this old-time mercantile. Sit out on in the porch swings or rockers on the back porch. This is where you should be sipping your ice-cold A& W or hot-and-spicy ginger ale. It certainly revved us up after lunch for more sight-seeing. Next door is The Annex, which was built in 1909 as a rival general store but is now part of the Mast Store. This place has quality seasonal apparel and camping and fly-fishing gear. A deli in the annex provides light refreshments that you can enjoy outdoors, and a candy store offers barrels of taffy, jaw breakers, horehound candy, licorice, and about a hundred other sweets sold by weight. Just take your basket around and fill it up.

# Yancey County

## Burnsville

The small-town charm here adds to the fun, especially if you're looking for a break from malls and megamarts.

## Annie's Boutique
**Jacks Creek Rd., Burnsville**
• **(828) 682-4172**

This amusing little shop sells popular brands of clothing for everyone in the family at discount prices. The shop also carries gold jewelry and precious stones.

## needle me this
**112 W. Main Street, Burnsville**
• **(828) 682-9462**

The region is famous for its fine handcrafts, so you will not want to miss the display of finished quilts at this little shop. You can order a custom-made quilt here too. For do-it-yourselfers, the shop carries fabrics and notions and offers sewing and quilting classes.

## Something Special Gift Shop
**102 W. Main St., Burnsville**
• **(828) 682-9101**

This is a place where the country crafts and gifts are abundant and unique. The shop carries pottery, wooden shelving, prints and home-decorating items.

### Micaville

While you're in the area, make a short side trip to Micaville. It truly is a "one-house" or one-store town. Barely more than a corner on the intersection of two country highways, Micaville is a typical country village.

## Ian and Jo Lydia Craven, Handbuilt Porcelain
**1692 U.S. 80 S., Micaville**
• **(828) 675-9058**

Pull into the private-looking drive of Ian and Jo Lydia Craven's studio. Take U.S. Highway 19 E. out of Burnsville and turn right on U.S. Highway 80 S., going another 2 miles before turning right on a dirt road. The Cravens' work has been exhibited in major galleries all over Europe — Marbella, Madrid, Paris, Munich and other major cities — and more recently in the United States.

The couple has worked together since 1972 and for most of that time lived in southern Spain, where they developed their distinctive style and colors, moving to the Loire valley of France for three years before settling in the North Carolina mountains. Work-

ing exclusively in porcelain and using antique lace for imprinting, Jo Lydia designs and builds the pieces and Ian fires them in a glaze-on-glaze technique. You can watch them work if they happen to be there when you stop by. The shop is open every day except Sunday April through December and by chance or appointment January through March.

# Central Mountains

## Buncombe County

### Asheville Malls and Shopping Centers

The Asheville area has long been known for its tradition of crafting talent and resourcefulness. Entrepreneurship is alive and well here also, and it's been aided by an influx of newcomers in the last 20 years who have added fresh ideas and culturally diverse backgrounds to an already interesting mix of creative people. Asheville has become a proving ground for individuals who have a business concept and a dream. The tourism-based economy here has spawned new growth and the revitalization of Asheville's downtown.

But if you hunger for mega-parking lots and busy shopping malls, we've got you covered. There are two large malls in the area: the Asheville Mall, (828) 298-5080, 3 S. Tunnel Road, anchored by Sears, JCPenney and Montgomery Ward; and Biltmore Square Mall, (828) 667-2210, 800 Brevard Road, anchored by well-know retailers such as Belk, Dillard's and Proffit's. And there are also bustling community shopping centers and other specialty shops at all points of the compass from Asheville.

One busy area shopping center east of Asheville, River Ridge Outlet Center, 800 Fairview Road, (828) 298-9785, devotes its entire 40 stores to outlet shopping. You can easily reach River Ridge from Exit 8 off Interstate 240, which loops around the city, or by taking Exit 53B off Interstate 40. Don't overlook the shops along the main streets of the area's small towns for some quaint alternatives. Some nearby towns have developed their own shopping districts that draw out-

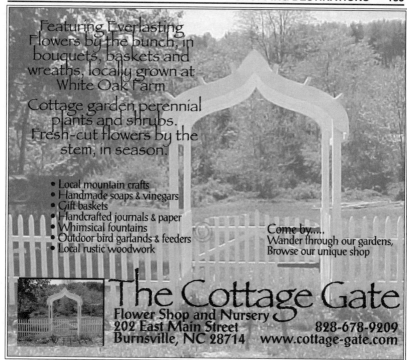
side visitors. One of these is the village of Black Mountain, 15 minutes east of Asheville, which has become known as a haven for antiques (see details in the Black Mountain section in this chapter). And if you look, you're apt to find a favorite shop out in the county that's noted for its special wares, personal service or both.

Another not-to-be-missed shopping experience is the western North Carolina Farmers Market, 570 Brevard Road southeast of Asheville (see our Attractions chapter). Its 36 acres of fresh produce, quality plants and garden supplies, crafts and just about everything you'd expect to find at an old market square.

## Downtown Asheville

The renaissance of Asheville's inner city as a shopping destination is a recent and welcome surprise. What is particularly pleasing to Asheville's visitors and residents alike is that the downtown has become a very pedestrian-friendly place. There are several municipal parking garages downtown, one on Biltmore Avenue south of Pack Square and the other on Rankin Street off Patton Avenue, west of The Square. There's also a city parking garage behind the Asheville-Buncombe Library at 67 Haywood Street near the Asheville Civic Center. If you're an energetic shopper, you'll want to make a day of it, with lunch at one of Asheville's charming downtown restaurants and bistros. The visual appeal of the city's architecture is an added bonus. Unique shops are a-plenty in downtown and we could fill the chapter on Asheville's antique shops alone; so please do take the time to stroll around and discover your own favorites.

You can start with the so-called "Renaissance Corridor" of Biltmore Avenue near Pack Square. What was once a decaying, questionable area lined with X-rated movie houses and blank storefronts only five or 10 years ago, is now a thriving avenue of upscale shops, art galleries and other venues. The sudden, unexpected growth of Biltmore Avenue set the tone for further downtown efforts and was a vital link to the revival of Pack Square as the elegant heart of the city it had been.

At the south end of Haywood Street is the intersection of Battery Park Avenue, anchored by the historic and architecturally interesting Flat Iron Building that was constructed during Asheville's boom period in the 1920s. This building also helps to shape what is known as Wall Street, the narrow, twisting alley behind the Flat Iron Building that has long been the address for interesting and artistically inclined entrepreneurs.

## A Far Away Place
**11 Wall St., Asheville • (828) 252-1891**

This is more than a store: Part gallery, part shop, it's a total experience. The talents of artisans from more than 40 native cultures are represented in this gallery/shop. Exquisite ancient artifacts hang alongside the work of present-day artists. An excellent array of music native to faraway lands is also on offer. Find jewelry, clothing, hats, bags, stationary, and books here, devoted to lands beyond our hemisphere. Owner Mark Fields is a world traveler who takes off for several months at a time to go hunting for the artifacts which will adorn the walls of A Far Away Place.

## Ad-Lib
**40 Biltmore Ave., Asheville**
**• (828) 285-8838**

This is a sister store to the one in Boone featuring women's clothing that emphasizes natural fabrics and colors. A collection of hats hangs on one wall and one section of the shop is devoted to unique leather shoe styles; comfort and quality are of the utmost importance here. Sweaters, jumpers, dresses, shirts, skirts, and pants in silks, linens, cottons, and wools in an array of magnificent natural colors set this clothing store apart from others. Ad Lib also sells artistic jewelry, candle holders, and one of a kind picture frames.

## Asheville Antiques Mall
**43 Rankin Ave., Asheville**
**• (828) 253-3634**

You could spend a day in these shops alone, which are stocked by independent dealers with an amazing assortment of furniture, decorative and household items, antique prints, paintings, jewelry and books. Some friends who just moved from Vienna, Austria, couldn't believe the assortment of wonderful antique furnishings. It was all we could do to drag them out of the place before they had committed their life savings.

## Asheville Wine Market
**60 Biltmore Ave., Asheville**
**• (828) 253-0060,**

You can take home an exquisite sampling of the grape from the Wine Market. Winemaster Eberhard Heide is the proprietor and will assist you in your choice of premium international wines and beers. The array is staggering, so you might be wise in choosing Eberhard's famous Wine Samplers, six international vintage wines specially priced and packaged. You can also buy specialty items for the wine connoisseur at the Asheville Wine Market.

## Bloomin' Art
**60 Haywood St., Asheville**
**• (828) 254-6447**

This is more than just a florist. Besides fragrant bouquets, baskets and unusual items of floral artistry, you'll find plant holders and flower pots.

## Celtic Ways
**14 Wall St., Asheville • (828) 254-0644**

Vivid tartans drape the windows of Celtic Ways, a shop with a true Scot's heart. Tartan kilts, shawls, scarves, tams, gloves and some jewelry — all can be found at this ethnic treasure chest.

## Constance Boutique
**62 Haywood St., Asheville**
**• (828) 252-4002**

This boutique is a most delightful gallery of elegant taste, clothing of unique textures and materials, jewelry, scarves, and hair accessories. The owner (a different Constance than the author) receives her distinctive inventory from New York City, where she does individual buying of her one-of-a-kind outfits and accessories. A small shop, Constance Boutique carries usually only a tiny selection of sizes, so pray you'll find your size in the lovely velvet party dresses, raw silk chemises, and exquisite leather shoes.

## Corner Cupboard Antiques Mall
**49 N. Lexington Ave., Asheville**
**• (828) 258-9815**

Here's another place to spend a few hours mulling about, browsing over people's old stuff. Why do we love doing this so much? Perhaps it's that slightly dusty, musty attic odor which attracts us, or the history that lies behind each item. Who knows? But here, you can indulge antiquing in this large mall. It houses many vendors under one roof; you'll be sure to find hats, jewels, furniture, paintings, books, mirrors and much much more.

## Downtown Books and News
**67 Lexington Ave., Asheville**
**• (828) 253-8654**

Toward the funkier north end of Lexington Avenue, you'll find this excellent book and magazine store. See close-up on Bookstores in this chapter for more details.

## The Earth Guild
**33 Haywood St., Asheville**
**• (828) 255-7818**

Its gorgeous storefront is a good indication of the quality of handcrafts you'll find inside. Weaving, pottery, handmade jewelry and other lovely wares are all visible behind large streetfront windows. You can also find supplies for the making of your own crafts here.

## Enviro Depot
**18 Haywood St., Asheville**
**• (828) 252-9007**

This great place teems with toys, games, puzzles, books, posters and scientific activities for the avid naturalist and the environmentally conscientious. It also offers lotions and potions made of natural ingredients, and our favorite Burt's Beeswax Chapstick and other items.

## King-Thomasson Antiques
**64 Biltmore Ave., Asheville**
**• (828) 252-1565**

This is a wonderful treasure trove of fine European country antiques. In business for almost 20 years, King-Thomasson also sells unique new and antique decorative pieces for the home.

## Kress Emporium
**19-21 Patton Ave., Asheville**
**• (828) 281-2252**

An architectural landmark, the Kress building in downtown Asheville was built in 1918 as a five-and-dime. Constructed of rich ceramic tile, the Kress building is only one of the many brilliant examples of art deco in the city. For years, the building fell into disrepair and its first floor was used for various flea markets. Today, this restored space is a showcase for over 80 artists, artisans, sculptors, hat makers, jewelry designers and many others devoted to artistic endeavors. Artists rent booths, decorate the walls, and add their works, so you are essentially strolling through 80 galleries under one roof.

Everything from Turkish kilims, heirloom stitched children's clothes, handmade dolls and shimmery velvet hats to paintings, handcarved furniture, antique tools, black-and-white art photos, glass sculptures, and much much more is on display in this high-ceilinged bright hall.

A small elegant cafe in the front of Kress Emporium serves coffee, espresso, cappuccino, and light snacks. In warm weather, a few sidewalk tables appear. The downstairs will also feature new space in the coming year.

## Lexington Park Antiques
**65 West Walnut St., Asheville**
**• (828) 253-3070**

Another fine sampling of the Asheville's antique district, Lexington Park Antiques specialize in . . . everything!

## Malaprop's Bookstore/Cafe
**55 Haywood St., Asheville**
**• (828) 254-6734**

Fascinating books, gifts, gourmet coffee and stimulating conversation mingle at Malaprop's new location, just a few doors down from the old one. This bookstore is one of the mainstays of downtown Asheville and a popular stop for visitors and locals. Visiting authors, special events, poetry readings and the spacious coffeehouse make Malaprop's much more than just a place to buy books. (See our close-up on Bookstores at the end of this chapter.)

## Mystic Eye
### 30 N. Lexington Ave., Asheville • (828) 251-1773

Amazing swirls of color — marbleized clothing, tie-dyes, batiks and blended silks — make this working studio store and gallery a treat for the eyes! Owner Laura Petritz covers her hardwood floor space with racks of flowing dresses and cloaks, jackets, pants, and scarves all manufactured by hand in the studios upstairs. Also on display are jewelry, crystals, funky accessories, hand made shoes, and much more. Every so often, the walls of Mystic Eye host a guest-artist's works.

## The Loft
### 53 Broadway, Asheville • (828) 259-9303

This eclectically funky shop filled with a menagerie of distressed furniture, paper lamps, candles, natural soaps, stationary, frames, handmade journals, and other gift and decorative items, is truly a local favorite. Handmade paper, beeswax soaps, picture frames, mirrors, sketch books, plush furniture, flowerpots and so much more grace this home designer's dream of a shop.

## Reunions
### 51 N. Lexington Ave., Asheville • (828) 236-0013

This newly expanded antique store takes up three buildings in downtown Asheville, and is under new ownership. The change has created a true anchor for "antique row" in this central location. Reunions carries old treasures large and small, including entire living room and bedroom sets. You can find hat boxes, chairs, lamps, dishes, cupboards, wooden shutters, trellises, vases, flowerpots, mirrors, and so much more. Not junky, Re-

unions carries many items, but has them neatly and charmingly displayed in home-like settings. Shoppers can even have a seat and wait while their friends look around.

## Tops For Shoes
### 27 N. Lexington Ave., Asheville • (828) 254-6721

This is another of those gutsy establishments that survived the decay of downtown and persistently worked to make the area a viable business district again. For more than 20 years, Tops has been known for quality footwear for the whole family, and the shop has a reputation for its service and large inventory. If you're shopping at Tops, parking is free at the city parking deck on Rankin Avenue.

## T.S. Morrison
### 39 N. Lexington Ave., Asheville • (828) 258-1891, 253-2348

An Asheville institution since 1891, the building is itself an architectural antique. This refurbished general mercantile store maintains a period atmosphere and has Victorian-era memorabilia and specialty gift items displayed in original store's cases. You can also find a variety of stamps and stamping accessories, stationary, crockery, baskets, glass gift items and much, much more. Traditional candy bins allow you to pick out your own sweets, which are sold by the pound. The store also carries some old-fashioned hair tonics, powders and soaps, so if nostalgia is what you are after, you may just find it in these interesting items. Spicy ginger ale, root beer, and cherry drinks are sold by the bottle. T.S. Morrison is more than just a gift shop, it's part of Asheville history, and yes, the old drawers still contain hardware-store items for sale, like nails, fasteners and nuts and bolts.

## Biltmore Village
Moving along to the south end of Asheville, near the entrance of Biltmore Estate, reached

Antiques abound in Asheville, where many shops cater to folks who prefer furnishings from days gone by.

# Buncombe County: Town Mountain Road

Wait until dark, when the lights of Asheville begin to twinkle, and drive along Town Mountain Road up the crest of the mountain. Start at Old Toll Road, which winds along behind Grove Park Inn and through residential areas and runs into Town Mountain Road. As you climb higher, you'll be able to see the lights of Asheville below, the view widening as you ascend the ridge. Soon, the other side of the ridge will open up so that the lights of Marion appear in the distance.

by taking Biltmore Avenue or McDowell Street south, you will find Biltmore Village. Geographically in Asheville, this junction of cobblestone streets and old buildings is an "incorporated town" (see our Overviews chapter). Therefore, we will discuss the Village separately.

When George Vanderbilt constructed his mansion in 1895, it was obvious that such a grand place would need a town at its gate to supply it. Vanderbilt didn't have to start from scratch; he merely purchased the existing village of Best, a good distance from the mansion on the outskirts of Asheville. Construction of suitable lodging for his craftsmen gave the new village a distinctively English-hamlet look that has been retained. The original cottages, which have the pebble-dash exterior used in some Asheville homes of the period, today form a cluster of specialty shops, restaurants and galleries. The creative spirit, it seems, has survived the century. Mr. Vanderbilt would be pleased.

Biltmore Village's cobbled sidewalks along such streets as Angle, Swan and All Souls will lead you past a delightful assortment of shops.

## The Angel Shoppe
**3 Brooks St., Asheville**
**• (828) 274-6940**

A host of heavenly gifts and collectibles awaits nearby at the Angel Shoppe. It features jewelry, stationery, lamps, bath and beauty items, garden products, art and more, all somehow connected to the store's angel theme.

## Bellagio
**5 Biltmore Plaza, Asheville**
**• (828) 277-8100**

This is a most-unusual shop devoted to wearable art. Richly colored, sensually textured fabrics are transformed into exquisite garments and then complemented by handcrafted jewelry.

## The Biltmore Magic & Costume Company
**1 Swan St., Asheville • (828) 274-9550**

If you've ever had a desire to make something or someone go "Poof!," check this out. Here, you can aspire to prestidigitation and buy the tricks of the trade, so to speak, while professionals demonstrate.

## Early Music Shop
**3 Biltmore Plaza, Asheville**
**• (828) 274-2890**

Here, you can find not only good music but also its source. Along with tapes, instructional books, videos and CDs, the Early Music Shop offers unusual musical instruments, such as hammered dulcimers, Celtic harps, psalteries, recorders and wooden drums for sale.

## Fireside Antiques and Interiors
**30 All Souls Crescent, Asheville**
**• (828) 274-5977**

Biltmore Village has several antique shops as well, though smaller and more intimate than Asheville's downtown stores. At Fireside, you'll find lots of brass and crystal, as well as pieces from England.

## Interiors Marketplace
**2 Hendersonville Rd., Asheville**
• **(828) 253-2300**

This market is one block north of Biltmore Village, near the former Asheville Train Depot. Asheville is one of only a handful of cities in the nation where this shopping concept, much like an Old World bazaar, has been brought to such successful fruition.

Interiors Marketplace, with its upscale pizzazz, has numerous vendor vignettes — merchandise artfully arranged in harmony as you might find it in your own home. Items generally are one-of-a-kind imported pieces, unusual handcrafted work, fine art and skillfully chosen domestic and imported antiques.

## Korth & Company
**30 Bryson St., Asheville**
• **(828) 252-0906**

Korth & Co. handles replicas of mahogany furniture of the 18th and 19th century — English, French and American. These fine reproductions are the store's mainstay.

## New Morning Gallery
**7 Boston Way, Asheville**
• **(828) 274-2831**

This gallery and shop occupies two stories and is surrounded by award-winning gardens. This is one of the South's premier arts and crafts shops, displaying the work of some of America's finest artists and craftspeople.

## Olde World Christmas Shop
**5 Boston Way, Asheville**
• **(828) 274-4819**

Unique gifts and yuletide items by Dee Cash Santas, Vaillancourt (folk art), Snow Village, Snowbabies, Anri (woodcarvings), Lilliput Lane and Hummel are among the eye-catching displays. The shop also sells homemade cream-and-butter fudge.

## Once Upon a Time
**7 All Souls Crescent, Asheville**
• **(828) 274-8788**

This is a splendid bookshop that will please your child with its thousands of books, toys, children's music, story tapes, artwork and more. See our Bookstore close-up at the end of this chapter for more information.

## Vitrum Gallerie
**10 Lodge St. Asheville**
• **(828) 274-9900**

This is North Carolina's only gallery dedicated to the fine art of studio glass. A colorful and creative selection of glass art jewelry, vases, goblets, paperweights and sculpture sparkle in this sunny, 2,000-square-foot gallery.

## Black Mountain

Only 15 minutes or so east of Asheville is Black Mountain, a picturesque village that is an antiques lover's delight. In the historic district anchored by Cherry Street, near the town's old train depot, is a cluster of shops that have fine antiques and collectibles. Black Mountain is an extremely walkable shopping town where everything from handcrafts, artwork, collectibles and antiques are available within a few tiny blocks. State Street is Black Mountain's main artery.

### Black Mountain Antique Mall
**100 Sutton Ave., Black Mountain**
• **(828)669-6218**

The BMAM has Southern primitives, folk art, vintage linens and displays an antique quilt collection. It is one of the older, more established antique malls here, and it offers many cases of small items for browsing as well.

### Black Mountain Drug Company
**101 W. State St., Black Mountain**
• **(828) 669-2511**

Don't leave Black Mountain without sticking your head in the door of the drugstore on the corner. This quaint, full-service pharmacy would look right at home in Mayberry. You can get your film here, as well as chapstick, shampoo, and other goods and sundries.

### The Cherry Street Antique Mall
**139 Cherry St., Black Mountain**
• **(828) 669-7942**

This antique mall sells items from many dealers. It's a great place to spend time browsing. Two floors house the wares of 18 dealers, with items as small as jewelry trinkets to large pieces of furniture. The mall also sells antique craft pottery.

### Howard's Antiques
**121 Cherry St., Black Mountain**
• **(828) 669-6494**

This shop sells those hot collectible antique toys and sturdy oak furniture. Especially fun are the inventive toys (compare these unique pieces with modern action figures and the other plastic stuff in malls today!).

### Song of the Wood Ltd.
**203 W. State St., Black Mountain**
• **(828) 669-7675**

Follow your heartstrings to the melodies of Song of the Wood Ltd. The talented musicians here play lively tunes on handcrafted hammered and mountain dulcimers and other traditional musical instruments. Selling instruments and tapes and CDs of their own music is a side business.

### Town Hardware and General Store
**103 W. State St., Black Mountain**
• **(828) 669-7723**

You can indulge your taste in nostalgia at this old-time hardware and general store. It sells old-fashioned housewares, bird feeders, gifts and reminders of yesteryear.

# Henderson County

## Flat Rock

### Secret Garden
**2720 Greenville Hwy., Flat Rock**
• **(828) 697-1331**

It's worth the short drive down the Greenville Highway (U.S. 25 S.) in order to pay a visit to this special shop — particularly if you or a loved one loves gardening and garden themes. In addition to flowers and plants, the shop is filled with small, decora-

---

**INSIDERS' TIP**

Bookstores may well be the first place you should look for information on a town. Whether you are moving to the area, vacationing, or looking for something interesting to do, check out the bulletin boards at the local bookstore. Places to rent, job opportunities, writer's conferences, literary evenings, concerts, items for sale — you will undoubtedly feel like an Insider once you are clued into this information.

tive garden sculptures and plaques, small fountains, garden flags, garden books, small framed flower prints, T-shirts, hats and tote bag with garden themes and flowery doormats just to name a few items found here.

For children there are stuffed critters like raccoons, turtles and insects found in the garden. Then there's a whole selection of floral scents, soaps and candles. Make sure, too, that you don't miss the downstairs shop. Besides a flower-bedecked patio, there's a "kitchen/dining" area with floral- and fruit-painted china, unique wine racks, canisters and so on. Another room holds tapestries, plant stands and fabulous rayon-chenille throws.

The next driveway south of the shop takes you to a cutting garden where you can select and cut fresh flowers and pay by the stem.

## Hendersonville

Over two decades ago, when main streets in most small towns were dying due to competition from big malls and discount stores, Hendersonville, which didn't even have a mall at the time, was taking steps to keep its downtown vital. The facades of historic buildings were exposed and refurbished, and Hendersonville's wide Main Street became a serpentine drive lined with trees and blooming plants. Park benches, too, became a permanent part of the Main Street scene. They are fine spots for resting tired feet, chatting with a friend or eating take-out in the sun-

shine while you watch the world go by. Few weeks pass without a downtown festival, art show or other event taking place here.

If there's any problem with downtown it's that the very popularity of the area sometimes makes finding a parking spot difficult. But if you don't mind walking a block or two, that problem can usually be solved by going to one of the large metered parking lots on Church or King streets, which run parallel to Main Street one block away in either direction. There are also parking areas on Fifth and Sixth avenues between Main and King. Though there are no meters on Main Street or its side streets, watch your 15-minute or two-hour limit if you want to avoid a ticket, because, again, due to the downtown's popularity, the limit is strictly enforced. That's a pity, in a way, because a couple of hours is never enough time to browse through all the places you'll want to visit, much less enjoy shop and enjoy lunch in one of the area's good restaurants.

Here's just a sampling of some of the places you might find interesting in Hendersonville.

### A Day in the Country
**130 Sugarloaf Rd., Hendersonville**
**• (828) 692-7914**

This store, just off Interstate 26 at the Hendersonville exit, has one of the area's largest selection of unique and unusual gifts, including Afghans, collectibles, gourmet foods, tapestries, antique and French country furniture, silk floral arrangements and more.

## Assembly Required
**340 N. Main St., Hendersonville**
**• (828) 692-9677, (800) 486-2592**

This full-service brew shop has all the equipment, books, kits and ingredients that you need for making your own beer, wine, liquors, cheese, vinegars and sodas. If you also need advice, owners Jack and Marilyn Bradt can provide plenty of that, too.

## Barbara's Antiques
**506 N. Main St., Hendersonville**
**• (828) 697-1550, (877) 793-7476**

Antiques and fine china exquisitely displayed is a hallmark of this lovely shop. China, in fact, is owner Barbara McCoy's specialty. Here you'll find beautiful examples of Wedgwood, Barvarian, Prussian, English and other fine china fit for the most elegant dining room.

## Banana Moon
**338 N. Main St., Hendersonville**
**• (828) 697-1941**

This is by far our favorite clothing store on Main Street, and one of our favorite sections here is the selection of outfits made of flax. In addition to all the dresses, sweaters, hats and handbags, there's everything wonderful for the bath and oodles of charming jewelry. Be prepared to buy.

## Beehive Resale Shop
**451 N. Main St., Hendersonville**
**• (828) 692-8882**

For nearly two decades the popular Beehive Resale shop has provided top-quality women's clothing at affordable prices. It carries some terrific brand-name women fashions and accessories at a fraction of the regular retail price, and the inventory changes daily.

## Blue Ridge Mall
**1800 Four Seasons Blvd.,**
**Hendersonville • (828) 697-1745**

Anchored by Belk, JCPenney and Kmart, this mall is full of boutiques and specialty shops and is the site of a number of special events, such as craft shows put on by the Henderson County Crafters Association.

## The Book Store
**238 N. Main St., Hendersonville**
**• (828) 696-9949**

Book lovers can browse for hours among the new and used books here. See our Bookstore close-up in this chapter.

## Brightwater Art Glass
**342 N. Main St., Hendersonville**
**• (828) 697-6842**

You're surrounded by all the colors of the rainbows when you enter this shop. Pick up a brilliant suncatcher for a few dollars or spring for a treasure-piece of stained-glass art, or have a, lamp, stained-glass door or window custom-made. Brightwater does restorations, sandblasting and beveling. It also carries books, stained glass and supplies.

## Carolina Mountain Artists
**444 N. Main St., Hendersonville**
**• (828) 696-0707**

One of the first things you notice about this artist co-op is the variety and high quality of the skills displayed here. The guild is made up 32 artists, who talents range from painting on canvas, wood, clay furniture, gourds, floor cloths and other fabrics to woodworking (including fine doll furniture), needlework, lovely quilts, wearable art, stained glass, pottery, jewelry, watercolors, baskets, bird and butterfly houses, silk flower arrangements and greenery. We were particularly taken with both the quality and the affordability of the fabric-decorated plates. In fact, the prices on much of this original art are very reasonable.

## The Consignment Gallery
**411 N. Main St., Hendersonville**
**• (828) 697-7712**
## Past-'N-Present
**351 N. Main St., Hendersonville**
**• (828) 697-1797**

By visiting these two North Main Street shops, owned by Tippy and Arthur D'Amato, you could furnish and decorate an entire home with quality antiques and still be able to adorn yourself or a loved one with some incredible estate jewelry.

Past-'N-Present is the place to go for a single piece or for whole sets of furniture. While the shop specializes in mahogany and oak, you also can find Victorian couches, marble-top chests, player pianos, antique telephones, mirrors, clocks, and lamps. You can also buy excellent wall decorations. In addition to paintings, there are prints, including those by Salvador Dali and second-edition Audubon prints.

The Antique Consignment Gallery has some furniture pieces but concentrates more on china, glass and collectibles. Here you'll find modern and antique jewelry, china by top names, sterling-silver plates, figurines by Lladro, Hummel and Armani and much more. And Arthur, who writes an column on antiques for a local paper, will be happy to give you some tips on distinguishing the real antique from the fake.

### The Curb Market
**221 N. Church St., Hendersonville**
**• (828) 692-8012**

The Curb Market started out on Main Street in 1924 with eight merchants selling their wares beneath umbrellas. It has mushroomed to 137 selling spaces, many staffed by third- and fourth-generation sellers. Merchants here are required to be Henderson County residents and to make or grow all items they sell. Among these are fresh vegetables, fruits, flowers, dairy products, baked goods, jams, jellies, pickles, relishes and handmade gifts of all kinds, including afghans, aprons, booties, dolls, folk toys, pillows, quilts, rag rugs, table linens, walking sticks, woodwork items and wreaths.

### Dancing Bear Toys, Ltd.
**418 N. Main St., Hendersonville**
**• (828) 693-4500**

In addition to almost every toy currently popular with children today, Dancing Bear carries a good selection of delightful puppets, costumes, puzzles and educational toys and books.

### Days Gone By
### Gifts and Collectibles
**303 N. Main St., Hendersonville**
**• (828) 693-9056**

Until a few years ago, this was downtown's oldest business, Justus Pharmacy, established in 1882. Retaining all its old-time flavor, it's now a place where you can find drugstore/soda-fountain collectibles. Afterwards, sit down for an old-time ice-cream soda or sundae at the Old-Fashioned Soda Parlor.

# Historic Hendersonville & Flat Rock Area

## 508 Main Street
508 Main St., Hendersonville
• (828) 696-4037

The diverse items you'll find inside this shop are as elegant as its green and gold exterior. Its owner, Bunny Collina, goes out of her way to find gracious gifts at prices that range from $2.99 to $199. These include, among many other things, seasonal florals and silk flowers, gold and sterling silver jewelry, decorative garden items, home-decor flags, pen-and-ink drawings, stationery, a locally made card line and locally made chocolates. She also carries the Aromatique home-fragrance line and Maralyce Ferree's line of Berber and fleece coats and drizzle-wear.

Bunny also creates gifts baskets of local foods and fragrance that are delivered anywhere in Henderson County and shipped nationwide.

## Four Seasons' Crafters
516 N. Main St., Hendersonville
• (828) 698-0016

A crafters cooperative, Four Seasons' Crafters is a year-round outlet for quality handmade arts and crafts. The artists here are as varied as the four seasons for which our area is famous. You'll find jewelry, fabric crafts, porcelain, ceramics, a kids corner, pierced lampshades, wreaths, tole-painted furniture, dolls and much more.

## The Goldsmith by Rudi, Ltd.
324 N. Main St., Hendersonville
• (828) 693-1030

Rudi Haug has been doing business in Hendersonville since 1975 and is now helped by both his son and daughter. This large, full-service jewelry store is so popular for new purchases, custom designs and jewelry repairs that there are five full-time jewelers working to fill the orders. The store does mounting, engraving and restyling.

At Rudi's, in addition of the finest is all kinds of jewelry, you can buy clocks, fine Swiss watches, a great line of pen sets and silver picture frames. Threre's also a fabulous array of gold and silver charms, including a popular Hendersonville charm that comes in three sizes in gold or silver.

## Honeysuckle Hollow
512 N. Main St., Hendersonville
• (828) 697-2197

Romance and nostalgia fill the air at Honeysuckle Hollow. Vintage clothing, linens, lace, scarves, fragrances, glassware, candles, antiques and jewelry turn this shop into an exciting treasure hunt. It's the place to go, too, for wonderful cards and relaxing contemporary, classical and traditional tapes and CDs.

## House of Towels
1971 Asheville Hwy. (U.S. Hwy. 25 N), Hendersonville • (828) 692-9489

People come from great distances to shop here. House of Towels has western North Carolina's most extensive selection of sheets, bedspreads, towels and tablecloths, brands like Fieldcrest, Cannon, Martex, Wamsutta, Croscill and Spring, all at discount prices.

## Jane Asher's Fourth and Main Antique Mall
344 Main St., Hendersonville
• (828) 693-0018

The antique and collectible lover will find 5,000 square feet of friendly, one-floor shopping here put together by 25 dealers. Though this is certainly the place to come if you like European clocks (you can get your clock repaired here, too), this store also carries a tempting array of fine china, glassware, art glass, dolls, Victorian quilts, toys, beaded Victorian bags, religious artifacts, costume and fine estate jewelry, old-fashioned sewing tools and lots and lots of buttons. Prices on the whole are moderate, but you can find the rare and expensive piece here, too.

## Little Elsie's
421 N. Main St., Hendersonville
• ( 828) 697-0664

Owner Sara Duvall has filled this store with surely every stuffed animal available today. Just to walk inside makes a shopper smile.

## Mast General Store
527 N. Main St., Hendersonville
• (828) 696-1883

True to its atmosphere, this beautifully restored 1905 emporium is chock full of old-time mercantile items, but you can also find quality outdoor gear, footwear and traditional clothing for all four of our seasons.

## Mehri & Company
**501 N. Main St., Hendersonville**
• **(828) 693-0887**

Opulence describes this unique store. Mehri & Company carries estate and antique jewelry, unique gifts, custom silk arrangements and antique furniture, tapestries and collectibles. You'll also fine wonderful table linens, plushly rich pillows and unique picture frames. If it's not of high quality, you won't find it here.

## Mountain Lore Books
**555 N. Main St., Hendersonville**
• **(828) 693-9949**

While specializing in regional, gardening, nature and children's book, Mountain Lore has all the bestsellers and a wealth of new paperbacks. See our Bookstore close-up in this chapter.

## The Paintin' Shed
**442 N. Main St., Hendersonville**
• **(828) 698-8088**

This is the place to come for arts and craft supplies and advice. You can also take any number of classes here, including decorative tole painting, working in sculpty clay, lampshade cutting and piercing, pen-and-ink drawing and much more. All the items sold here are handcrafted locally.

## Purple Sage
**416 N. Main St., Hendersonville**
• **(828) 693-9555**

This is the place to go if you're a gourmet cook, know one or would like to become one. You'll find pots, pans, knives, kitchen gadgets, coffee, cookbooks, gifts and imported and domestic wines. There's a wine cellar

downstairs, and Purple Sage also holds periodic wine tastings and cooking classes.

## Somewhere In Time
**514 N. Main St., Hendersonville**
• **(828) 693-5900**

You lose track of time in this shop's vast array of Victorian and country collectibles and antiques. It's the perfect place to browse and browse and, of course, buy. Be sure to check out the items on the "half-price table."

## Sweet Memories
**430 N. Main St., Hendersonville**
• **(828) 692-8401**

The focus here is on regional fine crafts, including a distinctive selection of Southeastern art glass, functional and decorative pottery, jewelry, wood, fiber, metalwork, china painting and handcrafted gifts.

## Touchstone Gallery
**318 N. Main St., Hendersonville**
• **(828) 692-2191**

We never go to Hendersonville without dropping in to see what beautiful art and whimsical creations are displayed at this gallery that specializes in contemporary American art and exceptional craft items. We seldom leave without being creatively inspired ourselves.

## Village Green Antique Mall
**424 N. Main St., Hendersonville**
• **(828) 692-9057**

It will take you a while to see all the quality antiques and collectibles here. The mall contains 12,000 square feet full of inventory brought in by 35 dealers from six states. Shipping and delivery service is available.

## Wickwire Gallery
**330 N. Main St., Hendersonville**
• **(828) 692-6222**

This fine art/folk gallery has just moved to

## INSIDERS' TIP

So, you've been shopping all day, your feet are sore, and you're near collapse . . . Why not revive yourself with an espresso or some soothing tea? Some area bookstores have cafes that serve snacks. Flip through a magazine or novel and let yourself be momentarily transported to another place and time.

new quarters from its old address on Main Street. It displays both established and emerging artists. See the Visual Arts/Henderson County section of our Arts and Culture chapter.

### The World of Clothing
**135 Sugarloaf Rd., Hendersonville**
**• (828) 693-4131**

This mammoth store has 102,000 square feet full of discount clothing from makers such as Cricket, J.G. Hook, Jantzen and 62 East, plus an Oriental rug department with 20,000 rugs, oil paintings, framed prints, mirrors and pillows.

# Transylvania County

## Brevard

A few years ago, the heart of Brevard was struggling to find itself. Many people predicted doom for downtown commerce after Kmart and Wal-Mart opened in separate shopping centers at about the same time and took Belk and other downtown businesses with them. Quite the opposite has happened. A wonderful new spirit has revitalized the area in the past three years, and Brevard's central district once again has become the heart of much of Transylvania County's social life.

Shopping here is certainly more attractive than ever. Brevard is perched on top of a high hill and is graced by an old, red-brick courthouse where Main and Broad streets meet. Lovely views of the mountains of Pisgah National Forest rise in the west. Here you have a choice of festivals, art shows and entertainment all year long. On summer weekends, there's nearly always music on the courthouse lawn, including programs by musicians from the Brevard Music Center. And an array of shops and restaurants, both new and old, have turned this into a delightful place to roam and enjoy.

Businesses stretch up and down Main and Broad and spill over onto all the side streets. Merchants and restaurateurs have even moved into some of Brevard's interesting old houses, transforming them into enticing shops and eateries. We've included a sampling of stores you can find in downtown Brevard. It's best to simply follow your nose in and out of all the pretty and fun shops. Stop in, too, at the Transylvania County Arts Co-op, 7 E. Main Street, across from the courthouse, to view original works by local artists. Down the street, the Chamber of Commerce, (828) 883-3700, 35 W. Main Street, is loaded with visitor information, and it has an art gallery too.

Anytime you get tired or hungry, there are any number of convenient places where you can drop in, sit down and get a bite to eat. A few of these, but by no means all of them, are listed in our Restaurants chapter. There are also some park benches scattered along Main Street where you can sit and take in the passing scene.

### Brevard Antique Mall
**57 E. Main St., Brevard • (828) 885-2744**

Brevard's largest antique shop has 20,000 square feet of quality antiques and collectibles featuring 60 booths on three floors. There are always really some beautiful pieces here with enough room to display them properly.

### Celestial Mountain Music and Folk Art
**16 W. Main St., Brevard • (828) 884-3575**

You're likely to find people making music when you walk into this store, and you're sure to encounter a fascinating array of musical instruments such as handcrafted mountain dulcimers, Celtic harps, guitars, dobros, mandolins, autoharps and crystal flutes — and you can schedule lessons to learn how to play them. The shop also records of traditional music and makes instrument repairs.

### D.D. Bullwinkle's
**38 S. Broad St., Brevard**
**• (828) 862-4700**

This unique shop, which specializes in Southern products, is practically impossible to describe — you'll have to see it for yourself. The shop sells dozens of kinds of penny candy, gourmet coffee, gifts, books, beautiful handmade furniture, jams, jellies, relishes, T-shirts (some with local logos) and — our favorite — very funny horse swings made from old tires.

Adjoining the shop is Rocky Soda Shop, where you can enjoy an old-fashioned milkshake, meal or snack (see our Restaurant chapter for more information on Rocky's).

Hudson River. You never know what you might find here.

## Madrigal's Interiors & Imports
**11 E. Main St., Brevard • (828) 833-3855**

A wonderfully eclectic shop of imported Mexican furniture and wonderfully unique antique pieces. Recently, they offered a huge, wood-carved mantelpiece that had come from a European castle via a mansion on the

## The Frame-Up
**4 W. Main St., Brevard • (828) 883-2385**

This is the place to go for fantastic archival framing. The store also carries one-of-a-kind jewelry, wood turnings, handmade furniture and beautiful (framed, of course) prints, as well as blown glass, porcelain and pottery.

Wall Street in Asheville was revitalized and restored some 15 years ago.
It's now home to many quaint boutiques and restaurants.

Lots of lovely little boutiques are just waiting to be discovered.

## Jeanie's Boutique
112 S. Broad St., Brevard
• (828) 884-9573

For super-feminine fashions at prices so low you won't believe the tags, go to Jeanie's. The shop sells stunning Indian clothing at a cost that's often less than you'd pay for discount dress stores. Stay and while and chat with the shop's interesting owner.

## Main Street Ltd.
224 E. Main St., Brevard
• (828) 884-4974

Housed in a grand, two-story, white house, this shop is filled with exquisite surprises including gift baskets, home accessories and camp care-packages for the many children who attend summer camps in the area. The store's unique gift-wrapping turns any purchase into a celebration.

## Mountain Rose Specialties
57 W. Main St., Brevard
• (828) 884-8579

Anyone who loves dolls will love Mountain Rose's large collection of little beauties of every size and type that little or big hearts could desire. It also stocks a wide selection of tea sets and plates.

## The Open Door Antique Mall
15 W. Main St., Brevard • (828) 883-4323

Fifteen or so carefully chosen dealers bring everything from the finest antique furniture to vintage comic books, all beautifully displayed. Here's the place to look for a rare book. If you've been looking for a special, specific something, put your desire on file with owners Greg and Sandy Wagner; they'll try to locate it for you. The mall specializes in antique fishing gear.

## O. P. Taylor's
2 S. Broad St., Brevard • (828) 883-2309

This store is a world unto itself. It carries, among other things, some beautiful, high-quality casual clothes. But the main attractions are the toys that fill its second floor, flow down the stairs and sometimes right out on the sidewalk. It's a place that delights children and adults alike.

## The Pink Flamingo
35 E. Main St., Brevard • (828) 883-4515

If you have a special party to attend or are feeling flamboyant, stop by The Pink Flamingo. You'll find super stylish — sometimes a little outlandish — ladies fashions at surprisingly low prices. The store also stocks some very pleasing jewelry and accessories too.

We always check "the backroom," for items on sale, and almost every week there will be a special half-price sale on, for example, "any dress with yellow in it," or "any article with sequins." You won't believe the buys!

### The Proper Pot
**44 E. Main St., Brevard • (828) 877-5000**

You'll find just the thing for the cook in your life. In addition to kitchenware, The Proper Post sells linens, gift baskets and gourmet teas and coffees.

### The White Squirrel Shoppe
**2 W. Main St., Brevard • (828) 877-3530**

This wonderful shop's jam-packed with collectibles, odds and ends of small, wonderful pieces of furniture, lamps, statues and gifts and crafts. There are also a number of its namesake white squirrels in all sizes and shapes. These make great souvenirs of the area, since there really are white squirrels in Brevard (see the White Squirrel Close-up in our Bed and Breakfasts and Country Inns chapter).

# Southern Mountains

## Haywood County

### Waynesville

Where downtown Brevard is built on a hill, Haywood's county seat sits on a high plateau. The mountains rise close all around so that you have a view of them no matter which way you face. And like Hendersonville, Waynesville, with its turn-of-the-century buildings, brick sidewalks, park benches and plants, has made its charming downtown one of the most popular shopping spots in the county. There's an interesting mix of more than 50 stores here: boutiques, galleries, specialty shops, family and service stores and restaurants. Here, too, is the place to find festivals and fun events, such as Razzle-Dazzle (a children's street festival) and the International Festival, which is a day of music, dance,

food and crafts held in association with Folkmoot, the International Dance Festival (see our Festivals and Annual Events chapter).

Twice a month in July and August, on Friday evenings, the street is blocked off in front of the courthouse for dances with live bluegrass bands, clogging demonstrations and dancing instruction, all free of charge. On Wednesday and Saturday in late summer and fall, when the harvest comes in, a farmer's market is set up downtown.

Even without these events, you can spend several hours or perhaps a full day browsing and eating — and probably still miss an interesting little place or two tucked in a side street or upstairs over another shop.

We've never had a problem finding a parking spot on Main Street, but if you do, there's free parking on Montgomery and Wall streets, both of which run parallel to Main Street one block in either direction. From Wall Street, a couple of walkways lead right down to Main. While you're here, take time to visit The Shelton House, (828) 452-1551, just off Main Street, home to the Museum of North Carolina Handicrafts (see our Mountain Crafts chapter).

If you don't shop yourself out in Waynesville, you should travel another 10 or 15 minutes to Maggie Valley. Here, along a 3-mile stretch of U.S. 19, you'll find a bonanza of craft and souvenir stores not included in this section among this little resort town's many lodgings, restaurants and other attractions (see our Attractions, Other Accommodations and Nightlife chapters).

### Blue Owl Studio and Gallery, Inc.
**11 N. Main St., Waynesville**
**• (828) 456-5050**

Hand-painted antique graphics of North Carolina's mountains are the mainstay of this gallery, but you'll find other interesting items here, too. See the Visual Arts Section, Haywood County in our Arts and Culture chapter.

### Candy Barrel
**55 N. Main St., Waynesville**
**• (828) 452-0075**

Its name explains it all. Barrels and bas-

# Bookstores

Close-up

When you're on the road, bookstores are almost as important as gas stations. They offer you a connection to the community through books on local legends, maps of trails and tours and cards of nearby places of beauty. Many include works by local authors who wax poetic about the mountains draw inspiration from the region. The following is a list of some of the stores available.

## Northern Mountains

### Blowing Rock

**Pleasant Papers**
**S. Main St., The Village Shoppes • (828) 295-7236**
More than a bookstore, this fine shop also includes quality papers, greeting cards and specialized gifts.

### Boone

**Blue Planet Map Company**
**487 W. King St. • (828) 264-5400**
Wanderlust to your heart's content with the wide range of local and worldwide travel books and a broad selection of atlases: road, travel, DeLorme topo, United States, world and historical. They even stock CD-ROM map software.

Photo: Constance E. Richards

You can spend hours in many of the area's bookstores.

## Waldenbooks
**1180 Blowing Rock Rd., Boone Mall • (828) 264-4084**

Waldenbooks is one of the country's leading chain bookstores featuring regional and outdoor books.

## Dancing Moon Earthway Bookstore
**703 W. King St. • (828) 264-7242**

Dancing Moon specializes in books and magazines of the healing and spiritual arts. This small shop also carries unique travel books, cards and posters, musical cassettes, candles, and even incense and oils. In other words, everything you might want to embellish your reading environment.

## Sparta

### Hemingway Book & Gift
**800 S. Main St. • (828) 372-6464**

Parents can browse through a good selection of books and maps while kids enjoy a large section devoted just to their interests at this shop that also carries local crafts, including the work of three area potters.

## Spruce Pine

### Spruce Pine Blue Moon Bookstore
**309 Oak Ave. • (828) 766-5000**

Blue Moon is the only general bookstore in this three-county (Mitchell, Avery and Yancey) area. It's a brand new and welcome feature in this town. The uncluttered space offers a sofa and table for browsing as well as a small cafe in the corner for sipping coffee and trying a muffin or giant cookie.

Located in the old Day's Drugstore, the red and white tiled floor and high tin ceiling make this more than a bookstore, but a gathering place as well. Blue Moon features a large children's book section, regional book selections and an array of handpainted notecards. Used books are in the back, and a selection of major U.S. papers help keep you up with national news.

A children story hour gathers here on the first Saturday of each month, and occasional live music keeps the shop open on certain evenings. Call for details.

# Central Mountains

## Asheville

### Accent on Books
**854 Merrimon Ave. • (828) 252-6255**

This store has good selection of quality magazines, cards and children's books in addition to a good selection of books on the great outdoors and the culture of the region.

### Blue Ridge Parkway Bookstore
**Mi. 382, Folk Art Center • (828) 298-0495**

Small but well-stocked, this bookstore offers the best selection in nature books, trail maps, books on regional culture and beautiful wildlife cards. (There are 11 other bookstores like it along the Parkway.)

— continued on next page

## Book Rack
### 485 Hendersonville Rd. • (828) 274-5050

Book Rack has a great selection of half-price used paperbacks that are sold and traded in a fresh and friendly environment.

## Books-A-Million
### 80 S. Tunnel Rd. • (828) 299-4165

This store bills itself as "a novel bookstore of epic proportions," and they aren't kidding. The megastore includes an excellent selection of regional and travel books as well as out-of-town newspapers. There's also a cafe and an area for frequent book signings by authors.

## Bookstore on Wall Street
### 18 Wall St. • (828) 252-2665

In addition to a fine selection of books of all kinds, this bookstore offers a generous section of books, kits and games. A good share of the shop's inventory is geared toward children — little wonder, since the shop's owner is also the author of picture books for children (if you have a child, ask about story times). This light and airy book shop does wonders for the imagination on a rainy afternoon, or any other day for that matter, and the cats in the window and asleep on the bookshelves are real.

## B. Dalton Bookseller
### 2 South Tunnel Rd., Asheville Mall • (828) 298-7711
### 800 Brevard Rd., Biltmore Square Mall • (828) 667-1293

B. Dalton is well-known throughout the country for its broad selection of books. This chain store includes many books of regional interest.

## Downtown Books and News
### 67 Lexington Ave., Asheville • (828) 253-8654

You can usually buy hard-to-find newspapers, periodicals and obscure book titles at this excellent and interesting combination news stand/used-book store. Foreign magazines, obscure fashion magazines, computer, food, art, photography, and alternative living are only some of the many subject of magazines you will find here.

## Little Professor Book Center
### 1378 Hendersonville Rd. • (828) 274-0990

The word "little" in the name is a bit misleading for Little Professor Book Center. There is a well-chosen selection of books, including magazines, maps and travel books. Owners Neil and Judy Meyer will help you find what you are looking for personally, and they send a newsletter to patrons in their database several times a year.

## Malaprop's Bookstore/Cafe
### 55 Haywood St. • (828) 254-6734

Malaprop's is simply an Asheville institution. We remember sipping our hazelnut coffee in the cafe, hunched over our high school homework dreaming of literary travels while ethereal music provided the background sounds for this haven of learned tranquility in the then-decayed Asheville downtown.

Owner Emoke Bracz, a writer, poet, and translator of Hungarian poetry and literature, fine-turned the art of the book trade in the 16-year life span of this once-small bookstore and cafe. Now two doors down from its original cramped-but-cozy space, Malaprops boasts shelves of fascinating fiction, alternative nonfiction, prose and poetry, as well as a large section with works of local authors and books on the region. Coffee table gift books, stationary, cards, journals, and artistic calendars make this one-stop shopping for all your literary gift needs.

And then there's the cafe! Author signings, prose readings, poetry readings, singer-songwriter evenings gather hoards of literati of all types into the spacious adjoining cafe. Local art and photographs adorn the walls, and cafe tables spill out onto the broad sidewalk in front of Malaprops, where an amalgam of adopted Ashevillians and visitors sip coffee and herb teas, and snack on fresh bagel sandwich combinations, muffins, cookies, and cakes. Malaprops will order any book for you they don't already have and sends out a seasonal newsletter filled with poetry, artful sketches, and literary news.

## Once Upon A Time
**7 All Soul's Crescent • (828) 274-8788**

This is more than a bookstore. It offers the area's largest selection of children's fiction and nonfiction, books, games, and tapes. It recently added children's clothing too.

## Waldenbooks
**800 Brevard Rd., Biltmore Square Mall • (828) 665-1066**

This respected chain bookstores offers a wide choice of books of interest to the traveler and the resident.

# Brevard

## The Book Nook
**15 S. Broad St. • (828) 883-9745**

The Book Nook has new and used books, that, as its proprietor proclaims, "contain only natural ingredients: sex, murder, adultery, joy, sorrow, passion and mayhem." If you don't see what you're looking for, they'll be happy to conduct book searches for you.

## The Cradle of Forestry in America Interpretive Association
**100 S. Broad St. • (828) 884-5713**

This nice store is stocked with nature-related books, gifts, prints, forest maps, literature and National Forest information. This nonprofit organization puts the money it makes right back into our area's magnificent national forests. It oversees another bookstore in the Cradle of Forestry itself in Pisgah Forest.

## Highland Books
**409 N. Broad St. • (828) 884-2424**

Highland carries the latest in new paperbacks and hardbacks in both fiction and nonfiction and a wonderful, large selection of greeting cards and gifts. The staff welcomes browsers. It has extensive gardening and children sections and travel and regional books, including nature books, field guides and maps.

There's a comfortable reading area, where you can peruse a book or preview some of the videos of local interest. Highland also has a wonderful selection of greeting cards and gifts.

# Hendersonville

## The Book Store
**238 N. Main St., Hendersonville • (828) 696-9949**

If you love books and bargains, don't drop in this store unless you have time to spare.

— continued on next page

Shelves crammed with used books of all kinds can keep you enthralled and more titles come in every day. In addition to buying, selling and trading, they will also do book searches.

## Mountain Lore Books
**555 N. Main St. • (828) 693-5096**

Formerly Carolyn's Book Shoppe, Mountain Lore has books for all ages and interests. In addition to popular bestsellers and paperbacks, this independent bookseller specializes in regional, gardening, nature and children's books.

## Waldenbooks
**1800 Four Seasons Blvd. (U.S. Hwy. 64 E.), Blue Ridge Mall • (828) 692-4957**

This popular chain store's books cover almost any subject that might interest you.

# Southern Mountains

## Cashiers

## Chapter 2
**U.S. Hwy. 64 E., Ingles Shopping Center • (828) 743-5015**

Chapter 2 carries new and used books and has a large selection of cookbooks, books of regional interest and children's books. Its real forte is, however, is fiction.

## Dillsboro

## Time Capsule
**N.C. Hwy. 441, Riverwood Oaks Gallery • (828) 586-1026**

This shop specializes in used, rare and out-of-print books, but it also has a good selection of hiking, flower and other nature books pertinent to the region. With more than 10,000 volumes, plan to stay a while. It's across the railroad tracks from Front Street.

## Franklin

## At Books Unlimited
**311 Westgate Plaza Rd. • (828) 369-7742**

You can buy new and used books here; the selection includes a great selection of hiking, nature and regional books. Books Unlimited also offers a fax service and is the headquarters for Western Union.

## Highlands

## Cyrano's Bookshop
**390 Main St. • (828) 526-5488**

Cyrano's describes itself as "cozy but complete." It's also defined by customer service, and the staff promises to track down hard-to-find titles.

## Fireside Books, Etc.
**383 Main St. • (828) 526-5454**

A full-range bookstore with fine sections on the Civil War, the Cherokee Indian Reservation and North Carolina authors, Fireside is also one of the best card shops in the area and has a line of unusual gifts.

# Murphy

## Book Cellar
**107 Tennessee St. • (828) 837-0315**

The Book Cellar is right across the street from Murphy's famous Hen Theater and sells both new and used books and new and used compact disks. While you'll find a little bit of everything in the way of reading material here, the most extensive section is made up of regional books. The Book Cellar will also do searches for special books.

# Sylva

## City Lights Bookstore & Cafe
**3 E. Jackson St. • (828) 586-9499**

City Lights offers new and used books, including great regional and children's sections as well as cards and calendars. Enjoy your book purchase with a specialty coffee, soup, sandwich, salad and/or dessert either in the store or at the outside seating area. On Friday and Saturday evenings, acoustic and folk musicians provide live entertainment.

# Waynesville

## Palmer House Bookshop
**125 N. Main St. • (828) 452-3932**

Palmer House is a general bookstore that carries both new and used books, including bestsellers and a large selection of children's books. It also offers a number of religious tapes, books and articles.

## Sloan's Bookshop
**Haywood and Depot Sts. • (828) 456-8062**

At the corner of Haywood and Depot streets, this bookshop is housed in a tobacco warehouse built in the 1780s, this full-service bookstore. In business since 1978, it has a broad range of new books with large sections of children's books, cookbooks and regional books. It also carries greeting cards, books on tapes and some delightful storytelling tapes. The shop's a great place to relax, browse and visit with the store's two aging but friendly dogs: a golden retriever and a poodle. There's also plenty of parking, which is sometimes a problem in the summer in Waynesville.

kets brimming with candies line the walls and run in a great aisle down the center, assailing you with scents of sweetness. Anything you find here sells for $4.59 a pound, so you can mix the flavors to your taste buds content. If that wasn't enough, there's a soda fountain in the rear, and you can enjoy its treats there or at the tables on the store's "front porch." There are various kinds of homemade fudge, too.

## Chloe & Co.
**113 N. Main St., Waynesville**
**• (828) 452-7792**

Housed in a small stone building that was Waynesville's first library, the selection at this upscale boutique is not large, but the items here are ever so tempting! There are stylish ladies fashions and accessories and a number of excellent pieces of fine antique furniture.

## Earthwork's Environmental Gallery
**21 N. Main St., Waynesville**
**• (828) 452-9500**

Earthwork's brings together arts and crafts of this county and Mexico's Native Americans. Africa is also represented. See the Visual Arts/ Haywood County section of our Arts and Culture chapter. The Earthwork's Frame Gallery, (828) 456-3666, is at 152 S. Main St.

## Gatekeepers
**4 N. Main St., Waynesville • (828) 698-5466**

Excellent taste is reflected in the home accessories, gifts and furniture found here. And the old building with its squeaky wooden floors and tin ceiling is almost as interesting. There's a fine garden shop in the rear.

## Home-Tech: The Kitchen Shop
**5 N. Main St., Waynesville • (828) 452-7672**

The items here can make cooking an adventure. This kitchen shop offers all the necessities to make a cook a chef. In addition to cookbooks, there's fine German-made cookware, small appliances, Burton burners and stove-top grills, gourmet coffees and all the items needed to brew it, handmade cutting boards and butcher-block tables, gift baskets made to order and much more.

## Mast General Store
**63 N. Main St., Waynesville • (828) 452-2101**

In addition to selling outdoor clothing and gear, this store also serves as a ticket office for local cultural events. The original fixtures of this early 20th-century store are still in place, including rocking chairs for its customers. Old-time housewares and other unusual items are stocked on the mezzanine. Periodic demonstrations by well-known regional craftspeople are also held here.

## O. P. Taylor's
**162 N. Main St., Waynesville • (828) 452-7212**

O. P. Taylor now has a branch of his toy store in Waynesville. See the Brevard listing in this chapter.

## Slow Lane
**71 N. Main St., Waynesville • (828) 456-3682**

If you need to decorate a home, this is not a bad place to start. While you won't find sofas and beds and the like at Slow Lane, you will find wonderful solid oak furniture made by craftspeople who live within 100 miles of town.

This big store also offers all kinds of gifts including clocks, baskets, lace, tons of teddy bears, large gold-framed prints of a nostalgic nature, furniture throws, place settings and table linens.

## T. Pennington Art Gallery
**15 N. Main St., Waynesville • (828) 452-4582**

To see Teresa Pennington's amazing skills at reproducing mountain scenes with colored pencils is worth the trip to this gallery. See our Visual Arts/Haywood County section in the Arts and Culture chapter.

## Twigs & Leaves
**98 N. Main St., Waynesville • (828) 456-1940**

David Erickson and his wife, potter Kaaren Stoner, whose studio is right in this craft gallery, call their shop "an adventure into the art of Nature," and it certainly is! Kaaren's leaf-enhanced pottery, arches and outdoor seating made of twigs and branches, nature photos and handmade fountains, meditation pools and organic plant vessels, whimsical lizards and many, many other artists' nature related items, plus reasonable prices, make its nearly impossible to leave this shop without making a purchase. For us, it wasn't possible at all.

## Ridge Runner Naturals
**33 N. Main St., Waynesville • (828) 456-3003**

River Runners carries nature-inspired gifts for all ages: birdfeeders, wind chimes, nature puzzles, T-shirts, books, games, walking sticks, maps and much more.

## Turnabouts
**142 N. Main St., Waynesville • (828) 456-4766**

This eclectic coffeehouse/gift shop with charming taste is a great place to stop, rest and feed the senses. While you sip a cappuccino or one of 20 varieties of coffees or a selection from the finest selection of teas, you can browse through a wonderfully wry collection of greeting cards, shop for a lovely natural fiber nightgowns, buy some European linens or Czechoslovakian crystal, purchase aromatherapy products and candles for your bath, select a gift for a special child, add to your gourmet food supply or select a gourmet food basket. You can order a gourmet picnic basket, too.

Turnabouts is planning to hold "Wine Nights" on Thursday, Friday and Saturday evenings, including cheeses, pates and fine desserts.

## Whitman's Bakery & Sandwich Shop
### 18 N. Main St., Waynesville • (828) 456-8271

Whitman's is one of the busiest stores in town. The wonderful smells wafting out the door tend to lure you right in. And believe us, the sandwiches layered between its freshly baked bread are hard to beat! It's another great place for sweet tooths too.

# Jackson County

## Dillsboro

Sylva is the county seat of Jackson County, and it's a bustling town stretched out along two busy one-way streets graced with a number of very nice shops and restaurants. But it's the tiny, doll-like town of Dillsboro, just a mile down U.S. 19-23. Business, that's the real shopping mecca for tourists and area residents alike. It's also one of the stops made by excursion trains of the Great Smoky Mountain Railroad, which brings even more visitors to Dillsboro.

With a shopping area approximately two blocks long and two streets wide (plus the railway that runs through the middle of town), you wouldn't think there could be so much to see, but there is. The following are only a few of nearly 50 shops and restaurants you'll find in this village. Most are open March through December, giving many of the crafters who supply and often own the shops here time to craft and restock during the winter months.

Dillsboro's is a delight at any season, but the fantasy finish to the Dillsboro shopping season takes place when, on the first two Fridays and Saturdays in December, the Christmas Luminaries is held. Thousands of candles light the way to extended evenings of musical entertainment and complimentary refreshments.

Here's just a brief sampling of the treats in Dillsboro.

## Bradley's General Store
### Front St., Dillsboro • (828) 586-3891

When you've visited all the stores listed below and a great many others, you'll find respite at Bradley's General Store, which has country gifts, home furnishings and — best of all — an antique, but working, soda fountain.

## CJ's
### Front St., Dillsboro • (828) 586-3198

For collectibles and gifts, most of them American-made, take a look at CJ's. They have an extensive inventory of figurines and decorative items for the true collector.

## Dogwood Crafters
### Webster St., Dillsboro • (828) 586-2248

Housed in a large, renovated log building around the corner from Front Street, this is one of our favorite stores in Dillsboro. We are particularly taken with the lovely, artistic cornhusk dolls here, but there also are hundreds of both contemporary and traditional handicrafts on display, including pottery, pillows, art and toys.

## Duck Decoy Inc.
### Front St., Dillsboro • (828) 586-9000

Some of the best duck woodcarvers in the country live in North Carolina, and Duck Decoy displays some of their works along with other distinguished gifts such as handmade oak tables and benches, backpacks, an array of knives, gourmet jellies, tin signs and T-shirts.

## Enloe Market Place
### Front St., Dillsboro • (828) 586-3603

Housed in an historic old home, Enloe carries fine gifts, prints, home accessories and offers a children's corner full of items to delight the kids. Want to impress your friends? Pick up a few bars of monogrammed soap.

## Front Street Company/Yarn Corner
### Front St., Dillsboro • (828) 586-0089

Needleworkers will love the variety they'll find here. Gifts, fine yarns, handpainted needlepoint and cross-stitch supplies are sold here. You can also take a class or receive assistance on your latest project. And for a respite before more shopping, you can dine at the Front Street Cafe or out in the courtyard. You can also purchase delectable gourmet items like teas and coffees plus jams and jellies, which make great gifts or personal indulgences.

## Gallery Z
**Front St., Dillsboro • (828) 586-3383**

The mountains are becoming world-famous for its studio glass, and at Gallery Z you can see some samples of it in the form of candle holders, lamps, vases and perfume bottles.

## Maple Tree Gallery
**Front St., Dillsboro • (828) 586-8021**

Here's a gallery that not only sells gems, jewelry and specimens but will also do gem mounting and repairs while you wait. The handmade wire-wrap jewelry, custom designs and gem-cutting make this an interesting stop.

## Mountain Pottery
**Front St., Dillsboro • (828) 586-9183**

At Mountain Pottery you can see pottery being made in an open studio. Its also got the town's largest selection of handmade porcelain, stoneware and raku pottery. The pottery is supplied by the more than 75 craftspeople from the region.

## The Nature Connection
**Front St., Dillsboro • (828) 586-0686**

This is a delightful store for both adults and children. It's full of home and garden accessories: fountains, metal sculpture, clocks, blown glass and birdhouses and feeders. Nature themes are also found in the books, guides, T-shirts, music, educational items and toys. And this doesn't begin to cover what you'll find here.

## Riverwood Pewter Shop
**N.C. Hwy. 441, Dillsboro**
**• (828) 586-6996**

The Riverwood Shops developed around a hand-hammered pewter business established in 1930. The Riverwood Pewter Shop is still here making hand-hammered pewter on the premises. You'll find the shop between the bridge, 1 mile south of U.S. Highway 74/23.

## Riverwood's Oaks Gallery
**N.C. Hwy. 441, Dillsboro**
**• (828) 586-6542**

Right next door to the Riverwood Pewter Shop, this cooperative of more than 80 Appalachian craftspeople is a showcase of weaving, jewelry, glass, wood, wearables and pottery.

## Southern Traditions
**Front St., Dillsboro • (828) 586-3943**

For a different kind of time travel, visit this charming old country home that's really a shop. At Southern Accent you can look for antiques, gifts, home accessories and counted cross-stitch supplies. The shop will gladly ship your purchases anywhere you like.

## Village Studio
**Front St., Dillsboro • 586-4060**

The talents that flower in these mountains is beautifully expressed in this gallery. It's filled with paintings and prints by area artists, handmade dulcimers, gifts and cards. The gallery-style shop also displays decorative accessories for home and office. The studio also does professional framing.

# Macon County

## Highlands

"There's just no place like Highlands," is a comment heard frequently. It's true, and the town has gone out of its way with rules and regulations to make sure that its small but busy downtown stays as nice as it is now. Highlands is also well-named. Its elevation of 4,118 feet provides pleasant summertime temperatures for roaming its Main Street and surrounding shopping areas. If you've never been to Highlands before, you might want your first stop to be at the Visitor Information Center, (828) 526-2112, 386 Oak Street, just above Town Hall on U.S. Highway 64. Not only will the staff give you the scoop on the whole area and a shopping guide that includes a map, but there are also public restrooms here.

On Main Street itself, you can spend hours

roaming in and out of the shops, where you'll find a wide variety of clothing, jewelry, art, gifts, handicrafts, toys, bird and bat houses, food, furniture, flowers and so on. If there's one overriding theme, it's quality. The residents who occupy some of the most expensive real estate in the mountains expect it and by the droves of shoppers who come here from other areas — the friendly merchants of Highlands aim to please.

Any first-time Highlands' shopper will be immediately drawn to Main Street's diverse shops. But don't stop with Main Street. Highlands has a number of distinctive shopping areas, including quite a few of its side streets. One example is Fourth Street; shops here are referred to as "on the hill." Other small Highlands shopping centers (all within walking distance of downtown) include Wright Square, Oak Square and Mountain Brook Square. There are also some great shops on the main roads leading into town.

Just keep in mind when contemplating a Highlands' shopping spree that some of these stores close after October or December or are open only on weekends. At this high an elevation, where winters can be bitter cold, a lot of residents and some storeowners spend the colder months in warmer climes.

### Highlands Wine and Cheese Co.
**U.S. Hwy. 64, Mountain Brook Center, Highlands • (828) 526-5210**

This wine and cheese shop offers pâté, imported cheese, a large selection of imported and domestic wines, deli trays and gift baskets.

### House of Lord
**Main St., Highlands • (828) 526-9147**

Long an elegant fixture on Main Street, House of Lord is the place to go for fine jewelry and art. The lines carried here are by internationally known designers.

### I'm Precious Too!
**Main and Leonard St., Highlands • (828) 526-2754**

As this store's name implies, it carries simply precious antiques, delicate linens, collectibles and some fine clothes.

### McCulley's
**Fourth St., Highlands • (828) 526-4407**

McCulley's, which has another shop in Aspen, Colorado, specializes in Scottish cashmere knitwear for women and men.

### Mirror Lake Antiques
**Fourth St., Highlands • (828) 526-2080**

This full-service antique store has a large selection of estate jewelry. It's the place to look for semiprecious stones, mineral specimens, gold jewelry, jewelry design and remodeling.

### Stone Lantern
**Main St., Highlands • (828) 526-2769**

This is one of our favorite shops in Highlands. It's not just the beautiful, well-chosen items from the Orient found here. It's the wonderful way in which they're displayed. Expect some high prices, but the quality is worth the cost.

### Tiger Mountain Woodworks
**N.C. 106S, Highlands**
**• (828) 526-5577**

Shopping for a rustic look? This shop sells handcrafted furnishings, including custom lodge furniture and country reproductions including beds, tables, dressers and other items for the entire house.

### The Toy Store
**Main St., Highlands**
**• (828) 526-9415**

We never go to Highlands without dropping in at The Toy Store to see the latest in toys and games. Here you'll find a old and new favorites, plus stuffed animals, dolls and so much more.

### Whiskers
**Main and Third Sts., Highlands**
**• (828) 526-3612**

Whiskers specializes in gifts for pets and their people. You'll find collars, catnip toys, biscuits, decorative leashes, bones, bowls, T-shirts and all manner of things pet lovers can't do without.

If we remember to respect that natural environment, our visits to these wood and park lands will be memorable for all the right reasons.

# Outdoor Safety

The mountains of North Carolina are known as being serene and ancient but subject to the unpredictability of nature. Breathtaking panoramas of misty mountains, rugged peaks, cascading waterfalls, deep forests, twisting trails dotted with wildflowers, cool sparkling mountain pools and streams seem to be at every turn. So when the mountains beckon, don't resist.

Just remember that nature, as spectacular as it can be, is also a powerful force and should be respected as such. There are basics of common sense and courtesy that are important to remember whenever you venture into the national parks and forests, as well as other wilderness areas. Be aware when you enter a primitive environment that you will be faced with the challenge of being entirely self-sufficient for whatever time you remain there. Often there will be no shelters, campgrounds, water spigots or restrooms, and wilderness trails are maintained to the most primitive standard. There will be few blazes or signs, so a compass and topographic map and knowledge of how to use them are essential.

Observe all park regulations. These rules are designed not only to protect the natural environment but also the health and safety of park visitors. Park officers are empowered to enforce the federal regulations on which these rules are based. You can look over a copy of these at park offices throughout the region (see the listings in our Forests and Parks chapter).

Careful planning is a must when you visit our national forests, the Great Smoky Mountain National Park or the Blue Ridge Parkway.

Know what you want to do and what your visit will require; know your surroundings and be aware of our often-changing weather. The mountains have much to offer enthusiasts of all ages, from beginners to experienced outdoors people. The following are reminders and tips in cases of emergency. Do take an interest in researching your outings further. These are the basic safety rules to follow, but educating yourself and training allows you to enjoy the wilds all the more. Books that we like include *Backpacking Tips* (by Bill and Russ Schneider); *Wild Country Companion: The Ultimate Guide to No-trace Outdoor Recreation and Wilderness Safety* (by Will Harmon); *Wilderness First Aid: When You Can't Call 911* (by Gilbert Preston, M.D.); *Reading Weather: Where Will You Be When the Storm Hits* (by Jim Woodmency); *Wilderness Survival: Staying Alive Until Help Arrives* (by Suzanne Swedo); and *Hiking North Carolina* (by Randy Johnson).

## Driving

When traveling by car on the Blue Ridge Parkway or the back roads of the national forests, make sure you observe all traffic regulations and drive a vehicle that's in good working order. Breaking down in some of the remote regions can spell disaster (or at least great inconvenience). Have enough gasoline to take you to your destination and back again, since gas stations are few and far between on the Parkway and can seem a world away when you're sitting by the wayside on a dusty back road. Bring along necessary auto tools and a good spare tire, and make sure your brakes and headlights are in good working order. (These mountains often have steep grades to negotiate, and the Blue Ridge Parkway's 27 tunnels require the use of headlights.)

When packing the car for the trip, include the following items: a first aid kit, flashlight, blanket, light jacket or sweater and a change of clothing, in case the weather changes (see our chapter on Climate). In case of a total breakdown, there's always AAA. For emergency road service, call (800) 477-4222; locally, you can also call (828) 253-5376. This is also the number of the local AAA travel office. (Nonmembers will be charged, but they will be helped in an emergency.)

# What to Pack

For any extended hiking or camping activities, something which will be longer than just a stroll to a waterfall, always have these essentials with you: a map, a compass, a flashlight/headlamp with extra batteries and bulbs, extra food, extra clothing, sunglasses, first-aid supplies, matches in a waterproof container, and fire starter.

When taking off into the woods, don't forget to take along a respect for the land and your own personal safety. Before you step foot on the trail, study a map of the area. (Maps are often available at visitors centers and ranger stations or posted on a bulletin board near park entrances). Know where you're going and don't stray from the trails, many of which are clearly marked. It's easy to become disoriented in deep woods. If you get lost, stay put; you're easier to find that way. It's good to have a pocket whistle when hiking; use three blasts on the whistle to alert those in search of you. If you get lost near a stream or creak, follow the water downstream; it will most likely lead to a community.

Dress properly for the season and wear sturdy worn-in shoes with thick, absorbent socks to prevent blistering. This helps in terms of comfort as well as navigation of rough terrain. Changes in elevation make for unpredictable weather. Be aware of the potential for change and be prepared.

When hiking or camping, never go alone.

Always tell someone your route (you are required to sign in with a park ranger for overnight hikes in national parks). And always make your whereabouts and intentions known to others.

Carry plenty of water. Streams may look sparkling and your thirst may be great, but, unfortunately, the water can be contaminated.

# Trails

Trails are rated by difficulty level, steepness, how obvious the trail is to follow and the roughness of the tread. Markers indicating difficulty are provided by the forest service and are usually at the beginning of the trail. The easiest trails have obvious routes and easy grades, with some pitches up to 20 percent maximum and a relatively smooth tread. They are indicated by a green mark with a slight curve. More difficult trails are marked with a curving blue line and have routes that are usually recognizable but are somewhat challenging with moderate grades, with some pitches up to 30 percent maximum and a smooth to rough tread. A most difficult trail may not be recognizable, requiring a high degree of skill, and may have a steep grade with some pitches greater than 30 percent and rough tread. The hardest trails will have markers with a black zigzag on them.

You should not leave any trail unless you have the equipment and survival skills to meet any condition of terrain, climate or exertion. Mechanical forms of transportation are not allowed in some wilderness areas. Although most trails are open only to hikers, some are designated for horse use in the Southern Nantahala and Shining Rock Wildernesses. Mountain bikes are not permitted, and you may not hike with a group of more than 10 people; we urge you to keep your party to no more than six. Check in at the ranger station before your hike.

# Food and Cooking

It's a good idea to bring a camp stove if you have one (or can borrow or rent one). They have improved in size and utility. If you must have a fire, make sure you control it.

Use existing fire rings when possible. Make sure the fire is dead before leaving, using sand or water to douse the smoldering embers thoroughly. Fires are prohibited in the Shining Rock Wilderness and Middle Prong Wilderness areas; therefore you must carry a backpack stove if you wish to cook in this area. Bring plenty of energy-rich, protein-packed edibles. You will be exerting a great deal of energy while hiking, swimming in mountain pools or rafting and kayaking. Any type of "bar," — be it granola, Power, fruit, oatmeal — packs easily and staves off hunger on the trail. Homemade trailmix with raisins, dried fruits, nuts, a few carob or chocolate chips, and sunflower seeds is fairly free of additives and added sugars. A handful can keep you going on those uphill climbs.

Carry plenty of water (squeeze bottles are the most easily accessible) and drink often, even when not thirsty. You may become dehydrated before you feel the urge to quench your thirst. Good foods to prepare over campfires or stoves include beans, pasta, couscous, instant soups, instant oatmeal, and hot cereals. Throw in any fresh vegetables you have brought along with you. If you have aluminum foil, steam fresh legumes by double-wrapping them with herbs, and place them in the embers of your fire. In ten minutes, enjoy steamed veggies. For breakfast, throw a handful of your trailmix in with the instant oatmeal or hot cereal. It can make a world of difference if you're camping for several days.

## What to Do with Waste

Remember the rule of seasoned campers and hikers: "Pack it in — pack it out." Leave no trace of your time in the woods, not only for the sake of future generations but for the benefit of the true residents of the woods —

the wildlife. Use thoughtful methods of sanitation. Bury all human waste and toilet paper in a hole six inches deep and at least 100 feet away from any water source. Tampons and pads should be carried back out with you in sealed containers — the scent of blood could attract bear or other wild animals. Do use biodegradable soap and a wash pan; scatter your wash water away from creek banks. Obviously, you should take all trash back out with you. Carry resealable bags that can be shut almost airtight for your food waste.

## Wild Animals

Be aware of your intrusion into the animals' woodland home. Leave all wild animals alone. Bears come out occasionally in the mountain park lands, particularly in the southern mountains near the Great Smoky Mountains National Park. Do not approach bears. They may look cuddly, but they can be dangerous. If one approaches your car, stay inside with the windows rolled up. Make noise on the trail or at your campsite — bears won't be interested in investigating foreign clamor. Before you sleep, take all food out of your tent. Seal your edibles as securely as possible in a backpack and hang it from a tree several yards from your sleeping area.

Snakes seldom bite unless disturbed or teased, but be aware of them and be able to identify poisonous snakes. Rattlesnakes and copperheads thrive in these parts. Dry conditions tend to bring snakes to water sources. Take note: Rattlesnakes do not always rattle their tails before striking, and can strike from any position, in any direction. If you are struck by a poisonous snake and have no suctioning kit, seek help immediately. Immobilize the limb, and keep the wound below heart level at all times. Try to identify the markings on the snake, so medical personnel will know

**INSIDERS' TIP**

**Raccoons are extremely cute, and those that have been fed by humans often seem friendly. However, it's best with all wild animals to give them their space. In 1996, North Carolina had over 400 cases of rabid raccoon.**

which antivenin to administer. Not every bite will require antivenin, but every bite does need medical evaluation.

Rabies can be carried by the common raccoon, another cute, cuddly looking creature you don't want to approach. The 1997 summer produced a rabies scare; squirrels and even a domestic kitten were affected by the disease. A rabid animal will generally foam at the mouth, act aggressively, and have wild eyes, often rolling back into the head. Stay far away from such animals. If bitten, seek medical treatment immediately.

## Insects

Ticks can be a problem in the warmer months. Infected ticks can cause Lyme disease. (Should a tick bite you, leaving a red spot that takes on the looks of a bullseye, itches and is accompanied by a fever, see a doctor as soon as possible. These are the indications of Lyme.) Check yourself after being in the woods and follow these tips: Wear light colored clothing so you can quickly spot ticks on you; tuck pant legs into socks; use insect repellent with DEET; and do not remove ticks with your fingers. Use pointed tweezers or splinter pickers. Lightly grasp the body of the insect, gently and slowly pull the body straight out, so as not to leave the head behind. Do not squeeze the tick, as this could push its bacteria directly into the victim's bloodstream. You should save the tick and take it with you when you seek medical help — enabling the physician to analyze it, and prescribe prophylactic antibiotics if necessary. Mosquitoes can flourish in the damp woods, so bring plenty of repellent.

## Plantlife

Foliage is abundant on the trails. One of these plants, poison ivy, a common bush, causes an itchy rash and more severe reactions in those allergic to it. It grows as a vine or short shrub with three glossy light-green leaves per stalk. Avoid this. If you feel you have been in poison ivy, wash your skin thoroughly with soap and warm water after contact. The oily sap this plant emits, known as

urushiol, can cling to pets' fur, clothing, shoelaces, even gardening tools for an extended period and plague you months after. Wash everything that may have come into contact with the plant.

## Hunting

Also be aware of hunting season. If you hike trails during hunting season, always wear bright "hunter-orange" for your protection. Deer season runs from early to mid-October and again from late November to mid-December. Bear season runs from mid-October to early November and again from mid-December to early January. These are very general time frames. Be sure to call for specific dates each year.

You can call the 24-hour phone line at the North Carolina Wildlife Resources Commission, (919) 662-4381, for information on hunting and fishing seasons and regulations in this region of North Carolina.

## Waterfalls

Waterfalls are another deceptively beautiful lure of nature here in the mountains. They have a magnetic quality, but they can be deadly. Each year someone thinks the view must be better from the top of the falls — a fatal mistake. There have been numerous deaths in the past few years due to slipping and falling from the tops or even sides of waterfalls. The rocks in any of our mountain streams are moss-covered and slippery, and the water rushing over falls is swift and cold. One misstep can be the last. View these wonderful waterfalls at the proper distance and from the bottom, looking up. Do not attempt to climb them. Use that zoom lens to get a closer look.

## Hypothermia

Hypothermia, the condition that causes a potentially fatal drop in body temperature, is a term you need to know. And contrary to popular belief, you don't have to be stranded in a snowstorm to experience this life-threatening condition. Whenever cold, moisture, and fatigue persist, it takes only a few hours to bring on the fatal results of hypothermia. Poor food intake, improper clothing, and alcohol can contribute to the problem.

Symptoms of hypothermia include exhaustion, uncontrolled shivering, confusion, loss of motor coordination, slurred speech, irrational behavior (like trying to disrobe in the cold) and unconsciousness. A victim of severe hypothermia, which occurs when the body core temperature falls below 92 degrees Fahrenheit, shivers in waves, cannot walk, curls into a fetal position to find the last remnants of warmth in the body and has rigid muscles. All forms of hypothermia must be treated immediately by drying and warming the victim.

For mild hypothermia, add more layers of clothing, put on dry clothes, increase physical activity and seek shelter.

Photo: Constance E. Richards

Always appreciate the view of waterfalls from the bottom.
Never try to scale a waterfall or stand at the top of one.

The Cashiers area boasts many stunning waterfalls.

For moderate hypothermia, add food and fluids, heat the victim with body contact and get the victim in a sleeping bag with another person who is wearing light clothing (to transfer body heat).

For severe hypothermia, create a shell of total insulation around the victim, and surround the victim with dry clothing, blankets, and multiple sleeping bags. Wrap all of the above in plastic to prevent heat loss as the core temperature rises and pushes warmer blood toward the extremities, and feed the victim warm sugar water a bit at a time.

Urinating will help conserve heat by emptying the bladder and concentrating body heat on the contracted inner organs. Do not expose the hypothermic victim to extremes of heat. Extremes of heat will burn the victim or can shock the heart. Remember that even a 50-degree day can bring on hypothermia if conditions are wet and windy. Keep your head covered in this kind of weather. Body heat may quickly be lost without a hat.

All victims of hypothermia should get medical attention.

# Heat Exhaustion and Heat Stroke

In warm weather, the sun can be intense at these higher elevations, especially in the summer months. Bring along enough sunblock for all exposed skin. We also recommend sunglasses to cut the glare, and a sun hat. Bring plenty of fluids along and drink them, whether you're thirty or not. You may become dehydrated even before you feel the urge to quench your thirst. Heat exhaustion, which can lead to heat stroke, must be taken care of immediately. A major increase in the body core temperature can kill a victim within minutes.

Signs to watch out for are sweating, increased pulse, weakness, dizziness, nausea, and thirst. Signs of heat stroke are hot skin, either very pale skin or very flushed skin, deceased urine output, increased temperature, and a change in mental status — disorientation and incapacity to reason or make judgments. Try to help relieve these symptoms immediately.

For heat exhaustion, rest in the shade, replace fluid loss with a water and salt solution (½ teaspoon salt per quart of water), remove all but the most necessary articles of clothing and refrain from further physical activity for the day.

For heat stroke, move the victim to a cool spot; remove the victim's clothing; pour water on the extremities and fan them, increasing air circulation and evaporation, or cover the victim with cool wet cloths and fan, or immerse victim in cool (but not cold) water. Do not allow victim to become cold or the body will begin shivering to produce more heat. Refrain from all physical activity and seek medical help.

# Coda

Nature can be formidable, but it can also inspire. Don't be afraid of challenging yourself, but do enter into your outdoor endeavors armed with knowledge, preparation, and training. If you're a wilderness novice, read outdoor magazines before your trip. (We love *Outside* and *Backpacker* magazines.) Brush up on basic first aid preparation with books specifically designed for the hiker and camper. We are fortunate in western North Carolina to be surrounded by a wealth of natural beauty. If we remember to respect that natural environment, our visits to these wood and park lands will be memorable for all the right reasons.

Whether you prefer the tamer environs of a city park or the wild-river adventure just over the ridge, you'll find just what you're looking for in these hills.

# Recreation

Leisure time reigns supreme here in the mountains. The quality and diversity of recreational opportunities are unparalleled. After you've been swept along in a whitewater raft, gone aloft in a hot-air balloon, come close to nature — and a backpacking llama — on a scenic hiking trail and reeled in a trophy trout on a mountain lake, you're still not finished. Whether you prefer the tamer environs of a city park or the wild river adventure just over the ridge, you'll find just what you're looking for in these hills.

Our mountains have the perfect places to fish from a boat on a peaceful lake, dive off a houseboat into crystal clear waters, take to tumbling waters in an inner tube, zip along behind a ski boat, canoe through placid or swift rivers or race over rapids in a kayak or a raft. (See our section on Outfitters at the end of this chapter for canoeing and rafting outfitters.) Swimming pools are included in the following "City and County Programs and Areas" section.) The suggestions below are just a few of the possibilities.

This chapter begins by highlighting the various city and county park areas and their accompanying recreation programs. Then we give you an overview of the Lakes, Whitewater Rafting and Kayaking, the Rivers, Canoeing, Fishing, Hunting, Mountain Biking, Rock Climbing, Hiking, Camping, Horseback Riding, Off-road Vehicle Trails and Other Recreation (like Airborne Rec, Llama Treks and Bowling). Listings of a few of the region's guides and outfitters are at the chapter's end. For a list of Ranger Stations and National Park Service Visitors Centers see our Forests and Parks chapter for contact information.

## County and City Programs and Areas

When time allows, we mountain folk tend to head for the fabulous recreation offered by the 1.5 million acres of public lands here (see our Forest and Parks chapter), often overlooking the many recreational opportunities right in our cities and towns. In this section, we describe some of those recreational possibilities. And we haven't even attempted to include the ever-so-many private clubs and spas that abound in the region.

### Northern Mountains

#### Alleghany County

**Crouse Park**
**Grayson and Cherry Sts., Sparta**
This city park provides a playground and covered picnic areas on the grounds of the

---

**INSIDERS' TIP**

How would you like to give both yourself and your horse a vacation in the mountains? You can at Las Praderas Stables and Cottages. Located on See Off Mountain Rd. off U.S. Highway 276 about 7 miles south of Brevard. It cost $20 a night for use of the stables and $130 a night for a fully furnished cottage with a fireplace. Las Praderas has trails, but it doesn't rent horses. Call (828) 883-3375 for more information.

Crouse House, the former home of one of Sparta's leading citizens. Basketball, volleyball and horseshoes are also popular here.

## Ashe County

### Ashe Park
**off Old Hwy. 16, Jefferson**

Centered in a lush green valley, Ashe Park is well equipped for fun with two tennis courts, two baseball fields, two covered picnic areas, a barn-like covered building that can house groups up to 75, four bathrooms, plenty of parking and a breathtaking view of Mt. Jefferson. It's also home to the county's Old Time Fiddler's Convention celebrated each year. See our Annual Events chapter for more on the Convention.

### West Jefferson Park
**Church Ave., West Jefferson**

West Jefferson's city park is a pleasant, grassy expanse on the rolling hills behind Main Street. Picnic tables are scattered by the creekside, and a basketball court crowns the hill.

## Avery County

### Banner Elk Town Park
**Hwy. 194, Banner Elk**

This city park is behind NationsBank, just north of the stoplight in Banner Elk. A few benches, flowers and a walkway add pleasant touches to this small city park.

### Sunset Park
**Beech Mountain Pkwy.**

This intimate little memorial park on half and acre gives visitors a lovely place to stop and reflect on the incredible natural beauty of mile-high Beech Mountain.

## Mitchell County

### Mitchell Family YMCA
**Summit Ave., Spruce Pine**
• **(828) 765-7766**

The Mitchell Family YMCA serves a three-county area. The focal point of the complex is a large ice-skating arena that draws school and camp groups from the region. Junior ice hockey, swimming, basketball, a fitness center, gymnastics and a variety of sports programs are offered here. Hours of operation vary seasonally.

## Watauga County

### Blowing Rock Memorial Park
**Main St., Blowing Rock**

Picnic tables, a children's playground and tennis courts fill this picturesque public park in the center of tiny Blowing Rock. Just off the main street, the park lends itself to outdoor lunches and ice-cream cone breaks. The park is also the center of village cultural events.

### Boone Greenway Pedestrian Walking and Biking Trail
**Boone**

The access point for this ambling trail is adjacent to the university parking lot on Dale Street and the Watauga County Parks & Recreation Complex on Complex Drive.

### Broyhill Park
**off Main St., Blowing Rock**

This serene, beautifully landscaped city park, highlighted by a small, placid lake, is just behind Main Street in Blowing Rock. A walking path, beautiful gazebo and ducks gliding across the water make this pleasant little park a favorite of local residents and visitors alike. A hiking path actually calls for some hearty climbing on the way back—during which you will pass leafy rhododendrons, a little waterfall, and forestation.

### Watauga County Parks and Recreation Department
**1012 State Farm Rd., Boone**
• **(828) 264-9511**

This county parks and recreation department oversees a number of area recreational attractions. Countywide schools are home to a number of park facilities such as lighted tennis courts, lighted athletic fields for football and soccer, outdoor basketball and volleyball courts and numerous children's play areas.

The Watauga County Swimming Complex on Complex Drive, (828) 264-0270, is a popular High Country recreation spot. In an area where winter can bring a definite chill, the indoor, heated 25-meter pool, diving pool and adjoining children's pool are welcome entertainment. It is open daily, year round, and the public is welcome. Modest fees vary according to age. Season passes are available. A changing schedule of Red Cross swimming instruction, aquacise, senior exercise and scuba classes are available upon request.

Tot Lot Park, in front of the Watauga County Swimming Complex, is a play area for all children. A picnic shelter, volleyball court and restrooms are nearby.

An outdoor county pool with a capacity for 60 swimmers is open seasonally from Memorial Day through Labor Day at Green Valley School off N.C. Highway 194 E. Hours are noon to 6 PM Tuesday through Saturday and 1 to 6 PM on Sundays.

Howard's Knob Park, open from April 1 to October 31, is at the highest elevation in the city of Boone. To get to this pleasant little park, head west on King Street, turn right across from the Daniel Boone Inn and proceed to the top of the hill. You'll find picnic tables, wildflowers and a great view of Boone at this 5½-acre park.

# Central Mountains

## Buncombe County

### Asheville Parks and Recreation
• (828) 259-5800

Asheville's parks and recreation facilities are scattered throughout the city and provide a multitude of recreational activities and cultural programs for all ages. Many of these are play areas, some with picnic tables and other amenities. The sites are open daily from 6 AM to 10 PM and can be used free of charge. Maps of park locations are available from the office of city parks and recreation.

Outdoor public swimming pools are found in Malvern Hills (Sulphur Springs Road), and also on Walton Street. They are open June through August and charge a moderate admission. The pools offer Red Cross Learn to Swim classes, fitness, and lifeguard certifica-

tion training. Approximately 20 public tennis courts dot the city for year-round use on a first-come, first-served basis. Some of these hard-surface courts are lighted for evening play.

### Lake Louise
**Lake Louise Dr., Weaverville**

Just under a mile from Main Street in this small town north of Asheville is Lake Louise, a man-made lake developed in 1911. The park once sported a dance pavilion on an island in the middle of the lake. Back then, a daily trolley line from the big city of Asheville brought dapper gentlemen and ruffle-skirted young ladies to Lake Louise for evening dance socials.

Today Lake Louise, with its central 40-foot-high fountain, is enjoying a new generation of visitors of all ages. Walkers on the popular lake path can observe an assortment of tree species cultivated by the Tree Board of the Town of Weaverville. You can identify more than 34 kinds, including sycamores, river birch, Japanese maples, flowering cherry, sugar maples, weeping willow, sweet gum, redbud and Virginia Pine, just to name a few. This place is popular with local schools groups with junior botanists in tow.

Lake Louise also offers a children's playground, an outdoor exercise facility, public restrooms and picnic shelters for visitors. Hours are 7 AM to 11 PM daily year round.

### Lake Tomahawk Park
**S. Laurel Circle Dr., Black Mountain**
• (828) 669-2052

This lovely little man-made lake and 20-acre park in a residential area of picturesque Black Mountain was a WPA Depression-era project. Visitors can enjoy the scenic water view, well-trod walking path, landscaping and resident waterfowl. A community center, public pool and play areas are part of Lake Tomahawk Park. The park opens around 5 AM and closes around midnight.

### Buncombe County Parks and Recreation
**205 College St., Asheville**
• (828) 255-5526

This comprehensive county recreation program includes a multitude of services and recreation sites throughout Buncombe County. Athletics is a big part of the program. Softball, soccer and tennis are available through a number of leagues, teams and associations in cooperation with or sponsored by the department.

The Aston Park Tennis Center on Hilliard Street, (828) 255-5193, offers memberships, clinics, private lessons and regular tournament play. The court facility is free to use and is open beginning in April Monday through Thursday from 9 AM to 9 PM and Friday through Sunday from 9 AM to 7 PM. After Thanksgiving, the center is open Saturday, Sunday, Tuesday, Wednesday and Thursday from 10 AM to 6 PM.

www.insiders.com

See this and many other **Insiders' Guide®** destinations online.

Visit us today!

Lake Julian District Park off Long Shoals Road is a thermal lake, used as a cooling agent for the CP&L electric facility at its shore. The lake, south of Asheville in the Skyland area, is a family recreation park open year round for fishing, canoeing, paddleboating and outdoor games. A children's play area and picnic shelters are also available. Fishing is allowed from shore or by boat for a rental fee. Patrons must provide their own electric motor — gas motors are not allowed. North Carolina fishing laws are enforced, and a local lake permit is required. Hours are 8 AM to 6 PM October to March; in April from 8 AM to 8 PM; from May through August, 8 AM to 9 PM; and in September from 8 AM to 8 PM.

The Buncombe County Parks and Recreation Department operates a variety of recreational park sites along the French Broad River and at numerous other points in the county. There are also many athletic fields, community centers and public pools.

The largest of these county public swimming pools is the 50-meter pool at Recreation Park in East Asheville on Gashes Creek Road. This park, a longtime Buncombe County favorite, has a privately operated, old-fashioned amusement park with Ferris wheel. A concession area, playground, restrooms and picnic shelters complete the park.

The Parks and Rec Department also sponsors a variety of county-wide enrichment classes in the arts and Red Cross swimming instruction. Call the main number provided above for more information.

## Henderson County

### Boyd Park
**Main St., Hendersonville • (828) 697-3079**
This city park is within walking distance of downtown. It has a miniature golf course and an activity building used for meetings and events such as local cat shows. There are also two tennis courts that are open until 11 PM year round.

### Dana Park
**Dana Rd., Dana • (828) 685-3546**
Dana Park's 6 acres contain a softball field, a children's playground and a community building with a fireplace and a complete kitchen, making it a popular spot for family reunions and gatherings. Classes in clogging, fitness and aerobics and other types of instruction also go on here. Call the park for more details on the classes. This park is 8 miles from downtown Hendersonville.

### Edneyville Park
**off U.S. Hwy. 64 E., Edneyville**
You'll find this 4-acre park tucked behind the Edneyville Volunteer Fire Department off U.S. Highway 64 E. about 10 miles from downtown Hendersonville. It has two tennis courts, a basketball court, a children's playground, a covered picnic shelter and restrooms. The Edneyville branch of the Henderson County Library is also here.

### Jackson Park
**Glover St. or Harris St., Hendersonville • (828) 697-4884**
Jackson Park's 212 acres on the southeast edge of Hendersonville make it the largest county park in western North Carolina. It has four lighted tennis courts, eight lighted softball/baseball fields, a soccer field, three playgrounds, restrooms, four covered picnic shelters for 50 to 150 persons and 20 woodland picnic tables that overlook the playing fields.

There's usually a lot of playing to watch in

this heavily used recreation area. The adult softball program usually involves around 76 men's and women's teams totaling 1,200 participants. The youth soccer, softball and baseball programs take place here too, along with the Four Season Senior Games. A summer day camp that includes crafts, organized games and planned activities is operated at Jackson as well as at other county parks for children ages 5 to 11. Call the above number for more information.

A 1.5-mile nature trail meanders through part of the park. This pretty, peaceful path takes you through hardwood and pine forests and wildflower and wetlands meadows. Dogwoods and silverbells bloom in the spring and sourwoods bloom in the summer. Self-guiding brochures that help with plant and tree identification are available.

The park also hosts a number of special events: On Easter weekend, 10,000 eggs are hidden for the children to find. Fourth of July is celebrated with softball and horseshoe tournaments, children's games, music, food and an impressive fireworks display after dark. On the first Saturday in October, Farm-City Day brings city and farm folks together here. There are displays of antique and modern farm equipment (including draft horses), tractor pulls, livestock exhibits, a petting zoo, a Civil War reenactment, chainsaw carving, demonstrations, live mountain music and much more. On the weekend before Halloween, a scary "Haunted Trail" winds through the woods, and there are games, treats and a costume contest. In December, the park is decorated with luminaries. See our Annual Evens and Festivals chapter or call the above number for more information.

The entrance gate is also accessible from Four Seasons Boulevard by turning onto Harris Street, or you can turn onto Glover Street from the Spartanburg Highway (U.S. Highway 176) to reach the park's Glover Street entrance. The park is open daily from 7:30 AM to 11 PM.

### King Memorial Park and Green Meadows Park
Seventh Ave., Hendersonville
• (828) 697-4968

The combined facilities of these two parks include the Mud Creek Nature Walk, a playground, a softball field, covered basketball courts and the Green Meadows Activity Building which hosts community meetings, pet shows and the like.

### Patton Park
off Fourth Ave., Hendersonville
• (828) 697-3081

The main attraction here is an outdoor Olympic-size swimming pool operated by the city. In May, the pool opens on weekends only; the regular schedule begins in June and runs until November. There is a small admission fee.

### Stoney Mountain Activity Center
Stoney Mountain Rd., Hendersonville
• (828) 697-4722

"Activity" is the right word for this center. All kinds of classes are taught here, including dance, tumbling, fitness and aerobics. To find the center, drive north out of Hendersonville on U.S. Highway 25, turn left onto Stoney Mountain Road and drive a mile; the entrance will be on the right.

### YMCA
810 Sixth Ave. W., Hendersonville
• (828) 692-5774

Just a few blocks from downtown, this complex is one of the more popular places in Hendersonville. It includes a gymnasium, four lighted tennis courts (two are Har-Tru composition courts) and a weight-training/wellness center with free weights and Nautilus and aerobic equipment. There is also a five-lane, 25-meter, heated indoor swimming pool as well as a whirlpool and sauna. The Y offers classes and activities for both children and adults.

## Polk County

### Polk County Recreation Department
Park St., Columbus • (828) 894-8199

The Recreation Department, which is dedicated to serving citizens of all ages, offers programs in aerobics, youth basketball, youth volleyball, line dancing, men's basketball and stretch-and-strengthen exercises at Stearns Gym on Walker Street.

Gibson Park on Park Street boasts a baseball field and swimming pool. The pool, open from June through August, offers family passes, swimming lessons and water aerobics.

## Transylvania County

### Brevard College
400 N. Broad St., Brevard • (828) 883-8292

Many of the recreation facilities at Brevard College, including the indoor swimming pool, are open to the public through inexpensive continuing education classes that include aerobics, water aerobics, beginning rock climbing and even golf tips. The campus is also a popular place for runners and walkers.

### Champion Park
Rosman • (828) 884-7977

The swimming pool here in Rosman is open from early June until September, seven days a week until dark. Champion Park also offers a softball field, a multipurpose court, a playground, a picnic shelter and a river access site.

### Franklin Park
Lakeview Dr., Brevard • (828) 884-6959

Brevard's public swimming pool, open in the summer, is within walking distance of downtown, just one block off East Main Street. You'll also find a fine new playground with slides, swings, modern monkey bars and a special area for younger children.

### Silvermont Park
E. Main St., Brevard

Open seven days a week from 8:30 AM until 10 PM, Silvermont has two lighted basketball courts, 3 tennis courts, a playground, a picnic shelter and a walking path located on the grounds of a historic mansion. Mountain Music Night with a live local artist is free of charge every Thursday from 7:30 until 10 PM. (See our Arts and Culture chapter for more on Silvermont.)

### South Broad Park
S. Broad St., Brevard

The small picnic area found at this arboretum is a lovely place to bring a lunch. It's right next to a large multi-purpose playing field.

### Transylvania Activities Center
1150 Ecusta Rd., Brevard
• (828) 884-3156

Headquarters of the Transylvania Parks and Recreation Department, this park also contains a gymnasium, two lighted softball fields, two soccer fields, a playground and a concession area with restrooms.

The parks program includes organized sports and fitness, including a children's soccer program, a softball league in the fall, aerobics and jazz-aerobics, kung fu classes, a ballroom dance club, senior games and silver arts, volleyball and children's tumbling and gymnastics. The county also sponsors youth dances, ballroom dances and summer day camps as well as Holiday Crafts Week and Halloween Fest.

# Southern Mountains

## Cherokee County

### Andrews Recreation Park
Andrews • (828) 321-2135

Andrews Recreation Park has a beach volleyball court, basketball and tennis courts, a softball field, playground equipment and an area for horseshoe games. In addition, there is a Little League baseball field, picnic areas, swimming pools and the Andrews Community Center that contains a large room with a stage, a smaller meeting room and kitchen and restroom facilities. The park is handicap accessible.

### Ferebee Park
Bristol Ave., Andrews
• (828) 321-2135

This park provides a quiet and restful picnic area, playground and restrooms just up from Main Street.

### Hall Memorial Park
First St., Andrews • (828) 321-2135

Right next to the Andrews Chamber of Commerce, this new park and its gazebo plays host to summertime country and gospel concerts and many other events. The Valleytown Cultural Arts Center built the park.

## Hiwassee River Park
**Murphy • (828) 837-6617**

The colorful displays of flowers, bushes and trees were planted and are maintained by volunteers with Cherokee County CARE. It features a walking path, benches and picnic tables.

## Konehete Park
**103 Konehete St., Murphy**
**• (828) 837-6617**

This large city park offers a swimming pool, four lighted tennis courts and four baseball/softball fields (three with lights). There are also areas for fishing, volleyball, two soccer fields and outdoor basketball courts.

Organized activities include swim teams, football, basketball, baseball, softball and soccer leagues for children, youth and adults. Wrestling, gymnastics, aerobics, line dancing, basketball and other events are held in the park's Old Rock Gym. Runners and walkers can use the trail or sidewalks throughout Konehete Park or use the running track at the Murphy High School.

## Murphy Garden Club Park
**Murphy • (828) 837-6617**

You'll find this park next to the Valley River near the post office. Its convenient location, picnic tables and barbecue stands make it a favorite spot to enjoy lunch or to just sit in a car and watch the river flow past.

## Valley River Park
**Andrews • (828) 321-2135**

On the banks of the Valley River right within the city limits of Andrews, this park offers fishing, a softball and baseball field and a picnic area.

# Clay County

## Clay County Recreation Park
**N.C. Hwy. 175, Hayesville**
**• (828) 389-3532**

This popular public park, not far from the 140-foot-high Chatuge Dam, is on N.C. Highway 175 on Lake Chatuge (see our information on this lake in the "Lakes" section of this chapter). The park has 25 campsites, picnic

and swimming areas, a boat launch and a ballpark.

# Graham County

## Graham County Recreation Complex
**Knight St., Robbinsville • (828) 479-7983**

The county has a large complex formed by the elementary and middle schools, the public library and the community and senior citizens center. All the buildings are located in the same area.

This complex also contains tennis courts and a swimming pool. The pool is open from June through August; there is a small admission fee.

# Haywood County

## Town of Canton Recreation Park
**Penland St., Canton • (828) 646-3411**

This city park, roughly 17 acres in size, contains three picnic sheds and numerous outside picnic tables, two outdoor basketball courts, four lighted tennis courts, play equipment both for small children and teenagers and two Little League baseball fields. The park's swimming pool and wading pool are open from the middle of May until the first of September; admission for kids 17 and younger is 50¢; 18 and older, $1. Concessions are available at the pool.

Canton also has an entertainment shelter and bandstand where summer programs are held. Around the park is a 1☐-mile walking and jogging trail along the banks of the Pigeon River. The parks department uses the sports fields at area public schools for team sports.

## Town of Waynesville Recreation Park
**128 W. Marshall St. • (828) 456-9541**

There's plenty of action at this park that consists of six hard-surface tennis counts, two outdoor basketball courts, a swimming pool, two picnic areas with shelters, a playground, three softball/baseball fields, two sand volleyball courts, a modified golf-driving range, soccer fields, shuffleboard, a quarter-mile track and fitness trail, a horse-show ring and a recreation building. The City Parks and Recreation Department that runs the complex also sponsors all kinds of youth and adult team sports and special events that include an open tennis championship, a trout fishing festival, an Easter-egg hunt and judo and bridge tournaments. For senior citizens, there are craft and exercise classes, trips, health programs and meals (see our Retirement chapter). There's a full complement of fitness, hobby and education classes for other adults and children too.

## Jackson County

The Jackson County Parks and Recreation Department, (828) 586-6333, operates the following eight areas. With 12 full-time staff members and an annual budget of around $250,000, it is able to offer lots of activities year round. Use the central phone number, above, to get more information on the following areas.

### Caney Fork Creek Park
**Caney Fork Rd.**

You'll find this little park 7 miles up Caney Fork Road next to the Caney Fork Community Center. It has a lighted basketball court, a softball field, shuffleboard courts, horseshoe pits and a picnic shelter and tables.

### Cashiers Community Center
**off U.S. 64, Cashiers • (828) 743-9990**

This small park and complex has a lighted ballfield, lighted tennis courts, an indoor basketball court and an outdoor swimming pool (open from June through August; admission is $2). Senior citizens' meals are served in the community center building, which is also available for meetings. The complex also includes the Cashiers Child Development Center that provides day care for 35 children ages 2 months to 5 years.

### Cullowhee County Park
**off N.C. 107, Cullowhee**

This 30-acre park has four soccer fields, two baseball fields, outdoor basketball courts, picnic shelters, a playground, a creek walk and nature trail and a parks' administration building that will also house a recreation center and gymnasium.

### Dillsboro River Park
**Dillsboro**

Canoers and kayakers can access to the Tuckasegee River through this 1½-acre park. The park has picnic tables.

### East LaPorte River Park
**N.C. Hwy. 107 S.**

The 7½ acres that form this park on the Tuckasegee River include river access for tubing, canoeing and swimming; restrooms; picnic shelters; a multipurpose basketball court; a beach volleyball court; and a greenway for free play and hiking trails.

### Fairview Youth Complex
**Fairview Rd., Sylva**

Three youth baseball fields, a concession stand, restrooms, a score tower and picnic facilities make up this complex between Sylva and Cullowhee.

### Mark Watson Park
**Old School Rd., Sylva**

This county park has four lighted tennis courts, two adult softball fields, a double-size asphalt basketball court, playground, horseshoe pits a picnic shelter and fairly large greenway for free play.

### Ralph J. Andrews County Park
**Glenville • (828) 743-3923**

Built on land near the Glenville dam donated to the county by the Nantahala Power

## INSIDERS' TIP

When horseback riding, always wear long pants and boots with a separation between shoe sole and heel. Wearing shorts on a leather saddle will chap and blister your thighs in no time. Shoes without any type of heel may cause your entire foot to slip through the stirrup and you could be dragged under the horse if thrown.

Company, this 78-acre park offers full RV hookups, tent camping, picnicking, hot showers and boat-ramp access to Lake Glenville. To reach it, go about 1.5 miles north of the Glenville post office until you come to Pine Creek Road on the left. Follow the signs to the park entrance, approximately 2 miles down the road.

## Sylva Swimming Pool
**Municipal Dr., Sylva • (828) 743-9715**

This outdoor, 185,000-gallon pool has high- and low-diving boards. It is open from June through August. Admission is $2 for those older than 12 and $1 for children 12 and younger.

## Western Carolina University
**N.C. Hwy. 107, Cullowhee • (828) 227-7317**

Recreation facilities at the university include the Reid Health and Physical Education Building, Breese Gymnasium, A.K. Hinds University Center and Ramsey Regional Activity Center. Among the indoor and outdoor sports available here are tennis, volleyball, basketball, swimming, bowling, handball, racquetball, softball, badminton, table tennis and

archery. The university also promotes extensive student intramural and athletic programs and offers Tiny Tot and Youth Swim programs in the summer. The swim program is open to the public. Also open to the public are continuing education courses in yoga, t'ai chi chuan, hydrorobics and other fitness classes.

## Macon County

## The Arrowood Pool
**S.R. 1310, Franklin • (828) 524-4446**

This pool, open to the public, is at the LBJ Civilian Conservation Center. To get there, go west out of Franklin for 3 miles and turn right at the "LBJ Job Corps/Wayah Bald" sign. Take the first left onto Wayah Road (S.R. 1310).

## Highlands Recreation Park
**U.S. Hwy. 64, Highlands • (828) 526-3556**

The recreation center here is open to the public from 8 AM to 10 PM Monday through Saturday and noon to 6 PM on Sunday. It offers swimming (admission is $2), a Nautilus Room ($5 a visit, $20 for a month), tennis courts ($1 per person per hour; courts may be reserved one day in advance) and aerobics ($4 a class). You can join a cardiovascu-

Photo: Cashiers Chamber of Commerce

Visitors from all over America come to the Cashiers area for sailing, boating, fishing, rock climbing and other sports.

# Macon County:
# The Blue Valley
# and Osage Overlooks

As viewed from this Macon County overlook, the mountains seem to go on forever in shifting hues of blues and greens. At certain times during the year, the mountains are totally shrouded in blue, which gives both the mountains and the Blue Valley Overlook its name. For a view you won't forget, drive 5.5 miles south of Highlands on N.C. Highway 106. Just a bit farther down this same highway, you'll come to the Osage Overlook with another great view of the Blue Valley.

lar program or play softball, baseball, volleyball, basketball, bridge and duplicate bridge here. Classes are taught in tumbling, repelling and wrestling. There is a picnic shelter with a playground nearby. The parks department also sponsors a Fourth of July Celebration complete with a parade and fireworks, as well as a summer playground program, various bazaars and a craft festival.

## Macon County Recreation Park
**U.S. 441 S., Franklin • (828) 349-2090**

The many attractions at this large and well-maintained park include softball fields, indoor and outdoor basketball courts, shuffleboard and tennis courts, horseshoes, a children's playground, a loop walking trail, a gymnasium, a swimming pool, two outdoor picnic shelters and four conference/party rooms. The community building here is open from 8 AM to 5 PM daily.

## Swain County

## Alarka Community Park
**Alarka Rd., Alarka**

A few years ago, when an old school building burned in this community west of Bryson City, the town used the land as the site for a fire department and a park with a playground, a picnic area, a nice jogging trail and a pavilion.

## The Bryson City Island Park
**Access on Island St., Bryson City**

As early as 1890, the editor of *The Swain County Herald*, the county's first newspaper, urged the county commissioners to strike a bargain for Island Park, as he called the seven-acre island in the Tuckasegee River, "where citizens may find a pleasant rendezvous far from the noise and bustle of city life." However, it wasn't until 1986, almost a century later, that Bryson City's downtown island, reached by a swinging bridge, finally became a park.

A lot of history has happened here. It's said, for example, that one of Jesse James' gang members lived on the island for a while (see "Iron-Foot of the Island" in this chapter).

A lighted trail circles the island, and tags identify many of the native plants and wildflowers along the trail. Boy Scouts who used the island for a camping site and headquarters in the 1930s and 1940s built the Interpretive Center. Island Park has a launching site for canoes and kayaks and areas for picnicking and fishing.

## River Front Park
**Island St., Bryson City**

This half-acre park that runs along the Tuckasegee is the site of the town's Riverfest (see our Festivals and Annual Events chapter). It also has a picnic area, including a covered pavilion and a walking trail. Another of Bryson City's parks, the small Ela River Park, also on the Tuckasegee, is used mostly for picnicking and fishing.

## Swain County Recreation Park
**W. Deep Creek Rd., Bryson City**
**• (828) 488-6159**

This attractive 34-acre park has a lighted field for baseball and softball, four lighted tennis courts, a basketball court, two playgrounds, shuffleboard and volleyball courts, horseshoe pits, a pavilion and picnic area and a jogging trail. There is also an outdoor swim complex with an Olympic-size pool, an intermediate pool and a kiddie pool. The pools are open June through August for a small admission price. Season tickets are available.

The list of organized activities includes several softball leagues, volleyball, soccer, aerobics, line dancing, tennis and swimming lessons. Youth programs feature karate, winter ski instruction, ball programs and a billiards league. The parks department also sponsors events such as the Christmas Extravaganza.

Plans for the next decade include the construction of a community center that will house an eight-lane bowling center, an Olympic-size indoor swimming pool, a double gymnasium, a teen center, racquetball courts, a fitness center, a commercial kitchen, a large multi-purpose room, arts and crafts classrooms, a large conference room and a walking track.

# The Lakes

Most of our mountain lakes are found in the central and southern mountains. Some of the smaller ones are private or in residential resort communities. Here we've listed some of the more popular lakes that have public access areas.

## Central Mountains

### Buncombe County

**Lake Julian**
**Overlook Rd. (extension access off N.C Hwy. 146)**
Lake Julian is a thermal lake used as a cooling agent for Carolina Power and Light. Therefore, the lake is deliciously warm, often reaching a scorching 95 degrees in summer! You might find the power plant that looms over one side of the lake a bit disconcerting, but the water never goes below 50 degrees in winter — the best time for fishing here is between October and March.

Several covered picnic areas make this a favorite spot for family reunions and company gatherings. Picnic shelters range in size from four to 10 picnic tables and can be rented for about $20 and $35 for Buncombe County residents. Nonresidents pay roughly $35 and $45. A children's playground, volleyball court and horseshoe pit provide some free landlubber entertainment. Paddle boats, fishing boats, or canoes for can be rented for under $10 an hour if you are a county resident. If not, then expect to pay about double. If you bring your own boat, there is a launch fee of under $5 per day. When there's room, a boathouse and dock can hold your sailboat for approximately $120 (residents) and $180 (nonresidents) per year. The lake is well-stocked with bass, crappie, catfish, brim, and talapia and the price for fishing is nominal.

Lake Julian Park is open from 8 AM to 9 PM April through August; 8 AM to 8 PM in September, and 8 AM to 6 PM October through March. It is closed on Thanksgiving, Christmas and New Year's Day. For more information, call the ranger station at (828) 684-0376.

### Lake Powhatan Recreation Area
**F.R. 3484 • (800) 280-CAMP**
Lake Powhatan is a popular destination with a lot to offer besides the pretty little lake for fishing (it also has a swimming beach and a lifeguard on duty). There are 96 sites for tents and trailers (no hookups), a trailer dump station, picnic tables with grills, restrooms with flush toilets, hiking trails, information hosts and a central supply of drinking water. The campground is open from mid-April through October, and the Forest Service provides numerous activities during the summer season. See the "Camping" section in this chapter.

Powhatan is in the Bent Creek Experimental Forest with a system of hiking trails that can get confusing, so pick up a map from the campground office at the entrance to the area. The Western North Carolina Arboretum with its 10 state-champion big trees is near Lake Powhatan.

### Rutherford County

**Lake Lure**
**U.S. 74**
This sparkling jewel is one of the most picturesque lakes you'll find anywhere —

Chimney Rock Park and other spectacular mountains tower over it and its 1,500 acres include 27 miles of shoreline. You'll find a number of marinas here, but before you haul your boat to the lake you should be aware that launch fees have been set high to lessen lake congestion. Also, because of its beauty, the shoreline here is quite developed. Still, you'll find a protected, sandy beach area for public use. It is in the center of the Lake Lure recreation area, across from Lake Lure Inn.

## Southern Mountains

### Cherokee County
**Lake Hiwassee**
**Access off U.S. 64**

Built in 1935, the TVA's 307-foot, 1,376-foot-long Hiwassee Dam is the highest overspill dam in the United States. It blocks the Hiwassee River to form the center of recreation and fishing in Cherokee County — the 22-mile-long, 6,090-acre Lake Hiwassee. Its 163-mile shoreline is almost completely surrounded by the Nantahala National Forest. In 1955, a second generating unit was added to the dam, along with the world's largest electric motor and reversible pump-turbine. This enables water from the dam to be used to generate electricity during peak hours. During off-hours, the water is then pumped 205-feet back into the Hiwassee reservoir for reuse.

The lake is known for its smallmouth bass and walleyes, but fishermen will also find largemouth bass, bluegill and crappie here.

The Hanging Dog Recreation Area (see "The History of Hanging Dog" in this chapter) is less than 4 miles northwest of Murphy off U.S. 64. The area features a 26-site campground, a picnic area, hiking trails and a boat-launching ramp. (See the "Camping" section

of this chapter for more information.) There are also a couple of marinas in the area.

### Cherokee Lake
**Access off N.C. Hwy. 294**

Operated by the Tennessee Valley Authority, this small lake, about a mile in circumference, is fed by the backwaters of the Lake Hiwassee. Its new pier is a great place to take children fishing, and the pier is designed for easy access for disabled individuals.

### Clay County

**Chatuge Lake**
**Access off U.S. Hwy. 64**

Stretching from Clay County into Georgia, Chatuge Lake, with its gradual 132-mile shoreline backed up by high mountain peaks, reminds us of a Swiss Alpine lake. It provides endless hours of water sports and fishing and presents some of the most beautiful views in the county. Thirty-two species of fish have been caught here; smallmouth and largemouth bass, spotted bass and sunfish are the important sport catches. Striped/white bass hybrids are also stocked annually to control the gizzard shad population, and threadfin shad are stocked periodically to augment the prey bass.

Built in 1941 by the Tennessee Valley Authority, Chatuge has been called the crown jewel of the TVA system because of its picturesque setting. It is also one of the most developed of those lakes, with more than 76 miles of shoreline in private hands. There are three commercial marinas in the area.

The popular Clay County Recreation Park, not far from the 144-foot-high Chatuge Dam, sits on the reservoir 6.2 miles from Hayesville on U.S. 64 (turn right onto N.C. 175). Here you'll find 25 campsites (see the "Camping"

---

**INSIDERS' TIP**

When whitewater rafting for the first time, pay attention to everything your guide says. Try not to panic if you get in trouble. Always remember the most important thing — if you fall in, keep your feet up and float. Do not try to stand — you may get caught in the rocks and drown in as little as 3 feet of water, under the rushing force of the current.

section of this chapter), picnic shelters, a ballfield, a swimming area and a boat-launch ramp.

Another good facility on the lake, this one in the Tusquittee Ranger District of the Nantahala Forest, is the Jackrabbit Mountain Recreation Area. It is on a pine-wooded peninsula that has three camping loops with 103 campsites, a swimming beach with shower facilities, hiking trails, two picnic areas and a boat-launching ramp. To get to the Jackrabbit Mountain Recreation Area, drive 2.5 miles down N.C. 175 from U.S. 64; turn right on S.R. 1155.

## Graham County

### Cheoah Lake
**Access along N.C. Hwy. 28**

This long and narrow Graham County lake is just a few miles west of Fontana Lake. Ly-

# Iron Foot Island

Iron Foot Island, Bryson City's 7-acre island park, is just downstream from the Cherokee's Old Mother Town of Kituhawa. Several Cherokee battles with other tribes and whites were fought in the island's immediate vicinity.

The most famous battle occurred in the 1700s and involved the Shawano, a tribe the Cherokees had fought for many years. A noted Shawano leader, Tawa-li-ukwanun, led a raid on the town of Tikwalitsi, near the present site of Bryson City, and a Cherokee conjurer named Dead-wood-lighter forecast that the raiders would set an ambush in the area of the island. Some of the Cherokee warriors took his advice and forded the river above the island and entered the site from the rear. But some didn't listen and went straight up the north bank of the river, where they were taken "like fish in a trap." After several bloody encounters, the Shawano were driven up Deep Creek and over the Smokies at Clingman's Dome.

Other skirmishes took place on and around the island during the Civil War. The most famous, known as The Battle of Deep Creek, occurred on February 2, 1864, when 600 Union troops crossed the high mountains in a daring surprise attack on Confederate Col. William H. Thomas' legion of Cherokee Indians. The Cherokee soldiers and their white mountaineer leaders "fought nobly until their ammunition gave out," according to press accounts. The Northern press claimed 200 Confederates had been killed, but the Southerners laughed and countered that they had killed 12 Union soldiers and had only lost five of their own.

But the island's most famous resident was called Iron Foot, because he had an iron stirrup attached to one foot. His real name was Ralph Clark, and some said the stirrup was to equalize the length of his legs, one being shorter than the other. Others said his foot had been shot off in a train robbery while he was with the Jesse James Gang. This made many local children apprehensive of the man as he clumped about the town and the river island, where he lived in an old shack. But Iron Foot minded his own business and most people thought well of him. Once, a flood caught him by surprise, and forced him up a tree; Neighbors had to send him food across the water on a wire attached to a limb.

When Iron Foot was dying, a man who went to help wrote that after Iron Foot's death, his belongings gave sure evidence "that he was one of the Jesse James Gang. He was the engineer when they took over a train. He recuperated from his wounds in Brazil."

ing tranquilly between steep green hills, it is reminiscent of a Scandinavian fjord. The water is so clear, you can usually see right down to the bottom. A turn onto U.S. 129 will bring you to the 225-foot Cheoah Dam that was built between 1917 and 1919 on the Little Tennessee River. In 1930, the Calderwood Dam farther down river in Tennessee formed Calderwood Lake, which is contiguous to its twin, Cheoah.

## Santeetlah Lake
### Access off U.S. 129 N.

This emerald-green lake in the center of Graham County is popular with both motorboaters and canoeists. Santeetlah has a reputation as one of the best bass-fishing lakes in the area, and pike and crappie are also plentiful. Three public boat ramps are located along its shores. A popular one is at Choeah Point off U.S. Highway 129N just outside Robbinsville near the ranger station (see the list of ranger stations in our Forests and Parks chapter). Choeah Point also has a campground with 26 camp sites, water, flush toilets, a picnic area and boat ramp. It is open from April 15 until October 31. (See our "Camping" section in this chapter.) To get to Choeah Point, take U.S. 129N for 7 miles, turn left at the sign and go 0.8 mile.

## Jackson County

### Lake Glenville
#### N.C. Hwy. 107

Lake Glenville Dam, four miles north of Cashiers, was built on the Tuckasegee River in Jackson County in 1941. It was renamed Lake Thorpe in 1951 after Nantahala Power's first president, J.E.S. Thorpe. Today, it's marked as Lake Thorpe on many, but not all, maps, but it's still Lake Glenville to most people in this area. The 6-mile-long lake covers 1,462 acres and offers 26 miles of shoreline. At an elevation of nearly 3,500 feet, it's the highest major lake in eastern America. Lake Glenville is a great place to cruise, canoe, swim, ski and fish. Mountain trout, walleye, brim, pike and largemouth and smallmouth bass are the fish you can expect to catch here.

Three marinas in the Glenville community rent pontoon, fishing and ski boats. These are well marked by signs on N.C. 107. The Ralph J. Andrews County Park (see the listing in the "County and City Programs and Areas" section above) also provides boat access to the lake. This reservoir is the source of water for a hydroelectric plant at the 1,200-foot level, said to be one of the highest facilities in the East. To visit it, turn off of N.C. Highway 107 onto Pine Creek Road and drive about 2 miles past the Ralph J. Andrews County Park to the power plant. The beach area near the dam is a favorite spot for swimming and sunbathing.

## Macon County

### Cliffside Lake Recreation Area and Vanhook Glade Campground
#### Access off U.S. 64 W.

Cliffside — a pretty and popular little lake in the Nantahala National Forest — is a great place to picnic, swim (the water is cold!), boat, hike and fish (mostly for rainbow and brook trout). Here you'll find 17 picnic tables, two picnic shelters, a bathhouse with cold-water showers and flush toilets and the Clifftop Vista Shelter.

There are numerous hiking trails in the area, including an interpretive loop around the lake. Cliffside Vista trail climbs 3 miles to an overlook of the lake. Tent camping used to be allowed here, but all camping has now been moved to the nearby Vanhook Glade Campground though campers may use Cliffside Lake and showers. (See our "Camping" section in this chapter for more information on the Vanhook Glade Campground.)

There is a $3 day-use parking fee at Cliffside from May 1 through October 31.

### Nantahala Lake
#### Access off Wayah Rd.

This large lake, which provides electricity for the Nantahala Power and Light Company, is in a remote area of Macon County reached by the paved-but-very-windswept, two-lane Wayah Road (S.R. 1310). The regular releases of water that supply the fast rides for rafters and kayakers on the Nantahala River cause the lake's water level to vary sharply. Nevertheless, fishing is good here. In fact, Nantahala Lake is the only lake in the state that contains

Kokanee salmon, a freshwater hybrid of the sockeye salmon. There are two public access sites: Rocky Branch, on the east side of the lake just off Wayah Road; and in the Choga area on the lake's western arm, off F.R. 440. There's a school and a volunteer fire department in the nearby Nantahala Community but no stores to speak of, so stock up ahead of time with what you need for an outing here.

## Swain County

### Fontana Lake
**U.S. 129**

At an elevation of 1,710 feet, this deep-water lake reaches 30 beautiful miles into the mountains, covering 10,530 acres when full. Much longer than it is wide (it has a 240-mile shoreline), Fontana runs east and west with the Great Smoky Mountains National Park on the north and the Nantahala National Forest on the south.

The lake was created in the 1940s by the Tennessee Valley Authority's Fontana Dam (see the Fontana Dam listing in our Attractions chapter). It's great for boating, water skiing, fishing and exploring. You'll find public boat launches on Fontana's south shore. There are also boat docks at the Fontana Village Resort (see our Resorts chapter), along with sightseeing cruises and boat rentals, including Wave Runners, bass boats, house boats, pontoon boats and ski boats. The lake is home to abundant smallmouth and large-mouth bass, native trout and walleye. You'll also find white bass, musky (some four feet or more in length) and a number of panfish.

# Whitewater Rafting and Kayaking

Western North Carolina and its adjoining states have some of the country's most thrill-

Photo: Mitchell County Chamber of Commerce

Whitewater rafting is one of the most popular activities in the North Carolina mountains.

ing whitewater. We've described some of the most popular rivers for rafting and kayaking in this section, listing them in alphabetical order.

Trips on all these rivers can be booked though any number of whitewater rafting companies that provide guides and instruction. Children must weigh at least 60 pounds before being permitted to raft (because that's how big they've got to be to fit into a life jacket safely). Some companies also rent rafts, canoes and kayaks and offer canoe and kayak clinics. Individual rates for rafting trips range from around $25 to $50. Rates are cheaper on weekdays and for groups. An overnight trip on the Chattooga that includes camping out on the river and four meals will run around $125. The following are just a few of the whitewater runners in the region. Some run trips in other states and other countries. (Also see our section at the end of this chapter for other outfitters, many of which include whitewater rafting in their services.)

**Nantahala Outdoor Center**
11044 U.S. Hwy. 19 W., Bryson City
• (828) 488-2175, (800) 232-7238
**Carolina Outfitters Rafting**
12121 U.S. Hwy. 19 W., Bryson City
• (828) 488-6345, (800) 468-7238
**Rolling Thunder River Company**
10160 U.S. Hwy. 19 W., Bryson City
• (828) 488-2030, (800) 344-5838
**Wahoos Adventures**
3385 U.S. Hwy. 321, Boone
• (828) 262-5774, (800) 444-RAFT

# The Rivers

## The Chattooga River

The Chattooga, made famous by the movie *Deliverance*, can produce some of the best whitewater in the Southeast and is one of our personal rafting favorites. Designated as a Wild and Scenic River by Congress in 1974, the Chattooga has its headwaters in the North Carolina Mountains and flows south to form the boundary between South Carolina's Sumter National Forest and Georgia's Chattahoochee National Forest. There is a 6-mile "floating section" from an access point on S.C. Highway 28 about 1.5 miles from its border with Georgia. This stretch

is also open to canoers and tubers, and, while it can be a real challenge, it's great for family rafting trips with children or for youth groups.

For a really exciting raft ride, ask about Section IV. You'll get great wilderness scenery, steep and technical rapids and frequent ledges and waterfalls, such as the super-rush of Five Falls.

## The French Broad River

The French Broad is one of the world's oldest rivers, and you seem to keep running into it or one of its many forks — including the North Fork, the East Fork, the West Fork and the Middle Fork — almost anywhere you travel in the valleys of the central mountains. It was not named, as some think, after a Parisian lady. The French Broad got its name in the 17th century when explorers realized that unlike the area's other rivers, this one flowed to the west toward the land claimed by the French. To the Cherokees, it was the "Long Man," and its many forks were called "Chattering Children."

Longer, warmer and wider than many mountain rivers, the French Broad offers rapids that range from Class II to Class V. How challenging the river is depends on the amount of rainfall and the season. High water and big waves occur most often in the spring and early summer; in midsummer and fall, it's usually a more gentle river that's better for canoeing and family outings.

## The Nantahala River

Because the Nantahala River is a controlled-release river from the Nantahala Dam upstream, it has usually consistent whitewater from spring until fall. Its clear and quite cold waters rush the rider for 9 miles through the spectacular Nantahala Gorge in the Nantahala Forest. This is one of the most heavily used whitewater rivers in the region, with a constant flow of rafters and kayakers who are fun to watch even if you don't care to join in the sport. Typical raft trips include Class III rapids at Nantahala Falls.

## The New River

The New River is one of the few north-flowing rivers in America. This river runs through the geographically remote Alleghany and Ashe Counties. Though one of the oldest rivers in the world, the New River was named by surveyor Peter Jefferson (Thomas' father) who was surprised to find this "new" river behind the mountains. The North and South Forks of the river flow over 100 miles through forested mountains and valleys. They join just south of the Virginia state line and the river continues through Virginia. Because of its scenic beauty and recreational value, a 26-mile stretch of the South Fork has been designated a National Scenic River.

The headwaters are shallow with a few mild rapids, allowing for easy paddling. This river is ideal for family fun — for large groups and less experienced canoers and kayakers. Tubing is great on this river; it allows you to meander downstream at a relaxed pace. Children love tubing and many outfitters can supply you with dual tubes, allowing mom or dad to share the tube with a smaller child. Fishing and swimming are also excellent in this river.

### The Nolichucky River

The Nolichucky River that runs through a gorge in the Pisgah National Forest in North Carolina and the Cherokee National Forest in Tennessee, has few rivals in the East during the high waters of early spring. Calm pools along the way allow you to catch your breath from some of the adrenaline-pumping rapids you'll have come through. The rafting season here is from March through October.

### The Pigeon River

The Pigeon River, in the heart of the Smokies near Gatlinburg and Pigeon Forge, Tennessee, has been considered a "dead" river for nearly 40 years, due to pollution and electric power generation. Now new regulations are restoring its health and requiring the power company to pump 1,200 cubic feet of water per second through the gorge. The upper part of the Pigeon offers exciting Class III and Class IV rapids; the lower section is better suited to the inexperienced and to families with children.

# Canoeing

Mountain lakes, including most of those mentioned earlier, are excellent places to go canoeing. Experienced canoeists also like to paddle the rivers listed under "Whitewater Rafting and Kayaking." (No canoeing is allowed, however, on the Chattooga until it crosses the Georgia-South Carolina line.) The New, Davidson and Green rivers are also popular, but the French Broad, along with its many tributaries, is probably the favorite and has been designated as a canoe trail by the state (see our French Broad River listing above). This river forms near Rosman, where the North, West, Middle and East forks of the French Broad meet; then it gathers force and, below Asheville, becomes a wide, sweeping waterway that at times can demand some solid canoeing experience.

If you are inexperienced or simply want assistance with your trip, several companies in the area are outfitters specifically for canoeing. Consult our "Outfitters" section at the end of this chapter.

# French Broad River Access Areas

### Blantyre River Park
**Old Blantyre Rd.**

This four-acre park that's on the western boundary of Henderson and Transylvania counties off U.S. 64 has river access and a canoe-landing ramp. Future plans call for picnic tables and an open recreation area.

### Buncombe County River Parks

There are several river parks in Buncombe County. South of Asheville, three parks — Hominy Creek River Park, Bent Creek River Park and Glen Bridge River Park — hug the French Broad along N.C. Highway 191 and offer easy access. The Ledge River Park is north of town off N.C. Highway 251. Water picks up speed here.

### Champion Park
**U.S. Hwy. 64**

You can put your canoe in at this park or access the river just west of Rosman, where U.S. 64 W. crosses the North Fork of the French Broad. These accesses put you in the quieter stretch of the French Broad as it meanders through woods and farms.

## Hap Simpson Park
### U.S. Hwy. 276

From Island Ford, it's 13 miles to this park, just south of Brevard. It's a small, pleasant park with picnic tables and river access. A 15-mile paddle from here will take you to the Blantyre River Park, mentioned earlier.

## Island Ford Access Area
### off U.S. Hwy. 64 W.

To reach this area 13 miles downstream from Champion Park, turn off U.S. 64 W. onto Island Ford Road just a short distance outside Brevard. There's a large sign marking the site at the bridge across the river on Island Ford.

## Tracking Station
### off N.C. Hwy. 215

During the spring and after a rain, sections of the North Fork of the French Broad are runnable but only by the very experienced canoeist. Cutting through a gorge on the eastern edge of the Nantahala National Forest, the trip is 7.2 miles from the access point by the bridge at the old Tracking Station just off N.C. Highway 215 (S.R. 1326) to the access point on U.S. 64 mentioned in the Island Ford description earlier. In that distance, the river drops 390 feet with a difficulty factor generally of 4 to 5 (two areas rate a 6). Before you attempt this run, make sure that the river gauge on the south side of the bridge at U.S. 64 is at least 3 inches above 0. You need that much water for a reasonably safe journey on the North Fork.

## Westfield River Park
### Fanning Bridge Rd.

There are plans to further develop this 19-acre park, which now has river access, a canoe landing camp and an open recreation area. Fanning Bridge Road is off N.C. 280 at the northern boundary of Henderson and Buncombe counties.

# Fishing

No matter where you are in the Western North Carolina Mountains, you're never more than a few miles from a fishing lake, a trout pond or one of our hundreds of miles of trout streams. However, with the exceptions noted below, North Carolina State fishing licenses and permits are required for all residents and nonresidents older than 16 who want to fish. Anyone younger than 16 may use a parent's or guardian's license. Licenses and permits are available at most discount stores, such as Wal-Mart and Kmart. The cost will range from $20 to $40 depending on the duration of the license and whether or not you are a state resident.

# Fishing in National Forests

Fishing in National Forest lakes is allowed year round, but fishing in the forests' rivers and streams is regulated and sometimes restricted. To fish in state-designated trout waters, anglers will need a North Carolina fishing license and trout permit. Streams located on game lands require a special-use permit as well.

Brook, brown and rainbow are the dominate species of freshwater trout in the area, and for management purposes, public mountain trout streams are designated as Wild Trout Waters (high-quality waters that sustain trout populations by natural reproduction) and Hatchery Supported Waters (waters that must be stocked periodically to sustain fishing and are usually closed in March). These are further classified as Catch and Release/Artificial Lures Only, Catch and Release/Artificial Flies Only and Delayed Harvest Waters. These designations are marked with specifically colored signs along the watercourses, but these colors can vary from area to area, so acquaint yourself with them.

Because regulations, including catch limits, change according to where you're fishing, it's up to you to know the rules. So before baiting a hook, contact the North Carolina Wildlife Resources Commission, (919) 662-4373, for full information, or pick up a copy of *N.C. Inland Fishing, Hunting and Trapping Digest* where licenses are sold.

## The Cherokee Indian Reservation

The Cherokee Indian Reservation has 30 miles of regularly stocked streams. State records for a brown trout (15 pounds, 8 ounces) and a brook trout (7 pound, 7 ounces) were caught in these waters. To fish in tribal water, you need no state license, North Carolina or otherwise. All you need is a Tribal Fishing Permit, available at nearly two dozen Reservation businesses.

The permit sells for $5 and is valid for one day, with a creel limit of 10. Permits for longer periods, such as three or five days, are also available. Children younger than 12 don't need a permit as long as they are with someone with the proper permit. Fishing is permitted on the reservation from a half-hour before sunrise to a half-hour after sunset. Most of March is closed to fishing with the annual season opening the last Saturday of March and continuing until the last day of February the following year.

Over 400,000 rainbow, brook and brown trout are added to the existing fish population each year, so some streams are closed on Tuesday and Wednesday for stocking. The reservation's "Fish and Game Management" brochure that is readily available almost everywhere gives the schedule for which streams are closed for stocking. If you'd prefer pond fishing, you'll find three well-stocked trout ponds on Big Cove Road in front of the KOA campground. A tribal permit is required to fish in ponds and streams.

### The Great Smoky Mountains National Park

The Great Smoky Mountains National Park has more than 600 miles of trout streams full

Photo: Cherokee Tribal Promotion Office

Thirty miles of streams, three ponds, and a regular stocking program make fishing on the Cherokee Indian Reservation in western North Carolina an angler's delight. Rainbow, brock and brown trout abound in reservation waters.

of rainbow and brown trout. Some of the more popular ones include Deep Creek, Noland Creek and the Oconaluftee River and its tributaries. Remote Forney, Hazel and Eagle creeks, all very good fly-fishing streams, can only be reached by boat over Lake Fontana, by horseback or by long treks through the park. In the park, you must have either a valid North Carolina or Tennessee fishing license; fishing stamps are unnecessary. Make sure you check park regulations at a ranger station or visitor center before you fish.

Possession of any native brook trout is prohibited. That's because that fish's range in the Smokies has declined by 70 percent since 1900 due to unsound logging practices before the park was established and from competition from rainbow and brown trout that were introduced into the waters.

## Trout Ponds

Other places where you don't need a state fishing license are the more than 35 trout farms scattered throughout the region. You can contact the North Carolina Agricultural Department, (919) 733-0635, or a local North Carolina Cooperative Extension Service for a trout farm brochure that lists the names, addresses and phone numbers of members of the North Carolina Trout Growers Association as well as a map to help you find the farms. Recreational trout fishing in these ponds requires no elaborate equipment, and there are no limits to the catch. Many places will clean your fish free of charge.

Rates at trout farms vary. You might pay $2 or $3 per pound or perhaps $10 per day with a catch limit.

# Hunting

Among the species of game available to hunters in North Carolina's mountains are deer, turkey, bear, squirrel, grouse, raccoon, wild boar, red and gray fox, rabbit, dove and waterfowl. The North Carolina Wildlife Resources Commission, (919) 733-0635, schedules such seasons as deer (bow and arrow), deer (gun), deer (muzzle-loading), black bear, squirrel, grouse, quail, wild boar and wild turkey.

To hunt in national forest game lands, you must have a hunting license and a game-lands use permit. A big-game license is required for hunting deer, turkey, bear and wild boar. Hunters entering game lands from the Blue Ridge Parkway must have a hunter parking and crossing permit, which is good for a one-year period and obtained in person from a park ranger (see the list of Ranger Stations in the Forests and Parks chapter). However, you must have a hunting license to get a parking and crossing permit.

Licenses and permits can be purchased at most discount stores such as Wal-Mart and at other sports-oriented places such as gun shops or camping supply stores. To help you with regulations, pick up a copy of *N.C. Inland Fishing, Hunting and Trapping Digest* where licenses are sold.

# Mountain Biking

Rugged root-covered forest floors, gradual but devastating hillside climbs, lush trails near rushing creek beds — this is the biking environment you will encounter in this region. Mountain biking is one of the fastest-growing sports in the mountains, and, while the

---

**INSIDERS' TIP**

The Sierra Club reminds its members that deer gun season (which usually runs from November to December) is the most dangerous part of the hunting season. Therefore, it's wise to stay out of both public and private game lands during such times. The game lands include the Pisgah and Nantahala national forests and the Shining Rock, Middle Prong, Linville Gorge and Southern Nantahala wilderness areas. Its advice: "Go to the Great Smoky Mountains National Park, where there is no legal hunting allowed. If you must go into the woods, wear blaze orange that is visible from all directions."

Nantahala National Forest and the Great Smoky Mountains National Park have their share of great riding trails, Pisgah Forest is gaining a reputation as the place to go for this sport. There are more than 400 miles of marked trails in Pisgah Forest alone, and the rugged and often difficult terrain on many of these paths makes them a sporting challenge even for the experienced biker. Not all trails, however, are that bad (or good, depending on how tough a biker you are!).

Some of the trails on our public lands are gated forest service roads that are closed to motor traffic and have good riding surfaces. Some are single-track forest trails with a great variety of rigorous turf. However, since such trails are shared with hikers, some of the more popular hiking trails, such as the Pink Beds Loop in Pisgah Forest, are only open to bikers from October 16 to April 14, when there are fewer hikers.

A list of biking trails is available from any of our national forest offices, and you can buy a number of good books on mountain biking that give detailed overviews of the trails and rate their difficulty. Some good sources are Lori Finley's series, *Mountain Biking the Appalachians*, published by John F. Blair, which covers the Highlands-Cashier and the Brevard-Asheville-Pisgah areas. One of our favorites is *Off the Beaten Track*, Volumes I and II, by Jim Parham (WNC Publishing, P.O. Box 158, Almond, North Carolina 28702, $12.95).

We want to stress that mountain biking is not a sport without danger. You should always wear a helmet, and when riding alone, always let someone know what trail you'll be taking and when you expect to be back. Jim Parham also stresses that you carry your bike over wet and boggy areas, stepping stones and steps and avoid skidding or spinning out on steep grades. Occasionally, trails can be confusing, so equip yourself with a good trail map, and take water along to keep from becoming dehydrated. Finally, watch out for and yield to the hikers and horses that may be sharing the trail with you. Be especially careful when going around blind curves.

Ski resorts are taking advantage of their slopes in the warmer months by opening them up to mountain bikers. Beech Mountain Ski Resort, (800) 468-5506, offers a variety of competitions throughout the warm weather and Wolf Laurel in Madison County, (828) 689-4111, is open most days during the summer and weekends after school starts. Call for exact times and an events schedule.

Some of the outfitters listed at the end of this chapter run bike trips into the mountains. These usually include the use of a 21-speed mountain bike, helmet and water bottle; an experienced tour leader; and transport service to and from trails. Half-day tours cost approximately $40; an all-day biking trip runs about $65. There is usually a discount when you bring your own bike, and group rates are available. Four days of touring — including all the above and accommodations, meals and more — will run more than $500. Bike rentals usually cost about $25 a day. Euchella Mountain Bikes give bike tours and can be contacted at (800) 446-1603, 488-8835, for Nantahala Forest tours.

# Rock Climbing

Rock climbing is not for the faint of heart, but for those intrepid few who have taken to this sport, the rewards can be exhilarating. North Carolina's mountains offer some spectacular granite outcrops, sheer cliffs and steep gorges that make for rock-climbers' heaven. Some of the experts even practice ice climbing in the region.

This high-risk sport requires knowledge, practice and focus. Bouldering, a good first start, allows you to apply climbing moves just a few feet off the ground. Anything more advanced should be done in the company of an expert rock climber.

The staff at a number of outdoor outfitters will lead rock-climbing expeditions to favorite climbing spots here in the North Carolina mountains (see the "Outfitters" section at the end of this chapter). Below we have listed several rock climbing spots favored for their ease (or difficulty, depending upon your experience). Obviously, there will be many more throughout the mountain region, so ask around, especially at the outfitter shops.

For rock climbers who want to seek out even more sites, we suggest you get a copy of *The Climber's Guide to North Carolina* by Thomas Kelley, who works at Black Dome

Mountain Sports, an outfitter. This company offers a rock-climb guide service too (see our listing of Outfitters at the end of this chapter).

# Northern Mountains

There are several climbing spots in the Linville Gorge area.

### Shiprock Mountain

Just outside Blowing Rock and behind Grandfather Mountain, Shiprock Mountain can be accessed off the Blue Ridge Parkway at Milepost 303, Rough Ridge parking area (do not park along the side of the Parkway). It offers a range of climbing for all levels and is a more traditional crack climbing area that does not require bolts.

### Table Rock

There are four access sites at Table Rock. To get there from Asheville, take U.S. Highway 221 N. to Linville Falls. At the Rock House Restaurant, turn right onto N.C. Highway 183, which turns into N.C. Highway 181. Follow the signs to Table Rock parking and picnic area. Paths will lead you down to the rock area. Another path from the parking/picnic area leads to three popular climbing faces: North Carolina Wall, The Amphitheater and The Chimneys. Don't try to climb around the waterfall, though; it's forbidden and dangerous.

# Central Mountains

### Devil's Courthouse

Off the Parkway at Milepost 422.4, this smaller rockface is a good climb for those just getting started. The climb is predominantly easy to moderate. Access is via a paved trail that leads up the mountain from the parking lot. Just before you get to the top, look for a rather obscure side trail that leads off to the right, travels back downhill through underbrush and ends at the base of the rock face.

### Snake's Den

Snake's Den is north of Asheville in Barnardsville. Take U.S. Highway 19/23 N. to the Barnardsville exit. Drive several more miles

to town, where you take the Dillingham Road to the right, a twisting, winding road that eventually becomes a graveled forest service road. Go about 5 more miles on this Forest Service road until you reach the rock face on your right, within two feet of the road. You can't miss it.

# Hiking

Hiking is a wonderful, easy, inexpensive way to enjoy the outdoors. You don't need much gear, and the rewards are priceless. Hiking, in its fundamental simplicity and solitary function, seems to evoke a primordial human connection with the forces of nature. Hiking in a peaceful wood with the gurgle of a mountain stream, a bird on the wing overhead, the comfort of a well-trod path and the vista before you, can have a profound effect on the human psyche. Best of all, most of our trails are easily accessible. No driving for hours; just a few minutes drive and you are up in the mountains ready for a few hours, or an all-day hike.

Here in the North Carolina Mountains, we are blessed with an amazing array of beautiful places to explore on foot. There's the spectacular Blue Ridge Parkway that runs almost the entire length of western North Carolina, and our proximity to major national forests such as Pisgah and the Great Smokies brings hiking possibilities virtually to our back doors. The Appalachian Trail runs right through our mountains. Numerous state and memorial parks in the region also have marked hiking trails. But be alert —the blazes on some trails are becoming faded and more difficult to see.

Safety should be foremost on your mind as you set off on a hike. Learn in advance about the topography you'll be covering, and let someone know your plans. Don't invite trouble: Hike with a friend. Be prepared with appropriate clothing and walking shoes or boots suited to the terrain, and take water and food along if you'll be traveling any distance into a remote area. Be aware of the sudden weather changes that can occur in these mountains. It's a good idea to carry a small flashlight and a whistle, in case you get lost. If you do get lost, stay put. Three periodic short bursts on your whistle will help alert others to your location (see our chapter on Outdoor Safety).

In this section, we point out just a few of the top hiking destinations, but you can find your own favorites by just heading into the horizon or along a dusty country road that runs through a forgotten wood. Numerous excellent books on the subject are available, including *Hiking North Carolina* by Randy Johnson, *North Carolina Hiking Trails* by Allen de Hart, *Walking the Blue Ridge* by Leonard M. Adkins, and *Waterfall Walks and Drives in the Western Carolinas* by Mark Morrison. And be sure an take advantage of another valuable resource — ranger stations in your area. (See our Forests and Parks chapter for a listing.)

## Northern Mountains

Hiking in the northern Mountains is centered around the Blue Ridge Parkway and the popular trails of Cumberland Knob, the 30-mile trail system of Doughton Park, the mist-shrouded trails of Mount Mitchell (see our chapter on Forests and Parks) or the family-outing trails of Moses Cone and Julian Price

memorial parks (see our chapter on the Blue Ridge Parkway).

Grandfather Mountain, near Linville, is another popular hiking area; a permit and fee are required (see our Attractions chapter). The 3,000 acre preserve is laced with 9 trails designated by the National Park Service as National Recreation Trails that vary in length and levels of endurance.

Glen Burney Trail skirts the cascading New Year's Creek in Blowing Rock as the stream falls into the John's River Gorge south of town. The 1.5-mile foot trail is steep — it descends some 800 feet below Blowing Rock — and provides breathtaking vistas of two substantial waterfalls: the 45-foot Glen Burney and the 55-foot Glen Mary. Take Laurel Lane off Main Street to the Annie Cannon Park parking area where a wooden trail map marks the trail head.

## Central and Southern Mountains

Even in the more urban central mountain region surrounding Asheville, there are plenty

Photo: Judy Scharns, Courtesy of Boone Convention and Visitors Bureau

A bright sun warms skaters at Appalachian Ski Mountain.

of easy-to-get-to hiking opportunities. Head out on the Blue Ridge Parkway where many trails intersect with parking and overlook areas, or stroll along the paths that follow the Swannanoa River on the Warren Wilson College campus just east of Asheville. The western North Carolina Arboretum also features many miles of wildflower-rich, wooded trails in its 426-acre park.

U.S. 276 from the Blue Ridge Parkway down to Pisgah Forest is a hiker's paradise. Some of the favorite trails originating off this highway include North Cove, Pilot Mountain, Art Loeb, Coon Tree, Looking Glass Rock, Cedar Rock and Black Mountain Trails. Stop by the ranger station/visitors center just a mile inside the forest's boundary for maps and information. There is also a 0.6 mile Pisgah Ecology Trail behind the center. For other great hiking trails in the central and southern mountains, see our "Three Famous Trails" sidebar in this chapter.

## Hiking Clubs

The North Carolina mountains have several organized clubs devoted to the sport of hiking and to maintaining the Appalachian Trail. Hooking up with one of these will extend your hiking experience and pleasure in the woods.

### Carolina Mountain Club
Asheville • (828) 667-1287

This venerable hiking club, formed in 1931, has a regional membership of about 468 from Buncombe, Henderson and Transylvania counties. The group has an extensive schedule of day hikes every Sunday and Wednesday and one Saturday a month. The club has also taken on the task of maintaining a 90-mile stretch of the Appalachian Trail. Retirees

and active professionals are among the club's members. The club's newsletter, *Let's Go*, is published quarterly. Prospective members must complete three hikes and provide two member recommendations. The membership fee is under $20 annually.

# Camping and Campgrounds

You can pitch a tent in the woods, down a creek prong of a wilderness area or within a designated forest campground here in the mountains of North Carolina.

## Blue Ridge Parkway

### Crabtree Meadows
Mi. 339.5 • (828) 675-5444

Seventy-one tent sites and 22 RV sites lie close to large grassy clearings. The lawn of wildflowers runs up to the forest edge, with mountains visible in the distance. The campground has the requisite picnic tables, grills, tent pads, but no showers. Water fountains and hand water pumps are centrally located.

This is a quiet, peaceful area awash with rhododendrons and hardwood trees and a good base camp for hiking in the Pisgah National Forest; trails lead to scenic falls on Crabtree Creek. Crabtree Falls Trail, a strenuous 2.5-mile loop begins near the campground entrance. A camp store, gas station, and restaurant/gift shop is also nearby.

### Doughton Park
Mi. 239.0

No reservations are needed here. It's first-come first-served; about $10 per adult, $5 for Golden Age Passport holders, and youths

**INSIDERS' TIP**

Especially if you are female, you shouldn't be hiking alone. Though rare, assault and murder on lone-hikers stories have made it into the headlines in the recent past. Take friends, or at the very least, a big dog, to enjoy the trail with. Let friends know where you are going, which trails you might be taking, and how long you will be gone.

younger than 18 stay for free. One-hundred-and-ten tent sites, including tent pads, picnic tables, grills, and lantern posts are scattered in wooded areas and around a grassy hillside. A smaller area with 25 RV sites lies across the road, though none of the sites have hookups.

Restrooms and water spigots are available, but no showers. This is camping as it was meant to be! The park itself covers approximately 6,000 acres in Alleghany and Wilkes County, and is the largest park on the Parkway. It was named after Robert Lee Doughton, a U.S. representative who served from 1911-1953 and who was an advocate for the construction of the Parkway.

### Julian Price
**Mi. 297.0**
• **(828) 963-5911**

Reservations aren't required for Julian Price. Like Doughton Park, it's first come first served; about $10 per adult, $5 for Golden Age Passport holders, youths younger than 18 free. This campground sprawls across both sides of the Parkway near Price Lake. One-hundred-and-twenty-nine tent sites lie fairly close together, divided by blossoming rhododendron bushes. Sixty-eight RV sites are also available, though with no plug-ins. Tent-pads, picnic tables, grills, and spigots provide adequate comforts.

There are restrooms but no showers; firewood can be purchased nearby. The Park is marked by mild terrain, covered by a dense hardwood forest. Poplars, chestnut trees, and maples make a pleasant canopy for hikers and campers. Canoes may be rented at the lake, and hiking trails nearby lead to two smaller lakes and creeks.

### Linville Falls
**Mi. 316.3 • (828) 765-7818**

Fifty-five tent sites and 20 RV sites are available in the campground of this 440-acre wooded park. Tent site 15 is the most secluded. The surrounding forest seems almost primordial with mossy-covered trees and waterfalls that plunge through the granite walls of Linville Gorge. Fishing in the nearby Linville River is allowed, and a visitor center and bookstore provides campers with plenty of area information.

### Mount Pisgah
**Mi. 408.6 • (828) 235-9109**

The entrance to Mount Pisgah Campground with its 70 tent sites and 70 RV sites lies directly across from Pisgah Inn on the Parkway. Small sites, close together are arranged in three landscaped loops. A dense forest adds privacy. There are no showers, but central hand water pumps and individual picnic tables, grills, and lantern posts are provided. Maps of the area, including hiking trails, are available at the camp. A picnic area lies in a meadow bordered by rhododendron.

# Great Smoky Mountains National Park

Of the 10 developed campsites in this national park, five are in Tennessee and five are in North Carolina. All have tent sites, picnic tables, fireplace grills and bathrooms with cold water and flush toilets, but no showers. There are a limited number of trailer sites but none of them have hookups. Sewage disposal stations are located at the Smokemont, Cades Cove, Deep Creek and Cosby campgrounds and across the road from the Sugarland Visitors Center about 5 miles south of Gatlinburg, Tennessee on U.S. 441. The stations aren't available for use in winter.

Three of the campgrounds —Elkmont and Cades Cove on the Tennessee side and Smokemont on the North Carolina side — take reservations between May 15 through October 31 and can be made by calling (800) 365-2267 up to five months in advance. All other campgrounds are on a first-come, first-served basis.

No more than six people may occupy a site (two tents or one RV and one tent). Group camping sites are available at Big Creek, Cades Cove, Cataloochee, Cosby, Deep Creek, Elkmont and Smokemont. Reservations at group camps are required and can be made by calling (800) 365-2267 or (423) 436-1266.

There is a seven-day limit at any campground between May 15 and October 31 and a 14-day limit between November 1 and May 14. Pets are allowed in the campground as long as they are on a leash or otherwise confined.

The following list of camping areas shows the number of campsites, fees per night, open/close dates and maximum RV lengths. To locate these camps, pick up a map or ask for directions at any of the park's visitors centers listed in our Forests and Parks chapter, which also contains additional information on The Great Smoky Mountain National Park.

## Abrams Creek
### Abrams Creek Rd.

There are 16 camping sites at Abrams Creek Campground on the northwestern edge of the park. It is reached from U.S. Highway 129 as it circles the eastern end of the scenic Chilhowee Reservoir in Tennessee. Some sites will take RVs up to 12 feet long and are open from March 21 to November 3. The cost is $10 a night.

## Balsam Mountain
### Balsam Mountain Rd.

When you camp here be sure to have a sweater handy even in the summer, because at 5,310 feet it's the highest and coolest of the Park's developed campgrounds. To reach it, turn off the Blue Ridge Parkway onto Balsam Mountain Road. Here you'll find 46 sites (some will take 30-foot RVs) and a ¾-mile, self-guided nature trail through alpine woods. Balsam Mountain is open from May 23 though September 29 and costs $12 a night.

## Big Creek
### Big Creek Park Rd.

This campground, which cost $10 a night, is just two miles off I-40. It has a ranger station, 12 camp sites and is open from May 21 through November 3. A very narrow, graveled, one-lane road leads from this area to the Cataloochee campground some 15 miles away, but should Cosby be full, don't attempt this road with trailers or RVs or in the dark. In fact, no RVs are allowed at Big Creek.

## Cades Cove
### Campground Rd.

One-hundred-fifty-nine sites capable of handling 35-foot RVs are available at this popular campground in Cades Cove, home to 700 people in the last century. (See our Forests and Parks chapter.) A few of these early buildings are still preserved, and the areas they originally cleared for farming are a wonderful place to spot all kinds of wildlife, particularly in the early morning and late evening.

This campground is open year round and the fee is $12 to $15 per night.

## Cataloochee
### Cove Creek Rd.

This is another campground in the area of two pioneer communities, Little Cataloochee and Big Cataloochee, that, with 1,200 people, was the largest settlement in the Smokies. Some buildings are still there (see our Forest and Parks chapter), and this area, too, is a good place to see wild turkey and deer.

The pretty campground, tucked into tall evergreens, has 27 sites and will take some 31-foot RVs. To reach it, take partly paved/mostly graveled Cove Creek Road off of U.S. Highway 276 for nearly 12 miles. We think you'll find the rather rough trip and sharp curves worth it. Cataloochee is open from March 21 through November 3 and cost $10 a night.

## Cosby
### Cosby Park Rd.

Even if you don't want to camp, this is a good place to go to hike. In addition to a self-guiding nature trail, there are trails that will take you through lovely woods and to waterfalls. (Ask folks at the camp office for some suggestions.)

If you do want to camp, you are likely to find room at one of the 175 campsites here when other campgrounds are full. You can reach Cosby Campground by taking U.S. Highway 321 and cutting south on Tenn. Highway 32. Turn onto Cosby Park Road. The campsites will take 25-foot RVs; cost is $12; and Cosby is open March 21 through November 3.

## Deep Creek
### Deep Creek Rd.

Deep Creek Campground, just outside Bryson City, rests on the site of yet another pioneer community and is a great place to go even if you don't want to camp here. It's only a short walk from the campground to Toms Branch, Juneywhank and Indian Creek Falls. In addition, Deep Creek is a popular place to go tubing.

The campground has 189 sites, some of which are suitable for 26-foot RVs, and the fee is $12 per night. In the summer, programs that are advertised on the camp's bulletin board are offered at the camp's amphitheater. The campground is open from April 11 through November 3 but is open to picnickers and hikers year round.

## Elkmont
### Elkmont Rd.

Elkmont Campground lies 1½ miles off Little River Road, one of the easiest (except for the traffic) and most popular drives in the Park. Early in this century, Elkmont itself was once a summer resort with dozens of cottages. Today it has 120 campsites, some suitable for 32-foot RVs, at $12 to $15 per night.

There is a self-guiding nature trail here, and park rangers offer programs for campers and noncampers alike. Elkmont is open from March 21 through December 1.

## Look Rock
### Foothills Parkway

Look Rock Campground, named for Look Rock Mountain, is a campground just off the Foothills Parkway. This is an 18-mile drive that follows the crest of Chilhowee Mountain between U.S. 321 and U.S. 129 on the western side of the Park.

Look Rock has 92 sites, some of which will take 35-foot RVs. It costs $12 per night and is open May 23 though November 3.

## Smokemont
### Newfound Gap Rd.

The site of this popular campground was once a small pioneer settlement and then a booming logging village. It was operated by Champion Fibre, which owned 93,000 acres of timber here prior to 1931. Today, second-growth timber has hidden old lumbering scars, but a stroll from the parking area will bring you to Mingus Mill, where corn has been ground into meal since 1886.

There is a short, self-guided nature trail along the stream in the campground that contains 140 sites, some suitable for 27-foot RVs. Smokemont is open year-round and cost from $12 to $15 per night.

# Backcountry Camping

A free backcountry permit is required for all persons spending the night in the park's backcountry. (Day hikers are not required to register or to obtain permits.) Backcountry permits are available at most park campgrounds, ranger stations and at Sugarlands and Oconaluftee visitor centers. Registration areas at ranger stations and campgrounds are accessible 24 hours a day. Visitor center registration stations are open from 9 AM to 5 PM.

# Three Famous Trails

Three famous trails cross the Western North Carolina Mountains.

### The Appalachian National Scenic Trail

This legendary trail runs through 14 eastern states from Mount Katahdin in Maine to Springer Mountain in Georgia and takes an average of four to five months to hike. As far as we know, close to 2,000 people have made this journey, but thousands of others have enjoyed shorter sections of it.

Almost 302 miles of the Appalachian Trail pass through our mountains. The trail crosses the Georgia–North Carolina line near Bly Gap in Georgia, runs through the Nantahala National Forest, crosses into the Great Smoky Mountain National Park at the Fontana Dam, cuts diagonally across the length of the park and weaves its way along the North Carolina–Tennessee border, exiting our state near Elk Park. It is blazed with white rectangles and a chain of shelters are spaced 8 to 12 miles apart throughout the entire trail.

You can access this famous trail at many points throughout its journey through North Carolina. Any good trail map of the region will show you where. You can also get detailed guidebooks at district offices or from the Appalachian Trail Conference, P.O. Box 807, Harpers Ferry, WV 25425-0807. For more information, call toll-free (888) 287-8673.

### The Mountains-to-the-Sea Trail

This relatively new trail, which was begun in 1985, will eventually run from Clingmans Dome, the highest point in the Great Smoky Mountains National Park, to the state's lowest elevation on the Outer Banks at Nags Head. This will be a travelway with various

— continued on next page

The Appalachian Trail crosses through Grassy Bald on Roan Mountain.

sections open to hiking, mountain biking, horseback riding and/or canoeing. It will cover almost 700 miles and is scheduled to be completed in the year 2020. However, 216 miles already cross our mountains from Blowing Rock on the Blue Ridge Parkway south to Balsam Gap, where the parkway crosses U.S. 19 north of Sylva.

This trail will take you through just about every ecosystem found in the Southern Appalachian Mountains, from high-elevation grass balds to cove hardwood forests and from mountain ridges to thickets of rhododendrons. It is generally blazed with three-inch white dots, except in areas such as the Middle Prong Wilderness, where routed wood signs point the way. Though mainly a foot trail, there are some sections open to mountain bikes. Contact the Pisgah District Ranger (the number is in our Forests and Parks chapter) for more information and maps.

### The Bartram Trail

From 1773 until 1777, William Bartram, a Philadelphia naturalist, traveled throughout the Southeast, writing exact and vivid descriptions of the plants and animals he saw and of the Native Americans he encountered. He published the writings in 1791 as *The Travels of William Bartram*, and they are still wonderful to read today.

Now, a memorial trail follows as closely as possible his original route across South Carolina, Georgia and the Nantahala National Forest of North Carolina. When finished, it will be around 100 miles long. The trail enters the state just south of Highlands, near Rabun Bald, curves in a north-to-west direction though Western North Carolina and will eventually link up with the John Muir Trail in Tennessee. Currently, it climbs from the Georgia line to the crest of the Blue Ridge Mountains before descending to the Little Tennessee River Valley south of Franklin. Here a canoe trail down the Little Tennessee River to Franklin is under consideration. At Franklin, it turns west and ascends the Nantahala Mountains to Wayah Bald, which at 5,385 feet is the highest point on the trail. It joins the Appalachian Trail briefly and descends to Nantahala Lake. Continuing mainly on private lands, it reaches Appletree Campground in the upper Nantahala Gorge then climbs up and over Rattlesnake Knob before reaching the "put in" on the Nantahala River. From the river, it ascends Tulula Gap and continues along the crests of the Snowbird Mountains. The trail has been constructed as far as Porterfield Gap, south of the Joyce Kilmer Memorial Forest.

To learn more about this trail, to order maps or to become a member of the society that is establishing the trail, write to the North Carolina Bartram Trail Society, Route 3 Box 406, Sylva, North Carolina, 28779. Maps are also available from the Forest Service.

---

Camping is permitted only at designated sites and shelters. The few backcountry campsites and all shelters require advance reservations. A Great Smoky Mountains Trail Map for backcountry campsite locations and information is available at visitor centers for $1. To make a reservation call (423) 436-1231 from 8 AM to 6 PM seven days a week.

For more information on the Great Smoky Mountain National Park, see our Forests and Parks chapter.

## National Forest Camping

Most national forest campgrounds have no hookups, but all developed campgrounds have at least one 25-foot parking spur, and many campgrounds have one or more campsites that can accommodate a large motor home or trailer that's 35 feet long or longer. Some sites provide pull-through drives. Primitive camps that are scattered all over the forests, including the wilderness areas, are for tents only. A few of those that offer some amenities, like drinking water, are listed below.

In addition to these listed campgrounds, there are also 10 group camps designed for organized groups of 25 to 100 people: Rattler Ford in the Cheoah District; Apple Tree, Kemsey Creek in the Wayah District;

Kuykendall, Cove Creek and White Pines in the Pisgah District; Silvermine and Harmon Den Horse Camp in the Appalachian French Broad District, Briar Bottom in the Appalachian Toecane District and Boone Fork in the Grandfather District. Group camps are available only by reservation through the district office where the site is located. (See our list of District offices in the Forests and Parks chapter.) The exceptions are the campgrounds located in the Pisgah District: Call toll-free (877) 444-6777 at least 10 days but no more than 360 days in advance for group camping and no more than 240 days in advance for family camping. The cost of a group camp ranges from $15 to $80. There is a $16.50 service fee charged per group reservation.

## Nantahala National Forest Camping

### Cable Cove
**F.R. 520 off N.C. 28 E.,**
**Cheoah District • (828) 479-6431**

Near Fontana Lake, this camping area that's open from April 15 through October 31, offers 26 sites, restrooms with flush toilets, a picnic area, water, fishing, trails and a boat ramp. The fee is $8 per night.

### Cheoah Point
**Off U.S. 129 N., Cheoah District**
**• (828) 479-6431**

At this area on Santeelah Lake, you'll find 26 sites, restrooms with flush toilets, water, a picnic area, a boat ramp, swimming, fishing and trails. It is open from April 15 through October 31, and the fee is $8 per night.

### Hanging Dog
**N.C. 1326 W., Tusquitee District**
**• (828) 837-5152**

A popular camping area on Hiwasee Lake, Hanging Dog has 67 sites, a picnic area, flush and vault toilets, water, a boat ramp, fishing and trails. The fee is $8 and it is open from April 15 through October 31.

### Horse Cove
**F.R. 415, Cheoah District**
**• (828) 479-6431**

Located almost 17 miles from Robbinsville

and open from April 15 through October 31, Horse Cove has 18 sites, water, flush and vault toilets, fishing and trails. The fee is $8 per night. There are also 5 sites open in winter at no fee, but there is also no water available at that time.

### Hurricane Creek
**F.R. 67, Wayah District • (828) 524-6441**

This is a primitive camp with undesignated sites and no drinking water. However, it offers vault toilets, fishing and horse and hiking trails. It is open from March 15 through January 1, depending on the weather, and the fee is $4 per night.

### Jackrabbit Mountain
**S.R. 1155, Tusquitee District**
**• (828) 837-5152**

Open from May 1 through October 31, this large camping area on Chatuge Lake has 103 sites and provides a dump station, a picnic area, flush toilets, amphitheater, showers, drinking water, swimming, a boat ramp, fishing and hiking trails. There are evening programs in season. The fee is $12 per night.

### Standing Indian
**Old U.S. 64, Wayah District**
**• (828) 524-6441**

There are 84 campsites at this campground located on the Nantahala River, along with a picnic area, restrooms, an amphitheater, shows, drinking water and hiking trails. Standing Indian is open from March 31 through December 1, and the fee is $10 per night. The charge for day-use is $2 per car.

### Tsali
**F.R. 521, Cheoah District • (828) 479-6431**

Made up of 42 campsites on Fontana Lake, Tsali has a picnic area, flush toilets, showers, drinking water, a boat ramp, fishing and hiking, biking and horse trails. Campsites are $15 a night. There also is a $2 trail-use fee in this popular area. It is open from April 15 through October 31.

### Van Hook Glade
**off U.S. Hwy. 64, Highlands District**
**• (828) 526-3765**

Since Van Hook is located just off pictur-

Photo: Cherokee Tribal Promotion Office

Crystal clear mountain streams make rafting and tubing popular summertime activities on the Cherokee Indian Reservation of western North Carolina.

# The History of Hanging Dog

The old community of Hanging Dog (you'll see a sign about 3 miles from Murphy when you travel northwest on U.S. Highway 64) got its name from Hanging Dog Creek, which was named by the Cherokees. One bitter winter ages ago when a failed harvest caused great hunger among the local Cherokees, only Deer Killer and his amazing hunting dog seemed to be able to bring down any game. But one day a buck, wounded by the hunter's arrow, fled across a creek. The dog followed, became hung up in fallen trees and debris and had to be rescued by his master. Once out of the icy water, the two chased down the deer and provided food for their village.

The creek was called Hanging Dog after that and its significance in history continued. In May 1865, Col. George W. Kirk's third North Carolina and Tennessee Federal Volunteers, whose assignment was to conduct guerrilla raids in western North Carolina during the Civil War, invaded Murphy and burned down the courthouse, a brick structure that had been built on the town square in 1844. (Many said the deed really was done by local ruffians and brigands in the unit who wanted to destroy the records of cases pending against them.) The Confederates, furious at this act, caught up with the raiders at Hanging Dog, and the conflict that ensued is thought to be one of the last battles of the war.

esque and popular U.S. 64 near Highlands and all its attractions, you might have to be a little lucky to get one of the 20 sites in this campground in high season. It has flush toilets, drinking water and hiking trails. Campers also have access to adjoining Cliffside Lake and can use the showers there. Van Hook is open from May 1 through October 31. The fee is $10 per night. Day-use at Cliffside Lake is $3 per car.

## Pisgah National Forest Campgrounds

### Black Mountain
**F.R. 472, Appalachian District, Tocane Station • (828) 682-6146**

This very attractive campground on the South Toe River has 46 sites, flush toilets, drinking water, an amphitheater and fishing and hiking trails. It's open from April 14 through November 1. The fee of $12 includes guided activities in season.

### Boone Fork
**F.R. 2055, Grandfather District • (828) 652-2144**

On Boone Fork, this 15-site campground

has a picnic area, restrooms, drinking water and hiking trails. Open from April 1 through December 31, the fee for the campground is $3.

### Carolina Hemlocks
**N.C. 80, Appalachian District, Tocane Station • (828) 682-6146**

Here you'll find flush toilets, drinking water, swimming, fishing, hiking trails and 32 campsites. There is also a picnic shelter that is available by reservation. The area is open from April 14 through November 1, and the fee is $12 per night.

### Curtis Creek
**F.R. 482, Grandfather District • (828) 652-2144**

This tents-only campground has no-charge, primitive, undesignated sites. There is, however, drinking water, vault toilets, a picnic area and fishing and hiking trails. It is open from April 1 through December 31.

### Davidson River
**U.S. 276, Pisgah District • (828) 877-3350**

One of the most popular campgrounds in North Carolina's mountains, Davidson River (situated along the beautiful river of the same name) has 161 campsites and is just 1.3 miles inside the Brevard entrance to Pisgah Forest. It offers a dump station, flush toilets, an amphitheater, showers, drinking water and fishing and hiking trails. There are also guided activities in season. It's open all year, and the fee is $15 to 18 per night. Reservations are available — and advisable — by calling toll-free (877) 444-6777.

## Lake Powhatan
### F.R. 806, Pisgah District • (828) 877-3350

This is another extremely popular campground on Lake Powhatan; it's less than 8 miles from Asheville and has 98 sites, a dump station, a picnic area, flush toilets, showers, drinking water, swimming and fishing and hiking trails. A lifeguard and guided activities are offered in season.

Lake Powhatan is open from April 7 through November 1, and the fee is $14 to $17 a night. You can also make reservations at this campground by calling (877) 444-6777.

## Mortimer
### N.C. 90, Grandfather District
### • (828) 652-2144

Mortimer has 23 sites, a picnic area, vault toilets, drinking water, hiking trails and fishing for a fee of $4 per night. In winter, there is no fee, but there is also no drinking water.

## North Mills River
### S.R. 1345, Pisgah District
### • (828) 877-3350

Located on North Mills River, this campground has 28 sites, a dump station, a picnic area, flush and vault toilets, drinking water, hiking trails and fishing. It is open from April 1 through November 15, and there is a 50 percent reduction in the $8 to $11 fees during the off-season.

## Rocky Bluff
### N.C. 209 S., Appalachian District, French Broad Station • (828) 622-3202

This campground on Spring Creek has 30 sites, a picnic area, flush toilets, drinking water, an amphitheater, hiking trails and fishing. It's open from May 1 through October 31, and the fee is $8 per night.

## Sunburst
### N.C. 215, Pisgah District • (828) 877-3350

Based at the site of an old logging town, Sunburst has 14 sites, a picnic area, flush toilets and drinking water. It's open from April 1 through December 30, and the cost is $7 per night.

# Horseback Riding

This is true "horse country." Beautiful horse farms — many specializing in Arabians, Appaloosas, Tennessee Walkers or other breeds — beautify our mountain landscapes. Riding stables and riding schools are scattered throughout. Many children have horses for pets instead of dogs or cats, and two horses in a pasture seem almost as common as two cars in a garage. "Watch for horses" signs dot the secondary roads, and somewhere in the region nearly every weekend, a horse show takes place.

## Where to Ride

Part of the reason for the popularity of horses here is that there are so many places to ride. In addition to private trails, fields and pastures, there are many quiet dirt and paved roads that are used for horseback riding. There are also designated riding trails in the Pisgah and Nantahala national forests and in the Great Smoky Mountains National Park. These are clearly marked with a horse sign, and you're not allowed on any other trails, though horses are permitted on many forest service roads.

The Tsali Recreation Area in the Nantahala National Forest (see our earlier information on Fontana Lake) is one of the premier riding areas in the Southeast. As of 1997, there is a $2 trail fee is charged. There is access to more than 18 miles of bridle trails, but be forewarned: Mountain bikes are also allowed here, and while hikers and bikers should yield to horses, riders should always yield to motorized vehicles. Meandering through pine and hardwood forests, the trails cover terrain as varied as wide-packed dirt paths and rocky ones that overlook the lake.

In the Pisgah Forest, two of the longer trails are the 12-mile South Mills River Trail in the Pisgah District and the rugged 18.4-mile Buncombe Horse Range Trail in the Appalachian Toecane District. The latter trail is suitable for overnight rides; on Community Hill, at 5,782 feet, you'll find a trail shelter with 10 wire bunks, a picnic shed, a horse corral and a nearby spring.

While most horse trails in the Pisgah District are for day rides or for primitive camping along the trails only, there is more developed camping at the South White Pines Group Campsite and the Harmon Den Horse Camp (tents only, open year round). See our preceding "Camping" section for more information.

# Rider Etiquette

To lessen the impact on trails, the park service staff asks that horseback riders travel in groups of six or fewer and that they stay on designated pathways, since cutting across switchbacks tramples plants and can cause severe erosion. Try to avoid tying your horse to a tree, but if this becomes necessary, use a rope or a tree-saver hitch to avoid damage. It's better to picket or hobble your horse, and move stock periodically to reduce trampling and prevent overgrazing.

To protect water quality, keep horses at least 200 feet from water sources and carry a water bucket and weed-free feed with you. Scatter manure and fill in pawed holes, especially when breaking camp. Horseback riders are required to yield to motorized vehicles, but bikers and hikers are supposed to yield to horses. Since trails are often narrow and some horses are skittish, it helps if you tell hikers where to wait while you pass.

# Riding Stables

Perhaps your involvement with horses only goes as far as wanting to take a trail ride. You can do that easily enough. There are many places in the mountains that rent horses, and most also provide a guide.

One-hour riding lessons cost between $20 and $30; one-hour rides are about $15 to $25; half-day trips are between $32 and $55; all-day trips range between $65 and $75; and a three-day, two-night camping trip by horseback costs around $300. Most riding stables are open from mid-April until the end of October. Most have age requirements for children. We've described a few of the stables in our mountain area.

## Northern Mountains

### Arrowmont Stable and Cabins
**1157 Pine Creek Rd., Glenville**
• **(828) 743-2762, (800) 682-1092**

Arabians, Appaloosas and Tennessee Walkers are featured here. There are five trails that offer a range of views, from mountaintops to picturesque valleys and streams. Lessons and a guide are included. The stables are closed on Mondays.

### Blowing Rock Stables
**N.C. Hwy 221, Blowing Rock**
• **(828) 295-7847**

Blowing Rock Stables is almost a mile outside the town of Blowing Rock in the northern mountains. Guided trail rides pass near Bass Lake and around the Manor House at beautiful Moses Cone Memorial Park. You can ride daily from April through December. The cost is $20 an hour ($35 for two hours) per horse. Boarding is offered at $300 per month seasonally and $250 a month yearly.

### Elk Creek Stables
**Elk Creek Rd., Boone**
• **(336) 973-8635, (800) 284-5542**

Elk Creek Stables located in the Leatherwood Mountains development 15 miles east of Boone on Elk Creek Road. Open year round, Elk Creek offers rental horses, boarding facilities and cabin rentals on 30,000 acres of land with more than 100 miles of trails. The cost is $15 for one hour or $25 for two. Day-rides are also available.

## Central Mountains

### Earthshine Mountain Lodge
**Golden Road, Lake Toxaway**
• **(828) 862-4207**

Earthshine specializes in two- and three-hour Western-style horseback and mule rides.

There's a two-rider minimum, a five-rider maximum, a minimum age of 12, and reservations are required.

Free corral kiddie rides are offered at scheduled time for guests.

### Etowah Valley Stables
**Brick Yard Rd., Mills River**
• **(828) 891-3340**

Guided horseback riding trips cost $50 a day or $15 an hour. Kids can ride for $10 an hour. Pony rides in a ring are available.

### Pisgah Forest Stables
**Avery Creek, Pisgah National Forest**
• **(828) 883-8258**

Explore the forest on half-day or full-day trail rides or excursions that last three days and two nights (four-person minimum). For rides of more than an hour, there is a two-person minimum. Reservations are required two days in advance. Children must be 6 years old to ride alone.

The cost for guided trips is $20 per hour.

### Pisgah View Ranch
**Rt. 1, off N.C. Hwy. 151, Candler**
• **(828) 667-9100**

Set in the shadow of Mt. Pisgah, this ranch offers breathtaking views and 2,000 acres of fields and forests. Horseback riding across this picturesque acreage is only $12 an hour for guests of the ranch and $18 for visitors. The ranch is open May 1 through November 1 and features delicious home-cooked meals in a large old-fashioned dining room. Reservations are required. Watch for the signs.

## Southern Mountains

### Cataloochee Ranch
**Rt. 1, Box 500, Maggie Valley**
• **(828) 926-1401**

Two-hour and all-day accompanied rides are available for adults and children older than 6. Reservations are required.

### Chunky Gal Stables
**10981 U.S. Hwy. 64 E., Hayesville**
• **(828) 389-4175**

This stable offers horseback riding, horse training, riding instruction and long- and short-term boarding. You can choose between one-, two- and four-hour rides. Arena riding is also offered for children and beginners. Chunky Gal is located 11 miles east of Hayesville.

### Fontana Village
**Hwy. 28, Fontana Dam**
• **(828) 498-2211, (800) 849-2258**

Horseback rides can be around the village (one hour), up a trail with lake views (1½ hours) or a journey to waterfalls (2½ hours).

### Hemphill Mountain Campground
**off Maggie Valley Rd., Waynesville**
• **(828) 926-0331**

Here you can get hourly or day rides, including trips into the Great Smoky Mountains National Park. There are also pony rides for children.

### Sapphire Valley Resort
**4000 Hwy. 64 W., Sapphire**
• **(828) 743-9574**

Sapphire Valley has miles of scenic trails, and trips leave on the hour at 11 AM and 12, 2, 3 and 4 PM. There is a minimum of two riders, who must be at least 8 years old and under 250 pounds. The cost is $20 per hour.

### Utah Mountain Riding Stables
**1200 Utah Mountain Rd., Waynesville**
• **(828) 926-1143, (828) 926-1740**

Explore hundreds of acres of trails on one- to three-hour rides. Children must be older than 5 to ride. Younger ones may ride double with an adult.

A one-hour ride is $12, 1½-hour rides are $18; two-hour rides are $30; and three-hour rides are $40.

# Clubs, Sites and Events

While horses are a part of the lifestyle in all areas of the western North Carolina, the heart of horse country is in the Central Mountain, particularly in Polk County around Tryon. In fact, it's the top area in the state for steeplechases and other equestrian activities. Below are just a few horse-lover activities. Check out our chapter on Annual Events and Festivals for others.

# Central Mountains

## Biltmore Saddle and Bridle Club Inc.
**Biltmore Estate • (828) 274-3757**

Since 1922, Biltmore Saddle and Bridle Club has offered members the pleasure of riding more than 75 to 100 miles of the hidden trails and venerable paths of George Vanderbilt's Biltmore Estate. This private riding club provides a 50-horse boarding barn, indoor arena, English riding instruction, jumping and dressage, horsemanship clinics and endurance rides. The club also actively hosts equestrian events such as the American Endurance Ride Conference.

Private riding lessons cost $25 per hour; group lessons are $20 per hour. Guided trail rides on some 100 miles of trail throughout the Biltmore Estate cost $25 per hour.

## Carolina Carriage Club
**Columbus**
**• (8280 894-5672, (828) 457-4038**

Anyone with an interest in the sport of pleasure and competitive driving may inquire about joining this club, which sponsors monthly pleasure drives and schedules driving and social events throughout the year.

## Foothills Dressage and Combined Training Club
**Columbus • (828) 863-4929**

There are no membership requirements other than an interest in the club's activities, which are devoted to promoting dressage and combined training. The club holds monthly mounted and unmounted meetings, has a drill team and sponsors several shows at the Foothills Equestrian Nature Center.

## Foothills Equestrian Nature Center
**500 Hunting Country Rd., Tryon**
**• (828) 859-9021**

The Foothills Equestrian Nature Center, or FENCE, presents over 18 various equestrian events during the year and provides interpretive nature study for adults and children

(see the FENCE listing in our Attractions chapter). The 330-acre preserve has equestrian facilities with stabling, a steeplechase course, three show rings, a cross-country course and access to the Foothills Equestrian Trails Association (FETA) trail system.

## Foothills Equestrian Trail Association
**500 Hunting Country Rd., Tryon**
**• (828) 894-5332**

Just to show you how big horses are in this county (and we don't just mean in hands), the equestrian industry contributes between $25 million and $30 million a year to the local economy. Not all that long ago it was possible for an area rider to follow a network of horse trails from Tryon to outlying settlements without crossing a paved road. But one of the very things that made this area so popular — horses — has helped destroy this trail system. As people moved in, the land was subdivided. The Foothills Equestrian Trail Association (FETA) was formed to preserve what's left of the network. It has obtained permission from local landowners for member riders to cross their property, and in exchange, FETA marks the trails with yellow diamond-shaped signs to ensure courteous use.

Membership in FETA is $50 a year for trail upkeep; the rider gets bridle tags to mark them as members. (Note: neither FENCE nor FETA offers horses for rent.)

## Green Creek Hounds Inc.
**Columbus • (828) 863-2171**

Green Creek Hounds promotes fox hunting and participates in horse and civic events in the Tryon area. The club was established in 1988 and is recognized by the Master of Foxhounders of America. The members hunt in Polk, Rutherford and McDowell counties.

## Tryon Hounds
**525 Racetrack Rd., Campobello, SC**
**• (864) 457-2346**

Recognized by the Master of Foxhound Association of America, this club was formed to participate in the sports of fox hunting, horseback riding, raising and breeding of fox hounds and the maintenance of trails and by-paths. Just over the North Carolina border, this group sponsors and participates in Tryon horse events.

### Tryon Riding and Hunt Club
Tryon
• (828) 859-6109, (800) 438-3681
For half a century, the Tryon Riding and Hunt Club has hosted the Spring Block House Steeplechase held next-to-the-last Saturday in April, and the Tryon Horse Trials, where horses perform dressage, stadium jumping and cross country in October.

### The Western North Carolina Agricultural Center
1301 Fanning Bridge Rd., Fletcher
• (828) 687-1414
There's a horse show here nearly every weekend, and most are free. The free shows start at 8 or 9 AM and finish around 9 PM. There is a charge for the occasional rodeo and gaited horse shows, which start at 6 or 7 PM. Admission for gaited shows is usually $2 to $5.

## Off-road Vehicle Trails

The late 1980s locked the Forest Service in conflict with the owners of off-road vehicles. Jeeps, four-wheelers, motorcycles and other all-terrain gadabouts were racing through the forests, creating erosion that polluted streams and endangered some trophy-trout waters, including the Lower Tellico.

Today, the Forest Service, off-road vehicle (ORV) owners, environmentalists and landowners whose property was being harmed have worked out a plan that sanctions areas for the sport and establishes rules and regulations to govern it. At this time, an individual does not need a permit to use an area set aside for ORVs (or ATVs, all-terrain vehicles), but that could change. A fee is charged for groups or commercial events. You don't even have to have a valid driver's license, but minors who operate these vehicles must be under the direct supervision of adults.

Trails in these areas range from a 15-percent pitch to a 50-percent pitch. You must know your vehicle and have good driving skills, and you should wear a sturdy helmet to lessen your chance of head injuries. Other tips for riders: Protect against erosion and stay on the road or trail, don't cut across switchbacks, and avoid wheel spin and wet trails. The following ORV areas are marked with symbols that show what kind of vehicles are allowed. Some old routes are badly eroded and have been closed to heal — don't ride on them.

### Brown Mountain
Brown Mountain has one four-wheel-drive trail in this area west of Lenoir. The other trails are open to ATVs and dirt bikes. There is no user fee.

### Roy A. Taylor ATV Trail System
This trail, in the Wayhutta section, east of Sylva, is open only to ATVs and dirt bikes — trucks and jeeps are not allowed. User fee is $3; a season pass costs $20.

### Upper Tellico
North of Murphy, Upper Tellico is open to all ATVs, dirt bikes and four-wheel-drive vehicles. User fee is $3; a season pass costs $25.

## Other Recreation

There are other things to do with your leisure time in the mountains, including some activities that could be considered a bit unusual.

### Airborne Recreation

### Mount Pisgah Balloons
1410 Pisgah Hwy., Candler
• (828) 667-9943
This operation began more than 15 years ago when ballooning was just catching on. Mount Pisgah Balloons, 30 minutes from Asheville, conducts pleasure tours over the mountains for around $110 per person. The company has found that hot-air travel attracts all ages: Its oldest balloonist was a local man in his 90s whose ride was a birthday gift from his children.

## Sky Tours
**76 Bear Creek Rd., Asheville**
- **(828) 251-5379, (800) 770-5379**

This Asheville-based ballooning service specializes in champagne balloon flights over the area. Weddings are popular in-flight events. Sky Tours hot-air balloon flights generally last an hour and are available daily (morning and late afternoon), weather permitting.

## Transylvania Balloon Rides
**40 Pole Miller Rd., Brevard**
- **(828) 884-5821**

To find the right conditions, most of these hot-air balloon flights begin just before sunrise or sunset, catching the mountains at their most spectacular. Flights usually leave from a field between Brevard and Hendersonville and last about an hour, often passing over Henderson County apple country. There's a champagne toast at the end of the flight, and each participant is presented with a flight certificate. The cost is $100 per person; the maximum capacity is two passengers and the pilot. They will also take on advertising promotions.

Transylvania Balloon is open seven days a week year round. Though summer is the busiest season, the visibility in winter is usually better.

# Llama Treks

## Avalon Llama Treks
**310 Wilson Cove Rd.,**
**Swannanoa • (828) 298-5637**

This unusual expedition service arranges one-day llama treks for groups of 6 to 10 people, two- or three-day wilderness adventures and other customized outdoor trips. Llamas carry all the gear; trip organizers serve up gourmet meals on the trail. Rates for one-day treks begin at $45 per person. Overnight rates run about $100 a day per person.

## WindDancers Lodging and Llamas
**1966 Martins Creek Rd., Clyde**
- **(828) 627-6986**

If you've never met a wooly llama, here's your chance! Soulful eyes, a dignified demeanor and personality make forming an attachment easy, especially during a long trek when the animals — much less damaging to the environment than other beasts of burden — not only carry your gear but become companions.

From April through November, WindDancers' llamas will tote the gourmet fixings for a lunch or dinner trek served by talented guides for $40 per person; an overnight adventure into Pisgah Forest will run $200 per person; three-day treks are $300 per person. Reservations and a four-person minimum are required.

# Bowling

## Tarheel Lanes
**3275 Asheville Hwy., Hendersonville**
- **(828) 253-2695, (828) 692-5039**

Western North Carolina's largest bowling center — featuring 32 lanes — is 2 miles north of downtown Hendersonville. It's a modern facility that also has a billiard and video game room, a pro shop and a snack bar. Tarheel Lanes hosts local, state and regional bowling tournaments. Summer hours are 11 AM to 11 PM; winter hours are 9 AM to 11 PM.

# Outfitters

The North Carolina Mountains are filled with recreation outfitters who provide services for outdoor enthusiasts. These services can be as comprehensive or specialized as you want, depending on the outfitter and what you want to do. Recreational clothing, customized adventures, specialty bike parts and canoeing supplies — these are some of the stock in trade at the region's outfitters, which are divided into two basic types: retail and full-service.

In most North Carolina mountain counties, you'll find retail outdoor outfitters that supply the fundamentals for fun but not guide services. These businesses have the gear for the outdoor types or people who just want to look that way. The shops can clothe you in sturdy foot gear, jackets, pants and vests to protect you from the elements, and they carry packs, from overnight frame backpacks to roomy day packs. Retail outfitters can provide hiking and camping food supplies, including a dehydrated five-course meal and the packable Sterno stove on which to cook it. And they have maps — detailed USGS topographical maps or basic day-hike trail maps — plus compasses and safety gear to get you there and back. Don't hesitate to ask questions. These people make a business of supplying recreation needs and can put you in touch with professional guides or just recommend a local day hike, fishing spot or swimming hole.

The popularity of mountain biking and river canoeing has created a demand for superior service and products for these two sports, and specialty shops have sprung up in some mountain counties to fill the void. These places concentrate on service and repair, but the owners, more often than not, know their merchandise from longtime experience. Rentals are usually also available, as are tours.

A full-service outfitter does it all, supplying everything from gear to guided treks. These businesses usually have top-of-the line gear, safety equipment, food supplies and major recreational vehicles, from bikes to kayaks. And a few even offer mail-order service. You get more than basics here: Your purchase can become a learning experience. For example, while you're being fitted for those incredible, molded rock-climbing shoes that seem to become part of your foot, you can get tips on top climbing spots. Or get advice on the best telemark skis and cross-country areas in the mountains. You can discuss the purchase of a kayak with someone who has taken one out more than once or select a pack sturdy enough to withstand the Alps. These people have been out there and can offer you expert advice and memorable guided trips.

But let's say you're one of those gung-ho, let-'er-rip outdoor types looking for a heart-pounding thrill. You can find instant gratification here with adventure expedition services. The primary focus is group adventure, often including the entire family in the white-knuckle thrills of whitewater rafting, canoeing, caving

or rock climbing, depending on the outfitter. Safety is given paramount consideration and detail. Gear is available as a sideline, or you can rent it for the trip.

Below, we've listed some of the well-known outfitters and adventure services here in North Carolina's Mountains.

# Northern Mountains

## Appalachian Adventures Rail Road
Grade Rd., off Hwy. 194, Todd
• (336) 877-8800

This company outfits for canoeing, kayaking, tubing and mountain biking on and along the New River. It is also a retail outlet for wilderness kayaks. Appalachian Adventures is based at an old train depot built in 1888. The landmark structure brims with a variety of gifts from the arts and crafts arena.

In spring, mid-April through mid-May, the outfitters are open weekends only. Beginning mid-May it's open seven days a week. All reservations require a 50 percent deposit. Call for a range of prices. Biking adventures take you through the back roads of Historic Todd and into green pastures, past old farms, and by the New River. The outfitters provide pre-mapped routes, ranging from flat easy to ride pavement, to more advanced rugged gravel and hilly terrain.

## Appalachian Challenge
## Guide Service
Hwy. 105 at Hwy. 104 and Tyncastle Hwy., Banner Elk • (828) 898-6484

This High Country adventure service assures you that "No experience is necessary." Experienced guides make the great outdoors accessible even to the novice adventurer. Excursions are designed for all ages, and safety is the prime consideration. These outfitters offer whitewater rafting down the Watauga River, French Broad River, and Wilson Creek. They also offer rock climbing and rappelling, backpacking and day hiking. They'll even pack you a lunch. Especially notable is the caving experience these folks will provide. The caves explored are in neighboring Tennessee and Virginia; this all-day adventure includes a lunch. Group rates are available.

## Boone Bike and Touring
**899 Blowing Rock Rd., Boone**
**• (828) 262-5750**

This full-service bike shop near Appalachian State University offers high-quality models, accessories, repair service and rentals.

## Edge of the World Snowboard Shop and Whitewater Rafting
**Hwy. 184, Banner Elk**
**• (828) 898-9550, (800) 789-EDGE**

Edge of the World guides rafting and canoeing tours on a portion of the Watauga River, in the northwest part of the county. They also supply caving and rock-climbing equipment. But here in the High Country of Watauga County, where skiing is king, no other outfitter covers the snowboarding scene as well as Edge of the World. The best quality equipment and advice are at your disposal here.

## Footsloggers
**553 W. King St., Boone**
**• (828) 262-5111**

This upscale outdoor retailer in downtown Boone is popular with both students and tourists in the High Country of the northern mountains. It carries a full array of high-quality outdoor clothing, hiking boots, rock-climbing and hiking equipment and camping gear (see our Shopping chapter for more details).

## High Mountain Expeditions
**Main St., Blowing Rock**
**• (828) 295-4200, (800) 262-9036**

For information and guide service for overnight camping, caving, trips, family float trips and whitewater rafting on the Nolichuckey and Watauga rivers and Wilson Creek Gorge, High Mountain Expeditions is one of the best places to go. When you stop for lunch, you will enjoy a gourmet feast by the river. All meals are prepared fresh daily by the Speckled Trout Cafe in Blowing Rock. They also outfit other popular mountain sports and offer kayak clinics, packages and specialty trips.

## Magic Cycles
**208 Faculty St., Boone • (828) 265-2211**

Magic Cycles is a specialty bicycle shop that also carries a large line of accessories. The staff repairs all types of bikes; rentals are also available.

## New River Outfitters & General Store
**10725 U.S Hwy. 221 N., Jefferson**
**• (336) 982-9193**

The historic New River General Store in Ashe County is the site of this well-known river outfitter, a seasonal adventure operation focusing on family tubing and canoeing along the New River. Camping and fishing areas are nearby.

## Riverside Canoe and Tube Rentals
**Garvey Bridge Rd., Chestnut Hill**
**• (336) 982-9439**

Riverside offers canoe trips by the hour, day, or weekend. Prices include paddles, lifejackets and shuttle service. Innertubes of all sizes are also available. At the facility itself, enjoy other recreation, including basketball, volleyball, and horseshoes.

## Rock & Roll Sports
**280 E. King St., Boone**
**• (828) 264-0765, (800) 977-ROCK**

Rock & Roll is a full-service bike and rock-climbing shop offering sales, service, rentals and tours. They also offer equipment for ice climbing.

## USA Raft
**off N.C. Hwy. 25/70, Marshall**
**• (828) 656-8148, (800) USA-RAFT**

USA Raft is one of the largest and most diverse professional rafting companies in the East. They run nine rivers in four states and have over 25 trip formats to choose from. But "big" doesn't make USA Raft any less personal than smaller organizations. On rafts or individual duckies, USA Raft allows the experience of the wild river.

Our all-day trip took us down the French Broad Section 9, which features two Class IV rapids and numerous Class IIIs. This thrilling

romp into the powerful and mesmerizing waters included a bus ride through winding mountain roads to reach our starting point. Experienced guides assuaged the fears of first-timers and educated them about the river itself. Wonderful catered picnic lunches, which we consumed in a forest clearing on the riverbanks, are provided on all-day trips. These master outfitters cover five rivers in our area: the Nolichucky, French Broad, Pigeon, Nantahala, and Ocoee.

USA Raft offers a variety of packages, such as Family Class Trips and Adventure Class Trips, that vary in degree of difficulty and length. It's on the way from Marshall to Hot Springs.

### Wahoo's Whitewater Rafting and Canoe Outfitters
3385 U.S. Hwy. 321, Boone
• (828) 262-5774, (800) 444-RAFT

Wahoo's — you can almost feel the whitewater spray in your face — is an apt name for this adventure-trek outfitter that emphasizes whitewater rafting. During the summertime, Wahoo's conducts rafting adventures down the Nolichucky River in nearby eastern Tennessee, several sections of the Watauga River, the French Broad and Pigeon Rivers near Asheville and the Ocoee in south-

eastern Tennessee which is the site of the '96 Olympic Games' canoe and kayak competition.

### Zaloo's Canoes
3874 N.C, Hwy. 16 S., W. Jefferson
• (336) 246-3066

Zaloo's is one of the oldest adventure operations in the High Country. These people know the New River like the back of their hand. For 15 years, Zaloo's has guided canoeists along the pastoral turns of the New River, one of the world's oldest and one of the few north-flowing rivers in America. Canoe season runs from mid-March to late October. Individual canoes and tubing rentals are also available.

## Central Mountains

### Backcountry Outdoors
U.S. Hwys. 64, 276 and N.C. Hwy. 280, Pisgah Forest • (828) 884-4662

This full-service outfitter is right at the Brevard entrance to Pisgah Forest. In addition to supplies, clothing and footwear, It sells and rents mountain bikes (front suspension), as well as bicycle accessories. You can also rent boats and get private instruction and guide service for rock climbing, mountain biking, kayaking, canoeing, hiking and whitewater rafting (for groups of 12 or more). In addition, Backcountry carries maps, will give you waterfall information and offers a drop-off service.

## B.B. Barns Inc.
**831 Fairview Rd., Asheville**
**• (828) 274-7301**

B.B. Barns is an upscale, outdoor retail shop with a quality line of recreational clothing. It also sells topo maps, books and some gear. The shop, which has a complete greenhouse, also caters to home gardeners.

## Black Dome Mountain Sports
**140 Tunnel Rd., Asheville**
**• (828) 251-2001, (800) 678-BDMS**

Black Dome is one of those shops that does it all. In operations since 1993, this outfitter store has an expert staff and nationally known brands of gear and outdoor clothing for mountain sports as well as bikes and kayaks. You can also make your purchases through the shop's mail-order service.

Black Dome's local mountaineering guide service offers an array of adventure trips throughout western North Carolina. Rock climbing is a specialty here, and the company's special-use permits allow excursions into Pisgah National Forest, not only for climbing, but also for caving, backpacking, and day hiking. Linville Gorge, Table Rock, and Wiseman's View are featured destinations. Also offered are guided flatwater trips for those who want to canoe.

## Blue Spruce Outfitters
**117-C Cherry St., Black Mountain**
**• (828) 669-6965**

This relatively new outfitter, 20 minutes east of Asheville, supplies top-name gear and is developing a guide service.

## ClimbMax Mountain Guides
**43 Wall St., Asheville • (828) 252-9996**

Obviously this outfitter's specialty is climbing. Experienced guides offer craggy rockface climbs to chilly ice cliffs. Climbing is taught in an indoor facility at the downtown Asheville location. Educational clinics and classes are

continued in the field for those who want to move beyond "bouldering."

ClimbMax offers customized guided backpacking, hiking, and rock-climbing trips to various destinations around western North Carolina. This outfitter reaches even beyond our borders, with trips to the American Northwest and volcano climbing in Mexico.

## Davidson River Outfitters
**U.S. Hwys. 64, 276 and N.C. Hwy. 280,**
**Pisgah Forest • (8280 877-4181**

Specializing in fly-fishing, this outfitter can supply all the clothing and equipment you'll want for this sport. The also have fly-tying material, rent fly rods and reels, and they offer fly-fishing lessons for $35 an hour. Guide services runs $20 for half a day for one person and $150 for two. A full day costs $175 for one person and $275 for two.

## Headwaters Outfitters Inc.
**Intersection of U.S. Hwy. 64 and N.C. Hwy. 215, Rosman • (828) 877-3106**

Headwaters provides canoeing, kayaking and tubing adventures. It specializes in trips on the French Broad River but will also provide canoeing on other rivers by appointment. A 10-mile trip for two people by canoe cost $36 and a 20-mile trip is $50; by kayak it's $20 for a 10-mile trip and $30 for a 20-mile trip. Expect a 10 mile trip to take three to four hours and a 20 mile trip to last six or seven hours. A favorite place to go tubing is on the North Fork of the French Broad. Headwaters provides a drop-off, and the lively, mountain waters will take you right back to their shop. The cost is $7. The company also offers a full-day "sea" kayak adventure on Lake Jocassee with an instructor/guide, transportation and a very nice lunch for $75. It can also arrange fishing trips, waterfall tours and other outdoor excursions. Headwaters is open from April through October.

## Hearn's Cycling & Fitness
**34 Broadway, Asheville**
**• (828) 253-4800**

Hearn's is a tradition in downtown Asheville. Since 1896, the name Hearn has been synonymous here with bicycles. From the turn-of-the-century elegance of bicycle touring to the mad dash and rugged individualism of mountain biking of a hundred years later, Hearn's has seen it all. This versatile shop has a wide variety of bikes, parts and accessories. They offer custom design and complete repair.

### Liberty Bicycles
**1987 Hendersonville Hwy., Arden**
**• (828) 684-1085, (800) 96-BIKES**

This full-service specialty bike shop is rated a Top 100 Dealer in the United States by the Bicycle Dealers' Showcase. Just south of Asheville, they offer sales, repair and custom frame work as well as a large selection of clothing, parts, accessories, maps and exercise equipment. The shop also rents mountain bikes.

### Looking Glass Outfitters
**U.S. Hwy. 64, 276 and N.C. Hwy. 280,**
**Pisgah Forest • (828) 884-5854**

Billed as an "outdoor shop," this store offers clothing, footwear and equipment for rock climbing, backpacking and hiking.

### Zippy Boat Works
**25 A Sweeten Creek Rd., Arden**
**• (828) 684-5107**

About 12 minutes south of Asheville is Zippy Boat Works, where you can buy canoes and kayaks. The shop also has rentals, instruction, paddling gear and guide books. In the business now for some 16 years, Steve Epps and his staff provide guided trips and paddling clinics on the French Broad River. The knowledgeable staff can also recommend solo trips to local lake sites and rivers.

# Southern Mountains

### Nantahala Outdoor Center
**13077 U.S. Hwy. 19, Bryson City**
**• (828) 488-6900, (800) 232-7238**

NOC, a long-established, employee-owned company, deserves its good reputation. The center can arrange food and lodging, provide canoe and kayak instruction, whitewater rafting, custom-designed programs, bicycle tours and rentals, and foreign and domestic adventure travel. It also has an outfitters store.

### Slickrock Expeditions Inc.
**P.O. Box 1214, Cullowhee 28723**
**• (828) 293-3999**

Slickrock specializes in recreational and educational backpacking, camping and canoeing trips in the southern wilds. The company's trips in the Southern Appalachians include North Carolina's Joyce Kilmer/ Slickrock Wilderness, Big Snowbird Wilderness, Bonas Defeat Gorge and Panthertown Valley. Slickrock also ran a number of canoeing trips throughout the Southeast, including ones in Georgia's Okefenokee Swamp and on the Big South Fork National River in Tennessee. The latest offerings are canoe trips on the Rio Grande Wild and Scenic River in Texas and backpacking trips in Oregon's Strawberry Mountain Wilderness. Trips are completely outfitted and led by a professional wilderness guide. Call or write for a brochure.

Ski resorts have learned to diversify, offering a wide variety of package deals, attractions, discounts and one-stop vacation planning.

# Skiing

It's been only 37 years since Western North Carolina's first ski resort opened at Cataloochee in the Maggie Valley area of Haywood County. That same year, Blowing Rock Ski Lodge became the first ski resort in the mountains' High Country. On its heels was Hound Ears, also in Blowing Rock, which opened during the winter of 1964-65, followed in the winter of 1966-67 by Seven Devils, now known as Hawksnest Golf and Ski Resort.

Beech Mountain Ski Resort opened in 1968-69, creating a new type of larger ski operation that would incorporate an Alpine village atmosphere. In the late '60s, the Blowing Rock Ski Lodge became Appalachian Ski Mountain. In the early '70s, Sugar Mountain Ski Resort, in Banner Elk near Boone, and Wolf Laurel, in Madison County about 45 minutes north of Asheville, were launched. Skiing in the mountains had finally arrived. Unfortunately, the industry stalled due to unseasonably warm winters and a downturn in the economy in the late '70s.

However, thanks to the latest advances in snow-making technology and some cold winters, skiers are back with a vengeance to enjoy the ski season, which generally runs from mid-November through March.

Lift tickets for area resorts usually run between $20 and $30 on weekends, depending on the resort, and drop by as much as $8 to $10 during the week. Ski rentals and lessons will add to that cost. Resorts have also learned to diversify, offering a wide variety of package deals, attractions, discounts and one-stop vacation planning. They also cater to newer trends such as snowboarding, which is currently taking the slopes by storm. Some resorts have incorporated snowboard parks to accommodate these slope surfers. Tubing, or sliding down a hill on a large innertube, akin to sledding, has also been introduced by several resorts. This is a great activity for the kids, and for folks who want to come along for the trip, but don't necessarily want to ski this time.

As families increasingly take more long weekend trips instead of lengthy vacations, these cool slopes within a few hours of most of Western North Carolina look extremely inviting. Cross-country skiing, another popular slant on the sport, is enjoyed along country roads and forest trails with every heavy snowfall. It's found mostly, however, in the High Country of the Northern Mountains, usually on restricted routes along Blue Ridge Parkway areas such as Roan Mountain (along the Tennessee and North Carolina border), Doughton Park (on the Parkway just outside the town of Sparta) and other Parkway links.

## INSIDERS' TIP

If the mountain weather fails to cooperate, and you find more grass than snow in the mountains on your trip, don't be disillusioned. The mountains in winter are excellent for hiking! Check with any local chamber of commerce or the National Forest Service for some easy trails, dress warmly and go out for a hike, weather permitting. The leaves that obscure many views in other seasons will be gone, and a frozen winterland can be yours for the viewing at the meandering pace of a hike, rather than a fast downhill run.

There's also some cross-country skiing on private trails at Beech Mountain Ski Resort. For more information on cross-country skiing, call the rangers' office of the Blue Ridge Parkway, (828) 295-7591.

# Northern Mountains

## Avery County

### Hawksnest Golf and Ski Resort
**1800 Skyland Dr., Banner Elk**
**• (828) 963-6561, (888) HAWKSNEST, (828) 963-6563 snow report**

This resort maintains 14 slopes: two beginner, six intermediate and six advanced, with a peak elevation of 4,819 feet. The vertical drop is 619 feet. Their newest slope, Top Gun, a.k.a. Ski Challenge of the South, is reported to be the best new slope in the Southeast. Two double chair lifts and two surface lifts get you to the top. The facility offers a restaurant and lounge, cafeteria, lockers, equipment and clothing rentals, ski lessons and a snowboard park. Kiddy Hawk is a great program available for children ages 5 to 12. Nighthawk, however, is way past their bedtime; this program gives avid skiers the opportunity to ski under the stars on Friday and Saturday until 2 AM. On these evenings, live music entertains guests in The Nest lounge. Discount rates are available for groups of 20 or more.

### Sugar Mountain Ski Resort
**1009 Sugar Mtn. Dr., Banner Elk**
**• (828) 898-4521,**
**(800) SUGARMT after Nov.**

Sugar Mountain Ski Resort sits at 5,300 feet above sea level. Among the 20 slopes at Sugar are seven beginner, ten intermediate and three expert runs. The vertical drop is 1,200 feet. The mountain is serviced by five chair lifts and three surface lifts. Sugar Bears is Sugar Mountain's ski program for children. The resort also offers equipment rentals, ski lessons, a tubing run, lockers, a nursery, a

game room, two cafeterias, a lounge restaurant, a deck grill, and a club called The Last Run Lounge. The resort offers discounts for groups of 15 or more. To get to Sugar Mountain, follow N.C. Highway 105 N. to N.C. Hwy. 184; after 1½ miles you will reach the turn for the resort.

## Madison County

### Wolf Laurel
**Wolf Laurel Rd., Rt. 3, Mars Hill**
**• (828) 689-4111, (800) 817-4111 (after Nov. 1)**

Wolf Laurel is just north of Asheville, a drive of about 40 minutes via U.S. Highway 19/23. The highways split about 20 miles from Asheville; follow U.S. 23 north and watch for signs that lead to the Rt. 3 (Wolf Laurel Rd.) turn-off.

www.insiders.com
See this and many other Insiders' Guide® destinations online.
Visit us today!

This resort is the newest of Western North Carolina's ski areas. Students from nearby Mars Hill College find it a convenient alternative to the resorts farther north, as do a number of Asheville's city dwellers.

The Wolf offers 54 acres of skiable terrain, in the form of 16 slopes, for beginners as well as more advanced skiers. Elevation is 4,600 feet, with a vertical drop of 650 feet. Three lifts and one high-speed, quad chair lift service the mountain. Ski lessons are offered hourly every day until 7 p.m. The lodge provides a ski shop, clothing and equipment rentals and a grill. Snow tubing has taken the Wolf by storm and the new Snow Tubing Park allows for all day and evening tubing. Even better, tubers don't have to hike back up the hill, but rather can hook their tubes up to a lift and ride their tubes back to the top, while enjoying the view. Lessons, season passes, discount packages, night skiing and a children's Wolf Cub program (for children 5-7) are also offered at Wolf Laurel.

Accommodations are available at the Wolf Cave Inn, within walking distance of the slopes. Special packages and group rates are available.

# Watauga County

## Appalachian Ski Mountain
**940 Ski Mountain Rd.,
Blowing Rock • (828) 295-7828,
(800) 322-2373, (828) 295-7828
(snow report)**

This family-owned ski resort, begun in 1962, continues to be a popular destination for vacationers. Appalachian Ski Mountain offers nine slopes: two beginner, four intermediate and three advanced, with a peak elevation of 4,000 feet. The vertical drop is 365 feet. You can get up the hill on two quad chairlifts, one double chairlift, one rope tow and one handle-pull tow.

A Bavarian-style 45,000 square foot lodge with a giant fireplace overlooks the slopes, housing a cafeteria, ski shop and gift shop. A 200-foot observation deck allows for generous views. Lockers and clothing and equipment rentals are available, as are adult lessons and a SKIwee instruction program for youngsters 4 to 12.

The second weekend in December marks Appalachian Ski Mountain's anniversary, which is always celebrated with 1962-vintage ski rates — bargains in anybody's book. Appalachian is also the home of the French-Swiss Ski College, one of the finest ski schools in the country.

Another fun celebration at Ski Mountain is the New Year's Eve fireworks display against the backdrop of a snow-covered slope. Two recent additions to the fun are the refrigerated outdoor ice skating arena and snow skating. Billed as America's newest winter sport, snow skating uses shoes with ski-like bottoms for skating or skiing down the slopes.

The only in-season closing times for the slopes are Christmas Eve night and all day on Christmas. The ice skating arena is open from Thanksgiving until the end of the ski sea-

Photo: Judy Scharns, Courtesy of Boone Convention and Visitors Bureau

Hitting the slopes at Appalachian Ski Mountain.

son, including Christmas. And on Valentine's night, after skiing, a grand fireworks display takes place. Group rates for 15 or more people are available upon request. The reservations department can book skiing and lodging for you.

To get to Appalachian Ski Mountain, take U.S. Highway 221/321 from Blowing Rock to Boone. You'll see a sign for the resort about 1.5 miles onto U.S. 221/321. Turn here on to Edmisten Rd. and drive 2 miles to the resort.

### Beech Mountain Ski Resort
1007 Beech Mountain Pkwy.,
Beech Mountain
• (828) 387-2011, (800) 438-2093

At 5,505 feet above sea level, Beech Mountain is the highest ski area in eastern North America. Established in 1969, the ski resort provides the complete winter sport experience from A to Z. Central to the resort is Beech Tree Village, a complex of facilities designed to anticipate the skier's every need. Its shops and services include equipment and clothing rentals, several gift shops, ski schools, a variety of restaurants, a nursery, video game facility, ski lessons, ski patrol and even an outdoor ice skating rink.

Beech Mountain has 14 slopes: three beginner, seven intermediate and four advanced. The vertical drop measures 830 feet. The mountain is serviced by one high-speed detachable quad chair lift, one J-bar and one rope tow, and every slope is within reach of the snow-making machines. A half-pipe run designed for snowboards was recently added along with snowboard rentals.

Through the resort rental offices, a variety of accommodations are available, including 650 privately owned townhomes and chalets,

four inns and a bed and breakfast. You can come to Beech Mountain for your vacation and never have to leave the resort. Multi-day packages and group rates are available.

# Southern Mountains

## Haywood County

### Cataloochee Ski Area
Ranch Rd., Maggie Valley
• (828) 926-0285, (800) 768-3588,
(800) 768-0285 snow report

Cataloochee, North Carolina's first ski resort, has long been one of the region's favorites. Its mile-high location provides fine conditions for making and keeping snow. "Omigosh," the area's longest advanced slope, plummets 2,200 feet from the very top of 5,400-foot-tall Moody Top Mountain and joins up with the 1,800-foot "Lower Omigosh," an intermediate slope. These along with seven other advanced, intermediate and beginner runs offer skiers plenty of options to match their skills. There are two double chair lifts and one surface lift, and night skiing is offered from Tuesday through Saturday. Snowboarding began at Cataloochee in 1984. There are now nine trails, and snowboard clinics are offered seven days a week, five times a day.

You can contact Cataloochee for discounted stay-and-ski packages with accommodations in the Maggie Valley area. After working up an appetite on the slopes, the lodge provides hot, home-cooked meals, or you can enjoy a toddy around the circular fireplace or on the deck that overlooks the ski runs.

### INSIDERS' TIP

If you are hitting the slopes near or on Beech Mountain and need to get away from the loud, post-skiing beer and burger crowd, take a peek into Jackalope's View Restaurant. It is not only a fine dining place, but also has an intimate bar with a familiar, friendly atmosphere. Make reservations for dinner, but if you desire a glass of quality wine, a cocktail or perhaps a plate of exquisitely prepared appetizers, stop in the cozy bar around dinner time. See our Restaurants chapter for more info.

# Jackson County

## Sapphire Valley Ski Area
**4350 Hwy. 64 W., Cashiers**
**• (828) 743-1164, (828) 743-1164**

Sapphire Valley Resort, which bills itself as "a resort for all seasons," has its own ski area for its property owners and resort guests, in addition to such outdoor sports as golf, tennis, horseback riding, canoeing, fishing, swimming and hiking. The ski area is composed of a novice hill with a rope tow and intermediate and advanced slopes served by a chair lift. There's a base lodge that contains a ski shop and rental shop; a ski school is housed in a separate building. Night skiing is available but cross country skiing is not. Snowboarding came to Sapphire in 1995 with two trails and clinics available. After a workout on the slopes, skiers can relax at the resort's health club with its indoor pool, Jacuzzi and sauna.

# Macon County

## Scaly Mountain Ski Area
**7420 Dillard Rd., Scaly Mountain**
**• (828) 526-3737 or (800) 929-SNOW**

The southernmost of the state's ski areas sits a few miles south of Highlands on N.C. Highway 106. Its elevations range from 3,800 feet to 4,025 feet. We think Scaly is perfect for beginners and children. In fact, at 1,800 feet, its beginners slope is actually its longest. The intermediate slope is 1,600 feet long, and Scaly's advanced slope, which makes up in steepness what it lacks in length, is only 1,200 feet. Served by one chair lift and a rope tow, these slopes are lighted for night skiing from Thursday through Saturday. Snowboarders will find four trails for their use, and clinics are available. Snowtubing is allowed Thursday through Sunday.

Though rates are subject to change, they're moderate when compared to many other areas and even cheaper when scheduled by a group of 25 or more. You can also get a good price by buying a rental equipment, instruction and lift-ticket package. Designed with families in mind, Scaly Mountain's lodge, which contains a huge, custom-made wood-burning stove, has windows that allow parents to keep an eye on the kids no matter which slope they are skiing. There is also a deck for outdoor viewing and a cafeteria for warm drinks and food.

During the dog days of summer, you can head for one of our higher-altitude courses for a decided drop in degrees. Later in the year, if a particular day seems too chilly for a game, you can play one of the courses in the warmer Thermal Belt.

# Golf

Cool summers and mild winters divided by long, rejuvenating springs and lingering, colorful autumns make "mountain golf," as it's commonly called here, a year-round pleasure. During the dog days of summer, you can head for one of the higher-altitude courses — up at 3,000 feet or more — for a decided drop in degrees. Or later in the year, if a particular day seems too chilly for a game, you can play one of the courses in the warmer Thermal Belt down around Tryon in Polk County, where the elevation is only 1,100 feet.

Wherever you play, you'll be surrounded by beauty and challenged by courses sculpted around undulating hills, deep mountain valleys, rivers, lakes, waterfalls and majestic rock formations, all kept lusciously green by some 50 inches of rainfall spread relatively evenly throughout the year. Because of the hilly nature of many of the courses, golf carts are popular. Some courses require them.

There are dozens of public, semipublic, resort and private courses scattered around the region. Some resort courses are open only to guests, but many offer reasonably priced golf packages that include accommodations and, often, meals. Others are open to the general public, but most require advance reservations. Here we give you a taste of the variety offered at our favorite courses that allow some public play.

Contact the Great Smoky Mountains Golf Association, P.O. Box 18556, Asheville, North Carolina 28801, or the chambers of commerce of individual western North Carolina counties for more detailed information.

# Northern Mountains

## Alleghany County

### New River Golf and Country Club
**611 Golf Course Rd., Sparta**
**• (336) 372-4869**

This 18-hole, par 71 rolling terrain course features front and back nines as different as night and day. The front nine is like a flatland course whereas the back nine is a true mountain course, with many hills. Yardages are 5601 and 5741 (women's and men's tees). The club is open to the public daily, and greens fees are $20 weekdays and $26 weekends, including cart. To get here, turn at the sign after Twin Oaks General Store on U.S. Highway 221.

## Ashe County

### Mountain Aire Golf Club
**1104 Golf Course Rd., West Jefferson**
**• (336) 877-4716**

This well-established public course offers 18 holes on well-maintained fairways complemented by the natural, rugged beauty of the Appalachian Mountains. Greens fees range from $28 to $32 per person including cart. Amenities include carts, club rentals and a driving range. Lessons and seasonal memberships are available, as are group rates. The club pro is Mark Hagel. The developers

---

**INSIDERS' TIP**

**Does your golf game improve in the mountains? Some players swear their shots travel higher and further here due to the thinner atmosphere.**

here also offer homesites in an adjacent golf course community called Fairway Ridge (see our Real Estate chapter).

# Avery County

## Blue Ridge Country Club
**U.S. 221 N., Linville Falls • (828) 756-7001**

This two-year-old semiprivate Championship Golf Course sits in a beautiful valley with wonderful mountain views. Four tee boxes allow for various skill levels and playing options. Yardage for this challenging mountain course ranges from 4800 to 6900. The course features subtle elevation changes, gentle terrain, and mountain vistas. Ongoing development is enhancing the course's lovely North Cove Valley location. It costs $39 to play on Mondays through Fridays and $48 to play on the weekend. The costs include carts.

Memberships are available. The Lodge at Blue Ridge operates as a 12-suite facility with all rooms including a private riverfront deck and a stone fireplace. Conference rooms are also available.

## Hawksnest Golf and Ski Resort
**1800 Skyland Dr., Banner Elk • (828) 963-6561**

Located off N.C. Highway 105, Hawksnest Golf Course is nestled high in the Blue Ridge Mountains. This par 72 course with large bentgrass greens offers the challenge of a true mountain course to golfers of all abilities. The thrill of playing this championship course is surpassed only by the majestic views from every hole (and the cool high-country weather). Facilities also include a well-stocked golf shop and full-service snack bar.

Yardage is 4799 and 5953. Weekend play costs $36 before 2 PM and $22 after; weekday play costs $20 before 2 PM and $34 after.

# McDowell County

## Old Fort Golf Course
**off I-40, Old Fort • (828) 668-4256**

This nine-hole, semiprivate course, established in 1962, lies southeast of Old Fort and is easily accessed off Interstate 40. This rolling course has a small lake, a few streams and a difficult dogleg on the third hole. The facility contains a driving range, pro shop and snack bar. Individual yearly memberships are available for $300; couples pay $375. Public greens fees are $12 and $16 for weekends and holidays. These fees are good for up to 27 holes of play.

# Madison County

## Wolf Laurel Resort
**Rt. 3, Mars Hill • (828) 689-9777, (800) 221-0409**

Wolf Laurel Resort offers an 18-hole championship course adjacent to "Ski the Wolf." Just 35 minutes north of Asheville, it offers many extras: a clubhouse and conference facility, pool, tennis, dining, putting greens and a croquet lawn. The course offers magnificent views. Golf and ski packages are available.

Wolf Laurel is on Route 3, 10 miles north on U.S. Highway 23 from the U.S. 19/23 divide. Costs are $40 per person and $15 for cart rental (which is a must).

# Mitchell County

## Grassy Creek Golf Club
**101 Golf Course Rd., Spruce Pine • (828) 765-7436**

This semiprivate championship 18-hole, par 72 course is just 4 miles from the Blue

---

**INSIDERS' TIP**

North Carolina rates second only to Florida in the number of deaths caused by lightning. It's not that we get more strikes than other states; it's just that people here don't seem to respect lightning as much as they should. So take shelter at the first approach of a thunderstorm — but do it indoors, not under a tree.

Scenic backdrops like this one make Asheville a golfer's paradise.

Ridge Parkway. A new 8,000-square-foot clubhouse includes a restaurant, meeting space and pro shop. There is also a driving range on site. Greens fees are $35 weekdays and $39 weekends and includes carts. Yardage is 6267 and 5773.

## Watauga County

### Boone Golf Club
**Fairway Dr. off U.S. Hwy. 321, Boone • (828) 264-8760**

This 18-hole course designed by Ellis Maples is a par 71. Level and gently rolling fairways and large bentgrass greens are features. Yardage is 6400. The club is open daily to the public and features electric carts and a restaurant.

Monday through Thursday, costs are $37; during the weekends, it costs $42 in the low season. Memorial Day through Labor Day, those costs change to $43 and $48, respectively, and include carts.

### Willow Creek Golf Course
**Bear Creek Rd., Boone • (828) 963-6865**

This challenging nine-hole, par 27 course is set in a valley. The course features a great deal of variety and offers senior citizens and student discounts during weekdays. Yardage is 1351 and 1574.

The golf course is 3 miles outside Boone, coming from Banner Elk on N.C. 105. Nine holes cost $8.50 walking, and 18 holes cost $14. With a cart, the costs are $13 and $21, respectively.

## Yancey County

### Mount Mitchell Golf Club
**7590 Hwy. 80 S., Burnsville • (828) 675-5454, (828) 675-4923 rentals**

This perfect vacation course is cradled in the valley below Mount Mitchell, the highest peak east of the Mississippi. Vacation rentals — privately owned houses and townhouses — are available around the perimeter of the course. Renters pay $42 weekdays for greens fees and cart rental. Regular greens fees are $48 weekdays and $59 weekends and holidays. This fee includes a cart. It is a lovely, scenic location. Yardage ranges from 5500 to 6500.

# Central Mountains

## Buncombe County

### Black Mountain Golf Course
**17 Ross St., Black Mountain**
**• (828) 669-2710**

This public course, operated by the Town of Black Mountain, about 20 minutes east of Asheville, boasts one of the country's longest par 6 holes at 747 yards. The course offers not only challenging fairways but marvelous views of the surrounding mountains. The quaint town of Black Mountain, noted for its antique shops, restaurants and musical tradition, is nearby.

Greens fees are $25 and $30, including the cart, for weekdays and weekends, respectively. This friendly, community golf course offers a multitude of discounts for senior citizens, Black Mountain residents, junior golfers (18 and younger whose parents are not members) and families. A pro shop and snack bar are also available.

### Brookwood Golf Course
**Mills Gap Rd., Arden • (828) 684-6278**

Tucked in a residential area off Sweeten Creek Road just 9 miles south of Asheville is Brookwood Golf Course. This semiprivate nine-hole, par 72/70 course has been in operation since 1963. (Nonmembers can play if they pay the greens fee.) The terrain is mostly level with a few gently rolling hills. A creek runs through much of the course. Yardage is 5653/5112/4730. The greens fee is a reasonable $10 for walking nine holes, $14 for with a cart; or $15 for 18 holes walking, $20 with a cart. This pleasant neighborhood course also has a grill and pro shop.

### Buncombe County Golf Course
**226 Fairway Dr., Asheville**
**• (828) 298-1867**

This public, county-operated 18-hole course has a long history. Begun in 1927, it was designed by noted golf architect Donald Ross, designer of the Biltmore Forest Country Club course and the Country Club of Asheville course. Buncombe County Golf Course is composed of a level front nine and rolling back nine. Yardage is 6000 and 6400. Greens fees are $23. Carts are not mandatory. The course also features a pro shop and snack bar.

### French Broad Golf Center
**5 French Broad Ave., Fletcher**
**• (828) 687-8545**

Off I-26 and less than a mile from the Asheville Regional Airport, this public golf facility transformed expansive pasture land into a sparkling 18-hole, par 72 course with level terrain, reshaped and interwoven with creeks and ponds.

The spectacular stone and wood clubhouse, reminiscent of arts and crafts style, houses a restaurant and pro shop. The greens fee for 18 holes, including cart, is $36 on weekdays, and $38 on weekends. Walking is allowed after noon Monday through Friday and after 1 PM on weekends. Rentals, lessons and clinics are available.

### The Grove Park Inn Resort
**230 Macon Ave., Asheville**
**• (828) 252-2711, (800) 438-5800**

The golf facility at Grove Park Inn is an experience unto itself. The golf course, originally called the Swannanoa Hunt Club, founded in 1893, later the Country Club of Asheville, was purchased in 1976 by Grove Park Inn. With the addition of the 18-hole course, swimming pool, tennis courts and historic clubhouse, Grove Park Inn became a complete resort in the 1980s (see our Resorts chapter).

The history connected to this course is incredible. Golf great Bobby Jones played here early in the century along with an amazing array of famous personalities visiting the adjacent Grove Park Inn. The course was a PGA Tour stop from 1933 to 1951.

The present course was redesigned in 1924 by famed golf architect Donald Ross. The layout of the front nine is level, leading into a rolling back nine and wonderful views as the course makes its way back up the hill to the Inn. Since 1989, the resort has made a substantial investment in rebuilding greens, landscaping and irrigation. The result is an impeccable course appealing not only to the avid golfer but the casual visitor to the inn as well.

The inn promotes various golfing events, including a fun event, Night Golf, for individuals and corporate groups. This nine-hole play starts at dusk with a three-hole rotation. Every rotation carries a musical theme — classical, country, or traditional mountain — with food and entertainment to match at each tee box. Special acrylic balls are used and fluorescent light sticks line the play area.

Grove Park Inn Resort packages are available.

### Great Smokies Holiday Inn/ Sunspree Resort
**1 Holiday Inn Dr., Asheville**
**• (828) 254-3211**

The golf course at the Great Smokies resort is 18 holes on rolling hills. Formerly the Great Smokies Hilton, this 120-acre resort, catering to corporate and tourist groups, is conveniently located right in the heart of Asheville off Patton Avenue and the interchange of Interstate 26 to the south and U.S. Highway 19/23 heading north from the city.

Greens fees vary seasonally but range from $22 to $32 for 18 holes of play, including cart. A fully stocked pro shop, rentals and lessons are available. Restaurants, conference areas, tennis courts and two swimming pools complete the resort experience. Golf packages are available, and seasonal children's activities are planned. Yardage is 5600.

### Reems Creek Golf Club
**36 Pink Fox Cove Rd., Weaverville**
**• (828) 645-3110 golf club, (800) 762-8479 real estate, 645-4393 pro shop**

This semiprivate course is part of the Reems Creek Golf Community, in a secluded, rolling mountain valley just 20 minutes north of Asheville. The Blue Ridge Parkway is nearby, easily accessed by Ox Creek Road, branching off Reems Creek Road, which is off U.S. 19/23 N.

The 18-hole championship course was designed by noted British golf architect Martin Hawtree. The course features bentgrass fairways. Yardage is 6464 and 4605. Greens fees are $39 weekdays and $44 on the weekend, including carts. Rentals and lessons, a pro shop and a restaurant are also available. Real estate information is available.

## Henderson County

### Crooked Creek Golf Course
**764 Crooked Creek Rd., Hendersonville**
**• (828) 692-2011**

This 18-hole, 6636-yard, par 72 championship course, situated just 1.5 miles from Hendersonville, is close enough for residents to take off for a quick game on a long lunch hour. Open to the public year round, the course has a wide-open feel with Bermuda grass fairways and bentgrass greens. There's a practice green, range, snack bar and pro shop. Crooked Creek provides both riding and push carts as well as lessons from a pro. Rates run $15 for 18 holes when walking and

---

**INSIDERS' TIP**

If golf is one of your main means of exercising, you may be tempted to bypass golf carts in favor of walking. On many of our hilly courses, that's likely to result in more exercise than you counted on.

$25 with a cart; nine holes are $10 walking and $15 with a cart.

## Cummings Cove Golf and Country Club
**3000 Cummings Rd., Hendersonville**
**• (828) 891-9412**

Designed by Robert E. Cupp, former on-site golf architect of Nicklaus Design Company, this Scottish-style course has been rated as one of the top 50 in North Carolina by *GolfWeek* magazine. Embankments flank many of the greens of this challenging 6008-yard, par 70 course, and woods border the entire course. Amenities include a modern clubhouse, pro shop, tennis courts and pool.

Cummings Cove is 8 miles from Hendersonville off U.S. 64 W. and is open to the public seven days a week. Tee times are required, and cart and green fee costs, which are subject to change, currently run $28 from Monday through Thursday and $34 from Friday through Sundays and on holidays. Eleven holes are $16.50 from Monday through Thursday and $19.50 from Friday through Sunday and on holidays. These prices do not include taxes.

## Etowah Valley Country Club and Golf Lodge
**U.S. 64 W., Etowah**
**• (828) 891-7022, (800) 891-7022**

Conveniently situated halfway between Hendersonville and Brevard in the small community of Etowah, this semi-private 27-hole championship course, designed by Edmund Ault and beautified by horticulturist Jean-Claude Linossi, has bentgrass greens measuring up to 9,000 square feet. Its three nine-hole courses and four tee positions allow for a variety of 18-hole combinations. For example, the rather flat south course plays from 2822 to 3507 yards (par 36); the west course, with its large greens and bunkers, from 2800 to 3601 yards (par 36); and the open, rolling north course from 2615 to 3404 yards (par 37).

Other amenities include modern lodges, lighted putting greens, a driving range, heated swimming pool, clubhouse, bathhouse, fitness center, pro shop, restaurant, lounge and meeting and banquet facilities for groups of up to 200.

For a different sort of challenge — or for non-golfing family members — Etowah provides a full-size, bentgrass greensward for croquet players and offers croquet packages along with a variety of golf packages. For example, a spring-through-fall, three-night weekend getaway golf package runs $321 per person, double occupancy, and includes lodging, breakfast, dinner, club storage and unlimited greens fees. Cart rentals, which cost $30 for 18 holes for two people, are not included in the package price.

Non-guests can play 18 holes for $46. (The price includes a golf cart.)

## Orchard Trace Golf Club
**942 Sugarloaf Rd., Hendersonville**
**• (828) 685-1006**

Night doesn't bring an end to golfing at this 18-hole, 2139-yard public course nestled in the heart of Henderson County's apple country. Seventy-two floodlights illuminate its entire 34 acres, making it the first fully lighted links in western North Carolina. The course is made up of bluegrass fairways and bentgrass greens meandering around a small pond and two winding creeks. Hole distances vary from 81 to 212 yards. Greens fees for 18 holes are $16 with a motorized cart, $11.50 with a pull cart and $10 for walking players. The clubhouse features a snack bar and a pro shop.

# Polk County

## Links O' Tryon
**11250 New Cut Rd., Campobello, S.C.**
**• (803) 468-4995, (888) 52-LINKS**

Nestled in rolling hills with a view of seven spectacular mountains, Links O' Tryon is the heart of a planned golf community with a lim-

---

**INSIDERS' TIP**

Due to frequent showers, it's wise to get a covered cart and stick an umbrella in your golf bag.

# Macon County:
# Sunset Rocks Overlook

For a stunning view of the town of Highlands in Macon County, drive to the Nature Center on Horse Cove Road just outside town. It's a 20-minute, moderate hike from there to the Sunset Rocks Overlook. In addition to Highlands, you'll be able to see the whole of historic Horse Cove. A sign, "Ravenel Park," marks the trail head.

ited number of nonresident memberships. The course, 8 miles south of Tryon, was designed by golf-course architect Tom Jackson on 275 acres and is ranked the number one semi-private golf course in the upstate by *GolfWeek* magazine. Its Golfer's Clubhouse is modeled after that of The Royal Burgess Golfing Society of Edinburgh, Scotland. Fences and bridges of imported field stone, white sand bunkers, Scottish-style grass bunkers and a large lake are some of the fine features of this 18-hole course.

Links O' Tryon also includes a restaurant, Golfer's Grill, an Olympic-size swimming pool, tennis courts and a traditional croquet lawn.

### Red Fox Country Club
**2 Club Dr., Tryon • (828) 894-8251**

The Red Fox Country Club, designed by architect Ellis Maples and opened in 1966, was quickly recognized as one of the top 100 championship courses in the country. Situated less than 2 miles from I-26, its 18 holes are serenely set amid mountain streams that wind to a 30-acre lake. Here you'll find wide fairways, large, sloping greens, a practice green and range, locker room, snack bar, rental clubs and pro shop.

For many years, Red Fox was operated as a private club, but it became semipublic in the mid-1980s. Memberships range in price from $1,000 to $4,000 per year, but the public is also permitted to play at a cost of $30 from 7:30 AM to 1 PM and $25 after 1 PM Monday through Friday. On weekends, the cost runs $35 until 1 PM and $30 after 1 PM. Prices include a required golf cart. Golfers who enjoy competition can sign up for Red Fox's mailing list and will be invited to play in its open golf outings held throughout the year.

# Transylvania County

### Glen Cannon Country Club
**Wilson Rd., Brevard • (828) 883-8175**

Glen Cannon, a semi-private course, is just 3 miles from downtown Brevard. This is one of the more established golf courses in the area, having been here for 32 years. Beautiful scenery surrounds this club, which offers a well-maintained 6270-yard, 18-hole championship course that's open year round. There's even a picture-perfect waterfall on No. 2. Amenities include tennis courts, a clubhouse and swimming pool.

Though it is a semi-private course, area visitors who live outside a 50-mile radius of Brevard may play on a per-day basis for $50 including a cart.

### Sherwood Forest
**N.C. 276 W., Cedar Mountain**
**• (828) 884-7825**

Sherwood Forest, a 1,000-acre community resort, sits on a high plateau in the Blue Ridge Mountains 8 miles south of Brevard on N.C. 276. Its 18-hole, par 54 golf course, open to the public, has Pencross bentgrass greens and stream-caressed fairways bordered with the area's marvelous rhododendrons and mountain laurel. A river runs through the course, whose relative flatness makes it one of the few mountain courses where you don't have to ride. The front nine is heavily wooded and the back nine is wide open. Water hazards on eight holes make up for the paucity of sand bunkers. In winter, greens fees are $11 during the week and $12 on weekends; in summer, they're $12 during the week and $13 on weekends. Students can play for $9.

# Jackson County:
# Whiteside Mountain

The top of this ancient Jackson County mountain, one of the oldest on earth, offers a fantastic view of Cashiers Valley, the upper Chattooga River watershed and the surrounding Blue Ridge Mountain peaks. A fairly easy 1.5-mile loop circles the summit with a half-mile side trail to Devil's Courthouse. From Cashiers, take U.S. 64 W. for 5 miles to Whiteside Mountain Road (S.R. 1690). Turn left onto this road and continue for about a mile until you reach the Whiteside Mountain parking area on your left (see our Forests and Parks chapter).

For longer stays, several cottages, villas and house rentals are available where you can enjoy amenities such as tennis, a heated pool, a number of lakes and miles of hiking trails. If you want to set up permanent residence, there are still a number of mountain lots available and occasional houses for sale.

# Southern Mountains

## Cherokee County

**Cherokee Hills Golf Course
and Country Club**
Harshaw Rd., Murphy
• (828) 837-5853, (800) 334-3905

Semiprivate Cherokee Hills, with its 18-hole championship golf course, lies in a picturesque mountain valley 3 miles east of Murphy. In addition to a 12-unit lodge, this community resort offers townhouses for rent or for sale, along with home sites, tennis courts, a pool, restaurant and complete pro shop. Golf packages start at $65 per night per person, double occupancy and include lodging and golf with a cart. Greens fees for non-guests are $15, and cart rentals are $10.60.

## Clay County

**Chatuge Shores Golf Course**
Myers Chapel Rd., Hayesville
• (828) 389-8940

This very attractive 18-hole, par 72 course serves the residents of several surrounding counties including Clay, Cherokee and Graham. Yardage is 6687. For residents of this area, annual family memberships are $340. Membership includes the use of the swimming pool and tennis courts. Cart fees (for both members and nonmembers) are $4 per person for nine holes and $7 for 18 holes. During the week Nonmembers pay green fees of $10 for nine holes and $18 for 18 holes; on weekends and holidays it's $11 for nine holes, $20 for 18 holes. There is a charge of $2 to use the pool.

## Haywood County

**Maggie Valley Resort
& Country Club**
1819 Country Club Dr., Maggie Valley
• (828) 926-1616, (800) 438-3861

This nationally acclaimed, 18-hole, par 72 course has been the site of four North Carolina Open Golf Tournaments and numerous other tournaments. *GolfWeek* rates Maggie Valley as one of America's best, and its bentgrass greens have been ranked among the top 15 in the nation. It's diverse and challenging: The first nine holes run through the rolling terrain of the valley, while the back nine winds through the mountains.

Accommodations include cozy guest rooms and mountainside villas surrounded by more than 35,000 square feet of well-tended gardens. There also are two all-weather tennis courts, a heated pool, a restaurant, a 32,000-square-foot event tent and a pub that offers resort-style nightlife. Call for special package rates.

## Springdale Country Club and Resort

200 Golfwatch Rd., Canton
• (828) 235-8451, (800) 553-3027

Springdale is another community resort centered around its excellent golf course. Eleven miles from Canton, not far from its entrance to the Blue Ridge Parkway and surrounded by the grandeur of the Great Smoky Mountains, the course measures a challenging 6812 yards from the championship tees. The 429-yard, par 4 No. 4, for example, has you punching your second shot through a narrow opening up to a trap-protected green. On the flatter and shorter back nine, the 417-yard, par 4 15th hole doglegs left and calls for a second shot across a pond.

But, while the golf may be exciting, this family-owned resort is casual and relaxed. Since golf is the name of the game here, you won't find pools, spas, tennis courts or fancy dress codes. You'll find family-style, home-cooked meals served overlooking the 18th green and cozy cottages with rocking chairs, a view and television. Other amenities include a practice green, range, chipping green, two restaurants, rental clubs and pro shop. Package tours include accommodations, breakfast, dinner, unlimited golf cart and unlimited golf. For permanent stays, one- and three-acre home sites and townhouses are for sale.

Cost for nonresidents is $45 per round, including a cart.

## Waynesville Country Club Inn

Country Club Dr., Waynesville
• (828) 456-3551, (800) 627-6250

Here, 27 holes of golf blend with mountain streams, ponds and the ever-present mountain views. The links, made up of lush fairways and picture-perfect bentgrass greens, consist of three separate and distinct par 35, nine-hole courses that start and finish at the clubhouse. Each hole offers three sets of tees, thus ensuring a pleasurable experience for golfers of all levels of play.

Guests can choose from lodge rooms, cottages or villas and several restaurants. You'll also find tennis courts, a pool and a pro shop. Be sure to ask about Waynesville's special Getaway Holiday Packages as well as

daily golf packages that start as low as $35 per person, double occupancy, during the un-crowded winter season. For nonresidents, the cost will run around $43.90 for 18 holes, including a cart. See our Resorts chapter for more information on the Inn.

# Jackson County

## High Hampton Inn & Country Club

N.C. 107 S., Cashiers
• (828) 743-2411, (800) 334-2551

Sitting at 3,600 feet, this 1,400-acre estate with its private 35-acre lake surrounds a historic country inn and its nearby cottages. All of these are just steps from the 18-hole, 6012-yard, par 71 golf course designed by George W. Cobb that provides a scenic mountain view from every hole. The cost, including a cart, is $48 (subject to change), $42 if you are a guest at the resort. In addition to the course, there are two putting greens and an excellent practice range with the tee area covered for protection against rain. High Hampton also offers a series of three- and four-day golf schools from April through October designed for beginners, intermediates and more advanced players. Each year, there are two tournaments, one in June and one in September, for seniors (age 50 to 64) and super-seniors (age 65 and older).

Facilities include tennis courts, a children's play area, an archery field and sports fields. An excellent children's activity program is offered from June 1 through Labor Day. There is also a well-equipped exercise room. The lake is popular for swimming, sailing, canoeing, rowing and pedaling boats. You'll also find an exercise trail and several walking trails, with guided walks weekly. All meals are served buffet style, and High Hampton's famous afternoon tea is offered from 4 to 5 PM. See our Resorts chapter for more information.

## Sapphire Mountain Golf Club

50 Slicer's Ave., Sapphire
• (828) 743-3441, (800) 533-8268

This challenging 6147-yard golf course, with water hazards on nine holes, plus a waterfall hole, is a part of the 5,000-acre, all-season Sapphire Valley Resort that grew

around the old Fairfield Inn, built in the late 1890s. This is the perfect place to go with non-golf-playing family members, because while you're out on the links, they can entertain themselves with horseback and canoe rides, fishing, swimming, hiking and tennis and join in supervised programs for children. A recreation complex offers a heated indoor pool with sauna and whirlpool, an exercise/weight room, table tennis and pool tables, game machines and minigolf.

Nonresidents can play here for around $50, including a cart. See our Resorts chapter for more information.

## Macon County

### Mill Creek Country Club
**U.S. 64 W., Franklin**
**• (828) 524-4653, (800) 533-3916**

Bordered on three sides by the incredible natural beauty of the Nantahala National Forest, the main attraction at this 380-acre community resort is still the 18-hole championship golf course. Rolling terrain, rippling creeks and thick stands of pine and willow trees interweave with the lush fairways and carefully manicured greens. As interesting as it is beautiful, this course can challenge players of any skill level. Half- and three-quarter-acre home sites and single-family homes are

for sale. Two-day, weekly and monthly rentals of deluxe villas also are available. Greens fees with a cart are $25 per person before 2 PM and $15 after 2 PM. On Mondays, the cost to those 55 and older is $16. Golf packages are available. Please call for rates.

## Swain County

### Smoky Mountain Country Club
**1300 Conley Creek Rd., Whittier**
**• (828) 497-4653**

In 1996 Swain County finally got a golf course that proved worth the wait. Since then the county-owned course, set in the beauty of the Smoky Mountains, has gone through several cosmetic changes to increase both its attractiveness and playability. The course was designed by J. Porter Gibson and modified by Brassie Gold Corporation. Each designer used the natural mountain terrain to develop a challenging place to play, and the resulting par 70, 6,500-yard championship course, with its change in elevation approaching 1,000 feet, gives each hole a different and delightful view of the mountains. Each hole also offers unique challenges. From the par 3s to the par 5s, no player is likely to get bored.

You'll find this fine golf experience a little more than a mile from the Smoky Mountains Expressway (U.S. 74) and seven miles from both downtown Bryson City and Cherokee. There are a number of pricing options that allow anyone to play at a reasonable rate. Many local hotels offer golf packages and a multi-play package can be purchased at the golf course clubhouse. Yearly memberships are also available.

The Great Smoky
Mountains' diversity can
accommodate everyone
from the casual tourist,
the weekend hiker to the
person searching for a
true wilderness
experience.

# Forests and Parks

If we had to pick one reason why we love living in western North Carolina, it would be its vast system of public lands. Few of us have to travel even an hour in order to be in a wild, natural, government-protected environment. For most residents, it's a matter of minutes. Even an avid outdoors person could spend a lifetime here and probably never see all that there is of these great natural treasures. If you could accomplish such a feat, you'd have to do it three more times, because even the same place is vastly different when altered by the dramatic changes brought on by fall, winter and spring.

Western North Carolina is home to more than half of the Great Smoky Mountains National Park and two huge national forests. The Pisgah National Forest and the Nantahala National Forest combined cover more than a million acres scattered over several tracts. In addition, the National Park Service oversees the large section of the Blue Ridge Parkway that crosses this region of the state (see our Blue Ridge Parkway chapter). There are also three very diverse state parks to be enjoyed: New River, Mount Jefferson and Mount Mitchell, plus two state forests: DuPont State Forest and Holmes Educational State Forest. In addition, there are the rugged 10,000 acres that make up the Green River Game Lands.

In this chapter, you will find a number of hiking and recreational possibilities, but there are many other suggestions in our Blue Ridge Parkway, Recreation and Waterfalls chapters for getting out and about in our parks and forests. Detailed camping information can be found in our Recreation chapter. As a handy reference, we have included here a special section that lists all ranger stations, their locations and phone numbers. They are a great source of information on forest trails, camping, plant life, wildlife, etc.

So let's jump right into some brief overviews of these mountainous public spaces as well as some of their, excuse the pun, high points.

## The Great Smoky Mountains National Park

This national park, with 276,063 acres in North Carolina and 244,345 acres in Tennessee, hosts 9 million visitors annually, making it the most heavily used National Park in the country. Congress authorized it in 1926, but because the land was difficult to acquire from both individuals and timber companies, it wasn't dedicated by Franklin Roosevelt until 1940 — and just in time, too! During the latter part of the last century, and even more so in the early part of this one, loggers were stripping these mountains bare, taking, at first, the most easily accessible trees from land that was later included in the park.

Lucky for us, the loggers hadn't gotten around to some of the steeper and more remote areas. As a result, we still have approximately 110,000 acres of old-growth forest within the 520,408-acre park. Some of these trees, such as poplar and spruce, are over 400 years old. However, in the more than half a century since cutting stopped, second-growth trees have made such a good comeback that most of us can't tell which areas are old growth and which are second growth.

As important as the park's trees are — and there are more than 130 species here — they are only one part of the area's unique ecosystems, which contain 1,500 varieties of flowering plants, 300 kinds of mosses and 2,000 different fungi. Among the wildlife that makes its home here are 200 species of birds, 60 species of fur-bearing animals, 48 different kinds of fish and 38 species of reptiles. Of the latter, the only two poisonous species are the timber rattlesnake and northern copperhead, the venoms of which are seldom lethal. Of the 27 species of salamanders that make the Smokies the salamander capital of the world, two of the most notable include Jordans Salamander, a subspecies found only in here, and the Hellbender, which can grow up to two and one-half feet long. Reintroduction efforts are bringing back the red wolf and river otter. Someday, a reintroduction of eastern elk, which were abundant in these mountains 200 years ago, could return that animal to the park.

**www.insiders.com**
See this and many other **Insiders' Guide®** destinations online.
**Visit us today!**

The most famous inhabitant here is, of course, the black bear. Around 1,700 make these mountains their home, giving it one of the country's highest bear densities. It's likely, therefore, that if you spend much time in the area that you'll come across a bear or two. To help make such an encounter fortunate instead of frightening, read *Bear Aware: Hiking and Camping in Bear Country*, by Bill Schneider.

Except for some fishing, it's against the park rules to disturb any of the plants and animals in this wildlife sanctuary. The park, however, is here to be enjoyed, and its diversity can accommodate everyone from the casual tourist, the weekend hiker to the person searching for a true wilderness experience. Despite its many visitors, you can still find solitude by getting just a little off the beaten track or by visiting the area in the winter.

The Great Smoky Mountains Park has 17 peaks more than 6,000 feet high. The highest in the park is 6,642-foot Clingmans Dome, which is accessible by trail and by car. Some 250 million years ago, these mountains, some

of the oldest on earth, stood more than 15,000 feet tall, but time and erosion have worn them down to the beautiful and often-dramatic forms they take today. The park is also enhanced by 700 miles of fishing streams. Many provide rainbow and brown trout all year long, but possession of any brook trout, our native trout, is prohibited. A Tennessee or North Carolina fishing license is required, but trout stamps are not. Check out the regulations at a ranger station or visitor center before you fish (see our Recreation chapter for more on fishing regulations).

For general information on the park, call (423) 436-1200. You can call or write to get a free catalog of books, maps, hiking guides and videos that you can purchase. Park headquarters is at 107 Park Headquarters Road, Gatlinburg, Tennessee 37738. In these days of budget cuts, it's particularly important to call ahead as services are changing and the folks at headquarters can keep you up-to-date.

## Getting Around by Vehicle

One-hundred-seventy miles of paved roads and 100 miles of gravel roads penetrate the park, some of them built by settlers in the 1800s, but there are no gasoline or automobile services, and speed limits are 45 mph or slower. U.S. Highway 441, which is closed to commercial vehicles, is the only highway that goes completely through the park. There are numerous scenic pullouts all along this route through Newfound Gap, and a 7-mile spur road (closed in winter) goes out to Clingmans Dome. Efforts are made to keep the highway open all year, but always check at the nearest visitor center for winter road conditions; sometimes it is closed due to snow or ice, and sometimes only vehicles with chains are allowed. While snow is fairly uncommon in the valleys, Newfound Gap receives an average of more than five feet a year.

Under normal weather and traffic conditions, it should take about an hour to cross the park on U.S. 441 if you don't make any stops, but during the peak visitor season from

May until October or in bad weather, it can take much longer. There are other spur roads, some of them unpaved and some of which are closed in winter, that lead to special areas of interest or campgrounds in the park. These "backroads" offer access to less visited areas and are often scenic in their own right. Most are one-way and can accommodate two-wheel-drive vehicles. Check on the conditions of these roads, however, before attempting them. A flash floods or mudslide sometimes makes one impassable.

Most park roads are open to bicycles. No off-road vehicles of any kind are allowed anywhere in the park.

## Getting Around by Foot

The park's vast area is crisscrossed by over 850 miles of hiking trails, over half of which are in North Carolina. Many of these trails were converted from old logging railroad grades or old logging roads. There are 51 official hiking trails and 11 self-guiding nature trails. You can pick up a leaflet about each nature trail as you enter it. For visitors just passing through, there are several trails right off of U.S. 441 that are marked by signs.

A relatively level trail in this area, the Kephart Prong Trail, is 9 miles north of Cherokee. It begins by crossing the Oconoluftee River on a footbridge and will take you 4 miles to the Kephart Prong shelter and back, passing the remains of a 1930s Civilian Conservation Corps camp along the way. The longest trail in the park is the 69 miles of the Appalachian Trail between Fontana Dam and Davenport Gap. (You must obtain a free backcountry overnight permit to camp at shelters along the Appalachian Trail, but no permits are necessary on those sections of the trail outside the park boundaries.) The second-longest trail is the 43-mile Lakeshore Trail on the north shore of the Fontana Dam.

If U.S. 441 is open, you can cross-country ski on the Clingmans Dome Road as well as other roads that are closed in winter. Horseback riding is permitted on designated trails. Saddle horses are available from about April 1 to October 31 at Cades Cove, (423) 448-6286; Smokemont, (828) 497-2373; Deep Creek, (828) 497-7503; Smoky Mountain, (423) 436-5634; and McCarter's, (423) 436-5354, near the park's headquarters at the Gatlinburg entrance to the park. Rates average about $15 per person an hour. Call the above numbers for more information.

Pets, on leashes or otherwise contained, are permitted in the park but are not permitted on trails or cross-country hikes. There are two exceptions: the Gatlinburg Trail and the Oconaluftee River Trail.

# Visitors Centers

You'll find visitors centers that offer free maps, information and exhibits at the entrances to the park. The informative park and nature books sold at the centers will enhance your visit. They're open from 8 AM until 7 PM, seven days a week.

**Oconaluftee Visitor Center**
**2 miles north of Cherokee on U.S. 441 • (828) 497-1900**
Open year round

**Sugarland Visitor Center**
**About 5 miles south of Gatlinburg, Tenn., on U.S. 441 • (423) 436-1200**
Open year round

**Cades Cove Bookstore**
**10 miles from Townsend, Tenn., on Cades Cove Loop Rd. • (423) 436-1200**
Open May though October
The 11-mile loop drive though this lovely cove is well worth taking (see Cades Cove in this chapter). There is no fee charged to enter the park.

# Places to Stay

Aside from the hundreds of motels, inns, cabins, bed and breakfasts, RV parks and campgrounds that offer accommodations just outside the park (some can be found in our Accommodations and Bed and Breakfasts and Resorts chapters), there are 10 developed campgrounds within the park itself. Five of them are on the North Carolina side (see our Recreation Chapter). From mid-May through October, nature walks and evening programs are offered at most developed campgrounds.

To camp in the backcountry, you need a permit. You can pick one up free of charge from any park ranger station, campground or at the Oconoluftee and Sugarlands visitor centers. However, some backcountry campsites and shelters are so heavily used that they require reservations. Call the Backcountry Reservation Office, (423) 436-1231, 8 AM to 6 PM daily, a month in advance if possible. You can only stay one night in a shelter and three nights in a backcountry campground.

For a map and guide of park trails, backcountry campsites and regulations, ask at a visitor center or send $1 to the Great Smoky Mountains Natural History Association, 115 Park Headquarters Road, Gatlinburg, Tennessee 37738, (423) 436-7318, and allow two weeks for delivery. This association has also put out an excellent book called *Hiking Trails of the Smokies* that sells for $16.95 and is available at visitor centers or by calling the association. See the write up under the "Organizations" section of this chapter for more information on this association.

LeConte Lodge, on 6,593-foot Mt. LeConte, is the only lodge in the park. It's open from mid-March to mid-November and is accessible only by trail. The shortest trail to the lodge is nearly 5 miles one-way, and reservations are required over a year in advance due to its popularity. Call or write LeConte Lodge, Gatlinburg, Tennessee 37738, (423) 429-5704.

# Some Points of Interest

## Clingmans Dome

At 6,642 feet, this is the park's highest peak, the third highest in eastern America, and the highest point on the Appalachian Trail. As we've mentioned, it can be reached by a 7-mile-long spur road off U.S. 441 at Newfound Gap. From the parking lot, a fairly steep half-mile trail takes you to an observation platform, which, if it's not a hazy day, offers an incredible panoramic view.

In addition to the Appalachian Trail, there are other nearby trails you can pick up at Clingmans Dome. One easy trail for a family hike is the 2.2-mile (4.4 miles roundtrip) Andrews Bald Trail. Look for the marked hiking trail at the west end of the parking lot. After about 1,000 feet the trail will fork. The right fork goes to Silers Bald. The left fork to Andrews Bald will take you down-slope through a spruce fir forest to a grassy bald with excellent views to the south toward Fontana Lake. It's especially nice when the flame azaleas bloom in late June or early July. This trailhead is not accessible by car from December 1 through April 1.

## Cades Cove

When these mountains were turned into a park, many of the people on small farms and in the communities here had to leave. Restored log cabins and barns in a number of areas remind us of these hearty settlers. Few places, however, are as beautiful and well

---

**INSIDERS' TIP**

The Smoky Mountain Field School is a cooperative effort between the University of Tennessee and the Great Smoky Mountains National Park that consists of intensive weekend and three-day field courses on topics such as geology, bears, stream life, birds, hiking, mushrooms, insects and fly fishing. For a free catalog, call (800) 284-8885.

preserved as Cades Cove, which contains more pioneer structures than any other location in the park. Pastures, old buildings and open vistas are a photographer's dream. And if you are in Cades Cove very early in the morning, you'll likely see deer and other wildlife feeding in the cove. There's an 11-mile, one-way loop that circles this scenic mountain valley and many of its historic buildings. Numerous ranger-led walks and lectures on a variety of subjects are held in Cades Cove every day of the week during the summer season.

There are also numerous hiking trails in the area, many leading to lovely waterfalls. Since many of these are in Tennessee, they are not included in our Waterfall chapter. One, Abrams Trail, begins in the back of Cades Cove loop road and is a moderate 5-mile, roundtrip hike. Abrams Falls has the largest water volume of any of the park's falls and is among the most photogenic. The 2-mile Cades Cove Nature Trail is great for families wanting an hour's outing. Pick up a brochure explaining the Cove's cultural and natural history before you take this hike. Surprisingly few people use this convenient trail.

To reach Cades Cove, take the Little River Road, a winding but relatively flat road that follows the Little River, from the Sugarlands Visitor Center on U.S. 441 near Gatlinburg. (See our listing of Visitor Centers in this chapter.)

### Roaring Fork Motor Nature Trail

Three miles from Gatlinburg, you can take this 5-mile, one-way loop through rich hardwood forests and past historic buildings and rushing mountain streams. To get to it, turn onto Airport Road in Gatlinburg. Enter the park and follow the Cherokee Orchard Road to the Roaring Fork Motor Nature Trail. No RVs, trailers or bicycles are allowed on this route.

### Cataloochee Valley

The most rugged peaks in the southeastern United States surround this 29-square-mile secluded valley, many over 6,000 feet tall. The valley was once the largest and most prosperous settlement in what is now the park with a population of about 1,200 residents. The churches, a school and several houses

and barns remain. Once known for its farms and orchards, today it's famous for its dense wildlife.

Cataloochee Valley is definitely off-the-beaten-track and requires a 10-mile drive on a winding, narrow, mostly gravel, relatively well maintained road that seems much longer than it is. To reach it, take U.S. Highway 276 toward Interstate 40. Just before it dead-ends into the interstate, turn left onto Cove Creek Road and follow the Cove Creek Missionary Baptist Church signs. There is a ranger station in the valley where you can get more information on the area. There is also a campground with 27 sites that is open from April to November. (See our Recreation chapter for more information on camping.)

### Mountain Farm Museum

At the park's southern entrance at Cherokee, from May through October you can walk through a collection of Southern Appalachian farm buildings with park interpreters who explain life as it existed here generations ago. These buildings, including a chestnut-log farmhouse, barn, apple house, springhouse and blacksmith shop, were built in the 19th century and assembled for various locations throughout the park in the 1950s. Admission is free.

### Mingus Mill

Mingus Mill is a half-mile north of the Mountain Farm Museum on the Newfound Gap Road. Built in the early 1800s, it's an excellent example of a water-powered gristmill, and it's still grinding corn. Hours vary, but the mill is usually open daily in the summer and on spring and fall weekends.

# Organizations

### Great Smoky Mountains Natural History Association
115 Park Headquarters Road, Gatlinburg, Tenn., 37738
• (423) 436-7318

This nonprofit organization is for people who care about the park and want to know more about its natural and historical resources. Authorized by Congress, it supports the park's educational and scientific programs in a number of ways, including producing publications such as the trail guidebook, funding special educational programs, purchasing river otters for the park and funding visitors center exhibits and artifact collections. Members receive the association's newsletter, discounts from other park associations (such as those at Yellowstone and Yosemite), a subscription to the park's quarterly newspaper and a chance to participate in annual meetings that include guided walks, guest speakers and entertainment as well as the annual guided day hikes to interesting destinations within the park. Members also have the satisfaction of helping promote the association's goals. Annual memberships are $25 per person and Lifetime Family memberships cost $500. Contact the association for more information.

The association also sponsors the Great Smoky Mountain Institute at Tremont, which provides photo workshops and environmental education programs in subjects such as Cherokee Earth Skills for everyone from school children to Elderhostel groups. Tuition, meals and lodging are provided for a minimal fee. Call (423) 448-6709 for more information.

### Friends of the Great Smoky Mountains National Park
**130 West Bruce Street, Sevierville, TN 37862 • (423) 436-2428, (800) 845-5665**

Over sixty years ago, a group of people joined together to establish a national park here to preserve and protect the natural wonders of the region. This organization is still dedicated to fund-raising and to restoring, preserving and enhancing the park. It has recently created a special license plate for North Carolina for a $30 special fee. For more information and an application call the above number. If you love the Smokies, this is a great organization to join.

## National Forests

As we mentioned earlier, the Nantahala and Pisgah National Forests cover more than a million acres in the North Carolina Mountains, including a number of wilderness areas. These vast forest lands of rivers, lakes,

waterfalls, spectacular views, wildlife and the richest plant life in the country can be accessed by federal and state highways, forest roads and trails. You'll find that they can easily be explored by car, on foot, by kayak or canoe and, in designated areas, by horseback, mountain bikes and off-highway vehicles. (See our Recreation chapter for more information on some of these outdoor sports and camping.)

You will find the maps and information you need to explore this vast region at the ranger districts listed in this chapter, and our chapter on Outdoor Safety will help to keep you well and happy while you're doing it. Since it will take a few lifetimes to get to know these two forests well, you should begin this delightful quest as soon as possible. It's your land. Enjoy it!

## Nantahala National Forest

This national forest, in the southwestern part of our mountains between Waynesville and Murphy, contains more than 516,000 acres, sometimes taking in huge chunks of land and sometimes consisting of relatively small plots. If you look at a map of the forest, it's so broken up in some places that it resembles a psychiatrist's inkblot test. When you travel in this part of Western North Carolina, you're going to constantly be entering and leaving the forest. While this might not make managing these public lands easy, it certainly makes for a lot of diversity.

Elevations in the forest range from a high 5,800 feet at Lone Bald in Jackson County to a low 1,200 feet in Cherokee County along the Tusquitee River below the Appalachian Lake Dam.

To get a better handle on this vast area, which is the largest of the four national forests in North Carolina, it's best to break it down into its four districts.

### Cheoah Ranger District
**U.S. Hwy. 129 N., Robbinsville • (828) 473-6431**

The Cheoah Ranger District is made up of 120,000 acres in Graham and Swain counties that adjoin four large reservoirs (Lake Fontana, Lake Santeetlah, Lake Cheoah and Calderwood Lake) and offer a network of 225 miles of hiking trails, including a 27-mile section of the Appalachian Trail. The Cheoah Ranger Station, adjacent to Lake Santeetlah on S.R. 1116 and 2 miles north of Robbinsville, is built on the site of a Civilian Conservation Corps campsite and contains an interpretive trail and a fine overlook of the lake. Here you can get forest information and maps.

Sitting to the southwest of the Great Smoky Mountains National Park, this part of the Nantahala Forest is often overlooked by visitors, but the slightly off-the-beaten-track district provides some incredibly beautiful places. First off, there is the 3,800-acre Joyce Kilmer Memorial Forest, which, maintained in a primitive state, has one of the nation's most impressive remnants of old-growth forest. The Gennott Lumber Company that started timber operations in the area in 1890 once owned the timber here, but — lucky for us — these trees were never cut. Now this memorial forest is a part of the 14,000-acre Joyce Kilmer-Slickrock Wilderness Area and contains magnificent examples of more than 100 species of trees, including yellow poplar, hemlock, sycamore, basswood, dogwood, beech and several species of oaks. Many of them are hundreds of years old, and some are more than 20 feet in circumference and more than 100 feet high. The area was set aside in 1936 as a memorial to Joyce Kilmer, the soldier-poet and author of the poem "Trees," who was killed in France during World War I.

The Joyce Kilmer National Recreation Trail is an easy 2-mile loop that takes you past some of these great giants, many felled by age or lightning. In some areas, the tree canopy is so thick that sunlight never reaches the ground. You'll also find a picnic area here and an outstanding variety of vines, ferns and early-spring wildflowers and shrubs, such as mountain laurels, rhododendrons and flame azaleas. No plants, living or dead, may be removed from this area. Wildlife is abundant in this undisturbed forest. The adjoining Slickrock Wilderness Area, with 13,100 acres in North Carolina, contains 60 miles of hiking trails that meander along streams and climb high ridges. It's home to bears, bobcats and

nonnative, environment-uprooting wild boars and has a number of dispersed, primitive, no-fee campsites. (See our Outdoor Safety chapter for tips on camping in such areas.)

For those who want more comforts, such as picnic tables, restrooms and water taps, there are two campgrounds, not very far from the memorial forest. Horse Cove Campground, which charges $8 a night, has 18 units and is by a rushing mountain stream called Little Santeetlah Creek. Rattler Ford campground nearby is reserved for groups.

To get to the Joyce Kilmer Memorial Forest, take U.S. Highway 129 out of Robbinsville to S.R. 1127 and follow the signs. Both the Horse Cove and Rattler Ford campgrounds are off S.R. 1127.

There are two forest recreation areas near Lake Fontana. The Tsali Recreation Area has 41 camping units with showers and flushing toilets, a boat-launching area and 38 miles of biking and horseback-riding trails. The popular trail network here now charges a $2 fee for horses and bikes. The Cable Cove Recreation Area also offers camping and hiking with boating access on Fontana Lake. It's 4 miles from Fontana Dam, the Appalachian Trail and the entrance to the Great Smoky Mountains National Park. The area also has a mile-long nature loop trail marked with placards that will help you identify the plants and trees growing along it as well as some historical features. The camping fee here is $8 a night. On Lake Santeetlah, the Cheoah Point Recreation Area has developed camping, picnicking, fishing and boating facilities. There is an $8 camping fee but no charge for day use. Nearby, the Wauchecha Bald Trail provides access to the Appalachian Trail (see our Recreation chapter for more information on all these recreation areas).

Of all the outstanding wild places in the Cheoah District, two great favorites with anglers, hunters and primitive camping enthusiasts are the Big Santeetlah Creek area and the 10,000 or so acres that encompass the headwaters of Big Snowbird Creek. The latter was one of the last areas to be settled by whites in North Carolina, and it was here in 1836 that a number of Cherokee Indians fled to escape exile in Oklahoma. For more information on these two areas, contact the

Cheoah Ranger Station (see our gray box on Ranger Stations).

## Highlands Ranger District
2010 Flat Mountain Rd., Highlands
• (828) 526-3756

The Highlands Ranger District covers more than 105,000 acres in Macon, Jackson and Transylvania counties. Within it, you'll find the 39,000-acre Roy Taylor Forest, which has some off-road vehicle trails (see our Recreation chapter) and Jackson County's rugged Tuckasegee Gorge.

The Highlands District also contains two national and wild scenic rivers, the Chattooga and the Horsepasture. The Chattooga, on which the movie *Deliverance* was filmed, is very popular with whitewater rafters, but only after it passes the South Carolina/Georgia border (see our Recreation chapter). No canoeing is permitted on either river within the district. The Horsepasture River is noted for its five waterfalls. Other famous waterfalls in this district include Whitewater Falls, Glen Falls, Dry Falls and Cullasaja Falls. (See our Waterfalls chapter for more information on all of these. Also remember that people die at such waterfalls every year. Please stay on trails and away from the water at the top of the falls.) Some of these cascades are found along the Cullasaja Gorge, another unbelievably rugged gorge in the area. You'll pass harrowingly close to it when you take U.S. Highway 64 from Highlands to Franklin.

One of the most famous mountains in the Nantahala Forest is Whiteside Mountain, between Highlands and Cashiers off U.S. 64 on the eastern Continental Divide. Said to be one of the oldest mountains on earth, it rises more than 2,100 feet from the valley floor to an elevation of 4,930 feet. Its spectacular north and south faces contain sheer cliffs ranging from 400 to 750 feet in height. They were formed of metamorphic rock commonly called Whiteside granite, gneiss containing a high content of feldspar, quartz and mica, along with such minerals as pyrite and rare monazite. The white streaks seen on its south face are feldspar and quartz. These don't show up on the north face due to lichens and mosses that cover the stone. The Cherokees called the mountain Sanigilagi, "the place where they

took it out," referring to where lightning "took out" the projecting rock on the mountain's western summit. What remained was said to have formed part of the great bridge a mythical monster named Spearfinger tried to build across the valley.

A 2-mile loop trail, designated as a National Recreation Trail, runs on the top of the mountain. It offers unparalleled views of the east, south and west, where you will see at least 27 other peaks, the Cashiers Valley and the upper Chattooga River watershed. To reach the mountain, drive 6.9 miles from the main Highlands intersection on U.S. 64 going toward Cashiers and turn onto Whiteside Mountain Road (S.R. 1600). From Cashiers, the turn is just past the Jackson/Macon county line. After about a mile, you'll arrive at the mountain's parking area and the trail that follows the edge of the cliffs. Use extreme caution here with pets and children. This is a popular place for rock climbing, but it's only suitable for experts. The rock face is closed to climbers from February 15th through July 15th to protect nesting peregrine falcons.

Cliffside Lake and the Van Hook Glade Recreation Areas, off U.S. 64 between Highlands and Franklin, form one of the district's most popular camping, swimming and fishing areas. Camping here is $10 a night, and day-use is $3 per car. This popular area fills up quickly, but there are also a number of primitive camping areas in the district. You can get information and maps at the district office off U.S. 64 just outside of Highlands or at the Highland Visitor Center in downtown Highlands. The visitor center is open daily from May through October; the office is open year-round from Monday through Friday.

## Tusquitee Ranger District
201 Woodland Dr., Murphy
• (828) 837-5152

Elevations in the 158,579-acre Tusquitee Ranger District range from 1,200 feet to 5,499 feet at Standing Indian Mountain. It's most famous for its "chain of lakes" — Appalachia Lake, Hiwassee Lake and Chatuge Lake — which offer opportunities to boat, water-ski, fish and swim. You can stay right on Hiwassee Lake at the forest's Hanging Dog Recreation Area, which has a large campground, a pic-

# Cherohala Skyway

For a beautiful perspective on our lovely mountains, travel the new, 51-mile Cherohala Skyway that connects the Tellico Plains in southeast Tennessee to Robbinsville, North Carolina. (In Tennessee, take Tennessee Highway 165 and in North Carolina take North Carolina Highway 143.) Called a mini-Blue Ridge Parkway, it travels through some of the best scenery of the Cherokee and Nantahala National Forests, thus the name which is a combination of Cherokee and Nantahala.

Much of the two-lane blacktop in North Carolina looks down on the Snowbird, Slickrock and Joyce Kilmer forests. On clear, unhazy days, you can see into the Great Smoky Mountains National Park. Restrooms, picnic areas and scenic overlooks are constructed along the way. Spirit Ridge, a lookout just east of Hooper Bald, is handicap accessible and offers one of most expansive views along the route.

# Ranger Stations

The offices of the National Forests in North Carolina are at 160-A Zillicoa St., Asheville, N.C., (828) 257-4200. To reach them, take the UNCA exit off U.S. 19/23.

You can contact the U.S. Forest Service for help and information in the following areas.

## Nantahala National Forest

**Cheoah Ranger District**
U.S. 129 N., Robbinsville • (828) 479-6431

**Highlands Ranger District**
2010 Flat Mountain Rd.• (828) 526-3765

**Tusquitee Ranger District**
201 Woodland Dr., off U.S. 64 E., Murphy
• (828) 837-5152

**Wayah Ranger District**
90 Sloan Rd., Franklin (turn at sign for U.S. 64 W.) • (828) 524-6441

## Pisgah National Forest

**Appalachian Ranger District,
French Broad Station**
88 Bridge St., Hot Springs • (828) 622-3202

**Appalachian Ranger District,
Tocane Station**
U.S. 19 E. bypass, Burnsville • (828) 682-6146

**Grandfather Ranger District**
At exit 90 (Nebo/Lake James Exit) off I-40, 9 miles east of Marion
• (828) 652-2144

# The Whiteside Mountain Legends

There was once a wicked ogress in these mountains who could pick up big boulders and meld them together by striking one against the other. Her skin had the appearance and feel of stone; any arrows or spears shot at her would just bounce off. Her name was Utlunta, but the Cherokees called her "Spearfinger" because of a very long forefinger that was shaped like a spear. Except for this finger, she was capable of appearing as a harmless old woman, and she would use this disguise to lure young children to her. Then she would use her spearfinger to stab them in the back of the neck or through the heart and dig out their livers — her favorite food.

One day, she began building a huge bridge from a point on the Hiwassee River some 4 miles from the Georgia line. First, she built a treelike rock, which even today looks like a tree, and then she started extending her bridge toward Whiteside Mountain with her rock-melding technique. But lightning destroyed it, scattering the rocks all along the ridge, where they too can still be seen. Finally, the Cherokee trapped her by digging a pit across a trail that she used. But, again, weapons were useless against her, until a chickadee lit on her finger, pointing out to its Cherokee friends her weak spot — the equivalent of an Achilles heel. Thus, the arrow they shot into it went straight to her heart, killing her.

Another myth says there is a cave in Whiteside Mountain where the devil had his throne. Others say it was in the nearby Devil's Courthouse — not to be confused with the Devil's Courthouse near the Blue Ridge Parkway. The one near Whiteside Mountain is considered to be the "supreme" throne room. The other is just a secondary "hall of justice."

nic area, hiking trails and a boat-launching ramp. At Chatuge Lake, the Jackrabbit Mountain Recreation Area has 103 camping sites, a swimming beach with shower facilities, hiking trails, picnic areas and a boat-launching ramp. (See our Recreation chapter for more information on these lakes and camping areas).

Just to the north of Chatuge Lake, you'll find the Fires Creek Bear Sanctuary, a 14,000-acre block of land that's been set aside as a haven for black bears. This area offers excellent trout, fishing, picnicking, hiking and camping. The most famous hiking trail in the area is the 25-mile-long Rim Trail, which follows the ridge around Fires Creek over several high-elevation balds that provide super-scenic vistas. There are several primitive camping areas here that include Huskins Branch, Hunter Camp and Bristol Fields.

The Leatherwood Falls Picnic Area provides picnic sites near Leatherwood Falls, plus a handicapped-accessible trail for wheelchair fishing along Fires Creek (see "Leatherwood Falls" in our Waterfalls chapter for more information). Another interesting place to visit in this district is the Beech Creek Seed Orchard west of Murphy off F.R. 307. This nursery supplies the southern Appalachian forests with genetically improved seeds of white, shortleaf and Virginia pines for reforestation. The orchard also has extensive hardwood clones banks of black cherry, oak and yellow poplar. You can get district information and maps at the district office off U.S. 64 east of Murphy.

## Wayah Ranger District
**90 Sloan Rd., Franklin • (828) 524-6441**

This Wayah District (Wayah means "wolf" in Cherokee) is centrally located in the

Nantahala National Forest. Its 134,000 acres are adjacent to the Cherokee Indian Reservation in the north and extend all the way down to the Georgia border on the south. Within these boundaries you'll find the Nantahala River Gorge, with opportunities for whitewater rafting and kayaking; two famous national trails, the Appalachian Trail and the Bartram Trail, which meet on Wayah Bald (see the Three Famous Trails gray box in our Recreation chapter); the Standing Indian Basin; and the Southern Nantahala Wilderness Area.

The 25,515-acre Southern Nantahala Wilderness Area, created in 1984, is managed by the Nantahala National Forest (10,900 acres are in North Carolina) and by the Chattahoochee National Forest in Georgia (where the remaining acreage is located). Elevations here range from 2,400 feet to 5,499 feet on Standing Indian Mountain with numerous peaks higher than 4,000 feet. The terrain, cut by streams, is steep and rugged. The forests are often dense, but there are grass-heath balds along many of the high ridges. All of the developed trails within this wilderness are rated "more difficult" to "most difficult." The Georgia portion of the wilderness has no developed trails. However, old roadbeds, which have been closed to vehicles, are suitable for hiking. Many of these old roads connect with trails in North Carolina. Several trails are open to horse travel. These are clearly marked by horse-with-rider signs.

Standing Indian Basin is a horseshoe-shaped drainage basin for the Nantahala and Blue Ridge Mountains. It's rimmed by several peaks that are more than 5,000 feet in elevation: Albert Mountain, Big Butt, Little Bald and Standing Indian Mountain. There is an abundance of wildlife and recreational opportunities here, particularly hiking. The nicely landscaped Standing Indian Campground, which is open from March 31 to December 1, has 84 camping sites, picnic areas, water and sanitary facilities for a fee of $10 a night. The Nantahala River, which flows right through the campground, offers fine trout fishing. No reservations are required.

Hikers and backpackers will find a special parking area at the Backcountry Information Center on F.R. 67, less than a half-mile from the campground and picnic area gate. The Appalachian Trail curves around the south and east ridge of the basin with various trails ascending off it. Trail heads can also be found all along F.R. 67, including the John Wasilik Memorial Poplar Trail that takes you to the second-largest yellow poplar in the United States (see our Attractions chapter).

The Big Indian Loop is a good horseback-riding trail — also shared with hikers, hunters and fishers. It begins at a wildlife field off F.R. 67 about 4 miles beyond the Backcountry Information Station and meanders through extensive rhododendron and birch thickets with good views of Big Indian Creek. Just follow the orange blazes.

And while here, you'll probably want to climb Standing Indian Mountain. To do so, take the Kimsey Creek Trail that begins at the Back-Country Information area off F.R. 67, where there's a bulletin board containing information about the area's many trails, then follow the blue blazes to the road bridge in the campground. Immediately after crossing the bridge, take the Park Creek Trail to the first blue-blazed trail leading to the left. This is the Kimsey Creek Trail, a moderately difficult trail that follows Kimsey Creek upstream, crossing it several times. Along the way, you'll go through three wildlife fields where you may see deer, grouse or other wildlife. When it ends at Deep Gap, you can turn left on the Appalachian Trail and continue a little more than 2 miles to Standing Indian Mountain. Backtrack (about a 7.5-mile round-trip) or return downhill on the rather strenuous Lower Ridge Trail, another popular but steeper trail that's also used to get to Standing Indian Mountain (about a 10-mile hike). You can also drive to Deep Gap on F.R. 71, thereby cutting the hiking distance to the summit to just more than 2 miles — a 4-mile round trip.

Among the other interesting hiking possibilities — and we've only mentioned a few — are trails to both Mooney Falls and Big Laurel Falls, which can also be reached from F.R. 67 (see our Waterfalls chapter). Speaking of water, the 9-mile stretch of the Nantahala River that runs from Beechertown to Fontana Lake is nationally known as a world-class whitewater river (see our Recreation chapter).

Area businesses situated along U.S. Highway 19 offer a variety of services, including outfitting and guiding, boat rentals, instruction and clinics, restaurants and overnight accommodations. Finally, visitors can drive through the Coweeta Experimental Forest to see forest management practices in silverculture, hydrology and engineering. A self-guiding brochure is available at the station office, which is open Monday through Friday from 7:30 AM until 4 PM. It's on U.S. 441, south of Murphy. This unit of the Forest Service's Southern Research Station was established in 1934.

## Pisgah National Forest

In 1889, George Vanderbilt came to this area and, like the authors of this book, fell in love with it. He bought several thousand acres of abused farmland near Asheville and built his famous Biltmore Estate, which still belongs to his family but is open to the public (see our Biltmore Estate and Winery chapter). To reclaim this used-up land, he hired Gifford Pinchot, a young American who had gotten his degree in scientific forestry in Germany, the only country that was teaching such an innovative concept at the time.

When the opportunity arose, Vanderbilt also began to buy up acreage in what is now Pisgah Forest. His dream, and that of Pinchot, was to create a vast estate where forest resources could be conserved for a continual supply of goods. Eventually, he owned 100,000 acres and named this vast tract after Pisgah Mountain, a prominent peak on his land. (In the Bible, Pisgah was the mountain from which God showed Moses the Promised Land. The Asheville area's 5,721-foot mountain is thought to have been named by Rev. James Hall, a chaplain who accompanied Gen. Griffith Rutherford on his punitive strike against the Cherokees in 1776.)

Pinchot left Biltmore Estate at the request

Photo: Tammy Hopkins

The Biltmore Campus Trail at the Cradle of Forestry.

# Nurturing Nature at the Cradle

One spring, summer and fall a few years ago, while working as an interpretive trail guides at the Cradle of Forestry, a National Historic Site in Pisgah National Forest, we looped over and over the same two 1-mile trails, describing the bountiful tree and plant life that flourish in these mountains and of the Biltmore Forest School. (The Biltmore Forest School had it's "campus" and began American forestry here.) Not once in all that time was there ever a minute of boredom. Wildflowers flowers blossomed and died; trees changed with the seasons; new exhibits appeared; educational programs and festivals excited the children. The new Forest Discovery Center that was under construction at that time, grew before our eyes. It was obvious that the Cradle's visitors, its staff and its many volunteers loved it here. You will too.

It doesn't matter if you're an adult or child; if the weather is bad or good; if you have an hour to spend or a whole day, the Cradle of Forestry can enrich, delight and enlighten you.

In April 1997 a wonderful array of 18 new exhibits opened in the Center. One lets you climb a replicated hillside, complete with rocks, trees, wildflowers and animals, through the different levels of a forest. Below the hill, you can crawl through a 30-foot, underground tunnel with roots for handholds to observe the creatures living there. A "Water in the Forest" exhibit teaches the dynamics of a watershed, from raindrops to faucet. You can play with interactive tumbling blocks to learn "The Habitat Game" that is so important to wildlife survival. Interactive computers let you manage a forest ecosystem and show you the consequences of your actions. A "Global Connections" exhibit and video focuses on issues facing forest managers throughout the world.

But the most popular exhibit by far is the "Fire-Fighting Helicopter Simulator," a sensory journey using visuals, sound, movement and smells for a flight into the depths of a wildfire to drop retardant to quench the flames. These are just some of the 18 exhibits inside the Center.

Here, also, you can view a very interesting 18-minute movie that recounts the history of the first forestry school, dine at the Forest Bounty Cafe and browse through an excellent gift shop full of charming toys and a fine selection of regional and outdoor books. Outside, two separate trails, which you can take with a guide or on your own, lead to some of the old buildings built by both early settlers and Dr. Schenck for his school and forest rangers. Modern-day crafters with last-century skills can often be found on the Biltmore Campus Trail: You might see toy maker Bob Miller, Gee Haw Whimmy Diddle Champion, and his wife Barbara, a weaver and a skilled open-hearth cook.

On the Forest Festival Trail, there's an 1915 Climax logging locomotive that children love to climb to ring the bell and talk to 86-year-old Preacher Rose, who burned a little coal on the train in the 1930s on Snowbird Mountain in Robbinsville. He comes to share his stories about logging trains Wednesdays through Saturdays. (The trails, the Forest Discovery Center and the exhibits are all wheelchair accessible.)

In addition to all this, there are many special programs and events that take place throughout the Cradle's season which runs from April 19 through November 2. These include the Appalachian Spring Celebration, which lasts from the end of April through

— continued on next page

Photo: Tammy Hopkins

The most popular exhibit at the Cradle of Forestry is the "Fire-Fighting Helicopter Simulator," a multi-sensory journey into the depths of a wildfire.

the end of May and concentrates on the diversity of wildflowers, birds and waterfalls and includes a wildflower photography contest; Bugs, Bogs and Beavers, which runs for over a week mid-July and offers guided hikes and ponds and streams explorations; Smokey the Bear's Birthday Party draws droves of children for all kinds of skits, games, music, a puppet show, birthday cake and, of course, Smokey; Forest Festival Day in early October brings over 50 crafters to the Cradle to demonstrate their skills at turning nature's bounty into art. At this festival you can learn to fly fish, try your hand with a crosscut saw, meet live animals and speak with archeologists who have uncovered artifacts in the Cradle area dating back 5,000 years.

On top of all that, for four evenings in late summer, the Waldenfest Summer Evening Concert series is held at the Cradle of Forestry; it's co-sponsored by Brevard College. Tickets for these musical events, which range from classical to jazz to show tunes, are $6 for adults and $3 for students. Season tickets are $16. (See our Arts and Culture chapter for more information on the concerts and on the Cradle of Forestry.)

The Cradle is located on U.S. Highway 276, 4 miles south of the Blue Ridge Parkway at milepost 412, or 11 miles from the intersection of U.S. Highways 64, 276 and North Carolina Highway 280 at the Brevard entrance to Pisgah Forest. It's open from 9 AM until 5 PM. Admission for adults is $4; students 6 to 17 years old are admitted for $2; children ages 5 younger are admitted for free. For more information called (828) 877-3130 or (828) 884-5713.

of Theodore Roosevelt to establish what would become the United States Forest Service. Vanderbilt replaced him with a German forester, Dr. Carl A. Schenck, who eventually started America's first school of forestry in the Pink Beds, a 20,000-acre parcel known for its lovely mountain laurels and other flowering plants. The area where the school stood is now a National Historic Site called The Cradle of Forestry. It still retains many of the school's structures, some of which were former buildings of the settlers who lived in the Pink Beds. The Cradle also offers guided trail walks and a great visitors center with a wealth of exhibits (for more specific information see our "Cradle of Forestry" Close-up in this chapter.)

In 1914, George Vanderbilt died at the age of 52 of complications from appendicitis. Shortly after that, his widow, Edith, wrote a letter to the Secretary of Agriculture of the United States that began, "Sir: I now confront the question of what disposal I shall make of Pisgah Forest, which, under the terms of my late husband's will, has passed to me without qualifications or condition." What she did was pass on 80,000 acres of the land to the Forest Service that her husband's former employee, Gifford Pinchot, now headed.

Over the years, other tracts have been added to this glorious forest so that it now contains 495,979 acres, which is more or less split across the middle by the Blue Ridge Parkway. It contains three wilderness areas: Shining Rock, Linville Gorge and Middle Prong. The Appalachian Trail runs along its border with Tennessee, and the relatively new Mountains-to-the-Sea Trail crosses through the forest (see the Three Famous Trails Close-up in our Recreation chapter). There are many other popular attractions here, such as the Fish

Hatchery, the Pisgah Center for Wildlife Education, Roan Mountain Gardens and Sliding Rock. (There are $3 parking fees at both Roan Mountain and Sliding Rock; $15 season passes are also available.) See our Attractions and Waterfalls chapters for more.

Pisgah Forest surrounds the east's tallest mountain, 6,684-foot Mount Mitchell, a state park unto itself. Pisgah has some 40 recreational areas that offer fishing, camping, hiking and so on. Some have developed campgrounds, but some provide only primitive camping in order to protect the environment, because this forest is a botanical wonderland. For example, the whole state has 55 species of orchids, and 39 of them are found in Pisgah. More than 200 species of plants grow on Roan Mountain alone. Pisgah is more of a whole piece than the Nantahala National Forest, but it still has some scattered boundaries and is divided into four districts. The most used, with more than 5 million visitors a year, is the Pisgah District, comprised heavily of the land that was originally owned by the Vanderbilts.

## Appalachian Ranger District, French Broad Station
### U.S. Hwy. 25/70 • (828) 622-3202

This is an area of Pisgah Forest that can almost guarantee you solitude. Mostly in Madison County with a little bit of the northeast section of Haywood thrown in, it contains 79,292 acres of some of the Appalachians' most isolated and craggy terrain. Many peaks here are more than 4,000 feet, the highest being Camp Creek Bald at 4,844 feet. This area is rich in botanical surprises, including a number of threatened or endangered species.

The district's only developed campground is the Rocky Bluff Campground and picnic area, on a tree-covered ridge a little more than

3 miles south of Hot Springs on N.C. Highway 209 S. There is also a primitive campground at Harmon Den and picnic areas at Murray Branch and Big Creek.

The district includes some 25 trails covering 127 miles, including three horse trails. Nearly 85 miles of the Appalachian Trail travels the mountain ridge forming the North Carolina-Tennessee state line. The famous trail can be accessed in many places, including on Max Patch Mountain (4,629 feet), where there are extraordinary views from its grassy summit. To reach Max Patch by car, drive south from Hot Springs on N.C. Hwy 209-S for 7.3 miles. Turn south of S.R. 1175 and drive 5.3 miles to S.R. 1181. Three miles on this gravel road will take you within a half-mile of the top. There you can take a 1.4-mile loops trail across its summit or a 2.4-mile trail around the top for great view from all sides.

For more information, contact the French Broad District Ranger Station listed in this chapter.

## Appalachian Ranger District, Tocane Station
**U.S. Hwy. 19 E. bypass, Burnsville**
• **(828) 682-6146**

The 74,458-acre Tocane Station is full of history. Even the name dates back to the Cherokees, because it comes from the Toe and Cane rivers that are in this area. According to legend, Toe was the nickname of an Indian princess, Estatoe, who wanted to marry a young brave from another tribe. Her people not only rejected the marriage proposal, but they killed the young man, after which the princess drowned herself in the river that came to be called Toe.

In 1913, the Forest Service purchased the first 25,000 acres that make up this district on the slopes of the Black Mountains. More than 55 miles of the Appalachian Trail meander in and out of North Carolina and Tennessee along a ridgeline to the north. The Craggy Mountain Scenic Area (not to be confused with Craggy Gardens on the Blue Ridge Parkway) is in the southwestern section of the district, where you'll find Douglas Falls, which is listed in our Waterfalls chapter.

One of the most renowned spots in this district is Roan Mountain Gardens, or simply "The Roan" as it's called around here. This 6,286-foot "bald" summit is the highest point of the Unaka Mountains, a range that forms a high barrier between eastern Tennessee and Western North Carolina. Even when it was nearly inaccessible, Roan Mountain was famous for its scenic beauty. In 1877, Gen. Thomas Wilder built a 28-room log inn on its summit and replaced that in 1885 with the 166-room Cloudland Hotel. His ads read: "Come up out of the sultry plains to the 'land of sky,' magnificent view above the clouds where rivers are born, a most extended prospect of 50,000 square miles in six different states, 100 mountain tops over 4,000 feet high in sight."

The hotel was abandoned after 1900 and burned just before World War I. After that, the old stands of spruce and balsam fir trees were cut, and the rootstock of the lovely purple rhododendrons that grew here was sold to nurseries, leaving only a few straggling bushes. But nature prevailed, and the flowering shrubs came back in neat clumps rather than in dense thickets, though some of these bushes grow from 15 to 20 feet tall and produce up to 800 blooms each. Today, like the guests of the Cloudland Hotel, you can enjoy the far vistas, stunning sunrises and sunsets and full-circle rainbows, plus 600 acres of rhododendron gardens and 850 acres of Fraser fir. The deep magenta-pink flowers are usually in full bloom during the last two weeks of June. You can learn much more about these and Roan Mountains' other wonderful plants on a self-guided trail through the gardens.

The name of the mountain is a mystery. Some say it came from a roan horse left on the summit by Daniel Boone. It may be from the red-berried "roan tree" that grows on its crest. Another mystery is the strange "music" heard here from time to time that sounds like the humming of thousands of bees. Scientists think that electrically charged air currents swirling by each other near the peak might cause it.

The gardens are on N.C. Highway 261, 13 miles north of Bakersville. The road to the gardens is open from approximately May 1 through October 31, depending on the weather. There is a $3 parking fee.

There are two family campgrounds in the

Tocane District: the Carolina Hemlocks Recreation Area and the Vlock Mountain Recreation Area. (See our Recreation chapter for more information.) There are areas for picnicking, fishing, swimming and hiking. A mile-long Hemlock Nature Trail begins at the swimming beach. Two others, Colbert Ridge Trail and the Buncombe Horse Range Trail, start nearby.

Three miles on up N.C. Highway 80, turn right on F.R. 472 and drive 3 miles to reach the Black Mountain Recreation Area. The Briar Bottom Group Camp (reservation required) is in the same area. From the group camp's gate, the 1-mile Briar Bottom Trail loops the campground, crossing two footbridges in the process. Both hikers and bikers use it. Another short trail goes up Setrock Creek to a waterfall. Both the Mount Mitchell and Lost Cove Ridge Trails are accessible from the campground. (See our Recreation chapter.)

## Grandfather District
**Rt. 1, Exit 90 (Nebo/Lake James exit) off of I-40, 9 mi. east of Marion**
**• (828) 652-2144**

This very scenic district's 186,735 acres cover parts of Avery, Burke, Caldwell and McDowell counties. Very near its center is the 10,975-acre Linville Gorge Wilderness Area, where you can still find virgin forests in deep coves and four different species of rhododendrons.

There are two campground/picnic areas in the district: The primitive, tents-only Curtis Creek Campground and the Mortimer Campground. The area also has two primitive camps in the Wilson Creek area at Chestnut and Kawana, and there are other picnic sites at Barkhouse on N.C. Highway 181 and at Mulberry, north of Lenoir. (See our Recreation chapter for more information.)

The Linville Gorge Wilderness Area offers a well-worth-it challenge to hikers and rock climbers. Here, the Linville River drops 2,000 feet in a 14-mile series of cascades between steep escarpments. Camping in the gorge is limited to three days and two nights. To control the numbers, a free camping permit that you can get from the Forest Service, (828) 257-4203, is required on weekends and holidays from May 1 through October 31. You

can get permits at the rangers office off I-40, 9 miles east of Marion or at the Linville Falls Visitor Center, (828) 765-1045 (milepost 316 at Linville) on Kistler Memorial Highway, which is open from 9 AM to 5 PM from April through November.

Famous Linville Falls is not a part of the Linville Gorge Wilderness Area. Just off the Blue Ridge Parkway, it's under the management of the National Park Service (see our Blue Ridge Parkway and Waterfalls chapters).

The Grandfather District has around 70 hiking trails, but many are not blazed or well maintained, so be sure to get information and good maps of the area before setting out. The one exception is the Mountains-to-the-Sea Trail, 46.5 miles of which run through this forest. (See our "Three Famous Trails" gray box in the Recreation chapter.)

## Pisgah District
**1001 Pisgah Hwy. (U.S. Hwy. 276)**
**• (828) 877-3350**

This district's 156,103 acres take in parts of Buncombe, Haywood, Henderson and Transylvania counties. It contains more than 275 miles of hiking trails that range from easy to very strenuous as well as horse trails and trails open to mountain bikes. The most challenging and the longest trails are the 31.7 miles of the Mountains-to-the-Sea Trail that runs through the district and the heavily used 30-mile Art Loeb Trail. The Pisgah District also has four campgrounds, plus three group campgrounds. Among the most popular are the Davidson River Campground right on the beautiful Davidson River, just 1.5 miles from the Brevard entrance to the forest on U.S. 276 and Lake Powhatan (see our Recreation chapter) on F.R. 3884 about 13 miles south of Asheville.

Definitely the most popular and used part of Pisgah Forest is the 16-mile stretch of U.S. 276 from the Brevard entrance to the Blue Ridge Parkway. This route brings you to the Davidson River Campground, the Pisgah District Ranger Station, the Fish Hatchery, the Pisgah Center for Wildlife Education (see our Attractions chapter), famous Looking Glass Falls and Sliding Rock, a natural waterslide (see our Waterfalls chapter) and the Cradle of Forestry next door to the Pink Beds picnic area. All along this route, you'll find picnicking spots by the Davidson River and numerous hiking trails. One very popular one is Looking Glass Rock Trail, a strenuous 6.2-mile round-trip hike to the top of a huge granite dome, which dominates the area and is very popular with rock climbers. Also try Moore's Cove, a 1.4-mile easy hike that ends at a lovely waterfall that you can walk behind (see our Waterfalls chapter).

Two of Pisgah Forest's three wilderness areas are also in the Pisgah District: the 18,500-acre Shining Rock Wilderness and the 7,900-acre Middle Prong Wilderness. Unfortunately, wilderness areas in this part of the country are in danger of "being loved to death." Certainly, if you are seeking solitude, these are not the places to find it. They have become so popular, and the impact of visitors on these areas is becoming so damaging, that you would do much better to visit other sections of the forest, where you occasionally might see some signs of past logging but can certainly have vast, beautiful areas of the woods almost totally to yourself.

# State Parks

## New River State Park
**Alleghany County access: by river only near Sparta, S.R. 1549 and S.R. 1308 Ashe County access: near Jefferson, S.R. 1590 (Wagoner Rd.) and U.S. 221 off N.C. 88**
• **(336) 982-2587 for both counties**

The New River, around which this state park is framed, is reported to be the oldest river in North America. It cuts a deep, twisting groove from the state boundary with Virginia and flows like a curling, satin ribbon through Ashe and Alleghany, the two northernmost counties of Western North Carolina. The beauty of this primeval river was almost lost 30 years ago when the Appalachian Power Company applied for a license to dam the New River and build reservoirs along its length. Fortunately, citizen opposition gained momentum, and in 1975, after extensive hearings and litigation, the North Carolina General Assembly acted to preserve a 26.5-mile

stretch of this historic river — from its confluence with the Dog Creek to the Virginia line — officially naming it a State Scenic River. The next year, the Secretary of the Interior moved to designate the same stretch as a part of the National Wild and Scenic River System, and Congress followed suit to affirm the action, thereby prohibiting the construction of dams and reservoirs on the river.

Thus the New River State Park was born. The park covers not only a scenic and tranquil waterway, but three designated parkland areas as well. The pastoral fields and forests along the New River also have their own historic interest: Indian activity here has been documented from 10,000 years ago by archaeological excavations that uncovered pottery shards, arrowheads, stone axes and other artifacts. This area of the New River Valley appeared to have served as a hunting ground for several neighboring tribes, Cherokees, Shawnee and Creek Indians, on their way north to hunting lands along the Ohio River.

Today, New River State Park is a popular destination for outdoor recreation. You can picnic at the river's access areas and at tables sheltered by a grove of trees or beneath a bonafide roof. Camping is facilitated at all three access points, but the Wagoner Road access off N.C. Highway 88 is the largest public area, offering restrooms, hiking trails, camp sites, picnic areas and put-in points for canoeing. The New River's placid waters are perfect for canoeing, which makes it an extremely popular sport here. In fact, the Alleghany County access area near the Virginia border can be reached only by canoe. This remote spot is bordered on one shore by an imposing rock face and on the other by a primitive camping area. Canoeing campers at this site must register at designated boxes or with a park ranger. Canoes may also be launched from the Wagoner Road access and U.S. Highway 221 access in Ashe County to the south and from numerous bridges that cross the New River.

You'll probably see more than one fisherman hip-deep in the well-stocked waters of this river. Area natives claim these waters provide some of the best bass fishing in the state. Anglers do need a license and should also be aware of fishing regulations of the N.C.

Wildlife Resources Commission. Check with park rangers for more information (and see our Recreation chapter).

The park is home to 14 species of endangered plants, including Carolina saxifrage, rattlesnake root and purple sage. Visitors are encouraged to help in the effort to protect this delicate fauna. River wildlife such as otters, beavers, muskrat, mink and raccoon abound along the shores.

A note of caution: During heavy rains, be aware that the New River is subject to heavy flooding. Canoeists are encouraged to wear flotation devices and to portage around all low-water bridges to avoid entrapment. Most importantly, know the river section you plan to traverse. Park information and maps of the river's course are available at ranger stations (see the Ranger Station grey box).

Park hours are 8 AM to 6 PM November to February; 8 AM to 7 PM in March and October; 8 AM to 8 PM during April, May and September; and 8 AM to 9 PM June through August.

## Mount Jefferson State Park
**Jefferson County access: S.R. 1152, off U.S. 221 • (336) 246-9653**

Mount Jefferson sparked interest as a park area in the 1930s when the Works Progress Administration constructed a rough 2-mile road to the summit of the mountain. It took another 20 years of local interest and persistence to reach state park status, which Mount Jefferson achieved in 1956.

Mount Jefferson is positioned geographically between the north and south forks of the New River and was once part of a broad plateau that formed much of the region. The drainage line formed by these two water sources played an important part in the formation of the mountain itself. Eons of weathering and erosion ultimately created Mount Jefferson, the majestic promontory that rises 1,600 feet from the rolling meadows and valleys below.

The drive up the mountain provides spectacular views, particularly at sunset, and you can see three states from the top (Tennessee is to the west and Virginia to the north). There are overlooks along the way and two moderately difficult trails at the top. The Summit Trail is just a fraction of a mile from the highest point on Mount Jefferson, and the 1.1-mile Rhododendron Trail that begins at the terminus of the Summit Trail is a delightful, self-guided, moderately difficult trek through the forest with stops at numbered stations. The lush beauty of the purple Catawba Rhododendron makes this trail a delight in early June. This trail also passes by a rock outcrop

Meadows and orchards carpet the high valleys of North Carolina's mountains.

Photo: Hugh Morton, Courtesy of Grandfather Mountain

called Luther Rock, made up of a volcanic amphibolite rock that gives Mount Jefferson its dark cast. The trail circles back to the picnic area parking lot below the summit.

Visitors to the high country can still see evidence of the once-abundant American chestnut in the building materials of area homes and rustic lodges that predate the 1920 blight that devastated this species of tree. And on Mount Jefferson, you can see American chestnut seedlings that continue to sprout in profusion. Sadly, the insidious blight continues to claim the trees before they can reach any significant height. Red maple, basswood, tulip trees and yellow birch also fill these woods, and you can spot a stand of big-toothed aspen below Luther Rock on the northern slopes of Mount Jefferson (only one other North Carolina county, Haywood, in the central mountain region, has these aspen trees).

Picnicking is popular at Mount Jefferson, which has a tree-shaded area with 32 tables and nine grills near the summit. Restrooms and drinking water are available nearby. There is no camping available here. Canoe-in and walk-in camping is available at nearby New River State Park.

Park hours are 9 AM to 5 PM November to February; 9 AM to 6 PM in March and October; 9 AM to 7 PM April, May and September; and 9 AM to 8 PM June through August.

Rangers urge you to call ahead before visiting Mount Jefferson during the winter. The weather in these northern mountains is often unpredictable, and roads can quickly become impassable.

## Mount Mitchell State Park
**N.C. 128, off the Blue Ridge Pkwy.**
**Mi. 355.4 • (828) 675-4611**

At 6,684 feet, Mount Mitchell is the highest peak in the eastern United States, and it also carries the distinction of being the site of North Carolina's first state park. The park covers part of the rugged Black Mountains, which were formed more than a billion years ago and soar higher than the nearby Blue Ridge range or the Great Smokies of Tennessee. This extreme elevation creates a climate more like that of Canada's, and many of the plants and animals found here are also more akin to their northern cousins than their neighbors down the hill.

Mount Mitchell State Park was formed in 1915, a reaction mainly to the effects of overcutting by the logging industry that had come into prominence at the turn of the century in North Carolina. The disappearance of much of the forests in the Black Mountains prompted Gov. Locke Craig, backed by concerned citizens, to preserve the last vestige of natural lands in this range.

Mount Mitchell is named in honor of University of North Carolina science professor Elisha Mitchell who, in 1835, made the rug-

## INSIDERS' TIP

One of our favorite hikes, which includes places where you pull yourself up by rocks and tree roots, is Mount Mitchell's Deep Gap Trail. This excellent but strenuous 8-mile round-trip hike covers four knobs on Mount Mitchell, the highest peak on the eastern seaboard (6,684 ft.). You'll see incredible wildflowers and coniferous forests, as well as ferns and lush mosses. To reach the trail entrance in this state park on N.C. Hwy. 128, off the Blue Ridge Parkway at milepost 355.4, leave your car in the picnic area parking lot. Walk directly through the picnic area until you reach a gravel trail with marker "Deep Gap Trail." This is a rough hike which will bring on a quick sweat with its straight uphill climbs: pack plenty of water and a snack. It gets very chilly (so bring a jacket) in this high elevation, and much of the trail is solid granite of the mountain. A walking stick and dependable shoes are a good idea. This is one of the most challenging hikes of the area.

ged trek into the Black Mountain Range to verify his conclusions that peaks here were indeed higher than Grandfather Mountain. Grandfather had long been thought to be the most prominent peak in the region. Mitchell, on a subsequent trip to the Black Mountain Range in 1857 to verify his measurements, which had again come under dispute, unfortunately fell from a cliff above a 40-foot waterfall, where he was knocked unconscious and drowned in the pool below.

This park has a marvelous array of 1,677 acres of woodlands, wildlife habitat, majestic views, trail systems and public camping and picnic areas. Because of the alpine-like climate, the weather here is always cooler, even in summer, than that in other parts of the state. It's a good idea to keep an extra jacket handy. The mists that roll over Mount Mitchell are a constant reminder of the extreme elevation and have historically been a hazard to small aircraft.

Mount Mitchell's summit has great sightseeing possibilities. On a clear day, the stone observation tower at the top of the mountain affords a 70-mile view. Dr. Elisha Mitchell is buried at the base of the tower, and a marker honors his work. A small nature museum halfway up the trail from the parking area to the tower is fun for children. In this rustic structure, dioramas and recordings give you a feel for the mountain's special plants and wildlife, and you can easily imagine the extremes of weather often found on lofty Mount Mitchell.

The parking area at the base of the summit is surrounded by a 40-table picnic area with stone grills and drinking water. Two sites have fireplaces under shelter and are often used for group picnics. Hiking trails branch off in several directions from the parking area. Look for the white-tailed deer that on occasion venture close to this area.

Stop at the Ranger Station at the entrance to the park for information on hiking, camping and maps of trail areas both along the ridge and down the mountain. At Mount Mitchell, you can camp family-style with a rustic ambiance at the nine-site campground that's open May 1 through October 31. This is tent camping only, no RVs. Restrooms are nearby, but no showers or hot water are available.

For day visitors who crave sustenance at this mile-high peak, try the concession stand at the summit for light snacks. For a more substantial meal and an inspiring view, you can dine at the park's restaurant a half-mile from the ranger's office. The sturdy stone-and-timber, lodge-like restaurant serves breakfast on weekends and holidays; lunch and dinner daily during park hours. Both food service locations have restrooms.

Hours at Mount Mitchell State Park are 8 AM to 6 PM November through February, 8 AM to 7 PM in March and October, 8 AM to 8 PM April, May and September and 8 AM to 9 PM June through August.

# State Forests and Game Lands

## Dupont State Forest
### Sky Valley Rd., Hendersonville
• (828) 251-6509

This is Western North Carolina's newest state forest. Its 7,600 acres in Henderson and Transylvania Counties were purchased in 1996 and 1997 from DuPont after the company sold its industrial operation and 2,700 acres of surrounding land holdings to Sterling Diagnostic Imaging. The forest is situated in an upland plateau of the Little River Valley with elevations that range from 2,300 to 3,600 feet. Its gently rolling land is bordered by moderately steep hills and mountains that are topped by exposed granite slabs and domes.

Soon certain forest's trails will be opened for horseback riding and bicycling. For now, a special permit is need for these activities. Registered as North Carolina Gameland, hunting in season is by lottery only and no hunting is allowed on Sundays. For fishing, streams here are classified as "wild." (Contact the North Carolina Wildlife Resources Commission, 512 North Salisbury Street, Raleigh, NC 27604-1188, (919) 733-7291, for more details on both hunting and fishing in this forest.) ATVs are forbidden in the forest.

At present, the land is open for hiking, and there are nearly a dozen very interesting trails that range from easy to strenuous. (A detailed, hand-marked color map is available at the Henderson County Travel & Tourism office, 201 S. Main St., Hendersonville, for $7.) For a short hike to 13-foot Hooker Falls, the site of a former gristmill, take DuPont Road (off Crab Creek Road for about three miles until you see the Little River bridge at the bottom of a long hill). Park near the gated Hooker Falls Road on the right just before the bridge. Walk around the gate and along the dirt road, bearing left at the fork and continuing parallel to the river. In a few minutes you will approach the top of Hooker Falls. Continue straight on the path to a good viewing location at the pool below.

If it's a hot day, and you'd like to cool off, continue on up DuPont Road for another 2.6 miles until it dead ends into Cascade Lake Road (Buck Forest Road on some maps). Drive almost a mile to a wide parking spot on the right. Walk across the road and go around the gate on the marked Corn's Mill Shoal Road. Walk past the intersection of Big Rock Trail to a crossing over Tom's Creek. Continue on the graded road to a fork. Take the right fork and after a short distance take the left fork (you'll still be on Corn's Mill Shoals Road) until your reach a gentle waterslide and

popular ford on the Little River where local residents have enjoyed swimming for years.

## Green River Game Lands
**Big Hungry Road (S.R. 1802), Hendersonville • (828) 733-7291**

Over 10,000 rugged acres in Henderson and Polk Counties make up these state-owned gamelands. There are 15 miles of beautiful trails here ranging from easy to strenuous, but because of the nature of the terrain, its recommended that you don't hike here alone. It's also wise to avoid the area during hunting seasons. Some of the trails offer great views of Tryon Peak and the Green River Gorge to the south. Others take you on a ridgeline next to the steep and dangerous Loobie Cliffs or for a view from Pace Cliffs. No vehicles or horses are allowed here. A brochure with a map and descriptions of the trails can be found at visitor centers in the area, or contact the North Carolina Wildlife Resources Commission, 512 North Salisbury Street, Raleigh, NC 27604-1188, (828) 733-7291. It is also your source for information on hunting here.

## Holmes Educational State Forest
**Crab Creek Rd., Hendersonville • (828) 692-0100**

Well-tended trails loop through 235 acres of mountain forests at this pretty state forest.

One of the most delightful, and educational, things about it is the Talking Trees Trail, which features different hardwood trees that, at the touch of a button tell stories about themselves, their sites and the forest history. Two new trails include the Soil and Water Trail featuring a 300-foot boardwalk over a wetland area and Crab Creek Trail spotlighting firefighting equipment displays and a walk through a pine stand. (Crab Creek Trail was built with wheelchairs in mind.) There is also a Forest Demonstration Trail that teaches actual forest practices. The Forestry Center houses audiovisual exhibits, and a natural amphitheater is available for special sessions or groups.

Holmes also has picnic tables and a group picnic shelter with a massive stone fireplace. For the hardy, there are walk-in tent sites in the forest that can be reserved by calling the above number. This pleasant state forest is open from mid-March through mid-November. It is 8.5 miles from Hendersonville on Crab Creek Road (S.R. 1127).

We've included attractions in this chapter that can keep even a whole family busy without costing a bundle — some are even free.

# Attractions

Most of the "attractions" in these mountains are the mountains themselves. There's not much of a need for artificial diversion, what with the natural activities inherent to this area. But if you tire of hiking, or tubing down mountain streams, fly fishing, mountain biking, kayaking, antiquing, and scouring the farmer's market for homemade preserves and string beans, then head over to these more organized attractions of the mountains.

It doesn't matter if rain is pouring through the treetops or sunshine is bursting over the rugged terrain, you'll always find something to do in North Carolina's mountains. We've included attractions in this chapter that can keep a whole family busy without costing a bundle — some are even free. One of the most alluring attractions in our mountains is the palatial Biltmore Estate in Asheville, to which we've dedicated an entire chapter. Other popular destinations, such as the Carl Sandburg Home in Flat Rock, have been included in other chapters. Details on the famous poet's lovely Connemara farm, where he spent the final 22 years of his life, can be found in the Arts and Culture chapter. The Festivals and Annual Events chapter is a good source of ideas for pleasurable outings, as are the Resorts, Rock Hounding and Waterfalls chapters. So pick your pleasure. But remember, these are only a few of the spontaneous, special ways to enjoy a ramble through the North Carolina highlands.

## Northern Mountains

### Ashe County

**Ashe County Cheese Factory**
**106 E. Main St., West Jefferson**
• **(336) 246-2501**
Did you know that it takes 10 gallons of milk to make one pound of cheese? That's one of the facts you'll learn as you watch cheese being made in this factory founded in 1930. The only cheese factory in North Carolina, it makes several varieties, including cheddar, colby and Monterey Jack. Guides escort groups through a viewing room, explain the process and answer questions. Sample your favorites and take a few home from the company cheese shop across the street from the factory. The plant is open 8:30 AM to 5 PM Monday through Saturday. Admission is free.

### Avery County

**Grandfather Mountain**
**U.S. Hwy. 221, outside Linville, a mile off the Blue Ridge Pkwy., Mi. 305**
• **(828) 733-2013, (800) 468-7325**
The rugged outline of this ridge that takes on the appearance of a bearded face — the "grandfather" — gives this mountain its name. Grandfather Mountain is the highest in the Blue Ridge chain. It is part of the International Network of Biosphere Reserves, "a special place where man and nature thrive in harmony." Of the 324 existing Biosphere Reserves, Grandfather is the only one privately owned. This wonderful oasis allows you to come close to the natural wildlife habitats of black bears, cougars, deer, eagles and river otter.

The nature museum offers valuable information. If you have no fear of heights, you might attempt the exhilaration of the famous Mile High Swinging Bridge (keep remembering to look at the view).

Work off those wobbly knees with 12 miles of hiking trails. The Grandfather Trail is a favorite, a rugged but beautiful trail traversing 2.3 miles. The Mountain also offers meandering footpaths and scenic walks for novice hikers. Once you've relaxed, spread a picnic and enjoy this majestic place, a reminder of the fragility of our relationship with this earth. The site is open daily except Thanksgiving and Christmas from 8 AM to 5 PM in winter, 8 AM to 6 PM in spring and fall and 8 AM to 7 PM in summer. A gift shop and restaurant are on the site. Admission is $10 for adults and $5 for children ages 4 to 12. Children younger than 4 are admitted free.

## Madison County

### Hot Springs Spa
**315 Bridge St., Hot Springs**
**• (828) 622-7676**

Does arthritis or rheumatism plague you? Do you seek relief from stomach, liver or gall bladder ailments? Historically, these mineral springs, maintaining a natural 100-degree temperature year round, have provided relief for visitors as early as the turn of the century. That was the heyday of this once-fashionable health resort. With the passage of time and a changing world, the springs fell into disuse, and the population dwindled away. But in 1990, the famous hot springs came into new ownership and are now back in business, offering a '90s version of "taking the waters."

Jacuzzis filled with the curative waters are available for hourly rates, determined by the number of people in your party. These run from $12 per hour for one person to $30 per hour for four people. Several resident massage therapists are available by appointment for a 30-minute session costing $30 or a one-hour session for $50. A half-hour foot Reflexology session will set you back $25.

A log fire in the central yard is perfect for lounging and communing with friends. The friendly employees at the spa make you feel like a long lost relative. The word "spa" may be a misnomer. This is a very casual place — don't expect luxury — but do expect to commune successfully with nature (leafy trees and the sky are your canopy). Tubs are set alongside the rushing French Broad River and Spring Creek.

The Hot Springs Spa is open year round

from 9 AM. Rates increase for evening sessions (after 7 PM). Lodging facilities are available in the RV park and campground, for which options include electric, water and sewer hookup and tent sites. A facility for hot showers is also available. Primitive camping cabins are also available, as is one fully furnished log cabin with a Jacuzzi on the back porch, fed from the natural spring, at a cost of $125 per night. When camping, children 6 or younger stay free. Special discounts and group rates are also available for the campground.

## McDowell County

### Linville Caverns
**U.S. Hwy. 221, between Linville and Marion, 4 miles south of the Blue Ridge Pkwy. • (828) 756-4171, (800) 419-0540**

These limestone caverns with marvelous stalactite and stalagmite formations were first explored in the late 1880s by H.E. Colton and his local guide Dave Franklin. However, the Indians had known about the caverns since 1822. Deep inside Humpback Mountain, these caverns were also hideouts for army deserters from both sides during the Civil War.

Today, in the company of experienced guides, you can take a path that leads along an underground stream filled with trout whose life in perpetual darkness has resulted in blindness. The limestone formations, suspended like jewels, have developed over eons into interesting shapes, such as the Frozen Waterfall, Natural Bridge and the Franciscan Monk. Did you ever wonder what absolute darkness looks like? You'll get your chance deep in these caverns. This must be the guides' favorite part — switching off those lights! You literally can't see your hand in front of your face.

The temperature underground is a constantly cool 52 degrees, so come prepared with a sweater or jacket. A gift shop is well-stocked, and items are reasonably priced.

Admission is $5 for adults and $3 for children ages 5 to 12. Seniors pay $4. Group rates are available. The caverns are open 9 AM to 6 PM June 1 through Labor Day; 9 AM to 5 PM April, May, September and October; and 9 AM to 4:30 PM November through March. They're open on weekends only in December, January and February and are closed Thanksgiving and Christmas.

# Mitchell County

### The Orchard at Altapass
#### Mi. 328.4 • (828) 765-9531
This historic orchard features fresh apples and peaches from July to November and is open only during these months. You can pick your own, or just buy the already-picked baskets and brown-paper bags of juicy fruits. Tours of the orchard are free. Come enjoy music, stories and hayrides on Saturdays.

# Watauga County

### The Blowing Rock
#### Off U.S. Hwy. 321, Blowing Rock
#### • (828) 295-7111
Fanciful tales about this beautiful spot are as interesting as the facts. This rocky granite outcrop is swept by a constant updraft from Johns River Gorge 3,000 feet below. Those are the facts.

The most familiar romantic legend of the Blowing Rock is that a beautiful Indian maiden was taken from the plains to Blowing Rock by her father, a Chickawaw chieftan who was fearful of a white man's adoration of his daughter. The daughter met an Indian brave wandering below the Blowing Rock and shot an arrow in his direction to capture his attention. They fell in love, but a reddening of the sky brought them back to the rock. It was a sign of trouble to the brave, commanding his return to his tribe in the plains. With the maiden's entreaties not to leave her, the brave, torn by conflict of duty and heart, leapt from the Rock. The maiden prayed to the Great Spirit every day until one evening, a gust of wind blew her lover back onto the Rock and into her arms.

The Blowing Rock claims a panoramic view of Mount Mitchell, Hawksbill, Grandfather and Table Rock mountains in the distance. The Rock is just outside the town of Blowing Rock and is open daily from March through November; it's open weekends in winter months, weather permitting. Hours are 9 AM to 5 PM March, April and November; 8 AM to 8 PM May through August; and 8 AM to 7 PM September through October. Admission fees are approximately $4 for adults, $1 for children ages 6 to 11 and $3 for seniors and groups.

### Daniel Boone Native Gardens
#### 591 Horn in the West Dr., off N.C. Hwy. 105 and U.S. Hwy. 321 and 421, Boone
#### • (828) 264-6390
The stone gatehouse bids you welcome as you enter the gardens through the handsome wrought iron gate, a gift made by Daniel Boone VI, a direct descendent of the great pioneer. Adjacent to Horn in the West, these beautiful gardens include an extensive collection of native plants covering 6 acres, informally landscaped with trails, split rail fences and a reflection pool at the Squire Boone

## INSIDERS' TIP

Before shopping at the Farmer's Market outside of Asheville, try The Moose Cafe, just above the market's entrance, for a hearty country breakfast (see our Restaurant's chapter for detailed information). Steaming hot biscuits grace your table before you even order and can be slathered with the honey, molasses, or homemade apple butter already provided. Lunches and dinners are traditional Southern fare; the menu includes a daily special and a four-vegetable plate. Prices are reasonable. Soak in the local atmosphere, try a piece of deep-dish pie and take a jar of apple butter with you.

Cabin. Many plants such as bloodroot, dog-tooth violet, yellow lady slippers and maiden hair fern are marked. A spring trickles through the enormous boulders of the Rockery, while a statue of St. Francis stands in the center of the secluded prayer retreat. There's even a meditation sanctuary that lets you pause and give thanks for such beauty. The gardens are open daily May through September and weekends in October 10 AM to 6 PM (until 8 PM when Horn in the West is running). A small admission is charged.

### Hickory Ridge Homestead
**591 Horn in the West Dr., off N.C. Hwy. 105 and U.S. Hwys. 321 and 421, Boone • (828) 264-9089, (828) 264-2120**

You'll swear you just saw Daniel Boone, but it was one of the costumed interpreters at Hickory Ridge Homestead on the grounds of Horn in the West. This living museum offers a glimpse into 18th-century mountain life and culture through a variety of activities including regular demonstrations in weaving and candlemaking, as well as presentations of other crafts. Try your hand at weaving on a 180-year-old loom, spinning wool or participating in other hands-on activities. Admission, only about $2 for adults and $1 for children, helps support the museum and its projects. Hours vary with the seasons, so call ahead. And while you're at it, ask about the intensive living history weekends and workshops.

### Horn in the West
**591 Horn in the West Dr., off N.C. Hwy. 105 and U.S. Hwys. 321/421, Boone • (828) 264-9089, (828) 264-2120**

This outdoor drama, one of several in this region, depicts the lives of North Carolina's early settlers — Daniel Boone among them — and their struggle for independence from Britain. This production, set in pre-Revolutionary 1771, lasts about two hours and is a one-of-a kind experience: history and excitement all rolled into one. Remember, this is an outdoor production. Summer evenings can be cool, especially at this elevation, so bring a light jacket just in case. The season is mid-June to mid-August, and the drama begins each evening at 8:30. There are no performances on Mondays. Admission is approximately $12 for adults and $6 for children 12 and younger.

### Mystery Hill
**Off U.S. Hwy. 321/221 between Boone and Blowing Rock • (828) 264-2792**

Mystery Hill explores the relationship of science, optical illusion and natural phenomena. See our Kidstuff chapter for a complete description.

### Tweetsie Railroad
**On U.S. Hwy. 321/221 between Boone and Blowing Rock • (828) 264-9061, (800) 526-5740**

Take a trip back to the Old West where there's plenty of old-fashioned fun for the whole family. This 30-year-old theme park features a 100-year-old locomotive, a petting farm, a Ferris wheel and musical shows. See our Kidstuff chapter.

# Central Mountains

## Buncombe County

### The Asheville Urban Trail
**Locations in downtown Asheville**

Asheville's formative period, the boom time from 1880 to 1930, left an indelible imprint on the character of the city. This was the era of George Vanderbilt (Biltmore Estate),

---

**INSIDERS' TIP**

For those Doubting Thomases out there who have to see for themselves why they call it Grandfather Mountain, head south on N.C. Highway 105 from Boone. In the heart of Foscoe look toward the mountain on your left, and, lo and behold, there he is, sleeping on his back. You can almost hear him snore!

E.W. Grove (The Grove Park Inn) and George Willis Pack (Pack Square), men whose taste for elegance produced a stunning blend of architectural styles that remains today.

To highlight and pay homage to this remarkable period in Asheville's history, the city has commissioned the development of The Urban Trail. This series of 50 stations is marked by plaques, sculptures and other interpretative visuals that bring the area's history to life. These museums in miniature line the length of a trail that runs 1.6 miles around downtown through five theme paths. The trail is still being completed, but a significant portion with remarkable stations is already in place. The walking benefits of the trail are free, along with the pleasure of the path. For free maps and information contact Asheville City Development on 29 Haywood St. downtown, or call them at (828) 251-9973.

### Asheville Tourists Baseball
**McCormick Field, off Biltmore Ave., Asheville • (828) 258-0428**
Professional baseball at McCormick Field has been a fixture in Asheville since 1924. Many of the all-time greats of the game, such as Babe Ruth, Ty Cobb, Jackie Robinson, Pete Rose and Nolan Ryan, played here en route to the majors. The Asheville Tourists are currently in their fourth year of affiliation

as a farm team with the National League's Colorado Rockies.

The new McCormick Field, a much improved facility, was completed in 1992. The old McCormick Field, with all its well-worn charm, was actually famous for a bit part as background in some of the final scenes for the popular baseball movie *Bull Durham* with Kevin Costner. The new stadium is grand, but it's Asheville's baseball tradition that keeps folks coming to McCormick Field to cheer on the Tourists.

The Tourists baseball season begins in April and runs through the first week in September. The Asheville team, a member of the South Atlantic League, plays about 72 home games. Box seats are about $6 for adults and $4 for children; general admission seats are $4 for adults and $2.50 for children ages 3 through 12. These prices are subject to change.

### The Botanical Gardens
**151 W.T. Weaver Blvd., Asheville • (828) 252-5190**
This wonderful 10-acre garden oasis in the middle of bustling north Asheville is adjacent to the campus of the University of North Carolina at Asheville. The gardens were begun in 1960 by the Asheville Garden Club and designed by Doan Ogden, a noted land-

scape architect, to preserve the heritage of native mountain plants and flowers. Today this mature garden has a wealth of beauty around every bend in the path and within every leafy bower. A bonus is the proliferation of birds and other small wildlife that have made this wonderful garden their home. You may spot a few rabbits at dusk; squirrels and chipmunks abound in the daylight hours. A meadow for sunning, a gazebo for lounging and a cool creek make this an oasis close to the city, perfect for those after-dinner walks. Many of the trees and other flora are marked with small tags, for identification. This site receives support from volunteers, donations and memberships. A botany center offers nature-related gift items. Admission is free. No pets are allowed.

## Buncombe County Recreation Park
Gashes Creek Rd. and U.S. Hwy. 81, Asheville • (828) 298-4311

On the banks of the Swannanoa River, this old-fashioned community recreation park offers families fun rides, picnic facilities and an Olympic-size pool. See our Kidstuff chapter for more.

## The Folk Art Center
Mi. 382, off I-70 east of Asheville
• (828) 298-7928

The Folk Art Center is home to the Southern Highland Craft Guild, an educational nonprofit organization founded in 1930 to give economic support and development to the craftspeople of the Appalachian Region. The guild serves nine states and has a membership of more than 700 crafts people who work to preserve and perpetuate the Appalachian

heritage as well as develop the contemporary face of craftsmanship.

The Center's century-old Allanstand Craft Shop offers for sale the work of guild members throughout the nine-state region. There is also a fine-crafts gallery on the upper level and a 250-seat auditorium that is the scene of workshops, programs and lectures by the Guild and Park Service. Craft demonstrations are held April through December in the foyer of the Center. Clay Day and Fiber Day are two of the special events also sponsored by the Guild at the Folk Art Center each year (see our Annual Festivals and Events chapter and Crafts in the Mountains chapter for more information on the Guild). Admission is free.

## Western North Carolina Arboretum
Wesley Branch Rd., Asheville
• (828) 665-2492

The North Carolina Arboretum is in an exciting phase of its young life. This 426-acre facility already boasts a 25,500-square-foot Visitor Education Center, the Horticultural Support Facilities and Greenhouses, the Plants of Promise Garden and the mile-long Natural Garden Trail, all of which are open to the public. The new Core Area Gardens include the Stream Garden, Spring Garden, Outdoor Events Garden, Appalachian Quilt Garden, Blue Ridge Court and Grand Promenade. Additional garden development here includes a conifer and holly garden, a landscaped parking area called the Auto Garden and the Entry Plaza in front of the Visitor Education Center. Numerous woodland trails lace the forested areas and follow the path of Bent Creek. Guided tours are available for groups if you

## INSIDERS' TIP

When traveling on the Great Smoky Mountains Railway, make your reservations as early as possible, especially for viewing the fall foliage. (Some people start planning their autumn-color train ride as early as April!) All advance reservations must be prepaid two weeks in advance, and all major credit cards except American Express are accepted. The most popular seating is in the open cars, which are by far the best for taking photos. If you sit here, however, you should bring a warm jacket or other wrap during cool autumn days.

call ahead. Educational lectures, tours and workshops are scheduled throughout the year.

Admission is free, and nominal fees apply for education programs. The outdoor areas are open seven days a week from 7 AM to 7 PM. The Visitor Education Center is open Monday through Friday from 8 AM to 5 PM and Saturdays from 9 AM to 5 PM. The greenhouse is open 8 AM to 4 PM Monday through Friday. The second and fourth Sundays of the month feature an open house from 1:30 to 4:30 PM.

To find Wesley Branch Road, turn off U.S. Highway 191 onto Bent Creek Ranch Road and bear left onto Wesley Branch Road.

## Western North Carolina Farmer's Market
**570 Brevard Rd., Asheville**
• **(828) 253-1691**

It's been described as shopping at a 36-acre roadside stand. The WNC Farmer's Market, southeast of Asheville, offers a bounty of fresh produce and quality plants, shrubs, trees and garden supplies. The retail area is reminiscent of an old market square with wooden tables overflowing with goods, fresh vegetables, crafts and other gifts from the farm. The garden center is operated by several gen-erations of garden specialists, Jesse Israel & Sons, supplying every flowering need.

The restaurant, The Moose Cafe, is on U.S. Highway 191 just south of the main entrance and serves good, basic home cooking. The truck stands are a feast for the eye and food for the soul too. The conversation from the back of the truck gives as much pleasure as the brown paper sack of red delicious apples you carry home with you.

Sections of the market are open 24 hours daily, and the retail buildings are open from 8 AM to 6 PM daily in summer and 8 AM to 5 PM winter.

## Western North Carolina Nature Center
**75 Gashes Creek Rd., Asheville**
• **(828) 298-5600**

From the moment you step through the door and a three-dimensional, full-size diorama of woodland creatures greets you, you know you are indeed crossing that bridge to the natural world. Exhibits such as weather forecasting, animal identification, a real working beehive, archaeological displays and zoological collections of live reptiles and amphibians make this a special stop. See our Kidstuff chapter for more.

Musicians and dancers representing spots from all over the world converge and perform at Folkmoot USA.

## Zebulon Vance Birthplace
**Reems Creek Rd., off Old U.S. Hwys.
19/23, Weaverville • (828) 645-6706**

This charming mountain homestead was home to one of North Carolina's most prominent political figures. Zeb Vance began his career as a lawyer, assuming public office by the young age of 24. He was elected governor of North Carolina three times, most notably during the Civil War. He served three terms as senator from North Carolina. At his death in 1894, this most capable public servant was admired by colleagues and beloved by his constituency. His life and career are profiled in an exhibit in the adjoining visitors center. But better yet, is the opportunity to see a period mountain home replete with old utensils, kitchenry, rope-spring beds and other objects whose uses are explained in the informative and free guided tours.

The two-story cabin and outbuildings are reconstructions, built from hewn, yellow pine logs around the original chimney with its two massive fireplaces. The furnishings and household items depict the period from 1790 to 1840 and include a few pieces original to the Vance family.

Pioneer Living Days are celebrated here each spring and fall. Costumed staff members demonstrate skills and occupations of earlier days. Military encampments and battle reenactments are frequently part of the events. Admission to the homestead is free.

# Henderson County

Information about some of Henderson County's attractions, including the Carl Sandburg Home, the Historic Hendersonville Depot and Model Railroad, the Historic Johnson Farm and the Western North Caroline Air Museum can be found in the Arts and Culture chapter.

## St. John in the Wilderness
**U.S. Hwy. 25 S., Flat Rock
• (828) 693-9783**

This charming chapel has an interesting background. In 1837, English-born Charles Baring, in search of a healthier summer climate, brought his beloved wife Susan, the former widow of a wealthy Charleston rice planter, to an area between the Watauga settlements in what is now Watauga County and Greenville, South Carolina, known simply as "the Wilderness." Thus began a migration of wealthy families from the coast that turned Flat Rock into "the little Charleston of the mountains." Baring bought hundreds of acres in the area and built a grand home called Mountain Lodge, developed on the order of an English country estate complete with a gatekeeper's cottage, a billiard house and a deer park. The hilltop private residence, hidden by tall pines on Rutledge Drive, is one of many grand old homes from this period still in the area.

Most of these homes are private dwellings, not open to the public. However, the Barings also built a private chapel that they donated to the Episcopal Diocese of North Carolina in 1836. Here many of the cream of Southern gentry worshipped together with their slaves and were buried together in the same cemetery. The chapel, partially built of now-yellowed bricks thought to have been made by Barings' slaves, was doubled in size in 1852. The beautiful structure is 2.25 miles south of Hendersonville on the west side of U.S. Highway 25. The site has a marker and can be easily seen from the road. Both the graveyard and the church are open to visitors daily from 9 AM to 4 PM.

Charles Baring's decision to move his family to this gentle mountain climate each summer must have been the right one, because Susan lived to be 83, and he died at age 92. They are buried in a vault inside the church under the spot where their pew used to sit.

## Wolfe's Angel
## Oakdale Cemetery
**U.S. Hwy. 64 W., Hendersonville**

Just a short distance from downtown Hendersonville on U.S. Highway 64 W., the cemetery plot of a local family, the Johnsons, is marked by an angel. She holds a stone lily in her left hand and extends her right hand upward. This statue, imported from Italy and sold to the Johnson family by novelist Thomas Wolfe's father, W.O. Wolfe, is prominently featured in the author's first novel, Look Homeward, Angel. Today an iron fence protects the famous angel, and a historical marker on the highway next to the cemetery notes its importance. You can enter the cemetery for a close-up look.

# Polk County

## Foothills Equestrian Nature Center
### 500 Hunting Country Rd.,Tryon
• (828) 859-9021

FENCE, as it is commonly called, is a 300-acre nature sanctuary dedicated to education, recreation and preservation. The state-of-the-art equestrian facility hosts more than 18 events each season, including two steeple-chases, hunter/jumper and dressage shows and driving rallies. The facility is home to the Carolina Carriage Club (see our Recreation chapter). It also has bridle trails.

Even if you aren't a horse person, FENCE has great hiking trails that are open to the public free of charge from dawn until dusk all year long. It also offers on- and off-site programs for school classes as well as adult classes in wildflowers and other nature subjects. Its Bird Center activities are outstanding. In addition to lectures and slide shows, there are frequent bird-watching outings. These include regular Thursday morning bird walks at FENCE or at nearby good birding sites in the spring and fall, as well as local, regional and international birding "ventures" throughout the year.

# Rutherford County

## Chimney Rock Park
### U.S. Hwys. 64/74-A in Chimney Rock
• (800) 277-9611, (828) 625-9611

Chimney Rock Park, in Hickory Nut Gorge, has been a favorite in the Southeast. Its unusual rock formations, spectacular Hickory Nut Falls dropping 404 feet to the gorge below, winding mountainside trails and delicate wildflowers draw a steady stream of visitors annually. From the parking area, take a 26-story elevator ride to the Sky Lounge, the park's snack and gift shop area. From the deck, just outside, you have a wonderful view

of the Park's landmark and namesake, Chimney Rock. Or try the steps to the Chimney — the rock formations and spectacular views along the way are well worth it.

This prominent rocky pedestal gives visitors a spectacular 180-degree view of the Hickory Nut Gorge area and beautiful Lake Lure just beyond. Make your way down a stairway from the chimney and choose one of several beautiful trails threading through the rocky outcrops, cliffs and mountainside of Chimney Rock Park. The Skyline Trail winds upward through the woods, hugging the mountain, leveling out after about a quarter-mile and proceeding along a flat, well-trod path to the top of incredibly beautiful Hickory Nut Falls.

The park is full of fascinating rocks, ledges and natural wildlife. You can squeeze through the crevice known as the Needle's Eye, visit the Grotto, the Rock Pile, the Moonshiner's Cave (with a replica of an old moonshine still) and journey up to the magnificent heights of Inspiration Point. If you get a little weak in the knees at the thought of high places, don't worry. Chimney Rock Park's Forest Stroll trail, leading from the parking area, is a leisurely three-quarter-mile walk to the base of Hickory Nut Falls. There is a viewing deck with a few picnic tables for your convenience.

The park is open year round and offers a number of annual and ongoing activities. A resident botanist and ornithologist offer several workshops and nature walks throughout the year.

The Sky Lounge snack and gift shop offers light lunch sandwiches and features a costume exhibit from *The Last of the Mohicans* film as well as theme-related gift items. A nature center, on the Meadows about halfway up the drive to the top of the park, is a pleasant stop. Picnic areas, grills, restrooms and play areas are nearby.

An annual pass to Chimney Rock Park is a wonderful investment at only about $17 for adults and $9 for children ages 6 to 15. Regular daily admission is $9.50 for adults and $5 for children ages 6 to 15. From November 15 to April 1, portions of the trail system are closed due to weather conditions. The reduced winter admission is $6 for adults and $3 for children ages 6 to 15. Children younger than 3 are admitted free. The ticket office of Chimney Rock Park is open from 8:30 AM to 5:30 PM (Daylight Savings Time) and 8:30 AM to 4:30 PM (Eastern Standard Time). The Park closes at 7 PM in the summer and one hour after the ticket office closes in the winter.

## Lake Lure Tours
### Lake Lure Marina U.S. Hwys. 64/74-A in Lake Lure • (828) 625-0077

Tour the lake *National Geographic* called "one of the 10 most spectacular man-made lakes in the world." A fleet of modern boats offers deluxe seats, full-length canopies and clear enclosures to keep you comfortable whatever the weather. Tours take 60 minutes, departing every hour from the Town Marina. Be sure to arrive early enough to enjoy the surroundings. Before hopping on board, stroll the wooden boardwalk along the lake or the mile-long walking trail to the gazebo and picnic area with swings for the kids. Even parking your car is a delight here — the rocky-faced mountains are exquisite (especially when the dogwoods are in blossom in the spring). Tickets cost around $5 for children 6 to 15 and $8 for adults. Tours operate March through November from 10 AM to 7 PM. For a special treat take the Sunset Dinner Cruise that includes a stop at Sunset Cove for wine and hors d'oeuvres (BYOB) and dinner at one of three lakeside restaurants. After dessert, climb back aboard for a romantic trip back to port under the summer moonlight. Tickets are approximately $12 plus dinner. Private charters are also available for all occasions.

# Transylvania County

## Brevard Music Center
### Probart St., Brevard • (828) 884-2011

The hills are alive with the sound of music for seven weeks each summer at this internationally famous music center. For more information see our Arts and Culture chapter.

## Cradle of Forestry
### U. S. Hwy 276, Pisgah National Forest • (828) 877-3130

The Forest Discovery Center and its trails and activities at the Cradle of Forestry are a "don't miss" attraction. For more information, see our Forest and Parks, Art and Culture and Kidstuff chapters.

## English Chapel
### U.S. Hwy. 276, Pisgah National Forest

This Methodist Church just a few miles from the entrance to Pisgah Forest is nothing fancy, but there's a lot of history here, and the setting by the Davidson River is lovely. The Rev. A.F. English who bought the land for $5 founded the church in 1860. It was built by local folks and continues to serve the community and forest visitors. However, it is usually locked except for Sunday 9:30 AM services. An exercise trail that borders the river's rushing, clear waters leads from the church to the Davidson River Campground. Unlike many trails in the forest, this one is wide and level, making for a relaxed stroll.

## Pisgah Center for Wildlife Education
### F.R. 475, Pisgah National Forest • (828) 877-4423

Situated adjacent to the Fish Hatchery (see the entry below), this educational facility, operated by the North Carolina Wildlife Resources Commission, has exhibits and programs that explain how human activities affect and are effected by wildlife and the natural environment. The center includes a paved walkway to outdoor exhibits focusing on wildlife and fish management, law enforcement and conservation education. Indoor exhibits feature aquariums containing coastal, Piedmont and mountain aquatic species and an auditorium. Wildlife educational programs are offered at the center throughout the year.

The center is open daily from 8 AM until 5 PM except Thanksgiving Day, Christmas Day and New Year's Day. Admission to both the center and its courses are free.

## Pisgah Forest Fish Hatchery
### F.R. 475, Pisgah National Forest • (828) 877-3121

First it was a logging camp, then a camp for the Civilian Conservation Corps during the Great Depression. Today, the Pisgah Forest Fish Hatchery, just off U.S. Highway 276 and at the base of John Rock, is operated by the

North Carolina Wildlife Resources Commission. It raises the thousands of trout that are released in area streams. Children really like this place. They particularly delight in the wild frenzies when the fish, which come in all sizes, are fed. Even more, they like to feed the fish themselves.

To get to the hatchery, drive several miles up U.S. Highway 276 from the Brevard entrance to Pisgah Forest and turn off on F.R. 475, which is well-marked and paved. The hatchery is less than a mile down this road. There are also a number of nice hiking trails in the area.

# Southern Mountains

## Cherokee County

### The Episcopal Church of the Messiah
Peachtree St., Murphy • (828) 837-2021

Murphy's "little church around the corner" was organized in 1855, when there were only two Episcopal families in the town. Much of the money, in 25¢ contributions, was raised by the mother of Lucy Morgan, who is herself renowned for her work at Penland School (see our chapter on Mountain Crafts). The church, the cornerstone of which was laid in 1896, is across the street from the blue-marble county courthouse. Its stained-glass windows executed by Tiffany's of New York, its handmade altar and the herringbone pattern of its heart-pine paneling make this church, which is open to the public, a small work of art.

### Field of the Woods
U.S. Hwy. 294, Murphy • (828) 494-7855

Field of the Woods is unique in the world.

Stretched over 200 acres, this Christian-themed park is made up of symbols and words taken from the Bible, often presented in a majestic form. One of the most spectacular displays is a 300-foot-wide marker listing the Old Testament's Ten Commandments in letters 5 feet high and 4 feet wide. Another is the representation of a huge open Bible that takes its text from Matthew 22:37-40, with the words painted in bold, black lettering that can be read from a great distance.

A 150-foot cross lies atop All Nations Mountain, surrounded by the flags of all the countries where Church of God of Prophecy, the park's owners, are active. There is a tomb, constructed in the likeness of the one in Jerusalem where many believe that Jesus' body was taken after his crucifixion. You'll also find a cafe, gift shop and Christian bookstore.

The park is open year round from sunrise to sunset. Admission is free.

# Cherokee Indian Reservation

The Qualla Boundary, home to the 10,000 members of the Eastern Band of the Cherokees, is one of America's most-visited tourist destinations. For more information see our Kidstuff chapter and our chapter on the Cherokee Indian Reservation.

### Cherokee Fun Park
U.S. Hwy. 441 N., Cherokee
• (828) 497-5877

This is a great place to drop off teenagers for a couple of hours while you pursue your own pleasures. The 4-acre park contains, among other things, minigolf courses, go-cart track, bumper boats, a large arcade and rides

**INSIDERS' TIP**

Look out! Heading southeast on U.S. Highway 74 just as you come into Chimney Rock is a view so beautiful you might miss a curve on this windy mountain road. Just take it slow and look to your right at the mountains above with shimmering rock faces and the Rocky Broad River with its swift current tumbling and cascading below.

designed for young children. See our Kidstuff chapter for more.

## Harrah's Cherokee Casino
**777 Casino Dr., Cherokee**
**• (828) 497-7777, (800) HARRAHS**

This big casino, three football-fields in size, is open 24-hours a day. Here, you'll find 2,300 video gaming machines, including video blackjack, video poker and video craps, plus many other games. When you've gambled up an appetite, you can satisfy it at three restaurants: the 125-seat Range Steakhouse, open nightly and specializing in steaks, seafood and chicken dishes; the 400-seat Fresh Market Square Buffet, open daily, featuring a wide array of cuisine and fresh bakery items; and the 60-seat Winning Streaks Grill, open daily, a quick and easy stop for sandwiches, appetizers and such.

Harrah's also contains a gift shop and a 1,500-seat multi-purpose entertainment center that offers big-time shows with big-name stars. And while you shoot for that new pair of shoes, a large, professional, culturally themed child-care center will keep your young ones entertained.

## Santa's Land Fun Park and Zoo
**U.S. Hwy. 19, Cherokee • (828) 497-9191**

Christmas comes alive in the summertime in this theme park with its Rudi-Coaster ride, Santa's Overland Express train and, of course, Santa himself. See our Kidstuff chapter for more information.

## Tribal Bingo
**U. S. Hwy. 19, Cherokee**
**• (828) 497-4320, (800) 410-1254**

While many gamblers head for the new Harrah's casino, thousands of others still prefer Tribal Bingo. Open nightly, seven days a week, this long-running enterprise of the Eastern Band of Cherokee Indians is housed in a newly renovated facility. Approximately two miles from downtown Cherokee, it has a seating capacity of 1,200. Evening and earlybird games offer $1,500 jackpots as well as progressive jackpots.

## Unto These Hills
**U. S. Hwy. 441 N., Cherokee**
**• (828) 497-2111**

From mid-June to late August each year, a cast of 130 brings to life the long-forgotten history of the Cherokee. Presented in a beautiful outdoor theater, this pageant captures the legends, rituals and dances of the tribe. See our Cherokee Indian Reservation chapter for more information.

# Graham County

## Chief Junaluska's Grave
**Off Main St., Robbinsville**

In 1814 a Cherokee leader joined the U.S. Army in a fight against the Creek Indians, vowing that he would kill all the Creeks. During that Battle of Horseshoe Bend, he saved Gen. Andrew Jackson's life but had to admit he left some of the enemy alive. It was then that he was given the nickname of Junaluska, which means "he tried repeatedly but failed." Despite his service to Jackson, who became the U.S. president, he also failed to stop the forced move of his fellow Cherokees and himself to Oklahoma on the infamous Trail of Tears. The chieftain reportedly remarked at the time that had he known what the future would bring,

---

**INSIDERS' TIP**

If you're going to Hot Springs Spa, why not make a day of pampering yourself inside and out? Call for reservations and reserve at least two hours in the tub for a good soak. Venture down the road a bit to the Bridge Street Cafe (featured in our Restaurants chapter) where a canopied deck overlooks Spring Creek for wonderful outdoor dining. Try the crisp Pinot Griggio with a "gorgonzola, caramelized onion and fresh rosemary open-fire grilled pizza." Superb!

he would have killed Jackson himself at Horseshoe Bend. Later, Junaluska walked from Oklahoma all the way back to the North Carolina, where he continued to struggle to keep the remaining Cherokees in their mountain home.

On January 2, 1847, the state legislature made him a North Carolina citizen and gave him a tract of land. When he died on November 8, 1858, he was more than 100 years old. His grave and that of Nicie, his wife, are on a hilltop just outside Robbinsville. To reach it, drive past the courthouse on Main Street and make a right turn toward the Stanley Furniture plant. The gravesite is on the left, clearly marked by a sign. A trail leads up to the two boulders that mark the graves, which are surrounded by an iron fence. It's said that it took eight yoke of oxen a half-day to pull

Junaluska's gravestone up the hill. Plans are underway to open a museum near the site devoted to Junaluska.

## Fontana Dam
**N.C. Hwy. 28, Fontana Dam**
**• (828) 498-2374**

You can drive across this 480-foot-high dam, the highest east of the Rockies, but don't be satisfied with that. Stop at the visitor's center for a breathtaking view and make use of the picnic tables there. Inside the center, you can take in a short video and other exhibits to learn about the dam's construction and history. After that, spend a dollar for a ride in the stainless-steel tram to the dam's base for a look inside the plant itself, where you'll get a lesson on hydroelectric power. This 2,365-foot-wide structure began providing power in

Photo: Cherokee Tribal Promotion Office

The Pioneer Farmstead, only one mile from Cherokee in North Carolina Mountains National Park, shows how early white settlers lived in this area in the 1800s. Demonstrations of 19th-century farm life are a regular feature during the summer months.

1942 to produce goods during World War II, and it closed in 1944. Today, it impounds the 10,600 acres of water that form 29-mile-long Fontana Lake. Historic Fontana Village, now a resort community, was built to house the workers who constructed the dam. The visitor's center is open from 9 AM until 8 PM and is staffed by volunteers who are former TVA employees.

# Haywood County

## Ghost Town in the Sky
**890 Soco Rd. (U.S. Hwy. 19), Maggie Valley • (828) 926-1140, (800) 446-7886**

This mountaintop family amusement park features a Wild West theme with gun fights, jail breaks, bank robberies, saloon shows, country music shows and authentic American Indian dances. See our Kidstuff chapter for more.

## Soco Gardens Zoo
**3578 Soco Rd. (U.S. Hwy. 19), Maggie Valley • (828) 926-1746**

Wild animals, an animal petting section, guided tours and two snake shows make this a great stop for families. See our Kidstuff chapter for more.

# Jackson County

## Great Smoky Mountains Railway
**119 Front St., Dillsboro • (828) 586-8811, (800) 872-4681**

There are few attractions more popular in Western North Carolina than this railway, and there's no better way to watch some of our area's great scenery glide by than from one of its passenger cars. When you catch a ride on the Great Smoky Mountains Railway, you have your choice of diesel-electric or steam locomotives, with seating in heated and air-conditioned coaches and open-sided cars. Some seating options at a small additional charge are the Club Car (for adults only) and the Crown Coach.

• **The Tuckaseigee River Excursion:** This is a 34-mile-long, 3½-hour Dillsboro-Bryson City round trip that follows the Tuckaseigee River past the spot where the train wreck in *The Fugitive* was filmed. It also takes you through the 836-foot-long Cowee Tunnel and over many trestles before reaching Bryson City, where you'll have a 45-minute layover for shopping, browsing and eating. The fare is $21.95 for adults and $9.95 for children 12 and younger by diesel-electric; $26.95 for adults and $9.95 for children by steam.

• **The Nantahala Gorge Excursion:** From Bryson City, you can take a 44-mile, 4½-hour round trip tour that brings you through the Nantahala Gorge, created by a river that's become one of North Carolina's prime spots for canoeing, kayaking and whitewater rafting. En route, you'll cross a portion of Fontana Lake on a trestle that is 791 feet long, on piers that are 180 feet tall. There's an hour layover in the Gorge for eating and viewing the whitewater activity. The fare is $21.95 for an adults and $9.95 for children by diesel-electric; $26.95 for adults and $9.95 for children by steam.

• **The Red Marble Gap Excursion:** This 38-mile, 4½-hour trip departs from Andrews and climbs east toward Red Marble Mountain. It passes through the hand-dug Will Sandlin Tunnel, crosses the 400-foot-long Hawksnest Trestle and descends a 4-plus percent grade from Topton down to Nantahala. Here, too, you have an hour for whitewater viewing and lunch. The mountain scenery on this excursion is particularly spectacular. Fares are $21.95 for adults and $9.95 for children on diesel-electric. There are no steam trains from Andrews.

• **Raft 'n' Rail Excursion:** This seven-hour trip offers a 22-mile train ride, an 8-mile guided raft trip, a picnic lunch and a return by bus for $54.95 for adults and $42.95 for children on a diesel train and $59.95 for adults and $42.95 for children on a steam train.

• **Twilight Dinner Train:** The most recently added excursion is the Twilight Dinner Train. It departs from the Dillsboro Depot for a luxurious, leisurely 2½-hour round trip that follows the Tuckaseigee River through the historic Cowee Tunnel to Whittier and back. A gourmet four-course dinner, elegant ambiance — candlelight, china and white linen — and old-fashioned attentive service is presented in the beautifully restored dining cars. You can select from four seasonal entrees at the time you make your reservations; cocktails and a selection of premium wines are available from the bar. The Dinner Train operates every Saturday evening from April through December and every Friday evening from July through October. The fare is $49.95 per person plus tax and gratuity.

## Judaculla Rock
### Off N.C. Hwy. 107

Judaculla (a name corrupted from the Indian tsulkalu, meaning "slant eyes") was a fearful giant of Cherokee lore whose farm was on Tanasee Bald at a point where Jackson, Haywood and Transylvania counties converge. One day, it's said, he jumped from his mountaintop home to a valley near what is now Caney Fork Creek, leaving the marks of his landing on a large, exposed piece of soapstone. These marks — pictographic writing on the rock — long predate the Cherokees. There are many theories as to their meanings. Is the rock a boundary marker? A battle commemoration? A peace treaty among unknown tribes? Or is it just ancient graffiti?

Judaculla Rock, well-marked by signs, is off N.C. 107 between Cashiers and Cullowhee on Caney Fork Road (S.R. 1737). A lovely 3-mile drive through a bucolic valley of scattered two-story, white frame farmhouses will bring you to the rock, which sits under an open-sided shed next to a cow pasture.

# Macon County

## Highlands Nature Center and Botanical Gardens
### Horse Cove Rd. (U.S. Hwy. 28 S.), Highlands • (828) 526-2623

Drive a short distance out of Highlands on East Main Street and you'll come to this interesting place. The Highlands Biological Station, one of the oldest research facilities in the country, operates both the center and the gardens. The center is a showcase for the animals and plants found on the Highlands Plateau, a unique ecosystem that attracts top researchers from around the world. Here you'll find user-friendly exhibits, American Indian

artifacts, mineral and rock specimens, snakes, salamanders and mounted specimens of area mammals and birds. In the Botanical Gardens, the trails, with their excellently identified plants and trees, will take you around Lake Ravenel, along a creek and up to a small waterfall.

The center is open from 10 AM to 5 PM Monday through Saturday from Memorial Day to Labor Day. Admission is free. The gardens are there for you to enjoy anytime. Even in winter, thick growths of rhododendron, galax and doghobble make it a deep-green little paradise.

## John Wasilik Memorial Poplar
### Nantahala National Forest, near Rainbow Springs

To see the United States' second-largest yellow poplar, named for a former Wayah District Ranger, drive west out of Franklin on U.S. Highway 64 and turn on F.R. 67 toward the Standing Indian Campground. Park a little more than a mile down the road at the "Rock Gap" sign before reaching the campground. It's a 1.5-mile, easy-to-moderate round-trip hike on the Wasilik Poplar Trail, which is lined with second-growth trees up to 8 feet in diameter. The giant memorial tree is 25 feet in circumference, and, until a storm blew off its top, it was 125 feet tall. The Ritter Lumber Company took the rest of the virgin timber out of this area in the early 1930s. They even cut down another yellow poplar of the same size. However, the oxen had such a hard time hauling it away that the lumbermen decided not to bother with this now-famous tree.

## Perry's Water Garden
### 136 Givson Aquatic Farm Rd., Franklin • (828) 524-3264

Even if you never intend to have a water garden, this 12-acre aquatic plant nursery — with its hundreds of lotuses, water lilies, blue-flag irises and other old and new water- and bog-loving plants — might change your mind. Claiming to be the largest such nursery in the country, it offers a tropical greenhouse, exotic Koi and goldfish, old-fashioned antique rose beds, picnic tables and walking trails. Perry's is open from 9 AM to noon and 1 to 5 PM Monday through Saturday and 1 until 5 PM on Sundays from March through September.

Trains, Ferris wheels, swimming pools, natural wonders, clowns and festivals all beckon as do seasonal activities such as Easter egg hunts, jack-o'-lantern carvings and Christmas decoration classes.

# Kidstuff

North Carolina's mountains are even more fun with kids in hand. Children seem to live with a sense of wonder that is heightened by the majestic mountaintops and surrounding natural beauty. They can see Daniel Boone behind every log cabin and wood nymphs playing in the shelter of rhododendron thickets. They can even see Santa Claus in the summertime (although there's a logical explanation for that one . . . read on).

Outdoor activities such as hiking are popular with families because the area is filled with trails appropriate for younger ages and abilities. Stop for a picnic along a mountain stream and watch your kids turn rocks and water into adventures only their uninhibited imaginations can know. Or teach them to ski before adult-size fear paralyzes their sense of adventure.

Organizations throughout the region offer exciting programs for little people. Libraries are always a rich source of activities, storytelling and, of course, books and tapes. Area arts councils provide opportunities for kids to explore their nascent creativity, setting it free with paints and clay, paper and yarn. Art exhibitions of their work are scheduled throughout the year.

Our Summer Camps and Rock Hounding chapters have additional resources for kid entertainment. Both offer kids a lifetime of memories. Parks and attractions in the mountains welcome pint-size visitors. Trains, Ferris wheels, swimming pools, natural wonders, clowns and festivals all beckon as do seasonal activities such as Easter egg hunts, jack-o'-lantern carvings and Christmas decoration classes. (See our Annual Events chapter.)

Many of our chapters offer lots of fun things to do with kids, but in this chapter we gathered some our favorites.

## Northern Mountains

### Watauga County

#### Magic Mountain Mini Golf & Gem Mine
**1675 N.C. Hwy. 105, Boone**
• **(828) 265-GEMS, (828) 265-GOLF**

The kids simply won't get bored here. Open every day from 9 AM to 11 PM, spring through fall, Magic Mountain is a kiddie paradise. Adults probably won't mind sifting through the enriched ore either, since there's a chance of finding a ruby, citrine, garnet, amethyst, aquamarine, sapphire, emerald, or other such rocks.

A sandwich and ice-cream parlor provide indoor or patio dining, and a video-game room provides entertainment for those members of the family who just don't want to get their hands dirty. The mini golf course is set on a mountainside amidst foliage and waterfalls.

#### Mystery Hill
**129 Mystery Hill Ln., between Boone and Blowing Rock • (828) 264-2792**

This is the place to go for interactive fun with your family or group of friends. Celebrating over 50 years in business, Mystery Hill explores the relationships of science, optical illusion and natural phenomena in a hands-on entertainment center. Defy gravity in the Mystery House where the ball rolls up hill or leave your shadow on the wall. (Just try getting the kids out of this one.) The Appalachian Heritage Museum and the Native American Artifacts Museum are included in the tour for one low price.

Open seven days a week, year round,

Mystery Hill is open 8 AM to 8 PM June through August, and 9 AM to 5 PM September through May. Admission is $7 for adults, $5 for children, $6 for seniors and free for kids under five. Group rates are available.

### Tweetsie Railroad
**296 Tweetsie Railroad Rd., between Boone and Blowing Rock**
• (828) 264-9061, (800) 526-5740

Long before there was a Carowinds or Six Flags, there was Tweetsie Railroad. A charming theme park now more than 30 years old, Tweetsie brings out the little kid in all of us. Not as overwhelming as those other parks, this one gives families a chance to go a little slower and savor the sight of their little pardner all decked out in cowboy hat and six-shooters, waiting for the bad guys on the train to be vanquished by the good guy sheriff and his deputies.

Remember when things seemed this simple? The innocence and measured pace of this park are its true charm, as is the 100-year-old Tweetsie locomotive, which still runs. Simple rides, a petting farm with deer, Mouse Mine No. 9, homemade fudge, caramel apples, a Ferris wheel and those souvenir shops where you have to spend a dollar or bust make Tweetsie a special, unhurried attraction that's hard to find these days. The amusement park also holds special events for certain holidays such as Halloween, July 4, and others.

Tweetsie Railroad is open daily from 9 AM to 6 PM from May through August. After Labor Day and through October, weekend hours (Friday through Sunday) are 9 AM to 6 PM. Tweetsie Railroad is also open some evenings in October for the Halloween Festival and Ghost Train. Admission is $16 for adults, $13 for children and senior citizens; children 2 and younger are admitted free. If you enter after 3 PM, the next day is free. Group rates and discounts are available.

# Central Mountains

## Buncombe County

### Pack Place Education Arts and Science Center
**2 S. Pack Sq., Asheville**
• (828) 257-4500

Four museums and a performing arts theater make this a must-see with kids, especially if the weather isn't cooperating. The Asheville Art Museum, The Health Adventure, Colburn Gem & Mineral Museum, YMI Cultural Center and Diana Wortham Theatre all offer special programs for children.

Health Adventure (meant to be enjoyed by the whole family), especially, is a blast for kids. Learn how the body works, with a life-sized torso — you put in the organs like solving a puzzle! Learn how the ear works. Learn about nutrition while "shopping." Learn mechanics and engineering with fun and games you can try. Check your eyesight; look at a bug, a hair, and other objects through a microscope. The ultraviolet light room will make your whites glow and your teeth green! Two floors of tactile fun can keep kids busy and entertained for hours. Mockingbird Theater Productions for children are also held at the center. See our Arts and Culture chapter for more information.

### Odyssey Center for the Ceramic Arts
**236 Clingman Ave. Asheville**
• (828) 285-0210

This recreational craft center offers some very special programs for children. Odyssey's kids' classes have been filling up quickly with

---

**INSIDERS' TIP**

When arriving at the Cherokee Indian Reservation, make sure you drop into the Cherokee Visitor Center on Main St. in downtown Cherokee. Not only can you get the latest information on lodgings, restaurants and attractions, but sometimes you'll be able to pick up money-saving coupons.

Photo: Judi Scharns, Courtesy of Boone Convention and Visitors Bureau

Skaters enjoy the facilities at Appalachian Ski Mountain.

eager faces and curious hands. Nine-week classes are offered for after school kids and homeschoolers. Kids of all ages learn basic skills in wheel throwing and handbuilding, making anything from animals, and castles to cups and bowls. Call for a detailed course schedule. For more information on general classes, see our Crafts in the Mountains chapter.

## Recreation Park
### Gashes Creek Rd. and U.S. 81, Asheville
• (828) 298-4311

Rec Park, as it's known in the area, is one of those old-time community recreation parks disappearing from the landscape in the wake of mega-theme parks. But, thank goodness, this park is in fine form. This delightful place on the banks of the Swannanoa River dates back to the 1920s, Asheville's boom era. A dance pavilion, boat rental and even a makeshift movie theater were set up in the middle of Lake Craig, which ran along the park's eastern edge. A Ferris wheel and carousel added to the prewar-era amusements. The lake became silted in the 1950s and was drained, but today the rushing waters of the Swannanoa River still hurry by the Ferris wheel, carousel, roller coaster, miniature train, Tilt-A-Whirl and kiddie boat rides. And a number of new rides and additional picnic facilities have been added to the recently landscaped site.

A county-operated Olympic-size swimming pool, an enduring feature of Recreation Park, has undergone reconstruction. This is a great place for families, church groups or birthday parties or anyone who remembers when riding to the top of the Ferris wheel was the scariest, most enduring feeling of all. The Nature Center is at the top of the hill, just above the park.

The amusement rides are open on the weekends April through May and mid-August through mid-September, and full time (Tuesday through Sunday) June through mid-August. Hours are noon to 8 PM, except Sunday, when it's open 1 to 8 PM. The swimming pool and rides can be enjoyed for a nominal fee. The tickets cost $1 to $1.50, less if bought in large sheets.

## Western North Carolina Nature Center
### 75 Gashes Creek Rd., Asheville
• (828) 298-5600

The Nature Center offers a remarkable

If you're of a certain state of mind, you don't need a sled.

blend of services to the area. Officially it's "an environmental educational resource, exhibiting and interpreting plants and animals native to the Southern Appalachian Mountains." But it is much more than that. From the moment you step through the door and a three-dimensional, full-size diorama of woodland creatures greets you, you know you are crossing that bridge to the natural world.

Well-planned exhibits in the educational facility offer a hands-on approach to everything from weather forecasting and animal identification to a real working beehive! In the next building are archaeological displays and zoological exhibits of live reptiles and amphibians. In another area, a special darkened room allows visitors to observe owls, bats and other nocturnal creatures.

Outside there's more: bobcats, raccoons, cougars, otters, foxes, bears, hawks, eagles, sheep, goats, chickens, peacocks and even wolves. The center has made spectacular use of limited acreage to create a special experience for the whole family. Make sure you walk along the boardwalk in the treetops; it takes you back to those days of childhood tree houses.

The Nature Center is open 10 AM to 5 PM, seven days a week. Admission is approximately $4 for adults, $2 for children ages 3 through 14 and $3 for senior citizens.

# Henderson County

## Carl Sandburg Home
**1928 Little River Rd., Flat Rock**
**• (828) 693-4178**

Be sure to let your kids pet the kids (and goats) at Connemara, the home of Carl Sandburg that is now a National Historic Site. See our Arts and Culture chapter for more information.

## The Historic Johnson Farm
**3346 Haywood Rd. (N.C. Hwy. 191)**
**Hendersonville • (828) 891-6585**

This well-preserved, 15-acre farm, its historic house, many outbuildings and nature trails will take children back to a lifestyle once common earlier in this century. See our Arts and Culture chapter for more information.

# Transylvania County

## Sliding Rock
**U. S. Hwy. 276, Pisgah National Forest**

Sliding Rock is just 7.6 miles from the junction of U.S. highways 276 and 64 outside Brevard. Here, you're invited to "take the plunge" down a 60-foot slippery cascade into the 50-degree to 60-degree, 6-foot-deep pool below. If you don't care to make the slide, it's fun to watch the action from paved viewing areas at the top or bottom of this natural, exhilarating ride that's fueled by 11,000 gallons of water a minute.

There's a large parking lot adjacent to Sliding Rock (the parking fee is $3) as well as a bathhouse. Lifeguards are on duty from 10 AM to 6 PM from Memorial Day through Labor Day. The rock, while slick, can take the bottom out of an ordinary bathing suit, so old jeans or cutoffs are best for this fast ride. Also, be care-

ful while getting in and out of the water. The surface of the rock, even where the water isn't flowing, can be slick and accounts for some hard tumbles.

## Pisgah Forest Fish Hatchery
**F.R. 475, Pisgah National Forest**
**• (828) 877-3121**

The Pisgah Forest Fish Hatchery raises the thousands of trout that are released into area streams. There are fish-food vending machines and your kids'll love watching the wild feeding frenzies when the fish, which come in all sizes, are fed.

To get to the hatchery, drive several miles up U.S. Highway 276 from the Brevard entrance to Pisgah Forest and turn off on F.R. 475, which is well-marked and paved. The hatchery is less than a mile down this road. (For more information see our Attractions chapter.)

## Pisgah Center for Wildlife Education
**F.R. 475, Pisgah Forest • (828) 877-4423**

This center focuses on natural habitats and how to preserve them. It offers exhibits and free programs on raising trout, trees, birds, streams and water quality, backcountry wisdom and more. (See the listing in our Attractions chapter.) Admission to the Center is free.

## Cradle of Forestry
**U.S. Hwy. 276, Pisgah National Forest**
**• (828) 877-3130**

Children of all ages love the Forest Discovery Center at the Cradle of Forestry. They can see a short movie about the first forestry school in America, which was situated here — and that's only the beginning. There are 15 educational exhibits on the workings of the forest ecosystem and what it takes to manage an ecosystem. For example, there is a replicated hillside complete with a forest summit. Below, a 30-foot tunnel lets one crawl underground through "The Great Tree and Burrow" exhibit, complete with all the animals that live there. Another exhibit explains the dynamics of a watershed, all the way to the household faucet. Adventure seekers can experience the "Fire-Fighting Helicopter Simulator" that flies into the depths of a wildfire to drop retardant to quench the flames, complete with visuals, sound, movement and smells.

Outside the building, there are two beautiful, mile-long paved trails, each with guided tours that will tell you of the Cradle's history and teach you a lot about the plants and trees along the way. The Forest Festival Trail has many forest demonstration projects, an old saw mill, the first little fish hatchery in Pisgah and an old Climax logging train. Children love to climb into the cab and ring the bell. The Biltmore Campus trail winds through the school's old campus of original and reconstructed buildings.

On Saturday and Sunday afternoons, craftspeople in period dress demonstrate crafts such as weaving, spinning, quilting, basketry, toymaking and life at the turn of the century. There are also a number of special events happening throughout the year, such as Fiber Arts Week and the huge Forest Festival Day held in October.

The Cradle, open seven days a week from 9 AM to 5 PM, is located on U.S. 276, 11 miles from the intersection of U.S. Highways 64, 276 and 280 at Pisgah Forest or 4 miles south of the Blue Ridge Parkway at milepost 412. The use fee is $4 for adults, $2 for students 6 to 12, and free for 5 years and under.

See our "Cradle of Forestry" close-up in the Forests and Parks chapter.

# Southern Mountains

## Cherokee County

### John C. Campbell Folk School
**1 Folk School Rd., Brasstown**
**• (828) 837-2775, (800) FOLK SCH**

This fine, 70-year-old craft school offers Little/Middle Folk School each June for one week for youngsters ages 7 to 17. The week is full of crafts, games and lots of fun. Classes fill quickly so early registration is essential.

Contact the Folk School to be included in a separate mailing for this program. See our Mountain Crafts chapter for more information on the school's other offerings.

## Haywood County

### Ghost Town in the Sky
**890 Soco Rd. (U.S. 19), Maggie Valley**
**• (828) 926-1140,**
**(800) GHOST TOWN**

You can take the incline railroad to this mountaintop family amusement park, or — for the more adventurous — try the chair lift. Once there, in keeping with the Wild West theme, you'll be treated to gun fights, bank robberies, saloon shows, country music shows and authentic American Indian dances. In all, there are 30 shows and rides, including the Red Devil roller coaster, and lots of food available.

The park is open from 9 AM to 6 PM from the first Sunday in May through the last Sunday in October. An admission price of $18.95 for ages 10 and older and $13.95 for ages 3 to 9 covers all rides, shows and amusements. Ages 2 and younger are admitted for free.

### Soco Gardens Zoo
**3578 Soco Rd. (U.S. 19), Maggie Valley**
**• (828) 926-1746**

In addition to many of the usual wild animals, this zoo allows touching and feeding in its petting section. There are guided tours, two snake shows (one venomous and the other nonpoisonous; in the latter visitors can touch or hold the performers) and a gift shop made for animal lovers.

Hours change with the season: 10 AM to 5 PM in May, September and October; 9 AM to dark in June, July and August. It is closed in the winter. Admission is $5 for adults, $4.50 for seniors and $3 for children ages 5 to 12. There is no charge for children 4 and younger as long as they are with the family and not a part of a children's group.

## Cherokee Indian Reservation

For more information on the reservation and other attractions here, see our chapter on Attractions and the Cherokee Indian Reservation.

Photo: Cherokee Tribal Promotion Office

Young and old enjoy the Rudi-Coaster, one of many family rides at
Santa's Land Fun Park and Zoo in Cherokee.

## Santa's Land Fun Park and Zoo
**U.S. Hwy. 19, Cherokee**
**• (828) 497-9191**

Christmas comes alive in the summertime in this theme park. We expect that young children will refuse to miss its Rudi-Coaster ride, Santa's Overland Express train and, of course, Santa. The family can also paddle boats around Monkey Islands in the lake, view Cherokee from the top of a Ferris wheel and visit a wealth of shops.

In the zoo, kids will enjoy petting baby bears and feeding deer and trout. A visit to the gristmill will show them how corn meal is made, and they can watch pork rinds being cooked. You'll also find a picnic and playground area in the park. It's open from early May until the first weekend in November.

Admission is $13.92 for adults and children ages 2 to 12. Children younger than 2 get in free. Prices are, however, subject to change.

## Cherokee Fun Park
**U.S. 441 N., Cherokee • (828) 497-5877**

This is a great place to drop off teenagers for a couple of hours while you pursue your own pleasures. The 4-acre park contains, among other things, two challenging miniature-golf courses, a go-cart track, bumper boats, a large arcade and rides designed for young children.

It opens daily at 11 AM on weekdays and 10 AM on weekends from May through October. Closing time is around 11 PM in midsummer and 8:30 or 9 PM in the spring and fall. Admission is free, but there is a charge of $4.25 for boats and go-carts and $3.50 for golf (play all day). After 6 PM it costs $3.50 for each golf game. Kiddie rides are $1.50 each.

## Cherokee Bear Zoo & Plaza
**Main St., Cherokee • (828) 497-4525**

When seeing a bear in the wild, it's always best to keep your distance (see our Outdoor Safety and Forests and Parks chapters), but here's a chance for children to get a close-up look at all kinds of bears, both big and small — and even feed them! This petting zoo also has monkeys, big cats, deer and other animals.

It's open at 9 AM on weekends and 10 AM during the week. Closing hours can be as late as 11 PM according to the season. The entrance fee is $2 with children 3 and younger admitted free.

Over one-third of the 250 rooms on the four floors of the estate — all lavishly furnished exactly as the Vanderbilts left them — are open to the public.

# Biltmore Estate and Winery

Amid the central North Carolina mountains, just outside of Asheville, you will see what appears to be a castle rising out of a mountainside. Biltmore Estate, the largest private residence in the United States, was home to George Vanderbilt, grandson of Cornelius Vanderbilt, founder of one of America's foremost shipping and railroading dynasties. George Vanderbilt first traveled to Asheville with his mother in 1888. Enchanted by the majesty of the mountains, he returned home to enlist the greatest designers and architects for the country estate he envisioned. Richard Morris Hunt, one of the foremost architects of the 19th century, patterned the magnificent 250-room mansion after 16th-century chateaux in the Loire Valley of France. Preeminent landscape architect Frederick Law Olmsted, noted for his design of Central Park in New York City, shaped the original 125,000 acres of the vast working estate. Vanderbilt's extensive personal collection of 70,000 objects from all parts of the world filled his country home, which was completed in 1895.

In 1914, after Mr. Vanderbilt's death, nearly 87,000 acres of the estate were sold to the U.S. government to form the nucleus of Pisgah National Forest, America's first national forest east of the Mississippi. The 8,000 remaining carefully and colorfully landscaped acres maintain much of the original Estate's grandeur. The 75-acre gardens are internationally renowned for annual and perennial displays of tulips, daffodils, roses, dogwoods and azaleas, among other plants. Each April, the Annual Festival of Flowers heralds spring with a Victorian celebration of renewal and floral majesty for a month of merry making.

Continuing the tradition of superlatives begun a century ago, William A.V. Cecil, grandson of George Vanderbilt and owner of Biltmore Estate, established the Biltmore Estate Wine Company in 1983. The first vineyards on the estate, planted in 1971, contained French-American hybrids and were planted in an area just below Biltmore House and behind the greenhouses, with vinifera plantings following a few years later. After years of experimentation and research, the winery opened in 1985 with state-of-the-art production technology. It is considered to be the most visited winery in the world, with over 500,000 visitors annually. It continues the tradition of Biltmore Estate as a self-sufficient working estate.

The turn-of-the-century mansion covers an incredible four acres of floor space. It took 50 servants to see to the needs of the Vanderbilts and their many frequent guests. These guests included famed writers Edith Wharton and Henry James, and presidents William McKinley and Woodrow Wilson.

More than 850,000 guests from all over the world visit this legendary home each year. Over one-third of the 250 rooms on four floors, lavishly furnished, often as the Vanderbilts left them, are open to the public. Describing rooms such as the Winter Garden, Banquet Hall, Music Room, Billiard Room, Tapestry Gallery, Louis XVI Room, Sheraton Room, Chippendale Room, Bowling Alley, Swimming Pool, Gymnasium, guest rooms and even the kitchens calls for a good thesaurus to avoid using words like "opulent" and "majestic" over and over.

The Winter Garden, a sunken room with marble floors and glass ceiling, is the first stop on the self-guided tour. The Banquet Hall, which hosted formal gatherings around a table large enough for 64 people, was designed specifically to house five hand-woven 16th-century Flemish tapestries depicting mythical characters. The 70-foot-high barrel-vaulted ceiling is worth a look. In fact, all the ceilings are notable, so don't forget to look up.

The Vanderbilt's daughter, Cornelia, and her husband, John Cecil, took over the Halloween Room in 1924 for a party during their wedding festivities. Some of their unusual decorations remain on the walls.

With so many spectacular rooms and gardens to choose from, the movie industry is drawn to the estate. A number of films have been shot here, including *The Swan* with Grace Kelly, *Being There* with Peter Sellers, portions of *Mr. Destiny* with Michael Caine and Jim Belushi, *The Last of the Mohicans* with Daniel Day-Lewis, *Richie Rich* with Macaulay Culkin, and most recently *My Fellow Americans* with James Garner, Jack Lemmon, and Dan Aykroyd.

A special tour called Behind the Scenes, which costs $11.95, takes you into the depths of the mansion. In the subbasement, for example, stand Mr. Vanderbilt's powerful boilers and power generators, which assured the estate's self-sufficiency. The tour includes the Butler's Pantry, which was the central command location for the servant infrastructure. Two new tours were added in 1999 — Rooftop Tours and Garden Treasure Walks, each costing $11.95.

After touring the main house, you can visit Victorian gift shops chock full of decorative accessories, books, toys and confections. Several dining opportunities await you at Deerpark Restaurant, The Stable Cafe and The Bistro, Biltmore's newest restaurant at the Winery (see a description later in this chapter).

Take a stroll in the many landscaped gardens just as Vanderbilt's guests did — strolling through the Azalea Garden and Spring Garden sheltered by a grove of white pines and hemlocks. The Walled Garden of four acres includes the Rose Garden with over 2,300 rose bushes in more than 350 varieties. Closer to the house, the Shrub Garden provides a "ramble" through flowering bushes on a small path. The Italian Garden is marked by three symmetrical pools, graveled paths and a manicured lawn reminiscent of Italian Renaissance landscape design. Benches and a classical statuary make this a peaceful and relaxing garden. Further along the estate's gladed road, notice the Bass Pond and Lagoon.

General admission to Biltmore Estate is $29.95 for adults. Children age 9 and younger are admitted free with a paid adult admission; youths ages 10 to 15 receive a discount. The estate is open from 9 AM to 5 PM daily, except Thanksgiving and Christmas. The Estate is open on New Year's Day. Hours and admission prices change on a seasonal basis, so call ahead for the most up-to-date information. Allow four to six hours to fully enjoy your visit. If you arrive after 3 PM, your ticket will

**www.insiders.com**
See this and many other **Insiders' Guide®** destinations online.
**Visit us today!**

---

**INSIDERS' TIP**

**Biltmore Estate is worth an entire day. You're welcome to drive along the meandering estate roads, stop off in the many gardens and meadows, have a rest by the lagoons and fishponds . . . take full advantage.**

also be honored the following day. During the Christmas season, take advantage of the Candlelight Evening Tours of Biltmore Estate. But call early — these popular, reservation-only tours book up quickly, and space is limited. Other special annual events include the Annual Easter Egg Hunt, Festival of Flowers, and Festival of Flowers Evenings (also reservations-only evening tours) in the spring and Summer Evenings Concerts in the summer.

Michaelmas: An English Harvest Fair is a new fall festival at Biltmore. Call (800) 289-1895 for reservations.

Biltmore Estate is on U.S. Highway 25 at the junction of Hendersonville Road and McDowell Street in Asheville. From I-40, Biltmore Estate is located just north of Exit 50 or 50B on U.S. Highway 25. For more information on the estate, gardens or winery, call (828) 274-6333 or (800) 543-2961.

Photo: The Biltmore Co.

Enjoy a glass of Biltmore wine with your dinner after you've toured the estate's grounds and gardens.

# Biltmore Estate Winery

To assure the success of the enterprise, a sixth-generation French winemaster, Philippe Jourdain of Provence, was chosen in 1977 as winemaster for the Biltmore Estate Winery. Mr. Jourdain was not only experienced in the operation of a family vineyard but was a respected teacher of viticulture and oenology, the sciences of grape growing and wine making. The winery flourished, and the first wine was sold in 1979. When he retired in 1995, Jourdain was replaced by Bernard Delille, a fellow Frenchman who has been winemaker at the Estate since 1986. The Biltmore Estate wine-making operation has evolved into a premier vineyard, producing approximately 75,000 cases of wine each year and garnering more than 160 medals at wine competitions nationwide.

The vineyard itself is located in the Long Valley where George Vanderbilt's dairy herd once grazed, across the French Broad River from Biltmore House. A 35-acre lake constructed near the vineyards provides irrigation and frost control. During the spring budding, cold spells often sweep through the mountains. Buds are sprayed with lakewater that turns into an icy sheath that incubates the buds and protects them from freezing internally. (Ongoing research and development at Biltmore Estate Winery are as essential as the grapes in producing fine quality wines.)

With more than 500,000 guests visiting the winery annually, the Biltmore Estate Winery has the distinction of being the most-visited winery in the United States. Officially opened for tours in 1985, the 90,000-square-foot facility is housed in the expanded original dairy barn and includes offices and the winery production works. The handsome pebble-dash building is crowned by a distinctive European-style clock tower from the estate. The expanded and renovated buildings feature a Welcome Center, The Bistro, Tasting Room and Gift Shop.

The Winery tour begins in the Welcome Center, an open area with hand-stenciled walls and Portuguese tiling that lend it a distinctly European flavor. Sample some of Biltmore's special seasonal wines or take advantage of the innovative menu at the newest restaurant on the estate, The Bistro (see our description later in this chapter).

An exhibit in the Welcome Center acquaints visitors with the ancient history of the grape and the more recent history of the building. A stylishly produced film runs daily at various times in a small theater just off the inner courtyard, beyond the main welcome area. From the theater, visitors can move to the wine-making operation and view fermenting, aging and bottling rooms, cool cellars, gleaming machinery and rows upon rows of barrels and bottles.

Your next stop is the Tasting Room, a relaxed, open room with several tasting bars. Wine stewards are eager to accommodate your taste buds with whatever sample you desire from the expansive wine list that includes white wines made from Sauvignon Blanc, Chardonnay and Riesling grapes and red wines from Pinot Noir, Cabernet Sauvignon, Cabernet Franc and Merlot. Zinfandel and Cabernet Sauvignon rosé wines are also available. For the children, a tasty Biltmore blend of grape juice is on hand.

Complete your visit to the Biltmore Estate Winery with a visit to the giftshop. Biltmore Estate wine is available for purchase in a multitude of package options. Wine accessories, gourmet foods, upscale kitchen and dining

**INSIDERS' TIP**

Try one, or more, of the restaurants after your stroll through the Biltmore House. These are not your standard bland and generic tourist-stops. Deerpark chefs have won awards, and the restaurant is often host to lavish wedding receptions. The Bistro is exceptional in flavor and freshness of the food. The atmosphere is comfortable and intimate. Don't forget to visit the eclectic shops as well.

accessories and other gifts with a Victorian flavor are attractively displayed. Biltmore Estate wines can also be found in fine wine shops and restaurants throughout North Carolina, South Carolina, Georgia, Tennessee, Virginia and Florida.

The Winery is open January through March from 11 AM to 6 PM Monday through Saturday and noon to 6 PM Sunday. April through December, the hours are 11 AM to 7 PM Monday through Saturday and noon to 7 PM Sunday. Hours change from season to season and year to year, so be sure to call before you visit. For general information on Biltmore Estate and Winery, call (828) 274-6333 or (800) 543-2961. The winery's self-guided tour is included in the price of admission.

# Dining on the Estate

You will certainly want to include dining as part of your Biltmore Estate experience. Deerpark Restaurant, The Stable Café and The Bistro offer creative menus that take advantage of the freshest and finest ingredients. Dining at all of the estate's restaurants is presently open to touring guests only.

## Price Code

Our price code is based on a two-person dinner, excluding drinks, dessert and tip. Please note that prices vary in all restaurants depending on the season and the time of day, i.e. lunch or dinner. All the restaurants in this chapter accept credit cards. (For more dining facilities in the area, see our Restaurants chapter.)

| $ | Less than $20 |
| $$ | $21 to $35 |
| $$$ | $36 to $50 |
| $$$$ | More than $50 |

## The Bistro
$-$$ • (828) 274-6341

The Bistro offers wild mushroom appetizers, seasonal entrees, wood-fired pizzas, fresh pasta creations and creamy desserts, which are enhanced by a wide selection of estate wines by the glass. A patio provides an exceptionally attractive setting for alfresco dining, weather permitting. Meals at The Bistro range from $15 to $25.

## Deerpark Restaurant
$$ • (828) 274-6260

Deerpark Restaurant is in an expanded and renovated old calving barn with a central courtyard framed by dining space. The menu changes each season and the chefs use fresh produce from gardens on the Estate. The Deerpark is open for lunch daily, serving a lavish buffet (under $15) which includes beef from the Biltmore cattle, pasta, a soup bar, a dessert bar and an expansive salad bar as well. A candlelight dinner buffet is offered here during the winter holidays, but due to its popularity, reservations are required and should be made as soon as your plans are set.

## The Stable Café
$-$$$ • (828) 274-6370

The Stable Café in the shopping area adjacent to the mansion underwent renovation and expansion for the 1995 centennial celebration. Rotisserie chicken, soup, salads, hamburgers and desserts are served in the quaint surroundings of the former carriage house and stable, just steps from the mansion itself. The Stable Café (with meals ranging from $7 to $13) is open for lunch daily, and in the evenings during Festival of Flowers and Christmas (with meals ranging from $22 to $30).

Cherokee legends live
on in the mountains,
valleys and coves where
we live and play.

# The Cherokee Indian Reservation

At the very end of the Blue Ridge Parkway, tucked next to the southern entrance to the Great Smoky Mountains National Park, is one of America's most visited tourist destinations: the Qualla Boundary, the 56,000-acre home of the 11,000 members of the Eastern Band of the Cherokees. The continuing influence of this once-mighty tribe on the life of today's western North Carolinians is more prevalent than most of us realize. Cherokee words flow easily off our tongues in the names given to our towns, rivers, mountains, resorts, real estate developments and businesses. Old folk remedies derived from Cherokee medicine still have their place in the homes of many longtime residents. Cherokee legends endure in the mountains, valleys and coves where we live and play. Their food — squash, beans, corn, potatoes and more — deliciously graces our tables. The natural dyes they discovered and their craft techniques color and shape our handmade heritage.

## Ancient Mountain Cultures

For more than 10,000 years, American Indians have roamed the western North Carolina Mountains. Artifacts of these prehistoric tribes — classified under names such as Upper Valley People, Middle Valley People, Hiawassee People and Dallas People — have been unearthed at their campsites, villages, battlefields and man-made mounds. At times, some groups coexisted in the same area but in separate villages. Yet, sooner or later, one would drive the others out and take control of

the rich hunting grounds. Then came the Cherokees, a group that had broken away from the mighty Iroquois countless centuries ago, perhaps around the time the group crossed the Mississippi River looking for permanent homes in the eastern United States. Linguistic analysis suggests this division happened at least 3,000 years ago. Despite similar languages and identical arrow types, the two groups were separate nations and bitter enemies by the time the Iroquois took over the territory north of the Great Lakes and moved into central New York.

## War with the Iroquois

Though it has never been proven, ancient legends of the Cherokees and other tribes indicate that the Cherokees once claimed a vast region that stretched from the Great Lakes to the Ohio River. But when they tried to move into New York from the south, a bitter war with the mighty Iroquois and their allies, the Delawares, ensued; eventually, the Cherokees were defeated. Thus, it is said, they began their slow retreat down the Ohio River and into West Virginia, fighting opposing tribes all the way. Eventually they moved south and west into the mountains of North Carolina and Tennessee. Here, they found a beautiful land with a favorable climate, rich in plants and game. Once conquered, the mountainous terrain was easy for this war-loving tribe to defend.

Some evidence suggests the Cherokee culture arose from the even older cultures that have been in these mountains from time out of mind. What we know for certain is that, by the time the Europeans arrived in the mid-1500s, the Cherokees might have been here for 1,000 years and were second only to the Iroquois federation in strength and population. Numbering around 25,000, they controlled some 135,000 square miles of territory, and they fought joyfully and successfully against the surrounding Catawbas, Sara, Cheraw, Tuscaroras, Creeks, Chickasaw and Shawnees to retain it.

This great Cherokee nation stretched from the Ohio River in the north all the way down into Georgia and Alabama, taking in parts of eight states, including all of western North Carolina, the eastern section of Tennessee, and parts of South Carolina and West Virginia. They claimed all of Kentucky as hunting grounds. Much of the area was used as a game preserve, while permanent settlements were built along rivers and streams in western North Carolina, eastern Tennessee, northern Georgia and northwestern South Carolina. These settlements were made up of as many as 100 small, rectangular log homes, and each town had a large council house and extensive communal agricultural fields. Even the smaller towns would have at least 200 acres planted in corn, along with potatoes, beans, squash and vast orchards of peach trees.

## Three Cherokee Regions

The nation itself was divided into three regions, each with its own dialect and principal town that also served as a religious center. The Over Hill Towns, which were found in Georgia and along the Little Tennessee and Tellico rivers, contained the major capital of the whole tribe. It was called Echota (Chota) and was regarded as a sacred city of refuge. The Middle Towns were found along the Tuckasegee River, the headwaters of the Little Tennessee River and along the Hiawassee and Valley rivers. Their principal town and religious center, a kind of sub-capital, was Nikwasi, built on the site of what is now Franklin, North Carolina. It has been said that the Cherokee regarded Kituwah, a large settlement in southeastern Swain County, as the "Mother Town." The Lower Towns, in South Carolina and farther east in Georgia, had a principal town on the Tugalo River called Keowee.

The Cherokees, unlike the Iroquois, had no strong central government. Until they had to make treaties with the English colonies, no single leader headed their nation, though there were wise men and women who wielded great influence among the entire tribe. Instead, town councils made up of male citizens elected their own town chiefs: one who presided over tribal affairs and one who was in charge of military matters. Each Cherokee was also a member of one of seven matriarchal clans. Children belonged to the clan of the mother, and one could not marry into his or her own clan. Divorce was fairly easy, and once divorced, the children stayed with the wife's clan, and the husband returned to his own clan.

A single town or clan could declare war, particularly acts of revenge, or it might be un-

---

**INSIDERS' TIP**

When visiting the Cherokee Indian Reservation, you're first stop should be at the Cherokee Visitor Center on Main Street in downtown Cherokee, (828) 497-9195 or (800) 438-1601. Here you'll find brochures and information on all Cherokee and area attractions, local restaurants and sightseeing. It's open daily from 8 AM to 9 PM from mid-June through late August; 8 AM to 6 PM from late August through October; and 8 AM to 4:30 PM from November through mid-June.

Although the popular "chiefs" are a photo attraction today in Cherokee, the Cherokee male of generations ago dressed much differently than their counterparts in the western United States.

dertaken by the entire Cherokee nation. It was the women, however, who had the vote on war or peace. The women chosen to announce such decisions were known as War Women or Pretty Women. Punishment of captives — including torture, death or pardons, as well as adoptions — also were decided by women.

## Europeans Arrive

The first contact with Europeans occurred in May 1540 when Hernando DeSoto arrived in Cherokee country in search of the gold and silver he had been told existed in the region. He, along with 300 horsemen, 300 footmen and a herd of 200 hogs, entered the area just east of Rabun Gap in Georgia, passed through what is now Highlands, North Carolina, and came to the town of Nikwasi (Franklin). From there, he went over the mountains to present-day Hayesville and on to Gauaxula, close to where the town of Murphy stands today. DeSoto's scribe called the people he met here Chalaque, a designation given to them by an eastern tribe. One hundred years later, a Frenchman wrote the name

Cheraqui, which the English later transformed into Cherokee. The Cherokees themselves, however, had always called themselves simply The People or The Principle People.

Finding only copper mines, DeSoto's expedition continued west toward the Mississippi River.

Twenty-seven years later, another Spaniard, Juan Pardo, led a more violent — and financially lucrative — gold-hunting expedition, coming into the mountains through present-day Toxaway. It is said that Pardo "left death, destruction and terror in his wake." For the next 125 years, Spaniards prospected quietly in the area, but life for the Cherokees went on much the same as it always had.

It wasn't until the late 1600s, when the English began to settle and explore the Carolinas, that everything changed. Between 1716 and 1743, trade between the Cherokees and the English flourished: More than 200,000 furs were exchanged for guns, blankets, broadcloth, calico, mirrors, tea kettles and other goods. But by the middle of that century, game was already growing scarce from years of overhunting to supply the demand for furs, and many Cherokees were in debt to unscrupulous traders.

Adding to the degeneration of what had been fairly decent relations between whites and natives, the English, French and Spanish drew the Cherokees, along with many of their longtime enemy tribes, into their own conflicts for territory, including the French and Indian War. During that conflict, the Cherokees' sympathies tended toward the French, but they were coerced into raising a force to fight for the British. As time went on, misunderstandings with and mistreatments of American Indians increased, and the Cherokees were frequently at war with the European settlers they found constantly encroaching upon their lands. In 1760, Col. Archibald Montgomery and 1,650 soldiers destroyed the Lower Towns along Georgia's Savannah River, forcing survivors to flee into the mountains. Montgomery and his men then advanced on the Middle Towns but were driven back. The following spring, however, another British force burned 15 of these settlements and destroyed 1,500 acres of crops, causing a widespread famine and the subsequent death of nearly half the Cherokee population.

Treaties were made and just as quickly broken, and intruding white settlers saw the Cherokees' sense of justice, which was like the old Hebrew concept of an eye for an eye, as savage. During the Revolutionary War, Britain provided the Cherokees with guns and offered bounties on the scalps of the rebellious American settlers on the east and west side of the Blue Ridge. Discovering this, the rebels, under Gen. Griffith Rutherfordton, marched through the Swannanoa Gap through present-day Waynesville and carried out raids throughout the Middle Towns, leveling 66 of them and burning crops and food supplies, while terrified populations fled into hiding. This scorched-earth policy forced the Lower Towns into a treaty that ceded away almost all their land in South Carolina. It was only one of many exchanges of land for a temporary peace, for by this time the Cherokees had little left to bargain with.

# Success and Tragedy

Though the size of their territory shrank drastically by the early 1800s, many Cherokees managed to prosper. One of their own, Sequoyah (George Gist), an illiterate, non-English-speaking child of a Cherokee mother and an absent white father, invented an alphabet so easy to use that in less than a year great numbers of Cherokees were able to read and write in their own language. A few years later, in 1828, the first Cherokee-language newspaper, *Cherokee Phoenix*, came into being. Some Cherokees, educated in mission schools, went on to get their degrees in higher education from American universities. Many owned large farms and slaves.

This success, however, only provoked resentment and covetousness in the surrounding white settlers. Then gold was discovered on Cherokee land in Georgia. Georgia refused to recognize the existence of the Cherokee nation and therefore disallowed them from owning land. They were given until June 1, 1830, to leave Georgia, and the state offered white settlers "gold lots" of Cherokee land by lottery. Though the Cherokees under Chief

Junaluska had helped Gen. Andrew Jackson's forces in their successful fight against the British in the War of 1812, President Jackson, as he had now become, failed to support the Cherokees against the State of Georgia. Instead, the federal government offered the Cherokees $4.5 million for their eastern territory and told them to move to Oklahoma. When they overwhelmingly rejected these terms, the Cherokees were forcibly removed from their tribal lands in the tragedy we now call The Trail of Tears.

One man in his sixties named Tsali, known to whites as Old Charley, was rounded up with his wife and family. Due to the mistreatment of his wife, he and his sons and son-in-law decided to overpower the soldiers and try to escape. In the skirmish, a soldier was killed, and Tsali and his family fled into the mountains to take refuge with others hiding there. The government soon realized there was no way to flush or starve out Tsali and other knowledgeable survivors from remote hiding places in their old hunting grounds. To save face, Gen. Winfield Scott said that if Tsali and his sons would surrender and stand trial for the soldier's murder, he would let the others stay where they were. Tsali and his sons,

hearing this, turned themselves in. His own people were forced to execute the old man, his oldest son and son-in-law by firing squad, but his youngest son, because of his tender age, was allowed to live.

# The Formation of the Qualla Boundary

After the American soldiers withdrew from the mountains, the ragtag remnant of the once-great Cherokees turned to William Holland Thomas, who was born on a farm near the what is now Waynesville. At the age of 12, Thomas had become manager of an Indian trading post at Qualla; by the age of 14, he owned it. He bought it from Felix Walker, a farmer, trader, land speculator and representative to Congress. He spoke and wrote Cherokee and studied American law on his own. Trusted and loved by the Cherokees, he was adopted by their old chief, Yonaguska. When Yonaguska died, Thomas, a white man, was elected chief of the eastern band of Cherokees, and he immediately went to Washington to obtain their share of the money that had been offered to the Cherokees for their

Photo: Cherokee Tribal Promotion Office

Pottery-making and several other ancient crafts are demonstrated at the Oconaluftee Indian Village in Cherokee. The cultural attraction is a re-created Cherokee village of the 1750s and is open from mid-May through the latter part of October.

land. After years of struggle, he was appointed Federal Agent to this eastern band of Cherokees, and the money was put in his trust. With it, he purchased 57,000 acres around the present village of Cherokee, plus a smaller tract known as the Snowbird Reservation near Robbinsville. Today, to those who come here by the thousands, this land is known as The Cherokee Indian Reservation, but to the people living on this acreage, it is the Qualla Boundary.

# The Present-day Qualla Boundary

And it is the nearly 11,000 residents of this region and their ancestors (who were, for many years, more isolated than the Western Band of Cherokees forced into Oklahoma) who have been largely responsible for keeping alive so much that is authentic and wonderful about the Cherokee culture. This may not be apparent immediately to the first-time visitor to the reservation, with its string of stores, motels, shops and tourist attractions that serve hordes of visitors each year. The tourist who simply comes for a relaxing vacation can enjoy hiking, swimming, trout fishing, river trips, shopping and attractions such as Tribal Bingo, Harrah's Cherokee Casino, Santa's Land Theme Park and Zoo and Cherokee Fun Park (some of these are listed in our Attractions and Kidstuff chapters).

You'll also find 44 motels and 84 cabins and 28 campgrounds with more than 2,200 sites at in-town locations as well as along the Oconaluftee River and tucked away on the mountain slopes. Several of these are associated with national chains. Not all facilities, however, are open in the winter. A visitors guide and directory that lists facilities, amenities and phone numbers can be picked up at the Cherokee Visitors Center on Main Street in downtown Cherokee, or call (800) 438-1601 to get a copy by mail. But even the casual visitor can learn a great deal about the history and the culture of the Cherokee People by including the following sites and events in your plans.

## Cherokee Heritage Museum & Gallery

Saunooke Village, U.S. 441 N., Cherokee • (828) 497-3211

This museum and gallery will be a particularly nice stop for those who appreciate the very best in contemporary Cherokee arts. The theme here is discovering the past through the present. It offers displays of art and cultural items such as masks, crystals, the uketena and more. The gallery presents a new exhibit each month. Cherokee Heritage also features educational taped tours, books and craft demonstrations. It is open daily from April through November. Admission is $2 for those 11 years and older; $1 for children ages 6 to 10; under 6 free. Group rates are available.

## The Museum of the Cherokee Indian

U.S. 441 at Drama Rd., Cherokee • (828) 497-3481

Plan to spend at least two hours at this museum, which has been called "a cutting edge" example of "how all museums should be." Outside the building is a 20-foot wooden sculpture of Sequoya (the Cherokee genius who is the only human to create a written form of language all alone), and inside you

---

**INSIDERS' TIP**

Do you have Cherokee ancestors? If so, and if you have some knowledge of your family tree, you may be able to expand on it by doing your own research in the library at the Qualla Civic Center on Acquoni Road. You can also check out Cherokee Roots, companion publications listing the rolls of the Eastern and the Western Bands of the Cherokee. To purchase the publications, write to Cherokee Roots, P.O. Box 525T, Cherokee 28719, or call (828) 497-9709. The books are also for sale in some area shops, such as the gift shop of The Museum of the Cherokee Indian.

can literally walk through Cherokee history. Interactive displays and multi-sensory exhibits allow you to experience the past. You can listen to storytellers, play the ancient butter bean game, travel the infamous Trail of Tears and much more.

The fine gift shop is loaded with a large selection of books, crafts, artwork and other Cherokee or Native American items. The museum is open year round except on Thanksgiving, Christmas and New Year's Day. Hours are 9 AM to 5 PM September through May and 9 AM to 8 PM June through August. Admission is $6 for adults, $4 for children. There are group rates, AA, AARP and other discounts available.

## Oconaluftee Indian Village
### Drama Rd., off U.S. 441 N., Cherokee
### • (828) 497-2315

Get ready to step back more than two centuries in time when you visit this re-created 1750s Cherokee village. Indian guides in native costumes will take you through the village, while others demonstrate such life skills as weaving, pottery, beadwork, food preparation, canoe construction, and arrow making and hunting techniques. You will see Cherokee homes, a sweat lodge and the important seven-sided council house. Cherokee history, culture and social customs will be explained, and you'll have ample opportunity to ask questions. Afterward, go back to the areas that interested you and spend as much time as you like exploring further. The village is open from 9 AM to 5:30 PM daily May 15 through October 25. Admission is $10 for adults and $5 for children 6 through 13 years old.

## Qualla Arts and Crafts Mutual Inc.
### U.S. 441 and Drama Rd., Cherokee
### • (828) 497-3103

Just across the street from The Museum of the Cherokee Indian you'll find a cooperative that displays the works of 300 Cherokee craftspeople and a section of American Indian crafts from other areas of the country. The store also has a large section of historical baskets, masks, pottery, fingerweaving, woodcarving and the like. It's open 8 AM to 8 PM June through August, 8 AM to 6 PM September through October, and 8 AM to 4:30 PM November through May. Admission is free.

## Unto These Hills Outdoor Drama
### Drama Rd. and U.S. 441 N., Cherokee
### • (828) 497-2111

Every summer from mid-June through late-August, one of the world's longest-running outdoor dramas takes the stage in the 2,800-seat Mountainside Theater just outside the town of Cherokee. In the half-century since the play opened in 1950, millions of visitors have watched the rich pageant of Cherokee legends, rituals, dances and history unfold before them. Even if you've seen this outdoor drama in years past, a recomposed musical score makes a return trip a new experience.

June and July performances, which run 2 hours and 15 minutes, start at 8:45 PM, with pre-show musical entertainment beginning at 8:10 PM. In August shows begin at 8:30 PM and pre-show entertainment at 7:50 PM. Reserved seating in the front half of the theatre is $14 for all ages; general admission is $11 per adult and $5 per child through age 12. Group rates are available for 20 or more people. Tickets may be purchased at the box office at the intersection of U.S. 441 and Drama Road from 9 AM to 6:30 PM Monday through Saturday. After 6:30 PM, you can buy them at the Mountainside Theater for that evening's performance. You can also order reserve tickets by calling the above number. Both the theater and the office are closed on Sundays.

At 411 feet, Whitewater
Falls in Transylvania
County lays claim to
being the highest
unbroken falls in the
Southeast.

# Waterfalls

Whether it's the roar of a great cataract forming rainbows in its drenching spray or a slender, misty stream of water musically splashing in a shallow pool, there are few places where the call of the falls can be so fulfilled as here in western North Carolina. There are literally hundreds in these mountains, more than 250 in Transylvania County alone.

Obviously, there are many wonderful waterfalls that aren't listed in this chapter. Some are on private property, and others can only be reached by long and strenuous hikes though rugged country. Most of the ones we've chosen are just a short jaunt away from a roadway, and some of these falls can be viewed simply by parking your car and taking a look. There are a few, however, we think are worth the extra effort required to reach them, even though it sometimes means traveling on a narrow, curvy, graveled secondary road (S.R.) or Forest Service road (F.R.).

But a few words of caution are in order: Water-drenched rocks can be extremely treacherous, and a number of serious accidents and deaths occur each year to people who slip and fall from the tops of these falls or from the spray- and moss-slick rocks, steps and trails nearby. (Even when fording mountain streams, extreme care is needed). If, however, you use common-sense caution, keep a sharp eye on children, stay well away from the tops of falls and never try to climb or walk across them, such tragedies can be avoided.

We also plead with you to stick to the trails and don't scramble around the stream and river banks, destroying vegetation and loosening the soil. Such impact from visitors, and often their carelessness with fishing lines, cigarette butts and other litter, endangers fish, wildlife and rare plants and plays a large role in destroying many of these lovely places.

Some of these sites attract so many visitors that, in 1997, a three-year pilot fee system was put in place at a few of the more popular waterfalls. The money collected is returned directly to each site to make improvements and pay employees. These include Sliding Rock ($3 per vehicle), Dry Falls ($2 per vehicle) and Whitewater Falls ($2 per vehicle). A season pass costs $15. However, one pass is needed for Sliding Rock and another is required for and provides access to Dry Falls and Whitewater Falls as well as nearby Whiteside Mountain. Both Golden Age and Golden Access Passports are honored.

# The Northern Mountains

## Avery County

### Elk Falls
**off U.S. Hwy. 19 E.**

Sixty-five-foot Elk Falls, just inside the Tennessee-North Carolina border, is one of the most beautiful waterfalls in the mountains. Its lovely pool, one of the largest and deepest around, makes this a super-popular swimming hole, but beware of the fast water here.

Elk Falls is easily accessible; just go north on U.S. Highway 19 E. to the town of Elk Park. A short distance up Main Street (S.R. 1303), turn right on Elk River Road (S.R. 1305), a residential street. Travel just over 4 miles to a parking area beside the Elk River. Here, a short trail leads to the top and on down to the base of the falls.

## Burke County

### Linville Falls
**Mi. 316.5**

Well-known Linville Falls, at the head of Linville Gorge, pours downward in several stages into one of the deepest gorges in the eastern United States. Its upper and lower cascades, we're told, used to be about the same height. But a heavy flood around the turn of the century broke off part of the ledge on the upper falls and deposited it at the top of the lower falls, decreasing the height of the former but increasing the height of the latter.

You can reach the falls by hiking from the Linville Falls Visitors Center at Milepost 316.3 on the Blue Ridge Parkway. For specific directions, check the maps posted at the center. The trails to various overlooks of the falls range from easy to difficult.

www.insiders.com

See this and many other **Insiders' Guide®** destinations online. **Visit us today!**

mer months). In winter, when the campgrounds are closed, you'll have to park outside the gate and walk in. A loop trail, lined with birch and hemlock and, in spring and summer, a great variety of wildflowers, leads to this beautiful 70-foot falls. To get to the falls by the shortest route, nearly a mile, descend the trail to the right. You can come back the same way for a trip of slightly less than 2 miles or continue on the 2.5-mile loop. If you do the latter, bear to the left to avoid trails leading into the campground.

## Upper Creek Falls
### off N.C. Hwy. 181

The main part of this cascade tumbles some 100 feet into a pool of thrashing water. This and the fact that it's moderately easy to get to make Upper Creek Falls a popular swimming and sunbathing area. To reach it, take N.C. Highway 181 south from the Blue Ridge Parkway for just more than 5.5 miles to a parking area on the left. A nearly mile-long, steep switchback trail descends through the woods to the falls.

# Yancey County

## Crabtree Falls
### Mi. 339.5

This 70-foot waterfall, considered to be one of the most photogenic in the state, is in the Crabtree Meadows Recreation Area (elevation 3,700 feet) on the Blue Ridge Parkway, 8.4 miles south of the junction of N.C. Highway 226 at milepost 339.5. The steep, rocky trail makes for a moderately difficult hike from the parking lot in the Crabtree Meadows camping area (you can pick up a trail guide at the campground's entrance during the sum-

## Setrock Creek and Roaring Fork Falls
### 3 mi. off of N.C. Hwy. 80 N.

On the Blue Ridge Parkway, exit onto N.C. Highway 80 N. (at milepost 344) and go approximately 2 miles north to Forest Service Road 472. Make a left onto F.R. 472 and drive 4.7 miles to the Black Mountain Campground. Inside the campground, you'll see a sign leading to the Briar Bottom group camp. Drive the short distance to a sign on the right that marks the way to this 75-foot cascade. When the trail forks, bear right. This is a round-trip excursion of a little more than a half-mile.

When you return to your car, continue your journey another 3.9 miles down F.R. 472 (when the road changes from gravel to pavement, it becomes S.R. 1205). At the Busick Work Center sign, turn right and park at the gate. The trail, an old logging road to the right of the gate, will take you to Roaring Fork River. Turn right on a path at the river. You'll find the falls, which drop in beautiful five-foot cascades, about ½ mile away.

The mossy rocks and leaves form alcoves worthy of the Garden of Eden! A trail running up the forested right side of the falls let you into a small pool at the top. Be very careful and use only the trail to get to the top.

## INSIDERS' TIP

Famous Linville Gorge and Linville Falls were named for William Linville and his son, Tom, who were killed by Indians. The Cherokees called the river "eeseeoh" or "river of many cliffs."

Photo: Asheville Convention and Visitors Bureau

Cascading waterfalls grace the mountainsides around Asheville.

### Waterfall on Big Creek
**off U.S. 19 W.**

This gushing waterfall, which can be viewed from the road, is reached by taking U.S. Highway 19 E. west out of Burnsville and then turning right on U.S. 19 W. toward the Tennessee border. Drive 17.5 miles to a marked pull-off on the left for a view of the 25-foot falls.

# The Central Mountains

## Buncombe County

### Douglas (or Carter Creek) and Walker Falls
**5 mi. south of N.C. Hwy. 197**

A journey into Pisgah's Craggy Mountain Scenic Area to view Douglas Falls offers an added attraction: The falls are surrounded by a stand of rare virgin hemlock. To reach the area, take U.S. Highway 19-23 out of Asheville for 13.5 miles and then go east on N.C. Highway 197 to Barnardsville. Turn south on Dillingham Road (S.R. 2173) about a half-

block past the post office. About 4 miles down this winding road, veer to the left and continue until it becomes graveled F.R. 74; stop for a view of two-tier 50-foot Walker Falls on the left.

Continue on another 5 miles or so until you dead-end at the Craggy Mountain Scenic Area parking area. Take the trail on the south end (right side) of the parking lot. It's a little more than a half-mile to a viewing area at the base of 70-foot Douglas Falls, named in honor of Supreme Court Justice William O. Douglas. Unless you are an experienced hiker armed with a good topographical map and compass, return the way you came. Most trail maps of this area are outdated and confusing. For the best viewing, visit both these falls after heavy rains.

### Glassmine Falls
**Mi. 361.1**

This waterfall is on private land, and its water flow can be thin when rain is scarce. (It's been know to dry up completely.) However, after heavy rains Glassmine Falls, with its immense slide downward, can be impressive. You can view the falls from Glassmine

Falls Overlook at milepost 361.1 on the Blue Ridge Parkway. This overlook is about 200 feet from the parking area, which is 5.7 miles south of N.C. 128, the road that leads to Mt. Mitchell's summit. It will be on the left when driving south from Mt. Mitchell and on the right when driving north. Look east to locate the fall's steep rock face (estimated at 800 feet), framed by stark skeletons of red spruce that have died from air pollution.

## Polk County

### Pearson Falls
**off Pearson Falls Rd. (S.R. 1102)**

There is a $1.50 fee for adults and 50¢ for children 6 to 12 (children younger than 6 are admitted free) to Pearson Falls Park, which is owned and maintained by the Tryon Garden Club, and it's well worth the price. Take U.S. Highway 176 south out of Saluda or north out of Tryon. Watch for a small sign on the Pacolet River side of the road that marks Pearson Falls Road (S.R. 1102). The entrance to the 250-acre park is slightly less than a mile down this road. This biologically rich glen with its profusion of wildflowers was purchased in 1931 and is now a North Carolina Natural Heritage Area. It's a great place for hiking, bird-watching and picnicking. The park is open from 10 AM to 6 PM daily in the summer. From November 1 to March 1 it's closed on Monday and Tuesday and is only open from 10 AM to 5 PM the rest of the week.

### Shunkawauken Falls
**White Oak Mountain Rd. (S.R. 1136)**

This cascade begins its tumbles practically from the summit of 3,102-foot White Oak Mountain, with the main portion measuring around 150 feet high. Though it's on private land, it can be viewed right from the roadside. From Interstate 26, drive east on N.C. Highway 108 for just less than a half-mile and turn

left on Houston Road (S.R. 1137). After another half-mile, take the fork to the left onto White Oak Mountain Road (S.R. 1136). You'll come to the waterfall in another 2 miles. There is a pull-off on the left just beyond it. If you continue on down the road for just a little more than a half-mile, you'll reach an overlook with a great view of Columbus and the surrounding area.

## Rutherford County

### Hickory Nut Falls
**Inside the park off U.S. Hwy. 64 E.**

This waterfall spilling 404 feet over a granite face is just over the Henderson County line at Lake Lure and can be seen from quite a distance. Hickory Nut Falls are located in the privately owned Chimney Rock Park (see our Attractions chapter). Admission ($9.50 for adults and $5 for children 6 to 15; children under 6 are free) includes a 26-story elevator ride up through solid rock and access to nature trails offering unparalleled views of the falls (the best is from Inspiration Point). It also offers a smashing view of Lake Lure, craggy-faced Rumbling Bald Mountain and the surrounding countryside. For a preview of the falls, you may want to rent the 1992 movie *Last of the Mohicans*, which featured the majestic falls prominently. To reach the park, take U.S. Highway 64 E. off I-26 and drive approximately 15 miles through Bat Cave to the park.

## Transylvania County

### Courthouse Falls
**off N.C. 215**

You'll have to walk a short distance to reach this waterfall, but it's one of our favorites and one of the most beautiful in the mountains. Take N.C. Highway 215 for 10.4 miles into Pisgah Forest from its junction with U.S.

# Jackson County:
# Richland Balsam

A self-guided, 1.5-mile loop trail will take you over the highest mountain in the Great Balsam Mountains, 6,410-foot Richland Balsam, and through a remnant of a spruce-fir forest. Drive to the Haywood-Jackson County Overlook at milepost 431 just north of the highest point on the Blue Ridge Parkway. The trail begins at the upper end of the parking lot and is paved at its start.

64 near Rosman. Turn right on F.R. 140 and drive approximately 3 miles to a small bridge that crosses a creek; you can park on the far side, on the right. Take the trail on the right for a few hundred yards to a narrow trail that bears left. This 300-foot, short, steep trail leads to the beautiful pool at the base of the falls.

## Daniel Ridge Falls
### F.R. 475

Two other fine cascades — Cove Creek and Shuck Ridge Creek Falls — are in this general area, but Daniel Ridge, also known as Toms Spring Falls, is the largest and easiest to find. Drive 5.2 miles up U.S. 276 to F.R. 475 and go 3.9 miles to a parking area on the right. From there, follow the logging road for less than a mile. You'll see the 150-foot falls on the left.

## The Horsepasture River Falls
### off N.C. Hwy. 281 S.

The series of waterfalls here are some of the most awe-inspiring in the region. To reach the falls, from the intersection of U.S. 64 and N.C. 281 in Sapphire, turn south on N. C. 281 and drive 1.8 miles to the Horsepasture River, 4.2 miles of which have been designated as part of the National Wild and Scenic River System. Find a parking spot along the guardrails near the bridge. Drift Falls, known to locals as "Bust Your Butt Falls," can been seen just down river. Unfortunately, it recently fell into private ownership, so you must not trespass on the property there. Parking is also a problem. There's a pull-off on the right for about three or four cars next to the trailhead, marked by a small green sign on the guardrail. (Make sure your vehicle is completely off

the road, or you may get ticketed.) From the trailhead, descend the trail for 100 yards until it joins the trail paralleling the river. Privately-owned Drift Falls will be to your right. Drop Off/Turtleback Falls is a few hundred feet further on your left, named for its dome-like rock. Through it looks like a great place for some slide-and-swim fun, don't attempt it; the currents in this pool have caused a number of drownings, and it's dangerously close to the top of Rainbow Falls. A few years ago, a girl was swept by the current over Rainbow and killed. Her two companions narrowly escaped the same fate.

Viewing the other beautiful falls along this wide, deep gorge will require a 1.5-mile steep descent on a sometimes-strenuous trail with precipitous ledges. It is not suitable for young children or those less than physically fit. Even if you're in shape, care is needed.

Continue down the gorge to the top of roaring, 200-foot Rainbow Falls, where you can often see rainbows in the thunderous spray. Again, *stay away from the brink of this waterfall!* Instead, take the trail to an upper overlook or descend to the lower overlook (if you don't mind a drenching) for a picnic or swim. Avoid these falls in winter, when the spray freezes and makes walking dangerous.

It's another fairly difficult half-mile trek to the base of Stairstep Falls where the river tumbles down seven 10-foot-tall, river-wide steps. If you're wise, you'll turn around and make the hike back to Turtleback Falls at this point; only the most experienced and intrepid should continue down the strenuous and dangerous 1.3-mile trail to Windy Falls. That series of nine violent cascades plunges 700 feet so mightily that they create their own wind through the narrowing gorge. We definitely advise not attempting this one. There isn't even a viewing place to see all of Windy Falls. A final word of caution: When visiting this wild-river gorge, one of the most beautiful and spectacular in the mountains, remember that accidents in the area have kept the local rescue squad busy through the years, and deaths have been a common occurrence.

## Looking Glass Falls
### U.S. 276

You barely have to get out of your vehicle to enjoy the most visited of Transylvania County's many waterfalls. This rushing 30-foot-wide, 60-foot-high cascade is set alongside U.S. Highway 276, 5.5 miles into Pisgah Forest from its junction with U.S. 64. A short flight of stone steps leads down to the base of the falls from a paved pull-off area right beside Looking Glass Creek.

## Moore's Cove Falls
### .7 miles off U.S. 276

One mile north of Looking Glass Falls on U.S. 276, keep a sharp eye out for the first bridge ahead and pull off in the wide, unpaved area just before reaching the bridge. (When driving south, it's 1.6 miles from Sliding Rock.) A wooden pedestrian bridge will take you across Looking Glass Creek to the lovely, easy .7-mile-long Moore's Cove trail, which is steep only for the first few hundred yards. At its end, a small stream tumbles over a deeply recessed ledge that allows you to walk behind the free-falling 50-foot falls. Avoid the steep path to the top of the ledge: It can be dangerous.

## Slick Rock Falls
### F.R. 475B

To reach this watery attraction just a short distance up the road from Looking Glass Falls,

follow the sign to the Pisgah Fish Hatchery (F.R. 475) on the left. Drive 1.6 miles and turn right on F.R. 475B. After 1.1 miles, you'll come to a sharp bend in the road. Park at the small pull-off on the right, where a trailhead leads up to the summit of Looking Glass Rock. The small but pretty 30-foot-tall Slick Rock Falls, some 50 yards away, spills over a rocky ledge of this rugged mountain. This waterfall well deserves its name "slick," so please don't try to climb it or any other falls.

## Sliding Rock
### U.S. 276

Just 1.6 miles farther up U.S. 276 (or 7.6 miles from its junction with U.S. 64) is Sliding Rock, one place where you're invited to "take the plunge" down a 60-foot slippery cascade into the 50-degree to 60-degree, 6-foot-deep pool below. If you don't care to make the slide, it's fun to simply watch the action from paved viewing areas at the top or bottom of this natural, exhilarating ride that's fueled by 11,000 gallons of water a minute. There's now a $3 fee per vehicle parking fee that helps pay for lifeguards, who are on duty from 10 AM to 6 PM from Memorial Day through Labor Day; the parking fee includes the use of a bathhouse.

The rock, while slick, can take the bottom out of an ordinary bathing suit, so old jeans or cutoffs are best for this fast ride. Also, be careful while getting in and out of the water. The surface of the rock, even where the water isn't flowing, can be slick and accounts for some hard tumbles.

## Toxaway Falls
### off U.S. Hwy. 64

In 1916, the first Lake Toxaway dam burst after a flooding downpour. The water from the lake washed away huge amounts of vegetation and soil and exposed a huge granite

## INSIDERS' TIP

While crime is not something we think much about when out exploring these mountains, there have been reports of vehicle break-ins from people stopping to take short walks into the woods or to enjoy forest beauty spots. Therefore, it's a good idea to lock your valuables in the trunk when leaving the car if you're going to be away for a period of time.

dome. Now, as you drive over this dome on a bridge, you get a bird's-eye-view of the great quantities of water, sometimes more than 300 feet wide, that pour 250 feet over this ledge into the valley below. In 1997, busy, twisting U.S. 64 was widened and an easier pull-off was created for the many people who wished to look down on and/or get a photo of the falls. (The bottom of the falls is on private land.) For a more leisurely view, you might want to stop for a meal at October's End, a nice Italian restaurant with a terrace overlooking the falls. (See our Restaurants chapter.)

## Twin Falls on Henry Branch
### 2.2 miles off F.R. 477

Since we sometimes are able to take this lovely hike to Twin Falls without meeting anyone else along the trail, we almost hesitate to risk jeopardizing such solitude by writing about it. Note that at 4.4 miles for the round trip, this is the longest trek in this list. While it's not a particularly difficult trail, it does involve negotiating a number of log bridges, so we always equip ourselves with a long, sturdy walking stick to help keep our balance, a good idea almost anytime you're walking forest trails that often have slippery and eroded sections.

To reach these two 100-foot waterfalls, drive 2.2 miles north on U.S. 276 from its junction with U.S. 64. Turn right on F.R. 477 and travel just more than 2.5 miles to a small parking area on the right side at the sign to Avery Creek Trail. Take this yellow-and-blue-blazed path for slightly more than a mile, until Avery Creek Trail crosses orange-blazed Buckhorn Gap Trail, which you should take to the right. In a little more than a half-mile, you'll come to a Trail Falls Loop sign. It's just a short distance in either direction of the loop to Twin Falls (the left loop is usually less overgrown), which are formed by two separate streams.

Our mountains offer hundreds of places to listen to the soothing sound of a cascading waterfall.

# Jackson County:
# Whiteside Mountain

The top of this ancient Jackson County mountain, one of the oldest on earth, offers a fantastic view of Cashiers Valley, the upper Chattooga River watershed and the surrounding Blue Ridge Mountain peaks. A fairly easy 1.5-mile loop circles the summit with a half-mile side trail to Devil's Courthouse. From Cashiers, take U.S. Highway 64 W. for 5 miles to Whiteside Mountain Road (S.R. 1690). Turn left onto this road and continue for about a mile until you reach the Whiteside Mountain parking area on your left (see our Forests and Parks chapter). There is a $2 per vehicle parking fee.

There is no trail to the very base of the falls. Don't try to make one. You'll only disturb the wonderful plants that live here.

### Whitewater Falls and Laurel Falls
#### off N.C. Hwy. 281

At 411 feet, Whitewater Falls lays claim to being the highest unbroken falls in the Southeast. To reach it, take U.S. 64 to N.C. Highway 281 and travel south for approximately 9.5 miles. Turn left at the Whitewater Falls Scenic Area for the short drive to the parking area, where there is a $2 per vehicle fee. From there, a .2-mile trail leads to the upper overlook. Be extremely careful when negotiating the steep trip down to a lower overlook for an even better view. An old roadbed leads to the top of the falls, but we don't recommend any close-up viewing, as a number of deaths occur in the area almost every year.

If you're in excellent shape, you can turn right on the trail that brings you to the middle overlook, and it will take you on a very strenuous hike of just less than a mile down to Laurel Falls, also known as Corbin Creek Falls.

When the trees have shed their leaves, you can view this waterfall from Whitewater. It's made up of a series of broken cascades that tumble about the same distance as Whitewater, but only the lowest one, which drops approximately 75 feet, can be easily seen. It's much too dangerous to try to get a close-up view of the others.

# The Southern Mountains

## Clay County

### Leatherwood Falls
#### F.R. 340

Compared to some falls, 25-foot Leatherwood is not particularly grand, but Fires Creek, which rushes past the falls' base, is great for swimming and fishing. To find it, go west out of Hayesville on U.S. 64 for just short of 5 miles and turn right on S.R. 1302. After 3.7 miles, turn left on S.R. 1344, which will become F.R. 340 as it enters the Nantahala Na-

---

**INSIDERS' TIP**

Some of the waterfalls listed here are deep in the area's forests, so be sure to take food and drink along with you and always wear comfortable shoes with nonskid soles. Packing a towel, a bathing suit and a change of clothing also isn't a bad idea, but be warned: The water will be chilly, to say the least, in any mountain pool. Make sure, too, that the pool you choose to swim in is absolutely safe. Currents near waterfalls can be treacherous. And as we've noted numerous times, never, ever wade above a waterfall where a slip can be fatal.

tional Forest. Drive 1.9 miles to the Leatherwood Falls parking and picnic area. You can view the falls from here or wade into the creek (it can be rushing and dangerous after heavy rains), or you can cross the bridge upstream and work your way back to the foot of the falls. Don't, however, be tempted to climb the cascade. It may not look dangerous, but it is. Less dangerous, but still for the daredevils, is jumping off the bridge into the creek. (Make sure the water is running deep enough for such sport.) From the picnic area, paved trails provide access for fly-fishing from wheelchairs.

## Haywood County

### The Graveyard Fields Falls
**Mi. 418.8**

Three waterfalls, Upper Falls, Second Falls and Yellowstone Falls (the largest of the three), are in Graveyard Fields, a vast area left nearly treeless by a devastating forest fire in 1925. Second Falls can be seen from the parking area at milepost 418.8 on the Blue Ridge Parkway, but most people prefer a closer look, making the Graveyard Fields Loop Trail almost too popular. The parking area is very crowded on weekends. Some parts of the trail are badly eroded, as are many side trails. Do Graveyard Fields a favor and stick to the main routes, avoiding the area altogether during wet weather. Check the information board at the parking area for the most direct routes to the falls, and be careful at the overlook at Yellowstone Falls, which can be treacherous (see our chapter on The Blue Ridge Parkway). As with all falls, stay out of the water at the top of the falls, and stay on the trails.

### Midnight Hole and
### Mouse Creek Falls
**1.5 and 2 miles off Waterville Rd.**

Seeing these falls requires a 4-mile round-trip hike, but it's an easy walk on a graded road that runs along beautiful Big Creek. To reach Big Creek, drive west on Interstate 40 to the Waterville exit (just before you reach the Tennessee border). Turn left on Waterville Road, which will enter the Great Smoky Mountains National Park. After approximately 3

miles and .8 miles past the ranger station, the road will end at a parking area of the Big Creek Campground. (In winter, the gate is closed at the ranger station, so you'll have to walk from there, adding 1.6 miles round trip.) Take the road (Big Creek Trail) just a few feet back from the parking area. A little less than 1.5 miles along this easy route, an obvious path will lead to Midnight Hole, where small (seven-foot) but gorgeous twin falls flow into a fantastic 80-foot-wide, 15-foot-deep swimming hole. Back on the road/trail, continue on slightly over another half-mile and you'll see Mouse Creek Falls, which drop a total of 50 feet, rushing into the creek.

For those with the energy, there is another series of waterfalls called Gunter Fork Cascades. The longest one drops 100 feet, making it one of the tallest waterfalls in the Park. They're 8.2 difficult miles from the parking area and are reached by a wonderful route that runs mostly along this beautiful creek then just over 2 miles up Gunter Fork Trail. That, however, is a hard 16.4-mile round trip, and you'll have to make a number of wet-stream crossings. You should get a trail map and specific directions if you want to see these falls.

## Jackson County

### Hurricane Falls and
### Glassy Creek Falls
**N.C. Hwy. 107 and Norton Rd. (S.R. 1145)**

Hurricane and Glassy Creek Falls are both on private property, but they can be viewed from the roadside on the same trip. To reach Hurricane Falls, drive north out of Cashiers on N.C. 107 for 1.8 miles and turn left on Norton Road (S.R. 1145). It's just more than a half-mile to a pull-off where you can see the waterfall, which has an average height of 40 feet that varies according to the height of Lake Thorpe into which it flows.

For Glassy Creek Falls, return to N.C. 107 and continue north for 8.6 miles to a pull-off on the left (because of the sharp curve at this location, you probably should pass the pull-off, turn around farther up the road and come back to park). The 100-foot curling falls is formed by the Little River Creek. The river you'll see in front of the falls is the West Fork of the Tuckasegee.

## Silver Run Falls
### N.C. Hwy. 107

Would you like a waterfall-fed pool to cool off in on a hot day? Then, from Cashiers, drive south on N.C. Hwy. 107 for just more than 4 miles and park at a graveled pull-off on the left with a utility pole at its corner. Follow the short path over a fallen log that bridges the creek or wade the water to this picturesque 20-foot waterfall. Its lovely, sandy beach and pretty pool make it a relatively safe and popular swimming area.

# Macon County

## Big Laurel Falls and Mooney Falls
### F.R. 67

Big Laurel Falls is a small but beautiful waterfall that plunges 30 feet in two stages into a tempting pool deep in the Southern Nantahala Wilderness Area. To get there, take U.S. 64 W. out of Franklin for about 12 miles and turn left onto Old U.S. Highway 64. In slightly less than 2 miles, turn right on F.R. 67, which is only partly paved, and drive for just short of 7 miles to a marked parking area. Take the easy trail (it's less than a half-mile) to the falls, bearing to the right each time the trail forks. Mooney Falls, actually a series of falls, is just more than a half-mile farther up the road on F.R. 67. Park at the Mooney Falls sign and take the very short trail for several different views of the falls. None of the cascades is more than 15 feet high, but the overall effect is exceedingly breathtaking.

## Bridal Veil Falls
### off U.S. Hwy. 64

Only a few dozen feet from U.S. 64, 2.5 miles west of Highlands, you can see this 120-foot, ethereal cascade right from your car. U.S. 64 used to run right behind the falls, but there was a problem with ice on the highway in winter, so the highway was moved. You can still use an old piece of the original highway to detour behind the falls. For a more leisurely view or to take a photograph, there's a pull-off just beyond the falls.

## Cullasaja Falls
### U.S. 64

The 250-foot Cullasaja Falls is one of the more majestic of the many cascades in the Cullasaja River Gorge, so it's unfortunate that U.S. 64 is so busy, narrow and dangerous at this point 8.8 miles west of Highlands, making more than a drive-by glimpse difficult. To get a good look, try to find a parking place in one of the narrow, frequently crowded, unmarked pull-offs on the highway's precipitous shoulder, keeping a careful eye on traffic when getting in and out of the car. Then be satisfied with a view and photo from the road. The primitive paths down to the base of the falls are much too dangerous to attempt.

## Dry Falls
### U.S. 64

Less than a mile from Bridal Veil Falls, Dry Falls drops 80 feet; 40 feet of that distance is free fall. The neat thing about this falls is that an easy, paved path leads down from the parking lot, taking you inside the recessed ledge behind the roaring and sometimes-drenching waters for a view from the other side. There is a $2 per vehicle fee.

## Glen Falls
### S.R. 1618

There are several beautiful falls and accompanying cascades here that drop 640 feet in only a half-mile. So, though the well-maintained trail to the 70-, 60- and 15-foot waterfalls in the Glen Falls Scenic Area is less than a mile long, it is steep and tough to hike back up. But, it's worth it! In addition, there are marvelous views of the Blue Valley as well as great picnic spots along the route. To reach the area, take N.C. Highway 106 just south of Highlands for less than 2 miles until you see the Glen Falls Scenic Area sign on the left and take S.R. 1618 immediately on the right. From there, it's a mile to the trail that leads from a parking area.

## Upper and Lower Satulah Falls
### off N.C. Hwy. 28

Upper Satulah Falls, which looks like a steep waterslide, is on private property, but you can see it easily from the road. From Highlands, drive south on N.C. 28 for 2.3 miles and

Mingo Falls, one of western North Carolina's most beautiful and least known waterfalls, is located on the Cherokee Indian Reservation.

Photo: Cherokee Tribal Travel & Promotion Office

look to your left at the foot of the vast rock face of 4,543-foot Satulah Mountain. Park at the overlook a short distance farther on the right side of the road. Continue on N.C. 28 for just more than a mile to view the high, narrow Lower Satulah Falls (also known as Clear Creek Falls). It's across the valley from a wide pull-off that also overlooks the Piedmont, including the Blue Valley, Rabun Bald and Scaly Mountain. This 100-foot, lower waterfall is best seen in the winter when the foliage is off the trees.

## Swain County

### Juneywhank Falls, Toms Branch Falls and Indian Creek Falls
**off Deep Creek Rd.**

All three of these popular falls in the Great Smoky Mountains National Park can be found by going out Deep Creek Road just outside Bryson City. However, you'll have to jog around several different streets as you pass through town to find this road, so the sim-

plest thing is to go to Bryson City and ask directions to Deep Creek Road. You'll travel 2.2 miles up this road before you enter the actual park. From that boundary, it's a little more than a half-mile to the parking area at the end of the road. The quarter-mile trail to 80-foot Juneywhank Falls begins about 100 yards from the picnic area.

To get to another 80-foot-drop cascade, Toms Branch Falls, go past the gate and take the gravel road (part of the park's popular Deep Creek Trail) a quarter-mile to the falls on the right. A half-mile upstream is the well-used tubing launch site, so expect to see hordes of tubers floating by in the summer. Actually, you can see the falls much better in the winter when the surrounding trees and bushes have lost their foliage.

Continuing on the Deep Creek Trail for less than a mile will bring you to Indian Creek Trail. The wide 25-foot waterfall known as Indian Creek Falls is just a few hundred yards down this path, where a side trail will take you to the base of the falls.

## Mingo Falls
### off Big Cove Rd.

Mingo, on the Cherokee Indian Reservation, is one of the most fabulous falls in the whole Smoky Mountains area, though the landscape around it has been somewhat marred in the past few years by storm damage. To reach it, take U.S. 441 out of Cherokee, where it becomes Newfound Gap Road once it enters the Great Smoky Mountains National Park. Just short of a mile after the junction with the Blue Ridge Parkway, turn right at the Jobs Corps Center sign. The road will end after a half-mile at Big Cove Road. Turn left and drive 3.3 miles to the Mingo Cove Campground and park. The trail is only a quarter-mile long, but the first part of it is very steep.

Touring the Blue Ridge Parkway is the most favored way of taking in the long sweep of fall color. From Boone and Blowing Rock to Asheville and Cherokee, each turn of the road offers a new horizon, a new definition of beautiful.

# The Blue Ridge Parkway

It's hard to believe this beautiful ribbon of roadway is only some 60 years old. The Blue Ridge Parkway is such a natural part of the landscape that it seems to have always wound through these mountaintops. This scenic highway was born in 1935 out of a need to provide work for people forced from their jobs by the Great Depression. The Parkway was conceived as a link between the Shenandoah National Park in Virginia and the Great Smoky Mountains National Park in North Carolina and Tennessee. After the political wranglings ended and financing was ironed out, the project employed thousands of workers and engineers. The inspiration of a particularly gifted young landscape architect, Stanley Abbott, and northern Italian stone masons contributed to the Parkway's beauty and grace.

The designers' goals were as lofty as the Parkway itself: to create for the traveler a sense of connection to the land and its history and to inspire future generations to preserve this connection. They succeeded. As you travel along the 250 miles of the Parkway in North Carolina, you pass sights that fill your soul and summon you to be part of this beautiful place. Scores of overlooks, designed for their grand vistas, invite you to pull over and stop. More often than not, a hiking trail will tempt you up the hill where wildflowers with colorful names such as Pink Lady's Slipper, Skunk Cabbage and Joe-Pye-Weed grow in abundance from April through October. Several endangered species live on Parkway lands, including wildflowers such as Gray's Lily, Heller's Blazing Star and Small Whorled Pogonia and animal species such as bog turtles, flying squirrels, salamanders and bats.

More than 100 bird species can be seen during the spring migration season. Picnic tables scattered along the Parkway make the slightest stopover a special occasion. Visitors centers and roadside historical markers bring to life the story of the mountains and regions, their people and natural beauty.

When the Parkway flows into North Carolina from Virginia at milepost 216.9, you find yourself in the rolling pasture land of Allegheny and Ashe counties. Those cows grazing in the northern meadows, the pioneer cabins just off the road and the lichen-covered split-rail fences are part of the Parkway by design. These farms in the northern stretches of the Parkway were welcomed, their owners encouraged to stay and work in harmony with the Park Service to preserve the look of a simpler time. It's as if you turned down a country road with no particular destination in mind and found yourself in a tranquil yesteryear.

As you get closer to Watauga, Avery and Mitchell counties, the mountains grow taller, the mountaintops stretch higher, and the horizon spreads farther. (Elevations on the Park-

## Emergency Contacts

The Parkway emergency number is (800) 727-5928 (PARKWATCH). For general Parkway Information call (828) 298-0398, which is a recorded message that updates Parkway travelers on road and weather information, park facility closings and general visitor services such as campgrounds and lodging.

way range from 649 to 6,047 feet.) The section of the Parkway known as the Linn Cove Viaduct, near Grandfather Mountain at milepost 304, is the newest link and an engineering marvel. This section swings 1,243 feet around the curve of the rugged mountain. Borrowing construction techniques developed in Switzerland, the viaduct was designed and built "from the top down" to create the least impact on delicate Grandfather Mountain. The structure was built of 153 precast concrete sections, no two exactly alike, and was completed in the 1980s.

Milepost 355.4 marks the entrance to Mount Mitchell State Park, where the highest peak in the eastern United States rises up to 6,684 feet. The mountainside becomes more rugged, the terrain more imposing and views even more panoramic. Misty blue mountains in the distance (yes, they really do have a blue hue) cradle the small towns in the valleys below. In recent years, the mountains and valleys have been unfortunate victims of traveling pollution blown in on the transcontinental jet stream. The result is reduced long distance visibility. The vistas are still remarkable, although compared with less-polluted times, the difference is sadly evident.

The Parkway changes again as it approaches Asheville and Buncombe County from the north. Many overlooks provide the opportunity to scan the communities down below. Asheville, the largest metropolitan area in the mountains, is a thriving small city with a unique mix of cosmopolitan and mountain flavors. Crossing over the French Broad River at milepost 393.6, look to the left for a glimpse of the Biltmore House in the distance, rising out of the trees and looking like a fairy tale castle.

Heading south, panoramas widen into vistas that surely must extend to the edge of the world. Many of the Parkway's 27 tunnels are in this section. Above Pisgah National Forest near Transylvania County stands the prominent peak of Mount Pisgah, milepost 408.6, at an elevation of 5,721 feet, taking its name from the Biblical mountain from which Moses first viewed the Promised Land.

Past Pisgah, the road winds around more incredible peaks and spectacular sights such as Looking Glass Rock, elevation 4,493 feet. This massive sculpted mountain of rock sits

majestically in the valley near the Pink Beds (pink with flowers in May) of Pisgah National Forest below. As the Parkway leads south, the names of the land take on a wilder, more mythical flavor — Graveyard Fields, Devil's Courthouse, Shining Rock, Big Witch. Many were derived from Indian legend and pioneer folklore. The road climbs to its highest point at Richland Balsam, elevation 6,047 feet, milepost 431, before beginning its descent to the terminus at milepost 469.1 near the entrance to the Reservation of the Eastern Band of the Cherokee Nation and the gateway to Great Smoky Mountains National Park.

There are so many places to stop, by whim or design, it's no wonder that the Parkway, with 25 million visitors annually, is the most visited of all the 367 territories in the National Park System. Visitors centers are equipped with amenities to make your trip easier, and you'll find accommodations, rustic inns and restaurants off many Parkway exits. Most are within easy driving distance from the Parkway. (Two outstanding choices right on the Parkway are Bluffs Lodge, (910) 372-4499, at milepost 241 and The Pisgah Inn, (910) 235-8228, at milepost 408.6; both are highlighted in our Other Accommodations chapter. Just across the Parkway from Bluffs Lodge is the Bluffs Lodge Coffee Shop, (910) 372-4744 where you can sip coffee and soak in the incredibly breathtaking vistas.) (See our Restaurants chapter for more eateries in the area.)

Plan on taking some extra time if you're traveling the Parkway — this is far removed from interstate driving. The speed limit on the Parkway is always 45 mph, though between the sharp mountain twists and turns and the plodding recreational vehicles, you'll often find yourself driving much slower than that. Just relax and enjoy the scenery of one of the most beautiful drives in the country.

# Friends of the Blue Ridge Parkway

For over 60 years the Blue Ridge Parkway has propelled countless thousands to inspirational heights. But in recent years, the federal government has drastically reduced crucial financial support for this national treasure.

# Autumn in the Mountains

Red, yellow and gold give green a rest. Fiery orange pumpkins and variegated gourds fill broad, fertile pastures. Shadows lengthen and days shorten. The first brisk breeze sweeps away summer's lethargy. Forget all those scientific reasons for seasonal changes,* autumn in the mountains is pure magic.

Sometimes gradually, sometimes overnight the verdant peaks and valleys do a slow burlesque, teasing with a hint of color here, a little more there, each stage more exciting until the grandest week of all when the mix of red and gold, green and yellow present their breathtaking finale. Somehow Mother Nature can wear colors you'd never put together — chartreuse and red, orange and green — and still look stunning. And even when the inevitable happens and the autumn color leaves us, usually no later than mid-November, something special is left behind. Like colorful wrapping paper torn away, the fallen foliage exposes a precious gift — the mountains themselves. Breathtaking vistas, obscured much of the year by the lush vegetation that flourishes in our diverse ecosystem, are revealed until spring works its way north again.

**Close-up**

The kaleidoscope of colored trees is more than a treat to the eye. It gives those of us who have forgotten our high school botany a break. We can easily identify hickories and poplars glowing their bright yellow against a Carolina-blue sky, or mountain favorites such as dogwood, sourwood, blackgum and maples turning deep red, sassafras a vivid orange. The various oaks turn russet and maroon, while some trees can't decide which color to turn, offering a rainbow-mix on the same tree.

It seems no one wants to stay indoors this time of year. In celebration of the fine weather and natural beauty, festivals and craft fairs abound. Harvest dances, apple cider pressings, mountain music and dances, special tours, steam-driven trains forging

— continued on next page

Photo: Tim Barnwell

In autumn, fiery orange, delicate yellow, deep crimson and other brilliant leaf colors sweep across the mountains.

through the red and gold are scheduled throughout the season (see our Annual Festivals and Events chapter).

A special breed of wildflowers bloom late in the year. Joe-Pye-Weed nods its foot-wide head high above the rest. Purple-blooming Blazing Star and Ironweed, golden Sneezeweed and lilac Aster bloom throughout the fall.

As you travel down the highways and byways, you'll pass fanciful Mr. and Mrs. Scarecrows, dressed in flannel shirts and jeans, hay for their body and jack-o'-lanterns for their heads. They sit in welcome at roadside stands selling pumpkins, gourds, honey, sorghum and cider. Take home colorful gourds and doll-size Indian corn for Thanksgiving table decorations. Many stands sell jams and relishes, dried apples and apple butter, pumpkin bread and pies in anticipation of the coming holidays.

Every year, thousands upon thousands of nature's admirers return to North Carolina's mountains to drink in the beauty. Touring the Blue Ridge Parkway is the most favored way of taking in this long sweep of fall color. From Boone and Blowing Rock to Asheville and Cherokee each turn of the road offers a new horizon, a new definition of beautiful. The ever-popular Mount Mitchell State Park area, just off the Blue Ridge Parkway, as well as the communities of Spruce Pine, Linville Falls, Little Switzerland and the North Carolina Minerals Museum, are other popular leaf-looking sites along the Parkway.

The fall foliage season generally reaches its peak in mid-October, but the degrees and intensity of color and peak for each area are determined by elevation. At 6,684 feet, Mount Mitchell, the highest peak in the eastern United States, enjoys the distinction of having the early jump on fall leaf color. The peaks of the High Country of the Boone area are next, about mid-October. And the Asheville area and southern stretches near Cherokee along the Parkway peak around the third and fourth weeks in October. But, if you choose the Blue Ridge Parkway as your vantage point for viewing fall color, you can pick any time in October. From Parkway overlooks high above, you can scan the valleys below to see autumn's transformation at many different elevations.

During that intense tourist trek in October, Parkway rangers suggest that you can get maximum enjoyment and avoid the crowds by making your trip here Monday through Friday, when traffic is less heavy. The weekends in October can quickly become a bumper-to-bumper snail's pace of leaf lookers, especially on Sunday afternoons.

If the you find the Parkway busier than you prefer during this time of year, get off the beaten track. Take one of the side roads that branch off the Parkway. These dirt and gravel roadways, maintained by the U.S. Forest Service, wind down the mountain to the valleys below. One word of caution: Check with the rangers at the visitors centers along the Parkway for information on these roads, their end points, and current driving conditions. Four-wheel-drive vehicles will have a better go of it on these twisting mountain roads, but front-wheel-drive is adequate. Just make sure your vehicle is in good working order and you have plenty of gas. There are no tow trucks or gas stations just around the bend back here in the mountain wilderness!

Other alternative routes include the major connecting highways to the Parkway or maybe a less-traveled two-laner just outside the major towns and cities. The State of North Carolina published a 90-page guide to North Carolina Scenic Byways featuring 11 mountain roads (31 statewide) that give visitors and residents a chance to experience the diverse beauty and culture of the Tar Heel State. Routes are clearly marked with signs stating NC Scenic Byway surrounded by green mountain and blue sea motifs. For more information contact the N.C. Department of Transportation, (919) 733-2520, P.O. Box 25201, Raleigh, NC, 27611.

U.S. Highway 194 is a good example of a scenic byway. This winding back-road passes near Valle Crucis on its way to Boone, then on to picturesque hilltop ridges near Todd in rural Ashe County. Another gorgeous option is U.S. Highway 321 from Boone to the rocky hills of west Watauga County and the charming country crossroad communities of Sugar Grove and Vilas on the way to the Tennessee state line. Schulls Mill Road off N.C. Highway 105 at Foscoe, outside Boone, is a locally used shortcut to Blowing Rock along a beautiful but very winding two-lane road. Cruising along U.S. 221 from Boone through Linville and the Christmas tree country of Linville Falls before heading down the mountain to the beautiful fields of the North Cove valley area near Marion is a lovely way to spend an October afternoon.

Farther south, take the Barnardsville exit off U.S. Highway 19/23 N. in Asheville for another quiet backroad lined with rural farms and old homesteads, or you could take N.C. Highway 151 up to the Parkway from the pleasant little farm community of Hominy Valley, west of Asheville. U.S. 276 from the Parkway down to Brevard is a very popular road in leaf season. It winds down past tumbling creeks and waterways, waterfalls and picnic areas and the well-known Cradle of Forestry area. The scenic winding roads around Highlands and Cashiers have always been noted for their breathtaking fall beauty. And the exquisite forests and country roads around Fontana Lake and Robbinsville are just being discovered by visitors to the North Carolina mountains.

A good many of those 1.5 million visitors to the Blue Ridge Parkway area during leaf season often decide to stay for a night or an extended family vacation. You can understand why local officials and innkeepers suggest booking your visit in advance for maximum satisfaction. Some veteran leaf lookers book as much as a year in advance for their favorite bed and breakfast inns or family hotels. If you're a spontaneous traveler and miss out on those hoped-for accommodations, check with local chambers of commerce for possible alternative accommodations that spring up during this busy tourism month. (The numbers for local chambers are listed in our Area Overview chapter.)

Whether you travel the Blue Ridge Parkway or the road less traveled, remember to guard and respect the fragile beauty of nature so that it remains a sight of miracle and majesty for generations to come.

*The scientific explanation of leaf changes: The intensity of the color season is determined by a number of weather variables that change from year to year. It is generally accepted, however, that more vivid leaf color is preceded by a weather year marked by long, dry spells in summer and cool, moist days in fall. When this happens, and the sunlight diminishes, the trees are "tricked" into quicker cessation of the process of photosynthesis. No sugar is produced to keep the lush green of the chlorophyll, so the underlying pigments emerge.

Now maintaining the Parkway in all its irreplaceable splendor has become an important issue. Taking up the gauntlet is a vigorous group, the Friends of the Blue Ridge Parkway, a nonprofit organization started in 1989. The grassroots support that characterizes the Friends has helped the organization flourish. The group's mission is to preserve and protect this national treasure through a series of initiatives focusing on the historical heritage of the Parkway and the region and by developing a wider environmental awareness and public education on the issues. The organization works to preserve historic sites and structures along the Parkway and lobbies Congress for the protection of scenic vistas and natural habitats.

The Friends of the Blue Ridge Parkway is composed of varying levels of membership and financial support. You can become a Friend for a contribution as small as $15 or as high as your pocketbook will allow. Corporate and group donations are welcome. Children can join Grover Groundhog's Nature, which offers special learning and fun events. All members receive the newsletter *High Vistas* and a subscription to *Parkway Milepost*, the official Blue Ridge Parkway news magazine. Programs and conferences are scheduled throughout the year. Memberships of $50

Photo: Asheville Convention and Visitors Bureau

In the morning light, the layered peaks of the Blue Ridge Mountains around Asheville take on a transparent hue.

or more receive special benefits. Financial gifts to the Friends of the Blue Ridge Parkway are tax deductible. Your time as a volunteer is also appreciated. Headquarters for this organization have recently moved to Roanoke, Virginia. You can call them at (540) 776-PARK or write to P.O. Box 20986, Roanoke, Virginia 24018. In North Carolina contact the satellite office by calling (828) 687-8722 or (800) 228-7275 or writing Friends of the Blue Ridge Parkway, 2301 Hendersonville Road, Arden, North Carolina 28776.

## Stops along the Way

In the pages that follow, we've described some of our favorite stops along the Blue Ridge Parkway in North Carolina, beginning at the state line at milepost 216.9 in Alleghany County and traveling south to the Parkway's southern terminus at milepost 469.1 at the Oconoluftee Visitors Center. Mileposts are markers that stretch the length of the Parkway, each posted a mile apart. Overlooks and other sites of merit are also noted by milepost numbers. This list is by no means exhaustive — there are literally hundreds of overlooks and other stops along the Parkway, and all have merit. But these are some of our favorites.

### Cumberland Knob
**Mi. 217.5**

Cumberland Knob, elevation 2,885 feet, was the first recreational area completed on the Blue Ridge Parkway back in 1937. The Civilian Conservation Corps, a government-authorized jobs program during the Great Depression, built the structures at this site and many like it along the Parkway and in surrounding areas. On the 1,000 acres at Cumberland Knob you can picnic, hike, listen to lectures by rangers or simply marvel at the view. A pleasant 20-minute loop trail starts at the visitors center and passes by Cumberland Knob. For the hardier hiker, try the two-hour loop trail from the center of the knob into Gulley Creek Gorge. Drinking water, restrooms, a book shop and a public telephone are also available.

### Little Glade Mill Pond
**Mi. 230.1**

This scenic stop overlooks a delightful pond near an old turbine-type mill. The water is smooth as glass, and a picnic area makes this a restful stop.

### Air Bellows Gap
**Mi. 237.1**

Air Bellows Gap, elevation 3,729 feet, is

designated as the Crest of the Blue Ridge. The spectacular vista includes a 180-degree view into the valley below, which is chock full of Christmas trees. The rich green of the tree farms stands out in a patchwork of patterns. Hawks soar on the updrafts of this windy gap and rich autumn colors turn this into a leaf looker's paradise!

## Brinegar Cabin
### Mi. 238.5

The Brinegar Cabin, an authentic mountain homestead covered in hand-hewn shake shingles, stands as testament to the harsh, isolated, self-sufficient life of mountaineers that lasted even into this century. This tiny cabin was home to Martin (1856-1925) and Caroline (1863-1943) Brinegar. The toll that mountain life takes can be seen in a simple photo portrait of Caroline at her mother's loom inside the cabin. The springhouse is still down a steep rocky path, and the garden patch that once yielded the necessities of life is now overgrown and barely discernible. The couple is buried nearby. (Admission into the cabin is free.)

The Cedar Ridge Trail (4.3 miles) and the Bluff Mountain Trail (7.5 miles) take off from points that begin at the end of the parking area.

## Doughton Park
### Mi. 234.8 to 238.6

This 6,000-acre park has picnic areas (milepost 241), a campground (milepost 239), trailer sites, comfort stations and drinking water. The park has 30 miles of trail over bluegrass bluffs (see our "Autumn in the Mountains" close-up in this chapter).

## Wildcat Rocks
### Mi. 241.1

This is the Caudill Family homestead, where visitors can get a glimpse into the rugged mountain life.

## Northwest Trading Post
### Mi. 259 • (336) 982-2543

Near Glendale Springs, this delightfully rustic craft shop of knotty pine with a genuine rock fireplace sells all kinds of items made by North Carolina residents in 11 neighboring counties. Home-baked goodies, handmade baskets, bowls, old-time wooden toys, quilts and jewelry made from antique buttons are just some of the wares offered by this nonprofit group that donates all profits to local charities. The trading post is open from April 15 to October 31, 9 AM to 5:30 PM. Restrooms (handicapped accessible) are also available.

## Cascades Parking Overlook
### Mi. 271.9

Here you'll find a picnic area and a self-guided trail to the Cascades pedestrian overlook (Falls Creek).

## E.B. Jeffress Park
### Mi. 272

A picnic area, comfort station and hiking trails fill this 600-acre park, named for one of the early advocates of the Blue Ridge Parkway. The Park is open year-round.

## Cool Springs Baptist Church
### Mi. 272.6

Religion was important to the early mountaineers, as evidenced by this reconstructed site that depicts church meetings and circuit-riding preachers of the late 1800s.

## Grandview Overlook
### Mi. 281.7

The Yadkin Valley stretches out below at this aptly named overlook.

---

## INSIDERS' TIP

Definitely stop at the Parkway information stations. They maintain an excellent supply of books and newspapers devoted to hiking, camping, waterfalls, and nature along the Parkway. The staffers are always well-informed on a plethora of Parkway information and lore.

# Finding Cold Mountain

Ever since Charles Frazier's *Cold Mountain*, a novel about a Civil War soldier's walk home to his beloved Ada, became a best seller, people have been wanting to know how to find this 6,030-foot peak located in Haywood County. There is a trail to the top, but only very experienced hikers should take it. It's steep, poorly marked and, according to how you go, 14 to 16 miles roundtrip. (For more information, contact the Forest Service in Pisgah National Forest.)

Those not so foot-worthy can take U.S. Highway 276 from the Blue Ridge Parkway toward Waynesville. This roughly follows along Wagon Road Gap along the east side of the mountain. Near Cruso, turn onto U.S. Highway 215, which will run along the western side of the peak. This 50-mile circle will take you past many of the coves, creeks and churches mentioned in the book and bring you back to the Blue Ridge Parkway not very far south of where you left it.

If you haven't time for this wonderful tour, just stop at the Parkway's Milepost 420. The massive peak in the distance is Cold Mountain.

## Boone's Trace
### Mi. 285.1

Daniel Boone passed by this site on his treks westward. An information marker provides details about his blaze to the West.

## Moses H. Cone Memorial and Visitors Center
### Mi. 293 • (828) 295-3782

Near the town of Blowing Rock, this former 3,600-acre estate of textile giant Moses Cone was donated to the Park Service in the 1950s. Today the rambling white manor house is home to a craft shop displaying the work of the Southern Highland Handicraft Guild. The mansion faces a picturesque lake, and the grounds are threaded with miles of hiking trails and include two trout ponds (check at the center for fishing information).

## Julian Price Memorial Park
### Mi. 295 • (828) 963-5911

This popular park of 4,344 acres includes a lake, campground, hiking trails, picnic area and limited boating. There's an easy 2.5-mile loop trail around the lakeside.

## Linn Cove Viaduct
### Mi. 304

Built around environmentally fragile Grandfather Mountain, this incredible bridge is a marvel of engineering and gives you the sense of flying over the valley below — breath-

taking! There's a visitor center and trails underneath the viaduct. Walking is not allowed on the bridge.

## Linville Falls and Gorge
### Mi. 316.5

An easy to moderate lower trail leads to the falls. A spectacular example of nature's power, these waterfalls were carved from massive quartzite rock millions of years ago. An upper trail with a steeper incline gives you quite a different view (see our Waterfalls chapter).

## Chestoa View
### Mi. 320.7

Chestoa is derived from the Cherokee word for rabbit. From this spot you can enjoy a scenic view of granite-faced Table Rock.

## Museum of North Carolina Minerals
### Mi. 331 • (828) 765-9483

Informative geology exhibits, rock and mineral displays, Parkway information, a book shop, gifts and restrooms make the museum a pleasant diversion for children and rock hounds of all ages (see our chapter on Rock Hounding).

## Crabtree Meadows Coffee Shop
### Mi. 339.5 • (828) 675-4236

You can get a good lunch here, as well as Parkway guidebooks, maps and the *Asheville Citizen-Times* newspaper. Facilities also include restrooms, a service station and a craft shop near Little Switzerland, a community on the edge of the mountain, that are open May 1 through November 1. The coffee shop is open 10 AM to 6 PM; the craft shop until 7:30 PM.

## Crabtree Meadows Recreation Center
Mi. 339.5-340.3, ranger kiosk
• (828) 675-5444

This 250-acre site includes a picnic area, numerous hiking trails and a campground. Primitive camping is available for tent and RV campers for approximately $10 per night for two adults; add about $2 for each additional adult. Children 18 and younger stay free. Comfort stations are also located here. The 40-minute trek to Crabtree Falls rewards you with a beautiful 125-foot waterfalls (see our Waterfalls chapter). Look for wildflowers in spring.

## Mount Mitchell State Park
Mi. 355.4 • (828) 675-4611

Take N.C. Highway 128 to the summit of Mount Mitchell, the highest peak in the eastern United States. Hiking trails, a memorial to Elisha Mitchell (for whom the peak is named), a small natural-history museum, comfort stations, a snack shop and a picnic area make this a pleasant stop.

Unfortunately you can see the dramatic evidence of acid rain on Mitchell's slopes from several vantage points. On a brighter note, keep your eyes peeled for the deer that dart through these woods. Bring a jacket since the weather is windy and cool up here, even in summer.

The massive stone-and-frame restaurant in the park is about two-thirds of the way up N.C. 128 leading to the summit, which makes it the highest restaurant in the eastern United States. Open from May 1 through October 31, the restaurant serves lunch and dinner daily and breakfast on weekends and holidays. It closes one hour prior to park closing, which varies seasonally. Call (828) 675-9545 for more information on the restaurant.

## Craggy Gardens Visitors Center
Mi. 364.4 • no phone

This popular stop offers nature exhibits, comfort stations and Parkway and national forest information. The center is open May through October. (See our "Autumn in the Mountains" close-up in this chapter.)

## Bull Creek Valley Overlook
Mi. 373.8

This scenic stop-off point overlooks what was once the home of the great bull buffalo.

## Folk Art Center
Mi. 382 • (828) 298-7928

Home of the renowned Southern Highland Handicraft Guild, this 30,000-square-foot contemporary structure of rock, timber and glass is an attractive complement to the natural woodland surroundings.

Visit Allanstand Craft Shop, America's oldest craft shop, on the main level for exquisitely crafted handblown glassware, functional pottery, handmade toys, handcrafted jewelry, handwoven coverlets and rugs. The Blue Ridge Parkway also maintains a book store and staffs an information center here. Up the sweeping ramp, the second-floor gallery houses the guild's permanent collection as well as changing exhibits by some of its 700-plus members. A library of handcraft and its history is also on the upper level. Craft demonstrations, interpretive talks and special events keep the Folk Art Center a vital and continuously interesting place for area visitors.

The center is open daily 9 AM to 6 PM April through December and 9 AM to 5 PM January through March. It's closed for Thanksgiving, Christmas and New Year's Day. The bustling city of Asheville is just off the next exit (see our Mountain Crafts, Attractions and Festivals and Annual Events chapters).

## French Broad River Overlook
Mi. 393.8

One of the few north-flowing rivers in the United States, this river figures prominently in the history and development of the Asheville/Buncombe County area and all of Western North Carolina. This overlook at milepost 393.8 spot is an especially good place to get a view of the river.

## Hominy Valley Overlook
Mi. 404.2

This pull-off from the parkway is a scenic

view of the pastoral mountain-valley farm community west of Asheville.

## Mount Pisgah
### Mi. 407.4

At 5,721 feet, Mount Pisgah is visible for miles around, holding court over the vast land once owned by George Vanderbilt that is now part of Pisgah National Forest. The summit can be reached by a moderate-to-strenuous winding trail from the parking area below. The junction of U.S. Highway 276 and the Parkway is just south of Mount Pisgah. Traveling down this winding and scenic road to Brevard in Transylvania County, you'll pass The Cradle of Forestry, the site of the first forestry school in America and also once a part of the Biltmore Estate (see the close-up in our Forest and Parks chapter).

## Looking Glass Rock
### Mi. 417

This spectacularly sculpted monolith in the valley below is one of the largest masses of granite in the eastern United States. Its name comes from the shimmering effects of sunlight on its surface when wet. Elevation is 4,493 feet. Though you can't get to Looking Glass from this stop, the view is fantastic. (A trail that leads to the top is off the road to the Pisgah Fish Hatchery, off U.S. Highway 276, just past Looking Glass Rock.

## Graveyard Fields
### Mi. 418.8

These flats were once overgrown with mounds of moss that inspired the name Graveyard Fields, but a fire destroyed the moss mounds in 1925. (See our "Autumn in the Mountains" Close-up.)

## Devil's Courthouse
### Mi. 422.4

The top of this rocky, rugged cliff can be reached by a steeply ascending, well-worn trail from a parking area below. Legend has it there is a cave inside the mountain where the Devil still holds court.

## Haywood/Jackson Overlook
### Mi. 431.0

This self-guided loop trail climbs with moderate difficulty 1.5 miles to the summit of Richland Balsam.

## Waterrock Knob
### Mi. 451

Adjoining this parking area, a short trail leads to an incredible four-state view (North Carolina, Tennessee, South Carolina and Georgia) with a panorama of the Great Smoky Mountains just ahead. Information and a comfort station are available here.

## Plott's Balsam Range Overlook
### Mi. 457.9

Yet another beautiful overlook, here you'll see the mountain range that's named for the German immigrant who settled here in the early 1800s.

## Big Witch Overlook
### Mi. 461.6

The interesting name honors one of the last of the great Cherokee medicine men. An exhibit tells of the early Cherokee eagle killers.

## Oconaluftee Visitors Center
### Mi. 469.1 • (828) 497-1900

This marks the terminus of the Blue Ridge Parkway, or its starting point, if you are traveling north. The popular visitors center (a half-mile north on U.S. Highway 441) hosts several events during summer, including Women's Day and the Mountain Life Festival, which celebrate the heritage of these mountains (see our Festivals and Annual Events chapter). Park information and restrooms are

---

**INSIDERS' TIP**

In summer, views of from the Parkway can be obscured by haze — partly natural and partly pollution. At those times, it's often best to visit the Parkway in the morning, before the day heats up and when the air is cleaner. This time of day provides the added beauty of ground fog curling up out of the valleys.

available. The center is open daily year round (except major holidays). Hours vary with the season.

Do be sure to visit Mountain Farm Museum, an open-air museum featuring historic farm buildings brought here from the surrounding area. The old cabin belonged to the nearby John Davis family and was built in 1901. It is a good place for children to see how things used to be. Watch out for the chickens, ducks and other farm animals strutting around the barns filled with antique farm implements. It feels as though the Davises have just gone down the road for a bit and asked you to set a spell and make yourself at home 'til they return.

Just ahead lies the Cherokee Indian Reservation and The Great Smoky Mountains National Park. For park information call (423) 436-1200.

# Camping

Camping is allowed along the Blue Ridge Parkway from May 1 through October 31. Designated camping sites require a daily fee of approximately $10 (subject to change) for adults, $5 for Golden Age Passport holders, free for youths younger than 18. Golden Age Passports (62 or older) and Golden Access Passports (blind or permanently disabled) can be obtained at any visitor center or campground along the Parkway. Each of these campgrounds has only primitive facilities, including a fireplace and table. Other amenities may include access to public telephones, water, picnic sites, gasoline, camping supplies and sanitary dumping stations. There are no electrical hookups. If you are a hardy soul, you can camp in winter, weather permitting. One of the campgrounds is open year-round, at the park's discretion. (The open campground rotates from year to year, so call to find out which one will be open this year.) No fee is required in the winter, but facilities are limited, so you'll need to call in advance. For general Parkway information and campground information, call (828) 298-0398.

Campground regulations are posted at campsites; additional copies are available at Parkway Visitors Centers. In case of emergencies, call (800) PARKWATCH.

See our Recreation chapter for additional campground listings.

# Campgrounds

None of the campgrounds along the Blue Ridge take reservations. All are filled on a first-come, first-served basis. Again, the cost is approximately $10 per adult, $5 for Golden Age Passport holders; youths younger than 18 stay for free.

### Doughton Park
**Mi. 239.0 • no phone**

One-hundred-and-ten tent sites, including tent pads, picnic tables, grills, and lantern posts are scattered in wooded areas and around a grassy hillside. A smaller area with 25 RV sites lies across the road, though none of the sites have hookups.

Restrooms and water spigots are available at this park, but no showers. This is camping as it was meant to be! The park itself covers approximately 6000 acres in Alleghany and Wilkes County, and is the largest park on the Parkway. It was named after Robert Lee Doughton, a U.S. representative who served from 1911-1953 and who was an advocate for the construction of the Parkway.

### Julian Price
**Mi. 297.0 • (828) 963-5911**

This campground sprawls across both sides of the Parkway near Price Lake. One-hundred-and-twenty-nine tent sites lie fairly close together, divided by blossoming rhododendron bushes. Sixty-eight RV sites are also available, though with no plug-ins. Tent-pads, picnic tables, grills, and spigots provide adequate comforts. There are restrooms but no showers, and firewood may be purchased nearby. The park is marked by mild terrain, covered by a dense hardwood forest. Poplars, chestnut trees, and maples make a pleasant canopy for hikers and campers. Canoes may be rented at the lake, and hiking trails nearby lead to two smaller lakes and creeks.

### Linville Falls
**Mi. 316.3 • (828) 765-7818**

Fifty-five tent sites and 20 RV sites are available in the campground of this 440-acre

The Blue Ridge Parkway near Asheville offers spectacular mountain vistas.

wooded park. Tent-site 15 is the most secluded. The surrounding forest seems almost primordial with mossy-covered trees, and waterfalls plunging through the granite walls of Linville Gorge. Fishing in the nearby Linville River is allowed, and a visitor center and bookstore provide campers with plenty of area information.

### Crabtree Meadows
Mi. 339.5 • (828) 675-5444

The 71 tent sites and 22 RV sites of Crabtree Meadows lie close to large grassy clearings. The lawn of wildflowers runs up to the forest edge, with mountains visible in the distance. The campground is rarely full and offers the requisite picnic tables, grills and tent pads but no showers. Water fountains and hand water pumps are centrally located. It is a quiet, peaceful area awash with rhododendrons and hardwood trees. This is a good base camp for hiking in the Pisgah National Forest; trails lead to scenic falls on Crabtree

Creek. Crabtree Falls Trail, a strenuous 2.5-mile loop, begins near the campground entrance. A camp store, gas station, and restaurant/gift shop are also nearby.

### Mount Pisgah
Mi. 408.6 • (828) 235-9109

The entrance to Mount Pisgah Campground with its 70 tent sites and 70 RV sites lies directly across from Pisgah Inn on the Parkway. The small sites, close together, are arranged in three landscaped loops. A dense forest adds privacy. There are no showers, but central hand water pumps and individual picnic tables, grills and lantern posts are provided. Maps of the area, including hiking trails, are available at the camp. A picnic area lies in a meadow bordered by rhododendron.

# Hiking

Towering trees, awe-inspiring vistas, gurgling mountain streams, colorful birds on the wing, flaming and delicate wildflowers and the comfort of a well-trod path mark hiking trails on the Parkway. This is all free for the taking when you leave the car behind and take advantage of the thousands of miles of trails winding in and around the Parkway. Hiking is an easy, inexpensive way to enjoy the outdoors: You don't need much gear, and the rewards are priceless. Just follow basic hiking rules to keep it safe and fun (see our chapter on Outdoor Safety). For additional hiking possibilities, see our Recreation chapter.

# Northern Mountains

## Cumberland Knob

The relatively easy trails of Cumberland Knob (mi. 217.5) allow you to walk where the Blue Ridge Parkway began back in 1935. Cumberland Knob Trail, an easy, paved half-mile walk, starts at the visitors center, swings through a picnic area and up to the Cumberland Knob overlook shelter. This is a good leg-stretching trail, especially if you've been riding the Parkway for a while without a stop. It's a good one for kids too. Gully Creek Trail here is a more strenuous two-hour hike along a mountain stream. Bring your wildflower field guides — these mountain springs give life to some amazing plants.

## Tanawa Trail

This 13.5-mile course, which runs more or less parallel to the Blue Ridge Parkway and Grandfather Mountain, from Beacon Heights (mi. 305.5) to Julian Price Park (mi. 297.1), deserves special mention. The trail offers a great deal of variety and plenty of access points along the Parkway as it winds along the ridge. One particularly popular section, noted for its breathtaking views, is the access just below the Linn Cove Viaduct (mi. 304.4) The Linn Cove information station and access spot are south of the viaduct. The trail passes directly under this bridge-like span and rises steeply up stone steps, then past a massive wall of rock. Next, the trail levels and leads into a shady stand of birch and beech trees, then traverses Wilson Creek to a clearing scattered with so many flat rocks that the

trail seems more like a flagstone path. The sharp rise to Rough Ridge is followed by the surprise of a 200-foot-long boardwalk. From this point, the view of the Piedmont below, which encompasses Linn Cove Viaduct, Table Mountain and Hawks Bill, is breathtaking.

## Craggy Dome Trail

The parking area just through the tunnel to the north of the visitors center (mi. 364.4) is the beginning of the trail leading to Craggy Dome. This well-marked path winds through beautiful rhododendron thickets and ascends to the breathtaking summit of Craggy Dome, a 360-degree sight to behold. The trail isn't strenuous, but it does have a continuously rising grade, so allow yourself plenty of time. Besides, seeing the unique wildflowers, velvety mosses and gnarled, lichen-covered trunks of the rhododendron is worth the extra time. Look for the colorless white stalks of the Indian pipes under cover of the rhododendron.

# Central and Southern Mountains

## Graveyard Fields

Take the hiking trails to Upper and Lower Falls (see our Waterfalls chapter) just off the parking area at milepost 418.8. This is a popular area for backpack camping and blueberry picking (which accounts for some of the many side trails) and includes Shining Rock Wilderness, just over the ridge to the southeast.

## Pisgah National Forest

Pisgah National Forest is a hiker's delight with its varying terrain: the steep slopes of Mount Pisgah, granite monoliths such as Looking Glass Rock and the level flats of the Pink Beds. There are also a number of relatively easy roadside jaunts along U.S. 276 to Brevard from the Parkway junction south of Mount Pisgah. This highway cuts a twisting path down the mountain along a creek bed leading to Looking Glass Falls. Many smaller trail spurs shoot off from the overlooks, and parking turnouts are always worth a look for different views and angles of the falls.

In 1992 a Haywood
County mine produced a
12.5-pound sapphire.

# Rock Hounding

We've all heard of fantasy cities with streets paved with gold and the Emerald City of Oz, but what about real highways paved with rubies? That's occasionally the case in Western North Carolina, where, if you look closely enough, you can see ruby-flecked gravel along the roadsides. That should give some idea of the copious amounts of gemstones in many sections of these mountains.

Important gems you might find are beryl (aquamarine, blue, golden and green), corundum (bronze sapphire, pink, ruby and sapphire), feldspar (moonstone), garnet (general, almandite and rhodolite), olivine, opal, quartz (agate, amethyst, chrysoprase, jasper and others), spinel, tourmaline, turquoise and zircon. Rock hounds collect at least 37 other minerals, some of which can occasionally be classified as gem quality. In the late 1800s, even a few diamonds supposedly turned up, but we know of none that have been found for more than 100 years.

It's rather ironic that, in 1540, Hernando De Soto visited the Cherokee village of Nikwasi (now known as Franklin, the county seat of Macon County) in search of gold, never realizing he was passing through an area awash in precious and semiprecious stones. Admittedly, most of the gems and semiprecious stones found in the mountains have no great commercial value, but many are attractive enough to be custom-set and taken home as special souvenirs of an exciting and rewarding afternoon of sluicing through buckets of rock and dirt.

Of course, there are the true tales of turning up a really big one! In 1989, a longtime Cherokee County rock hound found a 10.5-pound (18,000 carat) sapphire two feet underground in an undisclosed location that was cut and polished to a grapefruit-size 9,719.5-star sapphire worth several million dollars. In 1991 a 1,497-carat sapphire was found by a teenager in a Macon County mine, and in 1992 a Haywood County mine produced a 12.5-pound sapphire. Likewise, rubies of several thousand carats and a number of large emeralds have been found here over the years. Grandiose gems are surely there to be discovered by the lucky or inspired rock hound.

But even if these large and valuable stones are few and far between, it's not uncommon for even the most casual amateur to luck out on a gem worth a few hundred dollars while grubbing in a sluice box of mud and rocks. Gem mining, even when not richly profitable, is good fun, especially for children, whose eyes widen with amazement when they unearth a nice rock. It can be educational too, as school groups on field trips have discovered.

Gem mining can be wet and messy, so make sure you approach this exciting search in old clothes. Since you'll be standing at the flumes for a considerable length of time, a comfortable pair of shoes is a must. So is sunscreen. While many mines offer some shade in the form of shelters, tents or big, beach-type umbrellas, the sun reflecting off the water can give you an unexpected burn. Besides, this can be such a fascinating pastime that you may not realize how much time is passing. Certainly, if you find a fine gem in your first load or two of ore, you're likely to come down with rockhound fever — you'll be hooked.

www.insiders.com

See this and many other
**Insiders' Guide®**
destinations online.

Visit us today!

You don't necessarily have to go to a commercial gem mine to find precious and semiprecious stones — that is, if you know what to look for. A wide array of land, both public and private, contains igneous, sedimentary and metamorphic rock types, along with the individual minerals associated with such rocks. On private land, of course, you will have to get the permission of owners for any rock-hounding activities. On national forest lands (though not in national parks or wilderness areas) there is no objection, as a rule, to taking a handful of rock, mineral or petrified wood specimens from the surface of the ground.

There is no fee, special permission or permit required as long as such collecting doesn't conflict with existing mineral permits, leases or sales — and even if it does, you can seek the permission of the minerals' owners to do some collecting. These areas can be identified from maps in the ranger district offices. Any collected specimens must also be for personal and noncommercial use, and they cannot be of archeological value (artifacts, including projectile points, chips and flakes may not be collected).

Certain areas are designated as archeological sites or geologic interest areas, and ground disturbance of any sort is prohibited

in both these and any unrecorded archeological sites. You must also be sure that your rock hounding doesn't cause any significant surface disturbance to the land, air or water. Obviously, no explosives or mechanical equipment may be used.

The Forest Service's district ranger offices are the best sources for current rules, maps and information on local access and road conditions within the forests. (See our Forests and Parks chapter for a listing of these offices and phone numbers). While they don't normally keep information concerning minerals or collecting localities, they may have some knowledge about these subjects. For this information, it's best to contact the state's geological survey office, (919) 571-4000, university geology departments and libraries, mineralogical societies and rock-hounding and lapidary clubs.

# Gem Mines

While the heaviest concentration of gem mines by far is in the jewel-rich Cowee Valley of Macon County, there are other places scattered throughout the mountains where you can try your luck at finding a jewel or two.

The following list includes several gem-mining operations that are open to the public.

## Northern Mountains
### Mitchell County

### Blue Ridge Gemstone Mine & Campground
**626 McKinny Mine Rd., Little Switzerland • (828) 765-5264**

Established in 1984, this family-owned and operated mine maintains a 320-foot flume line. It is enclosed and heated in the spring and fall, so you can comfortably sift through buckets of dirt any time, May through December. It is open seven days a week. Inspect the rock and gift shop and bring a lunch for the picnic area, overlooking the mountains. Or, if you would like to camp, full hookups, water, and electricity are provided. For a small fee, the Blue Ridge Gemstone will cut, grind, and polish the stones you find. You can also have them set into handcrafted jewelry.

To get the Blue Ridge Mine, exit the Parkway at Little Switzerland. Take your first right before the stop sign. Turn right onto Chestnut Grove Church Road. Go under the Parkway and continue for 1 mile and then turn left onto McKinney Mine Road. The mine is 2 miles further, on the left.

### Emerald Village
**McKinney Mine and Crabtree Creek Rds., Little Switzerland • (828) 765-6463**

This mining attraction just 2.5 miles off the Blue Ridge Parkway in Mitchell County not only provides a guaranteed gem find at the Gemstone Mine but also has a mining museum underground in a genuine mine. The unusual antique displays are worth a look. A gift shop is filled with lapidary supplies, souvenirs, and attendants in the shop will answer your gemstone questions. Emerald Village is open from 9 AM to 5 PM April until the end of November. It costs $3.50 for adults, $3 for senior citizens and $2.50 for children to tour the facility. The cost of ore buckets ranges from $5 to $500, depending on the size.

### Gem Mountain
**N.C. Hwy. 226, Spruce Pine**
**• (828) 765-6130**

Open seven days a week, 9 AM to 5 PM March through December, and 9 AM to 7 PM June through August, this gemstone mine maintains modern gem-washing facilities and covered flumes. A picnic area by a nearby stream completes the outdoor hounding experience, or you can rest easy and dine in the e "Gem Mountain restaurant. There are ice-cream cones for the kids, and a gift and jewelry shop — fun for the adults in the group. Gem Mountain will cater birthday parties or

special events celebrations, and offers discounts on mining and lunches for these catered affairs. Call for details.

The cost is approximately $7 per bucket. Gem Mountain is located on N.C. Highway 226, between Spruce Pine (U.S. Highway Exit 19E) and the Blue Ridge Parkway.

### Rio Doce Gem Mine
**Hwy 226, Little Switzerland**
**• (828) 765-2099**

Open mid-April to Halloween, 3 AM to 5 PM, seven days a week, the Rio Doce mine is owned by the Jerry Call family. Jerry Call, a gemologist who worked in Brazil's Vale Rio Doce (Sweet River Valley) for over twenty years, is currently involved in large-scale mining operations in the Brazilian valley. Some of the fine gem exports from the Brazilian valley end up in Spruce Pine's Rio Doce flumes. Rock hounders may be unearthing Mitchell county gems or Brazilian stones! Jerry Call and his family are master gem cutters and offer a complete gemological laboratory and appraisal services. The adjacent gem and gift shop offers 14k gold, sterling silver, mineral specimens, and also provides gem cutting, rough and cut gems. There is also a picnic area. Rio Doce offers group rates.

The mine is located a half-mile north of the Blue Ridge Parkway and the North Carolina Mineral Museum.

## Watauga County

### Watauga County Magic Mountain Mini Golf & Gem Mine
**N.C. Hwy. 105, Boone**
**• (828) 265-GEMS, (828) 265-GOLF**

The kids simply won't get bored here. Open every day from 9 AM to 11 PM, spring through fall, Magic Mountain is kiddie paradise. Adults won't mind sifting through the enriched ore either, since there's a chance of

Photo: Hugh Morton, Courtesy of Grandfather Mountain

The southern end of the Blue Ridge Parkway connects with
the Great Smoky Mountains National Park.

finding a ruby, citrine, garnet, amethyst, aquamarine, sapphire, emerald, or other such rocks. A sandwich and ice-cream parlor provide indoor or patio dining, and a video game room provides entertainment for those members of the family who just don't want to get their hands dirty. The mini golf course is set on a mountainside amidst foliage and waterfalls. (See our Kidstuff chapter for more on this Magic Mountain.)

## Central Mountains

### Haywood County

#### Old Pressley Sapphire Mines
240 Pressley Mine Rd., Canton
• (828) 648-6320
Some of the world's largest sapphires, including the 1,445-carat "Star of the Caroli-

nas," have been found in this Haywood County mine. In addition to the opportunity to flume for sapphires and other gems, Old Pressley has picnic tables and a rock shop. Better yet, it's open all year, weather permitting, seven days a week from 9 AM to 6 PM. The flume is shut down during freezing weather, but people still can come here to prospect. There is a $5 entrance fee and a charge of 50¢ for each 10-quart bucket of ore. To get here, take Exit 33 off I-40 onto Newfound Road, then onto Willis Cove Road to the above address.

### Jackson County

#### Whitewater Trading
210 U.S. 64 W., Sapphire
• (828) 884-2711
This establishment, which is located 17 miles west of Brevard, in Transylvania County,

has enriched ore that's representative of most of the gems found in the region. Bucket prices are $3, $5, $10 and $25. Whitewater Trading is open from April 1 through Christmas, seven days a week from 9 AM until 7 PM in midsummer, closing earlier during the seasons of shorter daylight. Whitewater Trading's gift shop also sells gems, jewelry, colored glass, rugs and a large selection of T-shirts.

# Southern Mountains

## Macon County

This is the heart of gem mining in Western North Carolina. In Macon County's famous Cowee Valley you can go to more than a dozen gem mines where the entrance fee is usually $4 to $5 for adults and $1 to $2 for children ages 3 to 12. There is an additional charge of $1 to $5 for buckets or bags of gem-bearing gravel that you can sluice in search of that "find of the century." However, prices vary with the size of the buckets from mine to mine. Some in Macon County, as well as those in other counties, offer ore "enriched" or "seeded" with minerals not native to this locale; others offer strictly North Carolina stones.

Most gem mines, especially during the busy midsummer season, are open seven days a week from April 1 until October 31, and many are open from 8 AM until sunset, but times can vary. It's always a good idea to call before heading out to the mines; some closing times may vary according to the numbers of visitors and the weather during the season that you visit. Contact the Franklin Area Chamber of Commerce, 180 Porter St., Franklin, NC 28734, (828) 524-3161 for a listing of the county's many gem mines.

## Swain County

### Nantahala Gorge Ruby Mine
U.S. 19 W., Bryson City
• (828) 488-3854, (800) 245-4811
This Swain County mine, which uses enriched and native ore, has been known to

produce rubies of good color and clarity. It's open from mid-March or mid-April through the end of October or on into November, depending on the weather. Ten- to 12-pound bags of ruby ore run $3 a bag or two bags for $5; sapphire ore is $4 or two for $7; emerald ore is $5 or two bags for $9. More heavily enriched bags of ore (called "super ruby," "super-emerald" and "super-sapphire" bags) cost a bit more. There is no entrance fee.

### Smoky Mountain Gold and Ruby Mine
U.S. Hwy. 441 N., Cherokee
• (828) 497-6574
In addition to all the other attractions on the Cherokee Indian Reservation, you can come here to search for such gems as amethysts, garnets, sapphires, rubies, citrine, topaz and smoky quartz. Gem ore is $4 per bag or two for $7. Smoky Mountain also offers ruby and sapphire specialty buckets for $10 and a colored "fun bucket" for $5. Gold Ore is $5 per bag, $10 per bag for a bag with more ore and $25 for a one gallon bucket. Next to the shaded and covered water flumes is a gem shop that will also cut and mount your finds. The mine is open from 9 AM until 9 PM on Sunday through Friday and 9 AM to 11 or 12 PM from early spring through October.

# Gem Museums

Aside from small museums associated with some gem mines, there are some outstanding gem museums in the region. At these you can get the scoop on the history of rock hounding in North Carolina and a general education on gems and geology.

## Northern Mountains

### Museum of North Carolina Minerals
off Blue Ridge Pkwy. at Mi. 33
• (828) 765-9483
This museum is a great side trip off the Parkway. It displays a fascinating collection of minerals in various forms, from raw materials to the cut and polished items we know best. Spruce Pine, just down the road, and Little Switzerland, nearby, are both well known

Photo: Hugh Morton, Courtesy of Grandfather Mountain

Rugged beauty at Grandfather Mountain.

as sources of one of the highest and most varied concentrations of minerals in the United States. A gift shop offers a good variety of rock collections for any young rock hounds and enough material to keep them occupied quite a few miles down the road. Admission is free. The Mitchell County Chamber of Commerce, (828) 264-2120, is in the same building.

Place Education Arts and Science Center dazzles the eyes. The museum was founded in 1960 and highlights gems and minerals of all shapes and sizes from around the world. North Carolina-specific garnets, rubies, emeralds and gold deposits also feature heavily. Admission is around $3; children ages 4 to 15 and senior citizens receive a discount.

## Central Mountains

### The Colburn Gem and Mineral Museum
2 S. Pack Sq., Asheville
• (828) 257-4500
   This gem and mineral museum in the Pack

## Southern Mountains

### Franklin Gem and Mineral Museum
Phillips St., Franklin • (828) 369-7831
   The museum building, with its barred windows, is interesting in itself. It's the old county jail, located between Palmer and Main streets,

## INSIDERS' TIP

For 32 years, one of the biggest gem shows in the area, called Gemboree, is held at the Macon County Community Building (U.S. 441 S.) in Franklin each July and October. Call (800) 336-7829 for more information.

which was built in the 1850s and used for that purpose until 1972. Now converted to displays, the North Carolina Room contains a huge sapphire, a 49-pound corundum crystal and a baseball-size ruby crystal, all found at Corundum Hill Mine in Macon County, along with a rock collection, cut and faceted gems, an exhibit of mica types and so on.

The Fluorescent Room, a one-time solitary-confinement cell, displays the phenomenon of fluorescence and phosphorescence — what the narrative tape calls "nature's hidden rainbows."

The States Room contains specimens from each of the 50 states, including large specimens of fluorite that you can touch. There is also an Indian Artifacts Room with articles, many of which are centuries old, on loan from members and friends of the Gem and Mineral Society of Franklin.

A former high-security lockup known as The Slammer holds a display on rocks used in the manufacture of glass. The museum also has a nice collection of fossils and corals, as well as beautiful minerals from more than 30 nations.

In addition to all this, there is a fine library full of gems and mineral books and a special Writings in Stone exhibit. The small gift shop helps support the museum, which is open from 10 AM to 4 PM Monday through Saturday from May 1 through October 31. Admission is free.

## Ruby City Gems and Minerals
**130 E. Main St., Franklin**
• **(828) 524-3967**

There is any number of "rock shops" in and around the Franklin area, but this establishment also has a neat museum section, the result of more than 40 years of collecting specimens, artifacts, ivory carvings and rare gems. Here you'll find a 385-pound sapphire and a 162-carat gem-quality ruby. The shop carries jewelry, lapidary equipment and many rough stones. Other treasures found here include arrowheads, old tools, plus pre-Columbian Aztec and Inca vases and statues.

Get set to find a bit of everything: woolly worms, dogwood blossoms, gospel music, Scottish clans, Grandma's finest quilts and even "whimmy-diddles."

# Annual Festivals and Events

Our North Carolina Mountains are a celebration in and of themselves, and just living here seems to give rise to all manner of joyous, lively, enlightening, wondrous festivals. Here's a month-to-month sampling, broken down under the geographic regions of the Northern, Central and Southern Mountains. The events are free unless we've noted an entry fee. Please note, while we update these events with each new edition, it's still best to check with the chambers of commerce in each country to make sure events planned far ahead of time, are still scheduled.

Get set to find a bit of everything: woolly worms, dogwood blossoms, gospel music, Scottish clans, Grandma's finest quilt and even "whimmy-diddles" (Appalachian wooden toys) and washtub race cars. Have fun!

# January

## Northern Mountains

### Old Christmas Hickory Ridge Homestead
**591 Horn in the West Dr., Boone • (828) 264-2120**

A traditional Christmas celebration held annually on January 6, this community event is free and welcomes everyone to take part. A roaring bonfire (it's cold up here this time of year!) is built from the holiday trees and branches brought by the community as a good luck gesture for the new year. And the good luck begins when delicious food and beverages are provided at the event.

### Winterfest
**Beech Mountain Ski Resort, Beech Mountain • (828) 387-2011**

This town festival on Beech Mountain in the first week of January features an ice show, beauty contest and tube and box races. Nominal entrance fees ($1 to $5) are charged for the various events.

## Central Mountains

### Martin Luther King Jr. Annual Birthday Celebration
**Various locations, Asheville • (828) 259-5800, (828) 253-3714**

A variety of events in a five-day celebration at various locations around town honor the birth and contributions of the famed civil rights leader. It all begins the third Monday of the month. Events include a peace march through town, singing, poetry readings, lectures and music. The event is co-sponsored by the City of Asheville.

## Annual All That Jazz Weekend at the Grove Park Inn
290 Macon Ave., Asheville
• (828) 252-2711, (800) 438-5800

Hot jazz warms up a cold January weekend. This annual event features two evening concerts, Saturday afternoon jazz and legendary talents on Saturday night. Forty-six dollars will buy you a ticket for all the concerts over the weekend. Individual concerts from Friday to Sunday range from $7 to $25.

# February

## Central Mountains

### Black Mountain to Mount Mitchell Marathon Challenge
Black Mountain • (828) 669-2300

This is a 26-mile and a 40-mile foot race on the extreme sports level as it changes elevations drastically and is done in the middle of winter.

### Big Band Dance Weekend at the Grove Park Inn
290 Macon Ave., Asheville
• (828) 252-2711, (800) 438-5800

It's swing time at the famed Grove Park Inn. This annual event, on the first weekend in February, draws lovers of the Big Band sound of the 1940s and dancers from all over the country. The professional instruction and exhibitions — dancers sweeping across the ballroom in amazingly synchronized steps — are a special treat.

Friday's dance is $18 for one person; Admission to Saturday's dance costs $22.50, or buy a $34.50 ticket that covers both dances. Overnight packages run from $179 to $623.

### Winterfest Arts and Crafts Show
3 S. Tunnel Rd., Asheville
• (828) 252-3880

This annual regional crafts display fills the corridors of the Asheville Mall and offers a pleasant diversion from winter's chill for three days in early February. This show is sponsored by the High Country Craft Guild and features traditional mountain crafts such as quilts, ceramics, dolls and other items.

### Arts and Crafts Conference at the Grove Park Inn
290 Macon Ave., Asheville
• (828) 252-2711, (800) 438-5800

This annual professional conference in praise of the Arts and Crafts Movement of Gustav Stickley and his contemporaries working in furniture, pottery and metalware could have no better surroundings than the Grove Park Inn, a veritable shrine to the movement. The richness of the red-shingled stone resort and its fine collection of arts and crafts pieces exemplify the natural elements and clean lines of this radical design movement, which set the Victorians on their ears at the turn of the century. The conference is usually held the third week in February.

### Club Day at the Blue Ridge Mall
1800 Seasons Blvd., Hendersonville
• (828) 697-1745

The last week in February, local clubs and organizations set up booths to show the community what's offered within the groups.

# March

## Central Mountains

### Comedy Classic
290 Macon Ave., Grove Park Inn, Asheville
• (828) 252-2711, (800) 438-5800

Always a sellout, this popular weekend features an exciting lineup of top professional talent. It is always scheduled for the first weekend in March. Friday's concert costs approximately $20; Saturday's costs $25. A $40 tickets covers both concerts. One- and two-night packages run from $225 to $410 per couple on average.

Photo: Lake Eden Arts Festival

Celebrate the world of folk arts and the world of nature simultaneously at the Lake Eden Arts Festival.

## Saint Patrick's Day Celebration
**Various locations, Asheville**
• **(828) 253-0322**

Asheville's cobblestoned Market Street is the starting point for this lively celebration of the wearing of the green. Crafts, entertainment, food and an energetic parade complete the festivities for those with a bit of Irish in their soul.

## Western Carolina Home Show
**87 Haywood St., Asheville**
• **(828) 628-9626**

Always popular, this annual event fills the Asheville Civic Center with streams of visitors, merchants and an eye-popping array of the hottest items for the modern homeowner. It's fun to go, even if your dream house is still a dream. Parking is available in the municipal parking garage next door, just behind the public library. The cost of a ticket is $5.

## Horse Shows
**N.C. Hwy. 280, Western North Carolina Agricultural Center, Fletcher**
• **(828) 687-1414**

Throughout the month, WNC Agricultural Center hosts the Western North Carolina Quar-

ter Horse Show, the Roping Horse Show and the Carolina Mountain Arabian Horse Show. Call for exact dates.

Other horses such as palominos, saddlebreds and racking and walking horses are on parade throughout the year from March to November. Admission is free for most events. See our Recreation chapter for more information.

## Spring Craft Show
**1800 Four Seasons Blvd., Hendersonville**
• **(828) 697-1745**

The Henderson County Crafters Association brings handicrafts to the Blue Ridge Mall on Four Seasons Boulevard toward the middle of this month. Dolls, jewelry, pottery, homemade greeting cards and brooms are only part of what you'll see.

## Super Saturday
**Various locations, Tryon**
• **(828) 894-3051**

Downtown is transformed into a children's festival with puppet shows, theater performances, jugglers, magicians and arts and craft activities. The City of Tryon sponsors the event.

# April

## Northern Mountains

### Guided Bird and Wildflower Walks
**Grandfather Mountain, Linville**
• (828) 733-2013, (800) 468-7325

The third week in April commences bird and flower walks that are guided by experts at Grandfather Mountain. Learn about wildflowers just reaching bloom beginning at 2 PM Sundays. The bird walks are on Saturdays, beginning at 9 AM. The walks continue through May.

Hiking fees are $5 and regular entrance fees are $10. If visitors just want to go on the walk, the only have to pay the hiking fee. (See our Attractions chapter for more).

## Central Mountains

### Annual Easter Sunrise Service
**U.S. Hwy. 64/74-A, Chimney Rock Park, Chimney Rock**
• (828) 625-9611, (800) 277-9611

Deep valleys and craggy ridges are an inspiring backdrop for this service conducted by a guest minister, a free, ongoing tradition for more than 40 years.

### Biltmore Estate's Festival of Flowers
**1 Approach Rd., Asheville**
• (828) 274-6333, (800) 543-2961

Not only is Mr. Vanderbilt's 250-room mansion a magnificent sight, but the grounds and gardens, designed by noted landscape architect Frederick Law Olmsted, are just as breathtaking. This month-long festival celebrates the exquisite beauty of the estate's wildflowers, formal plantings and exotic blooms of the gar-

dens. The mansion itself is arrayed in Victorian floral design, while live music serenades you in the house and gardens. The house is also open for Festival of Flower Evenings, by reservations on Fridays and Saturdays during the event. The festival lasts from mid-April to mid-May, and the price is admission to Biltmore Estate. Admission is $27.95 for adults and $21 for children ages 10 to 15. (See our Biltmore Estate and Winery chapter.)

### Hickory Nut Gorge Dogwood Festival
**Lake Lure** • (828) 625-0204

Lake Lure shimmers, and a cascade of white petals dots the mountains of the gorge, providing inspiration for this festival in honor of the return of spring. Food, entertainment, tournaments and crafts abound. Saturday includes a parade and a 5K run. The festival, usually held the third weekend in April, runs from 10 AM to 7 PM, with entertainment going well into the evening.

### Pioneer Living Day
**911 Reems Creek Rd., Zebulon B. Vance Birthplace, Weaverville** • (828) 645-6706

Walk into the North Carolina mountains of yesteryear at the Zebulon B. Vance Birthplace. Pioneer Living Day at this state historic site is a fascinating event for the whole family, who can all become involved in demonstrations of the day-to-day life of early mountaineers at this country homestead surrounded by meadows and mountains. Cooking, candlemaking and spinning are just a few of the delights. This event occurs the third Sunday in April.

### Earth Day Celebration
**U.S. Hwy. 64/74-A, Chimney Rock Park, Chimney Rock**
• (828) 625-9611, (800) 277-9611

Join environmental speakers and guided nature walks in celebration of Mother Nature.

---

**INSIDERS' TIP**

Don't underestimate the popularity of the festivals and events in these mountains. Most attract hundreds, if not thousands, of visitors. Therefore, calling ahead to inquire about the best place to find parking is a wise idea. It can save time that'll be better spent enjoying a festival.

Outdoor festivals fill the mountain air with music of all kinds.

Programs, demonstrations and hands-on displays including animals, dulcimer music and magic shows compose this celebration.

## Old Depot Association Art & Crafts Show
Old Depot, Black Mountain
• (828) 669-2300

This is a juried art show held at the historic train station in downtown Black Mountain.

## Easter Egg Hunt
Jackson Park, Hendersonville
•(828) 697-4884

Just before Easter, you can bring the young and young-at-heart for an old-fashioned egg hunt in the area's largest park. This free, springtime event, when more than 11,000 eggs are hidden in the park for children to find, starts at 11 AM.

## Olde Tyme Music Festival
Downtown Hendersonville
• (828) 692-0183

On the second Saturday in April, acoustic musicians will entertain you from 10 AM until 5 PM on Appalachian and hammered dulcimers, fiddles, guitars, auto harps and banjos.

## The Block House Steeplechase
500 Hunting Country Rd., Tryon
• (828) 859-6109, (800) 438-3681

The year 2000 will mark the 54th running of the horses at this free mid-month event, one of the region's most famous and well-attended. It takes place at the Foothills Equestrian Nature Center (FENCE). Gates open at 10 AM.

## Revolutionary War Encampment at FENCE
500 Hunting Country Rd., Foothills
Equestrian Nature Center, Tryon
• (828) 859-9021

Experience revolutionary times with South Carolina's Second Regiment at the Foothills Equestrian Nature Center (F.E.N.C.E.). See demonstrations of period crafts, cooking, musket shooting and an authentic campsite. This free event is held near the end of April.

## Historic Johnson Farm Festival
3346 Haywood Rd. (N.C. Hwy. 191),
Hendersonville • (828) 891-6585

At the end of April, there are tours, an auction, demonstrations, arts and crafts and food at this old tobacco farm, a heritage edu-

# Folkmoot USA

A Russian youth, dressed in a traditional embroidered red tunic cinched at the waist with a gold rope and black pantaloon trousers tucked into black boots, tilts back his cap with a carnation pinned to the side. He observes the Spanish flamenco dancer, clasping her multiruffled emerald green skirt in her hands as she cocks back her black lace-covered head and moves her feet in lightning-fast tempo. He tries to follow her steps as she patiently repeats the cadence.

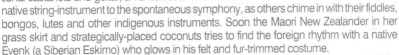

In the background, while the musicians play the traditional castanets and guitar, a Turkish strummer adds his native string-instrument to the spontaneous symphony, as others chime in with their fiddles, bongos, lutes and other indigenous instruments. Soon the Maori New Zealander in her grass skirt and strategically-placed coconuts tries to find the foreign rhythm with a native Evenk (a Siberian Eskimo) who glows in his felt and fur-trimmed costume.

This is the impromptu cultural exchange you might witness after a fabulous performance at Waynesville's Folkmoot USA festival. For 10 days every July, this small mountain town transforms itself into a miniature United Nations, melding folk music, dance and culture from around the world in an event much like one you would have to travel abroad to see. Each year 10 premier folk groups representing different parts of the world demonstrate their cultural heritages through colorful authentic and original reproduction costumes, lively dance and music played on unique instruments which are often handcrafted. Through the years, more than 70 countries have sent more than 130 groups to take part.

Folkmoot celebrates its 15th anniversary in 1998. It's amazing to look back at the humble beginnings of this festival in 1984. America was in the midst of the Cold War, apartheid ruled South Africa, and yet in one mountain village we could speak to our Russian guests one on one or have them visit in our houses. Poles, Kazakhs, Turks, Germans, Lithuanians, Kenyans and so many others joined together in song and dance,

Dancers from all over the world converge at Folkmoot USA.

music being the common language. Even today, the profound sensation of world peace this festival evokes is hard to mistake.

Folkmoot is patterned after classic European festivals. More than 300 musicians and dancers from around the globe descend on the Haywood County town and environs. They travel from their Waynesville home base, which is usually one of the public schools where they are housed hostel-style, to perform in city, college and school auditoriums around Western North Carolina. During intermission, the foyers turn into eastern bazaars, with the foreign visitors offering traditional souvenirs from their homelands.

International Festival Day is another opportunity to find a melange of international crafts and to watch some inspired street performances. This street fair was added to Folkmoot USA's lineup in 1986 and attracts 20,000 visitors who mingle among the 100 canopied handicraft and ethnic food booths along with the costumed performers who might just break into an informal sidewalk song and dance. Local artisans and vendors also join in.

The annual Folkmoot festival closes with a poignant all-group candlelight performance at the Lake Junaluska auditorium. Lights flicker on the water, crickets sing and a light dew descends on the cool night air as foreign friends bid us goodbye.

For more information on Folkmoot, including a performance schedule and admission costs, call (828) 452-2997. You can also write to Folkmoot USA, Post Office Box 658, Waynesville, NC 28786.

---

cation center and farm museum now owned by the Henderson County Public Schools. It's 4 miles north of Hendersonville on N.C. Hwy. 191. The festival runs from 10 AM until 4 PM.

## Appalachian Spring Celebration
**Cradle of Forestry, Pisgah National Forest**
**U.S. Hwy. 276, Pisgah Forest**
• **(828) 877-3130**

Starting the last week in April and running for a full month, the Cradle of Forestry celebrates our mountain's diversity of birds, wildflower and waterfalls with a variety of programs for both children and adults, including guided bird and wildflower walks and a wildflower photography contest. There is an entrance fee of $4 for adults and $2 for students.

## Southern Mountains

## Razzle Dazzle Saturday
**Various locations, Waynesville**
• **(828) 452-0593, (800) 334-9036**

Even the name sounds like fun. On the second Saturday in April, children of all ages enjoy a downtown, day-long celebration of arts and entertainment. There are live performances and hands-on art, food, face-painting and fun.

## Ramp Festival
**Various locations, Robbinsville**
• **(828) 479-3790**

On the last Sunday in April, the whole town celebrates the pungent ramp. This wild cousin of the onion is the star of this occasion sponsored by the local rescue squad. The day's activities feature a duck race, dinner with ramp-flavored dishes and a craft fair.

# May

## Northern Mountains

## Beech Mountain Hillclimb
**Beech Mountain**
• **(828) 387-9283, (800) 468-5506**

The torturous asphalt curves of Beech Mountain are the setting for this 1-mile automobile race to the top of the mountain. More than 80 cars participate in time trials and races over the two-day event. The race starts at the entrance of Ski Beech and climbs to the finish line at Fred's General Mercantile. Call early for lodging reservations. The Hillclimb is usually held on the first weekend of May. Ten dollars per carload gets you in to watch.

Photo: J. Pickering

The Lake Eden Arts Festival in the spring and fall offers music, dancing, crafts and fun.

# Jackson County: Wet Camp Gap

*GreatViews*

This 3-mile, round-trip hike to a lovely mile-high meadow with superb views of the Pisgah National Forest is not difficult. For part of the walk, you will be on sections of the Mountains-to-the-Sea Trail. Be sure to take a sharp left at the trail junction about 15 minutes from the start of your walk. To reach the trail, drive to the Bear Pen Gap parking overlook at milepost 427.6 on the Blue Ridge Parkway in Jackson County. The trail begins at the lower end of the parking lot.

## Spring Studio and Garden Tour
**Various locations, Spruce Pine**
• (828) 765-9483, (800) 227-3912

The first Friday and Saturday in May, the artists and garden businesses of Yancey and Mitchell counties open their studios and garden spots for informal viewing a week before Mother's Day. Fine handcrafted works and garden accouterments make for a delightful shopping mixture. The tour runs from 10 AM to 5 PM and is sponsored by the Toe River Arts Council. Pick up a map of studios on the tour at the Mitchell County Chamber of Commerce at the North Carolina Museum of Minerals, or the *Mitchell News Journal* in downtown Spruce Pine.

## Spring Arts Festival
**Town Sq., Burnsville**
• (828) 682-7413, (800) 948-1632

This young festival on second May weekend is only two years old. Saturday from 10 AM to 4 PM, the town square is home to artists and their works. Browse the booths for some creative gifts and fine art while the children paint and draw to their heart's content on the Expression Wall. Sponsored by the Toe River Arts Council and the Business Owners Association, this event is free.

# Central Mountains

## Spring Herb Festival
**off I-26, Brevard exit, Western North Carolina Farmer's Market, Asheville**
• (828) 689-5974

This event on the first weekend in May offers educational gardening programs as well as an opportunity to speak to herbalists and master gardeners. This festival is free, so you can save your money to buy herbs, books and herbal products.

## Folk Art Center Fiber Day
**Mi. 382, Asheville** • **(828) 298-7928**

The Folk Art Center, east of the city on the Blue Ridge Parkway, hosts a special day to celebrate the fiber arts in the middle of the month. The professional demonstrations attract large crowds, who get to watch how these folks spin thread and weave cloth out of the wool from sheep. This usually includes all the stages, from watching the sheep being shorn to the weaving on the loom.

## Lake Eden Arts Festival
**377 Lake Eden Rd., Camp Rockmont, Black Mountain** • **(828) 686-8742**

Lake Eden Arts Festival is a new event celebrating the world of folk arts. On the sprawling grounds of a boy's summer camp, this fest features dancing and music, drumming and handicrafts, poetry and storytelling over the three-day Memorial Day weekend in May, then again in October. There are also spiritual and healing workshops, a farmers' market, ethnic food booths, massage and aromatherapy and a vast and funky mixture of world music, folk and country sounds, all running concurrently on four different stages. This is one very hip festival — call for a brochure.

Day passes cost $15 for adults, $10 for children, on Friday and Sunday. Saturday's ticket costs $20 for adults, $15 for children. A weekend pass runs $70 for adults and $55 for children and includes tent or car camping.

With no overnight stay, tickets cost $30 (adult) and $20 (children) for the weekend.

## Garden Jubilee
**201 S. Main St., Visitors Information Center, Hendersonville**
• **(800) 828-4244, (828) 693-9708**

The last week in May brings arts and crafts, a plant sale, garden talks, food and more to the Visitors Information Center. The event is sponsored by downtown merchants who hold sidewalk sales and treasure hunts, a free flower drawing and bring in live music that day.

## Sunday Melodies in the Park
**Jackson Park Amphitheater, Hendersonville**
• **(800) 828-4344, (828) 697-1745**

A free summer concert series begins the second Sunday of the month. Call the above numbers for more information.

## Annual Main Street Antique Show
**Main St., Hendersonville • (828) 692-9057**

Seventy-five antique dealers show their wares on Main Street from 9AM until 5 PM.

## Brevard Music Center
**100 Probart St., Brevard**
• **(828) 884-2011, (800) 648-4523**

In mid-month the Brevard Music Center opens its series of more than 70 different concert events that last through mid-August.

## Carl Sandburg
## Folk & Poetry Festival
**1928 Little River Rd., Connemara, Flat Rock • (828) 693-4178**

One of the mountains' favorite people is the namesake and inspiration for this free entertainment. Carl Sandburg loved to sing, and music still graces Connemara, his farm, now a National Historic Site just outside Hendersonville. The last weekend in May, professional musicians and actors perform songs and poems from Sandburg's works from 10 AM until 5 PM.

## Flat Rock Playhouse
**2661 Greenville Hwy., Flat Rock**
• **(828) 693-0731**

From late May through early September, North Carolina's official state theater presents comedy, American classics, whodunits, mu-

Photo: J. Pickering

Bluegrass is one of the native sounds of the North Carolina Mountains.

sicals and farces. See our write-up in the Arts and Culture chapter for more information.

# Southern Mountains

## Ramp Convention
Various locations, Waynesville
• (828) 456-3021, (800) 334-9036

Early May brings a genuine mountain hoedown to again honor the ramp — a rare, wild onion-like plant — in downtown Waynesville. It adds zest to all the day's dishes. There'll be country and bluegrass music, square dancing and clogging too. But beware — it's been known to inspire a politician or two to make a speech.

## Great Smoky Mountain Trout Festival
Waynesville
• (828) 456-3021, (800) 334-9036

This Memorial Day event held in Recreation Park honors the greatest catch in the mountains with exhibitions, contests, crafts, food and entertainment. The Haywood County Chamber of Commerce sponsors this free event.

# June

## Northern Mountains

### Firefly Festival Arts and Crafts Fair
591 Horn in the West Dr., Boone
• (828) 264-2225, (800) 852-9506

Browse among great art and crafts, relive childhood memories as fireflies glow against the evening skies and listen to the finest flatpickin' musicians in the country. This free outdoor fest is on the first Saturday in June.

### Singing on the Mountain at Grandfather Mountain
off N.C. Hwy. 221 (entrance of Grandfather Mountain) McRae Meadows, Linville • (828) 733-4337

This traditional Southern gospel sing at magnificent McRae Meadows has been going strong since 1924. Drawing crowds in the tens of thousands, this event hearkens back to old-time preachin' when the message was delivered outdoors under the heavens and voices were lifted up to the skies. Lively gospel singing, entertainers, picnic lunches, preaching by well-known speakers and wide-open vistas create a joyful good time for the entire family. This event, which takes place on the fourth Sunday in June, is free.

### Yancey County Clogging — Art & Craft Show
Town Sq., Burnsville
• (828) 682-7413, (800) 948-1632

This dance festival runs for two days in mid-June. Burnsville's town square hosts a pig-pickin' the first night of the fest, serving succulent barbecue while cloggers dance the traditional mountain jigs handed down through the generations. The first evening culminates in a street dance. Saturday includes more clogging and arts and crafts booths.

### North Carolina Rhododendron Festival
Along Mitchell Ave., Bakersville
• (828) 765-9483, (800) 227-3912

For a half-century this festival has coincided with the blooming of the 600-acre Rhododendron Gardens atop Roan Mountain. A 10K road race, golf tournament, two pageants, historic tours, a car show and a street dance round out the three-day weekend in the third week of June. These events are free.

### Blue Ridge Mountain Fair Craft Festival
Crouse Park, Sparta
• (910) 372-5473, (800) 372-5473

Crouse Park in Sparta is the setting for an old-time mountain fair of food, fun, crafts and music held the last Saturday of the month.

## Central Mountains

### French Broad River Month
Various locations in Buncombe, Henderson, Madison and Transylvania counties • (828) 252-8474

June is French Broad River Month. This menagerie of events along the riverfront of the French Broad is sponsored by RiverLink, a nonprofit group devoted to improving the river and its banks. Boat races, a Bridge Party and Triathalon, whitewater raft trips, biking and rock climbing are all a part of this outdoors celebration. Activity charges vary, so call ahead.

## Annual Tryon Horse Show
500 Hunting Country Rd., Foothills Equestrian Nature Center, Tryon
• (828) 859-9021, (800) 4-EVENT 1

Sponsored by the Tryon Riding and Hunt Club at the foothills Equestrian Nature Center (FENCE) early in June, this is a free can't-miss event for horse lovers. Events include dressage, cross-country and jumping.

## Ice Cream Social/Spring Kickoff
Silvermont Mansion, Main St., Brevard
• (828) 884-5255

This early June benefit for the Brevard Little Theater, held at the Silvermont Mansion on Main Street, gives participants a preview of the community theater's coming season. Admission is free.

## The Blue Ridge Barecue Festival and NC State Barbecue Championship
Harmon Field, Tryon • (828) 859-6236

On a weekend in mid-June, the North Carolina state championship barbecue cook-off is held at Harmon Field, attracting even out-of-state barbecue specialists. There's non-stop bluegrass, Piedmont blues, rock and country music, crafts and children's activities. There is an admission fee of $5.

## Summer Nights at Fence Schooling Show
500 Hunting Country Rd., Foothills Equestrian Nature Center, Tryon
• (828) 859-9021, (800) 4-EVENT1

From late June through the middle of Au-

gust, a series of horse shows designed for family fun and friendly competition are held at the Foothills Equestrian Nature Center.

## Brevard Music Center
Probant St., Brevard
• (828) 884-2011, (800) 648-4523

The renowned music center opens for its summer run of more than 50 concerts.

# Southern Mountains

## Dillsboro Heritage Festival
Various downtown locations, Dillsboro
• (828) 586-3943

On the second Saturday in June, Dillsboro, one of the mountains' most crafts-filled towns, closes off its main shopping street for a festival full of food, arts, crafts and demonstrations.

## Bluegrass Festival
U.S. Hwy. 19 N., Happy Holiday Campground, Cherokee
• (828) 864-7203, (800) 438-1601

You can join in the foot-stompin' that goes on during this three-day, late-June event at the Happy Holiday Campground. Tickets are $25 for adults and $15 for children ages 6 to 13 per day. For three days, advance tickets are $60 for adults ($70 at the gate) and $30 for children.

# July

# Northern Mountains

## 4th of July Festival
Banner Elk Town Park, Banner Elk
• (828) 898-5605, (800) 972-2183

Games, a parade, bluegrass music, oldies music, crafts and traditional food all are offered at the Banner Elk Town Park.

## INSIDERS' TIP

Local newspapers print special supplements for larger events. Take these with you. They are excellent sources for information, schedules, and events locations.

Stake out a spot in front of the Jones House to watch the parades that pass through downtown Boone.

Photo: Judy Scharns, Courtesy of Boone Convention and Visitors Bureau

## Old-Fashioned July 4th Celebration on the Square
Town Sq., Burnsville
• (828) 682-7413, (800) 948-1632

The picturesque Town Square is the scene of a Fourth of July like our grandparents enjoyed. Don't miss the wagon-train parade, crafts, food and mountain music. When twilight falls, you would swear it's still 1900.

## Christmas in July Festival
West Jefferson • (336) 246-9550

This festival, which is held in mid-July, is heralded as a celebration of Ashe County's thriving Christmas tree industry. What better fun than to pretend its Christmas in the heat of midsummer! Christmas crafts, from roping and wreaths to decorated trees, are on display along with traditional mountain crafts. Music to suit just about everyone's tastes, including bluegrass, gospel and classic rock, fills the air. Helicopter rides, children's activities and all kinds of mouth-watering food round out the

fun. (The exact date of the festival varies from year to year, so call ahead of time.)

## Grandfather Mountain Highland Games and Gathering of the Scottish Clans
McRae Meadows, Linville
• (828) 733-1333

Expansive McRae Meadows on Grandfather Mountain is the gorgeous venue for a sea of kilts and tartans the second full weekend in July. For more than 40 years, this gathering has brought Scottish hearts together for ancient games, traditional food and bagpipes galore. Because there is no on-site parking, shuttle buses are provided from the entrance to the top of Grandfather Mountain for around $1 each way, per person.

Don't miss the spectacular Torchlight Opening Ceremony on Thursday evening, invoking the "spirit of the clans" upon the games. This stirring parade of torchbearers and traditional highland bagpipes and drums makes the centuries seem to fall away. A 5-mile foot race from the town of Linville to the top of Grandfather Mountain is also part of the opening night festivities. Evening activities continue throughout the weekend. Charges vary, so call for an informational brochure.

## Banner Elk Art Festival
### Various locations, Banner Elk
• (828) 898-5605,(800) 972-2183

This juried fine art exhibition and sale is held in the charming environment of this mountain valley village the third weekend in July. Stroll from gallery to gallery as you take in the array of artistic talent. Some artists set up shop outside in the balmy summer weather of Banner Elk.

# Central Mountains

## Old-Fashioned Grove Park Inn Family 4th of July
### 290 Macon Ave., Asheville
• (828) 252-2711, (800) 438-5800

Strolling music and sing-alongs, musical fireworks, a bingo scavenger hunt and tennis and golf clinics at this historic inn help celebrate our national birthday.

## 4th of July Gala
### Various downtown locations, Asheville
• (828) 259-5800

A spectacular shower of fireworks illuminates the skyline of historic City/County Plaza in downtown Asheville. Get there early for the food, music and fun. A variety of food booths, including Greek, Italian, German, Scottish and all the usual fair fare line the plaza. Funky tunes from zydeco to rockabilly to country grace the stage for an inspirational street dance.

## Shindig-on-the-Green
### City/County Plaza, Asheville
• (828) 258-6101

Every Saturday night in summer, starting the first weekend in July, old-fashioned mountain music thrives in the modern world on Asheville's central City/County Plaza. The Shindig-on-the-Green, now in its 29th year, is the best free entertainment in the region, drawn from the area's many talented musicians, singers and dancers. The program, co-sponsored by the City of Asheville Parks and Recreation Department and the Asheville Area Chamber of Commerce, began with the simple desire of a few dedicated area musicians to preserve our region's musical heritage. The first stage was set up on the steps of City Hall.

The traditional method of passing down mountain music is by playing it — here, banjo pickers, buck dancers, ballad singers, cloggers and fans fill the audience and the stage of this celebration of musical heritage. The City/County Plaza swells with a sea of mountain music lovers and spontaneous dancers who begin gathering at 6 PM. The fun usually goes on until 10 PM, or until the last banjo picker or guitar player goes home. A house band usually starts the action, followed by an invited team of cloggers or "smooth dance" square dancers. Musicians come from all over the area to be a part of the evening's entertainment. What began modestly almost three decades ago as a simple desire to keep the ancient strains of mountain music alive has become a living, breathing perpetuation of a unique cultural heritage.

## Guild Fair
### 87 Haywood St., Asheville
• (828) 298-7928

One of the most popular of the annual mountain crafts fairs, Guild Fair is sponsored by the Southern Highland Handicraft Guild. A juried craft exhibition, professional demonstrations and fine traditional mountain music set this fair apart from the rest. Artisans from nine different states in the Appalachians descend on the downtown civic center on the third weekends in July and October, offering every kind of craft from wood furniture to glassware to calico dolls and sofa cushions. Here, you can get a taste of both the traditional, simple craft and the high-end one-of-a-kind pieces. It's not just a place to observe: The Guild Fair also makes for excellent gift shopping for a special piece of craft heritage. Admission is usually $5.

## Swannanoa Chamber Festival
701 Warren Wilson Rd., Warren Wilson College, Swannanoa
• (828) 298-3325 ext. 316

This annual festival of chamber music is a rarity and a delight. From the campus of Warren Wilson College, a visiting contingent of classically trained professional musicians produces a series of five marvelous concerts. Traveling workshops and concert series for the Hendersonville and Waynesville communities are also part of this five-week-long musical celebration. The festival also combines lectures, demonstrations and a benefit recital into the regularly-scheduled program.

## The Asheville Poetry Alive Festival
UNCA, Asheville
• (828) 298-4927

This event is a treat. Poetry workshops and events, many featuring Pulitzer Prize winners, are held in Asheville the second weekend in July. Readings, lectures and seminars devoted to the written word are open to amateurs, professionals, and the general public. Come watch a "slam," write your own poems, listen to the masters . . . experiment. Admission is charged and varies for the whole event, workshops or individual days. There is a charge for the weekend pass. Call for event, workshop or day rates.

## Bele Chere
Various downtown locations, Asheville
• (828) 253-1009

This tremendously popular annual street festival has grown over almost two decades to become one of the premier events in the Southeast, attracting upwards of 350,000 people over its three-day span. This is western North Carolina's largest outdoor festival, featuring more than 100 national and regional entertainment acts. At least five different stages grace various key parts of downtown, and canopied booths line the main streets.

Multicultural crafts and food set the tone — the Greek Orthodox Church always sponsors a booth or two with excellent Mediterranean fare, and the fajitas, gyros, Indian samosas, Thai noodles and many other mouth-watering selections keep festival goers fairly content. Funnel cakes and shaved ice are sold every few steps. Local restaurants join in, often hosting booths in the central Pack Square.

The musical entertainment, as well as poetry and dance, is excellent, ranging from Andean pan flute music to throw-down gospel to reggae, rock and roll, Brazilian samba, Zydeco, Bluegrass, swing and much, much more. Street dances continue throughout the day and evening.

Vendors offer colorful batiks, jewelry, leather, pottery, and sundry handcrafted items. Special events like face-painting, puppet shows, kiddie concerts and numerous other activities are geared toward children, making this a terrific family outing. Bele Chere is always held the last Friday, Saturday and Sunday of the month. Many sophisticated shopping booths mingle with the more carnival-fare type, presenting had wrought furniture, clothing, hand made jewelry, and the popular Indian henna temporary tattoo art *mhendi*. Best of all, it's free!

## Summertime Saturday
Various downtown locations, Brevard
• (828) 884-2787, (800) 648-4523

On Saturday afternoons throughout July, Brevard's musicians and others from the area perform in the downtown shopping district.

## Harambee
Historic Depot and Seventh Ave. District, Hendersonville • (828) 884-3278

This multi-cultural festival takes place on

the first Saturday in July. Here you'll find arts and crafts, entertainment, food and more.

## Fabulous Fourth Metric Century Bicycle Tour

**Tryon • (828) 859-6042, (800) 440-7848**

As many as 300 participants and many visitors come from throughout the South to enjoy this 63-mile Independence Day tour that begins in Harmon Field in Tryon. The challenging course has ascents to almost 5,500 feet. After cheering the bicyclists on, visitors can go "next-door" to Columbus and enjoy that town's Fourth of July festival, an all-day affair that offers food, crafts, a street dance and evening fireworks.

## Coon Dog Day

**Various locations, Saluda**
**• (828) 749-2581**

This downtown celebration of the coon dog on the Fourth of July weekend is one of the more popular festivals in the region. It a great day for both dogs and their people, with contests and judging for the dogs and crafts, live music and a street dance for the people.

## Carnival!

**South Broad Park, S. Broad St., Brevard**
**• (828) 877-4777**

For four days in mid-July, carnival rides, pony rides, clowns, jugglers, food, prizes, a white elephant sale, dance lessons and free health screenings are offered, all to benefit the Transylvania Community Hospital. Admission is free, but there is a charge for the rides and some of the games.

# Southern Mountains

## Andrews Wagon Train

**Andrews to Franklin • (828) 837-6492**

Since the 1960s, this wagon train has wound its way through the mountains, leaving Andrews in late June and arriving in Franklin by the July 4 weekend.

## Mountaineer Antique Auto Show

**U.S. Hwy. 276, Maggie Valley**
**• (828) 926-1686, (800) 334-9036**

This is one of the largest gatherings of

spiffed-up vintage cars you're likely to see. It takes place over the Fourth of July weekend. There have been more than 500 participants in the past.

## Fourth of July Freedom Fest

**Town Square, Bryson City**
**• (828) 488-3681, (800) 867-9246**

Independence Day in Swain County is celebrated with a bevy of live entertainment, food, crafts and, of course, fireworks.

## July 4th Heritage Festival

**Various downtown locations,**
**Robbinsville • (828) 499-3790**

Join the downtown parade featuring local bands. The festival features lots of food and crafts too.

## Christian Harmony Singing

**John C. Campbell Folk School,**
**1 Folk School Rd., Brasstown**
**• (828) 837-2775, (800) FOLK SCH**

This annual gathering around the second weekend in July draws nearly 80 singers from much of the Southeast. The four-part unaccompanied shaped-note singing takes place from 10:30 AM until 3 PM, broken only by a covered dish dinner from 12:30 to 1:30 PM.

## Art Fest

**Downtown, Cashiers • (828) 743-5050**

On the second weekend of the month, several thousand people come to view and buy the best in local arts and crafts. Box lunches of tasty barbecue are for sale.

## Annual Snowbird Mountain Gospel Singing

**Jacob Cornsilk Community Center,**
**Robbinsville**
**• (828) 479-8984, (828) 479-3926**

This three-day event, which attracts singers from the entire Southeast, is held in the middle of July in the Jacob Cornsilk Community Center. The singing starts around 7 PM on Friday and Saturday and at 2 PM on Sunday.

## Mountain Heritage Day

**N.C. Hwy 107, Cullowhee**
**• (828) 227-7272**

This most "mountainy" day of the year

attracts some 50,000 people. You can watch chainsaw demonstrations, ax-throwing contests and cat and dog shows. There are also mountain arts and crafts and food. Favorites on the day's program are gospel, bluegrass and country music with lots of clogging, square dancing and line dancing.

## Mountain Artisans Summer Arts and Craft Show
**Macon County Community Bldg., U.S. Hwy. 441 S., Franklin • (828) 524-3405**

More than 70 exhibitors from six states show off their country and traditional crafts and fine arts in late July at this show.

## 33rd Annual Gemboree
**Macon County Community Center, U.S. Hwy. 441 S., Franklin**
**• (828) 524-3161, (800) 336-7829**

The "Gem Capital of the World" will show off its rough and cut gems, minerals, fine jewelry and equipment in late July. You can also shop for gem-related books and supplies, attend lectures and maybe win a door prize. Admission is free.

## Folkmoot USA
**Waynesville and other locations**
**• (800) 334-9036**

From late July through early August, beginning with a parade through downtown Waynesville, the mountains become the world's stage as musicians and dancers from different countries gather in a celebration of music, dance and culture. (See the "Folkmoot USA" Close-up in this chapter.)

# August

## Northern Mountains

## Mineral and Gem Festival
**97 Pine Bridge Ave., Pine Bridge Coliseum, Spruce Pine**
**• (828) 765-9483, (800) 227-3912**

A rock hound's dream come true, this week-long event draws crowds to its displays and sales booths. More than 50 dealers descend during the first week in August.

## Banner Elk Art Festival
**Hickory Nut Gap Rd., Grandfather Home for Children, Banner Elk**
**• (828) 898-5605, (800) 972-2183**

This juried fine art exhibit and sale is held the fourth weekend in August. It's sponsored by he Avery-Banner Elk Chamber of Commerce.

## Mount Mitchell Crafts Fair
**Town Sq., Burnsville**
**• (828) 682-7413, (800) 227-3912**

Here's a spectacular slice of Americana on the grassy Town Square in the quaint village of Burnsville. A splendid array of traditional mountain crafts, food and music make for an enjoyable day in mid-August.

## Central Mountains

## Village Art & Craft Fair
**Throughout historic Biltmore Village, Asheville • (828) 274-2831**

What a fabulous setting! Historic Biltmore Village and the grounds of the Cathedral of All Souls in south Asheville, just opposite the entrance to Biltmore Estate, come alive the first full weekend in August for this annual arts festival. The historic shopping district, once the village of Best, was purchased by George Vanderbilt in the 1890s to accommodate the army of crafters, artisans and laborers necessary to complete the five-year construction of Biltmore House (see our chapter on Shopping). More than 150 artists offer beautiful jewelry and fiber, pottery and metal works. Food and beverage sales benefit community charities.

## Mountain Dance and Folk Festival
**downtown Asheville**
**• (828) 259-6107**

This granddaddy of all U.S. folk music festivals started informally back in 1927 as just "a little pickin' and a-grinnin' and a-steppin'" at the home of Bascom Lamar Lunsford in Turkey Creek in Buncombe County. Today it has evolved into one of the most revered folk music festivals of its kind in the country.

Lunsford, the festival's founder, devoted his life to the perpetuation of our mountain musical heritage. He died in 1973, but his festival still retains the naturalness and spontaneity that gave it life 70 years ago on that porch on Turkey Creek. This toe-tapping, knee-slapping event, co-sponsored by the City of Asheville, begins in early August each year at various downtown locations.

## Sourwood Festival
**Various locations, Black Mountain**
**• (828) 669-2300, (800) 669-2301**

More than 150 art, craft and food vendors set up in this picturesque town, a 15-minute ride east of Asheville. A music tent, battle of the bands and carnival for children are just some of the fun in store Tuesday through Sunday on the third week in August. Stroll the old-fashioned main street and peek into the numerous galleries and antique stores. Many of them have special sales in conjunction with the festival. It features a lot of good old Americana — bring out the corndogs, watermelon and, of course, the sourwood honey.

## Goombay Festival
**Eagle St. and S. Market St., Asheville**
**• (828) 252-4614**

This spirited weekend festival celebrates African-American culture in exciting African and Caribbean style. Goombay is a West African term meaning rhythm, and this festival is based on a centuries-old celebration filled with music, dance and the joy of life.

For more than a decade, Goombay has personified joyous multiculturalism at the corner of Eagle and S. Market streets in downtown Asheville. Steel drums, jazz and reggae music, traditional African clothing, jewelry and decorations, and an incredible assortment of delectable food are all part of the fun. More than 50,000 visitors a year from all over the country step into the Goombay beat, many returning year after year. The festival takes place in late August.

## Summer Social
**Tryon Fine Arts Center, downtown Tryon**
**• (828) 859-8322**

The Fine Arts Council hold an all-day, outdoor arts and entertainment festival on the second Saturday of the month at the Tryon Fine Arts Center. It includes local and regional art, food, fun, dances, live music and magic.

## Annual Jazz in Brevard
**Brevard • (828) 884-2787**

The Transylvania Arts Council sponsors a day of world-class jazz. This mid-August event takes place in various locations. Tickets are $20.

# Southern Mountains

## J.C. Campbell Annual August Auction
**1 Folk School Rd., Brasstown**
**• (828) 837-2775, (800) FOLK SCH**

Spend the first Saturday of the month bidding on outstanding craft items. It's a great way to support this unique craft school.

## Annual Antique Show
**N.C. Hwy. 107, Blue Ridge School, Cashiers • (828) 743-5191**

Held the first weekend in August, this juried show at the Blue Ridge School draws dealers form all over the Southeast. Come early: The place fills quickly, and people do come to buy!

# September

# Northern Mountains

## Overmountain Victory Trail Celebration
**Mi. 331, Spruce Pine**
**• (828) 765-9483, (800) 227-3912**

Relive the lives of the "overmountain boys," who walked a trail toward history defending our rights and freedoms. Scheduled events are complemented by demonstrations of frontier cooking, leatherwork, beadwork, spinning and other Revolutionary-era lifestyle skills. The celebration is held on the 3rd weekend of the month at the N.C. Museum of Minerals.

## Olde Boone Streetfest
Various locations, Boone
• (828) 264-2225,(800) 852-9506

This country fair on the streets of Boone has the added appeal of the early fall leaf colors as a backdrop for fun. You can munch all day on traditional mountain foods or go for more modern tastes. The arts and crafts are excellent, and music sets a lively mood. The festival is held in late September.

## Music in the Mountains Festival
N.C. Hwy. 80, Toe River Campground Park, Burnsville
• (828) 682-7413, 682-7215,
(800) 948-1632

Mountain folk music and food at the Toe River Campground Park are a magical combination, especially with Mother Nature's beautiful backdrop. Various bluegrass and mountain music bands play at this all-day jamboree in late September, often jamming into the night with visitors who happen to bring along instruments. The small fee is usually under $5.

# Central Mountains

## Celebrate Folk Art Day
Folk Art Center, Blue Ridge Pkwy., Asheville • (828) 298-7928

Head for the Folk Art Center, east of the city on the Blue Ridge Parkway, for a day dedicated to those who carry on our Appalachian craft heritage. The early crafts of the mountains were made by combining local materials with skills brought over from England and Europe. Chairs, dolls, musical instruments, knives, quilts, weavings and carvings are all part of the show, plus musicians and storytellers.

## Fall Pioneer Living Days and Military Encampment
Zebulon Vance Birthplace, 911 Reems Creek Rd., Weaverville
• (828) 645-6706

The 1800s come alive at the Zebulon Vance Birthplace, a state historic site. Here mountain crafts and traditional cooking are demonstrated, and a 19th-century military encampment is reenacted on the grounds.

## Kituwah
87 Haywood St., Asheville Civic Center, Asheville • (828) 254-0072

This young festival celebrates the art and culture of the American Indian through dance, storytelling and arts and crafts. Admission will cost $7 to $15. Call for more detailed information, and for a schedule of performers and events. It is held for two days the last week of the month.

## Oktoberfest
290 Macon Ave., Grove Park Inn, Asheville
• (828) 252-2711, (800) 438-5800

This annual Oktoberfest happens during the last week of September at Grove Park Inn. Hearty German food, music and (of course) beer help to celebrate the time of harvest. This will be the festival's eighth year. Though it's not as raucous as the one in Munich, it can still quench your thirst for the real brew and taste for herb-infused sausages.

## Annual Apple Festival
Hendersonville
• (828) 692-1413, (800) 282-4244

For almost a half-century, this has been Henderson County's biggest event. It takes place from September's first Friday through Monday and includes a huge street fair, food, crafts, entertainment and sporting contests. There are 41 individual events and 25 kinds of entertainment taking place all over town, including the Mountain Music Jamboree, Sunday in the Park, a bike tour, a 10K run, Apple Jack and Apple Jill golf tournaments and the King Apple Parade.

# Southern Mountains

## Fireman's Day Festival
Town Sq., Bryson City
• (828) 488-9416

Held on the town square on the first Saturday of the month, this is a day and evening of festivities in the mountain tradition with music, entertainment and crafts.

## Smoky Mountain Folk Festival
**Stuart Auditorium, Lake Junaluska**
• **(800) 334-9036**

A freewheeling Labor Day celebration of the finest traditional and old-timey music and dance, this mountain festival is held in the cool, open-air Stuart Auditorium and on the surrounding grounds. There's even a separate show where kids can kick up their heels! Tickets are $7.50 at the door.

## Haywood County Fair
**Haywood County Fair Ground, Lake Junaluska**
• **(828) 452-0152, (800) 334-9036**

There are barbecues, cotton candy, gospel singings under the tent, old-fashioned horse and tractor pulls, a man's biscuit-making contest, a petting zoo, food and craft exhibits and more! The event takes place at the Haywood County Fair Ground in Lake Junaluska.

## Homecoming Parade
**Downtown Robbinsville • (828) 479-3330**

Remember the good ol' days? This is an old-fashioned homecoming the last Saturday of the month, complete with a football game at the high school and the crowning of a homecoming queen.

# October

## Northern Mountains

## Madison County Heritage Festival
**Various locations, Mars Hill**
• **(828) 689-9351, (828) 689-1424**

The first Saturday in October is set aside for this celebration of the community and family life of the people of "the Mountains of Madison." Traditional mountain crafts such as rug braiding, basket making, spinning and weaving and musical instrument making are among the exhibitions. This delightful, small college town opens up all of Main Street, serving a wonderful assortment of pies, cakes, breads

and home cooking. Forty craft booths, local musicians, clog dancers, storytellers and shape-note singers add to the festivities.

## Mountain Heritage Festival
**Various locations, Sparta**
• **(336) 372-5473, (800) 372-5473**

Enjoy an old-time celebration of early mountain life in the "unspoiled province" of Alleghany County, tucked up against the Virginia border. This is harvest time as it used to be. Sparta (population 1,957) serves up an energetic good time with all the ingredients that these events are noted for: food, fun, crafts and crowds.

## New River Festival
**Various locations, Todd**
• **(336) 877-1128, 877-1067**

Todd, a historic village in Ashe County, is the scene of a new festival on the ancient New River in early October. Once a bustling train town, Todd is now a quiet hamlet frequented by the traveler who wants a different, more leisurely getaway.

This festival offers an old-fashioned gospel sing, checkers playoff, horseshoe toss, arts displays, storytelling, a fishing tournament and much more. And don't miss the town's main attraction, the Todd General Store. And you thought community socials were a thing of the past. Admission: one smile.

## Valle Country Fair
**N.C. Hwy. 194, Apple Barn, Valle Crucis**
• **(828) 264-1299, (800) 852-9506**

When the colors of the autumn leaves set the mountains afire and the air carries a slight nip, you know it's time for the Valle Country Fair. This delightful mountain festival is the premier arts, crafts and mountain music event in the High Country, drawing upwards of 15,000 visitors annually for an entire weekend in mid-October.

Set on the grounds of the old Apple Barn near the Valle Crucis Conference Center in picturesque Valle Crucis, the event takes you back to simpler times when country fairs were the prime social events in the mountains. Every year more than 150 artisans unveil their handcrafted treasures.

The atmosphere is highlighted by the

Photo: Constance E. Richards

Many of the area's fairs and festivals come alive at night.

strains of mountain music, and you might even catch of a glimpse of old, buckskin-clad Dan'l Boone himself. It's actually actor Glenn Causey, who, since 1955, has played the venerable frontiersman in *Horn in the West*, the popular outdoor drama staged in nearby Boone (see our Attractions chapter). All proceeds from the fair benefit local High Country charitable organizations. Don't miss this one! Come early and stake out a parking spot.

To find the Apple Barn, take N.C. Hwy. 194 S. past the Mast General Store. You'll find the Apple Barn in just under 2 miles.

## Woolly Worm Festival
### Banner Elk
• (828) 898-5605, (800) 972-2183

A fuzzy weather prognosticator? Tradition says it's so. The woolly worm has earned this distinction here in the mountains, and people gather high up in Banner Elk to celebrate the fact every year during the third weekend in October, just before the winds blow chill. Stripes on the woolly worm are traditionally inspected by town elders. Depending on the color, the elders can predict what kind of winter it will be. Along with the honored woolly worm, more than 120 craft artists, races, entertainment and food make the festival a hit for the whole family.

## Fall Celebration of the Arts
### Spruce Pine
• (828) 765-9483, (800) 227-3912

This annual juried and invitational exhibition that takes place on the 3rd weekend in October features traditional and contemporary glass, fiber, ceramics, metal, wood, sculpture and jewelry by some of the region's finest artists. It's a good place to start a little early Christmas shopping.

## Apple Festival
### 591 Horn in the West Dr., Boone
• (828) 264-2225, (800) 852-9506

High in the Northern Mountains come apples, apples and more apples late in October. This annual festival celebrates the esteemed fruit with a traditional harvest-time good time. Crafts, entertainment and food, particularly the apples, "round" out the festival.

# Central Mountains

## Greek Festival
### City/County Plaza, Asheville
• (828) 253-3754

Asheville's Greek community has contributed richly to the multicultural fabric of the city for more than 100 years. This annual festival is a special treat for young and old alike. Ethnic music and crafts line the City/County Plaza downtown near Pack Square. And the food! Spanakopita, pastitchio, gyros, loumades, baklava — try one of everything! A cafe tent features Greek sweets and rich strong demitasses of finely ground Greek coffee; just don't swallow the dregs. It's held the first full weekend in October and is co-sponsored by the City of Asheville.

## Guild Fair
### Asheville • (828) 298-7928

One of the most popular of the annual mountain crafts fairs, Guild Fair is sponsored by the Southern Highland Handicraft Guild and features a juried craft exhibition, professional demonstrations and fine traditional mountain music. It's held in the downtown civic center on the third weekends in July and October (see previous listing).

## Lake Eden Arts Festival
### Camp Rockmont, Black
### Mountain • (828) 686-8742

The Lake Eden Arts Festival is a fun new event filled with dancing and music, drumming and handcrafts, poetry and storytelling. There are also spiritual and healing workshops and a farmers' market during the three-day weekend in late October and again in May.

## Thomas Wolfe Festival
### Various locations, Asheville
### • (828) 253-8304

The Thomas Wolfe Memorial Welcome Center and downtown Asheville host two days of events on the first weekend of October saluting Asheville's most famous writer. Included are readings, discussions, walking tours, a birthday party, music and theater events. Most events are free.

## Fall Quilt Show
### National Guard Armory, Hendersonville
### • (828) 891-5027

In mid-October, cozy covers transformed into works of art are on display at the National Guard Armory. The brilliant colors rival Mother Nature's fall display! Admission is $3.

## Farm City Day
### Jackson Park, Hendersonville
### • (828) 697-4884

The free, day-long event, held in Jackson Park, includes tractor pulls, plus sheep herding and shearing demonstrations. Here you'll find antique and modern farm equipment, square dancing, clogging, arts and crafts and food booths. The festivities end with a Civil War reenactment. A special children's section features activities such as a greased pig contest.

## Annual Any and All Dog Show
### Harmon Field, Tryon
### • (828) 859-6109, (800) 4-EVENT-1

Calling all dogs! Bring your people and join in the fun the second weekend in October at 1:30 PM. Categories include master and dog look-a-like, most unusual tail, best trick and more.

## Transylvania Art Guild Annual Fall Show and Sale
### Courthouse Lawn, Brevard
### • (828) 884-4366

Original art in all media including woodcarving and batik is for sale on the courthouse lawn on the second weekend in October.

## Pioneer Day at the Deaver House
### Deaver House, U.S. Hwy.
### 280, Brevard • (828) 884-5137

The Blue Ridge Mountains' oldest frame house, on U.S. Hwy. 280, is open for tours, food and entertainment. Admission is $6 for adults and $3 for children and includes dinner, served between 11:30 AM and 2 PM. Funds raised are used to preserve and restore the house.

## Annual Forest Festival Day
### Cradle of Forestry, Pisgah National Forest
### • (828) 877-3130

The Cradle of Forestry, a National Historic Site, celebrates our past and future forest resources with old-time demonstrations such as carding, spinning, natural dyeing, weaving, whittling, basket making, cross-cut sawing, fence-rail splitting and trail building. This popular event takes place the first week in

October. Admission is $4 for adults; $2 for students. Over 50 craftsmen, exhibitors and entertainers take part.

## Halloween Fest in Transylvania County
Various locations, Brevard
• (828) 883-3700, 884-3276

What better place for a fun and scary Halloween than in Transylvania. From 10 AM until 6 PM, there are food vendors, crafters, a musical competition, a bicycle rodeo and a mask-making workshop. In the afternoon, participants can sacrifice their blood, not to a vampire, but to the Bloodmobile, join or watch a costume parade, trick or treat in the downtown area, compete in a pumpkin-carving contest, enjoy a kids' carnival and much more.

## Southeastern Animal Fiber Fair
WNC Agricultural Center, Airport Rd., Fletcher • (828) 891-2810

The end of October brings a fair that features hundreds of fiber animals, including llamas, Angora goats, rabbits and many breeds of sheep. Demonstrations teach how to harvest and use such fiber "crops."

# Southern Mountains

## Annual Andrews Antique Car Show
Andrews • (828) 321-4411

For nearly two decades, 100 to 200 cars and trucks from as far away as Knoxville, Chattanooga and Atlanta are put on display at this huge show held the first Saturday of the month. The entry fee for vehicles is $15; spectators get in free. It's a lively event with all-day '50s music, car-related booths and lots of food. In years past, entries have included the world's fastest '57 Chevy.

## J.C. Campbell Fall Festival
1 School House Rd., Brasstown
• (828) 837-2775, (800) FOLK SCH

This is a two-day fair of food, crafts, children's activities, music, dance and good company, held the first weekend of the month.

## Church Street Art and Craft Show
Main St., Waynesville
• (828) 456-3021, (800) 334-9036

On the second Saturday of the month, Main Street is transformed into an arts and crafts marketplace that showcases the region's finest artisans. There are food booths and traditional mountain music. Only original works of art are accepted in this juried show.

## Maroon Devil Classic Band Contest
Lakeview Dr., Graham County High School, Bryson City • (828) 488-2152

On the third Saturday of the month, country and western bands from North Carolina, Tennessee and Georgia converge on this town, along with appreciative crowds.

## Bryson City Chili Cookoff
Everett St., Railroad Sta., Bryson City
• (828) 488-3681

Teams of chili cookers compete for trophies accompanied by live music on the last Saturday of the month. For $4 you get to sample everyone's chili.

## Pumpkin Fest
Various locations, Franklin
• (828) 524-3161, (800) 336-3704

On the last Saturday of the month, school children show off their decorated pumpkins and gourds during this town-wide celebration that also features costume contests, crafts and food vendors.

## INSIDERS' TIP

Before or after an event at Asheville's Civic Center or Thomas Wolfe Auditorium, we like to stop by the Gold Hill Espresso and Fine Teas at 64 Haywood Street, just across the way. The owners are Seattle transplants and have brought Seattle coffeeshop chic with them. The walls display fine art and the rack of magazines may just make you miss your show if you're not careful.

# November

## Northern Mountains

### Old Fashioned Christmas
**Various locations, Blowing Rock**
• (828) 295-7851

The town of Blowing Rock launches a series of seasonal festivities that continue through the end of December. It begins after Thanksgiving and includes a Christmas parade, "Christmas in the Park" with caroling in the town's Memorial Park, Christmas decorations throughout the town and various day and evening activities in conjunction with the season. Call the Blowing Rock Chamber of Commerce (number above) for a complete listing of Yuletide activities.

## Central Mountains

### Christmas Parade
**Various downtown locations, Asheville**
• (828) 251-4100

This is a vibrant, rousing, rollicking beginning to the fun of the Christmas season. Always held the Wednesday before Thanksgiving, Asheville's Christmas parade is alive with colorful floats, whirling Shriners, energetic marching bands, high-stepping steeds, tiny twirlers, raucous clowns and ol' St. Nick himself showering the throngs with candy canes and peppermints. This parade is always well-attended by young and old and swells downtown to bursting. Get there early to stake out your spot.

### Christmas at Biltmore Estate
**1 Approach Rd., Asheville**
• (828) 274-6333, (800) 289-1895

This magnificent re-creation of a Victorian Christmas of a century ago begins just before Thanksgiving and continues through December. Daytime visits to George Vanderbilt's mansion are wonderful, but make a point to include on your agenda this nighttime delight — the Biltmore House bathed in the glow of candlelight and blazing hearth fires. It's exquisite, but it's by reservation only, so book early. The cost is admission to the estate: $27.95 for adults and $21 for children ages 10 to 15.

### A Grove Park Inn Christmas
**290 Macon Ave., Grove Park Inn, Asheville**
• (828) 252-2711, (800) 438-5800

Here is a special place to fill your family with the Christmas spirit. In addition to beautifully decorated trees, there are gingerbread houses made by area artists, storytelling, caroling and craft demonstrations. The famed Grove Park Inn Staff Chorus performs daily in the Great Hall, with special appearances by the inn's ambassador, Major Bear. Holiday activities continue from late November through New Year's Day.

### Home for the Holidays
**Various locations, Hendersonville and Flat Rock**
• (828) 693-9708, (800) 828-4244

Concerts, exhibits, tours and special holiday events are scheduled beginning the day after Thanksgiving through Christmas. It starts with the mayoral downtown holiday lighting ceremony and includes tours of historic bed-and-breakfast establishments, Christmas carols, open house at the Curb Market, the Kris Kringle Kids Karnival and much more.

## Southern Mountains

### J.C. Campbell Annual Blacksmith Auction
**1 School House Rd., Brasstown**
• (828) 837-2775, (800) FOLK SCH

Taking place on the second Saturday of the month, this auction offers pieces by some the nation's greatest masters. Proceeds help keep the craft school's smithy one of the best.

### Annual Hard-Candy Arts and Crafts Show
**Macon County Community Building, Franklin** • (828) 524-9801, (800) 336-7829

In the old days, when times were hard, kids might receive only a few hard candies and perhaps a handmade gift for the holidays. This became known as a Hard-Candy Christmas. You get a free stick of peppermint at this popular show held just after Thanksgiving. The exhibitors are first-class: There are apple crafts, a children's section full of dolls and doll houses, a host of angels and other crafts reflecting the holiday spirit. Bring your Christmas list!

# December

## Northern Mountains

### Choose and Cut Weekend
**Sparta/Alleghany County**
**• (800) 372-5473**
**Ashe County • (336) 246-9550**
**Watauga County • (800) 852-9506**
  The Northern Mountains region is the land of Christmas trees, and fragrant masses of evergreens spread over remote hillsides begin to bustle with activity as Christmas nears. Choose and Cut Weekend provides the ideal opportunity to select the family Christmas tree. All locations offer tree-cutting festivities, including caroling and cider and cookie sampling in early December. After you tie the fir to the car roof, go have a mug of hot chocolate and join in the holiday events and festival fun. Christmas card memories!

### Boone Christmas Parade
**Downtown Boone**
**• (828) 264-2225, (800) 852-9506**
  The first Saturday in December is set aside to herald the holiday season in this picturesque college town. Choose a Fraser fir from the mountains and watch the magic of the holiday season begin at this old-fashioned parade.

### North Pole at Beech
**Various locations, Beech Mountain**
**• (828) 387-9283, (800) 468-5506**
  A lively old-fashioned holiday celebration starts at Fred's General Mercantile in this cozy ski village. You can ride on a caroling hayride and bring the little ones to see Santa in a real horse-drawn carriage. Christmas snow in the

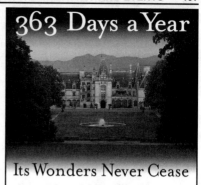

Northern Mountains comes more often than not.

## Santa and More
**Chimney Rock Park, Chimney Rock**
**• (828) 625-9611, (800) 277-9611**

Enjoy winter scenes of Hickory Nut Gorge, sounds of the season and visits with Santa throughout the month of December.

# Central Mountains

## Black Mountain Christmas Parade and Community Candle Lighting
**Downtown, Black Mountain**
**• (828) 669-2300, (800) 669-2301**

The unique village of Black Mountain just east of Asheville is the setting for a traditional parade down a picturesque Main Street to Lake Tomahawk, just a few blocks north of downtown. The event begins in late afternoon the first Saturday in December and is capped by the lighting of candles and carol singing around the rim of luminaria-lit Lake Tomahawk (where Santa has been known to make an appearance).

## Christmas With the Guild
**Folk Art Center, Blue Ridge Pkwy.,**
**Asheville • (828) 298-7928**

The Southern Highland Handicraft Guild displays Christmas decorations and holiday craft exhibits at the grand showcase venue of the Folk Art Center at the Blue Ridge Parkway entrance just east of the city. Free holiday concerts are featured on weekends throughout December.

## Kwanzaa
**39 S. Market St., YMI Cultural Center,**
**Asheville • (828) 252-4614**

The historic YMI Cultural Center (corner of Market and Eagle streets) in downtown Asheville is the setting for this African-American celebration of the holiday season. Kwanzaa is a Swahili word meaning "first" and signifies the first fruits of the harvest — a time when people come together to celebrate and give thanks for their good fortune. In 1966 these basic principles were adopted in America to create this celebration that includes lighting of the ceremonial Kinara candelabrum, traditional music, readings and a bounty of ethnic foods. The celebration takes place from December 26 to January 1.

## First Night Asheville
**Various downtown locations, Asheville**
**• (828) 259-5800**

Take to the streets and bring in the new year Asheville-style. First Night Asheville is an alcohol-free, community cultural arts celebration that is oriented toward families. Festivals are held throughout the town and are sure to please all ages. Music, entertainers, food and brilliant fireworks displays welcome the new year. Many galleries stay open late for a nighttime stroll, and if you are craving bubbly to toast at midnight, numerous taverns, cafes and restaurants in the downtown area are practically flowing with rivers of the liquid gold.

## Festival of Lights
**Jackson Park, Hendersonville**
**• (828) 697-4884**

Held on Friday and Saturday nights, from 5:30 until 9:30 PM on the second weekend of the month, includes the lighting of the Hospice Tree, Santa, hayrides and refreshments. On Saturday evening, 2,000 luminaries light up the park.

## Christmas at Connemara
**1928 Little River Rd., Connemara, Flat Rock • (828) 693-4178**

Follow the luminaria-lined path up the hill-

---

**INSIDERS' TIP**

**Even though many of the festivals throughout the region are free of charge, take a little extra cash with you. These events bring out some of the best and most original crafters in the region, and you're sure to spot some "must have" objects — not to mention the often tempting food usually available at such affairs.**

side to the Carl Sandburg Home and savor a simple time of Christmas past just as the Sandburg family celebrated it. The one-day event, usually held the third week in December, costs $3 for adults. Children younger than 16 are admitted free.

## Christmas Parade and Kris Kringle Karnival
### Downtown, Hendersonville
• (828) 692-1413, (800) 828-4244

In early December, after a traditional Christmas parade down Main Street, enjoy the Kris Kringle Karnival, which features Santa Claus, crafts, carnival games, entertainment and food.

## Twilight Tour and Dickens on Main
### Various locations, Brevard
• (828) 884-3278

During this evening event the first Saturday in December, horse-drawn carriages transport revelers through the twinkling lights and luminaria-lit streets of downtown past carolers, musicians and food vendors. Most stores are open and serve free hot cider and cookies. This event, regardless of the weather, is extremely popular with local residents.

## Festival of Trees
### E. Main St., Silvermont Mansion, Brevard
• (828) 883-3692

You can buy or just enjoy looking at the exquisitely decorated trees, Christmas cakes, candies, cookies and gifts prepared for this four-day event in early December that benefits The Children's Center. A raffle is also held. The admission fee is $3.

# Southern Mountains

## J.C. Campbell Fireside Sale
### 1 Folk School Rd., Brasstown
• (828) 837-2775, (800) FOLK SCH

This craft-sale extravaganza on the first Sunday in December is just one of many community events happening around the hearth and the big Christmas tree at the John C. Campbell Folk School.

## Luminaria in Dillsboro
### Various locations, Dillsboro
• (828) 586-3943

The first two weekends in December, all shops hold open houses with thousands of luminaria lighting up the streets and Christmas caroling filling the night. Complimentary refreshments are served.

## Holiday Tour of Historic Homes
### Various locations, Maggie Valley
• (828) 926-1686, (800) 334-9036

This is a feast for the senses in old-fashioned homes decked out in their Christmas best. It takes place the first week in December and is free of charge.

## Christmas at the Lake
### Lambuth Inn, Lake Junaluska
• (828) 452-2881, (800) 222-4930

From December 1 to Christmas Eve, enjoy this three-week celebration that includes self-guided tours of the Lambuth Inn's beautiful Christmas trees, gingerbread houses and nativity scenes.

These mountains are filled with a wealth of talent and creativity that turns and turns, reshaping the perception and expression of the beauty of our mountain home.

# Arts and Culture

A lone tobacco barn with a red tin roof perches on a bald hillside. Horses whip their tails lazily about in a wildflower-dappled meadow. Mountain ridges mist over blue in the evening, while the sun's setting rays cast splashes of angry pinks, oranges and golds across the puff-clouded skies. A town square comes alive with warm lights, as the silhouettes of dining patrons bob in silent conversations through picture windows.

No doubt, these scenes of life in the mountains, not to mention the powerful stimulus of the primordial visions of nature surrounding us, unleash a certain creativity within. The pure beauty of the natural canvas inspires. And the provocative mix of people who reside within these mountains enlivens the arts and creates refreshing debate.

The visual arts spring to life here in the pottery, glass, jewelry, fiber and wood that are so keenly attuned to the highland heritage. Artists' studios can be found in every hollow and each back road, side street and suburban neighborhood in Western North Carolina. Professional painters and sculptors have infused new energy into the contemporary art scene in the mountains. Community art leagues and artists' guilds nurture the growth of emerging artists in nearly every county and town. Even the proliferation of coffee shops and poetry slams and the changing face of this Southern region can be attributed to this new population focused on creative endeavor.

Theater arts are threaded through the fabric of our everyday life, giving breath to the personal dramas that drive us all and illuminating the joy of being human. In the moun-

tains, we find our humanity represented by scores of creative sources: neighborhood little theater, public school productions, university theater departments, readers' theater, experimental groups, semiprofessional little theater companies and Actor's Equity players.

Music, too, echoes a mountain heritage, derived in part from the historically isolated life of our early settlers. These mountaineers culled their music from the soul of the hills and from the melodies carried on the wind. Born of the first front-porch sing-alongs, with "banjo pickin' and guitar playin'" at sundown, and the bittersweet ballads rising out of the mountain coves, the musical legacy found in North Carolina's mountains continues to thrive. More interesting is that it flourishes alongside the strains of a classical symphony, delicate chamber music, inspirational choral music, fervent black gospel, lively barbershop harmony, jazz, swing, and contemporary folk music.

Dance is so effortless here in the mountains. We have a thousand images of inspiration right outside our doors: trees swaying in the wind, leaves whirling across the hill, water tumbling over a rocky creek bed. The mountains have numerous groups for ballet, contemporary dance theater, traditional mountain clogging and buck dance, international folk dance and Old World contra dance, and even country-and-western line dancing.

Museums document the history of these mountains. Some are more academic museums devoted to departmental disciplines and regional displays of traditional mountain life, while others are restored farmhouses, grand old homes and vast estates that stand as tributes to the virtues and careers of pioneering citizens. Best of all, these museums are not of the stodgy, cement-building stock. These home museums transport you into the past with the scent of aged wood, slightly musty attics and wildflower-filled surroundings. They welcome you to step onto the back porch and drink in the deep valley views just as the mountain settlers of yore did.

This chapter gives you a glimpse into the melting pot of artistic interests that mirrors the quality of life here — and helps define it. The abundance of arts and crafts in this region and their many similarities often make it hard to characterize what is an "art" and what is a "craft." Here, we have tried to differentiate between arts and craft galleries or artisans' studios; the latter are described in the Mountain Crafts chapter. Consult both chapters closely, as you may well find part of what you are looking for in both.

Some of the following organizations are operated out of private homes. If that is the case, we don't furnish the address. Do call the number that's provided to get more information.

# Organizations

## Northern Mountains

### Alleghany County

**Alleghany County Arts Council**
**Grayson and Cherry Sts., Sparta**
**• (336) 372-2578**
The Alleghany County Arts Council, housed in a charming historic house in Crouse Park in downtown Sparta, is a young organization that sponsors local artists in yearly exhibits held in the local public library. The council also puts on the annual Blue Ridge Mountain Craft Fair the last Saturday in June at the Justin Higgins Agricultural Center and Fairgrounds on U.S. Highway 21 in Sparta. See our Annual Events chapter for information about county fairs.

## Ashe County

**Ashe County Arts Council**
**W. Sixth St., off E. Main St., West Jefferson**
**• (336) 246-2787**
This organization is headquartered in a lovely old stone building known as the Ashe Arts Center. This structure, constructed as a community center during the Great Depression, was a Works Progress Administration project. The Ashe County Arts Council is an active organization that sponsors 32 in-school arts programs, numerous arts residencies in the school system and eight community concerts. The group also sponsors continuously changing exhibits of the work of local artists in its Ashe Arts Center gallery.

## Avery County

**Avery County Arts Council**
**Newland Town Sq., Old**
**Social Services Bldg., Newland**
**• (828) 733-0065**
The Arts Council of Avery County coordinates myriad cultural activities for county residents. The group sponsors numerous arts festivals during the year, such as a Christmas Craft Show and the Very Special Arts Festival in the spring.

## Watauga County

**Watauga County Arts Council**
**124 E. King St., Boone • (828) 264-1789**
This county arts council is housed in the Jones Community Center in downtown Boone, a building that's also home to two art exhibition galleries. The council is a vital part of the community, sponsoring a number of events during the year and promoting education in the arts with fund-raising for the support of art scholarships.

## Yancey County

**Toe River Arts Council**
**Town Sq., Burnsville • (828) 682-7215**
This incredibly busy arts council serves

two counties (Yancey and neighboring Mitchell) with an inordinate number of artists and craftspeople — in part due to the presence of the revered Penland School of Crafts in Mitchell County (see our Mountain Crafts chapter).

Services provided by the Toe River Arts Council include a winter arts program and a symphony program. After-school art classes are available to school children. The group also sponsors art and music festivals each summer, along with summer art workshops. The group has developed a map outlining the location of the numerous studios of Yancey County artists and craftspeople and a free directory listing all the cultural offerings in the two-county area served by the council.

# Central Mountains

## Buncombe County

### Arts Alliance
**11 Biltmore Ave., Asheville**
**• (828) 258-0710**

This nonprofit organization has been dedicated to the support and perpetuation of the cultural arts in the Asheville/Buncombe County area for more than 40 years. The group provides technical support, management assistance and allocation of grants and other funding to emerging artists and area cultural activities and organizations. The Arts Alliance works closely with the community in an effort to identify these needs. Regular exhibitions are displayed in the gallery space.

### Asheville Art League
**Asheville • (828) 255-7577**

This community art league serves amateur artists in the Asheville area, providing support and opportunities to showcase individual work through yearly exhibits.

### HandMade in America
**67 N. Market St., Asheville**
**• (828) 252-0121**

This evolving community organization is hard at work to make Western North Carolina a nationally recognized center for the fine handcrafts indigenous to our area. (See the

related Close-up in this chapter for more information.)

## Henderson County

### Camera Club of Hendersonville
**Hendersonville • (828) 891-1803**

For over 25 years, this club has brought together photographers who enjoy sharing and learning from one another. The inexperienced can learn from the experienced, and the latter can compare ideas, techniques, equipment, materials and results. The club meets the fourth Tuesday of each month at the Opportunity House (see the subsequent listing in the Visual Arts section) for talks and demonstrations by professional photographers and members. Classes, workshops and field trips are also offered, along with a quarterly club competition night with each photograph judged on its own merits by outside judges. Special events have included exhibitions of members' prints at the Four Seasons Arts Council Gallery on Main Street and showings at the Hendersonville Library.

### Four Seasons Arts Council (FSAC)
**538 N. Main St., Hendersonville**
**• (828) 693-8504**

FSAC, a super-active organization, sponsors special art events throughout the year, including the spring Jubilee Arts Festival and a performance of Folkmoot, the International Dance Festival. In cooperation with the North Carolina Museum of Art, the council promotes art education through its Art Appreciation School Slide Program in Henderson County schools. It's also responsible for the Mountain Arts Program, the Regional Arts Project Grant Program and the distribution of public and grant monies for the arts in the county. Individual memberships are $30 a year ($20 for teachers) and $50 for families.

### The Henderson County Art League
**1411 Asheville Hwy., Hendersonville**
**• (828) 692-0575**

The Art League was established in 1958 and is a tax-exempt, not-for-profit corporation. Its purpose is the promotion, development and the enjoyment of the visual arts.

Currently, over 250 members represent all levels of artistic achievement from professional to beginners. The League meets at the Opportunity House at the above address on the third Wednesday of each month at 1:45 PM. Each month, it offers a new exhibit of its members' work and a demonstration of techniques or methods by qualified artists. On the first Sunday of each month, the League holds a reception and exhibit for a guest artist. All of these events are open to the public. Nineteen-ninety-nine marks the 40th annual Sidewalk Art Show held on Main Street in downtown Hendersonville. This two-day event features over 100 artists from many locations. In 1998 the exhibiting artists reported over $80,000 in sales. During the summer, many members gather at interesting local sites for outdoor paint-outs. The League also has a program called Artists to Artists that benefits art students in the local high schools. An All Member juried show with cash prizes in held is November. For additional information call the above number Monday thorough Friday.

## Western North Carolina Quilters Guild
**P.O. Box 3121, Hendersonville, NC, 28739 • No phone**

This guild was founded in 1982 to promote the art of quilting and provide an opportunity for area quilters to get together — a modern-day version of the old "quilting bee." Meetings are held on the third Thursday of each month at the First Congregational Church, 1735 Fifth Avenue W. at White Pine Drive. The guild features lectures, workshops and quilt shows. An extensive lending library filled with current books, patterns, magazines and videos are available to all members, who also receive an informative newsletter called *Grainlines*. Dues are $15 a year.

# Polk County

## Carolina Camera Club
**208 Melrose Ave., Tryon Fine Arts Center, Tryon • (828) 894-3640**

Photography buffs in this group get to share their mutual interests and improve their skills at monthly meetings and through other programs. The club is affiliated with the Pho-

tographic Society of America and is one of more than 30 camera clubs in six states that form the Southeastern Council of Camera Clubs. A monthly newsletter is available, and there is an annual contest for members' photographs. Award-winning images are exhibited in the Tryon Fine Arts Center lobby in January and February. Anyone interested in photography may become a member, and visitors are always welcome.

## Tryon Crafts Inc.
**208 Melrose Ave., Tryon Fine Arts Center, Tryon • (828) 859-8323**

A nonprofit organization, Tryon Crafts sponsors classes that include weaving, silver making, enameling on copper, rug hooking, crewel and needlepoint, macramé, wood carving, knitting, chair caning, stained glass, lampshade making and oshibana. New classes are opened if enough interested students and qualified teachers are found. Tryon Crafts also has a weaving cottage on Tryon Fine Arts Center property called the Cate-Hall Weaving Center. Member shows are held each year at Christmas and in spring, and a newly remodeled shop is open next to the Tryon Crafts office on the lower level of the TFAC building. The organization also sponsors out-of-town trips to various craft centers, such as Penland School in Penland and the John C. Campbell Folk School in Brasstown.

## The Tryon Fine Arts Center
**208 Melrose Ave., Tryon • (828) 859-8322**

This is an amazing arts center for a town the size of Tryon, and it's 100 percent privately funded. Built in 1969, the center contains a 345-seat theater with a hearing-impaired system, an exhibition room called Gallery I, a Mural Room for meetings and receptions, art studios, a crafts room for classes and an outdoor garden. In addition to all the activities of its affiliates — the Tryon Concert Association, Tryon Crafts, Tryon Little Theater, Tryon Painters and Sculptors, Foothills Savoyard, Tryon Youth Center and Carolina Camera Club (see listings) — TFAC offers musical performances by local and professional artists, recounting of personal travel experiences, benefits, lectures, slide shows, Christmas song fests, summer socials, North

Carolina Shakespeare Festival performances, jazz bands, contemporary subject seminars and more.

## Tryon Youth Center
### N.C. Hwy. 176, Tryon • (828) 859-3192

This organization provides social, artistic, recreational, educational and cultural experiences for the young people of the area. Each year, the center puts on a Youth Center Summer Musical in the Tryon Fine Arts Center auditorium, but most of its activities are centered in a 5,300-square-foot building on N.C. 176 that's also available for rent by other community organizations and individuals.

# Transylvania County

## Brevard Camera Club
### Brevard • (828) 877-4038

This club, affiliated with the Photographic Society of America, meets on the second Tuesday of the month in Brevard's Parks and Recreation building on S. Main Street. Meetings are usually instructional or entertaining. Dues are $8 per year. A similar organization, the Connestee Camera Club, is made up mostly of photographers from the Connestee Falls residential community. They support the Amateur Photo Exhibition by TCarts in July and have an exhibition during May and June at the Connestee Club House. This organization can be contacted at (828) 884-4646.

## The Connestee Art League
### Connestee Falls, Brevard
### • (828) 885-7220

This art group has over 50 members, made up of talented inhabitants of the large residential development of Connestee Falls. They meet at 9:30 AM on Monday mornings at the Art Room in the Connestee Falls Overlook Lounge. Live models and art demonstrations are a part of these gatherings. Dues are $10 a year.

## Paul Porter Center for Performing Arts
### 400 N. Broad St., Brevard • (828) 884-8330

The Paul Porter Center for the Performing Arts at Brevard College has been a dream in the making for the past ten years. In August

1998, that dream became reality with the inaugural season of the Porter Center. An elegant and stately structure, the Center features the Concert Hall with superb acoustics, the Morrison Theater and the Institute for Sacred Music. Events range from orchestral, chamber and folk concerts to theatrical productions, art exhibitions and seminars. The activities are planned to match this distinctive milieu tastefully and to reflect the rich cultural diversity found in Western North Carolina. Tickets and information regarding upcoming events may be obtained by contacting the box office at the above number.

## Transylvania Art Guild
### P.O. Box 655, Brevard, 28712
### • (828) 884-8727

The guild's 65 or so professional and amateur members meet the first Thursday of each month at the Lutheran Church of the Good Shepherd, 808 N. Broad Street, for an art demonstration or lecture. Members of the group conduct classes in various painting media. Paintings by members of the art guild are exhibited in the Chamber of Commerce Gallery, at the Transylvania County Library and at the Transylvania County Arts Co-op, as well as various commercial establishments in Brevard. There are three shows each year — in June, August and October — held on the lawn of the county courthouse. Dues are $20 a year.

## Transylvania County Arts Council
### 7 E. Main St., Brevard • (828) 884-2787

"TCarts" is now headquartered at 321 S. Caldwell Street in Brevard. In 1998 the Arts Council purchased an old church and renovated it completely. This new Community Arts Center houses the Arts Council, an exhibition/performance hall (where exhibits change monthly) and an educational wing where classes are held throughout the year.

Operating as a program of the Arts Council, #7 Arts, an Artists Cooperative, now occupies the Council's former location at 7 East Main Street in downtown Brevard. This gallery offers shoppers a chance to view and purchase fine arts and crafts at reasonable prices.

In its effort to provide inspiration and sup-

Photo: Judy Scharns, Courtesy of Boone Convention and Visitors Bureau

The Watauga Arts Council is housed in the Jones Community Center in downtown Boone.

port to local artists, art groups and school children, TCarts oversees 30 art programs and services, including Grassroots Arts and Regional Artist Project grant programs. The Arts in the Schools and Take Art to Heart programs foster creativity by giving students the best possible experience through in-school performances, artists in residence and monthly visits from volunteers who use the visual arts to teach critical thinking skills to students.

TCarts also joins Brevard College in presenting the Performing Arts Series for the community.

The Council holds two gala fund-raising events each year, one in the fall and one in the spring. The annual Holiday Tour of Homes and Studios is held the second Saturday in December.

For 26 years, this organization has sponsored a summer Festival of the Arts, a weeklong celebration of the visual and performing arts, usually held the second week in July. TCarts also sponsors a juried show of regional artists from six Western North Carolina counties at the Transylvania Fine Arts and Crafts Exhibition, held at Brevard College's Spiers Gallery in July.

## Transylvania County Handcrafters Guild
**P.O. Box 7, Brevard, NC 28712**
• **No phone**

This friendly, active group of some 90 members welcomes newcomers with open arms. Meetings are held the second Tuesday of the month at 7 PM in the social hall of the Sacred Heart Catholic Church (4 Fortune Cove) in Brevard. A business meeting is followed by brief craft demonstrations. The guild also has shows in the summer and fall as well as a couple of Christmas shows, but you don't have to show to be a member. Nearly every type of craft is represented, including weaving, stained glass, basketry, batik, fabric painting and woodworking. Dues are $10 a year.

There are other guilds in the Brevard area, including the French Broad Weavers, the Western North Carolina Quilters Guild (see previous listing), the Mini-Quilters and the Laurel Chapter of the Embroiders Guild. For more information on these organizations, call the Transylvania County Arts Council, (828) 884-2787.

# Southern Mountains

## Haywood County

### Haywood County Arts Council
**114 Church St., Waynesville**
**• (828) 452-0593**

HCAC, in cooperation with the Friends of the Library, sponsors free concerts the fourth Sunday of each month at the Waynesville Library. These can include chamber music, bluegrass or jazz. Since 1995, it also has sponsored a series of five concerts called the Swannanoa Chamber Festival Concert Season.

Another group HCAC supports is Spotlight, a children's theater that stages monthly or bimonthly plays at Haywood Community College's new auditorium. Past plays have included *The Glass Slipper* and *The Beauty of the Dreaming Wood*. In addition to producing Razzle Dazzle, an annual street festival for children in April, HCAC sponsors an International Festival— a day of dance, music, food and a juried crafts show — each July in association with Folkmoot, the International Dance Festival. HCAC also is involved in Haywood's own production of *The Nutcracker* and the annual Holiday Tour of Homes.

The council brings the Atlanta Ballet to Waynesville for its two-week annual residency in late summer — one of the most popular arts events of the year. In addition to open rehearsals, the ballet holds workshops for area youth. One year, they worked with local football players; another time, they entertained 8th graders from across the county and the Cherokee Indian Reservation. The ballet group also offers at least two performances at the Haywood Community College auditorium.

The council also sponsors the Autumn Showcase of fine handcrafts of Haywood

County and the Smoky Mountain Folk Festival held each Labor Day at Lake Junaluska, where more than 250 performers play old-time music on the stage of the Stuart Auditorium and on the Auditorium's grounds.

## Jackson County

### Jackson County Arts Council
**Sylva • (828) 293-5458**

Whether its dance, literature, drama or the visual arts, this council lends its support to dozens of activities and performances each year, including lectures, concerts and exhibitions. Here are some examples that demonstrate the types of cultural events to enjoy in the county.

•For students: The council sponsors summer art classes for children, a storyteller program in the schools and two Jackson County Youth Solo Scholarships. It also brings many performers to the schools, including the North Carolina Symphony, theatrical groups and puppet shows.

•Music: The council sponsors the Valley Chamber Festival, the Western Carolina University Jazz Festival, the North Carolina Percussion Society Convention and two performances each by the Western North Carolina Community Chorus and the Western North Carolina Civic Orchestra.

•Art: The council sponsors the Jackson County Visual Art Association, Dillsboro Sidewalk Art Show, North Carolina Teachers-Only Art Show and the Best in Jackson County Art Show.

The council, which puts out a quarterly newsletter, is also responsible for distributing Grassroots grants and other monies.

### Jackson County Visual Arts Association
**Main St., Sylva • (828) 293-3407**

The approximately 60 member-artists of this group meet monthly and sponsor monthly exhibits (featuring mostly local artists) at Gallery One in Sylva. The association provides art classes for adults and especially for youth and children. A special Membership Show is held each November, and the association sponsors Art from the Jackson County Schools and Art in the Park shows. It also participates in other local and regional shows and events, such as Mountain Heritage Day at Cullowhee in September. The group takes several field trips each year to such places as the Campbell Folk School, Bob Jones University and the Greenville Art Museum.

The gallery, run entirely by volunteers, is closed in the winter except during special events, but from May through October, it's open on a regular schedule.

## Western Carolina University
**N.C. Hwy. 107, Cullowhee**
**• (828) 227-7211**

Western Carolina University provides a year-round showcase for artistic performances featuring WCU students and faculty and entertainers of national renown.

Its 8,000-seat Liston B. Ramsey Regional Activity Center regularly stages national-caliber sports and entertainment events. The university's Lectures, Concerts and Exhibitions Series brings music, dance and theatrical productions to campus each year, and the department of communications and theatre arts stages its own high-quality plays. Western's galleries regularly play host to art exhibitions.

Last Minute Productions, WCU's student-run programming organization, maintains a regular schedule of events that brings music groups, comedians and other acts to campus. The talents of Western's student body and faculty are highlighted in recitals held throughout the year, and the artist-in-residence programs of the art and music departments bring nationally recognized artists to WCU to share their expertise in classroom lectures and their talents through concert and exhibitions. The English department's Visiting Writers Series bring new voices and legendary names to WCU to share the written word with the WCU community and visitors.

Western's Mountain Heritage Center, located on the ground floor of the H.F. Robinson Administration Building, depicts the natural and cultural heritage of the southern Appalachian region through exhibitions, publications, educational programs and demonstrations. Mountain Heritage Day, WCU's annual celebration of the mountain spirit, draws more than 30,000 visitors to the campus on the last Saturday each September.

# Macon County

## Arts Council of Macon County
3½ E. Main St., Franklin • (828) 524-7683

Macon County's Arts Council, which is dedicated to getting people actively involved in the arts, describes itself as "extremely volunteer driven." Here, you'll find ongoing, year-round programs and performances, including concerts, lectures and other presentations. Regular monthly programs are given, and they often concentrate on a particular subject. A recent program, for example, included a slide show on women's art. During the summer, there might be two or three such presentations a month.

Two performances of Folkmoot, the International Dance Festival, are also under the council's auspices. In addition, it sponsors one-day craft classes and has an extension program that brings art into the schools.

## The Arts League of Highlands
Highlands • (828) 526-4949

The Arts League of Highlands, founded in 1980, is a non-profit association of artists and supporters of visual arts and serves the Western Carolina/North Georgia mountain areas. The league, with over 100 members, sponsors several shows a year, supports and helps publicize visual arts in the area and takes field trips to galleries, art shows and other places of interest. Monthly meetings are held on the last Monday of the month at the Bascom-Louise Gallery in Highlands from May through September. Off-season, members host informal luncheon meetings. For further information, please write to The Art league of Highlands, P. O. Box 2133, Highlands, NC 28741 or call the above number.

## Macon County Art Association
30 E. Main St., Franklin • (828) 349-6708

One of the oldest art associations in Franklin (1962) continues to grow and flourish. Members are artists of oil, pastel, watercolor, acrylics, mixed media and sculpture. These members run the Uptown Gallery for displaying and selling their artwork. Many of these originals depict the surrounding Appalachian Mountains, in addition to genres of all subjects.

Membership is by board approval and dues are $25. The association emphasizes participation in activities enhancing and encouraging a better understanding of the inclusion of the fine arts in society. This also includes support for the Macon County Art Association scholarship fund for students attending Western Carolina University. Through help from the Arts Council in Franklin, programs for children such as summer camps in art are encouraged.

Monthly meetings are held on the second Monday at the gallery with programs for members and the general public. Workshops in all media are scheduled during the year for all who wish to attend. Summer outdoor shows are on the first Saturdays of July, August and September at Our Lady of the Mountains Catholic Church in Highlands. Hours are from 10 AM to 4 PM.

The Uptown Gallery is open all year. Summer hours are 10 AM to 4 PM, Monday through Saturday. Winter hours are from 11 AM to 3 PM, Wednesday through Friday.

## Swain County

### Swain County Cultural Arts Council
Bryson City • (828) 488-9626

Because only a small group of people makes up this council, it concentrates its efforts as a funds and grants distributing agency for supporting existing groups, instead of sponsoring any special events itself. One exception is its co-sponsorship of some of the town's festivals, and it works with the local recreation department on a number of activities. One of the council's main areas of support is a countywide program that brings special teachers of arts, crafts and music into the schools.

# Visual Arts

## Northern Mountains

### Ashe County

#### Ashe County Studio Hop
Various locations, Ashe County
• (336) 246-2787

Rural Ashe County is full of wonderful artists working in all media, from pottery to glass, woodworking and painting. The easiest, and certainly one of the most enjoyable, ways to experience the artistry of this area is to participate in the Ashe County Studio Hop. This event is held during one weekend in early fall every year. Contact Jane Lonon at the above number for more information.

#### Silver Designs by Lou E and Art Gallery
Off N.C. Hwy. 16, Glendale Springs
• (336) 982-4102

Just a few steps down from Holy Trinity Church (one of the "Churches of the Frescoes;" see our Close-up in this chapter) lies this interesting little gallery/shop. Silversmith Lou Eremita, a member of the Southern Highland Handicraft Guild, made his way to the mountains about 18 years ago from New York City. Finding the solitude of rural Ashe County to his liking, he has been inspired to create wonderful hand wrought silver jewelry of all descriptions. You can watch him work in this open studio and also take in the interesting gallery of stained glass, crafts and paintings

## INSIDERS' TIP

When visiting Saluda Mountain Crafts in Saluda, take the time to visit the old-fashioned ice-cream parlor right next door. Fudge Mountain Ice-cream makes its own ice-cream and fudge and serves it up in an authentic atmosphere created with antique items from past ice-cream parlors, old RKO movie theater marquees and cabinets made from the lockers of the Virginia Senate Building.

(primarily watercolors) by Ashe County artists on display.

## Avery County

### The Art Cellar
**N.C. Hwy. 184, Banner Elk**
**• (828) 898-5175**

Along with a wonderful selection of fine art representing the work of local artists, The Art Cellar in Banner Elk features animation art and the latest wrinkle in the art world — "outsider art." It's folk art created by those outside the art world's mainstream.

### James P. Kerr, Gallery & Studio
**N.C. Hwy. 184, next to Louisiana Purchase, Banner Elk • (828) 898-8696**

The owner of this gallery is a master of painting the landscapes and seascapes of the American continent and the islands of the Caribbean. His paintings of the entertainment world of New Orleans are especially favored by those who collect his works. Kerr's paintings are exhibited in many prominent galleries throughout the country and are in hundreds of private and corporate collections throughout the United States, Canada, Europe and the West Indies. Hours vary, so call for an appointment.

## Madison County

### Brush Creek Mountain Arts and Crafts
**491 U.S. Hwy. 25/70, Marshall**
**• (828) 649-9259**

This gallery, in an old, renovated, red brick gas station on the Marshall Bypass next to Madison County Middle School, features a variety of items. Along with painting, jewelry, pottery and ceramic art, you can find hand-stitched quilts in traditional mountain patterns.

## Mitchell County

### Ken Sedberry Clay Studio
**Mine Creek Rd., off U.S. Hwy. 226, Bakersville • (828) 688-3386**

Trained at the Rhode Island School of Design, Ken Sedberry works in clay, drawing from his artistic intuition and a wealth of experience as an instructor in Helena, Montana, at the Archie Bray Foundation, and the Catholic University in Washington, D.C. Today he fills his studio, near Loafer's Glory, with marvelously imaginative decorative pottery as well as wood-fired, functional tableware, all illuminated with a brilliant palette of color.

### Penland School of Crafts Visitors Center
**Penland Road, off U.S. Hwy. 19 E., Penland • (828) 765-6211**

We discuss this wonderfully unique, historic school in greater detail in our Mountain Crafts chapter, but it bears repeating that this facility and staff play a crucial role in preserving North Carolina's mountain heritage of arts and handcrafts. You can visit the school's gallery, which has a collection of the works of students and former students. Blown glass, handcrafted jewelry, wood sculpture, weaving, watercolors and works in oil are all artfully displayed and available for purchase.

### Twisted Laurel Gallery
**333 Locust St. (Lower St.), Spruce Pine**
**• (828) 765-1562**

This charming gallery represents more than 140 artists in all media from the tri-county area of Mitchell, Yancey and Avery counties. You'll find exquisite hand-blown glass as well as colorful stained-glass work. Wood sculpture of all types, some featuring those fanciful, carved faces of wood sprites, is well-represented. Functional and decorative pottery, fiber art, handmade jewelry, watercolor, oil and acrylic pieces are also available at Twisted Laurel Gallery.

## Watauga County

### Art in the Park
**Town Park, Main St., Blowing Rock**
**• (828) 295-7891**

For 25 years, Art in the Park has been a central focus of the Blowing Rock tourist season. These monthly events are staged from May to November in Blowing Rock's Town Park off Main Street and offer an ongoing festival of arts and crafts, featuring work of artisans from all over the Southeast. You can browse any number of booths exhibiting wood works, sculpture, fine art, handmade silver and gold jewelry, photography and leather crafts.

## Blue Ridge Hearthside Crafts
### N.C. Hwy. 105 S., Foscoe
### • (828) 963-5252

Blue Ridge Hearthside lives up to its name. This gallery features the traditional mountain crafts (baskets, wood sculpture, etc.) of local mountain artisans.

## Bolick Pottery
### Blackberry Rd., off U.S. Hwy. 321, Blowing Rock • (828) 295-3862

You'll want to make the special trip to Bolick Pottery on Blackberry Road, just minutes south of Blowing Rock. Here you'll find a family tradition at work. The Bolick family pottery was begun in 1973 by Lula Owens Bolick and her husband, Glenn. Before locating near Boone, the Bolicks worked with Lula's potter father, M.L. Owens, near Seagrove, North Carolina, a place steeped in the pottery tradition.

These fifth-generation potters continue to fashion traditional pieces, candle holders, mugs, bowls, pitchers and miniature tea sets in the old-time colors of oatmeal, gray and cobalt blue. All pieces produced by the Bolicks are microwave and dishwasher safe.

## Creekside Galleries/Carlton Gallery-Woven Works
### N.C. Hwy. 105, Foscoe • (828) 963-4258

In a rustic building just down the path behind the Green Mansions specialty shops is Creekside Galleries. This building houses Carlton Gallery, The Potter's Gallery and the working studio of potter Tim Turner. An amazing array of fine art, sculpture, pottery, contemporary crafts, woven works and unique jewelry in all media by more than 300 local and regional artists can be found at this fine studio complex.

## Crestwood Galleries
### Corner of Main St. and U.S. Hwy. 221, Blowing Rock • (828) 295-0008

Crestwood Galleries can be summed up in three words: "finest quality" and "unique."

The antiques from around the world are exquisite and include a selection of outstanding bronzes and lamps with wooden shades. Original fine art — oils on canvas and boards — comes from around the world and contributes to the gallery's reputation as well.

## Doe Ridge Pottery
### 149 W. King St., Boone • (828) 264-1127

Doe Ridge is an appealing pottery gallery in downtown Boone. You can find both functional stoneware and decorative works here. Handmade Christmas ornaments are an unusual feature of Doe Ridge. Commissions are also accepted.

## Expressions Craft Guild and Gallery
### Main St., Blowing Rock • (828) 295-7839

This lovely gallery features a variety of glass pieces, prints, photography, stained glass, functional and decorative pottery, woven pieces, leather work and wearable art. Special exhibits are on display each season.

## Hands Gallery
### N.C. Hwy. 105, Foscoe • (828) 963-5338

This gallery has been a part of the Boone arts scene for more than 20 years. A consistently fine selection of wearable fiber art, wood sculpture and imaginative, functional and decorative pottery is featured here.

## Morning Glory Craft Gallery
### 904 W. King St. Boone • (828) 265-4888

Near the courthouse in downtown Boone, Morning Glory Craft Gallery honors excellence in contemporary crafts and fine art. The gallery features an interesting range of work, from batik clothing to Native American art, fantasy pottery and handcrafted jewelry.

## Parkway Craft Center
### Mi. 294, Blue Ridge Pkwy., Blowing Rock • (828) 295-7938

In the splendid Victorian-era home known as Flat Top Manor, this distinctive craft center offers room after room of traditional and contemporary crafts of the finest quality. Since 1951, the center has come alive every May through October with demonstrations and displays by members of the prestigious South-

# Macon County: Jones Knob and Whiterock Mountain

A fairly easy, round-trip hike of about 5.2 miles will reveal some special vistas of the Nantahala Mountains to the west. First, from the corner of Fourth and Main streets in Highlands, take U.S. 64/28 toward Franklin for 4.2 miles. Turn left on Turtle Pond Road (S.R. 1620) and drive for 1.1 miles to S.R. 1678. Turn right and drive 1.4 miles to the top of a hill. Turn left on Jones Gap Road (F.R. 4522) and drive 2 miles to the parking area.

The trail leaves the parking area on the right, goes on an access road and crosses a wildlife management field. At the end of the field, the trail spur marked in blue leads 0.3 miles to Jones Knob and views to the left and down from the flat rock area at the top. The right fork (yellow blazes) is the Bartram Trail. Take it 1.3 miles to Whiterock Gap for views to the west. Continue for almost three-quarters of a mile to the blue-blazed spur trail to the left. This trail ascends less than a half-mile to a spectacular rock outcropping and view. Keep in mind, however, that seasonal closure of the road may occur.

The place where the ancient Cherokee village of Guasili (near Murphy in Cherokee County) probably stood was at what is now known as the Peachtree Mound, because Peachtree Creek joins the Hiwassee River here. Hardly a mound any more, this ceremonial center was flattened by excavations in both 1885 and 1933. More than a quarter-million artifacts were removed from the site and are housed in the Smithsonian and the Valentine Museum in Richmond, Virginia. Peachtree Mound was occupied during the Archaic period (8000 to 1000 B.C.), right up until historic times. Hernando De Soto visited it briefly in 1540. To reach it, drive 5.5 miles out of Murphy on U.S. Highway 64 E. A historical marker provides information on the area.

---

ern Highland Handicraft Guild of works in clay, fiber, wood, fabric, metal and materials native to the mountains. Be sure to save some time to sit on a rocking chair on the expansive front porch and take in one of the most inspiring views in the mountains.

## Tumbleston Studio of Art
### 525 Harrison Rd., Boone • (828) 264-7147

Richard Tumbleston is one of the best-known artists in the High Country of North Carolina. He continues to produce exceptional work and take on new challenges, working in new media. His egg tempera still-life work is luminous. You may visit his personal studio/gallery by appointment.

## Yancey County

## Hayden Gallery
### 7 S. Main St., Burnsville • (828) 682-7998

Just a step down from Town Square is Hayden Gallery. More than 200 area artists are represented here. You can find all types of local art, including pottery, ceramics, paintings, furniture and jewelry. Hours are typically Monday through Saturday, 10 AM to 5 PM, but during the winter it is best to call first.

## The Pot Hole
### 390 Seven Mile Ridge, 7 mi. south of Micaville • (828) 675-5217

The Pot Hole features the functional pottery of Danielle LeHardy. Each handmade stoneware piece is freehand-painted in a range of colorful geometric designs. You can find this tucked away studio/gallery by driving 7 miles south of Micaville, turning left onto Seven Mile Ridge Road and following the signs.

## Toe River Crafts
### U.S. Hwy. 80 S., Burnsville
### • No phone

Six miles south of tiny Micaville, on U.S. Highway 80 S., is Toe River Crafts. This rustic crafts cooperative gallery represents the work of several nationally known Yancey County artists and craftspeople, many with work shown across the country. You will find finely crafted, one-of-a-kind works at Toe River Crafts, from prints to metals, fiber arts, paper, wood works, photography, pottery and watercolor.

# Central Mountains

## Buncombe County

### A Far Away Place
**11 Wall St. and 16 Battery Park Ave., Asheville • (828) 252-1891**

A Far Away Place is an alluring gallery/shop in the old 1920s Flatiron Building in downtown Asheville. The double entrance gives you convenient access to a fascinating display of antique artifacts and modern-day handcrafts of more than 50 native cultures from all over South America, Mexico, the American Southwest and Africa. Owner Mark Fields purchases many of the crafts directly from local villages. Clothing, jewelry, art and musical instruments attract customers from all over the country.

### Art International Asheville
**35 Patton Ave., Asheville • (828) 281-0288**

Art International Asheville has quickly developed as the base for international artists exhibiting in Asheville. The owners, Patrice Tappe and Clayton Wefel, have reconstructed much of Europe's traditional elegance within their gallery. Housed in a renovated 19th century building downtown, the gallery's sweeping expanse plays host to unique figurative sculpture from Germany, bronze sculpture from Greece, acid-etched mirrors from Vienna, Art Deco-inspired art, Art Deco furniture and fixtures, dazzling gouache-on-bamboo paper works from China, oil and mixed media paintings, lithographs and etchings from Poland, Hungary, Russia, and most recently from Cuba.

Art International now exclusively represents 20 distinguished artists whose works are exhibited in museums and private and corporate collections worldwide. Tappe, an internationally acclaimed opera singer, and Wefel bring with them the experience of organizing major international art exhibitions for the United Nations at the Vienna International Centre.

### Asheville Gallery of Art
**16 College St., Asheville • (828) 251-5796**

This downtown gallery represents a fine assortment of leading area artists, such as popular local watercolor artist Ann Vasilik, whose interesting impressionistic interpretations of Asheville are quite striking. The gallery is a co-op of sorts, where the artists run the gallery themselves. A fine variety is represented here, including oils, acrylics, lithographs, etchings, and sculpture.

### Bellagio
**5 Biltmore Pl., Biltmore Village, Asheville • (828) 277-8100**

Gallery entrepreneur John Cram continues his representation of fine art in the Asheville area with Bellagio. This shop in Biltmore Village is a venue for "wearable art." Exquisite handwoven, high-fashion clothing and handcrafted jewelry and accessories fill this wonderful corner gallery/shop.

### Blue Spiral 1
**38 Biltmore Ave., Asheville • (828) 251-0202**

The elegant and airy gallery space of Blue Spiral 1 in downtown Asheville is a masterfully planned multi-level showcase for fine painting and sculpture. Changing exhibits cover the expansive 15,000-square-foot space. A new wing was added in 1997 that includes pull-out display "walls" on wheels for more exhibition space. This is a true state-of-the-art gallery.

The Blue Spiral 1 is also home to the largest collection of paintings by Will Henry Stevens (1881-1949). Stevens was a renowned regionalist and modernist who worked in oils, watercolor, pastels and mixed media.

### Broadway Arts Building
**49 Broadway, Asheville • (828) 258-9206**

The Broadway Arts Building is dedicated

to the visual and performing arts. It houses exhibits of contemporary fine arts and handmade crafts and presentations of avant-garde theater, dance, music and poetry slams. The building dates from the early 1900s and is an award-winning restoration project featuring heart-of-pine flooring and tin-molded ceilings in the main gallery and exposed rock-wall foundation and ceiling joists in the "green door" gallery.

## Gallery of the Mountains
### 290 Macon Ave., The Grove Park Inn, Asheville • (828) 254-2068

Treasure hunting — that's what a visit to this gallery is all about. Here, amidst the grand setting of the historic Grove Park Inn (see our Resorts chapter), you can find a treasure at every turn, including charming handcrafted wearables, jewelry, pottery, Arts & Craft Movement lamps and accessories.

## Grovewood Gallery
### 111 Grovewood Rd., Asheville • (828) 253-7651

This fine gallery is in the 78-year-old former home of the Biltmore Industries' woolen homespun operation. The interior of this interesting English-style cottage adjacent to the Grove Park Inn has been wonderfully renovated as gallery and shop space without sacrificing the integrity of its origin. The Grovewood Studios, in the next cottage, houses 11 artists specializing in wood work, blown glass, stone carving, jewelry and furniture. Their work, along with the work of other area craftspeople, is represented by the Grovewood Gallery.

## High Country Arts & Craft Guild
### 108 Westgate Pkwy., Asheville • (828) 252-3880

The High Country Arts & Craft Guild represents the work of more than 160 artists and craftspeople at six annual shows — three in the corridors of local malls in February and October — and a new show known as the French Broad River Wildlife and Environmental Art and Craft Show at the French Broad River Park. The fourth show is a spectacular Christmas holiday event at the Asheville Civic Center. High Country also sponsors the Appalachian Folk Festival the first weekend in

August and Kituwah, the annual American Indian Exposition of Art and Culture held the last weekend of September. (See our Annual Festivals and Events chapter.)

## Jewelry Design
### 63 Haywood St., Asheville • (828) 254-5088

The imaginatively conceived jewelry pieces of Jewelry Design gallery are works of art wrought in gold and silver. Rings, pins and necklaces sport unusual features that will catch your fancy. The gallery is next door to Asheville's Pack Library downtown.

## Merrimon Galleries
### 365 Merrimon Ave., Asheville • (828) 252-6036

This gallery, minutes north of downtown Asheville, represents a number of outstanding local artists specializing in oils, watercolor, hand-colored etchings, graphics and limited-edition prints. The gallery also features custom framing.

## New Morning Gallery
### 7 Boston Way, Biltmore Village, Asheville • (828) 274-2831

Started in 1972 as a modest crafts gallery, the New Morning Gallery is one of the best showcases of fine handcrafts in the region. Owner John Cram describes New Morning Gallery as "art for living." You can enjoy browsing the 6,000-square-foot shop filled with lovely sculptural pottery, handmade jewelry, fine art glass and unusual furniture.

## Seven Sisters Gallery
### 117 Cherry St., Black Mountain • (828) 669-5107

The wonderfully rustic brick interior, original pressed-tin ceiling, hardwood floors and antique furniture — all serving as display space for gallery work — set the mood for this relaxed gallery that has been an integral part of Black Mountain for more than 16 years. Seven Sisters Gallery is an anchor for the Cherry Street Historic District in this quaint old resort town. Artists from all over the region and Western North Carolina in particular are represented in wood, pottery, beadwork, handcrafted jewelry, fiber arts and other lovely crafts. Thought-provoking, themed exhibitions (one recent exhibit was titled "The Human Form — In Dance and Repose") draw tourists and residents alike to this popular gallery of fine art and craft work.

## Southern Highland Handicraft Guild
**Mi. 382, Blue Ridge Pkwy., off U.S. 70 E., Asheville • (828) 298-7928**

The Southern Highland Handicraft Guild was founded in 1930 as an educational, non-profit organization to provide economic support for the many talented craftspeople in the Southern Appalachian region. Today the Guild is composed of more than 700 members in a nine-state Southeast region. Members submit applications and are selected by a board based on the merit of their work. The Allanstand Craft Shop in the Folk Art Center (milepost 382), east of Asheville, and the gift gallery of the Moses Cone Memorial and Visitors Center (828) 295-7938, milepost 293) near Blowing Rock in Watauga County, serve as retail outlets for members' works.

(See our Blue Ridge Parkway and Attrac-tions chapters for more about the Folk Arts Center and the Moses Cone Memorial.)

## Swannanoa Valley Art League
**1132 Old U.S. Hwy. 70, Black Mountain • (828) 669-7224**

This community arts group is the oldest in Western North Carolina, serving amateur artists in the Swannanoa Valley area surrounding Black Mountain, east of Asheville. Members meet monthly at the Black Mountain Library. Classes in oil painting, calligraphy, printmaking, piano, drawing and watercolor are available at the studio on Old U.S. Highway 70. Yearly exhibits at the library showcase members' work.

## Vadim Bora Studio Gallery
**30½ Battery Park Ave., Asheville • (828) 254-7959**

Vadim Bora Studio Gallery, Asheville's newest gallery, is small in size but unique in concept. This gallery allows you to enter the artist's "kitchen," so to speak. Visit with the artist, originally from the republic of Ossetia in the Caucases Mountains of Russia, while

Photo: Asheville Art Museum

The Asheville Art Museum is the only visual arts organization serving the 17 counties of western North Carolina.

he creates his sculptures, paintings, sketches, and unique jewelry designs, and exhibits them in this central studio space. Vadim Bora is a multi-media artist, also specializing in sculpture, painting, and jewelry design. The bright studio is located conveniently on a major shopping street, and just above a frame shop. Oil paintings and sketches adorning the gallery walls are for sale, but you can also request your own commissioned portrait, sculpture, or jewelry. Bora also teaches sculpture classes in this studio-gallery. Call for more information and gallery hours.

### Zone One Contemporary Gallery
37 Biltmore Ave., Asheville
• (828) 258-3088

Zone One is part of the arts renaissance of Biltmore Avenue. Housed in one of the oldest buildings in downtown Asheville (c. 1846), this gallery focuses on contemporary painting and sculpture. Changing exhibits feature the work of noted regional and national artists. The office of the Black Mountain College Museum and Arts Center is also in the gallery.

## Henderson County

### The Arts Center
538 N. Main St., Hendersonville
• (828) 693-8504

This is, indeed, the center for art information and a good starting place for getting involved in the arts in Henderson County. The center, founded by the Four Seasons Arts Council (FSAC) in 1992 (see previous listing under Organizations), houses the council's offices as well as those of the Hendersonville Symphony Orchestra. Here also is the D. Samuel Neill Gallery, with shows by local, regional and national professional artists that

change approximately every six weeks. The Hall Gallery (actually a long hallway) offers the works of local artists, students and art organizations. There are also two artist studios for rent and a classroom for lectures, children's art classes and other events.

### Brightwater Art Glass
342 N. Main St., Hendersonville
• (828) 697-6842

You're surrounded by all the colors of the rainbow when you enter this shop. Pick up a brilliant suncatcher for a few dollars or spring for a treasure-piece of stained-glass art, or have a lamp, stained-glass door or window custom-made. Brightwater also does restorations and carries books, stained glass and supplies.

### Calico Gallery/Gallery 30
317 N. Main St., Hendersonville
• (828) 697-2551

Hendersonville has attracted any number of fine artists and craftspeople, and here's a place where you can buy their paintings and handmade crafts. The shop also stocks antique dolls, furniture and jewelry and other items.

### Opportunity House
1411 Asheville Hwy., Hendersonville
• (828) 692-0575

The Opportunity House was established as an Arts, Crafts and Cultural Center in 1958. Exhibits of artwork done by members of The Art League of Henderson County and guest artists are presented monthly. The Art Gallery is open to the public for viewing and purchases Monday through Friday from 9 AM until 5 PM. The Opp House Gift Shop offers a wide selection of handcrafted items made by its members. In addition, many talented art-

---

**INSIDERS' TIP**

If old cemeteries fascinate you, check out the large one at Old Mother Church on Fort Hill, overlooking the town of Robbinsville in Graham County. Its exact date is unknown, but it probably dates back to the 1840s. The present building, constructed around 1875, has served as a one-room school and a court of justice as well as a place of worship.

ists and crafts people teach classes year round in basic drawing, acrylics, oils, sketching, watercolor, stained glass, lapidary, weaving, woodcarving, pottery and sculpture.

## Touchstone Gallery
**318 N. Main St., Hendersonville**
**• (828) 692-2191**

Touchstone has long been one of the more lighthearted contemporary galleries in town. In 1998, *Niche* magazine recognized Touchstone as one of the top 100 craft galleries in the country.

When it opened a number of years ago, it concentrated exhibits mostly on local artists. Now it has expanded its reach to the whole region and occasionally throws in an out-of-region artist to spice things up. Most shows last from 60 to 90 days.

With the wealth of talent available, even more popular artists usually wait for more than a year for a repeat show, so there's an ever-changing array of new items to enjoy here. You'll find exceptional art and craft works in a variety of mediums: pottery, fused and blown glass, wood, metal, ceramics, marble, acrylics, oils, watercolors and collages, to name a few. This is also one of the few shops in the area that carries UNICEF cards and calendars.

## Wickwire Gallery
**330 N. Main St., Hendersonville**
**• (828) 692-6222**

Wickwire, a fine art/folk art gallery, "seeks the bread that sustains the heart." It goes out of its way to display the visions of emerging local artists. At the same time, the gallery also represents some very well established names, including three Smithsonian artisans and two "North Carolina Living Treasures."

# Polk County

## Heartwood Contemporary Crafts Gallery
**Main St., Saluda • (828) 749-9365**

With a focus on a more contemporary collection, this gallery is the perfect place for anyone who not only enjoys fine crafts, but also likes to bask in the small town atmosphere that makes Saluda special. Regional and national crafts people of the highest caliber dis-

play their wares in a well-lit, comfortable shop that highlights the qualities of the work. You'll find delicate porcelain sculpture, pottery (one of the finest collections in the region), jewelry in all its forms, wood items, garden sculpture, wind chimes, stylish bird houses and feeders and original prints and painting by the area's finest artists. And this is just a sample list of the numerous arts and crafts on display.

## Tryon Painters and Sculptors
**208 Melrose Ave., Tryon Fine Arts Center,**
**Tryon • (828) 859-9755**

Composed of 160 amateur and professional artists, some of whom are nationally known, this organization presents 10 art show openings a year, including artists from all over the United States. The group's shows are held both at the Tryon Fine Arts Center and at the Arts Palette in the Farwell Annex next door. The Arts Palette holds an open house the second Saturday of the month. Workshops and regular art and sculpture classes are held in the studio, which also contains a retail store featuring members' creations.

## Saluda Mountain Crafts Gallery
**I-26 and Exit 28, Saluda • (828) 749-4341**

Despite its proximity to a busy interstate highway, this gallery has a country feel. It's housed in a two-story home built in the 1920s, complete with a wraparound porch. Inside you'll find pottery, jewelry, furniture, weavings, quilts, prints, some original paintings and a vast array of other items, 99 percent of which were made right here in the mountains by some 200 different artists, many of them from the Saluda area. The gallery is open all year.

## The Upstairs Gallery
**409 N. Trade St., Tryon • (828) 859-2828**

The Upstairs Gallery got its name from former upstairs locations. Now, 21 years later, though definitely in a downstairs space, the name has stuck. The Upstairs is a well-known contemporary art gallery that features fine arts and crafts, children's art, literary readings, musical performances (including a monthly Pickin' Parlor), art education, Southern Writers Summer Series and an annual Christmas Craft Festival. The gallery is run entirely by volunteers and is closed in July, August and

# The Frescoes of Ashe County

Remote Ashe County, in the far northwest corner of North Carolina's mountains, seems an unlikely place for a collection of religious frescoes. But, perhaps, it is the very best place. The serene, natural beauty of this unspoiled mountain county is appropriate for these works of remarkable talent that evoke such divine inspiration.

Noted American artist Ben Long, born in Statesville, has found his niche as an artist who keeps alive the ancient art of the fresco. Fresco painting is a tenuous art based on the immediate application of pigment to wet plaster. So quickly does the bonding of the two take place that great skill and meticulous planning must be maintained in order to achieve the beautiful result.

Close-up

In two amazingly picturesque Episcopal churches — St. Mary's in West Jefferson, on N.C. Highway 194, off U.S. Highway 221, and Holy Trinity, just off N.C. Highway 16 at Glendale Springs — are housed a collection of wonderful religious frescoes created by Long and his students, spanning a period of years from the mid-1970s to the mid-80s. The marvelous beauty of the work and the powerful subjects have drawn thousands of visitors from all over the country to witness firsthand the evocative frescoes that decorate the walls of these tiny churches.

Both churches date to early in this century, and each seats a congregation no larger than 100. The white frame buildings, trimmed in scrollwork, are described as Carpenter Gothic in style. Neatly trimmed lawns and carefully tended gardens surround these tiny islands of worship. Both are open day and night for prayer and meditation and accept only donations for the privilege of seeing these splendid works of art.

At St. Mary's, in West Jefferson, the smaller of the two churches, you can listen to an eloquently recorded description of the works that grace the altar and line the rich, chestnut sanctuary walls. Here, at the altar, you have the opportunity to see the exquisite portrayal of *Mary, Great With Child*. This luminous fresco, modeled by Long's wife and bearing the face of a local mountain girl, was completed in 1974. On the opposite side of the altar, *John the Baptist*, completed in 1975, is pictured standing on the banks of the Jordan River; the face of this subject speaks volumes. In the center is the powerful fresco *The Mystery of Faith*, completed in 1977. This fresco, rising the full height of the altar, depicts the crucifixion of Christ and the celebration of the Eucharist. Works by Long's students line the walls of the tiny church of St. Mary's. *The Laughing Christ*, completed in 1975 by then-19-year-old

Photo: Judi Scharns

St. John the Baptist Churches
of the Frescoes.

artist Bo Bartlett, is an unusual rendition of the face so familiar to the modern world.

Down the road, about 10 minutes away, is Holy Trinity Church at Glendale Springs. Sitting on a commanding hill, framed by the North Carolina sky, the little Gothic-style frame building is as much a work of art as the magnificent fresco of *The Last Supper*, which fills its altar wall. When you enter Holy Trinity, you are struck by the immediacy of this fresco, which truly does fill the entire end wall of the church altar. So strong are the personalities of the life-size figures, so vibrant is the texture, it's as if you have come upon that private meeting of Christ and his Disciples quite by accident. You can almost hear them speak. The luminous quality of the fresco is achieved by the sealant, which is a centuries-old mixture of white wine and fresh egg white.

Long came to Holy Trinity in 1980, completing this work that summer. He success-fully enlisted the aide of area residents, who served as his models, along with his wife, two children and an errant dog, who found a home at Holy Trinity for the duration and is included in the foreground of the piece. The white cloth at the apex of the fresco, fluttering heavenward, is described by Ben Long as the "mystery" — that inexplicable quality of life's force that is within all of us.

The Churches of the Frescoes are truly inspirational and should definitely be a destination included in your travels. If you visit the city of Charlotte (see our Daytrips chapter), you can see more examples of the spectacular fresco art of Ben Long. There in the lobby of the massive NationsBank Corporate Center downtown is another fantastic display of this incredible art form.

January. Exhibitions open on Fridays with a public reception and run for four weeks. Family Day with a gallery tour is held the first Sunday after an opening.

## Transylvania County

### The Frame-Up
**4 W. Main St., Brevard • (828) 883-2385**

In addition to fantastic archival framing, The Frame-Up also carries one-of-a-kind jewelry, woodturnings, handmade furniture and beautiful (framed, of course) prints, as well as blown glass, porcelain and pottery.

### Gallery on Main
**53 E. Main St., Brevard • (828) 885-7299**

You'll find originals and limited editions prints here as well as a lovely selection of collectibles.

### Brevard College Visual Arts
**400 N. Broad St., Brevard • (828) 883-8292**

Exhibitions of visual art at the College can be found in two locations: The Mezzanine Gallery in the Paul Porter Center for Performing Arts (see Organizations above) and the Spiers Gallery in Sims Art Center. In addition to displays of art produced by the faculty and students, visitors may enjoy the talents of regionally and nationally known artists. Exhibitions include work that spans the spectrum of the visual arts including ceramics, painting, sculpture, photography and installations. Recent exhibitions have featured work by Canadian sculptress Jocelyn Salem, as well as such nationally recognized artists as Joe Molinaro, Michael Mallard, Michael Voors, Olga Alexander and Darryl Halbrooks. Gallery hours are Monday through Friday from 10 AM until 5:30 PM.

Not only does this gallery provide exposure to some fine artists, it also serves as a teaching tool for the college's art department. (Visiting artists often spend a few days on campus interacting with the students.) The shows, which include both two- and three-dimensional art, change approximately every five weeks. The exhibitions are representative of both regional and national artists, traditional and nontraditional. The public is invited to opening receptions, which often include musical presentations and poetry readings.

The works of area artists can also be seen in the Transylvania County Library at 105 South Broad Street, the Brevard Chamber of

Special exhibitions from the Whitney Museum in New York come to the Asheville Art Museum through a long standing cooperation.

Commerce and the Transylvania County Courthouse, the latter two of which are on Main Street.

## Transylvania County Arts Co-Op
7 E. Main St., Brevard • (828) 884-2787

Occupying the former gallery and offices of the Transylvania County Arts Council and associated with that council (see Organizations above), this gallery gives shoppers a chance to purchase beautiful, locally made arts and crafts at wonderful prices.

# Southern Mountains

## Haywood County

## Blue Owl Studio and Gallery, Inc.
11 N. Main St., Waynesville
• (828) 456-5050

If you wonder how the cities and landscapes of the mountains appeared in yesteryear, you can relive some of those days in this gallery. Filled with antique graphics of the past, the artists at Blue Owl bring them to life in brilliant handpainted colors. Better yet,

the prices for these works of art are surprisingly affordable.

## Earthwork's Environmental Gallery
21 N. Main St., Waynesville
• (828) 452-9500

Earthwork's is one of our Waynesville favorites. Its goal is to "celebrate the beauty of the earth through the eyes of the artists." This large gallery covers Southwestern arts and crafts and Native American wildlife themes. You'll find rugs, pillows and runners from the Zapotec Indians of Mexico, woodturnings by local artists, gourd art, stone carvings from Africa and captivating paintings and prints by Native American artists. There are also jewelry, books, music and many other items of superb taste at reasonable prices. The Earthwork's Frame Gallery, (828) 456-3666, is at 152 S. Main St.

## T. Pennington Art Gallery
15 N. Main St., Waynesville
• (828) 452-4582

You'll be amazed by the excellent colored-pencil drawings of Western North Carolina created by Teresa Pennington. In addition to original works, the gallery also carries limited-edition prints of local mountain scenes.

# Jackson County

## Belk Art Gallery and Chelsa Gallery
**Western Carolina University**
**N.C. Hwy. 107, Cullowhee**
**• (828) 227-7327**

Both of these galleries on the University's campus offer art exhibits by local, regional and national artists on a year-round basis.

## City Lights Bookstore & Cafe
**3 E. Jackson St., Sylva • (828) 586-9499**

In addition to offering new and used books, good food and live entertainment, City Lights has an interesting gallery of rotating exhibitions.

## Dogwood Crafters
**Webster St., Dillsboro • (828) 586-2248**

Housed in a large, renovated log building around the corner from Front Street, this is one of Dillsboro's most charming stores. We are particularly taken with the lovely, artistic cornhusk dolls here, but there also are hundreds of both contemporary and traditional handicrafts on display, including pottery, pillows, art and toys.

## Gallery One
**Main St., Sylva • (828) 293-3407**

Operated by the Jackson County Visual Arts Associations, the gallery sponsors monthly exhibits, mostly by local artists, and has an artist-in-residence. (See Organizations above.)

## Gallery Z
**Front St., Dillsboro • (828) 586-3383**

The mountains are becoming world-famous for studio glass, and at Gallery Z you can see some samples of it in the form of candle holders, lamps, vases and perfume bottles.

## Mountain Pottery
**Front St., Dillsboro • (828) 586-9183**

At Mountain Pottery you can see pottery being made in an open studio. It's also got the town's largest selection of handmade porcelain, stoneware and raku pottery. The pottery is supplied by more than 50 crafts people from the region.

## Riverwood Pewter Shop
**N.C. Hwy. 411, Dillsboro**
**• (828) 586-6542**

The Riverwood Shops developed around a hand-hammered pewter business established in 1930. The Riverwood Pewter Shop is still here making hand-hammered pewter on the premises.

## Riverwood's Oaks Gallery
**N.C. Hwy.441, Dillsboro**
**• (828) 586-6542**

Right next door to the Riverwood Pewter Shop, this cooperative of more than 80 Appalachian craftspeople ishowcases of weaving, jewelry, glass, wood, wearables and pottery.

## Village Studio
**Front St., Dillsboro • (828) 586-4060**

The talents that flower in these mountains are beautifully expressed in this gallery. Area artists fill it with paintings and prints, handmade dulcimers, gifts and cards. The gallery-style shop also displays decorative accessories for home and office. Professional framing is available.

# Macon County

## The Bascom-Louise Gallery and the Highlands Center for the Visual Arts
**E. Main St., Highlands • (828) 526-4949**

The Bascom-Louise Gallery stages impressive showings of works by regional and national artists. Exhibitions change every three weeks from May through November and are accompanied by public receptions for the artists. Lectures are also held here. A new permanent collection gallery houses artwork by some of the finest regional artists along with a sales gallery of original fine arts and crafts. The new workroom in back of the Bascom-Louise Gallery is bright, spacious and well equipped. It contains audiovisual, painting and drawing areas, plus a darkroom and raku kiln.

Workshops, taught by some of the finest artists in the Southeast, are open to beginning artists and professionals at the Highlands Center for the Visual Arts. They include classes in painting, drawing, sculpture, photography, crafts and more. Class sizes are kept small for close interaction with instructors. The costs of these intensive workshops range from $85 to $200. Sometimes there's a small additional fee for materials or the use of equipment. The center and gallery both are closed during the winter.

## Half-Moon Gallery
**Fourth St., Highlands • (828) 526-2172**

Looking for something earthy? Half Moon carries chairs, tables and beds made of willow and rhododendron; folk and Native American art; and antler lamps, carvings, bowls, throws, pillows, home accessories and other gifts to add warmth to your environment.

## Maco Crafts Inc.
**652 Georgia Hwy., Franklin**
**• (828) 524-7878**

This huge craft cooperative and fabric shop has thrived for more than a quarter-century. It assures high-quality work from more than 200 local craftspeople through a jurying process, yet it is still able to maintain an average inventory of more than 10,000 items. It is particularly famous for its quality quilts and also offers all the supplies a quilter could ever need.

In addition to its craftworks, which include jewelry, wood, pottery, paintings, stained-glass art, dolls and toys, there is a Christmas room that's open year round. Maco also has the area's largest selection of fine cotton fabrics and the latest patterns and books. The co-op's craftspeople will create custom work in both traditional and contemporary designs. You can also enroll in one of the many craft classes offered. Maco Crafts is 2 miles south of Franklin on U.S. Highway 441.

## Munger Creek Artworks
**456 Dillard Rd., Highlands**
**• (828) 526-2820**

Have you ever had a yen to be a potter? Here's a good place to learn. Six years ago, Ibby Kenna and Cynthia Strain opened Munger Creek Artworks, an artist co-op that offers pottery courses and, according to demand, holds classes in such things as printing, jewelry, gourd-craft, flower pressing and marbling.

Munger Creek also provides a sales outlet for both experienced crafters and students. As a result, there are many fascinating art works sold here, including two-dimensional art in all media, photographs, clothing, handcarved and twig furniture, and jewelry. All are one-of-a-kind and locally made. Custom orders are taken for most crafts. The cooperative, with more than 80 members, is just south of town.

## Tiger Mountain Woodworks
**N.C. Hwy. 106 S., Highlands**
**• (828) 526-5577**

Tiger Mountain is another place offering a rustic look. This shop sells handcrafted furnishing, including custom lodge furniture and country reproductions including beds, tables, dressers and other items for the entire house.

## The Uptown Gallery
**30 E. Main St., Franklin • (828) 349-6708**

Members of the Macon County Art Association (see Organizations above) display their oils, pastels, watercolors, acrylics, mixed media and sculpture here on a year-round basis.

Photo: Cherokee Tribal Promotion Office

The colorful Eagle Dance is performed during the summertime
outdoor drama "Unto These Hills" in Cherokee.

# Theater

## Northern Mountains

### Ashe County

#### Ashe County Little Theater
**Various venues, West Jefferson**
**• (336) 246-ARTS**

Ashe County is well-represented by this
amateur theatrical group, which features local actors of all ages in an energetic annual
program of popular Broadway productions.
Past productions have included *Oliver!*, *The
King and I* and *The Sound of Music*.

### Avery County

#### Lees-McRae College
**Main St., N.C. Hwy. 194, Banner Elk**
**• (828) 898-5241**

Mile-high Banner Elk is the lovely location
for this dynamic little college (see our Education chapter). The college is innovative both
academically and culturally and promotes a
yearlong calendar of cultural arts events that
is amazingly diverse for a school its size. The
Lees-McRae College Summer Theater, established as a semiprofessional theater in 1984,
is one of the foremost theatrical attractions in
the High Country.

Past productions have included *Fiddler
on the Roof*, *Man of La Mancha* and *Guys and
Dolls*. The Performing Arts Series, sponsored
by the college's Performing Arts Department,
offers consistently interesting dramatic productions, one-act plays, traditional mountain
dance performance (clogging) and other concerts throughout the academic year. All are
open to the public. Shows are approximately
$5 to $7 for adults and $2 for students.

### Watauga County

#### Appalachian State University
**Boone • (800) 841-ARTS**

Boone's community-minded university offers a series of cultural events throughout the
year. The Department of Theater and Dance
at ASU presents a wide array of one-act plays,
full dramatic productions and dance performances, all of which are open to the public.

The ASU Forum series is the university's formal lecture series that, in the past, has featured national speakers addressing topics of national and international importance.

During the summer, the community is treated to An Appalachian Summer Festival offering the best in music, dance, theater, visual arts and symposia. The Performing Arts series also brings national and international performers to the campus. These events are also open to the public. (See the "Music" section in this chapter for information on recitals and concerts.)

## Blowing Rock Stage Company
**Sunset Dr., Blowing Rock Arts Center, Blowing Rock • (828) 295-9627**

In its 12th season, the Blowing Rock Stage Company is the High Country's resident professional theater, drawing the services of professional Actor's Equity players every summer. The artistic home of the theater company is the Blowing Rock Arts Center, adjacent to Blowing Rock Elementary School. Local and summer residents of the High Country, as well as scores of tourists, fill every performance of this fine theatrical company. Past productions have included *Love Letters*, *Steel Magnolias* and *Last of the Red Hot Mamas: The Sophie Tucker Story*.

## Blue Ridge Community Theater
**Various venues, Boone • (828) 264-7459**

For over 20 years, Blue Ridge Community Theater (BRCT) has brought the best in amateur theatrical production to the High Country. The 200 local actors who regularly participate in BRCT stage two yearly productions — a fall drama and a spring musical.

## Yancey County

### Burnsville Little Theater
**Various venues, Burnsville • No phone**

This is Yancey County's resident amateur theater group. Drawing talent from the surrounding area, the Burnsville Little Theater stages two or three productions a year. Check local listings for venues since this is an amateur theater with no home stage.

## Parkway Playhouse
**202 Green Mountain Dr., Burnsville**
**• (828) 682-4285**

Active since 1947, the Parkway Playhouse is one of the oldest theater companies in Western North Carolina. The busy summer season draws professional Actor's Equity performers and produces top-notch theater for enthusiastic audiences. Past productions include *Night Must Fall* and *You Can't Take It With You*.

# Central Mountains

## Buncombe County

### Asheville Community Theatre
**35 Walnut St., Asheville • (828) 254-1320**

This award-winning theater is ranked one of the best in the Southeast, consistently providing the Asheville area with the best in live theater since its inception in 1946. This long tradition of excellence includes a colorful heritage that includes an association with famed motion picture actor Charlton Heston. Heston was co-director of ACT in the 1947 season, making it his springboard to stardom the following year when he returned to New York.

The Asheville Community Theatre produces a six-show season that includes the best of Broadway musicals, comedies and classics. The 468-seat Heston Auditorium has continental-style seating in its air-conditioned space, is handicapped-accessible and equipped with an enhancement system for the hearing impaired. Local restaurants offer dinner and show packages. The Asheville Community Theatre is also home to the Second Stage Reader's Theater, The Asheville Youtheatre and the Autumn Players. Tickets for the 5-show season cost around $60. Single shows cost approximately $15 for adults on Friday and Saturday and $12 on Sunday.

### Mockingbird Theater Productions
**2 S. Pack Sq., Diana Wortham Theater, Park Place, Asheville**
**• (828) 285-0207, (828) 285-0207**

Mockingbird Theater Productions, headed by actor/director John Hall, is the resident

Celebrate the fine art of summer...

# AN APPALACHIAN SUMMER FESTIVAL

## JULY 5–31, 1999

Featuring the finest in music, dance, theatre and the visual arts nestled in the splendor of the Blue Ridge Mountains

ON THE CAMPUS OF APPALACHIAN STATE UNIVERSITY
BOONE, NORTH CAROLINA

## CALL 1-800-841-ARTS

appsummer.appstate.edu

100ʸ
Appalachian

children's theater company for Pack Place Education Arts and Science Center (see our "Museums" section in this chapter). This young, imaginative company, now in its fifth year, draws on favorite childhood fairy tales, giving them a unique, comic twist in original adaptations by playwright Richard Kinter. Kinter's bright, engaging, original and very singable songs enliven such favorites as *The King Who Lost Christmas*, *Lil' Red* and *The Golden Goose*, *The Velveteen Rabbit* and *The Emperor's New Clothes*. Each production is highlighted by a classic, antic chase scene through the audience. This is great fun for everyone. All performances (matinees) are in the Diana Wortham Theater, and the modest admission is approximately $6 for adults and $4 for children.

## Montford Park Players
**Montford Park Recreational Facility, Montford Ave. and Pearson Dr., Asheville • (828) 254-4540**

This legendary Asheville theater company grew out of one woman's fascination with the English Bard. Founder Hazel Robinson cre-

ated the Montford Park Players on a financial shoestring back in 1973, bringing the works of Shakespeare to the public. The plays in those days were performed in the natural, grassy amphitheater of old Montford Park, with costumes and props scavenged by Ms. Robinson and her loyal thespian followers. As the Great Man said, "The play's the thing." And so it was.

The performances of the Montford Park Players gained in popularity and attracted attention from city leaders, who provided a space in Asheville's Montford Park Recreational Facility nearby and enough free lumber to build a real stage. That was 1983. Every summer since, this vigorous and dedicated amateur company, with steadfast Hazel Robinson at the helm as artistic director, continues to be a favorite Asheville entertainment.

Two separate works by Shakespeare, usually one comedy and one tragedy, are performed each summer season. You can bring a blanket and a picnic and stake out your space on the hillside. There's nothing like Shakespeare under the night sky to set the

# HandMade in America

Long before the first tourists came to western North Carolina, quilts and baskets, tools and furniture were being crafted as necessities of life. Although they were rarely seen by anyone but family members, these handcrafts were created with an integrity that speaks volumes about the people who live here. Today thousands come each year to see the woodworking, pottery, blacksmithing and weaving that are now considered treasured keepsakes. They come, too, to reconnect with that part of themselves that longs to create.

HandMade in America is hard at work garnering national and international recognition for this creative heritage. The formal development of HandMade began with a three-year grant received from the Pew Partnership for Civic Change in December 1993. More than 360 people participated in a six-month regional planning process that shaped and defined its mission.

Working with three tourism-related organizations (Blue Ridge Hosts, High Country Hosts and Smoky Mountain Hosts), HandMade is guiding the development of a craft "heritage corridor" across 22 Western North Carolina counties. The Blue Ridge Parkway serves as the main link by which visitors can access a series of loop trails that take them to historic craft locations, scenic byways and other attractions. A 120-page guide book, *The Craft Heritage Trails of Western North Carolina*, takes you on seven exciting trails carefully designed to traverse 400 of the region's most fascinating and historical shops, artists, inns, restaurants, galleries and historical sites. Many were not open to the public before, but HandMade's careful planning and negotiations have created new opportunities. And training sessions for all participating sites mean that you are greeted by people knowledgeable not just about their speciality but all the stops along the way.

Photo: Vic Lukas

The mountains are home to many talented artists and artisans, and
*HandMade in America* is working to get them the recognition they deserve.

Consider the names of the trails: High Country Ramble, Circle of the Mountain Trail, Farm to Market Trail, Mountain Cities Trail, Cascades Trail, Shadow of the Smokies Trail and Lake Country Trail, and you learn of the diversity of the region, the scope of the project and the theme each has to offer. All destinations have been carefully researched, their authenticity as truly American and/or handmade scrupulously verified. Many of the sites in our book are included on HandMade's self-guided trails.

HandMade is also involved in programs to provide craftspeople with some of the advantages that employees of large corporations enjoy. There are, after all, 739 full-time and 3,369 part-time craftspeople in the region whose total economic contribution to the state in 1994 exceeded $122 million. To support this burgeoning industry, HandMade is establishing an investment bank that provides low-interest loans to craftspeople and crafts-related businesses, job training programs, a crafts registry, a teacher certification program and an Institute of Creativity, Research and Design. They are also working with Andrews, Bakersville, Chimney Rock and Mars Hill on a Mainstreet Program that pairs these small towns with similar towns already involved in and benefiting from revitalization.

*The Craft Heritage Trails of Western North Carolina* is available for only $11.95 plus tax and shipping. Contact HandMade in America at 67 N. Market Street, P.O. Box 2089, Asheville, North Carolina 28802, or call (828) 252-0121.

mood. The performances are free, but in the true tradition of early Shakespearean troupes, a hat is passed at intermission. You can find the Montford Park Players at the outdoor amphitheater of Montford Recreation Center, one block off Montford Avenue at the intersection of Montford Avenue and Pearson Drive.

A highlight of the Christmas season is the Montford Park Player's production of *A Christmas Carol*. This energetic production has been performed at the auditorium of Asheville High School and also at Diana Wortham Theatre at Pack Place. Admission is approximately $5 for adults and $2 for children.

## Henderson County

### The Belfry Players
**131 Fourth Ave. W., Suite 215, Hendersonville • (828) 698-8288**

Sherry Raker is the Artistic Director of this theatrical group, which began in 1988 with just a few participants using a small performance space at St. James Episcopal Church in Hendersonville. It now draws on a large paid membership and produces three plays a year in the Sumner Pingree Theatre at Christ School, 500 Christ School Rd. in Arden. While its base remains in Hendersonville, the group now draws both its membership and audi-

ence from Asheville, Tryon and Brevard. The Belfry Players productions cover a broad range of material from *Spoon River Anthology* to *Sylvia* to short opera. Single show tickets are $9; season tickets to all three productions are $24.

The players also maintain an outreach program called "Bits & Pieces" that presents programs to retirement centers and various organizations. These may include music as well as drama and readings.

### Flat Rock Playhouse, The State Theatre of North Carolina
**2661 Greenville Hwy., Flat Rock**
**• (828) 693-0721**

Flat Rock Playhouse, The State Theatre of North Carolina, is a professional theatre operating under a contract with Actors' Equity Association, the national union of professional actor and stage managers. Founded in 1937, the Playhouse entertains more than 65,000 guests each season. Eight productions are offered between late May and mid-October annually. A variety of comedies, musicals and dramas, which rage from World Premiers to the latest from Broadway and London to the Classics, compose the summer/ fall series. A special holiday production will be added to the 1999 schedule.

Flat Rock Playhouse endeavors to produce plays that have a wide range of appeal and are appropriate for the entire family. For example, included in the 1999 playlist are *The Last Night of Ballyhoo, Wrong for Each Other, Sugar Babies, The King and I, Sinners, The Honky Tonk Angels, Look Homeward, Angel, Grease* and for the first time, a special holiday production of *A Christmas Carol.*

The performance schedule is Wednesday through Saturday at 8:15 PM and Wednesday, Thursday, Saturday and Sunday at 2:15 PM. The box office opens in late April, and reservations can be made by calling the above number. Musical productions cost $25 and non-musicals cost $22. Discounts are offered for students, seniors and groups of 13 or more.

Flat Rock Playhouse is located three miles south of Hendersonville on U.S. Hwy. 25, or from Interstate-26, take exit 22 and follow the signs.

The Vagabond School of the Drama operates Flat Rock Playhouse and has two main educational divisions: the summer Apprentice/Intern Program and the fall through spring Theatre for Young People. Between these two divisions, classes are offered to students from the first grade through college graduates and pre-professional students. The summer programs are accredited through the University of North Carolina in Asheville.

### Hendersonville Little Theatre
**The Barn on State St., Hendersonville**
• **(828) 692-1082**

This all-volunteer group of players has entertained the town since 1966, putting on four shows in a refurbished barn from September to May. These usually include a couple of comedies, a mystery and sometimes a serious drama. There are more than 400 members in this organization, and a large number of them actively work on each production. Tickets are $8, but there are various memberships available that range from $25 for a season ticket for three plays to $500 for a life membership that entitles you to see the plays free for life.

## Polk County

### Tryon Little Theater
**208 Melrose Ave.,**
**Tryon Fine Arts Center, Tryon**
• **(828) 859-8322, (828) 859-3545 info. line**

Since 1969, this organization has produced more than 100 plays and musicals. The nearly 800 members create six productions a year at the Tryon Fine Arts Center, including at least one musical each season. There are more than 150 individuals participating in some facet of every production. Recent works presented have as disparate as *My Fair Lady* and *The Glass Menagerie.* It is not unheard of for such shows to be sold out and for popular demand to require additional performances. Tryon Little Theater also holds acting workshops and play-reading groups. It has sponsored various theatrical events, premiered original productions and won the North Carolina Theater Award. Tickets range from $10 to $15, depending on the show.

## Transylvania County

### Brevard Little Theater
**P.O. Box 544, Brevard • (828) 884-2587**

This theatrical group, which will celebrate its 50th season in the year 2000, is the official theater company of the city and county. It's also the Resident Community Theater Company at Brevard College. The Barn Theater, overlooking scenic King's Creek on the Brevard College campus, was renovated and refurbished for the 1999 season.

The group produces four plays per season that runs from October through August. It also puts on children's plays, including the very popular *The Nutcracker* in December. In addition, there's a very active "BLT To Go" group that provides benefit performances for community and charitable organizations.

Reservations are advised due to the limited seating in the Barn Theatre. Certain productions are also at the larger Dunham Auditorium on the college campus.

# Southern Mountains

## Cherokee County

### The Valleytown Arts Center
**Third and Chestnut Sts., Andrews**
**• (828) 321-3453**

This center, originally the First Baptist Church, has been renovated with the purpose of providing a facility for the community to stage performing and visual arts. It houses both the Community Youth Players, an ensemble of young local talent that has been active since 1986 and that performs a Christmas play in early December and presents another performance in the spring, and the Andrews Community Theater that offers plays throughout the year. Concerts and other events are also staged here. Call for information.

## Clay County

### Licklog Players
**Peacock Playhouse, Hayesville**
**• (828) 389-8632**

This volunteer organization was started as a small community theater in 1977 by Diane Teague, Jimmy Hicks and Susan King. In searching for a name that reflected this area, they thought of the Davis family, early settlers who felled trees and cut notches in the logs to hold salt for their cattle. This area became known as Licklog, and so the name was adopted.

Today, Licklog Players has grown into a regional theatrical group with talent drawn from several surrounding states. It's housed in the 250-seat, air-conditioned Peacock Playhouse with state-of-the-art facilities. Last year, for the first time, the Players offered productions year round, including comedies, farces, mysteries, dramas, musicals and children's performances. Recent productions included *Cabaret, Annie, The Sound of Music, A Delicate Balance, The King and I, Trip to Bountiful, A Tuna Christmas* and *Rumors*.

Members of the Board of Directors, a theatre manager, paid directors, choreographers and music directors produce the wonderful works seen here. Some 300 volunteers perform all the other jobs. Tickets for plays are $10 for adults and $6 for students and children; musicals cost $12 for adults and $7 for students and children. Each year, Licklog offers a summer theater workshop for youth, which includes instruction in acting, dance, music and other areas of theatre arts.

## Jackson County

### Kudzu Players
**P.O. Box 834, Sylva, 28779**
**• (828) 586-8133**

The Kudzu Players, a community theater group of around 50 people, offers popular plays on a regular basis in the former courtroom of the historic Old Jackson County Courthouse. Call the above number for information and ticket prices.

### Niggli Theatre and Studio Theatre
**Western Carolina University**
**N.C. Hwy. 107, Cullowhee**
**• (828) 227-7491**

The University's Department of Speech and Drama produces dramas, comedies and musicals throughout the year. Call the above number for information and ticket prices.

## Haywood County

### Haywood Arts Repertory Theater
**250 Pigeon St. (U.S. Hwy. 276 S.),**
**Waynesville • (828) 456-6322**

HART is the region's most active theater company, producing seven main stage productions each year and up to six "studio" shows, including major musicals, classics and new plays. In recent years the theater has hosted a production direct from Off-Broadway, sent a production to New York and staged a new play in its studio that won honors at the John F. Kennedy Center. The group moved into its new home, the Performing Arts Center at the Shelton House, in 1997. The Center, a summer-stock barn-style facility, sits in the middle of an eight-acre National Historic Site shared with the Museum of North Carolina Handicrafts. It includes a 250-seat auditorium, a visual arts gallery and a 75-seat studio theater. The Center is located just two blocks from Waynesville's pretty Main Street. In addition to an acoustically fine, all-wood interior, there are earphones for the hearing impaired, and the facility is wheelchair accessible.

The group has more than 700 season-ticket holders and involves hundreds of volunteers, with an annual budget of more than $130,000. Tickets for plays are $10 for adults, $8 for seniors and $6 for students; for musicals tickets are $15 for adults, $12 for seniors and $8 for students with special one-half-price student tickets available for Sunday and Thursday performances.

## Macon County

### Highlands Playhouse
**Oak St., Highlands**
• **(828) 526-2695 (tickets), (828) 526-9443 (information)**

This community theater has been active for 60 years and is still going strong. It has been housed in the same building for more than 50 years, and work is under way to place it on the National Register of Historic Places. The Playhouse stages four productions in a season that runs from June into August. It combines professional talent with outside equity guest stars. Showtimes are Tuesday through Saturday at 8 PM and Sunday at 2 PM. Tickets are $20 for adults and $7 for students. Group rates for 10 or more are available.

## Swain County

### Smoky Mountain Community Theater
**Main St., Bryson City**
• **(828) 488-2988**

The Smoky Mountain Community Theater presents four plays a year in an old movie theater on Main Street. The group itself refur-

Photo: Blake Madden

Asheville Community Theater delights patrons with classical and contemporary performances like The Crucible.

bished the more-than-50-year-old structure, installing a sophisticated lighting system, building dressing rooms and more than doubling the size of the stage. Members are undaunted by large-scale productions. In the past, they've presented *Oklahoma, Fiddler on the Roof, The Music Man, South Pacific, The Sound of Music, The Wizard of Oz* and *Into the Woods*. A summer children's theater has been established that offers a workshop and production. The group plans to expand this program.

# Music

## Northern Mountains

### Ashe County

#### Ashe County Choral Society
**First Baptist Church, West Jefferson**
• (336) 246-ARTS

This group of community singers works each year to stage both a holiday and a spring concert. The holiday concert in December features religious and secular music, while the spring concert consists of a blend of contemporary pops and religious music.

### Watauga County

#### Music in the Mountains with Joe Shannon
**Various venues, Boone**
• (828) 264-8118

This lively concert series is also a weekly television show taped every Friday evening at 8 PM in Boone. Remarkably entertaining, it's part traditional mountain shindig, part Appalachian cultural history lesson.

Every week a musical guest takes the stage, setting the tone for the evening's entertainment. Guests have provided gospel, bluegrass, banjo, fiddle, old-time string band music and even songs of the Civil War, accompanied by traditional instruments. The program is highlighted by a one-on-one interview with one of the "old masters" of our Appalachian musical and cultural heritage. What

an honor to listen to national treasures such as 83-year-old Sugar Grove fiddle player Ora Watson. The shows are taped and aired on local Boone Radio.

In the summer, the concert series takes place at various venues. During the fall, all shows take place at the Blowing Rock Arts Center on Sunset Drive. The cost to attend is approximately $8.

#### School of Music Faculty Recital Series
**Appalachian State University, Boone**
• (828) 262-4046, (800) 841-ARTS

The Appalachian State University School of Music Faculty Recital Series is an eagerly anticipated series of concert events in the High Country. These performances are scheduled monthly during the academic year and are also open to the public.

## Central Mountains

### Buncombe County

#### Asheville Chamber Music Series
• (828) 253-2579

This 46-year-old organization sponsors five concerts a year featuring nationally renowned artists of chamber music. The concerts are presented in the Unitarian Universalist Church, 1 Edwin Place, off Charlotte Street in north Asheville. You could have purchased a season ticket for $60 for all six concerts in 1998 (six because the series is celebrating its 45th anniversary in 1998) or individual tickets — about $15 for adults, $12 for seniors. Students are admitted free.

#### Asheville Choral Society
• (828) 669-8695

Founded in 1977, the Asheville Choral Society has a membership of about 60 to 85 amateur and professional singers. The society's choral director, Robert P. Keener, is also the retired Chairman of the Music Department of nearby Warren Wilson College in Swannanoa. The group performs concerts that include classical and contemporary masterpieces of choral literature. The Asheville

Choral Society has appeared with both the Asheville Symphony and the North Carolina Symphony orchestras.

A season ticket is roughly $24 for three concerts, $18 for seniors; tickets at the door are $10 and $8, respectively. Students with valid identification are admitted free.

## Asheville Community Concert Association
• (828) 252-6777

This venerable cultural arts membership organization, now in its 66th season, is responsible for bringing the finest in national and international ballet, jazz, choral groups and classical orchestral music to Asheville. The Thomas Wolfe Auditorium of the Asheville Civic Center is the location for all performances. Individual tickets are available, and a season membership for the entire series of five concerts is approximately $75.

## The Asheville Symphony Orchestra
**Asheville Civic Center, Asheville**
• (828) 254-7046

The distinguished Asheville Symphony Orchestra, led by maestro Robert Hart Baker, is celebrating its 38th season. This community orchestra consistently provides exceptional concerts and continues to set new challenges for itself each season. The popular Masterworks series, composed of six concerts, features distinguished, internationally known guest artists. In addition, the orchestra performs its annual Children's Concert in October, a holiday pops concert in December and a spring pops concert in May.

Tickets start from $5 for a single concert to $150 for a season subscription (six concerts).

## Mid-Day Musicals
**Pack Place, Park Sq., Asheville**
• (828) 285-0207

This lively musical series, co-sponsored by the City of Asheville, is highlighted by a feeling of spontaneity. For the past seven years, a changing cast of some of the areas most talented singers has been performing these free lunchtime mini-musicals Thursdays at 12:30, starting the last weekend in August through the first weekend of October outside

Pack Place on historic Pack Square. Each performance features a different theme. A variety of pieces, such as the music of famed Broadway composer Stephen Sondheim, light opera by Gilbert and Sullivan, the classic standards of sophisticated Noel Coward and legendary Broadway composers Rogers and Hammerstein, are performed by these energetic and talented performers. Lunchtime has never been so entertaining!

## Song O'Sky Chorus — Sweet Adelines
• (828) 253-9090

The Song O'Sky Chorus — Sweet Adelines group has been in Asheville since 1974. It's composed of about 32 members from all walks of life who have a basic love of singing, enjoy musical fellowship and thrive on the melodious strains of four-part harmony. The chorus competes in regional four-part harmony competitions and performs public concerts throughout the year featuring old standards, Broadway show tunes, gospel, country and traditional Christmas music.

# Henderson County

## Blue Ridge Community College Concerts
**Blue Ridge College, College Dr., Flat Rock**
• (828) 692-3572, ext. 306

On Monday nights in a season stretching from September to April, the college's Division of Community Services sponsors eight classical music concerts in the 150-seat auditorium of the Patton Building. Many of the performers have national reputations, and about half the concerts feature outstanding students from the North Carolina School of the Arts in Winston-Salem. One concert is reserved to display the talents of a local professional. In addition, around three times a year, special benefit performances are given to help support the college's music department. Tickets to the Monday night series are $6; season tickets are $45.

## The Hendersonville Chorale
• (828) 692-3211

This group was founded in 1974 and was incorporated as a nonprofit organization in

1979. Ever since, it has enriched the lives of the residents here, both singers and listeners, by presenting two concerts a year of quality chorale literature of all historical periods. Eighty-five to 100 voices strong, these volunteers (it's a non-audition group; no one is turned away) perform in December and May at the acoustically fine First Baptist Church. There is a membership charge of $5 per concert to join the chorale. Tickets to the performances are $6 for adults and $3 for students.

### Hendersonville Symphony Orchestra
**538 N. Main St., Hendersonville**
**• (828) 697-5884**

Talented guest artists from around the nation are delighted to perform with this jewel of an orchestra. Totally community supported, it's made up of 60 to 70 music professionals, talented retirees and students and is conducted by Dr. Thomas Joiner. This results in six vibrant concerts a year of a quality normally found in large cities. The group also gives pops and children's concerts and an occasional special benefit. Since 1978, it has been the mentor to a string of educational programs in the Henderson County Public Schools. The symphony supports a coaching program for youth ensembles, adult ensembles, a full youth orchestra, a young artist competition and a one-week summer string

camp. Tickets to the concerts, which are held in the Hendersonville High School auditorium (the Christmas concert is at the First Baptist Church), are $12 for adults and $5 for students.

## Polk County

### Tryon Community Chorus
**• no phone**

The Community Chorus is an all-volunteer group of people from the foothills. Two concerts are given each year: one during the Christmas season and another in the spring. Participation is open to all singers. Rehearsals are held on Mondays at Tryon Congregational Church beginning approximately ten weeks prior to performances. These are presented in the Polk County High School auditorium on a Friday night and Sunday afternoon. Proceeds from the concerts go toward scholarships sponsored by the Tryon Rotary Club. For further information write to Chorus, P.O. Box 54, Tryon 28782.

### Tryon Concert Association
**Tryon Fine Arts Center, 208 Melrose Ave., Tryon • (828) 859-8322, (828) 859-9050**

This association sponsors a series of quality musical programs featuring artists of note from October through May at the Tryon Fine Arts Center. Membership is by subscription and open to anyone who enjoys a wide variety of musical presentations. Volunteers manage all aspects of the concerts.

# Transylvania County

## Brevard Chamber Orchestra
P. O. Box 1547, Brevard, 28712
• (828) 884-2823

Established in 1978, this 55-piece orchestra of paid professionals from the Carolinas and Georgia has been conducted since 1980 by Virginia Tillotson, head of the music department at Brevard College. The five-concert season has performances scheduled in September, November, December, February and April. Two programs feature the full orchestra, while two showcase smaller, more intimate ensembles. Each concert highlights critically acclaimed guest artists. The fifth concert is a festive Christmas program featuring the orchestra and the choirs of Brevard. A benefit concert, always something special in the way of guest artists and themes, is held once a year, usually in March. The BCO is Orchestra in Residence at the Paul Porter Center for Performing Arts at Brevard College. Season tickets are available. Individual tickets for specific concerts are available in advance only at the Porter Center Box Office. That number is (828) 884-8330.

## Brevard College
400 N. Broad St., Brevard
• (828) 883-8292

Long known for its outstanding music curriculum, the college schedules a number of cultural events throughout the school year. These have been greatly enhanced by the new Paul Porter Center for Performing Arts. The public is invited to enjoy recitals, musicals, choral groups and instrumental ensembles as well as dance and drama that involve both students and teachers.

Through its Life and Culture Program, Brevard also sponsors lectures, concerts and writers and poetry series and has sponsored musical performances by such renowned groups as the Russian Folk Ensemble, the Audubon String Quartet, the Dutch vocal ensemble Quince, The National Opera and the Preservation Hall Jazz Band. Performances

by the likes of Sukay and the Nai-Ni Chen Dance Company are joint productions with the Transylvania County Arts Council. The college also brings in famous theatrical companies and lecturers. Many of the performances are free of charge.

## Brevard Music Center
1000 Probart St., Brevard
• (828) 884-2011, (800) 648-4523

On 140 beautiful acres just on the outskirts of town, the Brevard Music Festal had it beginning in 1936. Today it presents more than 70 different concert events from late June through mid-August in the Center's 1,800-seat, open-sided auditorium. Performances include symphony orchestra, opera, jazz, Broadway musicals, pops and internationally acclaimed guest artists. The 1999 season includes appearances by composer/entertainer Marvin Hamlisch, harpist Deborah Henson-Conant, pianist Garrick Ohlsson, Rhythm & Brass, the U.S. Army Orchestra and staged productions of Gilbert and Sullivan's *The Mikado,* Puccini's *La Boheme,* Massenet's *Manon* and Herbert's *Naughty Marietta.* In addition, an intimate chamber music series is scheduled on weeknights along with various student performances.

Integral to its impressive concert series, the Center provides a unique training experience for 400-plus gifted students from across the nation. They, along with teaching professionals from leading college/conservatories and performing organizations, perform beside internationally known guest artists, working together to present seven weeks of fabulous music.

More than half of the events are free to the public. Single tickets can range from free to $25 for adults and from free to $13 for children. For ticket information or to request a schedule of events, call the BMC Box Office at (828) 884-2019 or visit the Center's website at www.brevardmusic.org, where tickets may be purchased on-line.

## Calico Chorus and Men's Chorus
Brevard • (828) 883-2297

For more than 27 years, the Calico Chorus, founded and directed by Ruth Hunter, has presented spring and Christmas concerts.

In addition, this group of nine women entertains nursing home residents and community and civic organizations all over Western North Carolina with its delightful repertoire of mostly American popular music. About 11 years ago, eight male singers, called the Men's Chorus, were added for some of the performances, both to sing with the women and to do their own numbers.

The major concerts are usually held at the Brevard Presbyterian Church, 300 E. Main Street, or at the First Methodist Church, 500 N. Broad Street. The group has also proven very popular when participating in the town's Festival of the Arts and has performed in the Great Hall of the Grove Park Inn at Christmas.

### Transylvania Choral Society
**Brevard • (828) 884-2645**

This is a non-auditioned group of about 45 singers. Formed by Ruth Hunter about 20 years ago to offer church choir members in the community a forum for singing major sacred works, it's now open to anyone who loves to sing. It meets at Brevard-Davidson River Presbyterian Church weekly except during the

Wintertime in Asheville's Pack Square.

summer. Concerts of classical choral music are offered twice a year, in the spring and at Christmas. The concerts are usually at the Presbyterian Church. A Pops and Pasta Night on July 4 was started two years ago as a fund-raiser for the group. The conductor is Mary Kyle Link.

## Waldfest Summer Evening Concert Series
**Cradle of Forestry, U.S. Hwy. 276, Pisgah National Forest**
• **(828) 884-5713, (828) 877-3130**

For several summers now, the Waldfest Summer Evening Concert series at the Cradle of Forestry (see listing in this chapter under Museums and the Close-up in our Forests and Parks chapter) has been co-sponsored by Brevard College. The concerts begin at 6 PM in the outdoor amphitheater, or, if it rains, inside the Cradle of Forestry Education Wing.

For more information and ticket prices, call the above number.

# Southern Mountains

## Cherokee/Clay Counties

### John C. Campbell Folk School Concerts
**1 Folk School Rd., Brasstown**
• **(828) 837-2775, (800) FOLK-SCH**

Free Folk School Concerts are held most Fridays at 7:30 PM at the school's historic Keith House Community Room on Brasstown Rd. During late spring and summer, weather permitting, the event moves in the Festival Barn. (Bring a lawn chair and follow the signs from the Keith House parking area.) These concerts range from traditional gospel and bluegrass to music for handbells to western song and cowboy poetry.

### The Brasstown Concert Association
**P. O. Box 105, Brasstown, NC 28902**
• **(828) 837-8822**

Since 1927, this association has brought artists from the outside world to what, until a few decades ago, was a beautiful but remote area of the mountains. Today, it presents six concerts, three in the spring and three in the fall, of renowned artists that vary from flute to harp to string quartets to brass quintets to fabulous performers of ethnic music from around the world. These concerts, which takes place at 3 PM on Sunday afternoons, can be enjoyed at the John C. Campbell Folk School. (See our chapter on Mountain Crafts.) Season tickets are $40 for all six concerts; $20 for a series of three concerts. Tickets are usually $8 for a single concert, and discounts are available to students.

The association also occasionally sponsors dance and performance arts programs, and schedules music workshops in the local schools.

## Macon County

### Highlands Chamber Music Festival
**P.O. Box 1702, Highlands, NC 28741**
• **No phone**

Since 1981, the Highlands Chamber Music Festival has presented a stunning month-long series of chamber music. The July-August season features about 15 concerts held at the Episcopal Church of the Incarnation and the Highlands United Methodist Church. Write to the above address for current information on performers and ticket prices.

# Dance

# Central Mountains

## Buncombe County

### Asheville Contemporary Dance Theatre and
### The New Studio of Dance (The Loyd Agency)
**133 Forest Hill Dr., Asheville**
• **(828) 254-2621**

This fascinating, experimental dance/theater company presents lavishly produced original works adapted from ancient legends of different world cultures — particularly the richly imaginative Aztec and Mayan legends, such as the story of the feathered serpent

Quetzalcoatl. Meticulous research, typically taking as long as eight months, incorporates experimental movement, puppets, sword play, mime, traditional music and interpretive costuming (including some interesting ones of sculpted foam) for each production. The 6- to 15-member company has performed across the Southeast and in France and offers artistic exchanges with international dance theatre companies.

### Fletcher School of Dance/ Land of the Sky Civic Ballet
**177 Patton Ave., Asheville**
**• (828) 252-4761**
This distinguished school of dance, started more than 50 years ago by the late Beale Fletcher, is an institution in Asheville. The school's performing arm, the Land of the Sky Civic Ballet, annually produces a polished, well-received version of *The Nutcracker* for holiday audiences.

## Polk County

### Tryon Dance Guild
**Columbus • (828) 894-3051**
Twice a year, in the spring and fall, this guild, under the auspices of the Polk County Community Schools, presents performances by renowned national dance groups. Shows are held in the 700-seat Polk County High School Auditorium. Call the above number for ticket information. Free performances are presented to students throughout the county.

# Literary Arts

## Northern Mountains

### Ashe County

### Blue Ridge Writers Group
**148 Library Dr., Ashe County**
**Library, West Jefferson • (828) 246-9087**
This group supports the creative efforts of area writers of fiction, nonfiction and poetry. The Blue Ridge Writers Group sponsors literary contests, offers a critiquing service and provides tips on getting work published.

# Central Mountains

## Buncombe County

### Poetry Alive!
**20 Battery Park Ave., Asheville**
**• (828) 298-4927, (800) 476-8172**
Interaction is the life's blood of this arts organization, which was formed back in 1984 with the express purpose of popularizing poetry and making it more accessible to the general public, children in particular. The prime focus of Poetry Alive! is making poetry, education and fun synonymous, a feat accomplished over and over again by this innovative organization.

From five to nine teams of poets/performers travel the nation, bringing the richly illustrative world of poetry to all who will listen and watch. Transfixed audiences from kindergartners to college students watch as the words leap off the page, and all manner of poetry — epic poems, sonnets, classics from world culture, doggerel and humor — come to life before their eyes.

Team members are college graduates in fine arts or education. They also work with teachers to incorporate these materials into the classroom by providing workshops, scripted material and tapes. And fortunately, for the rest of us, Poetry Alive! offers performances for adults as well.

### The Writers' Workshop
**387 Beaucatcher Rd., Asheville**
**• (828) 254-8111**
This busy organization is geared to writers — amateurs, professionals and youthful budding scribes — of all ages. For the last 12 years, this membership group, in the historic old 1920s-era Flatiron Building downtown, has been dedicated to the promotion of all things literary.

The Writers' Workshop offers support, evaluation, competition and valuable workshops designed to enhance the spark of inspiration and help it grow. A quarterly newsletter and regular literary competitions are yearly highlights. Nationally known professional writers are judges for these contests and participate in an annual professional writers' forum in Asheville, sponsored by The Writer's Workshop. This special series is open to the public. Past participants have included such literary greats as Eudora Welty, Alex Haley, John Le Carre, E.L. Doctorow, Kurt Vonnegut and Peter Matthiessen.

## Transylvania County

### Transylvania Writers' Alliance
**c/o Michael DeNike, 92 Thunder Rd., Brevard 28712 • (828) 883-8688**

Both professional and amateur writers meet to share and critique their works and hear tips from successful authors. In addition to monthly meetings, there are weekly critique sessions. These sessions, for both poetry and prose, are held on separate days. There are also occasional workshops with professional leaders. For more information, call Mr. DeNike at the above number.

# Museums

## Northern Mountains

### Watauga County

### Appalachian Cultural Museum
**University Hall Dr., Boone**
**• (828) 262-3117**

You must visit this fine museum of Appalachian cultural heritage. Located in University Hall in Boone just off the campus of Appalachian State University, it is a fascinating collection of artifacts spanning eons — from prehistoric times to the present. You can view special exhibits depicting highlights of life in our mountain region. Groups can take advantage of the specially guided tours led by museum staff (call for a reservation). These personalized illuminations of history focus on all aspects of living in the mountains, now and in the past. University Hall also houses the Appalachian Collection, a wonderfully varied assortment of music, books and documents pertinent to the region. The offices of the Appalachian Consortium and the Center for Appalachian Studies are also here.

### Hickory Ridge Homestead
**591 Horn in the West Dr., Boone**
**• (828) 264-2120**

This living history museum, sponsored by the Southern Appalachian Historical Association, is composed of a series of log structures, a main log cabin, a weaving room and a smoke house, all depicting the period of the late-18th century in the Appalachian mountains. The homestead reflects the same period covered by the outdoor drama *Horn in the West*, also on the site. The Olde Christmas Celebration and the Hickory Ridge Homestead Apple Festival in October are two special events celebrated here.

## Central Mountains

### Buncombe County

### Biltmore Estate
**N.C. Hwy. 25, Asheville**
**• (828) 255-1700, (800) 543-2961**

Don't miss the spectacular private working estate established in 1895 by railroad heir George Vanderbilt. Vanderbilt chose his original 125,000 acres well and created a lavish 250-room mansion styled after his favorite chateau in France's Loire River Valley and it's filled with antiques and artifacts (for much more information, see our chapter on The Biltmore Estate and Winery).

### Biltmore Homespun Museum
**111 Grovewood Rd., Asheville**
**• (828) 253-7651**

Built in 1917, the English-style pebble-dash cottage housing the museum was one of the original Biltmore Homespun shop buildings. Photos and artifacts preserve the old weaving operation begun almost a century ago under the auspices of Edith Stuyvesant Vanderbilt, wife of railroad heir George Vanderbilt of Biltmore Estate. Artifacts such as bolts of cloth, antique handmade looms and an original, old-time clock bring back the flavor of the Biltmore Industries and Biltmore Homespun Shops of days gone by. During the week there are weaving demonstrations throughout the day. There's no entrance fee.

## Biltmore Village Historic Museum
**7 Biltmore Plaza, Biltmore Village, Asheville • (828) 274-9707**

The 100-year history of Biltmore Village and its integral connection to George Vanderbilt and his magnificent Biltmore Estate is displayed in an exhibit of period photographs and Victorian artifacts in this free museum in Biltmore Village (see our chapter on The Biltmore Estate and Winery for more information).

## Estes-Winn Antique Automobile Museum
**111 Grovewood Rd., Asheville • (828) 253-7651**

Next door to Grovewood Gallery (see previous listing in this chapter), in the massive original weaving shed that once housed 40 looms for the old Biltmore Industries, is the Estes-Winn Antique Automobile Museum. This delightful collection is a veritable history of how America took to the highway, from the first Model T to shiny post-World War II roadsters. You can fantasize about grand old autos such as a 1926 Cadillac and a 1927 La Salle convertible. There's even a 1922 La France fire engine on display that once was used by the Asheville Fire Department. They just don't make 'em like they used to!

## Pack Place Education Arts and Science Center
**2 South Pack Sq., Asheville • (828) 257-4500**

This spectacular, 92,000-square-foot complex is a monument to the determination of such leading Asheville citizens as the late Roger McGuire, whose vision was to realize the potential of downtown Asheville. The success of Pack Place has finally become reality, and visitors and citizens alike are discovering the delights of this diverse cultural center. Pack Place is the union, adaptation and renovation of several historic structures and is home to The Asheville Art Museum, the Colburn Gem and Mineral Museum, The Health Adventure, Diana Wortham Theatre and the YMI Cultural Center.

The Asheville Art Museum, founded in 1948, is contained on 3½ floors of the old Pack Memorial Library, now a part of Pack Place. This first-rate museum maintains a fine permanent collection of 20th-century American art, including the work of such renowned artists as Romare Bearden, Jacob Lawrence and George Inness; the sculpture of Louise Nevelson; and contemporary abstracts of Asheville natives Kenneth Noland and Donald Sultan. Tours are available for group visits.

The Colburn Gem and Mineral Museum is an exploration of the geological world around us. The museum, founded in 1960, highlights gems and minerals of all shapes and sizes from around the world as well as those specific garnets, rubies, emeralds and gold deposits that make North Carolina a rock hound's delight (see our chapter on Rock Hounding).

The Health Adventure, founded in 1968, is a marvelous hands-on learning center, providing children and adults special insights into the human physical condition and related applied sciences. Two theaters accommodate school groups for educator-led programs. Thoughtfully planned, hands-on exhibits such as Brain Storm, Body Works, Miracle of Life and the Creative Play Space (for children younger than 8) invite young curiosity.

The Diana Wortham Theatre is a gem of a performance space for audiences, performers and technicians. The 500-seat theater is an intimate, sophisticated setting with a full-size stage, exquisitely detailed woodwork, impeccable acoustics and accessibility for people with disabilities. Diana Wortham Theatre presents, produces and hosts performing arts events that range from Shakespeare to Mamet, classical ballet to modern dance, lectures to performance poetry, symphonies to Brubeck, and world-renowned storytellers to local school pageants.

The YMI Cultural Center, also a part of the Pack Place complex, is on the corner of Market and Eagle streets, southeast of Pack Square, in an architecturally rich, century-old structure commissioned by George Vanderbilt. This museum is the home of changing exhibits and a permanent collection of artifacts that focus on the local, national and international African-American heritage.

The Adventure Place is an imaginatively stocked gift shop designed to complement the various museums found at Pack Place. A fascinating lobby exhibit entitled "Here is the Square . . ." traces three centuries of Asheville history and the evolution of Pack Square itself.

Tickets are required for admission to each of the museums. A single adult ticket for each museum is $3.50, with a discount for senior citizens and students (with ID) and for children ages 4 to 15. Your best bet is a one-day pass covering admission to all museums at $6.50, $5.50 and $4.50, respectively. Children younger than 3 are admitted free. Hours are Tuesday through Saturday from 10 AM to 5 PM. From June through October, Pack Place is also open on Sundays from 1 to 5 PM. The Art Museum is open Friday night until 8 PM.

## Smith-McDowell House
### 283 Victoria Rd., Asheville
### • (828) 253-9231

This fine old Asheville residence is on the campus of Asheville-Buncombe Technical Community College. The stately, early Victorian-era home, built around 1840, is Asheville's oldest brick residence, furnished with period antiques. You'll enjoy the marvelous architectural details and appointments of this palatial beauty. Personalized tours are available. Admission is $5 for adults and $2 for children. Regular hours are Tuesday through Saturday from 10 AM to 4 PM and Sunday from 1 to 4 PM. Hours during January, February and March are Tuesday through Friday from 10 AM to 4 PM.

## Swannanoa Valley Museum
### 225 W. State St., Black Mountain
### • (828) 669-9566

The Swannanoa Valley Museum, open seasonally from April through October, is the guardian of a remarkable collection of artifacts of everyday life in Western North Carolina, from pioneer times to recent years. Local residents donated many of the items here. This unique museum is also home to an exhibit honoring Rafael Guastavino, architect and designer of the century-old Basilica of St. Lawrence in Asheville; displays spotlighting Billy Graham's crusades; the U.S. Navy artifacts of Rear Adm.

G.C. Crawford; and an extensive collection of wildflower photography. The museum is open Tuesday through Saturday, 10 AM to 5 PM and Sunday, 2 to 5 PM.

## Thomas Wolfe Memorial
### 48 Spruce St., Asheville • (828) 253-8304

Asheville's native son, noted author of the classic coming-of-age novel, *Look Homeward, Angel*, spent his boyhood here in his mother's rambling old boarding house on Spruce Street, just off legendary Pack Square. This old house figured prominently in Wolfe's work and is important for its ability to convey the forces that helped shape this remarkable American writer. Tragically, the house was badly burned in a fire in late 1998, and is presently undergoing renovations. The Thomas Wolfe Welcome Center adjacent to the house is still open and offers information about the house and the author.

## Zebulon Vance Birthplace
### Reems Creek Rd., off Old U.S. Hwys. 19/23, Weaverville • (828) 645-6706

This charming mountain homestead was home to one of North Carolina's most prominent political figures. Zeb Vance began his career as a lawyer, assuming public office by the young age of 24. He was elected governor of North Carolina three times, most notably during the Civil War. He also served three terms as a U.S. senator. At his death in 1894, this most capable public servant was admired by colleagues and beloved by his constituency. His life and career are profiled in an exhibit in the adjoining visitors center.

The two-story cabin and outbuildings are reconstructions, built from hewn, yellow pine logs around the original chimney with its two massive fireplaces. The furnishings and household items depict the period from 1790 to 1840 and include a few pieces original to the Vance family.

Pioneer Living Days are celebrated here each spring and fall. Costumed staff members demonstrate skills and occupations of earlier days. Military encampments and battle reenactments are frequently part of the events (see our Annual Festivals and Events chapter). Admission to the homestead is free.

## Henderson County

### Carl Sandburg Home
1928 Little River Rd., Flat Rock
• (828) 693-4178

Carl Sandburg — poet, author, lecturer, minstrel, onetime political activist, social thinker and winner of two Pulitzer Prizes for his four-volume *Abraham Lincoln: The War Years* and his *Complete Poems* — spent the last 22 years of his life at Connemara, a 240-acre farm 3 miles south of Hendersonville. The main house was built in 1838 as a summer home for Charleston's Christopher Gustave Memminger, who served as Secretary of the Confederate Treasury from 1861 to 1864. Like many mountain residents today, Memminger wanted to escape the heat and humidity of the coast, while Sandburg sought relief from cold northern winters.

Sandburg moved here in 1945 with his wife, three daughters, grandchildren and his wife's prize-winning Chikaming goats — a herd that grew as large as 200; the milk was turned into a successful dairy operation. The Sandburgs spent happy and productive years in a lovely setting of rolling pastures, ponds, lakes and wooded mountains. Sandburg died in 1967, and Connemara became a National Historic Site the following year. It's open daily except on December 25.

To reach the site, drive south on U.S. Highway 25 and turn onto Little River Road at the Flat Rock Playhouse. Park at the Visitors Information Center and, after viewing the exhibits there, take the lovely walk past a small lake up to the main house for a guided tour. (Access assistance for the handicapped is provided.) Later, stroll about the farm and pet the goats and other farm animals if you don't mind risking an occasional bite, peck or kick. Hike the 2.6-mile round-trip trail up to Glassy Mountain, one of Sandburg's favorite walks, for a mountain ridge and valley view.

In midsummer, there are free dramatic renditions of some of Sandburg's writings offered by the Apprentice Company of the Flat Rock Playhouse in the outdoor theater (call for performance times). Connemara is particularly festive during the Christmas season, which is celebrated in "Sandburg style" on Saturday evenings from Thanksgiving until Christmas. The park is closed only on December 25.

### The Historic Hendersonville Depot and Model Railroad
Seventh Ave. and Maple St.,
Hendersonville • (828) 693-0605

Hendersonville got its first train depot in 1879, which was replaced in 1902 by the present structure. Now the quaint building is under an ongoing restoration program. Dressed up in its original colors, it houses an operating, 420-square-foot model railroad in its old baggage room. The model features the Hendersonville, Asheville, Brevard and Saluda stations, including the Saluda Grade (the steepest grade in the country), plus mountains, waterfalls, lakes, towns and industries. The train runs over 500 feet of track and has more than 100 switches. It's open to the public free of change year round (donations are appreciated) from noon to 3 PM on Wednesdays and 9 AM until noon on Saturdays. For information about the model railroad or membership in the club, call Harry Bothwell at the listed number; Mike Carlin, (828) 697-0470; or John Kulamer, (828) 697-2540.

### The Historic Johnson Farm
3346 Haywood Rd. (N.C. Hwy. 191),
Hendersonville • (828) 891-6585

Located 4 miles north of Hendersonville on N.C. Highway 191, this late 19th century, 15-acre tobacco farm became a popular summer tourist retreat in the 1920s. Today, owned by the Henderson County Public Schools, an 1870s brick farmhouse, 1920 boarding house, barn-loft museum, 10 historic buildings and two nature trails are operated as a heritage education center and farm museum. Guided tours are available at 10:30 AM and 1:30 PM Tuesdays through Saturdays May through October, and Wednesday through Saturdays, November through April. A small admission is charged for guided tours.

### Western North Carolina Air Museum
1340 Gilbert St., Hendersonville
• (828) 693-9703, (800) 828-4244

It's appropriate that this air museum, in

the state where flight was born, is located at the Hendersonville Airport. That also enables it to feature spring and fall air shows. Award winning, beautifully restored airplanes as well as restored replica antique and vintage planes are on display here. They range from a 1917 Nieuport 11 (Bebe) replica to a 1950s Ercoup and a Corbin Ace. You can even view a 1510 Ornithopter designed by Leonardo Da Vinci. The museum is open each Wednesday, Saturday and Sunday from noon until 6 PM. Admission is free, but donations are welcomed. Gifts and souvenirs are available. Annual museum memberships are $25 for individuals and $35 for families. Lifetime memberships are also available.

## Polk County

### Polk County Historical Association & Museum
**1 Depot St., Tryon • (828) 859-2287**

Housed in the old but charmingly renovated Tryon railroad depot, the association exhibits household, agricultural and historical artifacts used by the early settlers and Indians in this area. There is also a collection of folklore, old maps, records and pictures, including important items in American history such as "the cannonball that started the Civil War," said to have been picked up at Fort Sumter by a young Union officer, Abner Doubleday. Monthly historical meetings are held, and the public is invited. The museum is open on Tuesdays and Thursdays from 10 AM until noon and by appointment. Admission is free but donations are appreciated.

## Transylvania County

### Allison-Deaver Historical House
**N.C. Hwy. 280, Pisgah Forest**
**• (828) 884-5137**

Just two days before it was scheduled to be demolished, Western North Carolina's oldest frame house west of the Blue Ridge Mountains was saved by the Transylvania County Historical Society. Built in Quaker or Federal architectural style in the early 1800s by Benjamin Allison, it housed his family of 11 children. In 1830, he sold the house and its 420 acres to William Deaver, who, In the early

1840s, remodeled the six-room, 1,100-square-foot structure into a Greek Revival house and expanded it. Then, in the 1860s, the roof was raised to make room for second and third floor Charleston-, or Low County-style porches. This "house-restoration museum" is open for tours from April through October from 10 AM to 4 PM on Fridays and Saturdays and on Sunday from 1 to 4 PM. There is no admission charge, but donations for this on-going project are appreciated.

The Allison-Deaver House is located on N.C. 280 just north of its intersection with U.S. Hwy. 64 in Pisgah Forest. It is adjacent to the Forest Gate Shopping Center and Taco Bell restaurant.

### Cradle of Forestry
**U.S. Hwy. 276, Pisgah National Forest**
**• (828) 877-3130**

There is an old story, though probably not true, that claims someone told George Vanderbilt that if he was going to build a baronial estate (Biltmore House and Gardens certainly qualifies), he should have a baronial forest — and that's how scientific forestry got started in America. True or not, in the late 1800s, George Vanderbilt hired Gifford Pinchot to restore and manage the forest on the 8,000 acres surrounding his famous estate. His holdings were later expanded to 125,000 acres that, after his death, became part of Pisgah National Forest.

In 1895, Dr. Carl Schenck, a brilliant German forester, succeeded Pinchot and was a magnet for young men wishing to learn the new sustainable-forest methods. As a result, in 1898 Schenck started the Biltmore Forest School, the first forestry school in America. For his campus, he utilized an old schoolhouse and abandoned farm buildings in a 3,200-foot-high valley that was named the Pink Beds, after its lush bloom of flowers. In 1964, 6,500 acres in this area were established as a National Historic Site and became known as the Cradle of Forestry.

Special interpretive programs and guided tours are offered here, and you can view an excellent 18-minute movie depicting the relationship between Vanderbilt, Pinchot, Schenck and the Forest School students. The Forest Discover Center has a Biltmore Forest

School exhibit with a collection of artifacts as well as "Schenck's Office," where you'll find period furniture and artifacts and can look through the windows and listen to a conversation between Dr. Schenck and a student. (See the Cradle of Forestry Close-up in our Forests and Parks chapter.)

There are two beautiful, mile-long paved trails, each with guided tours that will tell you of the Cradle's history and teach you a lot about the plants and trees along the way. The Forest Festival Trail has many forest demonstration projects, an old saw mill, the first little fish hatchery in Pisgah and a old Climax logging train on display — children love to climb on it and ring the bell. The Biltmore Campus Trail winds through the school's old campus of original and reconstructed buildings. In addition to the schoolhouse, there's a general store, a two-story frame house built in 1884, another farmhouse that was used as student quarters, a blacksmith shop, an old barn that Schenck converted to an office, two former ranger houses designed by Schenck (known as the Black Forest Lodge and the Cantrell Creek Lodge), an old-time vegetable garden and more.

On Friday, Saturday and Sunday afternoons, craftspeople in period dress demonstrate crafts like weaving, spinning, quilting, basketry and toy making and give you a glimpse of life at the turn of the century. There are a number of special events throughout the year, such as Fiber Arts Week and the huge Forest Festival Day, held in October. The Cradle, open seven days a week from 9 AM to 5 PM, is on U.S. Highway 276, 14 miles northwest of Brevard and 4 miles south of the Blue Ridge Parkway at milepost 412. The use fee is $4 for adults and $2 for children ages 6 to 17. Children 5 and younger are admitted free.

## Jim Bob Tinsley Museum and Research Center
### 20 W. Jordan St., Brevard
• (828) 884-2347

Transylvania County may seem an unlikely place to find a cowboy museum, but this is a great one. It houses the extensive collection of art, memorabilia and research records of Jim Bob Tinsley, a Brevard native and famous

author, educator and musicologist. He performed with Gene Autry in the late '40s and has received many awards for his work, including one from the National Cowboy Hall of Fame for his book (one of 10) He Was Singing This Song, a compilation of traditional American cowboy songs.

Here you'll find original art, lithographs, photographs and bronze statues by famous sculptors of the caliber of Frederick Remington. There is also, as you might expect, a lot about country-and-western music, including a large collection of records, tapes and CDs. There are reels and TV tapes of western movies and old television programs that are played during office hours. And there are all those other things connected to cowboys: saddles, spurs, branding irons from famous ranches, Florida Cracker cowboy whips and an original Zane Grey 30-foot riata, to name a few items.

But Tinsley's interests go far beyond cowboys. The museum contains his historic Transylvania County memorabilia, including one of only six known Gillespie rifles. The gun dates from the early 1880s and was manufactured at the Gillespie rifle factory in nearby South Mills River. You'll also find art and literature concerning two of his other passions: pumas and sailfish. And then there are Tinsley's waterfall photos, many of which appeared in his popular book The Land of Waterfalls: Transylvania, North Carolina.

The museum's summer hours are Tuesday through Saturday from 10 AM to 4 PM; in winter, hours are Tuesday through Saturday from 1 to 4 PM. Admission is free.

## Silvermont Mansion
### E. Main St., Brevard
• No phone

John Silversteen and his wife, Elizabeth, moved to Transylvania County in 1902. He opened the Toxaway Tanning Company, around which the town of Rosman grew, and later established the Gloucester Lumber Company. His enterprises, the largest in the county, provided work for several hundred people until the 1950s. He was active in and generous to the community, building the first brick elementary school in Rosman and donating the land for that town's high school.

# Little People and Fairy Crosses

Those of us steeped in Western culture know all about the Old World's fairies, elves, gnomes, trolls and the like, but few of us are acquainted with the Little People who reside in these mountains, though some of European-descent have encountered them over the years. James Mooney, in his classic work, *History, Myths, and Sacred Formulas of the Cherokees*, first published in 1900 by the Bureau of American Ethnology, identifies a whole pantheon of spirit folk, some of whom are mentioned in other legends in our book.

The Cherokee's name for Little People is *yunwi tsunsdi*. They usually live in rock caves on mountainsides, though one group of Water Dwellers called *yunwi amaiyinehi* lives in water (they are the ones fishing enthusiasts should try to please). When full-grown, yunwi tsunsdi are only as tall as a man's knee, but they are well-formed and handsome with long hair down to their heels. They love music and spend a lot of time singing and dancing.

They are also powerful workers of wonders. Generally speaking, they are kind and helpful (particularly to children or people lost in the woods) but not always. If you hear their drumming in the distance, don't follow the sound: If disturbed in their homes, Little People will cast a spell that will make you lose your way. Even if you are found, you may spend the rest of your life in a daze. If you find an object, such as a knife or other item in the woods, you must say, "Little People, I want to take this," because if you don't and it belongs to them, they will throw stones at you on your way home.

Like the busy elves in Western lore, they will sometimes come near a human house at night and, before morning, finish a huge task like clearing a field that would require the efforts of a huge work force. However, if you hear them at work, don't go out to see them, or you'll die.

Many little footprints were seen, and a number of encounters with these little folk were described in accounts by both Indians and whites (mainly hunters) at the end of the last century. Some of these took place near or at the head of the Oconaluftee River, which flows through the present-day Cherokee Indian Reservation. There is also a certain spot in what is now the Great Smoky Mountains National Park where yunsi tsunsdi came to the Cherokees during summer solstices to tell them, among other things, tales of the Cherokee nation's history.

One day, the Little People were near Brasstown, doing their favorite thing — singing and dancing — when a foreign "messenger" arrived and told them the sad tale of Christ's death on a cross. They were so moved, they cried. As their tears fell, they turned into little stone crosses that can still be found today. A wonderful collection of these Fairy Crosses can be seen in Murphy's Cherokee County Historical Museum, which is described in this chapter.

But he's most remembered for Silvermont, the 1917, 33-room, Colonial Revival house that still stands on its spacious grounds on E. Main Street. Here the Silversteens raised their three daughters — two went into business with their father; one became a noted singer who performed with the likes of Arturo Toscanini and Leopold Stokowski under the name of Adelaide van Wey.

Silvermont was willed to the county when the last daughter died in 1972. It was placed on the National Register of Historic Places in 1981. Full of interesting furniture and Silversteen memorabilia, its first floor is used for community club meetings, by private groups and as a senior meal and recreation center. The 8-acre grounds have tennis and shuffleboard courts, a basketball court, a playground and a picnic area. On summer evenings, square dancing takes place on Tuesday, ballroom dancing on Wednesday and mountain music "on the porch" on Thursday. Christmas at Silvermont features decorations by the Transylvania Council of Garden Clubs, usually involving musical performances.

The mansion is available for weddings, receptions, family reunions, class reunions and other special events, but is closed when not in use. For more information call Herman Rahn at (828) 877-3939 or Harley Raines at (828) 883-9223. For information about the park, call (828) 884-3156.

# Southern Mountains

## Clay County

### Historical Arts Museum
**U.S. Hwy. 64 business, Hayesville**
**• (828) 389-6814**
The museum, housed in the town's old jail, is devoted to local history and is sponsored by the Clay County Historical and Art Council. Here you'll see a cross-section of memorabilia — the first telephone switchboard and a kitchen from last century — from earlier time. Receptions and showings of local artists are also held here. It is open from June through September.

## Cherokee County

### Cherokee County Historical Museum
**205 Peachtree St., Murphy**
**• (828) 837-6792**
This museum is housed in the former Carnegie Library building, right next to the even grander county courthouse. Its largest collection is devoted to the life of the Cherokees during their many centuries in the mountains and their removal to Oklahoma. Murphy itself was established near the site of the ancient Cherokee village of Guasili (pronounced "gau-ax-u-le"), visited by De Soto in 1540, and was also the site of Fort Butler, the largest of the forts built in the area for the Cherokees' removal via "The Trail of Tears."

In the museum are leftover weapons from Spanish explorers and another large collection of tools, housewares and other items from the early pioneer days in the region. Some of the most interesting things among the mineral and rock collections are "fairy crosses" (see our Close-up, "Little People and Fairy Crosses," in this chapter). These naturally occurring little stone crosses, called staurlite (pronounced "starlight") crystals, are supposed to bring the finder good luck. Some can be as large as 3 inches across. They still turn up around Hyatt Creek southeast of Marble and around Fishermare Branch, Almond Creek, between Parsons Branch and Burnt Branch and around the Brasstown area.

The museum also houses a collection of more than 700 priceless dolls donated by Louise S. Kilgore. They include, among other things, representations of famous personalities (including Elvis and Princess Diana) and unique older dolls made in pre-factory days. The collection takes up about one-fourth of the space on the museum's top floor. The museum is open Monday through Friday from 9 AM until 5 PM. Admission is free.

## Haywood County

### Canton Area Historical Museum
**36 Park St., Canton • (828) 646-3412**
With its library of old family histories and historical documents, this city-run museum, housed in the town's old library building, is an excellent place to research local history. Displays include artifacts, records, heritage handicrafts and pictures from the past, all of which combine to tell the story of the settling of Canton and the Pigeon River area, Haywood County and Western North Carolina (in that order of importance). The artifacts include everything from Indian arrowheads and tools to butter molds, quilts, glassware and pottery.

Special shows, such as an exhibit of old medical equipment and an exhibit of local primitive painters, are frequently held. You can also explore a Champion display room, which features a video on the role of Champion paper in the area. The museum also participates in educational programs at local schools and civic clubs. It's open Monday through Friday from 10 AM until noon and from 1 PM until 4 PM.

## The Museum of North Carolina Handicrafts
**307 Shelton St., Waynesville**
**• (828) 452-1551**

The Shelton House, built in 1875 and listed on the National Register of Historic Places, is the setting for these comprehensive exhibits of 19th-century crafts. It also has an interesting exhibit of handicrafts made by artisans who have participated in the educational demonstration of heritage crafts in the North Carolina State Fair's Village of Yesteryear since 1951 (see our Mountain Crafts chapter for more information). New exhibits include a working Pioneer Village and a collection of railroad memorabilia. The museum is open from 10 AM to 4 PM, Tuesday through Friday, May through October. There is an admission charge of $4 for adults; for groups of 15 or more, it's $2 per adult.

## Jackson County

### Mountain Heritage Center
**Administration Bldg., Western Carolina University, U.S. Hwy. 107, Cullowhee**
**• (828) 277-7129**

If you're of Scotch-Irish ancestry, this museum is a must! Even if you're not, it's a very special place for learning about the land, culture and people of the Appalachian region. A large permanent exhibit, "Migration of the Scotch-Irish People," relates the saga of this group's departure from their native Scotland to settle in Northern Ireland and, in a later generation, its journey from Ulster to the New World. It also highlights the homes and culture that developed here in the coves and hollows of Western North Carolina. Murals and a life-size, 18th-century Irish cottage make the story come alive. Other exhibits illustrate the mountains' natural history and society, both past and present.

This section also preserves objects of historical significance, including the heirlooms

of hundreds of families who lived here. There are exhibits on cornshuck handcrafts and the traditions of milling, tilling and stilling corn. A good place to start your tour is in the museum movie theater, where nine-projector, multi-image shows complement the thematic exhibits. The center also publishes books and other materials on mountain culture. All these — the exhibits, the shows and the literature — are based on thorough and extensive research.

The Mountain Heritage Center is also the focus for Mountain Heritage Day, held in September, which attracts more than 35,000 visitors (see our Festivals and Annual Events chapter). During this event, the center puts together a folk festival featuring musicians and craftspeople who maintain authentic mountain traditions. The center also sponsors a variety of special mountain-heritage events in the schools and communities throughout the region. It is open year round, Monday through Friday from 8 AM to 5 PM, and from 1 to 4 PM on Sunday. There is no admission charge.

## Macon County

### Macon County Historical Museum
**36 W. Main St., Franklin • (828) 524-9758**

This museum, supported by the Macon County Historical Society, preserves the area's heritage through displays of artifacts, documents and photographs that illustrate the social, cultural and historical background of the county. The museum is open Monday through Friday from 10 AM to 4 PM.

### Scottish Tartans Museum and Heritage Center
**86 E. Main St., Franklin • (828) 524-7472**

If you can't get to Scotland this year, this museum, recognized and authorized by the Scottish Tartans Society (the official registry of all publicly known tartans), is the next best thing. Opened in 1994, the 3,200-square-foot facility includes exhibits of tartan and Highland dress from 1700 to the present and shows the evolution of the kilt and the weaving of tartan. It also traces the influence of the Scots and other settlers on Appalachian and Cherokee culture and the history of North Carolina. Those of Scottish ancestry can investigate the tartan research library and find their family's tartan in the Tartan Room. There is also a great gift shop full of Celtic and Scottish treasures. All tartan items are imported from Scotland and come in 100 percent new wool. You'll also find scarves, shawls, sashes, tams, men's ties, caps and children's items. Immediate delivery can be had on books, music, clan videos, jewelry, Highland dress items, dirks, skean dubbs, and Scottish weaponry. The museum is open year round from 10 AM to 5 PM Monday through Saturday and 1 PM to 5 PM on Sunday. Admission is $1 for adults, and children 10 and younger with an adult are admitted free.

# Other Cultural Events, Organizations and Information

## Northern Mountains

### Watauga County

#### An Appalachian Summer
**229 Rivers St., Boone**
**• (828) 262-6084, (800) 841-ARTS**

For one glorious month each summer, Boone comes alive with an intense, exciting celebration of the arts. This July explosion of theater, music, dance and art is Appalachian State University's annual arts blowout, drawing visitors from across the Southeast. Now in its 14th season, An Appalachian Summer is an interactive arts festival, with workshops, art competitions, concerts and exhibits designed to please the entire family.

Children can participate in their own special art and creative writing workshops. All tastes are satisfied during Appalachian Summer. Music ranges from the classic strains of the North Carolina Symphony to New Orleans jazz, traditional bluegrass and from well-known singer-storytellers to the country/folk stylings of musical artists. The Atlanta Ballet, the Parsons Dance Company, international folk dancers and mountain cloggers and buck dancers all perform during that one month in Boone. The excitement is contagious.

You can purchase individual tickets for different events, but your best bet is the subscription package that covers the whole shebang. A full season package costs approximately $230. You can purchase a series of six or more adult tickets at a variety of discounts, or pay $16 each for individual events. Student admission costs about $9 and children ages 12 and younger are admitted for $2.

## Madison County

### Mars Hill College
**Off U.S. Hwy. 19/23 N., Mars Hill**
**• (828) 689-1217**

Mars Hill College is a fundamental source for a variety of cultural activities in the Madison County area. The celebrated theater, art, history and music departments continually provide excellence in each of those disciplines.

The Southern Appalachian Repertory Theater (SART) at Mars Hill College grew out of the exceptional talent of the college drama department and has, for 22 summers, perpetuated the best in classic and popular theater. SART has also served as the premiere stage for a number of emerging playwrights. The college department of art maintains gallery space and features the exceptional talent of both students and faculty members.

The department of music at Mars Hill is well-known for the talent that continues to emerge from its academic program. Concerts and recitals by students and faculty are open to the general public. This department, in cooperation with the Student Activities department, has been instrumental in bringing the finest in musical concerts and dance performance (such as the Joffrey Ballet, among others) to the campus.

Mountain heritage is a vital focus of this college. To that end, Mars Hill's Rural Life Museum is devoted to the presentation and preservation of the history of the unique lifestyle of our pioneer forebears. The museum is also home to the William A. Barnhill Collection, a personal photographic legacy illustrating mountain life in Western North Carolina in 1914, seen through the eye of the young roving photographer. The college also features a series of public service forums and a variety of speakers during the year addressing current national and international issues.

# Central Mountains

## Buncombe County

### Fine Arts Theater
**36 Biltmore Ave., Asheville**
**• (828) 232-1536**

This newly restored movie theater (a triple-X cinema in the 1970s) screens award-winning independent and foreign films. The main theater is an ode to the finer days of cinema, with dimmed brass sconces, plush seats, a high ceiling and finely draped stage. The smaller upstairs cinema is as cozy as the main hall is elegant. More than just your regular Milk Duds and Goobers, the snacks at the Fine Arts range from beer to biscotti. Catch the excellent first-run films shown here, because it's the only place down town you can!

### University of North Carolina at Asheville
**1 University Heights, off Weaver Blvd., Asheville • (828) 251-6600**

This exceptional liberal arts university (see our Education chapter) provides the city of Asheville and the surrounding area with an incredibly diverse and continuously entertaining array of cultural arts offerings. The departments of music, drama and art and the UNCA Cultural and Special Events Committee coordinate everything from international and experimental music/theater to folk music and dance, Broadway touring companies and Shakespeare with the renowned North Carolina Shakespeare Festival company.

The in-house cultural arts departments of music, drama and art offer an equally impressive schedule of events — first-rate theater productions, Tanglewood Children's Theater, university gallery shows for both students and faculty and community-based organizations such as the UNCA Community Chorus, the UNCA Community Concert Band and the UNCA Community Jazz Band. These are open by audition to any musically trained or inclined citizens of any age in the Asheville area. The

groups present various public concerts during the year.

One of the best-received UNCA cultural events is the summer Concerts on the Quad series. These free performances on the grassy stage of the university quad in the center of the campus happen every Monday from 7 to 8:30 PM during June and July and are always well-attended by area residents as well as UNCA students. Get there early and be ready for incredible entertainment. Summer performances have included those avant-garde poetry slam artists who fill the air with alphabetical arias, the talent of international folk dance teams from the acclaimed Folkmoot international dance festival (headquartered in Waynesville), Big Band jazz and African-American ethnic dancing.

### WCQS-FM
**73 Broadway St., Asheville**
**• (828) 253-6875**

This is the Asheville area's exceptional public radio station. The community-based FM station began back in the 1970s on the campus of the University of North Carolina at Asheville and moved to its present location in 1984. Programming features classical, jazz, folk and traditional music, in-depth local news and information and National Public Radio. It's available on several frequencies in the Western North Carolina area: 88.1 FM in Asheville and Hendersonville; 89.7 FM in Waynesville, Clyde, Cullowhee, and Webster; 91.3 FM in Franklin and North Georgia; 90.7 FM in Brevard; 95.3 FM in the Cherokee and Waynesville area; and 104.5 on the Asheville InterMedia Cable FM.

## Henderson County

### The Blue Ridge Radio Players
**P.O. Box 993, Hendersonville, NC 28793**
**• (828) 692-0621**

These talented volunteers dramatize literary classics on audio cassettes for broadcast over the air and distribution free of charge to the visually impaired all over the United States, including Hawaii. A number of public radio stations air these tapes, and many libraries specializing in tapes for the visually impaired make them available.

Each year, the Radio Players put on An Evening with the Blue Ridge Radio Players, consisting of a comedy and a mystery at the Blue Ridge Community College auditorium. This gives the public a behind-the-scenes look at radio production and helps to let the community know what the group is up to. If you would like to contribute your talents to this fine group, or you wish to learn how to gain access to the cassettes, write to the above address.

## Transylvania County

### RiverRun International Film Festival
**Brevard College, 400 N. Broad St.**
**Brevard • (828) 884-8209**

The first annual RiverRun International Film Festival held at Brevard College in the fall of 1998 and co-sponsored by the Belle Visione Film Society adds a new dimension for the College and the region. Independent film makes have a venue for screening feature films, documentaries and shorts. Internationally known actors, filmmakers, directors, producers and cinematographers conduct professional labs/workshops.

Each week during the Festival, Brevard College and Cinema Paradiso screen independent films in Durham Auditorium. The public is welcome. Call for information at the above number.

With the advent of good roads in the middle of this century, the crafts of "makin' do" in the mountains were transformed into beautiful art forms.

# Mountain Crafts

All areas of the United States have their talented craftspeople, but few places have the fabulous hand-wrought heritage found in the southern Appalachians. Tucked away in our coves or working in downtown studios, there are cadres of citizens to whom "handmade" is a large part of both life and livelihood.

Many of these crafts flourished in the isolation caused by the lack of good transportation to and from the remote mountain regions. With the advent of good roads in the middle of this century, the crafts of "makin' do" were transformed into beautiful art forms. The Cherokee Indians who occupied the area for countless generations (see our chapter on The Cherokee Indian Reservation) influenced handcrafts, as did the Old World settlers, passing down skills that eventually evolved into their own style. And there's no doubt that many crafts were inspired by the wealth of natural resources. There were honeysuckle, river cane and white oak for baskets; willows for furniture; silver bell and rhododendron for making canes; and the country's largest variety of wood for carving bowls, spoons and statues.

Natural dyes were derived from wild poke berries, blueberries, black walnuts, yellow root and any number of other plants. Skilled hands transformed pinecones and weeds of the fields and roadsides into wreaths and stunning dried-flower arrangements. Corn shucks became dolls, flowers and fans. Handmade toys that amused our great-grandparents still delight our children today. Clay for pottery was there for the digging, and some of this malleable earth was of such high quality that it ended up as table settings for royalty.

The land surrounding Franklin in Macon County is most famous for producing rubies and other gemstones, but it also contains a more humble treasure: kaolin. In 1767 an English tableware manufacturer, Josiah Wedgewood, sent a South Carolina planter, Thomas Griffith, to make an arrangement with the Cherokees to export the high-quality clay. Huge amounts of kaolin were shipped to Wedgewood and transformed into the famous Queensware. A Wedgewood dinner service of Macon County clay graced the table of Catherine the Great.

Gemstones, too, can be found in abundance in our fields, mines and rivers (see our chapter on Rock Hounding). These, in turn, inspired generations of jewelry makers. To fend off cold mountain winters, craftswomen turned scraps of old clothing into quilts; many of these works of art can be found in national museums. While spinners and weavers kept old skills alive out of necessity, today's fabric artists delight in introducing new and beautiful creations for the sheer joy of it.

The abundance of hardwoods and the need to create entertainment spawned some of the finest instrument makers around. Their delicate fiddles and sturdy dulcimers have inspired a wealth of accomplished musicians, unique songs and joyous dances, a tradition that continues today.

Handmade is, in fact, such an integral part of our lives in Western North Carolina that we probably take it for granted. A visitor to this area will find this rich heritage everywhere: in our homes, museums, shops, and galleries, as well as at roadside stands and at our craft fairs and festivals (see our Festivals and Annual Events, and Arts and Culture chapters). That this fine legacy will continue is guaranteed by the hundreds of craft classes conducted by a variety of educational institutions, senior-citizens centers, summer camps and parks and recreation departments, to name a few.

Three of the country's best craft schools are found in the region, attracting hundreds of craftspeople to settle in places such as Brasstown, Asheville and Penland. In addition to large and highly influential guilds, such as The Southern Highland Craft Guild (see the Folk Art Center entry that follows), there are also numerous small local guilds for weavers, spinners, quilters and other crafters that meet in members' homes. And, thanks to the efforts of HandMade in America, many artists' studios are open to visitors for the first time (see our HandMade in America close-up in the Arts and Culture chapter).

Here we give you schools and our favorite studios devoted to the crafts in our mountains. We have also included crafts such as glass-blowing and ceramics here. Though they're not intrinsically "mountain crafts," they are indeed practiced to near perfection in the western North Carolina Mountains.

# Northern Mountains

## Creekside Galleries
**Aldridge Rd., N.C. Hwy. 105,**
**Foscoe • (828) 963-4258**

This group of galleries next to the Green Mansions shopping center houses the working studio of potter Tim Turner. You can watch Tim throwing clay at the potter's wheel in the mornings. Later he dries, paints, glazes and fires up his works. An abundance of bowls,

plates, and goblets in various forms of completion always line his long worktables. You can purchase his works right out of the kiln.

Additional galleries in this adobe-like building include the Carlton Gallery of find woven works, and the Potter's Gallery, which also features unique jewelry and media. (See our Arts and Culture chapter.)

## J & S Beaumont Pottery
**N.C. Hwy. 194, Valle Crucis**
**• (828) 963-6399**

Located in the Red School House behind the Mast General Store, this pottery studio and gallery makes for wonderful browsing and picking up those little hand crafted gifts to take back home.

Visitors can view turning, glazing, and decorating processes from a special area just a few feet away. We spent a good two hours mesmerized by the spin of the potter's wheel and the scent of fresh clay being manipulated.

Adjacent to the airy manufacturing hall is the retail store. Here you'll find handmade and hand-painted dinnerware, and other functional pieces for the home. The rich patterns are influenced by European and American art pottery styles. We found the soap dish and water cup combos especially charming. The colors and patterns on display could match just about any bathroom decor. Wonderful urns, pitchers, and salad bowls also tickled our fancy. A special shelf for "seconds" offers some perfectly gorgeous pieces with only slight flaws at reduced prices.

## The Penland School of Crafts
**Penland • (828) 765-2359**

Resting on the crest of a remote mountaintop in Mitchell County, The Penland School is one of the country's finest institu-

---

**www.insiders.com**

See this and many other **Insiders' Guide®** destinations online.

**Visit us today!**

---

# Swannanoa Gathering

Making music in the mountains is a natural occurrence. Birds sing year round, their rich summer choruses dwindling to delicate solos come winter. The wind plays a medley of tunes, at times whistling through the leaves, at times roaring through the  coves. Crickets, katydids and grasshoppers start their washboard bands when the weather gets warm, and, of course, the people make music too. From cabin porches to concert halls, we have a reputation for being home to some of the finest folk, bluegrass and country music — sounds influenced by the early Scotch-Irish settlers and distilled into a distinct style all its own.

In the heart of the summer, about the time the katydids crank up, folks from all over the country converge upon the Asheville area for The Swannanoa Gathering at Warren Wilson College (See our Education chapter). Celebrating its seventh season in 1998, these four weeks of music workshops run through July and into early August. The schedule is full of special weeks that focus on specific styles and disciplines such as Celtic Week, Performance Lab, Dulcimer Week, Dance Week, Old-Time Music & Dance Week, Contemporary Folk Week and Guitar Week. Some years include Blues Week as well. With an Advisory Board that reads like a Who's Who in Folk Music — Chet Atkins, David Holt, John McCutcheon, Fiona Ritchie, Billy Edd Wheeler and Asheville's own David Wilcox — it's no wonder the programming and attendance improves every year.

The workshops convene at various sites around the Warren Wilson campus. Classes are open to everyone and many are structured for beginners. Students are free to create their own curriculum for each week (with the exception of some restrictions by individual teachers), although concentration on one or two classes is recommended.

Children's programs are offered during certain weeks for children ages 6 to 12.

— continued on next page

There's magic in the air at the Swannanoa Gathering.

Classes in crafts, field trips to local attractions such as Pack Place and the Nature Center and swimming activities are scheduled during the daytime class sessions.

A typical week begins with supper, an orientation session and socializing on the Sunday before the courses begin in earnest. Most classes meet for morning or afternoon sessions Monday through Friday. Some may meet in the evenings for performance critiques, rehearsals or jam sessions. Other evening activities include concerts by staff instructors, dances, song swaps and impromptu happenings such as picking sessions and "slow jams" (tune-learning sessions). Especially popular are the "sippin' & pickin'" activities under one of the heavy-duty tents overlooking the college's rich farmland and postcard-perfect mountains.

Just for fun, most weeks feature a pub night midweek when the students and staff provide the music at Be Here Now, a 250-seat smoke-free music club in Asheville (See our Nightlife chapter). Students are serious about their fun, though, spending long hours practicing until they get the notes right, prompting one student to write and perform, "I've Got the Swannanoa Gathering Sleep Deprivation Blues." He received a standing ovation from sympathetic classmates, who then headed back to campus for a jam that lasted until 3 AM! It seems some things are worth losing sleep over.

For sports and recreation, the college's facilities include a gymnasium, weight room, aquatic center and tennis courts as well as a pond, nature trails, a working farm and a kayak run on the nearby Swannanoa River.

The musical traditions of Scotland and Ireland, possessing separate and distinctive personalities, nonetheless share a common heritage. Celtic Week acknowledges this dual heritage with a program featuring the best from each tradition. Irish flute, Irish Step Dancing, Uilleann pipes, Celtic harp, tin whistle, Scottish fiddle, hammered dulcimer, bodhran (traditional Irish frame drum), Celtic guitar and Bouzouki (like a large, long-necked mandolin) are just some of the courses offered.

Performance Lab Week is designed for those who have a serious interest in moving to a higher level in their performing activities. The first three class days are spent on the campus, working on performance skills in a lab setting. Then it's put-your-music-where-your-mouth-is time as the acts hits the road to perform three concerts in the region. They are presented as a revue, with each act doing a short set as a part of each show. Set in well-known acoustic music venues, they offer a tremendous opportunity to work in optimal situations before an appreciative audience.

Old-Time Music & Dance Week explores the rich music, dance, singing and storytelling traditions of the Southern Appalachian region. Last year's programming included 23 courses plus visits from local master musicians, ballad singers and buckdancers. Old-time fiddle is a popular course, as are old-time banjo, old-time guitar and the autoharp. Shaped-note singing, a fascinating musical tradition stretching back to the 16th century, is also offered. Combining the sacred music of the earliest New England colonists, Southern white spirituals and the gospel hymns of the great 19th-century camp meetings, shaped-note singing creates a remarkably democratic four-part harmony with each part a separate and engaging melody. The music is notated using differently shaped notes — squares, triangles, circles and diamonds — which make it easier and more fun for untutored folks to participate in a venerable old Southern tradition.

The Mountain Dulcimer program includes both the mountain dulcimer and one of the most appealing and accessible of folk instruments, the hammered dulcimer. Students have an opportunity to learn either or both instruments from the country's finest teachers and players. Four skill levels are offered in each instrument.

Contemporary Folk Week is a unique program of workshops for anyone who has ever had the desire to play music for other people. If you're a closet songwriter who likes to go to "open mike night" at your local folk club, if you've been performing for a while and are ready to make the commitment to a career, or if you'd just like to feel more confident when you pull that guitar out at parties, this week is for you. Programs are divided into broad subject areas covering a variety of related topics: Songwriting, Performance, Sound Reinforcement and Recording, and Vocal Coaching.

New since 1996 is Guitar Week. Contemporary fingerstyle guitar, flatpicking (taught by a three-time national champ!), blues and guitar accompaniment are featured.

Whether you are a musician or not, there's a magic in the air at the Swannanoa Gathering. A series of concerts showcasing workshop staff is scheduled at the end of each week and is open to the public.

The Swannanoa Gathering has earned a well-deserved reputation for its quality programming and careful attention to details.

For more information contact The Swannanoa Gathering at (828) 298-3325, ext. 426.

tions devoted entirely to the study of crafts. It was founded by Miss Lucy Morgan in 1929 after an inspirational sojourn to the craft haven of Berea, Kentucky, where she spent a summer learning to weave. Upon her return, Miss Lucy set forth with a twofold purpose: to revive the mountain tradition of weaving here at home and to help the economically distressed women add to their livelihood. Word spread; students wanted to learn to weave. Soon new crafts were added, and suddenly Miss Lucy found her project becoming a school.

Today the school has a 450-acre campus and boasts a broad curriculum that includes book arts, glass, photography, printmaking, wood, surface design, metals, iron, drawing, clay and fibers. The Penland community includes staff, resident artists and the students, who are comprised of a mix of college students and graduates, professionals looking for a different career and retirees who seek the arts as an avocation. This diversity of life experience only adds to the flow of creativity and the quality of Penland.

The purity of Miss Lucy's original idea is woven into the fabric of Penland School today. The beauty of the art, the love of the work and the preservation of the heritage are ingrained in every student who makes the trek up the mountain to Penland. A shared spirit for creativity permeates the log walls of

the old dormitory, the chinks in the studio sheds, the light-filled drawing spaces, the ordered looms, the steady forge and solid kiln.

This is a place where inspiration lives, high on the mountaintop close to the sky. Many of the light-filled classrooms overlook a grass-covered bald and ridge upon ridge in the gloaming. Guest teachers, like master Venetian glass blowers, fiber artists from Australia, and many others, conduct two-week workshops. A cozy dining room serves buffet-style meals — the menu changes each day to include wholesome preservative-free organic meals.

To receive information on classes, tuition or any other aspect of the school, write to The Penland School of Crafts, Penland, North Carolina 28765, or call the previously listed number.

### Bea Hensley & Son Blacksmiths
**Rt. 1, off Mi. 331, Spruce Pine • No phone**

There aren't many working blacksmiths around, especially in this country. That's what makes this three-generational blacksmithing studio so special. Bea Hensley, winner of the National Endowment of the Arts Heritage Award in 1995, maintains this successful forge with his son Mike. Grandson Luke is still in middle school but spends his vacations observing and learning bits of the trade. Schooled in the apprenticeship-style, which has not changed much from the 1600s, Mike Hensley does major smithing in wrought iron, fashioning elaborate made-to-order gates and other home ornamentation in this shop.

The sheer power and stamina of these men is staggering. Beefy forearms, callused hands, and thick back musculature are the working result of years at the anvil. Especially transfixing is the portion of smithing when the blacksmiths make the anvil "sing" while forging a particular piece of iron. The "teacher" moves his smaller hammer over the anvil and hot iron, beating out a rhythm and directions that the "apprentice" must follow with the powerful blows of a heavy mallet. Now that both elder Hensleys are past the apprenticing stage, they still make the anvil sing for visitors at times, or while working on a particularly intricate project needing the both of them. This trade is fascinating and rare in this modern world.

Don't miss this, you can't help but be mesmerized by the song of the anvil.

### The Weaving Room/Crossnore School
**205 Johnson Ln., N.C. Hwy. 221**
**Crossnore • (828) 733-4660**

The Weaving Room is a self-help project of Crossnore School. All proceeds benefit the boys and girls of Crossnore Schools, children from the Carolina mountains and foothills. These children from families in crisis find a stable environment on the school's 72-acre campus.

At the Crossnore School watch weavers at their looms, creating traditional patterns and contemporary wares. Since 1920, the school has kept alive the almost forgotten art of producing hand woven clothing and home furnishings in patterns used by the early settlers of the Appalachians. In The Weaving Room,

Photo: Cherokee Tribal Travel & Promotion Office

At shops such as Qualla Arts and Crafts in Cherokee, visitors will find a wide selection of Cherokee hand-crafted products such as "booger" masks, pipes, baskets, beadwork, jewelry and much more.

you will find throw rugs in the Lee's Surrender pattern, capes and stoles in a Honeysuckle pattern, and table runners and baby blankets in the Bronson Lace pattern. The weavers use all natural cotton, wool, and linen, as well as some easy-care materials like rayon, orlon and synthetics.

### Woody's Chair Shop
**110 Dale Rd., Spruce Pine**
**• (828) 765-9277**
All-in-the-family trade has spanned three generations at Woody's Chair Shop. Rocking chairs, made by hand and by special machinery constructed and designed solely by Woody are the specialty here. The front shop sells fabulous wooden doodads, from smoothly fashioned business card holders to gravity-defying wine bottle holders, old mountain children's games and adult chess sets to humidors and grand mirrors.

Woodys' chairs are his pride, though, and are sought the world over. Special deliveries are sent to Europe yearly. Ask Woody or his wife for a quick peek into the workshop and he might just oblige. Expect lots of sawdust, some fascinating machinery, and workers in deep concentration. Ask the master chairmaker to show you the machine that evens up irregular chair legs. Also, cast a glance at the workshop floor; under the sawdust there's an intricately placed wood floor.

# Central Mountains

### Asheville Tileworks & Pottery
**119 Roberts St., Asheville**
**• (828) 259-9050**
A workshop and small gallery located in the city's industrial warehouse district, known as the Historic River District, Asheville Tileworks is the place to go when you need that extra umph in your kitchen or bathroom.

The owner works on individual tiles, adorning them with various patterns — fruits and vegetable or herb motifs, and other designs.

The tiles are created in the maiolica style, which originated in the Middle East during the 10th century in an attempt to imitate Chinese porcelains brought to the Majorcan port on the spice-trade route. The clay is covered with an opaque white glaze and lavishly decorated. Custom-designed tiles are also available, as are historical reproductions.

Asheville Tileworks sells most of its creations through retail around the country. However, you are welcome to browse about the small display gallery and watch the artisans at work.

### Black Mountain Gallery
**112 Cherry St., Black Mountain**
**• (828) 669-2450**
This downtown gallery is the only one in the area primarily dedicated to lathing turned wooden bowls, both artistic and functional. In a workshop adjacent to the gallery, father and son artists, Eddie and Marshall Hollifield, transform Mother Nature's abnormalities—the knots of a tree, or dome-shaped growths in tree trunks, known as "burls"—into works of art. Feel free to watch this fascinating process. The gallery also features the works of other local artists.

### The Folk Art Center
**Mi. 382, Blue Ridge Parkway, in east Asheville • (828) 298-7928**
The Folk Art Center is the grand showcase for the work of the more than 700 members of the Southern Highland Craft Guild. The Guild was founded in 1930 as an educational, nonprofit organization to provide economic support to the many fine craftspeople of the southern Appalachian region. Guild members come from a nine-state region and produce some of the finest traditional moun-

# Fire on the Mountains

Artisans are throwing open their studio doors and allowing the public to watch. No

longer content with "creating" in solitude, crafts have become a spectator sport. The mountains of North Carolina are well-known for the studio crafters dotting their countryside. (See our Arts and Culture chapter for more information about studios in HandMade in America.)

We, the viewers, are no longer just satisfied with the finished product; instead, we crave and are given the opportunity to experience the sweat and the inspiration behind American craftspeople's creations. Asheville, in particular, has amassed a group of studios concentrated in one area of the city, which is now considered an established arts and crafts community. The River District Studios, located along the French Broad River in Asheville's old industrial area close to downtown, is home to no less than 34 working studios. Some include galleries, and all welcome visitors. Ceramics, printmaking, painting, woodworking, sculpting, garden art, photography, welding, candle making, and many other crafts can be found here. Twice a year the River District Studios host a "sunset stroll" through studios and courtyards. Feel free to wander and watch and make a purchase or two. You'll be sure to run into a bevy of local supporters. Strolls take place in the fall and summer. "Great Southern Glassworks is a must-see in our mountains.

Toiling seven days a week, close to furnaces ranging in temperature from 850 F to 2300 F, and sustaining blisters, calluses, and sometimes burns, sounds more akin to forced labor than a creative endeavor. Ask glassblowers what the appeal is, and they will answer quite differently: the speed, the fervor, the rush — creating a tangible object out of molten liquid.

Contemporary American glassblowers have somehow garnered an image of swaggering Rambo-esque proportions; wielders of a weapon of heat, fire, and air. In the

Photo: Constance E. Richards

Stop by and see Andy and Roddy of Great Southern
Glassworks cajole art out of molten glass.

industrial section of Asheville, amidst old brick warehouses and seldom-used train tracks, Andy Merrick and Roddy Capers of Great Southern Glassworks blow glass.

The studio doors are open most hours of the day as the two artisans tend to their craft. Eyes safe-guarded by protective dark glasses and hands sheathed with impossibly thick gloves, but with little else in the way of protection, they fire up the furnaces and blow molten glass into splashy vases, colorful bowls, cobalt-blue goblets and more. Never resting during the 1□-hour session it takes to mold, shape, color, and keep a glass creation from bursting into a thousand pieces if it cools too fast, the men are in constant action.

Both master craftsmen, the glassblowers built their Riverside Drive studio in 6 months. They constructed their own invested pot furnace that reaches a working temperature of 2100 F and a melting temperature of 2300 F, for beginning the process of working with molten glass. Also in the warehouse-like studio sit two annealing ovens into which the glass objects are placed immediately after they are finished. The computer-regulated temperature gauge allows the glass to cool over several hours, or even days, taking the stress out of the glass gradually. At 875 F glass remains solid, won't slump, and will retain its form. Hence, the sweltering heat you will encounter is a mainstay of this craft! Andy and Roddy admit that it does cut down on the heating bills in the winter, though.

Anyone wishing to visit this spectacular show should remember that this is a working studio. When Roddy and Andy work, they must be completely focused or they could loose a valuable creation, or worse, a finger or a hand. Guests are asked to stand well behind the work area, where liquid glass, scorching-hot tools, and waves of gaseous heat are the tools of the trade. See the artists' works lined up on the shelves of the studio. They also sell their wares in area galleries as well as out of the studio.

For unique vases, bowls, glasses, cups, and other utilitarian glassware, as well as decorative pieces, Great Southern Glassworks is a treasure trove. The artisans consider the North Carolina mountain environs to be the stronghold of glassblowing on the East coast, fed in great part by the popularity of the Penland School, where many craftspeople return year after year for new methodology, workshops, and seminars.

Be sure to call and see if the artisans are in before you venture out, (828) 255-0187. The River District Studios are concentrated on Riverside Drive, Clingman Avenue, and Roberts Street.

---

tain crafts as well as the outstanding contemporary craft work evolving today.

The Folk Art Center, Asheville's gateway to the Blue Ridge Parkway off U.S. Highway 70, welcomes 350,000 visitors annually from all over the country and the world. They come to see the fine traditional mountain heritage on display in the permanent collection as well as the traditional and contemporary crafts in the ever-changing exhibitions. Allanstand Craft Shop, America's oldest craft shop, is a feast for the eyes with its displays of glassware, blankets, dishware, wooden toys, exquisitely crafted jewelry, prints, brooms and baskets.

The main level houses a 250-seat auditorium that serves the Guild's educational purposes and is also used by the Park Service. Here, as well as in the foyer, demonstrations are produced throughout April through December. Special events, such as Clay Day and Fiber Day, involve the public with hands-on participation projects and provide fun for the entire family. (Call the phone number we've provided to find out about the special events.)

The essence of the Guild and the Folk Art Center is described by lifetime member, woodcarver and dulcimer maker Edsel Martin of Old Fort who in 1970 wrote: "The Southern Highland Handicraft Guild is not just a business . . . it is people. People who are proud, who live close to the earth, and who live with

Cherokee craftspeople are known worldwide for wood carvings, pottery, baskets, beadwork, stone carvings and much more.

an independence and dignity that money can't buy. The Guild is not people who stand behind or in front of each other; it is people standing side by side."

The Folk Art Center is open from 9 AM to 6 PM daily except Thanksgiving, Christmas and New Year's. 9 AM to 5 PM January through March. Admission is free.

### Great Southern Glassworks
**9 Riverside Dr., Asheville • (828) 255-0187**

This is a working glassblowing studio. Come witness the inspired "performance" of the "craft rogues" molding liquid glass into gorgeous and useful forms and then buy something to take home. See the "Fire on the Mountains" Close-up in this chapter.

### Odyssey Center for the Ceramic Arts
**236 Clingman Ave., Asheville**
**• (828) 285-0210**

This is another new studio that has found a home in Asheville's Historic River District. Close to the train tracks and the banks of the French Broad River, this large pottery center offers courses in clay crafts for beginners and advanced students. Nine-week classes are offered in pottery, hand-building and figura-

tive sculpture, as well as kid's classes for after school and home schoolers. (Read more about these in our Kidstuff chapter.)

Weekend and week-long workshops, along with frequent lectures, feature nationally and internationally-known ceramic artists. An independent study program gives returning students the opportunity to use the facility during open studio hours and work independently. The Odyssey Gallery markets and exhibits ceramic works from local and national artists, and serves as an educational tool for students as well as the public. Call for a detailed course brochure and workshop schedule.

# Southern Mountains

### John C. Campbell Folk School
**1 Folk School Rd., Brasstown**
**• (828) 837-2775, (800) FOLK SCH**

The John C. Campbell Folk School has been a mountain institution for 75 years, and there's really no other place like it. Though Brasstown is only 2½ hours from Atlanta, Chattanooga and Asheville, the school — set in a mountain-rimmed farming valley — seems to be from another century. Actually, it began in this one, when Indiana-born educator John C. Campbell took his new bride, Olive Dame, on a fact-finding survey throughout the Appalachian Mountains. While he investigated the agricultural practices, she studied the music and handicrafts.

After John's death in 1919, Olive Campbell and friend Marguerite Butler went to Scandinavia to study hands-on schools without credits, degrees, grades or competition. They returned to the mountains to see if such a school would be welcomed in the region. More than 200 enthusiastic people showed up at an organizational meeting at a Brasstown church. Fred O. Scroggs, the local storekeeper, donated 75 acres of land, and the people pledged labor, building materials and, most importantly, their heartfelt support.

Today, the 372-acre campus contains 27 buildings, some designed by Belgian architect Leon Deschamps in a romantic European style, while others are more typical of Appalachian farm houses. It has fully equipped craft studios, a saw mill, meeting rooms, a covered outdoor dance pavilion, a nature trail, a craft shop, a vegetable garden, rustic lodgings and the Community Room, which has one of the best dance floors in America. The National Register of Historic Places has declared the campus a Historical District.

Over the years, the school's role in the community has changed as many of the needs it served (such as healthcare and job training) have been taken over by public programs. It continues, however, to enrich and serve the local community. Its craft shop, for example, sells the work of more than 200 mountain craftspeople, including the famous Brasstown Carvers, whose delicately carved animals are all-time favorites.

Lifestyles and relationships to tradition have changed since 1925. Most of today's 3,000 annual Folk School students come from all over the U.S. for a week or two to learn a craft, pick up an instrument or learn to dance. But the individual expression and social interaction that have been encouraged by crafts, music and dance are still needed today — perhaps more than ever.

Regularly scheduled concerts of traditional music, along with dances are open to the public. For those who want to learn a new skill or improve an old one, there are literally hundreds of weekend and one- or two-week-long courses offered year round in basketry, bead work, blacksmithing, book arts, broom making, calligraphy, chair seats, clay, crochet, dance, dolls, drawing, dyeing, embroidery, enameling, felting, food, genealogy, glass, jewelry, kaleidoscopes, knitting, lace, leather, marbling, metalwork, music, nature studies, painting, paper art, photography, printmaking, quilting, recreation, rugs, spinning, stone carving, storytelling, thread art, tinsmithing, weaving, woodcarving, woodturning, woodworking and writing. Phew!

Tuition ranges from $136 for weekends and $258 for the average week, plus the actual costs of materials (such as the student's clay in a pottery course). There are discounts for students from a number of surrounding Georgia and North Carolina counties as well as for members of Elderhostel on most, but not all, courses. Three family-style meals are served each day. Lodging (meals included) is provided in a number of on-campus buildings. Costs vary but range from $212 for six nights in a dorm setting (three to eight twin beds per room, shared bath) to $285 (two twin beds and bath); or $72 and $100, respectively, for weekends.

There are 12 campsites with full hookups and modest bathroom facilities on campus. Campsites can cost from $110 for six nights for two persons, including all meals, to $40 for weekends. Each additional person at a campsite is $1 per night. Individual meals in

## INSIDERS' TIP

**If you are planning to attend one of John C. Campbell's regular concerts, why not enjoy a meal at the school's table beforehand? Make reservations at least one day in advance: call (800) FOLK SCH or (828) 837-2775. Then prepare yourself for a tasty repast!**

1997 ran $5.30 for breakfast, $7.42 for lunch and $8.48 for supper. The school is 7 miles east of Murphy, off U.S. Highway 64.

To receive a catalog, call the number above or write to the John C. Campbell Folk School, 1 Folk School Rd., Brasstown, NC 28902.

## Haywood Community College Craft Production Program
**1 Freelander Dr., Clyde • (828) 627-4670**

This two-year program in jewelry, pottery, weaving and woodworking is considered one of the finest in the nation. In addition to teach-

Handmade textiles are prominently featured in the Southern Highland Craft Guild's permanent collections.

ing technique and design, the school is noted for its marketing courses that help turn aspiration into reality for the craft artists. Students design their own graduation show at the completion of their chosen program. (See our chapter on Education for more information on Haywood Community College.)

## The Museum of North Carolina Handicrafts
**307 Shelton St., Waynesville**
**• (828) 452-1551**

If you're looking for crafting inspiration or if you'd simply like to see some of the skills demonstrated by past and present North Carolinians, this museum offers you both. The white-framed Shelton House, built in 1875 and listed on the National Register of Historic Places, is as interesting as the museum and offers a perfect setting for the comprehensive exhibits of 19th-century crafts.

Just a short walk from Wayneville's charming Main Street, the museum contains examples of furniture from the last century, a Victorian bed and shaving stand, a dining table, handcrafted cupboard, toys (including a handmade miniature farmstead) and a working pioneer village.

It also features an exhibit of handicrafts made by artisans who have participated in the educational demonstration of heritage crafts in the North Carolina State Fair's Village of Yesteryear since 1951. You'll see such once-necessary tools as Saxony spinning wheels and walking spinning wheels. There is also a fine collection of Cherokee Indian artifacts — dolls, baskets, pottery and woodcarvings — as well as the Will Shelton collection of Navajo rugs, pottery, jewelry and baskets.

A small gift shop carries pottery, braided rugs, hand-carved birds and other handcrafted items and a selection of regional craft books.

Allow yourself at least an hour to enjoy this step back into the past. The museum is open from 10 AM to 4 PM Tuesday through Friday, May through October. There is an admission charge of $4 for adults and $1 for children under 4; for groups of 15 or more, it's $2 per adult. Special arrangements for group tours may be made by telephoning the museum.

The staff of Eagle's Nest Camp believes that the big missing ingredient for American children is membership within a tribe within a village within a nature-based homeland. This sense of "belonging" is one of the missing links that they strive to create for their campers.

# Summer Camps

For generations, children and young people have delighted in the many summer camps that thrive in the Western North Carolina mountains. They often attend the same camps that their grandparents enjoyed.

There are 24 camps in Henderson County alone and another 17 in neighboring Transylvania County, plus a number of others in surrounding counties. Some camps are coed, others single sex. Some are privately owned while others have religious affiliations or are sponsored by Scout organizations or civic clubs. A number of camps have focused activities, such as music, drama, rock climbing, whitewater skills and horseback riding. So, with such a wide range of camping options available, how do you go about choosing the right one for your child? At the very least, you should ask the following questions.

• Is the camp accredited by the American Camping Association, and if so, when was it accredited?

• How many years has it been in operation?

• How long has the director been there, and what are his or her qualifications? Does he or she own the facility?

• What is the camp's philosophy?

• What are the staff members' qualifications? How thoroughly is staff interviewed and investigated? What percentage of the staff returns each year?

• What percentage of campers return each year?

• What is the camper-counselor ratio?

• Does the camp supply references from past campers' families?

• Does the camp maintain a safe environment concerning such things as fire prevention, emergency drills, first aid, medical procedures, and regular evaluations and inspections of the food and facilities?

• What kind of vehicles are used to transport children? Are they owned or leased? Are drivers trained in ongoing safety-awareness programs?

• Does the camp carry liability insurance?

• Does it belong to any organizations that can help it maintain and improve its professionalism?

Although summer camps can vary in size, price, duration and age ranges of the campers, most include such activities as hiking, camping, canoeing, swimming, archery, mountain biking, horseback riding, tennis, golf, team sports and nature studies — thanks in part to the vast recreational opportunities offered by the nearby public lands (see our Forests and Parks chapter). As the late Frank "Chief" Bell Sr., founder of Mondamin Camp, put it, "The wilderness can be a magnificent playground and a great university." The cultural heritage of the area's arts and crafts, such as drama, blacksmithing and pottery, play a big role in summer activities.

While most camps draw the majority of their participants from the Southeast, many come from as far away as Alaska, Hawaii and South America for this mountain experience. Campers have been known to spend every summer for five to 15 years at the same camp; many have come back as camp counselors and some have even become camp owners. A number of the camps have been in continuous operation for more than 70 years. We've included just a few of the long-established facilities. For complete camp listings, contact local chambers of commerce.

# Central Mountains

## Camp Hollymont for Girls
**475 Lake Eden Rd., Black Mountain**
• **(828) 686-5343 winter; (828) 252-2123 summer**

Founded by George W. Pickering, who has served in this Christian camp's ministry since 1946, Camp Hollymont's tradition is continued by the McKibbens Family. Located on the 300-acre campus of the private Asheville School, Camp Hollymont provides for a fun-filled summer for girls from age 6 to 15, in refined living conditions. Acres of rolling hills and lush green forests provide the perfect summer setting for sports, fun and games, and learning crafts and skills. Girls live in the lodges, in clusters divided by age and grade. A cluster consists of four rooms, with one of the four for the counselor. There are 120 campers per session.

Rocking chairs sit on the wide open-air front-porches for better viewing of the panoramic Blue Ridge Mountains. An air-conditioned dining hall, stone chapel, professional stage and theater, athletic center with a gymnasium and indoor pool facilitate an excellent camp atmosphere. Seven athletic fields, seven tennis courts, an archery range, a track, cross-country trails, horse stables with training ring and miles of riding trails through the woods offer the perfect backdrop for the recreation-filled weeks that campers will spend at Hollymont. Several registered nurses staff the well-equipped infirmary 24 hours a day, and an Asheville physician is available for campers. Creative and nutritionally sound meals are served family-style in the dining hall; campers can also visit the canteen for snacks. The food service sees that all dietary needs are honored.

Because it is a Christian camp, Hollymont closes each day with evening devotions — quiet, sharing moments, inspirational stories, and prayer. Most memorable to campers, however, will be the action-packed weeks of exploration, games, and recreation overseen by the youthful and energetic staff. Qualified instructors teach girls horseback riding, tennis, archery, gymnastics, ceramics, cheerleading, climbing, singing, photography, sign language, music, camping, and a number of other recreational skills and hobbies. Campers select five instructional skills per two-week session.

Buncombe county lends itself well to the pursuit of nature, and one of the special offerings of the camp is the Hollymont Ranger Program, emphasizing safety, leadership skills, teamwork, camping, hiking, and high-adventure trips. The camper Rangers hike and explore the Blue Ridge Parkway, the Great Smokies, and Pisgah National Forest. The Ranger Program is limited to 12 girls per session, ages 13 to 16. These campers will experience whitewater rafting, rock climbing, high ropes course, rappelling, water skiing, mountain biking, and caving and spend weekends at the camp, joining in the camp's regular activities. Whatever programs Hollymont campers choose, they will be nurtured and taught by well-educated counselors, who make an effort to extend the camp's motto to all children attending: "Living and Learning with Love and Laughter." In this atmosphere, the campers develop self-confidence, build lasting friendships and grow spiritually, all while having a whole lot of fun.

A two-week session costs $1,425 and a four-week session costs $2,900.

## Camp Rockmont for Boys
**375 Lake Eden Rd., Black Mountain**
• **(828) 686-3885**

Driving up a tree-shaded lane, you approach Camp Rockmont at the same time you cast your first glance over Lake Eden and the Black Mountains in the distance. The lake's central position on the 600-acres of the camp's secluded property is a telling symbol of days by the water to come. Only 15 miles east of Asheville, near the town of Black Mountain, Camp Rockmont welcomes boys ages 6 to 17.

Under Christian leadership, the camp carries a prestigious reputation with it, serving more than 1,200 boys in the Blue Ridge Mountains each summer. Ranging from 13-day to 20-day sessions, the camp is divided into Junior Camp, Intermediate, and Senior Camp; campers range in age from 7 to 16. Within each camp, the boys are further divided into two tribes according to age and grade. Junior campers live in large lodges with private baths and stone fireplaces in the cavernous lobbies, while Intermediate and Senior campers stay in spacious cabins tucked into wooded slopes and use newly constructed bath houses. Each camper chooses six instructional activities every two weeks. The recreational activities are sporty in nature — Red Cross swimming, riflery, archery, tennis, weight training, canoeing, sailing, climbing, horseback riding, kayaking, and team sports. More reflective activities include pioneering, crafts, and Bible study.

Rockmont places a spiritual emphasis on the whole camp experience. Counselors enjoy devotional times with their cabins, and a Morning Watch and Sunday services are times also set aside for worship through singing, learning and sharing. Every Sunday evening, each camp gathers at a respective Council Ring site on the mountainside to reflect upon the prior week. Boys are recognized according to personal performance as it applies to attitude, enthusiasm, and cooperation.

Also unique to this boys' camp is the Ranger Program, not unlike the program at Rockmont's sister camp Hollymont for Girls. A Rockmont Ranger keeps a daily journal of his outdoor experiences, learning to live in the wilderness, identify flora and fauna, maneuver rope courses, whitewater raft, hike, and camp. Each Ranger receives a patch of completion at the closing ceremony. Rangers must be at least 14 years old.

The Counselors-in-Training program is aimed at young men 16 and older, who would like to assert their leadership as future Rockmont counselors. Choosing between a 13, 20, or 27-day session, trainees act as assistants to the counselors in cabin life, in skills-class instruction, and in everyday camp life. They also attend leadership training classes where they learn special skills and leadership techniques that will last a lifetime.

Thirteen-day sessions cost $1,250, 20-day sessions (July through August) cost $1775, and 27-day sessions (June through July) cost $2,150.

## Camp Merri-Mac for Girls
**1229 Montreat Rd., Black Mountain**
**• (828) 669-8766**

Set in the lush Black Mountain area, Camp Merri-Mac offers two four-week sessions for girls aged 6 to 16. Since 1978, Spencer and Dorothy Boyd, parents of six children themselves, have operated Camp Merri-Mac. They have some forty years of professional camp experience. The Camp is located on a 150-acre tract of land in the Blue Ridge Mountains, at an elevation of 2,800 feet. Campers are divided by age groups into Junior, Intermediate, and Senior Camps and are housed in thirteen screened and shuttered cabins with adjoining baths. The front porches make for great gatherings at dusk. The dining hall, infirmary, laundry and camp offices are located in the Big House, a former private home. Between mealtimes, campers may purchase a limited amount of snacks and drinks. The Mike, or the gym, is a central place for recreation, including indoor volleyball, basketball, as well as musical and drama productions. Three tennis courts, volleyball courts, and sports fields assure physical fitness is a large past of the program.

A member of the National Riflery Association and the Camp Archery Association, Camp Merri-Mac teaches range and field safety in target sports. Merri-Mac teaches camp craft skills, with emphasis placed on woods safety, proper equipment and a real appreciation for the outdoors. Operating on a tribal system, life at Merri-Mac takes on a distinctly Native American air. Girls are assigned one of three tribes — Choctaw, Iroquois or Seminole — during the first session, and remain a member of the respective tribe during their future

## INSIDERS' TIP

Provide your children with a variety of fun stationery for letter writing. Should they get homesick, they may feel better writing you or friends on stationery that you picked out together expressly for this purpose.

Photo: Camp Hollymont

Summer camps are great places to commune with nature and new friends.

years at the camp. These tribes compete in various activities throughout the session and choose leaders, who plan and organize many tribal events with staff advisors. These groupings foster healthy competition and leadership qualities in young girls attending the camp.

A 15-minute chapel service is held each morning, before girls begin their busy days. Not only sports are on the schedule; fine arts classes taught by college art majors, drama programs, comedy, modern jazz dancing as well as traditional clogging are also offered. Girls have the opportunity to enjoy water sports — canoeing, diving, and just fun splashing around. Merri-Mac's riding program has drawn a good bit of praise. The Boyd family's experience with horses in national shows, circuit, and fox hunting has given them an outstanding group of school horses. The camper-staff ratio of 3.5-to-1 enables each girl to feel the individual attention of a college-level counselor who may have been a camper here once herself.

The cost per four-week session is $2,250 (June through July and July through August), while two-week sessions (throughout June, July, and August) cost $1,290.

## Camp Timberlake for Boys
**1229 Montreat Rd., Black Mountain**
**• (828) 669-8766**

Due to the popularity of Camp Merri-Mac for Girls, the Boyd family founded Camp Timberlake for Boys in 1983. Providing a challenging adventure for boys aged 6 through 16, Timberlake operates on the same campground as Merri-Mac but has a separate program run by its own staff of skilled young men. The two four-week sessions and a smaller two-week session allow boys to familiarize themselves with the outdoors, and with a variety of sports they may not have access to in school.

The backpacking program, geared toward learning safe independence in the wilderness, provides instruction on how to plan a trip, what to bring, and how to set up camp. Experienced instructors lead overnight trips into the Pisgah National Forest. Swimming, diving, wrestling, tennis, horseback riding, archery and riflery are taught by qualified instructors, as are canoeing, climbing, and fencing, a unique sport for a summer camp. Fencing, which the Timberlake describes as "physical chess," enables each boy to use his own distinct skill — be that athletic ability and quickness or a strategic approach. Climbing is practiced on one of the three climbing walls before moving out to the fine granite of the Southeast. The camp also offers instructions in mountain biking and guitar. Lodging and board costs are similar to Merri-Mac's. The infirmary, also like Merri-Mac's, is staffed 24 hours a day by a registered nurse and assistant.

All activity and recreational equipment is checked before each day's use, and instructors are highly skilled at the activities they teach as well as in first aid. Services in a chapel by the lake begin each day with rousing singing and reflective Bible study. Two hours of free time a day give each boy the chance to make his own decisions about pursuing an extra activity, resting, reading, or playing.

Three four week sessions (June-July and July-August) cost $2,250, and four two-week programs (running June, July, and August) cost $1,290.

### Camp Mondamin for Boys
Lake Summit, Flat Rock
• (828) 693-7446,
(800) 688-5789 information
### Camp Green Cover for Girls
Lake Summit, Flat Rock
• (828) 692-6355
(800) 688-5789 information

In 1922, Camp Mondamin, for boys ages 7 to 17, was established by the late Frank "Chief" Bell Sr. on the then-new 350-acre Lake Summit. It has been owned and operated by the Bell family ever since. The lake and surrounding 800 acres of private woodlands make sailing and nature studies a large part of the curriculum. The camp also includes five tennis courts, a crafts shop, an indoor rifle range, a gymnasium, a barn and three riding rings.

Camp Green Cove, for girls ages 8 to 17, was founded by the Bells in 1945 at Rockbrook Camp in Brevard (see the Rockbrook Camp entry). In 1949 the Bells moved the camp to the upper end of Lake Summit. The buildings surround a beautiful cove where a dammed-off stream forms a smaller, private lake for swimming and canoeing. The main building houses the dining room, lounges, offices and craft shops where such subjects as weaving, pottery, macrame, copper enameling, silk-screen printing and drawing are taught. This building and the camp cabins are on one side of the lake. On the other side are four tennis courts, an archery field, a ball field, a barn and five riding rings, including a jumping course.

Each of these adjoining camps has its own infirmary with two nurses on staff; one physician in residence serves both camps. Sailing, horseback riding and woods skills are emphasized, and both offer swimming, canoeing, backpacking, rock climbing, a ropes course, wilderness camping, mountain biking, tennis, crafts and nature studies. Minor activities include archery, riflery, photography, volleyball and, at Mondamin, an amateur-radio program. Mondamin has a gymnasium; Green Cove offers gymnastics and dramatics.

These camps are unique in that they maintain a long, unbroken camp session of 6 weeks and don't accept campers for shorter times during that session. (They do have separate three- and one-week sessions.) These long-term camps accommodate a strong wilderness trip that gives participants the time to build skills and use them in the woods and on the water. The whitewater canoeing program here — headed by Gordon Grant, technical editor for *Canoe* magazine, former head of

---

**INSIDERS' TIP**

To prevent bugs in cabins, most summer camps now have policies that ask friends and families not to send care packages containing food. You might instead order a "Camp Pack" from Main Street Ltd., 22 E. Main St., Brevard, (828) 884-4974, (800) 248-CAMP. It'll custom-make a gift pack and deliver it locally or ship it nationally. (See our Shopping chapter for more on Main Street Ltd.)

instruction at the Nantahala Outdoor Center and a Mondamin camper in the '60s and '70s — has been recognized as one of the best of its kind.

The Bells' philosophy that it is not necessary to inflict a defeat in order to win a victory guides the camps' noncompetitive programs — an advantage for participants who aren't the best athletes. Programs are structured but unregimented to encourage self-direction and initiative.

The camps have a combined capacity of 185. The camper-counselor ratio is 4-to-1. The three-week June session costs $1,470, the six-week main sessions in July and August cost $3,145, and the one-week August session for ages 6 to 10 is $370 (participants must have finished 1st grade). There are discounts for early registration for main sessions.

## Camp Arrowhead for Boys
## Camp Glen Arden for Girls
off Green River Rd., Tuxedo
• (828) 692-8362

Arrowhead is a Christian camp for boys 7 to 15 years old. Set along sparkling Rock Creek, a tributary of the Green River, it has more than 1,000 acres of woodland, streams, meadows and trails that offer endless opportunities for playing, exploring, camping and riding. J.O. Bell Jr. started the camp in 1937, and it's been owned and directed by the Bell family for more than 50 years. In 1951, its sister camp, Camp Glen Arden for Girls joined it. The vast grounds contain two lakes, a swimming pool, archery fields, tennis courts, a gym, stables, a woodworking shop, a blacksmith shop and a great variety of other facilities and cabins. Just inside the Glen Arden gate, a towering 300-foot waterfall greets campers. Both camps offer almost all the activities found at the other camps mentioned in this chapter. The camps believe in providing moderate structure, but with enough free time to "watch a hawk circling above against fluffy clouds."

These two affiliated camps have a 4-to-1 camper-counselor ratio, although in the youngest camper cabins the ratio is 2-to-1. Camp Arrowhead holds two four-week sessions, which cost $1,650 each, and two two-week sessions, which cost $900 each.

## Falling Creek Camp
off Bob's Creek Rd., Tuxedo
• (828) 692-0262

Though conveniently close to Interstate 26 and the Asheville airport, Falling Creek's home in a hidden cove deep in the mountains seems incredibly remote. Its campus spreads over 1,000 acres. The main section surrounds two lakes with many miles of trails and outpost cabins between its mountaintop and the river pastures in the Green River Valley.

This camp for boys offers many competitive activities while realizing it's more important for a boy to work and cooperate with others than to consistently try to outrank his peers. The facility's 220 participants are divided into three age groups — Cherokee, Catawba and Iroquois — with about 12 cabins in each division. Each boy lives with seven cabinmates and one or two counselors. Care has been taken in the construction of all Falling Creek's building to preserve the natural beauty of the surroundings.

Each boy selects six different activities in which to participate on a daily basis. These include archery-riflery, sailing, water skiing, swimming, canoeing, horseback riding, track and field, land sports, lacrosse, soccer, mountain biking, hiking, rock climbing, nature programs, photography, crafts, woodcrafts, tennis, basketball, Indian lore, weightlifting and radio (the camp has its own radio station: WFCC-640 AM). The camp also has its own camp doctor and dietitian and is the brother camp to Camp Greystone for Girls, about 7 miles away on Lake Summit.

There is a three-week June session ($1,800), a short two-week session in June for seven- to 14-year-olds ($1,300), a five-week July main session ($2,850), and a 10-day August session ($1,030).

## Rockbrook Camp for Girls
N.C. 276, Brevard • (828) 884-6151

Rockbrook Camp, which serves girls ages 6 to 16, has been in existence since 1921. The 200-acre site, 4 miles from Brevard on the French Broad River, is replete with beautiful forests and waterfalls, all of which are accessible by numerous hiking trails. It is also just minutes away from Pisgah National Forest, which is used for day hikes, overnight backpacking trips and rock-climbing trips. Rockbrook has excellent in-camp rock-climbing facilities as well. These include a 70-foot climbing tower, an indoor climbing wall and rock faces.

Campers chose weekly from many fun-filled activities in a non-competitive environment. Emphasis is placed on canoeing, rafting and kayaking (Rockbrook is a licensed outfitter on the Nantahala River and has an outpost at this location near the Great Smoky Mountains). Other sports include tennis, swimming, soccer and horseback riding, with all levels of hunter-jumper instruction. Creative outlets include drama and pottery (the camp has a year-round commercial pottery operation that's devoted entirely to campers during the summer).

Campers live eight to a screened cabin with two counselors per cabin. The main buildings are comprised of a dining hall, gym, three stone lodges, a barn, two log cabins and the pottery studio. There are five tennis courts, a rifle range, an archery range and a lake. The camper-counselor ratio is approximately 4-to-1. A full-time registered nurse is on duty in the health lodge, and a licensed physician is on call. All staff members are trained in CPR and first aid.

The camp can accommodate 190 campers per session; the girls are organized into three age groups. The first session lasts three weeks and costs $1,750. The second session is four weeks and costs $2,150. The third session of camp is two weeks and costs $1,300.

## Camp Carolina for Boys
**Lamb's Creek Rd., Brevard**
**• (828) 884-2414**

Though Camp Carolina is only 2.5 miles from Brevard, its 22 acres feel far from town life. It's bordered by mountain ridges and on two sides by the Pisgah National Forest, and it's only a half-mile from the forest's entrance. The camp, established in 1924, has three streams and a 4½-acre lake for swimming, canoeing, kayaking and fishing for mountain trout. Both group and individual tennis instruction is provided on six tennis courts. Other

activities include riflery, archery, soccer, table tennis, basketball, football, baseball, lacrosse, hang gliding, mountain biking, skateboarding, weightlifting and arts and crafts. Horseback riding in Western and English saddles, forward seat and jumping are taught, and campers take day and overnight rides in Pisgah Forest.

Younger campers who have proven their skills on the camp's lake take river trips on Mills River and the upper French Broad. More advanced campers tackle the Green and Tuckasegee rivers, and the skilled have the opportunity to challenge the Nantahala, Pigeon and Chattooga rivers. All ages have the opportunity to experience whitewater rafting. In addition to Pisgah Forest camping, more challenging hiking and camping trips go deep into the Nantahala National Forest, Linville Gorge Wilderness Area and Mount Mitchell State Park. All campers may participate in rock climbing and rappelling, starting on the camp's wall.

Carolina's nature program involves collecting and identifying area plants and animals and pioneering projects include using hand tools to build tree houses, forts, dams, bridges and cabins.

The camp, which is open to boys ages 7 to 17, has a capacity of 200. It provides an average of one counselor for every four campers. For younger groups, there is one counselor for every three boys in a cabin. There is a lodge for each age group where meetings, evening programs and rainy-day activities take place. The camp's infirmary is staffed by two registered nurses, and a doctor is on call. The three-week June session costs $1,650; the four-week July session, $2,000; and the 2½-week August session, $1,450.

## Camp Illahee
**Illahee Rd., Brevard • (828) 883-2181**

Illahee means "heavenly world" in the Cherokee language, and this camp for girls ages 6 to 16 that was established in 1921 abounds with natural beauty and high spirits. The grounds are beautifully landscaped. They contain 30 cabins, a dining hall, a new recreation lodge that includes a stage and gymnastics area, an infirmary, a crafts shop, a barn, a canoe lake, tennis courts, an open-air woodland chapel, riding rings, rifle range, two climbing walls and many other facilities.

Each camper sets her own schedule, which can include such activities as riflery, team sports, archery, dance, drama, gymnastic, aerobics, painting, drawing, weaving, stitchery, ceramics, printing, woodworking, synchronized swimming and diving, tennis, horseback riding, hiking, whitewater canoeing, rappelling, backpacking and kayaking.

Illahee holds two two-week sessions that cost $1,375 each; two three-week sessions that are $1,915 each; and a four-week session for $2,510.

## Camp Gwynn Valley
### 1080 Island Ford Rd., Brevard
### • (828) 885-2900

Camp Gwynn Valley is somewhat newer than some of the other camps in this chapter and is also different than the others in that it provides a special, sheltered environment for younger children, ages 5 to 12. Mary Gwynn established the camp in 1935, and it has been in continuous operation ever since, attaining an international reputation for dealing with the needs and interests of the younger child. Camp Gwynn Valley, altitude 2,240 feet, sits in a secluded cove that opens onto a sunlit valley with a view of the Pisgah Range.

The camp's 300 acres are comprised of 250 acres of woods and a 50-acre working farm, where children can take turns feeding the animals, weeding and hoeing the garden and milking the cow and goats. Cabin cookouts often begin with a trip to the farm to gather fresh eggs and pick vegetables in season. Baby animals — lambs, rabbits, calves, piglets and kittens — are favorite members of the camp's "family."

Swimmers gain confidence in the pool before graduating to the camp's lake. Most boating and canoeing also take place on the lake, although older children who meet the requirements take short trips on the nearby French Broad River. They can also fish for bream and bass in the lake and for trout in the millpond, where a historic mill has been renovated and is once more grinding corn and wheat, providing electricity and performing other functions such as churning ice cream.

Children get to participate in the entire food-producing process — from field to table — picking, shelling, sifting, bagging, baking and eating the cornbread.

Horseback-riding instruction concentrates on the basic skills of English saddle seat; advanced riders do some open field and trail riding on the property. Campers also learn something of the care of tack and horses, including Loeb, the draft horse that pulls the wagon for after-supper hay rides. Cookouts and sleep-outs are conducted mostly on camp property. The younger children use closed-in, fixed tent sites, while older ones backpack to more remote areas.

Crafts include ceramics, weaving, copper enameling, tie-dyeing, macramé, puppetry, mosaics and broom- and candle-making. There is no formal arts program, but in the relaxed time after supper, children can choose to learn Braille, plan a play with their cabinmates or learn mountain and international dances in the lodge. Sketching, painting and collage are also taught. Campers participate in campfire readings of poetry and children's classics, and the children are encouraged to write about their camp activities.

Children are placed in cabin groups according to grade completed in school, with six to 10 children in a cabin, depending upon their ages (the younger ones are in smaller groups). The camper-staff ration is 3-to-1. Younger children have inside bathrooms in their cabins. The older children heat water with wood and have battery-powered lights in their cabins — lessons in energy conservation and resource management. Home-cooked meals are served in an open-air, screened dining room. A physician and nurses are in residence.

Five-day sessions at Camp Gwynn Valley cost $400; nine-day sessions, $700; 13-day sessions, $950; and 19-day sessions, $1,400. If the parents' combined gross income is below $60,000, they may request a discount.

## Eagle's Nest Camp
### 43 Hart Rd., Pisgah Forest
### • (828) 877-4349

The staff of Eagle's Nest Camp believes that the big missing ingredient for American children is membership within a tribe within a village within a nature-based homeland. This sense of "belonging" is one of the missing links that they strive to create for their campers. One way they achieve the goal is through the joy children gain in knowing that they are, according to the camp's brochure, "responsible and viable parts of a greater idealized whole."

This journey to wholeness takes place in a "village" setting surrounded by the natural beauty of a serene, mountain-enclosed valley. Its quadrangle is bordered on one end by an open-air dining room, where whole and natural foods have been served family-style for the past 20 years, and at the other by the 60-year-old lodge with a stone fireplace and stage. Many of the rest of the camp's buildings have been rebuilt in the last 15 years, and the kitchen, infirmary, laundry and offices are brand new.

Activities — including, swimming, lake and whitewater canoeing, fishing, rock climbing, backpacking, dance, Native American ceremonies, dramatics, musical instrument instruction, ceramics, weaving, woodworking photography, sewing, crafts, sketching, sculpture and nature skills — meet in large open-air buildings, in the meadows, by the lake, at the horse-riding ring and stable, on the athletic or archery fields, on the tennis court, in the theaters, at the canoe dock, in the garden, and in the apple orchard. The camp's three hilltops provide plenty of breathing room, and the surrounding forests, trails, river, streams and mountains offer opportunities for adventure and development of wilderness skills. An Indian Village brings children to the heart of the mythic story and ceremony each week. Full-stage musical productions can involve one-third of the camp. Campers and counselors alike share in the chores of keeping Eagle's Nest running smoothly.

This coed camp, now in business for 72 years, is designed for children age 6 through high school and offers three three-week sessions. It has a camper-counselor ratio of 1 to 4. The 1999 fee is $1,600 for ages 6 to 12 and $1,675 for campers ages 13 to 15. Those who have completed the 10th or 11th grade may apply to be Junior Counselors, who come to the camp at half-fare.

Eagle's Nest also offers expanded wilderness adventures to teenagers, such as 100-mile hikes on the Appalachian Trail.

# Southern Mountains

### Camp Merrie-Woode
**100 Merrie-Woode Rd., Sapphire**
**• (828) 743-3300**

In 1999, Camp Merrie-Woode opened for it's 81st season; all sessions will be filled long before that time. It was founded in 1919 by Mrs. Jonathan C. "Dammie" Day, born of English parents, who founded the camp on "English traditions and Christian principles" as a place where girls could come for adventure and discover the strength in themselves. Since 1978, when former campers bought the operation, Merrie-Woode has been run as a non-profit foundation.

Though only a mile off U.S. Highway 64, the camp, nestled at the foot of Old Bald Mountain and overlooking the headwaters of Lake Fairfield, sits secluded at 3,300 feet among rhododendron, hemlock and hardwood forests. Instruction is offered in archery, arts and crafts, canoeing, ceramics, dance, dramatics, horseback riding, jewelry, kayaking, hiking, climbing, land sports, music, nature, photography, sailing, swimming, tennis, tumbling and weaving. Special emphasis is given to hiking, backpacking, wilderness camping, trail riding, rock climbing, whitewater canoeing and kayaking. Emphasis is placed on the process by which a girl attains skills or grows in self-confidence, rather than on competition or the final product.

Many camp traditions have developed over the years, not the least of which is the camp uniform. The gray "middy" and green ties and shorts are the same as uniforms used in the past that link present campers to generations before them. All except the oldest campers live four to a cabin plus a counselor.

Merrie-Woode offers three sessions: a three-week session for ages 7 to 16 for $1,780; a five-week session for ages 8 to 17 for $2,835; and a two-week session for ages 6 to 14 for $1,150.

One of the things that makes this area so inviting is the likelihood that your property will be blessed with a crystal-clear river, lake, pond, stream or spring.

# Real Estate

Whether you want a simple log hideaway, a grand estate or something in between — a condo, a horse farm, a lakefront lodge or a classic Victorian with stained-glass windows and turrets — you can find it here in wide range of prices.

There are, however, a few things to be aware of when buying property in this region. Out in the countryside, zoning is practically nonexistent, so a $200,000 house can wind up next door to a rundown home. Because of this, people moving to the area often favor housing developments, resort properties and golf communities, all of which have deed restrictions and amenities. You can also expect prices in such places to be considerably higher than you would pay for similar unrestricted properties. When buying into a development, make sure you know what the arrangements are for road maintenance, water and sewer upkeep and covenants. Some restrictions might affect your future plans, such as adding a swimming pool or detached garage. When buying outside developments, make sure the road access to your new home is clearly yours.

Another way buyers get around zoning problems is to buy large tracts of land to form buffers around their homes, but with so much of western North Carolina devoted to public lands, large tracks, while still to be had, are getting harder to find at reasonable prices. Much of the remaining undeveloped land is on steep mountainsides. While such places can offer spectacular views, they often require extensive foundations and retaining walls just to keep a house from sliding or washing away. Remember, too, that the higher up you are, the windier your site is likely to be. The old-timers, who nestled in coves, knew such places offered protection from storms and were easier to reach in bad weather.

That brings up another caution: When you're buying land that you intend to build on, make sure it has a site that will be approved for a septic tank and that the ground perks adequately. As we mentioned in the Climate chapter in this book, one of the things that makes this area so inviting is the likelihood that your property will be blessed with a crystal-clear river, lake, pond, stream or spring, and local laws against polluting them are — thank goodness — strict.

Speaking of water, don't let anyone convince you that it's perfectly safe to build on one of our 100-year flood plains. It could be that you wouldn't have to worry about such a flood in your lifetime. However, we came very close to having a 100-year flood in August 1994 when a tropical storm moved up from Florida and into the mountains, causing landslides, washing out roads, polluting wells and flooding out more homes than we thought possible. That storm moved through rather quickly, but high-pressure systems to the north can cause Gulf-produced weather to occasionally stall out in the mountains. We were lucky that time! Remember too that our rich bottomlands got that way because seemingly peaceful rivers or creeks overflowed their banks to deposit all that good soil there.

Finally, if you don't know where to begin

---

**INSIDERS' TIP**

**The local Chamber of Commerce will always have a stash of real estate newsletters and newspapers. Pick one up to familiarize yourself with the offerings of particular companies.**

looking for your spot in the mountains, read our County Overviews chapter and combine it with the real-estate information below. We have listed a few of the many Realtors doing business in each county. Contact the chamber of commerce in the area you're considering. You'll find such phone numbers in our County Overview Chapter. They will send you information and put you in touch with all the local Realtors.

But don't wait too long to make your move if you like a good deal. Newcomers are flocking to the region, and real estate prices are rising—fast!

# Northern Mountains

## Alleghany County

Alleghany County still is a treasure waiting to be discovered. This largely undeveloped county owes its pristine state to the geographical isolation imposed on it by the limited road system here. It is the northernmost county in North Carolina's mountains and is bordered by Virginia to the north and the Blue Ridge Parkway to the east. Access into the county from any direction is by twisting two-lane roads. However, this isn't necessarily a drawback. If you like the feel of wide-open, rolling land without urban clutter, then Alleghany County is for you.

Real estate is still reasonably priced in this county of 11,550 residents, and a surprising variety of properties are available, but as the general populous discovers the pastoral beauty of this area, the prices go up. It is still possible to find a $40,000 fixer-upper bungalow, and also a $300,000-plus executive home in the southeastern part of the county. A four-bedroom home near Sparta, the county seat, sells for an average of $150,000. The land outside the town is sparsely populated; homes perch on mountaintops surrounded by views of farmland valleys that spread toward the Virginia border. No-frills homesites up to an acre in size run between $8,500 and $15,000. If you crave the extras — the mountains, by a creek or river or a spectacular view, then boost that price to about $20,000 and more.

Here and there, in the more remote areas of the county, little communities are clustered around a typical crossroads and a convenience store. In this rural setting, farmland can be found for roughly $5,000 to $6,000 an acre.

Alleghany County, for all its rural charm, also has the allure of old money. Southeast in the county is Roaring Gap, a spectacular ridge with an unbelievable 180-degree view of metropolitan Winston-Salem, about 75 miles away in the valley below. This area was settled in the 1930s as a summer retreat by prominent Winston families such as the Bowmans, Hanes and Grays. The grand homes here, many with the chestnut-bark siding characteristic of the era, are nestled along the ridge with the confidence of established tradition. Adding to the landscape of this venerable region are the occasional private club, placid mountain lake or old stone church. When homes in Roaring Gap do become available, they tend to change hands quietly, without ever reaching the open market. Inquire about these areas with a local realtor.

### Boyer Realty
**1246 U.S. Hwy. 21 S., Sparta**
• **(336) 372-8888**

In business for over 20 years, Boyer Realty is owned by James and Shirley Boyer. The company deals with a variety of properties, from land to residential homes and some commercial properties.

### Dixon Auction and Appraisals
**27 N. Main St., Ste. A, Sparta**
• **(336) 372-8642**

Since '79 Boy Man Dixon, founder and owner of Dixon Auction and Appraisals, has dealt in the sale, appraisals, and auctioning of properties. The company handles private and some commercial sales.

### Miles Realty
**565 S. Main St., Sparta**
• **(800) 553-2322, (336) 372-5646**

Donald W. Miles and his family have been in real estate since the early '70s. He's a licensed building contractor, and deals in lots and homes, commercial lots, farmland, town and country properties, seasonal retirement homes and seasonal vacation homes.

Photo: Hugh Morton

Walk above the clouds in North Carolina's mountains.

### Reeves Auction & Realty Co.
**349 S. Main St., Sparta**
**• (800) 682-5804**

Reeves Auction & Realty was established in 1972 and is a member of the Alleghany County Listing Exchange Service. The company features properties along the Blue Ridge Parkway and the New River, including vacation homes, lots, acreage tracts or farmland.

## Ashe County

Ashe is a rural county on the move. Like its neighbor, Alleghany County, Ashe has been isolated in the past by an undeveloped road system. Roads have improved and city leaders are seeing more interest from outside business. Businesses aren't the only ones attracted to this area, though; the rolling countryside is becoming more and more intriguing to individuals and families, retirees and couples. This could make a real estate investment now in Ashe County a glowing prospect.

Riding north from Boone along U.S. Highway 221, you'll see the hills of Ashe County rise out of the valleys. Instead of the haphazard residential growth you might see else-

where in the region, you see geometric plantings of Christmas trees — a big business here — and unmarked pasture land dotted with cows and horses. Fairly large expanses of acreage are still available, mostly in 100-acre parcels that sell for $3,000 to $6,000 an acre. You can even be a gentleman farmer if you can find one of the county's many marvelous old two-story farmhouses down a gravel road or restored mills on a waterway.

Most of Ashe County's population is gathered around the towns of West Jefferson and Jefferson. In either of these pleasant communities separated by less than a mile, a modest two-bedroom, one-bath bungalow can be bought for around $70,000, or if you prefer, you can buy an executive home for as much as $200,000 and up. Some apartment complexes and condominium units are also scattered over the two towns.

The virgin land out in the county has also attracted luxury golfing communities. Both Mountain Aire Golf Club and Jefferson Landing are upscale recreation-centered developments with condominiums, town houses and single-family residences. At Jefferson Landing, homesites are available starting in the

$30,000s; condos, townhouses and single-family residences here start at $135,000. A scenic mountain backdrop is the setting for the Jefferson Landing 18-hole golf course, and a section of three community villages that include townhouses, patio homes and single-family dwellings. They range in size from 1,400 square feet on up and in price from $150,000 on up.

At Mountain Aire Golf Club, just off old U.S. 221, Fairway Ridge offers year-round residence or a seasonal retreat alongside a new golf course. Large homesites, cleared or naturally wooded, offer breathtaking mountain views; most of the sites overlook the fairways. Paved roads and underground utilities are additional features.

Heading south toward Boone on N.C. Highway 194 you'll pass Stone Bridge. This executive development is composed entirely of new homes constructed from antique logs. The homes range in price from $60,000 to $250,000.

## Ashe High Country Realty
**7 S. Jefferson St., West Jefferson**
• **(336) 246-6348, (800) 729-0735**

Ashe High Country Realty provides abundant information on available real estate in the lush and peaceful countryside of Ashe County. Business is continually growing for this popular company which now employs five buyer agents. Ashe High Country Realty offers a wide choice of properties from one- and two-story log cabins to chalets, traditional homes, and the occasional old mill or mini horse-farm. Properties along the meandering New River, near trout springs in the forest and with delightful long-range views, are just some of the offerings. The company also offers acreage, building lots, farms, and commercial properties.

## Blue Ridge Mountain Realty, Inc.
**911 S. Jefferson Ave., West Jefferson**
• **(336) 246-8600, (800) 533-3721**

In business for 17 years, Blue Ridge Mountain Realty handles a variety of properties in a very rural area. Vacation homes are big sellers, as are riverfront lots and tracts. These offices deal in everything from permanent residences to resort properties, small acreage to commercial property and vacation rentals.

## Dogwood Realty
**592 S. Main St., Jefferson**
• **(336) 246-7455**

Founded by Cheryl and Phillip Lewis in 1977, Dogwood Realty provides a full range of real estate services, from the sale of resort properties and vacation homes on the New River to residential log cabins and larger homes.

## Fleetwood Falls Inc.
**3108 Railroad Grade Rd., Fleetwood**
• **(336) 877-1110**

Fleetwood Falls Inc., run by the Milton King family for some 30 years now, handles real estate sales, land development, chalet rentals and general contracting. The offices also offer property management. Milton King, his wife and two sons operate the company together and pride themselves in presenting properties in accordance with the natural mountain setting. They offer mainly chalets and cozy log cabin-style houses.

# Avery County

From the Christmas tree farms sprawling over the hillsides like vineyards in the southern part of the county to the seasonal activity of the ski areas and the multimillion dollar exclusivity of the Linville area, Avery County offers a diverse real estate market. Building lots range from $7,000 to $40,000 — even more in resort areas or private residential clubs, where you can expect to pay up to $200,000 for restricted land. The median price for a home in Avery County is $87,000, but this does not indicate availability nor reflect the high-end homes of the seasonal community.

Closer to Boone, bordering N.C. Highway 105, is Linville, a resort area that has attracted seasonal visitors and moneyed jet-setters for about 100 years. Today's seasonal guests,

from all over the country, make their second nest in several exclusive developments such as Linville Ridge and Grandfather Golf and Country Club. These gated communities all have spectacular views (some 360 degrees!) and executive custom homes that can cost from $200,000 to more than $1 million.

Banner Elk, northeast of Linville, is home to Lees-McRae College; Sugar Mountain, a ski resort; and Elk River Country Club, a gated community. In town, comfortable houses can be purchased in long-established neighborhoods surrounding the college for between $70,000 and $150,000. But the prime real estate focus here is seasonal rentals. Modern condos, mountain chalets and rustic one-bedroom bungalows are among the places rented in season, winter or summer, typically for about $100 per night or $400 to $600 per week. Timesharing is also a popular concept here.

For retirees in Avery County, resident-controlled communities such as Linville Land Harbor are appealing. A sense of community and cohesion is evident in this development 20

miles from Boone, where RVs, executive homes and vacation bungalows stand side by side. Recreational facilities that include an 18-hole golf course, a boating lake, tennis courts, a heated pool and shuffleboard courts are also available to members who pay a one-time fee. Most residents of Linville Land Harbor are seasonal, but a number of permanent families have also made this development their home, perhaps drawn by its unhurried pace, recreation options, security and sense of community.

The county line runs through the center of Beech Mountain, a ski community, making it a part of both Avery and Watauga counties. See Watauga County for information on Beech Mountain.

### Braswell Realty
**320 Linville St., Newland**
• **(828) 733-5800**

Specializing in mountain properties with spectacular views, Braswell Realty is only 10 minutes from Grandfather Mountain. Whether you're looking for a vacation home where you can relax or an old farmhouse to renovate, the sales staff can show you every nook and cranny of the high country. Braswell is the exclusive Realtor for the new Blue Ridge Country Club, where lots are for sale if you're looking to build.

## High Country Realty
**N.C. Hwy. 105, Grandfather Business Center, Linville**
• **(828) 963-6521, (800) 227-6521**

Located in the Grandfather Business Center in Linville, High Country Realty deals in area property just minutes from the popular golf and skiing areas of Seven Devils and Sugar Mountain. Handling the sales and rental of vacation homes and condominiums, the small, experienced staff has helped customers find just the right property in Avery County for more than 15 years.

## Lacey Realty
**Main St., Newland • (828) 733-2151**

Avery County's oldest real estate office helps make sure the buyer is aware. "Get a lawyer. Get a real estate broker. Get a survey and get title insurance," the owners say. The company provides prospective buyers with thorough information, including a pamphlet of real estate jargon definitions, to familiarize buyers with all aspects of their purchases.

# Madison County

The allure of mountain hollows, coves, winding country roads and rushing water make Madison County, only 35 minutes from Asheville, a great retreat for all ages. This county remains largely rural and features some of the most remote, undeveloped mountain areas available in western North Carolina.

There is still a considerable amount of acreage to be had in Madison County, some of it rather steep and densely wooded, such as Shelton Laurel and Walnut, communities near the Tennessee line. You can buy land here beginning at $2,000 an acre. In some areas closer to Buncombe County, there is also a pleasing variety of long hilltop pasture lands for $2,000 to $5,000 an acre depending on the size of the parcel and how usable the land is.

Largely undisturbed, the principal towns of Marshall and Hot Springs are basically much as they were in their heyday at the turn of the century. Hot Springs was once a fashionable resort, famous for its curative springs. As a result, many of the area's grand old homes are waiting to be rediscovered. Hot Springs is also home to seasonal residents and a vital resting point off the Appalachian Trail.

Mars Hill, home to Mars Hill College, is a quaint Main Street hamlet with only a few traffic lights, but the expansion of the campus has impacted the town, bringing in more diverse groups and a growth in businesses along the road that links the town with U.S. Highway 19/23. The completion of a massive interstate corridor link over the mountains with Tennessee is expected sometime after the turn of the century and should significantly open up this area for development.

Modern residential housing is in a state of transition in Madison County. The average basic three-bedroom home sells for about $100,000, and rentals are few and far between. There are a few planned subdivisions in Madison County, but not many.

## Blue Ridge Realty
**Main St., Mars Hill**
• **(828) 689-9898, (888) 689-9898**

Owner and founder Ginny Todd opened the Blue Ridge Realty offices in 1993. This fairly young company specializes in "environmentally pleasing properties," that is, matching clients with exactly the environment they would like to be surrounded with. Want a house with a mountain ridge view? Or perhaps a river and a valley? A secluded forest home by a creek? Blue Ridge Realty aims to grant wishes. The company's properties include small-town as well as rural acreage, homes, farms, farm houses, mountain hideaways, and commercial properties.

## Hoffman & Associates, Real Estate
**105 Anderson St., Mars Hill**
• **(828) 689-4599, 689-5039,**
**(800) 937-2157**

Owner and founder Jeanne Hoffman has been in the real estate business some 20 years. This company handles commercial, as well as residential properties. The full-service office also offers appraisals and has a variety of parcels and homes to choose from, including farms, mountain acreage, land and lots.

### Northland Properties at Wolf Laurel
**424 Wolf Laurel Rd., Mars Hill**
• **(828) 689-2100**

Specializing in Wolf Laurel homes and land, this office is run by broker Mercer Davis. Northland Properties at Wolf Laurel is a private, gated community with excellent mountain views and forests and streams nearby.

### Roberts Real Estate
**Main St., Marshall**
• **(828) 649-2535, (800) 852-9112**

Frank Roberts, a lifelong resident of Madison County, established Roberts Real Estate 14 years ago. This company deals in a variety of properties, including farms, homes, acreage, investments, commercial, and rentals. Roberts Real Estate is across from Court House.

# Mitchell County

If you want your own special place in the woods or at the top of a mountain, and you enjoy simple outdoor pleasures, Mitchell County will delight you. Tucked back in these high woods and atop spectacular mountain peaks are some of the more reasonably priced getaway properties you'll find in the mountains.

The influence of Little Switzerland, a community with a decidedly Swiss architectural flavor that was settled in the early 1900s, is evident in the many nearby gingerbread-trimmed chalets and cabins. A three-bedroom, completely furnished chalet in the woods near Spruce Pine sells for a relatively modest $90,000. And even properties with a view are surprisingly reasonable here. In Little Swit-

zerland, a large furnished Swiss chalet on three levels, with two fireplaces, a deck and the famous Little Switzerland view runs $135,000.

The mountaintop views are not the only appealing land parcels in Mitchell County. Down winding mountain back roads, you can find acreage with your own personal waterfall or trout stream for $6,000 an acre. Mini-farms with barns, outbuildings and quaint old homesteads sell for $60,000. And 30 private acres of gentle meadowlands along the picturesque Old North Toe River runs around $107,000.

The hamlets of Spruce Pine and Bakersville are reminiscent of a bygone era. Here, marvelous old homes can be purchased at incredibly low prices — $60,000 for a two-story house, for example. More modern homes are also moderately priced. Upscale homes, such as a three-bedroom, two-story cedar with vaulted ceiling and stone fireplace are also tucked away in the mountains of Mitchell County.

If you prefer even more seclusion, a few properties with some acreage are still available near the border of the Pisgah National Forest and the Blue Ridge Parkway. These properties range from 34 acres near the forest with a stream and an old homestead for $150,000 to a choice 16-acre mountaintop tract near the Parkway with a meadow, woods and mountain springs for $80,000.

People who settle in Mitchell County seem to prefer the rustic seclusion, but when the urge for city comforts arises, they take solace in the easy driving distance to Asheville and Boone.

### Real Property People, Inc.
**113 Mitchell Ave., Bakersville**
• **(828) 688-3921, (800) 806-6725**

In business since 1982, Real Property People helps you find homes, mountain farms, cabins, acreage, and lots to suit your needs.

## INSIDERS' TIP

**People moving to our mountains from crime-ridden cities often pay premium prices to be in gated, security-conscious communities. While rules in such places do protect property values from unwanted developments in the neighborhood, longtime residents have to smile at what they consider unnecessary paranoia.**

The office is also open on Saturdays, in addition to regular business hours.

## Howell-Sparks Real Estate
### 408 Oak Ave., Spruce Pine
### • (828) 765-7477, (800) 443-6295

Ray Howell's and Billy Sparks' Howell-Sparks Real Estate has been in business for some 25 years. The company specializes in condos, residential land and homes, mountain land lots, wood-sided houses, and a few mountain log cabins.

## Yellow Bird Realtors
### 188 N.C. Hwy. 226 S., Bakersville
### • (828) 688-3064, (800) 332-2374

Over the past 12 years, George Thomas, owner and founder of Yellow Bird Realtors, has dealt in residential and commercial real estate. Rentals, cabins and farm houses also make up the wide variety of choices offered by this company.

# Watauga County

Tourism, a university and geography play equal parts in the development of property in Watauga County. The mountain communities of Boone, Blowing Rock, Beech Mountain and Valle Crucis have grown up around the tourist trade. This is ski country, and the character of home design — much of it log — and property prices reflect the influx of seasonal money. New homes on individual building sites with long-range views typically start at $100,000 here and range as high as $500,000, depending on the cachet of the location.

Many of the exclusive gated communities in the area are populated by seasonal residents who build homes costing from $200,000 to several million. Here, homes built with natural materials — stone, timber, and a wealth of glass — perch on the mountaintops with views that seem to go on forever. The upscale Mayview section of picturesque Blowing Rock,

Photo: Judy Scharns, Courtesy of Boone Convention and Visitors Bureau

Snow on the rooftops, downtown Boone.

15 minutes southeast of Boone, commands a breathtaking view and equally breathtaking home prices — $250,000 and higher.

A basic three-bedroom, two-bath bungalow on about 2 acres, which was available 10 years ago in Watauga County for about $60,000, today sells for $85,000. This makes it tough for first-time home buyers, whose problems are worsened by a scarcity of year-round rentals. When you add to the mix the 13,000 students at Appalachian State University, who are only guaranteed one year of campus housing, coupled with the reality that seasonal tourism doubles the population, the scarcity is understandable.

Acreage in Watauga is at a premium. The tourism industry has created a lack of prime farmland, and large tracts held through the generations are particularly difficult to locate on the market. No acreage of any kind, if it becomes available, is priced less than $3,000 an acre. The best possibilities for this type of real estate are generally found a good 20 minutes north and west of Boone.

Tourist rentals and timeshare options are popular in the resort sections of the county. Beech Mountain, the mile-high ski community that evolved from the tourist trade, straddles both Avery and Watauga counties, but the major portion of its active real estate lies on the Watauga side. In this tiny community with a year-round population of only 300 or so, there are three subdivisions and about 600 seasonal rental units. Private homes in Fox Run or the Woodland Meadows of Beech cost anywhere from $200,000 to $350,000. Most of these are seasonal homes, but there are also a few hardy year-round residents. Rentals are available either as condominiums or individual chalets and cottages. Summer rental prices can range from $85 per night for a one-bedroom unit to $125 per night for a six- or seven-bedroom unit. In winter these

rates jump to $125 and $400, respectively. These rental units are good investment properties available for as little as $40,000 for a one-bedroom condo unit to an upscale $500,000 for a seven-bedroom home with great amenities and an awe-inspiring view.

### Advanced Realty Inc.
**2575 N.C. Hwy. 105 S., Boone**
**• (828) 264-5111, (800) 264-6144**

This five-year-old company, located in the Highland Commons Shopping Center and run by business partners Vivian Woodard and Ada Webster, can supply just about any property at any time. Advanced Realty deals with all properties and styles of homes. Long-term vacation rentals, from 6 months to a year, may also be found here.

### Beech Mountain Slopeside Rentals Inc.
**503 Beech Mountain Pkwy.,**
**Beech Mountain**
**• (828) 387-4251, (800) 692-2061**

Slopeside Rental features are numerous. Chalets, contemporary condos, ski lofts, townhouses, and family homes are all either slopeside or within walking distance of the Beech Mountain ski slopes. Fully equipped kitchens, Jacuzzis, and washers and dryers make this a no-worry vacation every time. Color TV with cablevision and grocery delivery mean you'll only have to leave the house to hit the slopes.

### Blowing Rock Properties
**1059 Main St., Blowing Rock**
**• (828) 295-9200**

This real estate firm in downtown Blowing Rock is a town mainstay. Come visit the conveniently located offices to find out about hot properties in the Blowing Rock area, as well as the surrounding mountains. The company

---

### INSIDERS' TIP

There's a lot to be said for a house sitting high on a plateau or mountainside with a spectacular mountain views. But while these higher elevation homes are cooler in summer, they are also much colder in winter. Hilltops, too, are often subject to high winds, while homes snuggled in a protected valley or cove may experience little or no wind at all.

is a full-service firm, dealing in private and commercial properties.

## Blowing Rock Realty
### 1150 Main St., Blowing Rock
### • (828) 295-9861, (800) 255-9861

This full-service real estate agency is the oldest in the area, established in 1924. This company deals in homes, condominiums, land and commercial properties.

## Boone Realty Inc.
### 764 U.S. Hwy. 105, Boone
### • (828) 264-5267, (800) 392-5263

Ira J. Bingham, Jr., owner of this 25-year-old company, offers residential sales and property management, as well as some commercial properties. Conveniently located in the Watauga County hub of Boone, this office is a good stop for browsing over hot properties on your way in or out of town.

## Jenkins Realtors
### 452 Sunset Dr., Blowing Rock
### • (828) 295-9886

This Blowing Rock real estate firm not only handles residential and commercial properties, lots and condominiums but also has a number of rentals in the delightful Blowing Rock area and environs. These include spacious vacation rentals, seasonal rentals, and long-term rentals. Call the company for a free brochure.

## Leatherwood Realty
### Rt. 2 off N.C. Hwy. 286, Ferguson
### • (828) 973-4142

This real estate firm offers a "country place in the Blue Ridge." Leatherwood has been a family-owned company for over four generations of the R.B. Johnston family. It will give you over 40,000 acres of Blue Ridge High Country to choose from and it offers not only

properties to purchase but also short and long-term rentals of cozy cabins and wooden homes.

## Sherry Garris Properties
### 1005 Beech Mountain Pkwy., Beech Mountain • (828) 387-2579

Self-professed "new kid on the block" Sherry Garris Properties offers sales and rentals in this delightful area. Founder and owner Garris has worked in real estate and lived on Beech Mountain for more than ten years, and recently opened her own office. With great energy and enthusiasm, Garris prides herself in "matching the right home with the right price with the right people." If you're looking for a ski-weekend rental, or perhaps something for the whole season, the chalet and townhouses offered are fully furnished and include color TV, kitchen, and phone.

# Yancey County

Variety is the draw for newcomers to Yancey County. This lushly wooded county has high peaks — Mount Mitchell is here — as well as the wide sweep of valleys. Prices for desirable acreage (parcels of 10 to 100-plus acres), can vary in price from $3,000 to $15,000 an acre. Individual lots varying in size and price are spread throughout the county.

The average three-bedroom, two-bath home in Yancey County sells for about $85,000, but there's a variety of nice homes on either side of that figure. These include old two-story farmhouses with the mail-order gingerbread trim of a century ago as well as modern versions of the log cabin and contemporary classics of timber and glass.

The area has numerous seasonal residents and a growing retiree population. The pace is slower here, and the charm of Burnsville, the county seat established in 1833,

---

## INSIDERS' TIP

Jackson County has a number of historic homes, churches and commercial buildings. If you'd like to check some of them out, call the Jackson County Travel and Tourism Authority at (800) 862-1911 and ask them to send you a free tour brochure and map. This self-guiding driving tour will take you to 29 sites, 10 of which are listed on the National Register of Historic Places.

with its picturesque town square, recalls a simpler era.

An exclusive new development, Mountain Air Country Club, is now in its first phase of development on a 500-acre mountaintop site 35 minutes northeast of Asheville and 4 miles west of Burnsville. This private equity country club community features an 18-hole, par 71 golf course designed by Pete Dye associate Scott Pool (see our Golf chapter); a private paved airstrip located 4,400 feet above sea level; and homesites for approximately 264 single-family dwellings. There will also be about 336 cluster homes, townhomes and luxurious condominiums. For more information on living at Mountain Air, call (800) 247-7791.

## Common Ground Realty
### 2 West Main St., Burnsville
### • (828) 682-6416, (800) 830-6166

A short walk up the street from the Chamber of Commerce Visitor Center in Burnsville, Common Ground Realty may well be the most convenient place to begin the search for area properties. Owned by Bill Thomas, this office is a member of the National Association of Exclusive Buyer Agents, mandating that the agents pledge in writing to represent only buyers.

## Lunsford Realty
### 725 West Bypass, Burnsville
### • (828) 682-7408

Lunsford Realty deals in anything from small modern one-story homes to older farm houses on vast acreage. Founded by owner Doris Lunsford 20 years ago, the company encompasses a variety of styles. Lunsford Realty is the area representative for log cabin homes. Large country homes and farmhouses are also on the list, as is acreage, commercial and residential properties.

## Mount Mitchell Realty
### 7590 N.C. Hwy. 80 S., Micaville
### • (828) 675-4414

This real estate firm, located on N.C. Highway 80, a few miles from Burnsville. The full-service firm will put you together with the property of your choice in the Burnsville area, Mount Mitchell and in between. Mount Mitchell Realty is located in the pro-shop of the Mount Mitchell Golf Club.

## Thurston Associates
**155 N.C. Hwy. 80 S., Micaville**
**• (828) 675-5038, (800) 675-5074**

Founded in 1992 by Jacquie Thurston, this real estate firm specializes in mountain properties of all types. The owner has 15 years experience in selling mountain properties. The firm is located inside the historic Micaville General Store in downtown Micaville, four miles east of Burnsville.

# Central Mountains

## Buncombe County

This is the site of the largest private real estate sale in America: George Vanderbilt purchased 125,000 prime acres 100 years ago and created the incomparable Biltmore Estate. You can't buy anything of that magnitude here today, but Buncombe County does have an amazing array of property. The unique character of the county is visible in its real estate landscape: classic turn-of-the century country farmhouses, the Queen Anne "ladies" of old Asheville, French Country cottages from the 1920s, lavish homes of Biltmore Forest, stately Georgian-columned domiciles and pastel Victorian dream houses in historic Montford, and contemporary timber and glass aeries hugging the mountainsides.

The influx of newcomers from all over the country has boosted the market price of building lots and residential properties. The spectrum is broad. Acreage, found more easily in the western and northern sections of the county, sells at a premium. Generally, Buncombe's larger parcels are available for about $5,000 per acre. In the rural areas; lots with views start at about $12,000. You have to be cautious about your selection of a hilltop in Buncombe County — especially if you plan to enjoy that view in the future, since zoning is variable.

Homes run the gamut from a fixer-upper for $20,000 to the grandeur of multimillion dollar places in the exclusive Biltmore Forest. There are many upscale subdivisions planned for all points of the county. Still, the average three-bedroom, two-bath home in Buncombe County sells for about $107,000, and there's much variety on both sides of that figure.

Each end of the county reflects a distinct character, and builders and developers are quick to accommodate these varying tastes. The northern part of the county is more rustic with log homes and refurbished farmhouses. Cedar homes are popular throughout the county. The western end of Buncombe is punctuated by quaint bungalow homes of the 1940s and an array of modern rustic-style homes. In the east are Black Mountain and Montreat, tourist spots since the early 1900s. Classic homes here reflect the 1920s and '30s rustic camp look as well as the classic white frame of the 1940s.

But it's the south end of the county that seems to be experiencing the most rapid growth. The terrain here is more level and the mountains more open, making the land more conducive to development. Stretching toward the Asheville Regional Airport off Interstate 26 are numerous new upscale subdivisions geared to the young urban professional. These modern, mostly cedar or traditional brick homes range from $140,000 for a three-bedroom, two-bath home on three-quarters of an acre to the $350,000-plus executive home with all the expected amenities. Also in south Buncombe, several country-estate subdivisions offer acreage or run along the crest of a mountain, commanding much higher prices: from $450,000 to $1 million. A new posh subdivision, Biltmore Park, on the edge of the Biltmore Estate, sells building sites for $50,000 and higher.

## Appalachian Realty
**72 Arlington St., Asheville**
**• (828) 255-7530**

With sixteen brokers, Appalachian Realty has a lot packed into a little office. Offering unique properties in Asheville, especially old Victorian homes in downtown or nearby neighborhoods, this company also deals in land adjoining the Parkway. The diversity of the agents lends a bit more to buying or renting real estate than your average suit-and-tie office. Clients enjoy this casual atmosphere.

### Beverly-Hanks & associates
**300 Executive Pk., Asheville**
• **(828) 254-7221, (800) 868-7221**
**1940 Hendersonville Rd., Arden**
• **(828) 684-8999**
**400 Beverly-Hanks Ctr., Hendersonville**
• **(828) 697-0515**
One of western North Carolina's largest real estate companies, with three offices — downtown, South Asheville, and Hendersonville — maintains more than 500 properties. Beverly-Hanks & associates also offers sales associate profiles and relocation information. All of these may be found on their Website, as well. Open daily, including Saturdays and Sundays, the company offers a variety of styles and sizes of homes in several counties, Asheville neighborhoods, and mountainsides.

### Century 21 Carroll & Demos
**50 Orange St., Asheville**
• **(828) 254-7733, (828) 277-7773, (888) 951-5400**
One of the largest Realtors in Asheville with some 30 brokers, this company specializes in manor estate and luxury homes. Each

property is displayed on the World Wide Web, as well as being published in the international distributed *Unique Homes* magazine. Besides sprawling estates, however, Carroll & Demos also offer downtown apartments and historical log cabin homes. The company also has a Certified Homes Program that is designed to get the maximum value for a home while providing the buyer with all the necessary information. It includes a home inspection by a licensed contractor, a termite report, an appraisal by a state licensed appraiser, and a one-year home warranty.

### Northland Properties
**U.S. Hwy. 25/70, Weaverville**
• **(828) 254-2500**
This real estate firm, with another branch in Wolf Laurel, offers a diverse choice of properties in the central mountain area. These include tracts of land and lots in the valleys and mountains and other countryside properties.

### Preferred Properties
**39 Woodfin St., Asheville**
• **(828) 258-2953, (800) 951-4646**
This 28-year-old full-service company deals in residential and commercial acreage in Buncombe and Henderson Counties. The owners are Ellen Ford, Edward Gibson, Juanita Wright, and Jan NcNeil.

# Henderson County

Back in the early 1830s, wealthy planters from Charleston, South Carolina, were already building majestic summer homes in this cool, mountain-ringed county. Because it sits on a high plateau, much of Henderson County is made up of lovely, rolling hills — as opposed to the steep, mountainous terrain found in many other areas — so there's ample opportunity for residential developments, horse farms, grand estates and golfing communities. And while retirees find perfect spots throughout western North Carolina to live out their golden years, Henderson County has long been the retirement mecca of the region.

This has driven up prices, relatively speaking, but the county is still affordable, with real estate in all price ranges. The median price of a single-family home, for example, is around $115,400, but you can still find small, older, one- or two-bedroom older home in town or out in the country for $65,000. If you'd like, you can also pay $1 million-plus for a grand old estate or one of the modern ones on several acres.

Among developments, Champion Hills, a relatively new golfing community, is the most expensive, where the average price of a home ranges from $350,000 to $500,000 and up. Kenmure, another golfing community near fashionable Flat Rock, is slightly less expensive, as are nearby residential developments, where houses on one acre range from $200,000 to $400,000 and more. The Mills River area, between Asheville and Hendersonville and handy to the Asheville Airport and I-26, was mostly devoted to farming two decades ago. It still manages to maintain a rural atmosphere, although it's become upscale and pricey.

Some of the best buys — and some beautiful country to boot — are to the east of Hendersonville. Like it or not, this prime apple-growing region probably is destined to go as suburban as much of the rest of the county has done in the last 20 years as its popularity continues to grow.

## Beverly Hanks & associates
**1450 Asheville Hwy., 400 Beverly Hanks Ctr., Hendersonville**
• **(828) 697-0515, (800) 868-0515**

Beverly Hanks, over the last two decades, has grown into western North Carolina's largest full-service realty firm. For less than $1.5 million the firm currently can sell you a 9,800-square-foot home with 8,600 feet of columned porches grandly placed on almost 19 acres. It also offers any number of three-bedroom, two-bath houses that range in price from around $80,000 to $150,000. This company has it all, including nice two-bedroom single homes that start under $60,000.

## Judy Gibbs Real Estate
**421 S. Church St., Hendersonville**
• **(828) 696-1942, (800) 640-1809**

A Henderson County native with 22 years experience, Judy Gibbs, broker/owner, and her associates can find you a brand new three-bedroom, two-bath home for under $140,000 or sell you Champion Hills home overlooking a lake and golf course for a bit over $400,000.

## Kenmure Enterprises, Inc.
**10 Kenmure Dr., Flat Rock**
• **(828) 693-8481, (800) 345-1860**

Kenmure is a long-established, prestigious, guarded residential community located in historic Flat Rock just four miles south of Hendersonville on U.S. Highway 25. With 1,400 acres, the development is centered around a Joe Lee-designed 18-hole championship golf course. Overlooking it stands the Kenmure Mansion, a stately, carefully restored

**INSIDERS' TIP**

Downtown properties are hitting a boom in cities experiencing revitalization, like Asheville and Hendersonville. Get in on the "ground floor" by looking at lofts and warehouse space. They can be purchased for still-reasonable prices. Future business owners or downtown dwellers are viewing these areas with more and more interest, so act fast.

Southern home dating back to 1850 that serves as the clubhouse. Inside is an informal grill room, a formal dining room, banquet facilities, a pro shop and administrative offices. Other amenities include a heated swimming pool and a tennis court.

Prices in the architecturally controlled community start at $325,000 for homes and $160,000 for freestanding condominiums and villas. Homesites range from $39,900 to $250,000.

## Preferred Real Estate
### 222 Seventh Ave. E., Hendersonville
• (828) 696-9900, (800) 442-0098

The 11 realtors that make up this firm handle homes, lots or land in any section of the county. They recently offered a three-bedroom, three-bath home with a large workshop and garage on 21 acres with a waterfall, streams and views for $285,000. Or how about a townhouse (including a two-car garage) in a country setting with a huge master suite with a spa for under $109,000?

## Coldwell Banker Harold & Associates, Realtors
### 1611 Asheville Hwy., Hendersonville
• (828) 692-0222, (800) 827-2408

This large real estate firm sells everything from small starter homes for $35,000 on up to $500,000 homes in the best developments, with a vast amount of property at all prices in-between. One really interesting property they offered recently was a wonderful stone house in historic Flat Rock with two additional cottages for $160,000.

# Polk County

The area around Saluda, Tryon and Columbus on the edge of the Blue Ridge has all the great scenery and laid-back charm of the rest of the region. This area boasts two additional attractions: the thermal belt — the warm microclimate found here — and horses, for Polk County is true horse country. This horse-country land, an area filled with old and established horse farms, is going to be expensive, even on its perimeter. If, for example, you wanted to create your own horse farm in the heart of horse country, you'd probably pay $10,000 to $20,000 an acre, while you might get much the same amount of land elsewhere for $3,000 an acre. An existing horse farm of 20 to 60 acres with a nice house, barns, riding arena and good board fences runs around $600,000 in prime horse country; outside, it might be almost half that price.

For those buyers not into horses, this is not the least expensive area in which to buy, but you do get good value for your money. You might be able to find a one-bedroom house on a small lot for $65,000, but the average for a fine three-bedroom, two-bath home on a nice lot is anywhere from $95,000 to $165,000. You can also find grand estates or large historic homes for $1,500,000 and up.

## Century 21 Tryon Real Estate
**Tryon • (828) 859-9715, (800) 321-9722**

Located in an office in the heart of downtown Tryon, this company recently offered a newly remodeled two-bedroom, two-bath cottage full of charming nooks and crannies for $119,000. For the horse lover with a limited income, there was a reasonably priced three-bedroom, two-and-a-half-bath ranch home on six-plus acres with views and horse pastures.

## Remax
**803 N.C. Hwy. 108, Columbus**
**• (828) 894-0859, (800) 849-0859**

Here's another firm that can fulfill your dream of a horse farm. It was recently showing a five-acre plot in a great equestrian area with trail access. It came with a 4-bedroom, two-bath home, plus a guest house for $217,900. Five additional acres were also available. For the person who prefers town life, there was a three-bedroom, two-bath home convenient to everything for $112,500.

# Transylvania County

Few places have been chosen so many times as the best place to retire or live as Brevard, the small county seat of this pretty, tree-covered, river-filled county known for its 250-plus waterfalls. Brevard forms a triad with Hendersonville and Asheville. Now a five-lane

connector to I-26 and the Asheville Airport has brought the three towns even closer together. It's also increasing development and land prices, which have jumped dramatically in the last two years. Simple summer cottages are now in the $85,000 range. A more substantial house starts at about $120,000 and can go up to $250,000 with most of the homes in this upper price range found in developments such as Connestee, Glen Cannon and Ilahee Hills, where home prices can range up to $400,000. In such developments, lots can go from $7,000 to $170,000.

In Straus Park, a new development on 315 acres just minutes from downtown, homesites start at $60,000 and homes start at $280,000. (See the listing below.)

Raw land (and there's not a whole lot of it in this county because so much is taken up by Pisgah National Forest) is running from $5,000 to $10,000 an acre, whether you're buying eight acres or 80. Prices around Lake Toxaway (reached by a steep, sharply curved section of U.S. Highway 64 W.) match or surpass those in the Highlands-Cashiers area. (See our information on Jackson and Macon counties in this chapter). While there are houses tucked along back roads and coves that are still affordable, homes that sell for $500,000 and up are common here. A lakefront lot on Lake Toxaway, if you can find one, can go for $150,000 to $200,000. A two-bedroom, two-bath condo costs well over $100,000, and a two-bedroom, two-bath chalet recently sold for $190,000.

## Century 21/Kaiser Realty
**3100 S. Greenville Hwy., Brevard**
**• (828) 884-8848, (800) 232-7172**

Dick Smith, broker, and Jean Ann McMurry, Realtor, specialize in homes and lots in the 4,000-acre Connestee Falls Development. They have a large selection of building sites, including lakefronts, golf lots and nicely wooded property, as well as homes with prices ranging for $95,000 to $400,000.

## Lake Toxaway Realty Company — Breedlove-Nichols
**U.S. Hwy. 64, Lake Toxaway**
**• (828) 966-4029**

Susan Breedlove and John L. Nichols, Jr.,

both owner-Realtors, specialize in two fine country club developments: Lake Toxaway Estates and Sapphire Lakes. Both have 18-hole golf courses, tennis facilities and fine dining. In addition, Lake Toxaway Estates enjoys the largest private lake in North Carolina. It also boasts of some of the most expensive property in the region running from $150,000 to $600,000.

### Straus Park
**1175 Asheville Hwy., Brevard**
**• (828) 885-2525, (888) 640-2525**

Brevard's newest development will contain a 15-acre park, six miles of walking trails and a six-acre lake with a social center. Park Place, within the development, will feature banking, physican and other professional services, and Market Place will contain shops and restaurants.

# Southern Mountains

## Cherokee County

One of the most desirable areas around Murphy, the county seat, is within 10 to 15 miles of town. Here, for around $90,000, you can buy a two-bedroom, two-bath mountain cabin featuring a stone fireplace, hardwood floors and tongue-and-groove ceiling in the great room, and two covered porches. In fact, many delightful homes are priced under $100,000. At the Cherokee Hills golfing community, a one-acre lot with, say, a three-level Cape Cod with four to five bedrooms and a full basement will cost around $139,000 to $250,000. For undeveloped land near Murphy, the average one-acre, wooded lot with views and underground utilities runs about $14,500. Five acres will cost between $3,000 and $5,000 an acre.

Very few farms or farmettes are available, but they too would cost around $5,000 an acre. Large tracts of land run from $3,500 to 10,000 an acre. One-acre lots (if you can find one) on Lake Hiwassee will set you back $100,000 to $125,000. There is less property for sale around the historic old railroad town of Andrews, but you can still find some good buys. A beautiful, 470-acre Valley River farm

of rolling hills, ridges, creeks, streams and the Valley River was asking $10,000 an acre. Lots with some amenities also are going for $10,000 and more. There are, of course, still small summer places that are bargains if you don't need anything fancy.

### Valleytown Realty
**Chestnut St., Andrews**
**• (828) 321-4133, (800) 632-2212**

This firm offers some charming properties. Consider a four-bedroom, two-and-a-half-bath contemporary home with such amenities as a marble fireplace in the bedroom situated on one-and-a-half acres with a creek and professional landscaping for $177,000. Valleytown also offered 99 acres with stair-step waterfalls down a lovely creek with frontage on the Valley River for $3,500 an acre.

### David Hilton Realty
**58 Hiawassee St., Murphy**
**• (828) 837-1910, (800) 871-1910**

David is a native of the mountains with over 25 years real-estate experience. He has homes and lands in every price range, from a $45,000 fixer-upper in a quiet country setting to a spacious chalet with mountain views for $189,000.

## Clay County

You won't find smokestacks in this mostly rural county, but you will find a wide price range in real estate. You can pay as little as $35,000 for a one-bedroom cottage on a half-acre in the country or as much as $250,000 to $300,000 for a four-bedroom, four-and-a-half-bath home on 10 to 12 acres. Property on Lake Chatuge is probably the most expensive, where half-acre lots sell for around $90,000 to $150,000 and half-acre creekfront lots go for $30,000 to $80,000. On the other hand, large tracts of 25 acres and more elsewhere in the county can be as low as $3,000 an acre.

### Mountain Streams Real Estate, Inc.
**267 Hwy. 64 W., Hayesville**
**• (828) 389-8631, (800) 845-2067**

Offering land, homes and vacation rent-

# Macon County: Wayah Bald

On a clear day from the 5,200-foot Wayah Bald in Macon County, you can see north to the Great Smoky Mountains in Tennessee and south into the rolling hills of Georgia. You can also climb an old fire tower, built in the days of the Civilian Conservation Corps. To reach Wayah Bald, take S.R. 1310 out of Franklin. Turn on to F.R. 69 (a steep, gravel road) to the bald. This is also where the Appalachian Trail and the Bartram Trail join and briefly merge. Visitors are also welcome at the 1916 Wilson Lick Ranger Station, situated along F.R. 69, where you can view the history of the first Ranger Station in the Nantahala National Forest.

als in the mountain lakes region of North Carolina and North Georgia, this firm, headed by John McLauchlin, can set you up in your dream home or find the perfect spot to build it. Recenlty he offered a three-bedroom, four-bath Cape Cod-style home on nearly seven acres with 230-degrees of mountain views for $235,500.

## Mountain Country Realty
**U.S. Hwy. 64 West, Hayesville**
• **(828) 389-8898, (800) 433-9307**

Dick Osborn is Broker/Manager of this four-partner firm with seven agents. It handles houses, acreage, farms and seasonal rentals. Currently Mountain County lists a wide range of properties in both Clay and Macon Counties — from lots on Lake Chatuge in the $100,000 range to a cabin on a couple of acres for about $60,000. Some of their best sellers are at Rainbow Falls and Rainbow Mountain, environmentally protected developments with minimum tracts of five acres and underground utilities. These properties are located at elevations of 3,500 to 5,000 feet and start at $34,000.

## Graham County

Though national forest land covers nearly 60 percent of Graham County and Lake Fontana and Lake Santeetlah cover a lot more, good buys abound in this beautiful lake-and-mountain region. An average three-bedroom, two-bath home on a half-acre goes for around $85,000. We ran across a secluded home with three bedrooms, three baths, a large porch and a full basement on a wooded two-acre lot for $94,000. Twenty acres within 15 minues

of Robbinsville was going for $19,000 with owner financing. Building lots run from around $5,000 up to $160,000 for property on Lake Santeetlah.

There are, as in other counties, what we locals think of as high-priced properties. Both a seven-bedroom and a two-bedroom on 1 acre on deep water on Lake Santeetlah were selling for $395,000, and the asking price of a nearby three-bedroom on one acre on a creek was $315,000. These prices are headed skyward.

## Cherokee Realty
**U.S. Hwy. 129 bypass, Robbinsville**
• **(828) 479-6441, (800) 343-7635**

Cherokee Realty has been in business in Graham County for more than 20 years. They can sell a 10-acre mini-farm with a two-bedroom home and a guest cottage for $139,000, or a lakefront lodge with five bedrooms, three baths and two large porches overlooking Lake Santeetlah for $175,000.

## Southland Realty
**U.S. Hwy. 129 bypass, Robbinsville**
• **(828) 479-3991, (800) 249-2207**

With over 70 percent of the land in Graham County federally owned, finding your perfect spot in this unpolluted environment could be daunting. Southern Realty, however, can show you existing homes in all prices ranges and sizes. It also handles lake property, land with small streams, rare large-acreage tracts and lots in subdivisions. It can even arrange owner financing on selected properties. One intriguing property recently on the market was a mountaintop, log-home estate overlook a lake. With two stone fireplaces and

20-plus acres, it seemed a great buy at $359,000.

# Haywood County

This beautiful mountain county with its easy access to Asheville and the Great Smoky Mountains has long been popular — and is becoming more so — with retirees moving in from out of state. A small, older, two-bedroom, one-bath home in Waynesville can run as low as $65,000, while summer cottages, which tend to be in nice locations with views and/or streams, are likely to cost $90,000 or more. In the upper range, a four-bedroom, three-bath home near the Waynesville Country Club or the Laurel Ridge Country Club will cost around $275,000.

Nice homes on 10 acres or so will also be in the $250,000 price range. Raw land begins at about $7,500 for a half-acre lot to $75,000 for the same size lot in one of the upscale development such as The Sanctuary. Near Clyde, 2- or 3-acre tracts in the Summerset development run $55,000 to $60,000.

Some of the best buys in the county are in Canton. The area has been held back for a long time because of the odor emitted by Champion Paper, a company that practically built the town. In recent years, however, Champion has worked on its water and air pollution problems, and a fairly new Interstate 40 interchange on the eastern side of Canton has made access to Asheville and other parts of the region easy. There are some darling older homes in Canton at extremely reasonable prices. On the whole, homes are 10 to 14 percent less expensive than in the western part of the county — if you take the time to look, you might come up with a super bargain.

## Pioneer Realty
### 1510 Dellwood Rd. W., Waynesville
• (828) 923-3025, (800) 923-3025

Pioneer Realty, with offices both in Waynesville and Maggie Vally, covers the area with 15 agents. They recently offered a three-bedroom, two-bath home with a workshop for $129,000; a three-bedroom on four acres with an office and two outbuildings for $174,000 or a 6.1-acre horse farm with a

charming and spacious log home for $298,000.

## Haywood Properties
### 1082 N. Main St., Waynesville
• (828) 456-7244, (877) 574-0883

The four agents of this firm represent a great range of properties, from a fully furnished, contemporary, little two-bedroom, two-bath summer house in Maggie Valley for $82,900 to a modern three-bedroom on 18 acres with a gazebo and sauna connecting to another three-bedroom guest house. They were asking $223,500 for the latter.

# Jackson County

In this mountainous county, relatively flat land is at a premium and is priced accordingly. Around Sylva, the median cost of a three-bedroom, two-bath house runs between $80,000 and $150,000. The upper end is found in well-built developments, such as Marion Forest near Sylva, where houses go for $200,000 plus. However, you can still find older two- or three-bedroom homes with one or two baths for between $75,000 and $85,000. In charming Dillsboro, just a hop, skip and a jump away from Sylva, these same houses might sell for $100,000 and up. Simple mountainside summer cabins can range from $65,000 to $90,000.

As mentioned before, the price of raw land varies according to its steepness, but the average is from $2,000 to $3,000 an acre for 10- to 20-acre tracts, while a one-acre, fairly level lot is between $10,000 and $15,000. The Cashiers-Highlands area is a whole different — and more expensive — story. While you can still find a two-bedroom, two-bath house on a small lot with no view for as low as $60,000, the cost for a fairly fine house will start at $150,000 and go up to $1 million or more for an estate of 15 to 50 acres with views, a stream, a pond, horse trails and other such amenities.

The main real estate market, however, is in the club resorts in areas such as Sapphire Lakes, Fairfield-Sapphire Valley, High Hampton, Highland Falls, Highland Country Club and Wildcat Cliffs that offer sought-after amenities, restrictions and a secured gate.

In such developments, a two-bedroom, one-bath apartment or condo will start at $85,000, and a one-acre lot can sell for as much as $250,000. Outside such developments, you may be able to find a lot for around $10,000. Houses in the area run $1 million and up. Cashiers is still a "bargain" compared to prices in Lake Toxaway to its east or Highlands to its west, but property values here have sometimes doubled in the last two years. Lakefront lots on Lake Glenville start around $100,000. A home there can run $500,000 or more.

## Lee Realty
**N.C. Hwy. 107 S., Cashiers**
**• (828) 743-2484, (800) 225-3762**

Estate communities like Forest Ridge, Zachary's Gap, Table Top, Burt's Farm, Sheepcliff Crossing and Bald Rock are the focus of this realty company. Prices generally range from around $90,000 to $500,000.

## V. C. Smith Real Estate
**U.S. Hwy. 64 andN.C. Hwy. 107,**
**Cashiers • (828) 743-2427,**
**(800) 345-6492**

V. C. Smith serves Cashiers, Highlands, Lake Glenville and Lake Toxaway areas. They handle lake front, lake view, residential, country club, mountain view and stream and creekside properties. They recently marketed a 10-acre mountaintop with 360-degree views of Lake Glenville, the Blue Ridge Parkway, and range after panoramic range of mountains for $329,000.

Photo: Hugh Morton

Hikers on Rough Ridge at Grandfather Mountain, North Carolina.

# Macon County

Here you'll find everything from open valleys to steep, rugged terrain, and elevations from 1,900 feet to 5,500 feet. Highlands, at 3,838 feet, is one of the highest incorporated towns east of the Mississippi. You also have your choice of houses and land in all price ranges, most of them very reasonable for what you get. Around Franklin, it's not hard to find a very nice three-bedroom, two-bath house with a view for $80,000 to $120,000. If you're willing to pay between $130,000 and $180,000, you're going to get a few acres of land and quite a bit more square footage or other amenities. You'll spend approximately $250,000 for a fine farm with barns and 20 or so more acres with views in every direction. Raw land costs between $5,000 and $10,000 per acre for 1 to 10 acres, but for large tracts the price can fall as low as $1,500 an acre.

Property prices around the historic resort village of Highlands are much higher. Large resort developments have driven costs up in this spectacularly scenic region — Heavenly Highlands, it's called. Prices soar heavenward too, being even higher than those around Cashiers, which was discussed in the Jackson County section. Homes costing more than $3 million are not uncommon here.

## Preferred Properties of Highlands
**West Main St., Highlands**
• **(828) 526-5589, (800) 255-2101**

Because Highlands is a small plot of limited land surrounded by National Forest, you won't get as much house for your money here as in Franklin, but this company still offers some charming "deals." They recently offered a two-bedroom, two-bath cottage with vaulted ceilings, a dining room, a stone fireplace, and a covered deck with a view for $96,000. They also offer homes in the $1 million-plus range.

## The Prudential – McClure Henry Realtors
**144 Porter St., Franklin • (828) 524-9000**

The variety of listings — and bargains — carried by this firm would please almost anyone's tastes and bank account. We saw a secluded two-bedroom, two-bath home with two separate living levels and two kitchens along with two extra lots and a creek for $114,900. A well-built, close-in, two-bedroom, two-bath furnished home on two-acres with a stream was just $110,000. Or they could sell you a fully furnished bungalow near a river for $59,500.

# Swain County

People who like the outdoors will like Swain County. Surrounded by the Cherokee and Nantahala national forests and the Great Smoky Mountains National Park, residents have access to some of the largest expanses of wilderness in the eastern United States while still living an easy drive from Asheville, Knoxville and Atlanta. The price of an acre depends on how many acres you purchase: One-half to 2½ acres run $3,000 to $15,000 an acre; from 3 to 5 acres, $3,000 to $6,000; 5 to 15 acres, $2,500 to $4,500; 15 to 40 acres, $1,500 to $3,000; and 40 acres and more, around $1,000 to $2,000 an acre.

House prices run the gamut too. You might find a one-bedroom, one-bath cottage on one acre for $30,000, or you can buy a five-level, four-bedroom house on 5 acres with two Jacuzzis and a four-car garage close to town but without city taxes, for $425,000. On the average, however, a three-bedroom, two-bath house on an acre costs between $100,000 and $250,000.

## Foxfire Realty
**266 Everett St., Bryson City**
• **(828) 488-1515**

This small but efficient company was recently marketing, among other interesting properties, a three-bedroom, two-bath home for $99,500 and a four-bedroom, three-and-a-half bath home on four-plus acres for $250,000.

## Swain County Realty
**On the Square, Bryson City**
• **(828) 88-6169, (800) 554-4312**

Representing one of the fastest-growing real estate companies in the county, brokers Bill Alexander and Pat Fortner deal in land, vacation and year-round homes, commercial property and rentals.

When moving to the
North Carolina
mountains, you won't
feel like you are retiring,
but rather beginning a
second career of
healthy recreation,
travel, cultural
enrichment, culinary
arts, entertainment, and
the discovery of nature.

# Retirement

North Carolina's mountain towns and cities have been at the top of leading publications' lists of "top places to retire" for some time now. But many retirees discovered this area years ago, long before the lists were a twinkle in publishers' eyes. Some of us locals were once visitors or summer vacationers who were so delighted with the beauty, the climate, the amenities, the price of properties and the services offered that we ended up moving here permanently. Another important factor that makes this area attractive for retirement is the low crime rate and active lifestyle offered here.

This large and vital segment of the mountains' population is growing by leaps and bounds. By the year 2010 Henderson County, one of the fastest growing retirement regions here, will have a population of which 40 percent is older than 65. This county, along with others in the region, is responding by making long-term plans to assure that essentials such as healthcare, housing, transportation and social support services are adequate to meet this growth. While the majority of older adults in the area have ample income (Henderson County's poverty rate is one of the state's lowest), the costs of such services are more than offset by the talent, wisdom, life skills and energy senior citizens bring to our area.

But what draws people here for retirement anyway? When moving to the North Carolina mountains, you won't feel like you are retiring, but rather beginning a second career of healthy recreation, travel, cultural enrichment, culinary arts, entertainment, and the discovery of nature. Whether settling down in the placid seasonal community of Blowing Rock, where fine and unique restaurants line the main street along with quality antique stores, bakeries, and sweet shops, or the rolling green countryside of Valle Crucis, where your visitors will adore the many bed and breakfasts they will encounter in this rural valley, you will not go wrong in choosing to continue your lives here. With all the cultural treats of the area — universities and music schools, museums and galleries, mountain craft schools and studios, unique shops and arrays of excellent restaurants, botanical gardens, and nearby forests and waterfalls — you would be hard pressed to find time to while away the hours sitting in a rocking chair!

A number of counties around North Carolina hold Senior Games competitions, which were founded in 1983 to create a year-round health promotion and educational program for North Carolinians 55 and older. Today, over 36,000 seniors participate in 52 local games that serve all 100 counties across the state. For example, in Transylvania County, these qualifying games are sponsored each spring. To participate, you must be 55 or older and reside in the county for at least three months out of the year. Competitions include the running and standing long jump, a 1,500-meter race walk, men's and women's tennis (both singles and doubles), men's and women's horseshoes, bowling, billiards, a basketball shoot, table tennis, a football and softball throw, spin casting, golf, swimming events, cycling, racquetball and badminton. Gold, silver and bronze medals are awarded in each age category in each event. All winners are eligible to participate in the North Carolina State Senior Games in Raleigh, during the autumn. For more information, call North Carolina Senior Games, (919) 851-5456.

At the same time, Transylvania and other counties also sponsor the Silver Arts Competition. Entries must be the original work of the artist, must be work created after the age of 55 and must have been completed within two years of the local games' qualifying date. First-place winners in each visual and heritage arts subcategory are entered in the state finals.

If help is needed, it's available. In counties that have long dealt with seniors' needs — such as Buncombe and Henderson — such services are broad and highly organized. In some of the more rural counties, what may be lacking in highly organized structures is more than made up for in small-town and community caring. (See our Healthcare chapter for information on the health services in the area.) Here — aside from the usual government agencies, such as health departments, departments of social services, the public libraries, parks and recreation departments (which coordinate annual Senior Games) and commercial in-home health services that can be located in the Yellow Pages — is just a partial list of places you may call upon for support systems, socializing and just plain fun.

# Regional Services

## Northern Mountains

### Area Agency on Aging
**155 Furman Rd., Executive Arts Building, Region D Council of Governments, Boone • (828) 265-5434**

This agency serves senior citizens in the seven northwestern counties of North Carolina. The agency directs a Long Term Care Ombudsman Program for the region and serves as a funding and information resource for agencies involved in senior care, education, and public awareness in Alleghany, Ashe, Avery, Mitchell, Watauga and Yancey counties to the north. Senior Centers in each of these locations offer a variety of programs that include group meals at the centers as well as home-delivered meals, In-Home Aide, recreational programs, legal services, health screening and nutrition guidance. Transportation and adult day care are also provided through some locations.

### Legal Services of the Blue Ridge
**171 Grand Blvd., Boone**
**• (828) 264-5640, (800) 849-5666**

Senior citizens can get advice for problems with Social Security, Medicaid and Medicare, food stamps, housing, institutional care and consumer issues.

## Alleghany County

### Alleghany Council for Aging Inc.
**Greyson and Whitehead Sts., Senior Center, Sparta • (336) 372-4640**

This organization oversees In-Home Aide, group meals, home-delivered meals, health promotion, Senior Games, AARP, recreation and educational classes.

### American Association of Retired Persons (AARP)
**Greyson and Whitehead Sts.**
**• (336) 372-4640**

This branch of the national organization meets the fourth Tuesday of each month at 6 PM at the Alleghany Senior Center, for discussion, support, counseling, and social time.

### Blue Ridge Opportunity Commission
**1747 U.S. Hwy. 21N., Sparta**
**• (336) 372-7284**

The BROC provides information and referral, housing weatherization and repair.

### Cooperative Extension Service
**90 S. Main St., Sparta • (336) 372-5597**

This office provides advice on energy resources conservation, homemaking and personal financial management counseling for Alleghany County senior citizens.

### Department of Social Services
**182 Doctors St., Sparta**
**• (336) 372-2411, (336) 372-2414 food stamps**

The Department of Social Services can help you arrange for health support services, Medicaid, protective services, senior citizens transportation, emergency assistance programs and nursing home placement. Food stamps are also available through this office.

# Ashe County

### American Association of Retired Persons (AARP)
**• No phone**

This group meets the first Wednesday of each month from 12 to 4 PM at the public library in Jefferson to discuss issues concern-

ing seniors in the area and to provide mutual support.

### Ashe Services for Aging Inc.
**180 ChattyRob Ln., West Jefferson**
**• (336) 246-2461**

This agency oversees programs for transportation, In-Home Aide II, group and home-delivered meals and educational classes. Senior Tar Heel discount cards, the Health Insurance Information Program, adult daycare and daily activity programs are some of the benefits available here for Ashe County's older residents.

### Blue Ridge Opportunity Commission
**169 Warrensville School Rd., Warrensville • (336) 384-4543**

The group offers assistance with weatherization and repair, housing and community action and crisis intervention regarding fuel and electricity.

Winter's white cloak at Grandfather mountain.

Photo: Hugh Morton, Courtesy of Grandfather Mountain

## Department of Social Services
303 E. Main St., Jefferson
• (336) 246-7125
This public agency offers senior citizens resources, information, aid for medical expenses, adult protective services, food stamps and (home-heating) fuel assistance.

## Foster Grandparent and Senior Companion Program
707 Ray Taylor Rd., West Jefferson
• (336) 246-4898
This volunteer program brings senior citizens together in community service with children in the public schools who have special needs.

## Health Department, Senior Companion Program
707 Ray Taylor Rd., West Jefferson
• (336) 246-4898
Companionship is key to the success of this in-home service that involves active senior citizens working with disabled or less active senior citizens in the community and provides assistance with light housekeeping, meal preparation, laundry, bookkeeping, bill-paying and transportation.

## USDA Rural Development
525 E. Main St., Jefferson
• (336) 246-8818
Low- and moderate-income grants for senior citizens for housing and home repair are available through this agency.

# Avery County

## Avery Senior Services Senior Center
165 Shultz Cir., Newland
• (828) 733-8220
Transportation, In-Home Aide I, group and home-delivered meals and health promotion are a few of the many services provided by this active senior center.

## Senior Companion Program
707 Ray Taylor Rd., West Jefferson
• (336) 246-4898
Avery County senior citizens are also served by this in-home assistance program headquartered in Jefferson in Ashe County.

## Emergency Management Office
205 Administrative Bldg., Newland
• (828) 733-8213
This local office assists veterans with claims to the Veterans Administration for such things as education, medical care, insurance and loans.

## W.A.M.Y. Community Action
260 Eastotoa Ave., Newland
• (828) 733-0156
This group provides community center crafts, weatherization and home repair, job training, a garden program and transportation assistance. (W.A.M.Y. stands for Watauga, Avery, Mitchell and Yancy Counties.)

# Madison County

## Department of Social Services
Main St., Marshall • (828) 649-2711
Food stamps and assistance with Medicaid and fuel bills are provided though this office.

## Madison County Senior Center
25 Long Branch Rd., Marshall
• (828) 649-2722
This site is the central location for a network of county centers that offers recreational activities, health screening, chore services, nutrition information and home-delivered meals as well as congregate meals on-site and information on other vital services of interest to Madison County senior citizens.

## Mars Hill College Programs for Senior Citizens
Mars Hill • (828) 689-1166
Mars Hill College participates with Elderhostel, a worldwide continuing education enrichment series for senior citizens. Programs from history and music to science and art are part of this learning opportunity offered 22 weeks each year. The college also provides a regular continuing education program linked with the Mars Hill Curriculum. The Summer Alternative Vacation Program

and the Learning Institute for Elders (LIFE) have learning tours on a variety of subjects.

## W. Otis Duck Fitness Trail
**Mars Hill College • (828) 689-1243**

This mile-long walking trail is ideal for active senior citizens. It passes through 20 exercise stations on a course that gently winds up and down over the Mars Hill College campus. Also funded by private donations, this trail is open to the entire community.

# Mitchell County

## Cooperative Extension Service
**County Office Bldg., Bakersville**
**• (828) 688-4811**

This county extension service provides senior citizens with advice on energy resources conservation, financial management and homemaking.

## Department of Social Services
**Hemlock St., Bakersville**
**• (828) 688-2175**

Senior citizens around Bakersville can find resource information, In-Home Aide services, food stamps, energy assistance, health support services, transportation and home improvement assistance through this agency.

## Mitchell Senior Center
**152 Ledger School Rd., Bakersville**
**• (828) 688-3019**

Transportation, In-Home Aide I, group and home-delivered meals and health and nutrition assistance are some of the services provided by this center.

## Veterans Service Office
**126 School Rd., Bakersville**
**• (828) 688-2200**

This local office assists veterans with claims to the Veterans Administration for such

things as education, medical care, insurance and loans.

## W.A.M.Y. Community Action Inc.
**108 Crystal St., Spruce Pine**
**• (828) 766-9150, (828) 688-5832**

Transportation, weatherization and home repair, elderly nutrition and gardening programs are some of the services provided by this office. (W.A.M.Y. stands for Watauga, Avery, Mitchell and Yancy Counties.)

# Watauga County

## American Association of Retired Persons (AARP)
**Boone**

This group for Boone-area retired folk meets the third Monday of each month at 11:30 AM for a Dutch-treat lunch at a local Shoney's. This AARP chapter is active in legislative lobbying and in local and regional issues.

## AppalCART Transportation
**274 Winklers Creek Rd., Boone**
**• (828) 264-2280**

AppalCART provides county and town transportation service to seniors. Call for schedules and arrangements.

## Cooperative Extension Service
**971 W. King St., Boone • (828) 264-3061**

Homemaking and housing information as well as energy resources conservation and financial management counseling are provided through the county extension service.

## Department of Social Services
**769 W. King St., Boone**
**• (828) 265-8100**

Health support services are among the many types of aid available through this department.

## INSIDERS' TIP

When visiting or living in a mountain county that lacks a daily newspaper, buy or subscribe to the county weekly. These are great, up-to-date sources for our cultural events, educational opportunities and other activities.

## Veterans Service Office
**Room 100, Courthouse Annex, Boone**
• **(828) 265-8065**

This local office assists veterans with claims to the Veterans Administration for such things as education, medical care, insurance and loans.

## W.A.M.Y. Community Action Program
**Main Office, 679 W. King St., Boone**
• **(828) 264-2421**

Watauga County senior citizens benefit from the active participation of this office in the areas of weatherization and home repair, transportation for elderly and job and gardening programs. (W.A.M.Y. stands for Watauga, Avery, Mitchell and Yancy Counties.)

## Watauga County Project on Aging
**783 W. King St., Lois E. Harrill Senior Center, Boone • (828) 265-8090**

Transportation, In-Home Aide I and II, group and home-delivered meals and health screenings are provided to Watauga County senior citizens.

# Yancey County

## Cooperative Extension Service
**10 Orchard St., Burnsville**
• **(828) 682-6186**

Financial management counseling, housing information, homemaking services and information on energy resources conservation, agriculture and home horticulture are offered by the county extension service.

## Department of Social Services
**Lincoln Park, Burnsville**
• **(828) 682-6148**

Health support services, transportation and aid for medical expenses are some of the services of this department.

## Veterans Service Office
**Room 8, Courthouse, Burnsville**
• **(828) 682-2136**

This local office assists veterans with claims to the Veterans Administration for such things as education, medical care, insurance and loans.

## W.A.M.Y. Community Action Program
**W. Main St., Burnsville • (828) 682-2610**

Above Pollard's Drug Store, the W.A.M.Y (Watauga, Avery, Mitchell and Yancy) programs offers limited home repair assistance as well as elderly transportation.

## Yancey County Committee on Aging
**10 Swiss Ave., Senior Center, Burnsville**
• **(828) 682-6011**

This lively place offers In-Home Aide I, group and home-delivered meals, transportation and health promotion like blood pressure and cholesterol checks. Senior Tar Heel Discount cards and the Senior's Health Insurance Information Program (SHIIP) are also part of the services offered here.

## Yancey Transit
**Room 6, Courthouse, Burnsville**
• **(828) 682-6144**

Yancey Transit offers senior transportation assistance through a contract with the Senior Center.

# Central Mountains

## Buncombe County

## Buncombe County Council on Aging
**Community Services Center, 50 S. French Broad Ave., Ste. 141, Asheville**
• **(828) 258-8027, (828) 258-8028**

This private, nonprofit corporation, a United Way agency, is composed of senior citizens groups and organizations providing services to Buncombe County senior citizens. Outreach services include friendly visitation, senior companionship, home repair, weatherization and fan distribution. The agency coordinates various countywide programs that offer nutrition assistance, congregate meals at 17 locations, the Senior Tar Heel discount program and volunteer opportunities for older citizens.

Senior transportation is assisted by the BOOST system, (828) 254-3887, and C.A.R. (Call-a-Ride, which can be reached through the Council on Aging number), door-to-door service for shopping, medical appointments and meal sites. The council also coordinates the Hearing Aid Bank, income tax assistance and educational programs. The age requirement is 60 or older.

## Buncombe County Sheriff's Department Reassurance Program
**393 Hendersonville Rd., Sheriff's Dept.**
**• (828) 277-3131**

This helpful program, staffed by citizen volunteers, provides daily telephone check-in service for a number of Buncombe County's elderly. This program also works in connection with Visiting Health Professionals, Social Services and the Meals on Wheels program. The Buncombe County Sheriff's Department makes home visits when needed.

## North Carolina Center for Creative Retirement
**Univ. of NC at Asheville**
**• (828) 251-6140**

This innovative university program, begun in 1988, offers learning, leadership and community-service opportunities for older adults. Among these are the College for Seniors, a peer learning and teaching program; Schools and Campus Volunteer Programs, a variety of student/mentor learning experiences; Leadership Asheville Seniors, a series of day-long sessions geared toward community service; and a continuing program of research into issues concerning older adult education.

# Henderson County

## American Association of Retired Persons (AARP)
**P. O. Box 692, Hendersonville**
**• (800) 411-2277**

This organization offers a 55 Alive/Safe Driving Course for senior citizens, Bridge Club, tax aid services and is the coordinator of Senior's Health Insurance information Program (SHIIP). It informs and educates seniors regarding relevant issues through speakers and literature and is one of the sponsors of the Widowed Persons Services (see below). Currently, it is in the process of organizing AARP's "Connections for Independent Living."

## Blue Ridge Community College
**College Dr., Flat Rock • (828) 692-3572**

BRCC offers many continuing education courses and cultural events. Most importantly for retirees, it operates the Center for Lifelong Learning, which provides adults older than 50 the opportunity to buy a lifetime membership for continuing education classes.

## Council on Aging
**304 Chadwick Ave., Hendersonville**
**• (828) 692-4203**

The council provides a variety of services that help older adults cope with physical, social or other aging problems. Specific programs include Meals on Wheels, Service Advocates for the Elderly (SAFE), Elder Neighbors, minor home repairs, installation and repair of smoke alarms (Fire Alert) and an Information and Referral Helpline, (828) 697-4357. Other services include lending out heaters and fans, a hearing-aid bank, a thrift shop (213 Church Street, (828) 693-7756) and Living Wills.

## FISH Volunteer Medical Transportation
**P.O. Box 2411, Hendersonville**
**• (828) 693-5100**

FISH provides roundtrip transportation within the county and, when medical services are not available, to Asheville for health-related appointments. While the organization does not provide emergency medical transportation, it will take patients home from the hospital after outpatient surgery. Clients must call to make arrangements at least two days prior to an appointment. Office hours are from 8 AM until noon from Monday through Friday.

## Lifeline Personal Emergency Response System
**Pardee Hospital/Lifeline**
**715 Fleming St., Hendersonville**
**• (828) 692-9061**

This program offers round-the-clock, professional monitoring of every emergency call for help, direct to Pardee Hospital.

## New Life Center (Adult Day Care)
**Hendersonville • (828) 696-4219**

This adult day-care facility has planned activities to meet an individual's specific needs It provides educational, recreational, social, diversional, and volunteer programs.

## Volunteer Center
**Opportunity House, 1400 Asheville Hwy., Hendersonville**
**• (828) 692-8700**

The Volunteer Center recruits interviews and refers volunteers to non-profit, for profit and government agencies, which have volunteer opportunities. It also provides guidance and support to volunteer programs, does volunteer and staff training, board training and is an advocate for volunteerism.

## Widowed Persons Service of Henderson County
**Opportunity House, 1400 Asheville Hwy., Hendersonville • (828) 687-3776**

The newly widowed find outreach here on a one-to-one basis. There are also group sessions which bring together the widowed to discuss problems and provide mutual assistance, as well as a telephone service that the widowed can call for referral and assistance.

## Opportunity House
**1411 Asheville Hwy., Hendersonville**
**• (828) 692-0575**

This arts, crafts and cultural center is a nonprofit organization that opened its doors in 1958. Now, as then, it continues to offer fellowship and learning opportunities to individuals of all ages and faiths. Activities include bridge, crafts, dance, golf, ladies club, seminars and smoke-free bingo. In addition, The Arts League and The Volunteer Center of Henderson County are headquartered here. The gift shop on the premises features many handcrafted items and is open to the public. Opportunity House is open Monday through Friday, 9 to 5 PM, and visitors are always welcome. The annual membership fee is $25 for singles and $45 for couples; a lifetime membership fee is $200 for singles and $380 for couples.

(See our Arts and Culture chapter for more information.)

## Seniors Health Insurance
**Hendersonville • (828) 692-4600**

Personal insurance counseling provided by the N.C. Senior Health Insurance Information Program (SHIIP) is available at Pardee Hospital's Health Education Center in the Blue Ridge Mall. The trained SHIIP volunteers provide free counseling to older adults on long-term care insurance, Medicare and Medicaid Supplement insurance. Contact the Pardee Health Education Center at the above number, 1800 Four Seasons Boulevard, Hendersonville, for more information.

## Western Carolina Community Action
**526 E. Seventh St., Hendersonville**
**• (828) 693-1771**

This organization develops and administers programs of interest to older adults that include weatherization, a heating appliance replacement and repair program (HARRP), FISH medical transportation answering and dispatch, a variety of transportation services, emergency assistance, emergency fuel, plastic for windows, a garden program, a food closet, job placement with supportive services, liquid nutrient supplement (Ensure) and Section 8 Housing Assistance, to name a few.

## YMCA
**810 Sixth Ave. W., Hendersonville**
**• (828) 692-5774**

Adult programs include fitness classes, health enhancement programming, swimming classes, volleyball, basketball, special events and workshops. Specifically for older adults, the "Y" offers a Water Exercise program, an Arthritis Water exercise program, a Senior Pep Exercise program and a Deep Water Aerobic program.

# Polk County

## The Meeting Place
**500 Carolina Dr., Jervey-Palmer Bldg., Tryon • (828) 859-9707**

Housed in the old St. Luke's Hospital building, this center serves both congregate and in-home lunches Monday through Friday. It also offers classes in exercise, quilting and

Photo: Cathy Ciucevich

Even snow doesn't stop the area's retirees from enjoying golf.

sewing, but one of its biggest draws is its ceramics workshop. The products made here are sold in The Peppermint Shop, housed in the same building; they produce much of the income for the upkeep of the center.

The Meeting Place also has a pool room, a television lounge and frequent games of cards, bingo and checkers. It has it's own library and is visited regularly by a bookmobile. There is also a regular Wednesday music session. Other services include regularly scheduled transportation for shopping and medical appointments, and special holiday trips are offered. Seniors may also take advantage of nutrition education programs, legal services and tax services. There are satellite centers with many of the same services in both Saluda and Green Creek.

### Polk County
### Transportation Authority
Columbus • (828) 894-8203

The authority provides transportation to senior centers and elsewhere by appointment.

# Transylvania County

### American Association of
### Retired Persons (AARP)
P. O. Box 1336, Brevard 28712
• (828) 883-8486

AARP meets at 10 AM on the fourth Tuesday of each month in the Fellowship Hall of the First United Methodist Church in Brevard to hear speakers and participate in other programs of interest to the retirement community.

### Brevard College
### Community Education
400 N. Broad St., Brevard
• (828) 884-7400

Reaching beyond the college-aged population, Brevard has a wide variety of continuing education programs for adults. The Office of Community Education currently offers more than 200 courses annually, with an enrollment for nearly 2,000 participants that include intellectual and academic subjects, cultural experiences, local orientation, hobbies and self-improvement, and health and physical fitness

classes. All classes are noncredit. In addition, musical performances, dramatic presentations, art gallery exhibits and lecture series are presented throughout the year and are open to the public.

The Brevard College library is also an integral part of the intellectual life here. It has over 45,000 books, over 200 periodical subscriptions, valuable electronic resources available on CD-ROM, World Wide Web and access to nearby colleges through the Mountain College Library Network.

### Koala Adult Day Care
19 Carolina Ave., Brevard
• (828) 884-2980

Care-givers can leave loved ones here while they work or just take time for themselves. It offers its clients crafts, remotivation, reminiscing, fun and games, medication and a hot lunch. The fee is $22 a day and grants are available to those unable to pay the full amount.

### Lifelilne: Emergency Response
Transylvania Community Hospital: Home Care Hospital Dr. • (828) 883-5254

Lifeline provides 24-hour access to emergency help when a person is at home alone or with a caregiver who may be unable to provide necessary assistance in an emergency. It links, via telephone and specialized electronic equipment, with continuous emergency assistance at Transylvania Community Hospital.

### Meals on Wheels of Brevard
Transylvania Community Hospital, Hospital Dr., Brevard • (828) 883-8776

Like so many other of these programs, MOW provides hot, well-balanced noontime meals, weekdays, to shut-ins without age or income restrictions. Volunteers deliver the meals, and the cost based on the client's ability to pay.

### Med-Drive
Transylvania Community Hospital: Home Care Hospital Dr., Brevard
• (828) 883-5254

Med-Drive volunteers provide transportation to medical appointments for people over

60 within Transylvania County. Limited out-of-county transportation is available for chemotherapy, radiation and renal dialysis. Med-Drive doesn't accommodate emergency medical transportation.

### Telephone Reassurance Program
**Brevard Police Dept., City Hall,**
**Brevard • (828) 833-2212**

This 24-hour service is for people who live alone. They can leave their name, age, address, doctor's name and who to call in an emergency. Every morning, these people call or are called by the Police Department to make sure everything is okay. If there is no response or if help is needed, a police officer is sent to the address and proper steps are taken.

### Western Carolina
### Community Action
**299 S. Broad St., Brevard**
**• (828) 844-3219**

A branch of the WCCA in Henderson County, Transylvania's office serves congregate lunches Monday through Friday at both Silvermont in Brevard and in Quebec on Highway 64 W. and provides transportation to both sites as well as out-of-county medical transportation. It joins with the AARP in providing trained tax preparers to assist with tax returns and oversees the Senior Health Insurance Information Program (SHIIP), job-training for those older than 55, a weatherization program for both renters and homeowners with limited incomes, emergency assistance, liquid nutrient supplement (Ensure) program, plastic for windows, spring and fall garden supplies, a heating appliance repair and replacement program and rental assistance. Program eligibility is based on income.

# Southern Mountains

## Cherokee County

### Cherokee County Senior Services
**105 Alpine St., Murphy • (828) 837-2467**

Many activities take place at the Penland Senior Citizens Center, including craft classes and exercise programs conducted by the health department. A Friendly Visitor Program visits homebound seniors for "cheers and chores," and there's a congregate meal program at the center Monday through Friday, as well as a home-delivered meals program. It also offers information and referrals to various community services.

The organization's red vans offer regularly scheduled runs into each section of the county. Out-of-county trips are also scheduled for shopping, recreation and medical appointments. SHIIP (the Senior Health Insurance Information Program) is active here with trained counselors helping senior citizens with health insurance information. It also supports annual Senior Games and holds an annual picnic. In the Andrews branch (The Sunshine Club, 19 Business, Andrews, (828) 321-4505), there is also a nutrition program, an exercise program and a classes.

## Clay County

### Clay County Senior Center
**Ritter Rd., Hayesville • (828) 389-9271**

The center provides a congregate "Meals with Friends" and Meals on Wheels, Monday through Friday, as well as transportation for "any necessity of life." It also holds classes in painting, wood carving, crocheting, exercise and has popular Thursday-Morning Music Sessions.

## Graham County

### American Association of
### Retired Persons (AARP)
**Robbinsville • (828) 389-9271**

This group meets at the senior center (see the following entry) on the second Monday of the month for refreshments and to hear speakers talk about a variety of topics.

### Senior Citizens Center
**Moore Branch Rd., Robbinsville**
**• (828) 479-7977**

A congregate lunch is served at the center five days a week with home-driven meals to homebound seniors. A transportation service provides medical transportation to doctors and hospitals all over Western North Carolina as well as occasional shopping trips to places such as Asheville and Knoxville, Tennessee. There are also art and basket-weaving classes and bingo.

# Haywood County

## Canton Senior Center
1 Pigeon St., Old Canton Armory, Canton • (828) 648-8412

The center promotes wellness in older adults through group socialization, special activities, crafts, speaking, educational opportunities and organized trips.

## Council on Aging
1271 East St., Waynesville
• (828) 452 2370

The council provides information and referral, resource directory, advocacy, coordination of services, special programs, and the Senior Games. The council is also the lead agency for CAP/DA, which serves elderly adults needing care in an in-home setting.

## Haywood Community College
1 Freelander Dr., Clyde
• (828) 627-4500

Tuition is free to persons older than 65, except for the cost of materials in arts and crafts classes. See the HCC listing in our Education chapter.

## Intentional Growth Center
959 N. Lakeshore Dr., Lake Junaluska • (828) 452-2881, ext. 720, (800) 482-1442

The center, an Agency of the United Methodist Church, is a nationally accredited provider of continuing education courses and programs of clergy and laity. It also serves as a popular center for the National Elderhostel program and for church-related older adult events such as Fall Flings and Christmas at Lambuth Inn.

## Meals on Wheels
Department of Social Services, 486 E. 486 E. Marshall St., Waynesville
• (828) 452-6620, ext.356

Meals are provided five days a week based on need. Fees are based on income.

## Mountain Projects Inc.
2251 Old Balsam Rd., Waynesville
• (828) 452-1447

This organization is a community action agency serving Haywood and Jackson Counties. It operates numerous programs for low-income and disadvantaged persons. These currently include housing rehabilitation, Head Start, a congregate nutrition program, foster grandparents, a retired senior volunteer program, section 8 rental assistance, Haywood Public Transit, employment and training programs, and in-home chore services for the elderly. The eligibility for program participation is determined by the particular grant funding the program.

## Waynesville Recreation Center
44 Boundary St., Old Waynesville Armory, Waynesville • (828) 456-9207

Senior citizens meet here for lunch Monday through Friday. The center, which serves the entire community, also offers special activities, crafts, lectures and organized trips.

# Jackson County

## American Association of Retired Persons (AARP)
Sylva • (828) 586-9434

This active chapter holds a monthly breakfast, lunch and covered-dish supper. Aside from a monthly meeting at the Golden Age Club (see the following entry) and programs that present topics of interest to senior citizens (such as a seven-week course that teaches personal financial management to women), the organization holds frequent fundraisers to support such services as Lifeline.

## INSIDERS' TIP

**Many local restaurants, museums and movie theaters offer Senior discounts — inquire and bring proof of age!**

## Cashiers Senior C.A.F.E.
**Cashiers Community Building, off Hwy.**
**64 W. Cashiers • (828) 743-9215**

This center provides congregate meals, home delivered meals and social activities for senior citizens in the Cashiers area. Seniors can also use and receive instruction on the center's public access computer with Internet access.

## Golden Age Club
**1 Central Ave., Sylva • (828) 586-4944**

This is one of the more active senior citizen centers in the mountains. Its 300 members enjoy classes in exercise, beginner and advanced line dancing, square dancing, tai chi exercise, wood carving, basic computer instruction, tennis, hiking and creative writing. There are coffee klatsches for men and women, organized card games and co-ed softball games. A philosophy group uses the center for its discussions. Another group is devoted to bowling. There is also a singing group and a line-dancing group that give performances around the area. Other activities include income tax preparation, a walking program, Senior Games, shuffleboard, horseshoes, billiards, fundraisers and intergenerational programs. A covered-dish supper is held once a month with dancing afterward. The fourth Saturday of every month, the center serves an "All You Can Eat" Country Breakfast for $3. The public is invited. Membership fees for those 50 and over are $5 a year, and seniors get a lot for their money!

## Jackson County Department on Aging
**30 Central St., Sylva • (828) 586-8562**

This active agency provides programs and resources for county seniors. In addition to coordinating services with other agencies and councils, it provides information and referral services on a variety of subjects and health issues, initiates new services and is a senior advocacy group. It also publishes a monthly newsletter, *Jacksonian,* with information about local senior events and happenings.

## Jackson County Transportation
**• (828) 586-0233**

This organization fills a need that many residents in rural counties encounter. It provides on-call transportation for medical visits to nutrition sites. One day a week, it follows established routes in outlying areas to take people shopping, to banks and to doctors. It also visits the county's rehabilitation center and offers low-cost, zoned transportation to the general public.

## Mountain Projects, Inc.
**23 Schulman St., Sylva • (828) 586-2345**

For information on this agency's services, see our Mountain Projects, Inc. entry in this chapter under Haywood County.

## Southwestern Community College
**Hwy. 116, Sylva • (828) 586-4091**

SCC's Continuing Education program — serving Jackson, Macon, Swain and The Qualla Boundary — offers classes in everything from computers to crafts. You can reach the center nearest you by calling the Sylva campus number above, the Cherokee Center, (828) 497-7233, the Macon County Center, (828) 369-7331, or the Swain County Center, (828) 488-6413.

## Sylva Senior C.A. F. E.
**Community Services Building**
**538 Scots Creek, Sylva • (828) 586-6710**

A congregate lunch is served here Monday through Friday, and the Home-Delivered Meals Program delivers hot, nutritious meals daily to Jackson County's homebound elderly seven days a week. This center has a public access computer with Internet connection for seniors in the Sylva area and Instruction is available. It also offers occasional programs, including exercises, bingo and adventurous outings, but simply socializing is one of the biggest attractions.

## Western Carolina University
**N.C. Hwy. 107, Cullowhee**
**• (828) 227-7397**

In addition to all the arts and culture found at a large university, this institution offers an outstanding continuing education program. It's also super-active in Elderhostel, offering a program on campus every summer and in the spring and fall at selected off-campus locations. Elderhostelers live in a residential setting and attend three classes each day for a week. They enjoy various types of entertainment in the evening. The weekly fee includes room, board, classes and extracurricular activities. A limited number of commuter spaces are available in each session. The commuter fee is $150 for one week and includes the courses, lunches, field trips, banquets and all scheduled evening activities. (See the WCU entry in our Education chapter for more information.)

## Macon County

### American Association of Retired Persons (AARP)
**various locations • (828) 524-5391**

This chapter has been active in the county for more than 20 years. Meetings are held at noon the second Thursday of each month.

### Macon County Department of Aging
**125 Hyatt Rd., Franklin • (828) 349-2058**

The department is the only full-service agency to serve anyone older than 60 west of Hickory. A sampling of the services provided: transportation, congregate meals, home-delivered meals, chores, respite care services, an Alzheimer's support group, an Alzheimer's day respite center, overnight respite, case management, information and referral, SHIIP, a lending library on dementia and medical equipment for loan.

## Swain County

### State of Franklin Services to Senior Citizens
**Courthouse-On-The-Square, Bryson City • (828) 488-3047**

The Swain County Senior Center provides an Elderly Nutrition Program for people older than 60 at noon Monday through Friday as well as transportation to the center. Transportation is also provided for medical appointments and shopping. On certain days of the month, there are regularly scheduled trips for out-of-town medical appointments.

Through the National Council of Senior Citizens, a Senior AIDES Program provides an employment service for people older than 55 for 20-hour-week jobs with nonprofit organizations. Other activities include line-dancing and classes through Southwestern Community College. Bingo is played on Wednesdays and Fridays, and there's a health screening at the center once a month.

## Retirement Communities

Because western North Carolina is so popular with retirees, it naturally follows that many retirement communities have sprung up here. While most are concentrated in the Asheville-Hendersonville area, others are sprouting in surrounding areas. They offer everything from an independent living style to total life care. They also offer a wide range of options to fit various retirement needs and budgets: manufactured homes, cluster or attached homes, townhouses, condominiums, apartments and luxurious life-care facilities.

Some offer basic services, such as lawn care, at the option of individual residents. Others take care of all maintenance. Some include a variety of recreational amenities. A number provide meals, housekeeping, social activities, transportation and nursing care.

Most counties have low-cost retirement apartments through their departments of social services that are priced according to income levels, though there is often a waiting list for these. Here are a few examples of what is available. For more information, contact local chambers of commerce.

## Northern Mountains

### Appalachian/Brian Estates
**163 Shadowline Dr., Boone • (828) 264-1006, (800) 333-3432**

This 91-residence community for older adults is unique in that it offers both annual and seasonal apartments. Appalachian/Brian Estates is strictly a rental retirement community developed as a cooperative venture between Appalachian State University Foundation and Don Beaver of Beaver Sports Properties. Since residents are not required to liquidate their assets and no endowments or purchase plans are required, the rental option is a big drawing card.

Modern facilities, including a variety of thoughtfully designed floor plans for studio, one- and two-bedroom residences, a community dining room and several recreational areas cater to the carefree retirement lifestyle. Lounges, a club room for parties, exercise facilities, a professional hair salon, library and sundry store are all on-site. A guest suite is provided for visiting family members. Services are well-planned and involve community outreach. At nearby Appalachian State, the "A/BE" residents enjoy university programs geared toward retirees. The university library is also open to the residents.

Community security includes a 24-hour emergency call system and smoke detectors and sprinkler systems in every residence. Staff members are available around the clock. Prices start at $1,200 per month for an unfurnished studio apartment and vary depending on the six different floor plans, annual or seasonal.

# Central Mountains

## College Walk
**Neely Rd., Brevard**
• **(828) 884-5800, (800) 280-9600**
At College Walk you'll find a stimulating community planned exclusively for your pleasure and customized to your lifestyle. Whether you relish long, solitary walks in picturesque woods, love learning and broadening your horizons or simply prefer a busy schedule of activities, there's something that will satisfy you here.

On a 25-acre site, College Walk borders Brevard College and is convenient to the Brevard Music Center, shopping and Pisgah National Forest.

This community offers two- and three-bedroom cluster homes, studio, one- and two-bedroom apartments and a state-licensed assisted-living facility. Apartments, which can range in size from 430 to 1,020 square feet, have no entry fee. Monthly fees range from $1,130 to $1,985 and include one meal daily, housekeeping, maintenance, transportation, linen service, utilities, a 24-hour emergency call system, security and a large number of activities.

The two- and three-bedroom cluster homes all have screened porches and garages and range from 1,250 to 1,650 square feet and cost $120,000 to $150,000. Owners pay a one-time, nonrefundable membership of $5,000 and a monthly fee of $585 for one person, $800 for two people. The fee includes one meal daily, land lease, outside maintenance, security patrol and use of the clubhouse, library, game room, auditorium, workshop and other common areas.

## Crescent View
**2533 Hendersonville Rd. Asheville**
• **(828) 687-0068**
This Lutheran-sponsored planned community in Buncombe County has a variety of studio, one- and two-bedroom apartment homes for retired seniors. Fine dining, housekeeping, and linen services are available here, as well as 24-hour security and transportation. Crescent View also offers assisted-living residences. On the south end of Asheville, it is close to major supermarkets, movie theaters, shopping, and easy access to the Blue Ridge Parkway.

## Deerfield
**1617 Hendersonville Rd., Asheville**
• **(828) 274-1816, (800) 284-1531**
This pleasant Episcopal retirement community on Asheville's south end offers apartments and cottages for seniors. The attractively landscaped estate maintains a health center, a central formal dining room with wait service, and a community center with a host of amenities. Deerfield maintains Life Care assisted living and will be expanding over the next few years. Just off a main thoroughfare on Asheville's south side, Deerfield is close to shopping, restaurants, cinemas, and access to the Blue Ridge Parkway.

## Givens Estate United Methodist Retirement Community
**2360 Sweeten Creek Rd., Asheville**
• **(828) 274-4800**
This United Methodist retirement community is spread over 160 wooded acres in South Asheville. The retirement village has residential options that include apartments, duplexes and individual houses scattered across the

campus. Asbury Hall, in the community's center, offers congregate living with dining and recreational facilities. Also within this facility is Sales Health Care Center, designed to provide domiciliary or skilled nursing care to residents who can no longer live alone. A campus nurse and 24-hour emergency call system and housekeeping are additional services. The purchase price of houses, duplexes, villas and congregate-living apartments range from $47,500 to $165,000. Apartment rental under the federal government's HUD program is based on income.

## Highland Farms Retirement Community
**200 Tabernacle Rd., Black Mountain**
**• (828) 669-6473**

Highland Farms was one of the first retirement communities in Western North Carolina. This beautiful spot, nestled in the mountains in Buncombe County near the village of Black Mountain, has drawn retirees since the 1970s. Cluster homes, condominiums, apartments, individual homes, a residential lodge, a healthcare center and a rest home are spread over a lovely campus with the mountains in view.

Residents enjoy a number of services and activities. A library, music area, art and craft studio and even a vegetable garden keep those at Highland Farms active. Seminars and on-campus workshops foster a close relationship with the surrounding communities of Asheville and Black Mountain.

## Lake Pointe Landing
**333 Thompson St., Hendersonville**
**• (828) 693-7800, (800) 693-7801**

Lake Pointe Landing is Henderson County's newest retirement community. It requires no endowment or entry fees. Though the 32-acre complex has easy access to I-26 and is less than a mile from Hendersonville's restaurants, shopping, banks and medical offices, the lush landscaping and 1½-acre lake make it seem more a "country place."

Lake Pointe is made up of patio homes known as the Villas, where retirees can enjoy 100 percent equity ownership. There are two- and three-bedroom units, each with a second-floor loft to use as a study or for extra

storage. Both units come with two baths, a living room, a fully equipped, all-electric kitchen, a fireplace, a screened-in back porch and an enclosed garage. For more space, there are special homes with a lakeside view, retirement center proximity, or seclusion and privacy.

Homes range in price from $164,000 to $208,400. The monthly service fee is $450 and includes the use of the Club House, which has an arts and crafts room, an auditorium, a library, a general store, an exercise room/spa, a swimming pool, a beauty and barber shop, a billiards room, a bridge room, a woodworking shop and garden plots. Dining service for one dinner meal a day is $240 a month. Lake Pointe Landing homeowners are give priority places into the Health Center and independent/assisted living apartments.

Rental apartments, called The Harbor, are also available. Residents here have biweekly maid service and evening meals in a full-service dining room. All utilities except cable TV and personal telephone service are included in the rental fee, along with maintenance and a full calendar of activities with scheduled transportation and use of the Club House. Special guest suites are available for family and friends when they come to visit. Alcove apartments range from $1,050 to $1,085 per month, while a three-bedroom can run $2,495 to $2,695. A second-person monthly fee is $500. There is also a $1,000 non-refundable application fee; a $1,000 non-refundable smoker's fee and a $1,000 non-refundable pet-owners fee.

In addition, there are assisted living apartments at The Inn at Lake Pointe Landing with a choice of alcove and one-bedroom apartments. A licensed staff provides help in monitoring medications, grooming, housekeeping and access to transportation and other assistance.

Lake Pointe Landing also offers an on-site, long-term-care facility, Life Care Center of Hendersonville. It provides rehabilitation, skilled and long-term care services.

## Pine Park Retirement Inn
**2601 Hwy. 64 E., Hendersonville**
**• (828) 692-1911**

Pine Park is a month-to-month rental retirement center with no "buy in" or long-term lease. There is, however, a $500 nonrefundable processing fee ($200 for the second person) that is paid in advance of occupancy.

The center has 110 units: 63 independent-living units and 47 assisted-living units. One-bedroom apartments range in price from $1,623 to $2,115 per month, and a two-bedroom apartment is $2,060 per person. (A second person adds $450 to the cost.) This includes three meals a day, a social activities program, once-a-week housekeeping, including linens, all utilities and cable television, two-way intercom service, 24-hour attendant services and transportation to medical services, shopping and other outside activities.

Additional services associated with the activities of daily life — such as bathing, supervision of medications and personal laundry service — are available in assisted-living units, which range in price from $1,919 to $2,273, with an additional person adding $450 to the base rate. There is a charge for using the on-site beauty/barber shop. Pets are allowed for a $25 per month pet charge.

## Riverwind Adult Community
### 100 Riverwind Dr., Hendersonville
• (828) 891-2010, (800) 452-3058

This community of manufactured homes, created by the Oakwood Homes Corporation, is just off U.S. Highway 64 W. in Etowah between Brevard and Hendersonville. It's also just a mile from two championship golf courses (Etowah Valley Country Club and the Cummings Cove Golf Course; see our Golf chapter for more info) and is convenient to medical facilities and shopping (including groceries). Riverwind offers Freedom, Oakwood and Virginia homes in two and three bedroom, two bath models with brick/block foundations that contain approximately 1,000 to 1,700 square feet. The prices begin at $69,900 and include the property that the home is on. Its cable, city water, electricity, natural gas and telephone lines are all underground. The Homeowners Association dues are $50 a month and include sewer service, street and entrance lights, common area maintenance,

garbage collection and use of the recently built clubhouse, swimming pool and whirlpool spa.

## Tryon Estates
### 617 Laurell Lake Dr., Columbus
• (828) 894-3083, (800) 633-2718

Tryon Estates — owned and operated by ACTS, Inc., a not-for-profit corporation — lies on a 215-acre wooded site in Polk County's Thermal Belt. It offers both one-, two- and three-bedroom apartments and two- and three-bedroom villas with all buildings connected by covered walkways. Chef-prepared gourmet meals are served each day in an elegant central dining room. There are also private dining rooms. It has a regular activity schedule and a full-time activity director. Other amenities include a theater-style auditorium, library, woodworking shop, billiard room, an activity-craft room, a card room, a beauty/barber shop, a pharmacy, banking and postal services, a gift shop and an indoor, heated swimming pool. Outside, you'll find garden plots, walking and biking paths, a stocked fishing pond, croquet and shuffleboard. Maid service is available.

Residents are also offered portable emergency-call buttons, home healthcare and a state-licensed, Medicare-approved healthcare center with a medical staff on duty 24 hours a day. This community includes 44 personal-care units (assisted living) and 52 skilled-nursing units. There is a dining room/activity area in the healthcare center with three meals served daily. Healthcare costs are covered under the monthly fee. The cost also covers daily breakfasts and dinners, all utilities except telephone, weekly bed-linen laundry, maintenance, transportation, landscaping, activities and security. The entrance fees to this life-care community — which provides a lifetime apartment lease, guaranteed access to all medical care and use of all community facilities — currently range from $99,900 to $155,900 (a second person's entrance fee is $5,000). The monthly service charge for one person ranges from $915 to $1,145. Overnight guests/children are welcomed, and pets are allowed.

Savvy consumers like
the fact that hospitals in
western North Carolina
are still nonprofit and
focused on quality.

# Healthcare

Even before the turn of the century, when these mountains became a haven for sufferers of tuberculosis, healthcare held a prominent position in Western North Carolina. Carriage upon carriage of visitors arrived to "take the air" and enjoy the healthful climate at local spas. Many of these visitors remained as permanent residents. Today, the legacy of these early mountain sanatoriums forms a strong foundation for the rapidly expanding modern medical facilities found in each county of the region.

Increased national focus on healthcare and technological advancements is one important reason that the latest medical services are available to residents of even the most remote mountain counties. Innovative pooling of related or crossover medical services is also a growing trend here. Buncombe County's Memorial Mission Hospital and St. Joseph's Hospital, for example, have merged. Asheville and Buncombe County, especially, boast a thriving and continually growing medical community.

In addition to the major hospitals and healthcare centers, private physicians' practices line the two major thoroughfares of the city. Although the Buncombe County (especially Asheville) region often seems like a magical resort, untouched by American urban life, the level of medical care available is equal to that of a major university research center — with some important differences. Savvy consumers like the fact that hospitals in Western North Carolina are still nonprofit and focused on quality. State-of-the-art medical care is delivered with individual concern and friendliness. The patient, not the stockholder, comes first.

Throughout the region, services ranging from large, centrally located full-service hospitals, 24-hour emergency treatment centers, urgent-care and outpatient centers to community hospitals, community medical centers and special private clinics directed to the needs of the underinsured can be found. Special medical concerns, such as cancer treatment, heart care, women's services, orthopedics, pediatric medicine, psychiatric services, rehabilitative therapy and veterans' services are a major focus at many of the region's medical facilities. The latest diagnostics services, including ultrasound, mammography, CT scan and MRI (magnetic resonance imaging) are available at all the region's larger medical facilities. With the increasing accessibility of technology, even some of the smaller community hospitals in the region can offer this level of medical service.

In this chapter we offer you an overview of the region's larger medical facilities, the community hospitals, a number of the community clinics and their basic and specialized services. To find out more about the many services that each of the healthcare outlets offer, call the general numbers that we've provided.

If you unfortunately encounter a medical emergency in Western North Carolina, all our counties offer 911 emergency telephone service. For non-emegencies, check the front of the local phone book for other important phone numbers.

## Northern Mountains

### Alleghany County

**Alleghany Memorial Hospital**
**233 Doctor's St., N.C. Hwy. 18, Sparta**
• **(336) 372-5511**

Just off the intersection of North Carolina Highways 21 and 18 N., in the heart of Sparta,

Alleghany Memorial Hospital has served this rural, northern county since 1951. Personalized service and quality care are the mission of the 150-member staff at Alleghany Memorial. Comprehensive services are provided 24 hours a day. These include a well-staffed emergency room; radiology services such as CT scanning, mammography, ultrasound, MRI and fluoroscopic services; rehabilitation services; obstetrics; and restorative, respite and terminal care. An additional primary care clinic handles specialty services like urology, orthopedics, cataract surgery and everyday health problems. An In-Home Aide program, home-care program and Lifeline provide outreach services to the community.

# Ashe County

### Ashe Memorial Hospital
**200 Hospital Ave., Jefferson**
**• (336) 246-7101**

About 40 minutes from Boone, this small rural hospital maintains a sophisticated level of care for a county population of just 23,000. The hospital, established in 1939, is licensed for 76 beds and has a staff that includes two general surgeons, nine family practitioners, one radiologist, two ophthalmologists, one pediatrician and one internist. A full-service hospital, Ashe Memorial offers general, laparascopic and orthopedic surgery; complete eye care including cataract treatment and laser surgery; diagnostic imaging; pediatric medicine; cardiopulmonary therapy and testing; nutritional counseling; Lifeline emergency response program; and a 24-hour emergency unit. The hospital has also runs

the Mountain Hearts Cardiac Rehabilitation Center and Segraves Care Center, a 60-bed skilled nursing home.

# Avery County

### Sloop Memorial Hospital
**101 Crossnore Rd., Crossnore**
**• (828) 733-9231**
### Charles A. Cannon, Jr. Memorial Hospital
**805 U.S. Hwy. 184, Banner Elk**
**• (828) 898-5111**

The Sloop Memorial and Charles A. Cannon hospitals have merged and operate under the umbrella of the Avery Health Care System, (828) 733-4410, 1955 Newland Hwy. Both are full-service facilities serving small rural communities. Cannon, with a 79-bed capacity, was founded in 1908 and is in Banner Elk, just 17 miles from Boone. Sloop, with 38 beds and a staff of 15 doctors, was founded in 1929 and is in Crossnore, 25 miles from Boone.

Both offer a wide range of modern services, including critical-care units, obstetric services, radiology departments featuring CT scanning, nuclear medicine and MRI services. A 24-hour emergency service is available in both hospitals. Cannon also houses an inpatient psychiatric unit.

Three community clinics — Foscoe Family Health Center, (828) 963-7161, N.C. 105, Sugar Grove; Newland Family Medical Center, (828) 733-9276, 358 Beech St., Newland; and Kalmia Community Health Center, (828) 265-2400, 869 N.C. 105, Suite 8, Boone — serve as outreach affiliates of the hospitals.

---

**INSIDERS' TIP**

The Ducky Derby takes place every September to benefit cancer services for children at The Ruth and Billy Graham Children's Health Center in Asheville. The Health Center "sells" yellow rubber duckies before the Derby. On the day of the event, the sponsored duckies are dropped into a pool by a crane. Other events include 5K races, local school band performances and the Ducky Derby Dive. Prizes (like a new car or a weekend getaway) are given away. It's fun and it's for a good cause. Call (828) 254-4701 for more information.

# Madison County

## Mars Hill Medical Center
**1 Chestnut St., Mars Hill**
• **(828) 689-3507**

Mars Hill Medical Center is in the small college town of Mars Hill, roughly 20 minutes north of Asheville. This private medical group, founded in 1971, serves the primary healthcare needs of the remote rural communities of Mars Hill, Marshall, Hot Springs and Laurel in Madison County.

The Mars Hill location is the coordinating site for the various community services encompassed by the Hot Springs Health Program, and caregivers spend a great deal of hands-on time in the community. The 150 healthcare professionals and support staff of the Hot Springs Health Program all work with a high degree of mobility, providing primary medical care, pharmacy and dental services, home health and hospice care, occupational and physical therapy and social services.

This group is professionally affiliated with the schools of medicine of the University of North Carolina at Chapel Hill, Duke University, the Mountain Area Health Education Center of Asheville and Bowman-Gray in Winston-Salem, acting as a teaching site for each. The experience in this rural community offers young medical students a perspective different from the usual city hospital internship.

The Marshall/Walnut Medical Center, (828) 649-3500, is at 8625 U.S. Highway 25/70. The Hot Springs facility, (828) 622-3245, is on Highway 25/70 close to the BP gas station. The Laurel Medical Center is at 400 Cook Farm Road off N.C. Highway 208 that leads to Greeneville, Tennessee.

# Mitchell County

## Bakersville Community Medical Clinic
**86 North Mitchell Ave., Bakersville**
• **(828) 688-2104**

The tiny, rural community of Bakersville is served by this private clinic of five family physicians, one chiropractor and one nurse practitioner. The clinic offers a wide range of primary care services, including obstetrics and gynecology, flexible sigmoidoscopy, orthopedic medicine, drug screening, pediatrics, sports and industrial medicine, geriatrics and nutrition counseling. The clinic is affiliated with the Spruce Pine Community Hospital.

## Spruce Pine Community Hospital
**125 Hospital Dr., Spruce Pine**
• **(828) 765-4201**

Founded in 1955, this 80-bed community hospital is within the town of Spruce Pine, in the mountains north of Burnsville. The hospital serves Mitchell, Avery and Yancey counties. Spruce Pine Hospital is also a member of the Mission St. Joseph's Health System. The full-service Spruce Pine facility also staffs a 24-hour emergency room. Social workers assist the hospital in arranging nursing home care.

# Watauga County

## Blowing Rock Hospital
**416 Chestnut Dr., Blowing Rock**
• **(828) 295-3136**

This 100-bed, full-service community hospital is located in the village of Blowing Rock, north of Boone. It is a private, nonprofit hospital, with an adjacent doctor's-office complex. Facilities include acute and long-term care; surgery, x-ray and lab facilities; on-call physicians; and an emergency room. The hospital and long-term care unit are fully accredited by the Joint Commission of Accreditation of Hospitals.

## Watauga Medical Center
**336 Deerfield Rd., Boone**
• **(828) 262-4100**

Watauga Medical Center started in 1936 as a humble medical clinic on the campus of Appalachian State Teacher's College in Boone. The clinic quickly developed into a regular 50-bed hospital and by 1967 had expanded to an 83-bed facility at its present Deerfield Road site. Watauga almost doubled its capacity by 1979 and by 1985 began an expansion project to house an enlarged imaging department. In the early 1990s, the Medical Center also completed an outpatient facility. Today the hospital is licensed as a

Autumn on the slopes, and winter at the peak.

147-bed complex. There are 73 physicians on staff. To reflect the expanding services, the hospital changed its name in 1993 to Watauga Medical Center.

Some of the services at Watauga Medical Center include a critical care center; a complete surgical suite covering general and specialized surgery; an imaging unit offering CT scanning, MRI, x-ray, mammography and ultrasound; a birthing suite featuring relaxed birthing rooms, Cesarean section rooms, two well-baby nurseries, a level II neonatal intensive-care nursery and an isolation nursery; and a well-equipped, well-staffed pathology department for routine and special procedures, including forensic pathology. A special kidney-dialysis unit and a regional cancer center are also part of Watauga Medical Center's comprehensive medical complex. The center has a 24-hour physician-staffed emergency room and has air access via heli-

copter to Sanger Clinic in Charlotte for heart patients, and Baptist Hospital in Winston-Salem for head trauma patients.

## Yancey County

### Yancey Community Medical Center
**320 Pensacola Rd., Burnsville**
**• (828) 682-6136**

Serving the Burnsville area, this primary care clinic is open Monday through Friday, 8 AM to 5 PM with evening hours on Thursday until 8. X-ray facilities are available, and there's a lab operated by Spruce Pine Community Hospital on the premises. The clinic is affiliated with Mission St. Joseph's Health System. This medical center will see walk-ins with emergencies. After hours, it's best to go to the Spruce Pine Community Hospital, (828) 765-4201, 125 Hospital Drive.

# Central Mountains

## Buncombe County

### The Asheville Veterans Affairs Medical Center
**1100 Tunnel Rd., Asheville**
• **(828) 298-7911**

The Asheville VA Medical Center is in the Oteen area, in east Asheville and just minutes from an entrance to the Blue Ridge Parkway. The facility has a 76-year history of service to veterans in the mountains of Western North Carolina, beginning in March 1918 when it became U.S. Army General Hospital No. 19, a cantonment-like collection of 104 frame buildings accommodating 1,200 beds. The first patient was admitted in September of the same year. Treatment of tuberculosis was the primary focus.

In 1920, administration of the hospital was transferred to the U.S. Public Health Service. It was during this period that the Cherokee Indian term oteen, meaning "chief aim," was proposed for use with the hospital as an encouragement to every patient to adopt as his chief aim "to get well."

The mission of the USPHS hospital continued to be the treatment of tuberculosis. More permanent buildings were constructed on site from 1924 to 1936 to help provide better treatment facilities for this disease. Modernization of these structures was completed and capacity expanded during World War II. The 40-year mission as a tuberculosis treatment center was enhanced and the scope of treatment broadened when the hospital was officially designated as a General Medical and Surgical Hospital in 1961. It now contains 220 beds and a 120-bed on-site Nursing Home Care Unit.

Asheville's VA Medical Center is recognized as a major general medical and surgical hospital. The Center is known for its strong programs in vascular, thoracic and cardiac surgery. Its successful cardiac surgery program is the longest-running, continuously cost-effective program of its kind in the VA system and serves veterans from Virginia, West Virginia, upstate South Carolina, east Tennessee and western North Carolina.

The VA Medical Center provides a number of special programs, including cardiac catheterization, nuclear medicine, respiratory care, audiology and speech pathology, geriatric evaluation and management, mental health programs, a 25-bed substance-abuse program, a residential rehabilitation treatment program, a community nursing program and a hospital-based Primary Care program. The VA Center also has a mutual-use sharing agreement with the region's major hospitals in certain specialized medical areas.

A nonprofit research corporation administers an ongoing research program here. It currently consists of nine projects, most of which are clinical trials.

### Charter Asheville Behavioral Health System
**60 Caledonia Rd., Asheville**
• **(828) 253-3681, (800) 522-3695**

The history of this facility is really two histories: one of a hospital providing professional mental health services and the other of an architectural structure known as the Kenilworth Inn.

The Kenilworth Inn was built around 1890. After several reconstructions and metamorphoses, the structure which was the Inn opened for business in 1918 as U.S. General Army Hospital #12. The Army operated the hospital until 1922, until it reverted back to the original owner and was re-opened as an inn once again. It operated until 1929 when the stock market crashed caused the owner to lose the property.

In October of 1931, a group of physicians purchased the facility and moved their mental health service operation, Appalchian Hall, onto the premises. It continued as a family operation until 1981, when the facility was purchased by National Medical Enterprises. The current incarnation is a combination of the services of Appalachian Hall and Highland Hospital.

Highland Hospital was founded in 1904 as "Dr. Carroll's Sanitarium." Dr. Robert S. Carroll established the facility the next year as a training school for nurses. The sanitarium moved to its well-known location on nine acres on Zillicoa Street in what is now the Montford historic district. In 1939 Dr. Carroll gave 100 percent interest of Highland Hospital to Duke University. The facility as a whole was purchased by National Medical Enterprises (NME) from Duke in 1993.

Perhaps the hospital's most famous resident patient was Zelda Fitzgerald, married to F. Scott Fitzgerald, author of *The Great Gatsby*. Zelda spent her last days here: She died in a fire at Highland in the 1940s.

Charter Asheville provides a fully integrated system of mental health services for children, adolescents, adults and families experiencing emotional, behavioral and addiction problems. The hospital offers inpatient partial hospitalization, intensive outpatient and outpatient services for all ages. Woodhill Treatment Center is the hospital's adult chemical dependency program.

Charter Asheville offers free, confidential evaluations in its Needs Assessment & Referral Center which can be reached at the same address and phone number as the hospital. The hospital is open 24 hours a day, seven days a week. A licensed, qualified professional administers this service. Charter Asheville Behavioral Health System is licensed by the state of North Carolina to operate 139 hospital beds and is accredited by the Joint Commission of Accreditation of Hospitals.

## Mission + St. Joseph's Health System

Residents of Western North Carolina can choose from a strong network of excellent community hospitals. The largest of these is Mission St. Joseph's in Asheville, the regional referral center. It offers a level of sophistication of medical care found at large university medical centers.

Mission St. Joseph's was formed by combining Asheville's two private acute care hospitals, Memorial Mission and St. Joseph's. As a system, Mission St. Joseph's has 5,000 employees, 800 beds, and more than 500 physicians. The health system is private, not for profit, and governed by a board of volunteer leaders. Costs compare favorably with similar health systems. The system operates under continuing governance from the state, which monitors changes, excellence of care, and commitment to service and community outreach.

Virtually every medical specialty is available at Mission St. Joseph's. Programs emphasize prevention, cost control, logistical and financial access, and excellent care.

The partnership was the first of its type in North Carolina and one of the first in the nation. Combined, the two large hospitals cover more than 2 million square feet. The 500 physicians — primary care doctors, specialists, and sub-specialists — care for patients in the hospitals as well as in the new critical care, heart, genetics, and women's and children's centers. Medical Services are organized according to clinical specialty: the Owen Health Center provides for cardiology and heart surgery, and a cardiac rehabilitation program. It's also a national leader in minimally invasive and valve replacement surgery. The Ruth and Billy Graham Children's Health Center is an inpatient hospital, pediatric intensive care unit and neonatal ICU for newborns. Orthopedic care ranks among the top 35 hospitals in the country in the number of joint replacement surgeries done. The Helen Powers Women's Health Center educates and supports women of all ages, including high-risk obstetrics patients. The Fullerton Genetics Center diagnoses, provides laboratory testing and counseling for individuals and families who may be affected by inherited health problems. Services include Copestone behavioral medicine unit, including geriatric, adolescent, psychiatric and substance abuse programs

Surgical services include one-day and laser assisted surgery and a soon-to-be dedicated vascular center. Neurosciences, adult medicine, and oncology are, of course, included in the comprehensive hospital program. Emergency trauma services are staffed 24 hours a day and include hospital-operated air and ground transportation services. Programs for Seniors include Golden Care to help manage medical paperwork, and a 24-hour free Senior Healthline. For more information about the Mission St. Jospeh's, call Healthline at (800) 321-6877.

# Polk County:
# White Oak Mountain

Polk County's topography varies from rolling foot-hills to level plains on one side and high timber-clad mountains on the other. You can see a great example of all this from what has been called "the greatest view east of the Rockies." Drive east on N.C. Highway 108 for just less than 5 miles to Houston Road (S.R. 1137). Turn left and drive a half-mile to a fork. Bear right for just more than a half-mile, turn left onto White Oak Mountain Road and drive 2 miles to "The Brow," fronting the White Oak Condominiums near the top of Shunkawaken Falls (see our Waterfalls chapter). From this height of 3,000 feet on a clear day, you can see fields and farmlands stretching for 50 miles, and it's a very pretty at night with all the lights twinkling below. Another great vista lies across the relatively flat mountaintop westward to the base of the last incline of Tryon Peak, which is the highest of a number of summits on the White Oak Mountain massif. It's called Sunset Rock, and it's a popular Polk County picnic spot with a view of rugged, steep mountain ranges flowing into each other.

The following are two separate addresses but are one healthcare system.

## Memorial Mission Hospital
### 509 Biltmore Ave., Asheville
• (828) 255-4000

This private not-for-profit medical facility began more than 100 years ago, in 1885, as the Asheville Mission Hospital. Today, this nearly 500-bed hospital and the staff of 390 physicians and 2,000-member support staff provide medical expertise and high-quality care. Most specialties are represented at Mission, which has expanded in the last 20 years to cover virtually an entire hilltop in downtown Asheville.

Mission manages the Yancey Community Medical Center in Burnsville and operates EMS services in neighboring Yancey, Madison and Mitchell counties. Mission provides regional air and ground transportation through its ambulance helicopter (MAMA) and a ground transport unit, freeing up community EMS services to remain closer to home in case of need.

## St. Joseph's Hospital
### 428 Biltmore Ave., Asheville
• (828) 255-3100

Established in 1900 by the Catholic Order of the Sisters of Mercy, St. Joseph's Hospital serves all of western North Carolina. This 331-bed facility offers comprehensive general, diagnostic, surgical and acute care with a staff of more than 350 physicians and a 1,400-member support staff.

Special services include a physician-staffed 24-hour emergency care unit, intensive and coronary-care units, a restorative-care unit, an outpatient surgery center, an imaging center, a diabetes center, respiratory care/cardiology services, physical and occupational therapy services, a pathology lab, a kidney stone treatment center, a pharmacy, social work services and chaplain services.

St. Joseph's telephone assistance programs provide community services through Ask-A-Nurse, (828) 255-3333, Cancer Connection, which provides free information for cancer patients, and Lifeline. Lifeline, (828) 255-3678, is for maintaining contact with people who might need instantaneous assistance or who need to be checked on frequently.

## Thoms Rehabilitation Hospital
### 68 Sweeten Creek Rd., Asheville
• (828) 274-2400

Established as the Asheville Orthopedic Home in 1938 by the Rotary Club and the Junior League of Asheville, Thoms Rehabilitation Hospital was originally a facility for

# The Invisible Warriors

The town of Franklin was built where the Cherokee settlement of Nikwasi once stood. Nikwasi was one of the oldest Cherokee towns and an important ceremonial center. In the old days, Indians built their town lodges on large man-made mounds, and Nikwasi's was one of the few that possessed the "everlasting fire," or spiritual connection, hence the lodge was used in religious ceremonies.

Once, long ago, a powerful, unknown tribe invaded the land, destroying the villages and killing the people. One morning at dawn, the intruders were seen approaching Nikwasi. The villagers rushed to defend their town but were eventually forced to retreat.

Suddenly, a stranger appeared. He spoke and dressed like a chief from the Overhills settlements. The villagers thought he had come to their aid with reinforcements. He shouted to the Nikwasi chief to call off his men — he would defeat the enemy. As the Nikwasi villagers fell back toward the lodge, they saw hundreds of warriors, armed and painted for battle, streaming out of an open doorway in the side of the mound where no doorway had existed before. It was then the villagers recognized the warriors as *nunnehi* — "Immortals," or the "people who live anywhere."

Theirs was a race of spirit people, fond of music and dancing, who lived in the highlands and had a great many town lodges, especially on mountain balds. As soon as the nunnehi got a short distance from the mound, they became invisible. The invaders could see the weapons but could not see who wielded them; frightened, they began to flee. They tried to hide behind large rocks as they retreated, but the nunnehi's arrows flew around the boulders and killed them. When only six or so of the invaders were left alive, they were so upset they just sat down and cried. Since that day, the Cherokees have called that spot at the head of the Tuckasegee River *dayulsunyi*, "Where They Cried."

It was Indian custom to spare a few warriors to return home and tell of their defeat. Thus, the invaders went home to the north and the nunnehi returned to the mound.

There are countless Cherokee stories involving this spirit race who, when they chose to show themselves, look like ordinary people. They also appeared to whites during the Civil War. It's said that a large troop of Union soldiers came to Franklin to surprise a small number of Confederates posted there but, upon seeing so many soldiers guarding the town, they turned away.

handicapped children from the remote areas of the mountains of western North Carolina. Thoms is now a nonprofit regional referral center offering acute care, day treatment and transitional outpatient rehabilitation services to those with physical, cognitive, and developmental impairments. Traditional and specialized rehabilitation programs are offered for all ages. The hospital has a total of 100 beds: 80 beds at a comprehensive outpatient center at the main campus located in the Biltmore sec-

tion of Asheville and 20 beds at Memorial Mission Hospital.

The hospital works with brain trauma cases, spinal cord injuries, stroke and developmental disabilities, pain and industrial injuries and conditions of amputation and neuromuscular disorders.

The staff is composed of physicians, psychologists, nurses, and physical and occupational therapists and speech/language pathologists, among other professionals. Thoms is a founding member of Community CarePartners, a post-acute continuum of care.

# Henderson County

## Blue Ridge Dental Practice
1801 Asheville Hwy., Hendersonville
• (828) 696-0512
## Blue Ridge Health Center
U.S. Hwy. 64 E. and Howard Gap Rd.
Hendersonville • (828) 692-4289
## Druid Hills Family Practice
1801 Asheville Hwy., Hendersonville
• (828) 696-0545
## George Bond Memorial Health Center
U.S. Hwy. 74, Bat Cave • (828) 625-9141
## Kate B. Reynolds Women's and Children's Center
U.S. Hwy. 64 E. and Howard Gap Rd.
Hendersonville • (828) 692-7057

Blue Ridge Community Health Service is a private, not-for-profit community health center with five locations in Henderson County. A staff of board-certified family practice physicians, internists and pediatricians, along with physician assistants, family nurse practitioners and certified nurse-midwives, work as a team to provide personalized comprehensive health care for the entire family, from newborns to the elderly. Doctors are on 24-hour call and enjoy staff privileges at Margaret R. Pardee Hospital in Hendersonville.

Maternal Outreach and Child Service Coordination programs support the obstetrics and gynecology services. A nutritionist provides dietetic education and counseling, and home-health nursing services are available for homebound patients.

Board-certified dentists, along with hygienists, provide restorative and preventive dental care to children and pregnant women, and emergency care for established Blue Ridge patients. The new dental facility will be a teaching site for dental students from the University of North Carolina School of Dentistry.

Blue Ridge Community Health Services leads the way in providing access to health care and dental care – a major concern for many people throughout Western North Carolina. The doors are open to "everyone" without regard to financial status. Their focus is providing quality health care at affordable rates with an emphasis on the medically underserved. Most insurance plans are accepted, including Medicare and Medicaid. A sliding fee schedule is available for those who qualify, and payment plans can be arranged.

All locations can be reached after hours by calling (828) 692-4289.

## Margaret R. Pardee Memorial Hospital
715 Fleming St., Hendersonville
• (828) 696-1000

Founded in 1953 with the help of a $100,000 donation from Ivor Pardee in memory of his aunt, Margaret R. Pardee, this 100-bed facility has grown through the years to its present 222 licensed acute-care beds, which include 21 psychiatric beds. In addition, there are 40 skilled nursing beds.

The recently completed hospital surgical facilities house six large operating rooms, 22 day-surgery rooms and a 13-bay recovery room. Pardee's advanced diagnostic equipment and treatment facilities include a sleep-disorder lab, MRI, CT scan, echocardiograms, advanced angiogram equipment, nuclear medicine, endoscopy, mammography, ultrasound, kidney stone lithotripsy and bone densitometer.

Pardee Hospital dedicated the Kayden Radiation Oncology Center in 1993. The Center was built to meet the needs of cancer patients who require radiation therapy five days a week for six weeks or more. The addition of radiation therapy means that that all three major treatment modes are available at Pardee: surgery, chemotherapy and radiation therapy. The American College of Surgeons certified Pardee as a Cancer Center in February 1997. The certification process takes three years and involves a cancer registry, which records and reports cancers and treatments to the N.C. Central Cancer Registry. This data becomes part of the national database on cancer care. Local Cancer Conferences, held twice a month, are attended by physicians, nurses, social workers, the chaplain, pharmacists and others who treat or work with cancer patients. These conferences review cases and share treatment and support possibilities for each patient.

Family-centered, one-room birthing in the Family Way unit allows families to fully appreciate the childbirth experience. Pardee's day-surgery unit, freestanding outpatient radiology department and large emergency department make treatment more convenient. Express Care (same address as above) is open evenings, weekends and holidays for care of minor emergencies and illnesses without the waiting time that is sometimes seen in the Emergency Room.

Pardee's Home Care includes OB and pediatric nursing, psychiatric nursing and personal care services. Other services include cardiac and pulmonary rehabilitation, respite care of dependent adults, geriatric evaluations and adult day care. In the summer of 1996, Pardee launched the Hendersonville Family Practice Residency Program in conjunction with the Mountain Area Health Education Center (MAHEC) in Asheville and the University of North Carolina in Chapel Hill. Designed to train family physicians who wish to practice in a rural area, the three-year program trains two residents annually. The program is community-based, conceived and initiated by community physicians who want to share their medical expertise and knowledge with doctors in training and to bring excellent family practitioners to our area. The Hendersonville Family Health Center is one immediate benefit of the Residency Program. As part of the program, the clinic is always accepting new patients.

Pardee provides health education to the community through a variety of means. The Pardee Health Education Center at the Blue Ridge Mall on Four Seasons Boulevard has served the community in health promotions and wellness since 1989. Free or low-cost screenings, seminars by doctors and healthcare professionals, support groups and a wealth of literature and videos on health topics are available at the Center. The Henderson County Breast Cancer Initiative that is sponsored by Pardee provides education on breast cancer, bringing services such as mobile mammography, breast self-examination education and a breast cancer awareness speakers bureau to neighborhoods, community organizations and business.

Pardee Care Center is a 130-bed nursing home on land adjacent to Blue Ridge Community College. It shares space with both the college and Four Seasons Hospice. Locating the nursing home and 12-bed home for Hospice patients adjacent to the campus provides additional clinical spaces for students in the College's allied health programs, fosters skill upgrading and certification of health-care professionals and facilitates cross-training of staff through the expansion of conferences and seminars to serve all partner organizations.

## Park Ridge Hospital
**Naples Rd., Fletcher • (828) 684-8501**

First opened in 1910, the Mountain Sanitarium eventually evolved into Fletcher Hospital. Then, in 1986, its new 103-bed facility was opened, and this not-for-profit facility, operated by the Seventh-day Adventists, became the Park Ridge Hospital. The facility is a full-service general, acute-care hospital that has a 24-hour emergency department, OB/GYN and psychiatric services. With 150 physicians and more than 450 employees, it averages about 23,000 patient visits per year, with a focus on "the well-being of the whole person" that includes a vegetarian option for all hospital meals.

Park Ridge offers the latest in healthcare technology, including a CT scanner, a mobile MRI unit and nuclear medicine. Specialized spine and orthopedic surgery capabilities are available at Park Ridge. Comprehensive ophthalmology services also are provided. Approximately 750 cataract surgeries are performed every year. Park Ridge also provides a variety of educational and rehabilitative programs that include child and adolescent psychiatry, occupational health, cardiac and pulmonary rehabilitation, wellness, smoking cessation, classes for expectant parents and HOPE, a woman's program that treats eating and psychological disorders.

The emergency department operates 24 hours a day. The Home Health Agency provides skilled nursing care and rehabilitation

Photo: Historic Hendersonville and Flat Rock Area

Breath deeply and let the mountains help heal.

# Alternative Healthcare in the Mountains

Ever had an ache or unhealthy condition that you'd like to get rid of without scads of medication? Or have you exhausted all medical avenues and don't seem to be getting better? Do the fluorescent lights of hospital corridors and the rubbing alcohol smell of austere clinics make you cringe? And how do you feel about a waiting room full of weary, sour faces and tattered magazines? Many Americans are venturing down another path to wellness these days. Healing of the whole body — rather than an ache, or just one body part — is increasingly becoming an alternative or addition to established medical treatments. "Alternative" or "holistic medicine," practiced in a soothing aesthetic atmosphere, is becoming more and more widely accepted, even by the media.

Close-up

"Alternative Medicine: Not So Alternative Anymore" was the headline of a leading news magazine article. More than one-third of Americans now use alternative therapies such as chiropractic, acupuncture, and massage. For a number of years, the Asheville area has been drawing alternative healing practitioners to these mountains. The population has been receptive enough to create an abundance of newsletters, several weekly and monthly newspapers, magazines and web pages devoted to the subject, just in this area alone.

The mountains have drawn alternative healers and educators for many reasons — the air, the climate, the calming landscape, the natural beauty, community interest and even a spiritual calling. A shiatsu (pressure point) massage therapist originally from Mexico moved her practice from California to Asheville because she felt "drawn to the

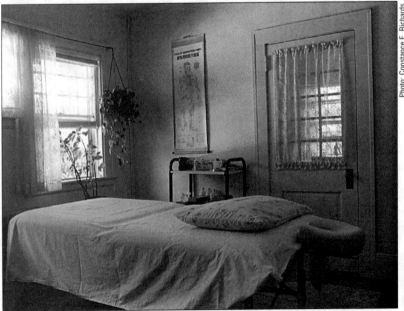

Photo: Constance E. Richards

Many alternative healing practices involve bodywork.

mountains like a magnet. There is an incredible power in these mountains, it is a wonderful place to practice," she says. Carolyn Ball, a psychotherapist and founder and president of The Center for Wholistic Health in Asheville, moved her lucrative 13-year-old business from Houston to Asheville. "I woke up one morning with the word 'Asheville' in my head," Ball says. "I had never been here, but something drew me to this place."

Nathan Boniske, a certified Rolfer (the practitioner of a form of deep-tissue manipulation that realigns the body and releases emotional and physical stress) moved his successful practice from New York's SoHo to his childhood home of Asheville. His practice takes up part of his own large Victorian house to the delight of clients.

"The conditions were excellent for coming here — people are open and receptive, and in need of alternative types of healthcare for physical and mental wellness," says Boniske.

Holistic medicine, another term that describes the art and science of healing through natural means, includes a wide range of methods for treating various ailments, or for simply making the body function better. Various forms of massage, Rolfing, acupuncture, chelation therapy, herbology, reflexology, aromatherapy, biofeedback, acupressure, hypnotherapy, ear coning and homeopathy are only a few of the therapies that make up the lingo of alternative medicine.

Many of the treatments are ancient in their histories, involving the use of plants and herbs to successfully combat ailments; others are newer derivations of old folk remedies. Rolfing, for example, is a relatively new discipline. It's the popular name for Structural Integration, developed by Dr. Ida Rolf in this century, based on the idea that human function is improved when segments of the body are properly aligned. Acupuncture, on the other hand, originated in China more than 5,000 years ago. The World Health Organization recognizes the use of acupuncture in the treatment of a wide range of medical problems, including digestive disorders, respiratory disorders, neurological and muscular disorders, urinary and muscular problems and PMS.

If you are interested in using alternative therapies but put off or confused by the holistic health jargon, consult the bible on the subject: *Alternative Medicine — The Definitive Guide.* It will familiarize you with various forms of holistic therapies. In your search for local practitioners and centers, pick up free locally published newspapers and newsletters in bookstores and cafes in Asheville for current articles and listings. Some of the most well-known are *The Re:Source, Spirit in the Smokies, New Frontier Magazine,* a national magazine which has relocated to Asheville, *Celestine Journal,* and the Web magazines *NC Natural* and *Asheville Holistic Alternatives. AHA* offers a complete listing of alternative healthcare centers and individual practitioners, as well as events and shopping opportunities for those interested in natural health. If you are an alternative practitioner, you can be listed for free. Another good resource is the *Serenity Press Guide to Cosmic Commerce in WNC,* a comprehensive guide to alternative healers and merchants in western North Carolina.

---

at home. The hospital also has birthing rooms and a large physical therapy department that's part of its cardiac rehabilitation and occupational health program for area industry. Blending faith and technology Park Ridge Hospital provides the highest quality healthcare.

# Polk County

## St. Luke's Hospital
**220 Hospital Dr., Columbus**
• **(828) 894-3311**

St. Luke's, founded in 1929, is a private,

nonprofit, 73-bed facility serving 34,000 patients annually from Polk, Spartanburg and Greenville Counties. It offers primary, emergency and outpatient services including a geriatric psychiatric unit, a Center of Behavioral Medicine for psychiatric outpatients, a restorative care unit, and ICU and a 24-hour, physician-staffed emergency department. St. Luke's also offers state-of-the-art diagnostics, including a new CT scanner, new GE mammography equipment, a new heart-monitoring system for both the ER and ICU, nuclear medicine and a new bone densitometer, among others. It also offers physical, occupational, respiratory and speech therapies.

St. Luke's staff specialties include general, orthopedic and pain-management surgery, ophthalmology, family practice, gerontology, internal medicine, pathology, psychiatry, urology and radiology.

## Transylvania County

### Transylvania Community Hospital
Hospital Dr., Brevard • (828) 884-9111

Transylvania Community Hospital is a 94-bed, not-for-profit community facility. The hospital, formed in 1933, is fully accredited and offers a wide range of services including preventative care, wellness programs, inpatient and outpatient medical/surgical services, a complete physical/occupational/speech therapy department, cardiac and pulmonary disease rehabilitation and follow-up care. Services include: Bridgeway, an inpatient and outpatient alcohol and substance abuse unit; Work Well, an occupational health program that helps injured workers get back to work; and the Living Well with Diabetes program, a comprehensive diabetes management and education service. The Wound Care, Ostomy and Continence department offers special are for patients with non-healing wounds or infections, temporary or permanent ostomies, or incontinence.

The medical staff at TCH includes specialists in emergency medicine, ENT, internal medicine, family practice, pediatrics, sports medicine, ophthalmology, oncology, orthopedics, radiology and urology, among others.

# Southern Mountains

## Cherokee County

### District Memorial Hospital
71 Whitaker Ln., Andrews
• (828) 321-1200

Nationally accredited by the Joint Commission on Accreditation of Healthcare Organizations, DMH is a state-licensed, 60-bed, acute-care facility located in the beautiful valley town of Andrews. Its growing medical staff of more than 20 physicians includes specialists in cardiology, critical care, emergency medicine, family practice, gastroenterology, general surgery, internal medicine, ophthalmology, orthopedics, pathology, pulmono-logy, radiology and urology.

District Memorial's 24-hour emergency department is complemented by its 24-hour laboratory, respiratory and x-ray services. It has a fully equipped intensive care unit and a growing surgical unit for both in-patient and outpatient procedures. DMH also has a Convalescent Unit and offers occupational physical and speech therapy.

### Murphy Medical Center
4130 U.S. 64 E., Murphy
• (828) 837-8161

Five miles from Murphy on the Hiwassee River, the Murphy Medical Center opened in 1979 and is one of the more modern facilities in the region. A full-service hospital with 50 beds and a 120-bed nursing home, MMC serves the residents of Cherokee, Clay and Graham counties and adjoining counties in Georgia and Tennessee with 24-hour emergency room and can respond to most medical needs.

It provides services in the fields of family practice, general surgery, internal medicine, orthopedics, pediatrics, radiology, ophthalmology, urology, obstetrics, gynecology and oncology. The hospital also provides a personal-response emergency system.

# Haywood County

## Haywood Regional Medical Center
### 262 Hospital Dr., Clyde
• (828) 456-7311, (800) 834-1729

Established in 1927, this is the largest hospital west of Asheville serving the westernmost counties as the provider of primary, acute hospital care and numerous medical specialty services.

The facility's expanding medical staff includes more than 65 physicians and medical professionals representing almost every medical specialty.

The modern 200-bed facility, built in 1979, is a full-service regional hospital utilizing the most advanced technology, equipment and staff to provide high-quality patient services. Available services include lithotripsy, cardiac care, a cancer center, reference laboratory, rehabilitation services, an osteoporosis center, a diabetes education center, occupational health services and a home-health/home-service center.

Recent additions involved the opening of a 20-bed restorative care center to provide transitional care to patients who require continued hospital care before returning home; a $3 million radiology renovation project, which included the highest level technology available in western North Carolina for CT scans, nuclear medicine and ultrasound; a Women's Care Center; a modern OB/GYN and wellness resource for families and women of all ages; and a new building housing the growing home-health services staff and expansion of the hospital's rehabilitation programs and services.

Key preventive programs and services include occupational medicine, mammography, an osteoporosis center, cardiac rehabilitation, a diabetes treatment center and numerous ongoing support groups.

## Home Care Services of Haywood Regional Medical Center
### 90 Hospital Dr., Clyde
• (828) 452-8292, (888) 456-0011

Now serving all the counties included in this book, Haywood County's Home Care Services' certified nursing assistants provide home care under the supervision of a registered nurse. CNAs perform personal care tasks such as bathing, essential housekeeping and home management, while a team of RNs and pharmacists provide infusion therapy, skilled nursing, rehabilitation services and medical social work.

Home Care Services also provides hospice services. Haywood Regional Medical Center also has designated beds for Hospice respite care and in-patient use. In addition, the organization offers many specialized services, including maternal/infant, psychiatric, respiratory, bereavement and Lifeline programs.

# Jackson County

## WestCare Health System
## Harris Regional Hospital
### 69 Hospital Rd., Sylva • (828) 586-7000
## Swain County Hospital
### 45 Plateau St., Bryson City
• (828) 488-2155

WestCare Health System was established in 1994 by Harris Regional Hospital to meet the expanding health needs of a growing Western North Carolina population and to enhance the delivery of healthcare in the region. Swain County Hospital and its affiliated services joined the System in 1997. WestCare Health System — through Harris Regional Hospital, Swain County Hospital and affiliated medical resources — offers clinical services, acute care inpatient serves, outpatient services, cardio-pulmonary services, emergency departments, an Urgent Care Center, emergency medical services, Home Health and Hospice, imaging services, laboratory services, a medical resource Center, nutrition services, wellness services, occupational health management, rehabilitation services, surgical services and women's and children's services. WestCare Health System and its affiliated hospitals and services and its associated medical staff are widely recognized as a provider of choice in the healthcare field.

# Macon County

## Angel Community Hospital
### Riverview St., Franklin • (828) 524-8411

The 25 doctors at this modern, multipurpose 59-bed facility specialize in allergies, orthopedics, family practice, internal medicine, pathology, emergency medicine, urology, ophthalmology, OB/GYN and pediatrics. Angel provides 24-hour emergency service and outpatient surgeries. The Home Health Agency is fully accredited, and the American College of Radiology certifies its mammography unit.

ACH also offers, among other services, physical therapy, diet/nutrition classes, MRI, CT scanning, nuclear medicine, speech therapy, pathology, chemotherapy, cardiopulmonary services, family services and an occupational health program for business and industry.

Two new services are the Urgent Care Center, (828) 524-9800, at the intersection of U.S. 23 and 441 that treats non-emergency medical problems and the 24-hour Angel Medical Answer Line, (828) 369-4455, which is staffed by nurses.

## Highlands-Cashiers Hospital
### Hospital Dr. and U.S. 64 E., Highlands
### • (828) 526-1200

A private, non-profit healthcare provider, Highlands-Cashiers Hospital has served the medical needs of the people of southern Macon and Jackson Counties and western Transylvania County for nearly half a century. A new 24-bed hospital and 80-bed nursing facility opened its doors in 1993. It offers a wide range of diagnostic services, state-of-the-art medical technology, and a board-certified medical staff of nearly 30 physicians, including specialists in cardiology, gastroenterology, general surgery, plastic and reconstructive surgery, urology, rheumatology, orthopedic surgery, ophthalmology, podiatry and pulmonary medicine. The hospital has a 24-hour emergency room and offers Saturday morning Urgent Care. It's affiliated with both Mission/St. Joseph's Health System in Asheville and Emory Healthcare System in Atlanta, Georgia.

The Fidelia Eckerd Nursing Center, a part of the hospital, offers long-term nursing care, respite care and assisted living.

## Macon County
## Public Health Center
### 189 Thomas Heights Rd., Franklin
### • (828) 349-2081

Opened in 1980, this health center offers a wide range of public health services, including family planning, prenatal, child and adult health screenings, orthopedic and hypertension services. The health center's laboratory offers support for the public health programs and may file forms for Medicare, Medicaid and some insurance companies. Routine vaccinations are given free; other services are also free or provided at low cost. While no appointments are necessary, Monday and Thursday are generally considered the center's walk-in days. The Macon County Public Health Center also holds clinics in Highlands and Nantahala on a regular schedule.

The center also provides environmental health services, such as water testing, issuing septic system permits and food and lodging inspections.

## General Emergency Numbers

All Emergencies, 911
Alcohol and Drug Abuse, (800) 234-0420, (800) 333-2294
Ask-A-Nurse, (800) 321-6877
Center for Missing Persons, (800) 522-5437
Domestic Violence / Sexual Abuse, (800) 268-1488
Highway Patrol, (800) 445-1772
Mental Health/ Suicide Prevention, (828) 264-4357
NC Wildlife Resources Commission, (800) 662-7137
Poison Control, (800) 542-4225
Runaway Hotline, (800) 621-4000
Teen Crisis Hotline, (800) 367-7287
Toxic Spills, (800) 424-8802

## Northern Mountains

### Alleghany County
EMS, (336) 372-5217
Police, (336) 372-4252

### Ashe County
EMS, (336) 246-2768
Police, (336) 246-9368

### Avery County
EMS, (828) 733-8287
Fire Marshall, (828) 733-8210
Police, (828) 898-4300, (828) 733-2023

### Madison County
EMS, 911

### Mitchell County
EMS, (828) 688-2014
Police, (828) 688-2113, (828) 765-2233

### Watauga County
EMS, (828) 264-9486
Fire, (828) 262-4516
Police, (828) 262-4500, (828) 295-5210

### Yancey County
EMS, (828) 682-2512
Fire, (828) 682-2414
Police, (828) 682-3260

## Central Mountains

### Buncombe
EMS, 911
Crime Stoppers, (828) 277-1000

— continued on next page

Police, (828) 252-1110
Rape Crisis Center, (828) 255-7576

## Henderson County
EMS, Fire, Police, Rescue Squad, Sheriff, 911
Ask-A-Nurse, (828) 697-2829
Domestic Violence (Mainstay), (828) 693-3840
Lifeline Emergency Response, (828) 692-1846
Mental Health, (828) 693-5741
Rape Crisis Program and Sexual Abuse (The Healing Place), (828) 692-3931

## Polk County
EMS, Fire, Police, Rescue Squad, Sheriff, 911
Crime Stoppers, (800) 847-7119
Domestic Violence and Sexual Abuse (Steps to Home, Inc.), (828) 894-2340
Mental Health, (828) 859-6661

## Transylvania County
EMS, Fire, Mental Health, Police, Rescue, Sheriff, 911
Domestic Violence (Safe), (828) 885-7233
Lifeline Response, (828) 883-5251
Mental Health (Trend), (828) 884-2027
Rape Crisis, (828) 883-2872

# Southern Mountains

## Cherokee County
EMS, Fire, Police, Rescue, Sheriff, 911
Domestic Violence/Rape/Sexual Abuse (REACH), (828) 837-8064

## Clay County
EMS, Fire, Police, Sheriff, Rescue, 911
Domestic Violence/Rape/Sexual Abuse (REACH), (828) 837-8064

## Graham County
EMS, Fire, Police, Rescue, Sheriff, 911
Domestic Violence/Rape/Sexual Abuse (Dept. of Social Services),
(828) 479-7911
Mental Health (Smoky Mountain Center), (828) 479-6466

## Haywood County
EMS, Fire, Police, Rescue, Sheriff, 911
Child Abuse and Neglect, (828) 452-6613
Crisis Counseling, (828) 454-6610
Mental Health (Smoky Mountain Center), (828) 524-8946

## Macon County
EMS, Police, Fire, Rescue, Sheriff, 911
Angel Medical AnswerLine, (828) 369-4455
Ask-A-Nurse, (828) 586-7675

**Jackson County**
EMS, Fire, Police, Rescue, Sheriff, 911
Domestic Violence/Rape/Sexual Abuse (REACH), (828) 586-8969
Mental Health (Smoky Mountain Center), (828) 586-4646

**Swain County**
EMS, (828) 488-6655
Fire, (828) 488-2621
Police, (828) 488-3650
Rescue Squad, (828) 488-2197
Sheriff, (828) 488-2194
Ask-A-Nurse, (828) 586-7675
Domestic Violence/Rape/Sexual Abuse (Swain-Qualla Safe), (828) 488-6809

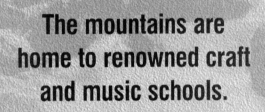

The mountains are home to renowned craft and music schools.

# Education

Formal education came to the mountains in 1793, only 10 years after the first settlers moved west of the Blue Ridge. Scotch-Irish Presbyterians established the first school here, an academy called Union Hill in what is now the city of Asheville. Only two years later the University of North Carolina, the oldest state university in the nation, opened its doors in Chapel Hill.

Today, the University of North Carolina, as well as a number of other colleges and prep schools, offer a wide range of educational and cultural options. They provide a wealth of affordable continuing-education courses that draw on the skills of the area's large number of talented retirees.

In addition, the mountains are home to renowned craft and music schools. Penland School of Crafts is the oldest and largest school for high-quality mixed-media arts and crafts in North America. For some 70 years the John C. Campbell Folk School has offered outstanding courses in traditional crafts, music and dance (see our Mountain Crafts chapter). At the Brevard Music Center, approximately 300 gifted students from across the nation have the opportunity to join teaching professionals and famous guests in the performance of 50 summer concerts (see our Arts and Culture chapter).

In-state tuition at most of the state institutions is considered reasonable, but costs are subject to increases as specified by state legislation.

As in other chapters, we have divided our discussion of education into three geographic regions. At the end of the chapter, we give a brief overview of public school systems in the North Carolina mountains.

## Northern Mountains

### Universities

#### Appalachian State University
**River St., Boone • (828) 262-2000**

From its beginnings as a teachers academy, Appalachian State University has grown into one of the top comprehensive universities in the South. Today, students major in a variety of fields, including graphic arts, business, exercise science, criminal justice and teacher education. University programs, such as Freshman Seminar, have received national recognition. Innovative partnerships with public schools, community colleges, business and industry, retirement centers and others provide students opportunities to translate classroom learning into real-world experience. Off-campus properties in Washington, D.C., and New York City provide opportunities for special learning experiences.

Appalachian offers approximately 100 undergraduate majors, more than 75 graduate majors and a doctorate in educational leadership. The university consistently has ranked among the top 15 comprehensive regional universities in the South since *U.S. News & World Report* began ranking colleges and universities in 1986.

Appalachian's enrollment is approximately 12,300 students, representing 89 of the state's 100 counties. Beautifully set in the rugged Watauga County mountains, Appalachian attracts students from the state's larger cities as well as its hometown of Boone.

Appalachian prides itself in creating the

# Macon County: Slick Rock

Slick Rock is a granite rock outcrop on an eastward facing slope, the summit of which offers an impressive view of far-off mountains. From Highlands, take Horse Cove Road to the end of the pavement, then take the right fork onto Bull Pen Road and drive about 1.5 miles. When you reach a sharp left curve, look for a pull-off and a steep, unmarked path on the right (if you pass a road that intersects Bull Pen on the right at a 45-degree angle, you've gone too far; turn around and go back). This timber-sale road runs right beneath Slick Rock. The hike to the top is less than a quarter-mile, and it's a great place to watch a sunrise.

right climate for undergraduate learning, bringing together the most advanced resources, a dedicated faculty and a comfortable living environment.

When it's time for a study break, students can take advantage of many cultural and recreational activities offered on campus and in Watauga County. The University's Performing Arts and Lecture Series, and An Appalachian Summer, its summer arts festival, bring world-class music, art, drama and speakers to Boone year round.

## Four-year Colleges

### Lees-McRae College
**375 College Dr., Banner Elk**
• **(828) 898-5241**

Lees-McRae College is a coeducational liberal arts institution that, at 4,000 feet above sea level, boasts the highest elevation of any college east of the Mississippi River.

This private college is affiliated with the Presbyterian Church (U.S.A.). Its beginnings go back to 1900 and the Rev. Edgar Tufts, who founded what was then a high school as an outgrowth of his ministry in the Appalachian Mountains. Elizabeth A. McRae was the teacher for the first class of 14 girls. In the ensuing years, the school grew, thanks in great measure to the generosity of the school's benefactor Mrs. S.P. Lees. The efforts of these two women were not forgotten when the school was chartered in 1907 as the Lees-McRae Institute. It was renamed Lees-McRae College in

1931 when it gained accreditation as a coeducational junior college.

The college attained senior college status in 1990. The attractive campus has 30 buildings, many built of native stone. There are 13 residence halls, two classroom buildings, an 89,000-volume library, auditorium, student center and physical education center. The 32-member faculty reflects a variety of religious, ethnic and national origins. Enrollment is 470, and the student-faculty ratio is 15 to 1. More than 90 percent of the students received financial aid in 1998. Scholarships are also available in academics, athletics and performing arts.

Lees-McRae offers both bachelor of arts and bachelor of science degrees as well as course work in a number of pre-professional areas. The school also maintains study-abroad and community service programs, as well as an honors curriculum.

This "campus in the clouds" has Beech Mountain at its front door and the fabled Grandfather Mountain at its back. The climate is cool in summer and frosty in winter, making it a popular choice for lovers of winter sports. The resort area of Boone is just 17 miles away, and the Appalachian Trail passes only a few miles from Banner Elk.

### Mars Hill College
**124 Cascade St., Mars Hill**
• **(828) 689-1201, (800) 543-1514**

Mars Hill College is tucked away on a ridge in rural Madison County, just over the mountain from Tennessee. This four-year, private coeducational college has the distinction of being the oldest educational institution in Western North Carolina. It was founded in 1856 as the French Broad Baptist Academy by a group of citizens descended from the original settlers of the area. The school was chartered officially as Mars Hill College in 1859 by the North Carolina General Assembly.

The Civil War brought hard times to the South, and Mars Hill College felt its share. Struggling with the deprivations of war, the college was able to stay in operation for the first two years of the war but was forced to close from 1863 to 1865. For much of its history, the school operated as an academy or boarding school, one that provided some college-level courses. In 1921, Mars Hill was reorganized as a junior college and became a pioneer in that field of education. This Baptist-affiliated college subsequently became a four-year institution, awarding the first baccalaureate degrees in May 1964.

The campus lies on 194 acres of rolling hills with a panoramic view of Mount Pisgah, Clingman's Peak and the Craggies. It's hard to tell where the campus ends and the town of Mars Hill begins, so closely are they linked in every way. The pace is a little slower here, more conducive to inspiration. (Only in the last 15 years was a second stoplight added to Main Street.) And when the need for city life arises, Asheville is just 18 miles south.

For all its bucolic charm, Mars Hill College is recognized today as educationally progressive in the fields of innovative curriculum development, continuing education, regional cultural studies, the arts and international education. The campus houses The Rural Life Museum, which facilitates the collection, preservation, exhibition and interpretation of rural life artifacts in the southern Appalachian region. The Southern Appalachia Center at Mars Hill College provides a structure through which the social and cultural preservation of the region is enhanced. The college maintains a significant number of regional collections, most notably the Bascom Lamar Lunsford

Folk Music Collection, a veritable treasure trove of memorabilia, sound recordings and other items pertaining to the "father" of mountain folk music. The arts hold a significant position at Mars Hill College.Started in 1976, the Southern Appalachian Repertory Theater, first operated as a vehicle for the college summer theater program, has evolved into a theater company of national renown, annually staging productions by new playwrights as well as old favorites.

With an enrollment of nearly 1,300 students, Mars Hill College offers a 13-to-1 student-teacher ratio. The college offers 31 majors in its curriculum but also provides students the opportunity to pursue specially designed courses of study, available through three interdisciplinary programs: communications, international studies and regional studies. The student-to-computer ratio is 6-to-1, which far exceeds the national average at colleges of 13-to-1. Approximately 50 international students come to the campus each year, and out-of-state students comprise 40 percent of the student body. Mars Hill's athletic program includes 13 NCAA Division II sports.

# Two-year Colleges

## Mayland Community College
**U.S. Hwy. 19E., Spruce Pine**
**• (828) 765-7351**

This small community college offers a unique family atmosphere in a natural mountain setting in the Blue Ridge Mountains on 41 acres just east of the town of Spruce Pine. Nearby is Mount Mitchell, the highest mountain east of the Mississippi; a little to the north is world-famous Grandfather Mountain. The Blue Ridge Parkway also winds its way through this scenic area.

The college, established in 1971, takes its name from the initials of the Tri-County area it serves: Mitchell, Avery and Yancey. With an enrollment of around 800, this coeducational institution can provide personal student-instructor interaction. Mayland is accredited by the Commission on Colleges of the Southern Association of Colleges and Schools to award the associate in arts degree, diplomas and certificates.

In addition to curriculum programs, Mayland also provides a wide variety of classes under the umbrella of continuing education. Included in this division are classes in occupational extension, community service, Small Business Center and Human Resources Development.

The Basic Skills Program offers adults opportunities to develop basic and computational skills necessary to function in employment in the community. Two outreach facilities, the Avery Learning Center in Newland and the Yancey Learning Center in Burnsville, complete the campus of Mayland Community College.

## Watauga Campus of Caldwell Community College and Technical Institute
**2887 U.S. Hwy. 421 N., Boone**
**• (828) 297-2185**

This satellite college of nearby Caldwell Community College and Technical Institute provides quality continuing education opportunities for residents of Watauga County. Both two-year degrees and one-year diploma programs are available. Occupational programs offer one or two years of training in vocational and technical subjects. College parallel programs provide freshman and sophomore courses for students who may wish to transfer to four-year institutions.

Established in 1973, the CCC&TI offers instruction leading to completion of certificates, diplomas, and degrees, as well as continuing education courses. A permanent Watauga Campus was established in 1998 with the addition of a 23,000 square foot instructional facility. In addition to this 39-acre site, classes are also taught at four other locations in the county. A range of training and degrees are offered, among others: Aviation Ground School, Emergency Medical Service Training, Fire/Rescue Training, Massage Therapy, Real Estate Training, and Accounting.

Grants, scholarships, loans, work-study programs and veterans' benefits are available.

# Central Mountains

## Universities

### The University of North Carolina Asheville
**1 University Heights, Asheville**
**• (828) 251-6600**

The University of North Carolina Asheville is the designated public liberal arts university of the 16-campus University of North Carolina system. The university sits on a wooded 265-acre site a mile north of downtown Asheville. UNCA opened in 1927 as Buncombe County Junior College, and through an ongoing community commitment, has evolved into a small, distinguished public liberal arts university.

Recently named a "best buy" by the Fiske Guide to Colleges, UNCA offers four-year undergraduate degree programs in the arts and humanities, the natural and social sciences and selected pre-professional and professional programs. UNCA also offers an undergraduate "2-plus-2" program in engineering with North Carolina State University in Raleigh. Undergraduates spend two years at UNCA and two years at NCSU. The Asheville Graduate Center offers graduate degree programs from N.C. State, UNC-Chapel Hill, UNC-Greensboro and Western Carolina University, as well as UNCA's Master of Liberal Arts program.

UNCA is the home of the North Carolina Center for Creative Retirement, including its College for Seniors, an additional avenue for continuing education.

The newly renovated D. Hiden Ramsay Library is the cultural and architectural heart of the campus. It houses nearly 318,000 volumes on open shelves, approximately 50,000 government documents and several hundred audio and video tapes. A computerized, one-day library network with sister universities extends the collection to more than a million volumes.

The arts figure prominently in UNCA campus life. The proximity of cosmopolitan Asheville is a definite influence, and the two frequently intertwine. Access to the university is a prime benefit to the citizens of Asheville.

The university's theater programs, concerts, dance performances, arts exhibits and lecture series enrich the community.

The colorful University Botanical Gardens lie adjacent to the campus and provide vast meadows for sunning and trails for walking. This 10-acre preserve, maintained by the non-profit Botanical Gardens at Asheville since 1960, features thousands of labeled plants native to southern Appalachia and small wildlife creatures that occasionally make an appearance. Lovingly landscaped paths wind around a flowing creek and over quaint bridges. Students often use the lush meadows as a prime sunning spot, and couples chat quietly in the romantic gazebos dotting the broad lawn. It's obvious why this is a popular spot for weddings. Volunteers staff a small gift shop.

Ongoing construction at UNCA provides for the growth of this increasingly popular campus. UNCA has about 3,100 students and an average class size of 21.

# Four-year Colleges

## Brevard College
**400 N. Broad St., Brevard**
• **(828) 884-8300, (800) 527-9090**

Brevard College offers an innovative, interdisciplinary course of study culminating in a four-year degree. Located on a beautiful mountain campus, the college has a faculty:student ratio of 8:1. Environmental studies, wilderness leadership and experiential education, ecology, music, art, theater and organizational studies (business) are just some of the majors offered here. A strong affiliation with the United Methodist Church dates back to 1853 when the college was established as the first Institution of higher learning in Western North Carolina. A small liberal arts residential college, Brevard has approximately 670 students representing 30 states and 15 foreign countries.

Long recognized for its outstanding tradition in music, the college now features the Paul Porter Center for Performing Arts with the acoustically impressive concert hall, Blackbox Theater and Institute of Sacred Music. Opened in the fall of 1998, the Porter Cen-

ter provides excellent venues for nationally known performers as well as BC's own student ensembles, choirs and thespians.

With numerous national championships from competition in the NJCAA, the colleges mail and female athletes now compete in the NAIA in such sports as soccer, baseball, softball, volleyball, cross country, track and field and more. Intramural sports are available and adventure-based sports such as kayaking, climbing, rappelling and mountain biking are offered through the college's wilderness leadership program. The college runs a variety of "immersion" educational experiences for academic credit, including the 1997 Voice of the Rivers Expedition – a 2,000-mile kayaking experience on the French Broad, Tennessee, Ohio and Mississippi rivers to the Gulf of Mexico, where participants have taught some 6,000 students along the way about environmental issues.

The philosophy of Brevard College is that service be a vital part of the classroom experience, so the Center for Service Learning coordinates service activities in the surrounding community. BC's summer program, Creekside, offers courses for college credit; professional workshops, athletic camps and Summer BrainStorm, a program for gifted high school students in the arts and environmental studies. Community education classes are provided throughout the summer and the rest of the year and are attended by more than 2,000 adult learners.

## Montreat College
**310 Gaither Cir., Montreat**
• **(828) 669-8011**

Seeming to emerge from the woods, Montreat College is a unique, four-year liberal arts college affiliated with the Presbyterian Church (U.S.A.). This lovely, small college has a 79-year heritage of quality education founded on Christian beliefs.

In 1916 the Montreat Normal School for women was founded. In 1934 during Dr. Robert C. Anderson's tenure as president, Montreat Normal School was renamed simply Montreat College. The college grew as its academic program expanded. It began a four-year degree program in 1945. After 14 years as a four-year women's college, the college was restructured in 1959 as a coeducational junior college and was given a new name, Montreat-Anderson College. In 1985 the college board of trustees realized the demands and changing circumstances in higher education and made the decision to again become a baccalaureate institution, re-creating the dream of Dr. Anderson. The recent name change back to Montreat College returns the 79-year-old school to its original vision and identity.

Students benefit from Montreat's small classes, and they grow through one-on-one interaction with professors and classmates. Studies challenge them to integrate faith and learning while considering subjects in ways never thought possible. Hands-on experiences in the majors (internships, field studies, mission programs, community service, and independent research) enable students to gain practical career and life preparation.

Montreat College is tucked within the wooded paradise of the community of Montreat, near Black Mountain, 15 miles east of Asheville. The campus follows a tree-lined valley, woven through with numerous streams. This beautiful campus features buildings constructed of native stone whose interiors are uniquely highlighted by wide use of flint, colorful mica, granite, sandstone and marble. The facilities of the Mountain Retreat Association and the Presbyterian Department of History are also in Montreat.

Montreat College offers majors in American studies, Bible and religion, business administration, English, environmental studies, history, human services, liberal arts, mathematics and outdoor education. A teaching certification program is available on the secondary school level. The college's School of Professional and Adults Studies offers associate's, bachelor's and master's degrees for working adults with campus facilities in Charlotte and Asheville.

A significant aspect of Montreat College is the fact that the college provides extensive financial aid to enable any qualified student to get a college education. More than 80 percent of the student body receives some form of financial aid through a variety of federal and state grants.

## Warren Wilson College
### 701 Warren Wilson College Rd., Swannanoa • (828) 298-3325

Warren Wilson College has always combined academic rewards with a strong work effort and service to the community. In 1894 the national Presbyterian Board of Missions started the Asheville Farm School to provide education for boys of the Appalachian mountain area. In the early 1940s, the college merged with the Dorland-Bell School for Girls in Hot Springs in Madison County. At that time, it became Warren Wilson High School, named in honor of a young sociologist who worked with the school through the auspices of the Presbyterian Church. The year 1942 saw the addition of a junior college division, and in 1966 Warren Wilson finally became a four-year, liberal arts college.

Of the school's 700 students, 25 percent come from North Carolina, 5 percent from outside the United States, and the remainder from 40 other states. The college is known for its unusual curriculum that combines in equal measure strong academics, work for the school and service to the community. Each student works 15 hours per week on one of 105 essential work crews. These crews range from plumbing and landscaping to farm labor and administrative support. Students also must perform a minimum of 100 hours of community service while they are enrolled. Students generate service projects to fill any needs they see. Projects are also offered through the campus center for service learning.

The 1,100-acre campus sits in the Blue Ridge Mountains just east of Asheville. The campus features a 300-acre working farm, an archeological site and 600 acres of forest. Dormitories built of native stone dot the intimate main campus, and 25 miles of hiking trails are available to students right on campus, along with a campus whitewater paddling location.

Ties to the land are evident in the fact that the most popular major at Warren Wilson is environmental studies. A highly touted, low-residency program awarding an M.F.A. in creative writing as well as a widely respected program in traditional Appalachian folk music are two additional facets of this creative school.

During the summer, the college sponsors several art and humanities events; two of the most popular are The Swannanoa Gathering, started in 1991, and The Swannanoa Chamber Festival, in institution since 1969. The Gathering is a series of week-long workshops and clinics in a festival atmosphere offering all kinds of folk music, such as Celtic, old-time, contemporary folk, blues and mountain dulcimer. The Chamber Festival features a resident woodwind quintet, a pianist and a guest string quartet. The players offer workshops for local school children and perform everything from world-premiere compositions to Russian folk songs to classical favorites.

# Two-year Colleges

## Asheville-Buncombe Technical Community College
**340 Victoria Dr., Asheville**
• **(828) 254-1921**

A member of the North Carolina Community College System, A-B Tech offers associate degrees, diplomas or certificates in 48 curriculum programs through four academic divisions: Allied Health and Public Service Education, Arts and Sciences, Business and Hospitality Education, and Engineering and Applied Technology. A fifth division, Continuing Education, offers opportunities for specific job training and retraining, basic skills education, and vocational courses for individual enrichment.

A-B Tech celebrates its 40th anniversary in 1999. Established September 1, 1959, the college was originally funded by a bond election and called the Asheville Industrial Education Center. Over the years, community support has helped A-B Tech grow and expand its services so that it currently enrolls approximately 20,000 curriculum and continuing education students annually.

The campus has undergone a metamorphosis over the years, acquiring land from surrounding parcels as they became available.

The main campus is made up of 144 acres off Victoria Road, and 22 buildings house academic programs and campus services. Included are three historic homes: Sunnicrest, one of George Vanderbilt's villas renovated to house the college's Business and Industry Services; the Smith-McDowell Museum, the oldest brick house in Buncombe County, which is leased to the Western North Carolina Historical Association; and Fernihurst, a circa-1875 mansion A-B Tech plans to renovate for its nationally-recognized culinary program. The college also operates a campus in Madison County that offers adult education and college credit courses.

## Blue Ridge Community College — Flat Rock Campus
**College Dr., Flat Rock**
• **(828) 692-3572**

BRCC was established in 1969 with campuses in both Henderson and Transylvania counties (see next entry). The college offers academic credit programs leading to associate degrees, vocational diplomas and vocational certificates as well as a college transfer program. It enrolls approximately 1,600 curriculum students and serves around 12,000 with both job-related and continuing education courses. In 1997, BRCC opened its Allied Health and Human Services Building. This 66,000-square-foot building houses the Associated Degree Nursing, Surgical Technology, Health Unit Coordinator, Certified Nursing Assistant, Emergency Medical Technician, Cosmetology and Early Childhood Development Center. The Office for Student Services anchors the building.

The college works closely with area businesses to develop special programs needed by new industries, and its Small Business Center holds workshops, seminars and classes to aid new and existing businesses and professions.

The college also provides the community with various cultural programs. One of the most popular is the Blue Ridge Concert Series, which brings outstanding artists to the college at affordable prices. For more information on these events, see our Arts and Culture chapter.

## Blue Ridge Community College — Brevard Campus
**Asheville Hwy. and Osburn Rd., Brevard**
**• (828) 883-2520**

In the fall of 1997, BRCC in Transylvania County moved to its new, conveniently located campus on the north side of Brevard. The building, which once housed an elementary school, was renovated to become the college's Transylvania Center and include a student center, a science lab and computer labs. The space also houses an adult high school program, an industrial maintenance program and classrooms for curricula programs and continuing education classes. Information Systems replaces the Computer Operations program with not only a new title but also with Internet, networking and system-management courses. Carpentry has added a planning and estimating course and an OSHA safety certification course. Also, a six-month Paramedic continuing education class is offered in cooperation with Transylvania Emergency Service. Other continuing education courses are the popular nursing assistant course and law enforcement training updates.

Regular curricula programs include business administration, health unit coordinator, horticulture, office systems technology and college transfer. In addition, the college offers all prerequisites for any BRCC program, including the Associate Degree Nursing program.

## Cecils College
**1567 Patton Ave., Asheville**
**• (828) 252-2486**

Until moving to an eight-acre site west of the city in 1977, Cecils College had been a landmark in downtown Asheville. Founded in 1905 by Robert Talmadge Cecil, the college was well-known as a business school, primarily providing secretarial training. Mr. Cecil owned the college until his death in 1956. Through the years, Cecils College was owned by a succession of out-of-state corporations operating similar small business colleges elsewhere. In 1972, Cecils College finally returned

to ownership by a North Carolina-based, family-owned corporation, Executive Schools Inc. On November 1, 1998, the college was acquired by a family member who formed a new ownership corporation, South College of North Carolina.

The college is accredited as a junior college by the Accrediting Council for Independent Colleges and Schools and is licensed by the Board of Governors of the University System of North Carolina to confer the degree of applied science. The associate of applied science degree is awarded to Cecils graduates in the areas of business administration, computer information systems, medical assisting, office administration, accounting, and paralegal studies.

## Isothermal Community College
**902 U.S. Hwy. 108 W., Columbus**
**• (828) 894-3092**

This two-year institution, chartered in 1964 to serve the people of Polk and Rutherford counties, offers associate of arts and associate of science degrees in 22 areas of study transferable to four-year colleges and universities. It also serves its communities with technical, vocational and continuing educational programs, and its libraries are open to the public.

The main 132-acre campus, which serves almost 58,000 students, is at Spindale in Rutherford County. It is outside the geographic scope of this book, but our coverage does include the 11-acre Polk County satellite campus, located on property adjacent to St. Luke's Hospital in Columbus, that serves some 1,500 students. It offers curriculum classes in business administration, administrative office technology, computers and liberal arts. There is also a wide range of continuing education classes, which include training for nurse aides, emergency medical technicians, and fire and rescue personnel. Lifelong learning enrichment courses include art, piano, jazz, languages, genealogy, Appalachian/North Carolina history and folklore, other history-related subjects, investing, fitness, classic films and English as a second language classes. The College also sponsors periodic special events for the community.

# The Legend of Standing Indian Mountain

Many years ago, say the Cherokee, a great winged monster swooped down and carried off a child playing near the village and took him to a cave high in the cliffs of a nearby mountain. Frightened people from all around came together and prayed to the Great Spirit for help in getting rid of the huge beast. After days and nights of prayer, a dazzling lightning bolt and a booming thunderclap came out of a clear sky and shattered the mountain, killing the creature and its offspring.

The lightning was so powerful, though, that it destroyed all the trees on the mountain's summit, producing the "bald" top that it has to this day. It also turned a warrior, who was posted on the mountain to keep an eye on the beast, to stone. Some said it was his punishment for being a poor sentry. Over the hundreds of years since this event occurred, this "standing Indian" has been worn away to a pillar of stone with an ill-defined head on top. In fact, you may even have some trouble distinguishing the stone pillar from the jumble of rock that surrounds it, but you will be able to see the cliffs that were torn asunder by the Great Spirit's lightning bolt.

---

# Southern Mountains

## Universities

### Western Carolina University
**NC Hwy. 107, Cullowhee**
• **(828) 227-7317, (800) 928-2369**

Founded by Professor Robert Lee Madison in 1889 as a semipublic community school to train teachers, Western Carolina University has grown and evolved over the years to become one of the most technologically advanced campuses in the country. The approximately 6,500 students that make up Western's student body hail from North Carolina's mountains and from other regions of the state, the country and the world.

Undergraduate students may choose from more than 80 majors in one of the four colleges: applied sciences, arts and sciences, business, and education and allied professions. Students interested in careers in engineering, law, medicine, dentistry, optometry, veterinary medicine and pharmacy may enroll in pre-professional programs. The graduate school offers more than 50 programs leading to a master's degree, educational specialist degree and the doctor of education degree.

A faculty of 330 leads WCU's rigorous academic program. Classes are small enough that individual effort can be recognized and encouraged. The residential Honors College offers a rare learning environment for gifted students.

Numerous service and research centers at WCU serve Western North Carolina, including the Mountain Resource Center, Highlands Biological Station and the Mountain Aquaculture Research Center. Western's centers in Asheville and Cherokee extend graduate and undergraduate programs to the region.

In the fall of 1998, Western Carolina became one of just 12 public universities nationwide and the first in The University of North Carolina system to require freshmen to come to campus with personal computers. Two computer ports in each residence hall room make it possible for students to connect to the Internet and university computer network from the comfort of their rooms. The use of nine multimedia electronic classrooms puts WCU at the national forefront in the use of educational technology, leading Cullowhee to be called the "most wired" small town in North Carolina.

Western's 230-acre main campus in Cullowhee sits in a beautiful valley between the Blue Ridge and Smoky mountain ranges, with world-class outdoor recreation opportunities just minutes away. The 8,000-seat Liston B. Ramsey Regional Activity Center regularly hosts national-caliber sports and entertainment events. The university's Lectures, Concerts and Exhibitions Series brings music, dance and theatrical productions to campus each year. WCU's own department of communication and theatre arts stages its own high-quality plays, and Western's galleries maintain a regular schedule of art exhibitions.

Western's Mountain Heritage Center depicts the natural and cultural heritage of the southern Appalachian region through exhibitions, publications, educational programs and demonstrations. Mountain Heritage Day, WCU's annual celebration of the mountain spirit, draws more than 30,000 visitors to the campus on the last Saturday each September. See our Festivals and Annual Events chapter for more information.

The university's Division of Continuing Education and Summer School offers an Elderhostel program for people 55 and over. Elderhostel participants take part in a variety of extracurricular activities while they are engaged in exciting and challenging courses. On-campus groups are housed at Madison Hall, a historic building that's been renovated to create a comfortable and convenient meeting facility. WCU also offers Elderhostel programs throughout the year at a number of off-campus locations, including the Waynesville Country Club Inn, Balsam Mountain Inn and the Nantahala Village Resort and Inn.

WCU's Listener Program opens the classrooms of Western Carolina University to the people of the region. Individuals not currently enrolled in a college have an opportunity to sit in on designated undergraduate classes and sample many subjects from accounting to zoology.

## Two-year Colleges

### Haywood Community College
**185 Freelander Dr., Clyde**
**• (828) 627-4500**

Haywood's facilities are impressive. The 83-acre campus features a student center with a 1,100-seat auditorium and the Regional High Technology Center — one of only two in the state. The Learning Resource Center houses more than 25,000 books, 167 serial subscrip-

Photo: Judy Scharns, Courtesy of Boone Convention and Visitors Bureau

Winter's favorite pair — a child and a sled.

tions and 38,000 microfiche, and offers video and audiotaping services. Computerized searches of indexes and abstracts are available, as well as an online interlibrary loan service. The beautiful campus also includes a horticulture complex with greenhouses, a dwarf conifer garden, a millhouse with a fishpond, a rhododendron garden, an extensive arboretum, a commercial sawmill and dry kiln and a 320-acre teaching forest.

Programs take from one semester to two years to complete and lead to a certificate, diploma or an associate degree in such fields as business administration, engineering technologies, natural resources, human services and professional crafts. (See our Mountain Crafts chapter for more on the crafts program.) Students also learn skilled trades like welding, plumbing and electrical installation.

Continuing education programs include GED certification, business and industry training courses, crafts and emergency medical training. The college also offers small business and occupational training courses.

## Southwestern Community College
### 477 College Dr., Sylva • (828) 586-4091

Established in 1964 to serve Swain, Jackson and Macon counties and the Cherokee Indian Reservation, SCC combines a strong vocational-technical program with general education. Its student body of 1,700 attends classes both on its main 57-acre campus between Webster and Sylva on N.C. Highway 116 and at centers in Bryson City, Cashiers, Cherokee and Franklin.

The programs, courses and activities, given both in day and evening classes, prepare students for the workforce by helping them qualify for jobs in new or existing industries and by providing specific skills training. There are also courses leading to the college's degree programs and transfer courses as well as GED and continuing education classes in such subjects such as basic investment, weaving, computers, CPR certification, law enforcement, fire-and-rescue training and a National Park Service program. In 1999, SCC added programs in speech and language, pathology assistant and environmental science technology.

## Tri-County Community College
### 2300 U.S. Hwy. 64 E., Murphy
• (828) 837-6810

This Murphy-based college was originally an extension of the Asheville-Buncombe Technical College, but in 1967 it became an individual unit called the Tri-County Industrial Educational Center. When the state approved its college-transfer program in 1978, its status was upgraded to the Tri-County Community College.

The college serves students primarily from Cherokee, Clay and Graham counties at its two campuses in the Peachtree community of Cherokee County and in Robbinsville. It offers college-transfer and technical and vocational programs, including certificates in real-estate appraisal and horticulture, diplomas in cosmetology and welding and associate in applied science degrees in accounting and nursing. The continuing education department offers basic skills programs, occupational extension courses, firefighter training and community service classes including cooking classes, craft and painting courses and many others. A small-business center has opened at the college to help increase the success rate and number of small business in the area. Many services and seminars are offered here at little or no cost.

The newest addition to TCCC's Peachtree campus is a childcare center that offers a model daycare program care for 45 children.

# Preparatory Schools

## The Asheville School
### 360 Asheville School Rd., Asheville
• (828) 254-6345

Set on a commanding hill sheltered by woods, The Asheville School is the personification of tradition. This venerable preparatory school was founded in 1900 on the western edge of Asheville. The campus is dotted with majestic trees and graced with architecture from another era, each building having a distinct history. Stately, rambling structures, known in the early days simply as the "House" and the "School," were the heart of the campus, providing basic student housing and classroom instruction. Anthony Lord, an Asheville native and noted architect, designed three of the most beautiful structures on the campus: the Crawford Music House and the Howard Bement House in 1937 and Memorial Hall in 1947. The newest additions to Asheville School architecture in the '80s and '90s maintain the artistic integrity of existing structures. The school was named to the National Register of Historic Places in 1996.

The rich heritage of this traditionally male boarding school has seen a number of additions brought on by a changing society. The Asheville School is now coeducational, with 200 students, 60 percent male and 40 percent female. Seventeen states and 13 foreign countries are represented.

One thing that has never changed through the years is the commitment to a rigorous academic program designed to foster excellence. The overall student-faculty ratio is 4-to-1, and the average class has 11 students. Study is closely supervised, each day's schedule strictly guided. A full range of advanced-placement courses are offered for college credit. Graduating seniors of the Asheville School are routinely accepted into outstanding colleges and universities, both in this country and abroad, including Brown, Columbia, Duke, Harvard Oxford, and Stanford.

Extracurricular activities are encouraged and include clubs, publications, philanthropic organizations, chamber choir and dramatic society. The mountaineering program is a special feature of the Asheville School. Designed to build teamwork and group communication skills, a new Alpine tower and ropes course on campus enable students to learn the fundamentals of climbing, belaying and rappelling before heading to the mountains surrounding the school. A strong Equestrian Program has also recently been included.

The school is celebrating its centennial in 2000. The celebrations will begin in September 1999 and continue through September 2000.

## Christ School
### 500 Christ School Rd., Arden
• (828) 684-6232

This Episcopal prep school for boys in grades 8 through 12 is 9 miles south of Asheville, 12 miles north of Hendersonville and 20 miles northeast of Brevard. There are 160 boarding students from 15 states and eight foreign countries. With 18 of the 30 faculty members living on campus, Christ School offers a true sense of community.

The school prides itself in the statement that "teachers at Christ School are instructors, advisors, coaches, mentors and friends." The core campus and faculty homes make up a small part of the beautifully landscaped, 500-acre wooded campus. Chapel bells ring out daily, reminders of the school's strong emphasis on spiritual growth. The extensive campus acreage encourages a variety of team sports and outdoor activities, including cross country, soccer and football. Weekend trips to the surrounding mountains include Outward Bound-style rock climbing, backpacking, kayaking, rafting and mountain biking as part of the regular outdoor program.

The school work program involves every student and fosters a sense of contributing to the community. Each student is responsible for maintaining upkeep of his personal dorm room, for performing a daily 20-minute task and for joining in the regular Friday total campus cleanup.

The academic program at Christ School is designed to prepare boys for rigorous college programs. Advanced placement courses are offered in a comprehensive range of subjects. The learning resource program offers academic support in English, math and study skills within the context of a rigorous college preparatory curriculum. The newly expanded library is completely automated and connected to the North Carolina Information Network, which also connects the school to DIALOG with access to major university libraries such as the UNC-Chapel Hill and North Carolina State University. Christ School graduates are accepted by some of the finest colleges and universities in the nation, including Duke, Sewanee, University of North Carolina-Chapel Hill, Dartmouth and Williams.

## Carolina Day School
### 1345 Hendersonville Rd., Asheville
• (828) 274-0757

Carolina Day School, on 28 acres just 15 minutes south of Asheville, is a nonsectarian, coeducational, independent school with approximately 500 students, ranging from pre-kindergarten to grade 12. The present school, formed by the merger in 1987 of Asheville Country Day School (founded in 1936) and St. Genevieve/Gibbons Hall (founded in 1905) carries on traditions of both schools.

A rigorous academic discipline is carried throughout all grades and subject areas at Carolina Day. The pre-kindergarten and kindergarten groups are exposed early to literature, number concepts, hands-on science and computers as well as vital social skills. Grades 1 through 5 build on this foundation, with emphasis on reading, writing and mathematics. Social studies, science, Spanish and the arts enrich the lower school experience and prepare students for the middle grades. In the middle school (grades 6 to 8) students are encouraged to become both autonomous learners and contributing members of a group. Academic expectations increase and students take part in sports, modern languages, the arts and projects using multimedia technology. The upper school offers advanced-placement college-level courses, access to information technology and additional options for fine and performing arts. Carolina Day School graduates are accepted in many of the country's most competitive colleges and universities.

# Public Schools

To register a child for school in North Carolina, a parent or legal guardian must present the child's birth certificate, up-to-date immunization record and previous report cards, if the child was enrolled in another school system.

Western North Carolina public schooling ranges from larger urban schools to small country schoolhouses. Outside of Buncombe County however, the schools tend to be smaller, and obviously, more rural. Classes are usually small — 20 students being the average. Each system offers advanced placement courses, honors programs and classes for the academically gifted. County and city schools are fully accredited by the state of North Carolina and the Southern Association of Colleges and Schools.

The Buncombe County school system also operates an alternative program for students in grades 7 through 12 who have been identified as "at risk," keeping them in school and focused on life beyond graduation. The county system operates the Progressive Education Program, which offers special education curricula for students. The Career Education Center is an extension of the high school curriculum, offering classes beyond those offered in the "home" schools, like cosmetology, electronics, graphic communications, masonry and welding. The city school system operates the Accelerated Learning Center for middle grade students. Here, a low pupil-teacher ratio (10-to-1) and emphasis on parent involvement encourage students to reach their maximum academic potential. Most schools offer after-school child care, and all elementary schools in the Asheville City school system offer after-school care.

The schools in the smaller communities, especially, are highly supported by the community. The schools in Blowing Rock, for example, maintain a community-sponsored web page, newsletter, and programs involving the community in the life of the school and the children.

For more detailed information on the school of your interest, contact the information offices of your school system at the numbers we have provided.

The following are brief descriptions of school systems in the North Carolina mountains, divided regionally. Enrollment figures are based on the 1997-98 school year.

# Northern Mountains

## Alleghany County School System
**1 Peachtree St., Sparta • (336) 372-4345**
There were 1,443 students enrolled in Alleghany County's one high school and three elementary schools serving kindergarten through 8th grade.

## Ashe County Public School System
**320 South St., Jefferson**
**• (336) 246-7175**
There are three high schools, four elementary schools and a career center for remedial

and at-risk students, adding up to a school population of 3,347.

## Avery County School System
**775 Cranberry St., Newland**
**• (336) 733-6006**

The 2,343 students in Avery County are divided among one high school, one middle school and seven elementary schools.

## Madison County School System
**2 Blannahassett Island Rd., Marshall**
**• (828) 649-9276**

One high school, one middle school and six elementary schools serve the needs of the 2,453 students in this county. As with most counties in North Carolina, Madison has an exceptional-children's program and other special-needs services. An elementary school is on an island in the French Broad River, along with the school system's administrative offices.

## Mitchell County School System
**115 School Rd., Bakersville**
**•(828) 688-4432**

There are 2,280 students in this county. Mitchell has one high school for grades 9 through 12, two middle schools and five elementary schools.

## Watauga County School System
**175 Pioneer Trail, Boone**
**• (828) 264-7190**

A student population of 4,753 is spread among the one high school and eight elementary schools.

## Yancey County School System
**100 School Cir., Burnsville**
**• (828) 682-6101**

A high school, two middle schools and six elementary schools bring the total enrollment to 2,372 students.

# Central Mountains

## Asheville City School System
**16 S. Biltmore Ave. • (828) 255-5304**

For its student population of 4,414, the city has a system of 10 schools, including one high school, one middle school, six elementary schools, one preschool and the Accelerated Learning Center. An innovative dropout prevention program, the Accelerated Learning Center, was established to assist students with their school work and return to the regular classroom if they fall behind due to absences, disciplinary action or other reasons.

## Buncombe County Public Schools
**175 Bingham Rd. • (828) 255-5925**

Buncombe County has by far the largest concentration of students, 23,343, in the North Carolina mountains. The system supports six high schools, six middle schools, 20 elementary schools and the Buncombe Community School (for at-risk students). In addition, there are special programs in place at Roberson High School, Valley Springs Middle School (which added a wing to serve physically and mentally handicapped students) and Estes Elementary School to meet the needs of the county's 431 handicapped students. The Career Education Center provides students special vocational courses such as cosmetology, graphic arts and computers, which are not offered at their individual high schools.

## Henderson County Public Schools
**414 Fourth Ave. W., Hendersonville**
**• (828) 697-4733**

The Henderson County Public School System, with a student population of 11,000, is a K-12, 20-school district with four high, four middle and 11 elementary schools plus one alternative school, which serves middle and

---

**INSIDERS' TIP**

**Mountain children keep an eye on the sky in winter. It doesn't take much snow to keep school buses from running on icy mountain roads and for the schools to close down for a "snow day." Of course, children pay for too many snow-day holidays with an extended school year.**

Grandfather Mountain affords vistas of neighboring peaks.

high school students. A new elementary school is under construction and is expected to open in the summer of 1999.

This school system has an impressive history of academic excellence. Six of its schools were recently named Schools of Distinction by the North Carolina Department of Public Instruction for academic growth in 1997-98; while 17 of its schools attained Exemplary Growth status due to achievement in the state testing program. The class of 1998 averaged 1019 on the SAT, two points above the National average and 37 points above the state average.

Henderson County Public Schools are strongly supported by the community at large. The business community offers financial support, scholarship opportunities and JobReady programs. Over 1,400 adult volunteers serve students regularly.

## Polk County School System
**202 E. Mills St., Columbus**
**• (828) 894-3051**

Polk County's six schools serve 2,380 students and employ 180 teachers; more than half of the teachers hold advanced degrees. The high school, completed in 1992, boasts a 750-seat theater, modern athletic complex, up-to-the-minute science labs and vocational department, and a high-tech media center. Since 1994 the system has invested more than $1 million in technology: each school has a computer lab staffed by a technology specialist; all schools are connected to the state computer network; every 9th grade English student gets a laptop computer. Eighty percent of the 1998 graduates are pursuing advanced degrees: 103 seniors earned $495,361 in scholarships and awards. Polk County High was rated 5th highest statewide in academic growth during 1998; Tryon Elementary made the "Top 25" as a "School of Excellence," with 90 percent of students performing at or above grade level. Saluda is an "A-Plus" school where the arts are integrated throughout the curriculum. Based on 1998 end-of-grade/end-of-course test scores, all six Polk County schools were rated "Exemplary" by the State Board of Education.

## Transylvania County School System
**400 Rosenwald Ln., Brevard**
**• (828) 884-6173**

Transylvania's system is made up of a high school, middle school and elementary school in Brevard; elementary schools in Pisgah Forest, Rosman and Lake Toxaway; and another high school and middle school in Rosman. The schools employ around 550 people and serve just under 3,900 students. The county is currently engaged in a $26 million building upgrade and expansion program. It has also added an alternative school, Davidson River School, for middle and high school students with placement by referral only. The Transylvania school system consistently scores among the top systems in the state on all North Carolina tests.

# Southern Mountains

## Cherokee County School System
**100 Hickory St., Murphy**
**• (828) 837-2722**

The Cherokee County system is composed of 12 schools: three high schools, two independent middle schools, three middle schools connected to elementary schools, six elementary schools and one alternative school. They serve almost 3,500 students. There are also pre-kindergarten programs available at all the elementary schools.

## Clay County School System
**Yellow Jacket Dr., Hayesville**
**• (828) 839-8513**

Clay County has three schools—one each to serve elementary, middle and high school students—all on one campus. All have been built in the past few years. Total enrollment is around 1,250, and there are over 150 school employees. The system is one of only four in the state that had all their schools classified as exemplary, with students exceeding state expections in all areas of achievement and performance. It has also posted the lowest dropout rate in the state. Both elementary and middle schools have consistently been ranked in the top 10 in physical education.

## Graham County School System
**Main St., Robbinsville • (828) 479-3413**

All three of Graham County's schools are in Robbinsville. Enrollment in the elementary, middle and high schools totals just more than 1,250 students. There are approximately 225 employees, of whom 108 are teachers.

## Haywood County School System
**1615 N. Main St., Waynesville**
**• (828) 456-2400**

This system serves more than 7,000 students in 10 elementary schools, three middle schools and two high schools. It employs a staff of 1,049, including 525 teachers and 142 teaching assistants. The students habitually exceed the state and national norms. In addition to traditional core requirements, students are exposed to art, music, physical education, media, computer technology and a second language beginning in kindergarten.

## Jackson County School System
**398 Hospital Rd., Sylva • (828) 586-2311**

The county has four elementary schools, one combined school (kindergarten through 12th grade) and one high school. Total enrollment is approximately 3,540 students. The system has around 450 full-time employees, including 254 teachers. More than 50 percent of the teachers hold graduate certificates. In 1997 Jackson County Schools were third in the state for SAT scores and were one of eight North Carolina systems to score above the national average.

## Macon County School System
**1202 Old Murphy Rd., Franklin**
**• (828) 524-4414, (828) 524-3314**

The school system encompasses seven elementary schools, one middle school and one high school in the Franklin area and two schools for kindergarten through 12th grade in Nantahala and Highlands. The schools teach a total of 3,953 students.

## Swain County School System
### 280 School Dr., Bryson City
### • (828) 488-3129

This system consists of two elementary schools, a middle school and a high school and serves around 1,600 students. The schools employ 247 people, including 143 teachers. Its elementary students are consistently among the leaders in the region and the state on the "end of grade test" scores in reading and math and has received a "Governor's Award for Excellence in Education" for two of the past three years. Seventy-three percent of Swain County's high school students enter two- and four-year colleges and 31 percent of graduating seniors receive a scholarship. The average class size in the high school is 12.7.

# Index of Advertisers

| | |
|---|---|
| 23 Page Restaurant | 57 |
| A Bed of Roses | 117 |
| Alpen Acres Motel | Insert |
| Alpine Village | 153 |
| Applachian Realty Associates | 497 |
| Applachian State University | 435 |
| Apple Inn | 125 |
| Ashe High Country Realty | 489 |
| Asheville Community Theater | 443 |
| Asheville Symphony | 443 |
| The Baird House | Insert |
| The Banner Elk Inn | Insert |
| Barbara's Antiques | 196 |
| Biltmore Estate | 407 |
| Biltmore Village | 193 |
| The Black Mountain Inn | 115 |
| Blake House Inn | 117 |
| Blowing Rock Realty | Insert |
| Blowing Rock Stables | Insert |
| Blowing Rock Stage Company | Insert |
| Blue Ridge Rentals | Insert |
| The Book Store | 196 |
| Brookside Inn | Insert |
| Cabin Fever | Insert |
| Carolina Mountain Artists | 196 |
| The Castle Hotel | Insert |
| Chetola Resort | Insert |
| The Claddagh Inn | 125 |
| The Cottage Gate | 185 |
| The Goldsmith by Rudi, Ltd. | 197 |
| Dancing Bear Toys, Ltd. | 196 |
| Deer Brook Inn | Inside front cover |
| Dereka's Sugar Mountain Accomodations | Inside front cover |
| DeWoolfson Down | Insert |
| Diamond Brand Camping Center | 247 |
| Echo Mountain Inn | 125 |
| ERA Resort Real Estate and Rentals | Inside front cover |
| Eseeola Lodge | Inside front cover |
| Fall Creek Cabins | Insert |

Fleetwood Falls Resort ............................................................................ Insert
Flintlock Family Campground .................................................................. Insert
Gatekeepers ................................................................................................. 196
Gideon Ridge Inn ....................................................................................... Insert
Grandview Lodge ......................................................................................... 137
Grandfather Mountain Resorts ............................................. Inside front cover
Grovewood Gallery ..................................................................................... Insert
Haywood Park Hotel .................................................................................... 161
Hemlock Inn .................................................................................................. 145
Herren House ................................................................................................ 137
High Country Inn ........................................................................................ Insert
High Country Realty .............................................................. Inside front cover
The Highlands at Sugar ......................................................... Inside front cover
Hillwinds Inn ............................................................................................. Insert
Historic Hendersonville and Flat Rock Area .............................................. 195
Holiday Inn Sunspree Resort ..................................................................... 159
Humpback Hollow ................................................................. Inside front cover
Incredible Toy Company ............................................................................ Insert
The Inn Around the Corner .......................................................................... 115
Inn on Main Street ....................................................................................... 117
The Inn on Mill Creek ................................................................................. 115
Jefferson Landing ..................................................................................... Insert
Kenmure Enterprises, Inc. .......................................................................... 499
Kress Emporium ....................................................................................... Insert
Liberty Bicycles ........................................................................................... 263
Linville Cottage Bed and Breakfast ....................................... Inside front cover
Linville Ridge Country Club .................................................. Inside front cover
Mast General Store ...................................................................................... 179
Maple Lodge Bed and Breakfast ................................................................ 111
Mehri and Co. of N.Y., Inc. ......................................................................... 197
The Monte Vista Hotel ................................................................................. 119
Mountain Creek Bed and Breakfast ........................................................... 137
Mountain Home Bed and Breakfast ........................................................... 125
Mountain Lore Books ................................................................................... 197
Mountain Retreats Realty ....................................................... Inside front cover
Mountain Spring Cabins and Chalets ........................................................ 163
The New French Bar ...................................................................................... 57
Old World Galleries .................................................................................... Insert
The Paintin' Shed ......................................................................................... 196
Paramount Realty Company .................................................. Inside front cover
Parkview Lodge ...................................................................... Inside front cover
Peacock Ridge Cabins .............................................................................. Insert
Pixie Inn and Tartan Restaurant ............................................ Inside front cover
Purple Sage ................................................................................................. 197
Radisson Hotel Asheville ............................................................................ 148
Recreation Park ........................................................................................... 313
Rocksberry Inn Bed and Breakfast .......................................................... Insert
The Red Rocker Inn ..................................................................................... 115
Renee Allen House Bed and Breakfast ...................................................... 115
Rustic Barn ............................................................................................... Insert
Serves You Right ...................................................................................... Insert
Shadylawn Motel and Restaurant .......................................... Inside front cover

South Marke on Main Street ............................................................................ Insert
Sourwood Inn ............................................................................................ 117
Sugar Mountain Resort Accomodations ............................................... Inside front cover
Sugar Ski and Country Club ................................................................. Inside front cover
Sugar Top Resort Reservation Service ................................................. Inside front cover
Sycamores .............................................................................................. 117
Tanger Outlet Center ................................................................................ Insert
The Swag ................................................................................................ 137
T.S. Morrison .......................................................................................... 191
Ten Oaks Bed and Breakfast .................................................................. 137
Thurston Associates ............................................................................... 495
Times Square Inn and Restaurant ........................................... Inside front cover
Tree Haven Bed and Breakfast .............................................................. 115
Tuft's House Inn ..................................................................... Inside front cover
The Waverly Inn ...................................................................................... 125
Westglow Spa .......................................................................................... Insert
Wickwire Fine Art/Folk Art ....................................................................... 197
The Woodlands Barbeque Pickin' Parlor ................................................. Insert
Works of Wood – Destination Pointe Apartments ................................. Inside front cover
The Yellow House .................................................................................... 137
Yonahlossee Resort and Club ................................................................ Insert

# Index

**A**

Abrams Creek campground 248
Accent on Books 205
Ad-Lib 178, 186
Advanced Realty Inc. 493
Air Bellows Gap 366–367
airports 33–35
Alarka Community Park 232
Alibi's 76
Alleghany Council for Aging Inc. 508
Alleghany County
    arts councils and organizations 412
    bed and breakfasts and country inns
        101–103
    golf 273
    healthcare 525–526
    motels and hotels 149–150
    nightlife 74
    overview of 5–6
    parks 223–224
    public schools 557
    real estate 486–487
    restaurants 44–45
    retirement and senior services 508–509
Alleghany County Arts Council 412
Alleghany County School System 557
Alleghany Inn 149
Alleghany Jubilee 74
Alleghany Memorial Hospital 525–526
Allison-Deaver Historical House 452
Almost Rodeo Drive 175
Alpine Village 158
Alpine Village Inn, The 153–154
alternative medicine 536–537
ambulance 541–543
American Association of Retired Persons 508,
    509, 511, 513, 516, 517, 518, 520
Andrews-Murphy Airport 34–35
Andrews Recreation Park 228
Andrews Wagon Train 398
Angel Community Hospital 540
Angel Shoppe, The 190
Annie's Boutique 184
Annual All That Jazz Weekend at the Grove
    Park Inn 384
Annual Andrews Antique Car Show 405
Annual Antique Show 400
Annual Any and All Dog Show 404
Annual Apple Festival 401
Annual Easter Sunrise Service 386
annual events. See festivals and annual events
Annual Forest Festival Day 404–405

Annual Hard-Candy Arts and Crafts Show
    406–407
Annual Jazz in Brevard 400
Annual Main Street Antique Show 392
Annual Snowbird Mountain Gospel Singing
    398
Annual Tryon Horse Show 394
Appalachian Adventures Rail Road 261
Appalachian/Brian Estates 520–521
Appalachian Challenge Guide Service 261–
    262
Appalachian Cultural Museum 448
Appalachian National Scenic Trail 250
Appalachian Ranger District 299–300
Appalachian Ranger District, Tocane Station
    300–301
Appalachian Realty 496–497
Appalachian Rustic Furnishings 175–176
Appalachian Ski Mountain 269–270
Appalachian Spring Celebration 389
Appalachian State University 433–434, 545–
    546
Appalachian Summer, An 457
AppalCART Transportation 511
Apple Festival 403
Applegate Inn Bed & Breakfast 140
Apple Inn 123–124
Archer's Mountain Inn 104
Area Agency on Aging 508
Arrowmont Stable and Cabins 256
Arrowood Pool, The 231
Art Cellar, The 420
Art Fest 398
art galleries. See visual arts
Art International Asheville 423
Art in the Park 420–421
arts. See under specific art form
Arts Alliance 413
Arts and Crafts Conference at the Grove Park
    Inn 384
Arts Center, The 426
Arts Council of Macon County 418
arts councils and organizations
    Alleghany County 412
    Ashe County 412
    Avery County 412
    Buncombe County 413
    Haywood County 417
    Henderson County 413–417
    Jackson County 417–418
    Macon County 418–419
    Swain County 419
    Watauga County 412

Yancey County 412–413
Arts League of Highlands, The 418
Ashe County
    arts councils and organizations 412
    bed and breakfasts and country inns
        103–104
    golf 273–274
    healthcare 526
    literary arts 447
    motels and hotels 150
    music 441
    nightlife 74
    overview of 6–7
    parks 224
    public schools 557–558
    real estate 487–488
    restaurants 45–47
    retirement and senior services 509–510
    special attractions 309
    theater 433
    visual arts 419–420
Ashe County Airport 34
Ashe County Arts Council 412
Ashe County Cheese Factory 309
Ashe County Choral Society 441
Ashe County Little Theater 433
Ashe County Public School System 557–558
Ashe County Studio Hop 419
Ashe High Country Realty 488
Ashe Memorial Hospital 526
Ashe Park 224
Ashe Services for Aging Inc. 509
Asheville, shopping in 184–188, 190–191
Asheville Antiques Mall 186
Asheville Art League 413
Asheville-Buncombe Technical Community
        College 551
Asheville Chamber Music Series 441
Asheville Choral Society 441–442
Asheville City School System 558
Asheville Community Concert Association 442
Asheville Community Theatre 434
Asheville Contemporary Dance Theatre 446–
        447
Asheville Gallery of Art 423
Asheville Parks and Recreation 225
Asheville Poetry Alive Festival, The 397
Asheville Regional Airport 33–34
Asheville School, The 555–556
Asheville Symphony Orchestra, The 442
Asheville Tileworks & Pottery 467
Asheville Tourists Baseball 313
Asheville Urban Trail, The 312–313
Asheville Veterans Affairs Medical Center, The
        529
Asheville Wine Market 186
Assembly Required 194
At Books Unlimited 208
autumn, in the mountains 363–365
Avalon Llama Treks 260
Avery County
    arts councils and organizations 412
    bed and breakfasts and country inns
        104–106
    golf 274
    healthcare 526
    motels and hotels 150–152
    nightlife 75
    overview of 7–8
    parks 224
    public schools 558
    real estate 488–490
    restaurants 47–49
    retirement and senior services 510
    skiing 268
    special attractions 309–310
    theater 433
    visual arts 420
    waterfalls 347
Avery County Airport 34
Avery County Arts Council 412
Avery County School System 558
Avery Senior Services Senior Center 510
Azalea Inn, The 104

**B**

B. Dalton Bookseller 206
Backcountry Outdoors 263–264
Baird House 106
Bakersville Community Medical Clinic 527
balloning 259–260
Balsam Mountain campground 248
Balsam Mountain Inn 68–69, 141
Banana Moon 194
Banner Elk, shopping in 175
Banner Elk Art Festival 396, 399
Banner Elk Inn Bed & Breakfast 104–105
Banner Elk Town Park 224
Barbara's Antiques 194
Barley's Taproom 76–77
bars. See nightlife
Bartram Trail 251
Bascom-Louise Gallery and the Highlands
        Center for the Visual Arts 431–432
B.B. Barns Inc. 264
Bea Hensley & Son Blacksmiths 465–466
beansTalk 75
Beanstreets 77
Bear Trail Lunch Counter 47
Bed and Breakfast at Turbyvilla 101–102
bed and breakfasts and country inns
    Alleghany County 101–103
    Ashe County 103–104
    Avery County 104–106
    Buncombe County 114–123
    Cherokee County 134
    Clay County 134–135
    Graham County 135
    Haywood County 135–140
    Henderson County 123–128
    Jackson County 140–142
    Macon County 142, 144–146
    Madison County 106

Mitchell County 107–108
Polk County 128–130
Rutherford County 130–131
Swain County 146–147
Transylvania County 131–134
Watauga County 108–112
Yancey County 113–114
*See also* motels and hotels
Bed of Roses, A 114
Beech Alpen Inn 150–151
Beech Mountain 48
Beech Mountain, shopping in 175
Beech Mountain Hillclimb 389
Beech Mountain Ski Resort 270
Beech Mountain Slopeside Rentals Inc. 493
Beech Mountain Street Dances 75
Beehive Resale Shop 194
Be Here Now 77
Bele Chere 397
Belfry Players, The 437
Belk Art Gallery 431
Bellagio 190, 423
Best Western 167
Best Western Central 159
Best Western Eldreth Inn 150
Best Western Great Smokies Inn 170
Best Western Smoky Mountain Inn 167
Beverly-Hanks & associates 497, 498
Big Band Dance Weekend at the Grove Park
    Inn 384
Big Creek, Waterfall on 349
Big Creek campground 248
Big Laurel Falls 356
Big Lynn Lodge 152–153
Big Witch Overlook 370
Biltmore Estate 333–335, 448
Biltmore Estate's Festival of Flowers 386
Biltmore Estate Winery 336–337
Biltmore Homespun Museum 448
Biltmore Magic & Costume Co., The 190
Biltmore Saddle and Bridle Club Inc. 258
Biltmore Village, shopping in 188, 190–191
Biltmore Village Historic Museum 449
Bistro, The 337
Black Diamond Bistro and Grill 47
Black Dome Mountain Sports 264
Black Mountain, shopping in 192
Black Mountain Antique Mall 192
Black Mountain campground 254
Black Mountain Christmas Parade and
    Community Candle Lighting 408
Black Mountain Drug Company 192
Black Mountain Gallery 467
Black Mountain Golf Course 276
Black Mountain Inn 116
Black Mountain to Mount Mitchell Marathon
    Challenge 384
Black Walnut Bed and Breakfast Inn, The 114
Blaine House 142
Blake House Inn 116
Blantyre River Park 239
Bless Your Heart 176

Block House Steeplechase, The 387
Bloomin' Art 186
Blowing Rock, shopping in 175–178, 181–182
Blowing Rock, The 311
Blowing Rock Antique Center 181
Blowing Rock Hospital 527
Blowing Rock Memorial Park 224
Blowing Rock Properties 493–494
Blowing Rock Realty 494
Blowing Rock Stables 256
Blowing Rock Stage Company 434
Bluegrass Festival 394
Blue Moon Bakery and Cafe 55
Blue Owl Studio and Gallery, Inc. 203, 430
Blue Planet Map Company 178, 204
Blue Ridge Barbecue Festival and NC State
    Barbecue Championship, The 394
Blue Ridge Community College 513
Blue Ridge Community College—Brevard
    Campus 552
Blue Ridge Community College Concerts 442
Blue Ridge Community College—Flat Rock
    Campus 551–552
Blue Ridge Community Theater 434
Blue Ridge Country Club 274
Blue Ridge Dental Practice 533
Blue Ridge Gemstone Mine & Campground
    376–377
Blue Ridge Health Center 533
Blue Ridge Hearthside Crafts 421
Blue Ridge Mall 194
Blue Ridge Motel 159
Blue Ridge Mountain Fair Craft Festival 393
Blue Ridge Mountain Realty, Inc. 488
Blue Ridge Opportunity Commission 508, 509
Blue Ridge Parkway
    camping on 246–247, 371–372
    description of 361–362
    Friends organization 362, 365–366
    hiking on 372–373
    recommended stops 366–371
Blue Ridge Parkway Bookstore 205
Blue Ridge Radio Players 458–459
Blue Ridge Realty 490
Blue Ridge Writers Group 447
Blue Spiral 1 423
Blue Spruce Outfitters 264
Blue Valley Overlook 232
Bluffs Lodge 149–150
Bogart's Restaurant and Tavern 81
Bolick Pottery 421
Book Cellar 209
Book Nook, The 207
Book Rack 206
Books-A-Million 206
Book Store, The 194, 207–208
Bookstore on Wall Street 206
bookstores
    Asheville 205–207
    Blowing Rock 204
    Boone 204–205
    Brevard 207

Cashiers 208
Dillsboro 208
Franklin 208
Hendersonville 207–208
Highlands 208
Murphy 209
Sparta 205
Spruce Pine 205
Sylva 209
Waynesville 209
Boone, shopping in 178–181, 181–182
Boone Airport 34
Boone Antique Mall, The 178
Boone Bike Touring 262
Boone Christmas Parade 407
Boone Fork campground 254
Boone Golf Club 275
Boone Greenway Pedestrian Walking and Biking Trail 224
Boone Realty Inc. 494
Boone's Trace 368
Boston Pizza 60–61
Botanical Gardens, The 313–314
bowling 260
Boyd Park 226
Boyer Realty 486
Bradley's General Store 211
Brasstown Concert Association 446
Braswell Realty 489–490
Brevard, shopping in 200–203
Brevard Antique Mall 200
Brevard Camera Club 415
Brevard Chamber Orchestra 444
Brevard College 228, 444, 549
Brevard College Community Education 516
Brevard College Visual Arts 429–430
Brevard Little Theater 438–439
Brevard Motor Lodge 164
Brevard Music Center 318, 392, 394, 444
brewpubs. See nightlife
Bridal Veil Falls 356
Brightwater Art Glass 194, 426
Brinegar Cabin 367
Broadax Inn Bed and Breakfast 134–135
Broadax Inn Restaurant 67
Broadway Arts Building 423–424
Brookside Inn 154
Brookwood Golf Course 276
Brown Mountain 259
Broyhill Inn & Conference Center, The 154
Broyhill Park 224
Brush Creek Mountain Arts and Crafts 420
Bryson City Chili Cookoff 405
Bryson City Island Park, The 232
Bull Creek Valley Overlook 369
Buncombe County
    arts councils and organizations 413
    bed and breakfasts and country inns 114–123
    dance 446–447
    golf 276–277
    healthcare 529–532

kidstuff 326–329
lakes 233
literary arts 447–448
motels and hotels 159–163
museums 448–450
music 441–442
nightlife 76–80
overview of 13–14, 16
parks 225–226
public schools 558
real estate 496–497
resorts 88–89
restaurants 55–58, 60–61
retirement and senior services 512–513
special attractions 312–316
theater 434–435, 437
visual arts 423–426
waterfalls 349–350
Buncombe County Council on Aging 512–513
Buncombe County Golf Course 276
Buncombe County Parks and Recreation 225–226
Buncombe County Public Schools 558
Buncombe County Recreation Park 314
Buncombe County River Parks 239
Buncombe County Sheriff's Department Reassurance Program 513
Burgiss Farm Bed and Breakfast 102
Burke County, waterfalls in 347–348
Burnsville, shopping in 183–184
Burnsville Little Theater 434
buses 35

C

Cabin Fever 176
cabins. See motels and hotels
Cable Cove campground 252
Cades Cove 288–289
Cades Cove Bookstore 287
Cades Cove campground 248
Cafe Nostalgia 49
Cafe on the Square 55
Caldwell Community College and Technical Institute 548
Calico Chorus and Men's Chorus 444–445
Calico Gallery/Gallery 30 426
Camera Club of Hendersonville 413
Camp Arrowhead for Boys 480
Camp Carolina for Boys 481
Camp Glen Arden for Girls 480
Camp Green Cover for Girls 479–480
Camp Gwynn Valley 482
Camp Hollymont for Girls 476
Camp Illahee 481–482
camping and campgrounds
    Blue Ridge Parkway 246–247, 371–372
    Great Smoky Mountains National Park 248–249, 251
    Nantahala National Forest 252, 254
    national forest camping 251–252
    Pisgah National Forest 254–255

Camp Merrie-Woode 483
Camp Merri-Mac for Girls 477–478
Camp Mondamin for Boys 479–480
Camp Rockmont for Boys 476–477
camps 475–483
Camp Timberlake for Boys 478–479
Candy Barrel 178, 203, 209
Caney Fork Creek Park 230
canoeing 239–240
Canton Area Historical Museum 455–456
Canton Senior Center 518
Cardinal Drive-In 65
Carl Sandburg Folk & Poetry Festival 392
Carl Sandburg Home 329, 451
Carnival! 398
Carolina Camera Club 414
Carolina Carriage Club 258
Carolina Day School 556–557
Carolina Hemlocks campground 254
Carolina Mountain Artists 194
Carolina Mountain Club 246
Carolina Nights 81
Cascades Parking Overlook 367
Cashiers Community Center 230
Cashiers Senior C.A.F.E. 519
Castle Hotel, The 154
Castle Inn on English Knob 107
Cataloochee campground 248–249
Cataloochee Ranch 67–68, 96–97, 257
Cataloochee Ski Area 270
Cataloochee Valley 289
Cecils College 552
Cedar Crest 49–50, 118–119
Celebrate Folk Art Day 401
Celestial Mountain Music and Folk Art 200
Celtic Ways 186
Century 21 Carroll & Demos 497
Century 21/Kaiser Realty 500
Century 21 Tryon Real Estate 500
Chalet Inn, The 142, 144
Chalet Motel and Apartments 167
Champion Park 228, 239
Chapter 2 208
Charles A. Cannon, Jr. Memorial Hospital 526
Charter Asheville Behavioral Health System 529–530
Chattooga River 238
Chatuge, Lake 234–235
Chatuge Cove Complex II 166
Chatuge Mountain Inn 166
Chatuge Shores Golf Course 280
Chelsea Gallery 431
Cheoah Lake 235–236
Cheoah Point campground 252
Cheoah Ranger District 290–292
Cherohala Skyway 293
Cherokee Bear Zoo & Plaza 331
Cherokee County
    bed and breakfasts and country inns
        134
    golf 280
    healthcare 538–539
    kidstuff 330
    lakes 234
    motels and hotels 165–166
    museums 455
    music 446
    nightlife 80
    overview of 21, 23
    parks 228–229
    public schools 560
    real estate 501
    restaurants 67
    retirement and senior services 517
    special attractions 319
    theater 439
Cherokee County Historical Museum 455
Cherokee County School System 560
Cherokee County Senior Services 517
Cherokee Fun Park 319–320, 331
Cherokee Heritage Museum & Gallery 344
Cherokee Hills Golf Course and Country Club
    165, 280
Cherokee Indian Reservation
    fishing on 240
    kidstuff 330–331
    nightlife 81
    Qualla Boundary 343–344
    special attractions 319–320, 344–345
Cherokee Indians, history of 339–344
Cherokee Lake 234
Cherokee Realty 502
Cherry Street Antique Mall 192
Chestoa View 368
Chetola Resort 75, 84–85
Chianti's Italian Restaurant 65
Chief Junaluska's Grave 320–321
children, activities for. See kidstuff
Chimney Rock Park 317–318
Chinquapin Inn 107
Chloe & Co. 209
Choose and Cut Weekend 407
Christian Harmony Singing 398
Christmas at Biltmore Estate 406
Christmas at Connemara 408–409
Christmas at the Lake 409
Christmas in July Festival 395
Christmas Parade 406
Christmas Parade and Kris Kringle Karnival
409
Christmas With the Guild 408
Christ School 556
Chunky Gal Stables 257
Church Street Art and Craft Show 405
City Lights Bookstore & Cafe 209, 431
CJ's 211
Claddagh Inn, The 124
Clay County
    bed and breakfasts and country inns
        134–135
    golf 280
    lakes 234–235
    motels and hotels 166
    museums 455

music 446
nightlife 80
overview of 23–24
parks 229
public schools 560
real estate 501–502
restaurants 67
retirement and senior services 517
theater 439
waterfalls 354–355
Clay County Recreation Park 229
Clay County School System 560
Clay County Senior Center 517
Clear Creek Guest Ranch 87–88
Cliffside Lake Recreation Area and Vanhook
    Glade Campground 236
climate 37–40
ClimbMax Mountain Guides 264
Clingmans Dome 288
Club Day at the Blue Ridge Mall 384
coffeehouses. See nightlife
Colburn Gem and Mineral Museum, The 380
Cold Mountain 368
Coldwell Banker Harold & Associates, Realtors
    499
colleges and universities 545–555
College Walk 521
Colony Lake Lure Resort at Fairfield
    Mountains 90–91
Comedy Classic 384
Comfort Inn 165–166, 167–168
Comfort Inn—Asheville 159
Comfort Suites 159–160
Common Ground Realty 495
Connestee Art League, The 415
Consignment Gallery, The 194–195
Constance Boutique 186–187
Contra Dancing and Traditional American Folk
    Dancing 75
Cool Springs Baptist Church 367
Coon Dog Day 398
Cooperative Extension Service 508–509, 511,
    512
Corner Bistro, The 65
Corner Cupboard Antiques Mall 187
Corner Palate, The 47
Cosby campground 249
Cottage Inn 168
cottages. See motels and hotels
Cottages of Glowing Hearth, The 155
Council on Aging 513, 518
Country Charm & City Elegance 174
Country Farmhouse 181
Courthouse Falls 350–351
Crabtree Falls 348
Crabtree Meadows campground 246, 372
Crabtree Meadows Coffee Shop 368–369
Crabtree Meadows Recreation Center 369
Cradle of Forestry 297–298, 318, 329–330,
    452–453
Cradle of Forestry in America Interpretive
    Association, The 207

craft galleries. See visual arts
crafts, mountain 461–473
Craggy Dome Trail 373
Craggy Gardens Visitors Center 369
Creekside Galleries 462
Creekside Galleries/Carlton Gallery-Woven
    Works 421
Crescent View 521
Crestwood Galleries 176, 421
Crooked Creek Golf Course 277–278
Crouse Park 223–224
Cullasaja Falls 356
Cullowhee County Park 230
Cumberland Knob 366, 373
Cummings Cove Golf and Country Club 278
Curb Market, The 195
Curtis Creek campground 254
Cyrano's Bookshop 208

D

Daily Grind, The 47–48
Dana Park 226
dance (performing art)
    Buncombe County 446–447
    Polk County 447
dancing. See nightlife
Dancing Bear Toys, Ltd. 195
Dancing Moon Earthway Bookstore 178, 205
Daniel Boone Inn Restaurant 50
Daniel Boone Native Gardens 311–312
Daniel Ridge Falls 351
David Hilton Realty 501
Davidson River campground 254–255
Davidson River Outfitters 264
Day in the Country, A 193–194
Days Gone By Gifts and Collectibles 195
Days Inn 164, 167
Days Inn—Blowing Rock 155
D.D. Bullwinkle's 200–201
Deep Creek campground 249
Deerfield 521
Deerpark Restaurant 337
Department of Social Services 509, 510, 511,
    512
Devil's Courthouse 244, 370
DeWoolfson Down 182
Diamond K. Dance Ranch 81
Dillsboro, shopping in 211–212
Dillsboro Heritage Festival 394
Dillsboro River Park 230
District Memorial Hospital 538
Dixon Auction and Appraisals 486
Doe Ridge Pottery 421
Dogwood Crafters 211, 431
Dogwood Inn 130
Dogwood Realty 488
Don's Mountain Aire Seafood & Steak House
    45
Doughton Hall Bed & breakfast 102–103
Doughton Park 367
Doughton Park campground 246–247, 371

Douglas Falls 349
Downtown Books and News 187, 206
drama. See theater (performing art)
Druid Hills Family Practice 533
Dry Falls 356
Duck Decoy Inc. 211
Duckett House Inn & Farm, The 106
Dupont State Forest 305–306

**E**

Eagle's Nest Camp 482–483
Early Music Shop 190
Earth Day Celebration 386–387
Earth Guild, The 187
Earthshine Mountain Lodge 65, 80, 93–95, 256–257
Earthwork's Environmental Gallery 209–210, 430
Easter Egg Hunt 387
East LaPorte River Park 230
E.B. Jeffress Park 367
Echo Mountain Inn 61–62, 124
Edge of the World Snowboard Shop and Whitewater Rafting 262
Edneyville Park 226
education. See schools
Elk Creek Stables 256
Elk Falls 347
Elkmont campground 249
Elk River Airport 34
Emerald Village 377
Emergency Management Office 510
emergency medical services (EMS) 541–543
emergency phone numbers 541–543
English Chapel 318
English Shopper, The 182
Enloe Market Place 211
Enviro Depot 187
Episcopal Church of the Messiah, The 319
Eseeola Lodge 105
Essence of Thyme 66, 80
Estes-Winn Antique Automobile Museum 449
Etowah Valley Country Club and Golf Lodge 278
Etowah Valley Stables 257
Eve's Leaves/J.W. Tweed's 175
Expressions 62
Expressions Craft Guild and Gallery 421

**F**

Fabulous Fourth Metric Century Bicycle Tour 398
Fairfield Mountain Resort 164
Fairfield Sapphire Valley 99
Fairview Youth Complex 230
Fall Celebration of the Arts 403
Fall Creek Cabins 155
Falling Creek Camp 480
Fall Pioneer Living Days and Military Encampment 401

Fall Quilt Show 404
Falls Landing Restaurant, The 66
Famous Louise's Rock House Restaurant 48
Far Away Place, A 186, 423
Farm City Day 404
Farmers Hardware 178–179
Farmers Hardware Ski Shop 179
Ferebee Park 228
Festival of Lights 408
Festival of Trees 409
festivals and annual events
        January 383–384
        February 384
        March 384–385
        April 386, 387, 389
        May 389, 391–393
        June 393–394
        July 388–389, 394–399, 457
        August 399–400
        September 400–402
        October 402–405
        November 406–407
        December 407–409
Field of the Woods 319
Fine Arts Theater 77, 458
fire 541–543
Firefly Festival Arts and Crafts Fair 393
Fireman's Day Festival 401–402
Fireside Antiques and Interiors 190
Fireside Books, Etc. 208
First Night Asheville 408
fishing 240–242
FISH Volunteer Medical Transportation 513
508 Main Street 198
Flat Rock, shopping in 192–193
Flat Rock Inn 124–126
Flat Rock Playhouse, The State Theatre of North Carolina 392–393, 437–438
Fleetwood Falls Inc. 488
Fletcher School of Dance/Land of the Sky Civic Ballet 447
Flying Frog Café 58
Folk Art Center, The 314, 369, 467, 469–470
Folk Art Center Fiber Day 391
Folkmoot USA 388–389, 399
Fontana Dam 321–322
Fontana Lake 237
Fontana Village 257
Fontana Village Resort 95
Foothills Dressage and Combined Training Club 258
Foothills Equestrian Nature Center 258, 317
Foothills Equestrian Trail Association 258
Footsloggers 179, 262
forest lands, state 305–307
Forest Manor Inn 160
Foscoe, shopping in 182–183
Foster Grandparent and Senior Companion Program 510
4 1/2 Street Inn 144
Four Seasons Arts Council 413
Four Seasons' Crafters 198

Fourth of July Freedom Fest 398
4th of July Festival 394
4th of July Gala 396
Foxfire Realty 505
Foxtrot Inn, The 128
Frame-Up, The 201, 429
Franklin 532
Franklin Gem and Mineral Museum 380–381
Franklin Park 228
Fred's General Mercantile Company 175
French Broad Golf Center 276
French Broad River 238, 239–240
French Broad River Month 393–394
French Broad River Overlook 369
frescoes 428–429
Friends of the Blue Ridge Parkway 362, 365–366
Friends of the Great Smoky Mountains
National Park 290
Front Street Company/Yarn Corner 211–212
Fryemont Inn 146–147

**G**

Gallery of the Mountains 424
Gallery One 431
Gallery on Main 429
Gallery Z 212, 431
Gamekeeper Restaurant, The 50
Garden Deli 54
Garden Jubilee 392
Gatekeepers 210
Gazebo Creekside Cafe, The 70
gem mines
      Haywood County 378
      Jackson County 378–379
      Macon County 379
      Mitchell County 376–377
      Swain County 379
      Watauga County 377–378
Gem Mountain 377
gem museums 379–381
George Bond Memorial Health Center 533
Ghost Town in the Sky 322, 330
Gideon Ridge Inn 108–109
Givens Estate United Methodist Retirement
Community 521–522
Glassmine Falls 349–350
Glassy Creek Falls 355–356
Glen Cannon Country Club 279
Glendale Springs, shopping in 173–174
Glendale Springs Inn & Restaurant 45–46, 74, 103
Glen Falls 356
Glenville, Lake 236
Golden Age Club 519
Goldsmith by Rudi, The, Ltd. 198
golf
      Alleghany County 273
      Ashe County 273–274
      Avery County 274
      Buncombe County 276–277

Cherokee County 280
Clay County 280
Haywood County 280–281
Henderson County 277–278
Jackson County 281–282
Macon County 282
Madison County 274
McDowell County 274
miniature 325, 377–378
Mitchell County 274–275
Polk County 278–279
Swain County 282–283
Transylvania County 279–280
Watauga County 275
Yancey County 275–276
Goodwin Weavers Showroom, The 181
Goombay Festival 400
Graham County
      bed and breakfasts and country inns
       135
      lakes 235–236
      motels and hotels 166
      overview of 25
      parks 229
      public schools 560
      real estate 502–503
      resorts 95
      retirement and senior services 517–518
      special attractions 320–322
Graham County Recreation Complex 229
Graham County School System 560
Grandfather Mountain 309–310
Grandfather Mountain Highland Games and
Gathering of the Scottish Clans 395–396
Grandfather Ranger District 301
Grandview Lodge 68, 135–136
Grandview Overlook 367–368
Grapevine Music 179
Grassy Creek Golf Club 274–275
Graveyard Fields 370, 373
Graveyard Fields Falls, The 355
Graystone Lodge 155–156
Great Smokies Holiday Inn Sunspree Resort
160, 277
Great Smoky Mountains National Park
      accommodations 288
      backcountry camping in 249, 251
      camping in 248–249, 251
      fishing in 241–242
      history of 285
      special attractions 288–289
      support groups 289–290
      traveling in 286–287
      visitors centers 287
      wildlife in 286
Great Smoky Mountains Natural History
Association 289–290
Great Smoky Mountains Railway 322–323
Great Smoky Mountain Trout Festival 393
Great Southern Glassworks 468–469, 470
Greek Festival 403–404
Green Creek Hounds Inc. 258

Green Door 77–78
Greenery Restaurant & Lounge, The 61
Greenfield Resort 150
Greenhouse Crafts 173–174
Green Mansions Village 183
Green Meadows Park 227
Green Park Inn & Resort 85
Green River Game Lands 306
Greens, The 80
Greyhound Bus Line 35
Greystone Inn, The 91–92
Grove Park Inn Christmas, A 406
Grove Park Inn Resort 88–89, 92, 276–277
Grovewood Gallery 424
Guided Bird and Wildflower Walks 386
Guild Fair 396, 404

## H

Half-Moon Gallery 432
Hall Memorial Park 228
Halloween Fest in Transylvania County 405
Hampton Inn 163–164, 164
Hampton Inn—Asheville 161
Hampton Inn of Cherokee 170
Ham Shoppe, The 183
HandMade in America 413, 436–437
Hands Gallery 421
Hanging Dog 254
Hanging Dog campground 252
Hanna's Oriental Rugs & Gifts 176
Hap Simpson Park 240
Harambee 397–398
Harrah's Cherokee Casino 81, 320
Hathaway's Cafe and Market 60
Hawkesdene House, The 134
Hawk & Ivy, The 118
Hawksnest Golf and Ski Resort 268, 274
Hayden Gallery 422
Haywood Arts Repertory Theater 439–440
Haywood Community College 518, 554–555
Haywood Community College Craft
    Production Program 472–473
Haywood County
    arts councils and organizations 417
    bed and breakfasts and country inns
        135–140
    gem mines 378
    golf 280–281
    healthcare 539
    kidstuff 330
    motels and hotels 167
    museums 455–456
    nightlife 81
    overview of 25–26
    parks 229–230
    public schools 560
    real estate 503
    resorts 95–98
    restaurants 67–68
    retirement and senior services 518
    skiing 270
        special attractions 322
        theater 439–440
        visual arts 430–431
        waterfalls 355
Haywood County Arts Council 417
Haywood County Fair 402
Haywood County School System 560
Haywood/Jackson Overlook 370
Haywood Park Hotel 161
Haywood Properties 503
Haywood Regional Medical Center 540
Headwaters Outfitters Inc. 264
healthcare
    Alleghany County 525–526
    alternative medicine 536–537
    Ashe County 526
    Avery County 526
    Buncombe County 529–532
    Cherokee County 538–539
    emergency phone numbers 541–543
    Haywood County 539
    Henderson County 533–534, 537
    Jackson County 539–540
    Macon County 540
    Madison County 527
    Mitchell County 527
    Polk County 537–538
    Transylvania County 538
    Watauga County 527–528
    Yancey County 528
Health Department, Senior Companion
    Program 510
Hearn's Cycling & Fitness 264–265
Heartwood Contemporary Crafts Gallery 427
Hemingway Book & Gift 205
Hemlock Inn 71, 147, 156
Hemphill Mountain Campground 257
Henderson County
    arts organizations 413–417
    bed and breakfasts and country inns
        123–128
    golf 277–278
    healthcare 533–534, 537
    kidstuff 329
    motels and hotels 163–164
    museums 451
    music 442–443
    overview of 16–18
    parks 226–227
    public schools 558–559
    real estate 498–499
    resorts 89–90
    restaurants 61–64
    retirement and senior services 513–514
    special attractions 316–317
    theater 437–438
    visual arts 426–427
Henderson County Art League, The 413–414
Henderson County Public Schools 558–559
Hendersonville, shopping in 193–200
Hendersonville Airport 34
Hendersonville Chorale, The 442–443

Hendersonville Little Theatre 438
Hendersonville Symphony Orchestra 443
Heritage Cottages and Villas 168
Heritage Inn Bed and Breakfast 144–145
Herren House 136
Hickory Nut Falls 350
Hickory Nut Gorge Dogwood Festival 386
Hickory Ridge Homestead 312, 448
High Country Arts & Craft Guild 424
High Country Inn 156–157
High Country Realty 490
High Hampton Inn & Country Club 69, 90, 98–
    99, 281
Highland Books 207
Highland Farms Retirement Community 522
Highland Lake Inn and Conference Center 62,
    89–90
Highlands, shopping in 212–213
Highlands-Cashiers Hospital 540
Highlands Chamber Music Festival 446
Highlands Inn, The 146
Highlands Nature Center and Botanical
    Gardens 323
Highlands Playhouse 440
Highlands Ranger District 292
Highlands Recreation Park 231–232
Highland Suite Hotel 168
Highlands Wine and Cheese Co. 213
High Mountain Expeditions 262
hiking 244–246, 250–251, 372–373
Hillwinds Inn 157
Historical Arts Museum 455
Historic Hendersonville Depot and Model
    Railroad, The 451
Historic Johnson Farm, The 329, 451
Historic Johnson Farm Festival 387, 389
Hiwassee, Lake 234
Hiwassee River Park 229
Hoffman & Associates, Real Estate 490–491
Holiday Inn Cherokee 170
Holiday Inn Express 157
Holiday Inn of Banner Elk 151
Holiday Inn—Tunnel Road 161–162
Holiday Tour of Historic Homes 409
Hollywood Cinemas 78
Holmes Educational State Forest 306–307
Home Care Services of Haywood Regional
    Medical Center 540
Homecoming Parade 402
Home for the Holidays 406
Home-Tech: The Kitchen Shop 210
Hominy Valley Overlook 369–370
Honeysuckle Hollow 198
Horn in the West 312
horseback riding 255–259
Horse Cove campground 252
Horsepasture River Falls, The 351–352
Horse Shows 385
hospitals. See healthcare
hotels. See motels and hotels
Hot Springs Spa 310
Hound Ears Club 85–86

House of Lord 213
House of Towels 198
Howard's Knob Park 50
Howard Street Grille and Cottonwood Brewery
    50–51, 75
Howell-Sparks Real Estate 492
Hubert's 62
Hummingbird Lodge 145
Humpback Hollow 151–152
hunting 242
Hurricane Creek campground 252
Hurricane Falls 355–356

I

Ian and Jo Lydia Craven, Handbuilt Porcelain
    184
Ice Cream Social/Spring Kickoff 394
Imperial Motor Lodge 165
I'm Precious Too! 213
Incredible Toy Company, The 181
Indian Creek Falls 358
Inn Around the Corner, The 119
Inn at Brevard, The 131
Inn at Ragged Gardens, The 112
Inn at the Taylor House, The 109
Innisfree Victorian Inn 141–142
Inn-on-Mill-Creek, The 119–120
inns, country. See bed and breakfasts and
    country inns
Intentional Growth Center 518
Interiors Marketplace 191
Iron Foot Island 235
Island Ford Access Area 240
Isothermal Community College 552

J

Jackalope's View 51
Jackrabbit Mountain campground 252
Jackson County
        arts councils and organizations 417–418
        bed and breakfasts and country inns
            140–142
        gem mines 378–379
        golf 281–282
        healthcare 539–540
        lakes 236
        motels and hotels 167–168
        museums 456
        overview of 26–27
        parks 230–231
        public schools 560
        real estate 503–504
        resorts 98–99
        restaurants 68–70
        retirement and senior services 518–520
        skiing 271
        special attractions 322–323
        theater 439
        visual arts 431
        waterfalls 355–356

Jackson County Airport 35
Jackson County Arts Council 417
Jackson County Department on Aging 519
Jackson County School System 560
Jackson County Transportation 519
Jackson County Visual Arts Association 417–418
Jackson Park 226–227
James P. Kerr, Gallery & Studio 420
Jane Asher's Fourth and Main Antique Mall 198
Jarrett House, The 70, 142
J.C. Campbell Annual August Auction 400
J.C. Campbell Annual Blacksmith Auction 406
J.C. Campbell Fall Festival 405
J.C. Campbell Fireside Sale 409
Jeanie's Boutique 202
Jefferson, shopping in 174
Jefferson Landing Lodge 150
Jenkins Realtors 494
Jewelry Design 424
Jim Bob Tinsley Museum and Research Center 453
John C. Campbell Folk School 330, 470–472
John C. Campbell Folk School Concerts 446
John C. Campbell Folk School Dance Events 80–81
John Wasilik Memorial Poplar 323
Jones Knob 422
Jordan Street Café 66
J & S Beaumont Pottery 462
Jubalo's 44–45
Judaculla Rock 323
Judy Gibbs Real Estate 498
Julian, Lake 233
Julian Price campground 247, 371
Julian Price Memorial Park 368
July 4th Heritage Festival 398
Jump Off Rock 76
Juneywhank Falls 358

**K**

Kate B. Reynolds Women's and Children's Center 533
kayaking 237–239
Kenmure Enterprises, Inc. 498–499
Ken Sedberry Clay Studio 420
Key Falls Inn 131–132
kidstuff
    Buncombe County 326–329
    camps 475–483
    Cherokee County 330
    Cherokee Indian Reservation 330–331
    Haywood County 330
    Henderson County 329
    Transylvania County 329–330
    Watauga County 325–326
King Memorial Park 227
King-Thomasson Antiques 187
Kituwah 401
Klondike Cafe 75

Koala Adult Day Care 516
Konehete Park 229
Korth & Company 191
Kress Emporium 187
Kudzu Players 439
Kwanzaa 408

**L**

La Caterina Trattoria 55–56
Lacey Realty 490
Lake Eden Arts Festival 391–392, 404
Lake Lure Inn 64–65, 130–131
Lake Lure Tours 318
Lake Pointe Landing 522
Lake Powhatan campground 255
Lake Powhatan Recreation Area 233
lakes
    Buncombe County 233
    Cherokee County 234
    Clay County 234–235
    Graham County 235–236
    Jackson County 236
    Macon County 236–237
    Rutherford County 233–234
Lake Tomahawk Park 225
Lake Toxaway Realty Company—Breedlove-Nichols 500–501
La Paz Restaurante—Cantina 60
Laughing Seed Café, The 57–58
Laurel Falls 354
Leatherwood Falls 354–355
Leatherwood Realty 494
Lee Realty 504
Lees-McRae College 433, 546
Legal Services of the Blue Ridge 508
Lexington Park Antiques 187
Liberty Bicycles 265
Licklog Players 439
Lifeline: Emergency Response 516
Lifeline Personal Emergency Response System 513
Lindridge House Bed & Breakfast 109–110
Links O'Tryon 278–279
Linn Cove Viaduct 368
Linville Caverns 310–311
Linville Cottage 105
Linville Falls and Gorge 347–348, 368
Linville Falls campground 247, 371–372
Lion and the Rose, The 120
literary arts
    Ashe County 447
    Buncombe County 447–448
    Transylvania County 448
Little Elsie's 198
Little Glade Mill Pond 366
Little People 454
Little Professor Book Center 206
llama treks 260
lodges. See motels and hotels
Loft, The 188
Lomo Grill 68

Lone Dove Saloon 78
Looking Glass Falls 352
Looking Glass Outfitters 265
Looking Glass Rock 370
Look Rock campground 249
Louise, Lake 225
Louisiana Purchase 46, 75
Lovill House Inn 110
Lower Satulah Falls 356, 358
Lulu's Cafe 69–70
Luminaria in Dillsboro 409
Lunsford Realty 495
Lure, Lake 233–234

**M**

Maco Crafts Inc. 432
Macon County
    arts councils and organizations 418–419
    bed and breakfasts and country inns
        142, 144–146
    gem mines 379
    golf 282
    healthcare 540
    lakes 236–237
    motels and hotels 168, 170
    museums 456–457
    music 446
    overview of 28–29
    parks 231–232
    public schools 560–561
    real estate 505
    restaurants 70–71
    retirement and senior services 520
    skiing 271
    special attractions 323
    theater 440
    visual arts 431–432
    waterfalls 356, 358
Macon County Airport 35
Macon County Art Association 418–419
Macon County Department on Aging 520
Macon County Historical Museum 456
Macon County Public Health Center 540
Macon County Recreation Park 232
Macon County School System 560–561
Madison County
    bed and breakfasts and country inns
        106
    golf 274
    healthcare 527
    overview of 8–9
    public schools 558
    real estate 490–491
    resorts 84
    restaurants 49
    retirement and senior services 510–511
    skiing 268
    special attractions 310
    visual arts 420
Madison County Heritage Festival 402
Madison County School System 558

Madison County Senior Center 510
Madrigal's Interiors & Imports 201
Maggie Valley Opry House 81
Maggie Valley Resort & Country Club 95–96,
    280
Magic Cycles 262
Magic Mountain Mini Golf 325
Main Street Inn, The 145–146
Main Street Ltd. 202
Majdi's Tent 62–63
Malaprop's Bookstore/Cafe 187–188, 206–
    207
Maple Lodge 110–111
Maple Spring Observation Point 98
Maple Tree Gallery 212
Margaret R. Pardee Memorial Hospital 533–
    534
Marion's Old Homeplace 44
Market Basket, The 69
Market Place, The 58
Mark Watson Park 230
Maroon Devil Classic Band Contest 405
Marshall House Bed & Breakfast Inn 106
Mars Hill College 457–458, 546–547
Mars Hill College Programs for Senior Citizens
    510–511
Mars Hill Medical Center 527
Martin House 176
Martin Luther King Jr. Annual Birthday
    Celebration 383
Mast Farm Inn, The 111–112
Mast General Store 179–180, 183, 198–199,
    210
Mayland Community College 547–548
McCulley's 213
McDowell County
    golf 274
    special attractions 310–311
McGuffey's Bar and Grille 78
Meadowbrook Inn, The 157–158
Meals on Wheels 518
Meals on Wheels of Brevard 516
Med-Drive 516–517
medical care. See healthcare
Meeting Place, The 514, 516
Mehri & Company 199
Melange Bed & Breakfast 126
Memorial Mission Hospital 531
Merrimon Galleries 424
Micaville, shopping in 184
Mid-Day Musicals 442
Midnight Hole Falls 355
Miles Realty 486
Mill Creek Country Club 282
Mimosa Inn, The 128–129
Mineral and Gem Festival 399
mines. See gem mines
Mingo Falls 359
Mingus Mill 289
Mirror Lake Antiques 213
Mission + St. Joseph's Health System 530
Mitchell County

bed and breakfasts and country inns 107–108
gem mines 376–377
golf 274–275
healthcare 527
motels and hotels 152–153
overview of 9–10
parks 224
public schools 558
real estate 491–492
restaurants 49–50
retirement and senior services 511
special attractions 311
visual arts 420
Mitchell County School System 558
Mitchell Family YMCA 224
Mitchell Senior Center 511
Mockingbird Theater Productions 434–435
Monte Vista Hotel 120
Montford Park Players 435, 437
Montreat College 549–550
Mooney Falls 356
Moore's Cove Falls 352
Morning Glory Craft Gallery 421
Mortimer campground 255
Moses H. Cone Memorial and Visitors Center 368
Moss & Lace 183
motels and hotels
Alleghany County 149–150
Ashe County 150
Avery County 150–152
Buncombe County 159–163
Cherokee County 165–166
Clay County 166
Graham County 166
Haywood County 167
Henderson County 163–164
Jackson County 167–168
Macon County 168, 170
Mitchell County 152–153
Polk County 164
Rutherford County 164
Swain County 170–171
Transylvania County 164–165
Watauga County 153–158
Yancey County 158–159
See also bed and breakfasts and country inns
Mountain Aire Golf Club 273–274
Mountain Artisans Summer Arts and Craft Show 399
mountain biking 242–243
Mountain Breeze Restaurant 54
Mountain Brook Cottages 168
Mountain Country Realty 502
mountain crafts 461–473
Mountain Creek Bed & Breakfast 136–138
Mountain Creek Cottages 168
Mountain Dance and Folk Festival 399–400
Mountaineer Antique Auto Show 398
Mountain Farm Museum 289

Mountain Heritage Center 456
Mountain Heritage Day 398–399
Mountain Heritage Festival 402
Mountain Home Inn 126–127
Mountain Lore Books 199, 208
Mountain Music Jamboree 74
Mountain Pottery 212, 431
Mountain Projects, Inc. 518, 519
Mountain Rose Specialties 202
Mountain Springs Cabins & Chalets 162
Mountains-to-the-Sea Trail 250–251
Mountain Streams Real Estate, Inc. 501–502
Mountain View Log Cabin Rentals 171
Mount Jefferson State Park 303–304
Mount Mitchell Crafts Fair 399
Mount Mitchell Golf Club 275–276
Mount Mitchell Realty 495–496
Mount Mitchell State Park 304–305, 369
Mount Pisgah 128, 370
Mount Pisgah Balloons 259–260
Mount Pisgah campground 247, 372
Mouse Creek Falls 355
movie theaters. See nightlife
Munger Creek Artworks 432
Murphy Garden Club Park 229
Murphy Medical Center 538–539
Murphy's Restaurant & Pub 51–52, 75–76
Museum of North Carolina Handicrafts, The 456, 473
Museum of North Carolina Minerals 368, 379–380
Museum of the Cherokee Indian, The 344–345
museums
Buncombe County 448–450
Cherokee County 455
Cherokee Indian Reservation 344–345
Clay County 455
gem 368, 379–381
Haywood County 455–456
Henderson County 451
Jackson County 456
Macon County 456–457
Polk County 452
Transylvania County 452–455
Watauga County 448
Music in the Mountains Festival 401
Music in the Mountains with Joe Shannon 441
music (performing art)
Ashe County 441
Buncombe County 441–442
Cherokee County 446
Clay County 446
Henderson County 442–443
Macon County 446
Polk County 443–444
Transylvania County 444–446
Watauga County 441
Mustard Seed Market, The 181
Mystery Hill 312, 325–326
Mystic Eye 188

**N**

Nantahala Gorge Ruby Mine  379
Nantahala Lake  236–237
Nantahala National Forest
    camping in  252, 254
    ranger districts  290–292, 294–96
    ranger stations  293
Nantahala Outdoor Center  265
Nantahala River  238
Nation's Inn  150
Nature Connection, The  212
needle me this  184
New French Bar, The  57
New Life Center  514
New Morning Gallery  191, 424
New River  238–239
New River Festival  402
New River Outfitters & General Store  262
New River State Park  302–303
New Studio of Dance, The  446–447
Niggli Theatre and Studio Theatre  439
nightclubs. See nightlife
nightlife
    Alleghany County  74
    Ashe County  74
    Avery County  75
    Buncombe County  76–80, 458
    Cherokee County  80
Cherokee Indian Reservation  81
Clay County  80
Haywood County  81
Transylvania County  80
Watauga County  75–76
Nolichucky River  239
North Carolina Center for Creative Retirement
    513
North Carolina Rhododendron Festival  393
Northland Properties  497
Northland Properties at Wolf Laurel  491
North Mills River campground  255
North Pole at Beech  407–408
Northwest Trading Post  367
Nu-Wray Inn  54–55, 113

**O**

Oak Barrel Restaurant, The  67
Oaks, The  129
Oconaluftee Indian Village  345
Oconaluftee Visitors Center  287, 370–371
October's End  66
Odyssey Center for the Ceramic Arts  326–
    327, 470
off-road vehicle trails  259
Oktoberfest  401
Old Christmas Hickory Ridge Homestead  383
Old Depot Association Art & Crafts Show  387
Olde Boone Streetfest  401
Old Edwards Inn, The  146
Olde Tyme Music Festival  387
Olde World Christmas Shop  191

Olde World Galleries  176
Old Fashioned Christmas  406
Old-Fashioned Grove Park Inn Family 4th of
    July  396
Old-Fashioned July 4th Celebration on the
    Square  395
Old Fort Golf Course  274
Old Pressley Sapphire Mines  378
Old Stone Inn, The  68, 138
Old Teneriffe Inn  127
Once Upon A Time  191, 207
On The Verandah  70
O.P. Taylor's  202, 210
Open Door Antique Mall, The  202
Opportunity House  426–427, 514
Orchard at Altapass, The  311
Orchard Inn, The  64, 129
Orchard Trace Golf Club  278
Osage Overlook  232
O'Sullivan's of Asheville  78–79
Our Daily Bread  52–53
outfitters  260–265
Overmountain Victory Trail Celebration  400

**P**

Pack Place Education Arts and Science Center
    326, 449–450
Paintin' Shed, The  199
Palmer House Bookshop  209
Papa Nick's  49
Park Deli Cafe  63
Park Ridge Hospital  534, 537
parks
    Alleghany County  223–224
    Ashe County  224
    Avery County  224
    Buncombe County  225–226
    Cherokee County  228–229
    Clay County  229
    Graham County  229
    Haywood County  229–230
    Henderson County  226–227
    Jackson County  230–231
    Macon County  231–232
    Mitchell County  224
    Polk County  227–228
    state parks  302–305, 369
    Swain County  232–233
    Transylvania County  228
    Watauga County  224–225
Parkview Lodge  152
Parkway Craft Center  421–422
Parkway Playhouse  434
Past-'N-Present  194–195
Patton Park  227
Paul Porter Center for Performing Arts  415
Pearson Falls  350
Penland School of Crafts, The  462, 465
Penland School of Crafts Visitors Center  420
Perry's Water Garden  323
Pigeon River  239

Pinebridge Inn 153
Pine Crest Inn 64, 129–130
Pineola Inn and Pineola Motel 152
Pine Park Retirement Inn 522–523
Pink Flamingo, The 202–203
Pioneer Day at the Deaver House 404
Pioneer Living Day 386
Pioneer Motel and Cottages 171
Pioneer Realty 503
Pisgah Center for Wildlife Education 318, 329
Pisgah Forest Fish Hatchery 318–319, 329
Pisgah Forest Stables 257
Pisgah Inn 165
Pisgah National Forest
      camping in 254–255
      hiking in 373
      history of 296, 299
      ranger districts 299–302
      ranger stations 293
Pisgah Ranger District 301–302
Pisgah View Ranch 257
Pleasant Papers 176–177, 204
Plott's Balsam Range Overlook 370
Poetry Alive! 447
police 541–543
Polk County
      bed and breakfasts and country inns
            128–130
      dance 446
      golf 278–279
      healthcare 537–538
      motels and hotels 164
      museums 452
      music 443–444
      overview of 18–20
      parks 227–228
      public schools 559–560
      real estate 499–500
      restaurants 64
      retirement and senior services 514, 516
      special attractions 317
      theater 438
      visual arts 427, 429
      waterfalls 350
Polk County Historical Association & Museum
      452
Polk County Recreation Department 227–228
Polk County School System 559–560
Polk County Transportation Authority 516
Possum Trot Grill 58
Pot Hole, The 422
Powhatan, Lake 233
Preferred Properties 497
Preferred Properties of Highlands 505
Preferred Real Estate 499
preparatory schools 555–557
Pretty Place, The 86
Proper Pot, The 203
Prudential-McClure Henry Realtors, The 505
public schools 557–561
Pumpkin Fest 405
Purple Sage 199

Purveyors of Art and Design Materials 180

Q

Quality Inn, The—Biltmore 162
Quality Inn and Suites, The 164
Quality Inn Appalachian Conference Center
      158
Qualla Arts and Crafts Mutual Inc. 345
Qualla Boundary 343–344

R

radio stations 458
Radisson Hotel—Asheville 162–163
Rainbow Lake Resort 165
Ralph J. Andrews County Park 230–231
Ramada Plaza 163
Ramp Convention 393
Ramp Festival 389
Razzle Dazzle Saturday 389
real estate
      Alleghany County 486–487
      Ashe County 487–488
      Avery County 488–490
      Buncombe County 496–497
      buyer precautions 485–486
      Cherokee County 501
      Clay County 501–502
      Graham County 502–503
      Haywood County 503
      Henderson County 498–499
      Jackson County 503–504
      Macon County 505
      Madison County 490–491
      Mitchell County 491–492
      Polk County 499–500
      Swain County 505
      Transylvania County 500–501
      Watauga County 492–494
      Yancey County 494–496
Real Property People, Inc. 491–492
recreation. See under specific activity
Recreation Park 327
Red Fox Country Club 279
Red House Inn and Bed and Breakfast 132–
      133
Red Onion Cafe, The 53
Red Rocker Inn 121–122
Reems Creek Golf Club 277
Reeves Auction & Realty Co. 487
Regal's Litchfield Cinemas 76
Relia's Garden Restaurant 71
Remax 500
Renee Allen House 120–121
resorts
      Buncombe County 88–89
      Graham County 95
      Haywood County 95–98
      Henderson County 89–90
      Jackson County 98–99
      Madison County 84

Rutherford County 90–91
Transylvania County 91–95
Watauga County 84–86
Yancey County 87–88
restaurants
Alleghany County 44–45
Ashe County 45–47
Avery County 47–49
Buncombe County 55–58, 60–61
Cherokee County 67
Clay County 67
Haywood County 67–68
Henderson County 61–64
Jackson County 68–70
Macon County 70–71
Madison County 49
Mitchell County 49–50
Polk County 64
Rutherford County 64–65
Swain County 71
Transylvania County 65–67
Watauga County 50–54
Yancey County 54–55
retirement and senior services
Alleghany County 508–509
Ashe County 509–510
Avery County 510
Buncombe County 512–513
Cherokee County 517
Clay County 517
Graham County 517–518
Haywood County 518
Henderson County 513–514
Jackson County 518–520
Macon County 520
Madison County 510–511
Mitchell County 511
Polk County 514, 516
regional services 508
Swain County 520
Transylvania County 516–517
Watauga County 511–512
Yancey County 512
retirement communities 520–523
Reunions 188
Revolutionary War Encampment at FENCE 387
Richland Balsam 351
Richmond Hill Inn 122
Ridge Runner Naturals 210
Rio Burrito 61
Rio Doce Gem Mine 377
River Front Park 232
River House 46–47, 103–104
RiverRun International Film Festival 459
rivers 238–239
Riverside Canoe and Tube Rentals 262
Riverwind Adult Community 523
Riverwood Pewter Shop 212, 431
Riverwood's Oaks Gallery 212, 431
Roaring Fork Falls 348
Roaring Fork Motor Nature Trail 289

Roberts Real Estate 491
Rockbrook Camp for Girls 480–481
rock climbing 243–244
rock hounding 375–381
Rock & Roll Sports 262
Rocky Bluff campground 255
Rocky's Soda Shop & Grill 66–67
Roy A. Taylor ATV Trail System 259
Ruby City Gems and Minerals 381
Rustic Barn Bed & Breakfast 112
Rutherford County
bed and breakfasts and country inns 130–131
lakes 233–234
motels and hotels 164
resorts 90–91
restaurants 64–65
special attractions 317–318
waterfalls 350

S

safety, outdoor
around waterfalls 218
cooking 216–217
driving 215–216
emergency supplies 216
heat exhaustion/heat stroke 221
hiking and camping 216–217
during hunting season 218
hypothermia 218–219
insects 218
poisonous plants 218
waste disposal 217
wild animals 217–218
Saint Patrick's Day Celebration 385
Salsa 56
Saluda Mountain Crafts Gallery 427
Samovar Cafe, The 63
Santa and More 408
Santa's Land Fun Park and Zoo 320, 331
Santeetlah Lake 236
Sapphire Mountain Golf Club 281–282
Sapphire Valley Resort 257
Sapphire Valley Ski Area 271
Saratoga's Café 81
Sassy Goose, The 133
Scaly Mountain Ski Area 271
School of Music Faculty Recital Series 441
schools
four-year colleges 546–547, 549–551
preparatory schools 555–557
public schools 557–561
two-year colleges 547–548, 551–552, 554–555
universities 545–546, 548–549, 553–554
Scottish Tartans Museum and Heritage Center 456–457
Secret Garden 192–193
Senior Citizens Center 517–518
Senior Companion Program 510
senior services. See retirement and senior

services
Seniors Health Insurance 514
Serves You Right! 177
Setrock Creek 348
Seven Sisters Gallery 424–425
(Shag Club at) Geno's 75
Shephard's Thunder Ridge 81
Sherry Garris Properties 494
Sherwood Forest 279–280
Shindig-on-the-Green 396
Shiprock Mountain 244
shopping
    Asheville 184–188, 190–191
    Banner Elk 175
    Beech Mountain 175
    Biltmore Village 188, 190–191
    Black Mountain 192
    Blowing Rock 175–178, 181–182
    bookstores 204–209
    Boone 178–181, 181–182
    Brevard 200–203
    Burnsville 183–184
    Dillsboro 211–212
    Flat Rock 192–193
    Foscoe 182–183
    Glendale Springs 173–174
    Hendersonville 193–200
    Highlands 212–213
    Jefferson 174
    Micaville 184
    Todd 174
    Valle Crucis 183
    Waynesville 203, 209–211
Shunkawauken Falls 350
Silver Designs by Lou E and Art Gallery 419–420
Silvermont Mansion 453–455
Silvermont Park 228
Silver Run Falls 356
Sinbad Restaurant 63
Singing on the Mountain at Grandfather Mountain 393
skiing
    Avery County 268
    Haywood County 270
    Jackson County 271
    Macon County 271
    Madison County 268
    Watauga County 269–270
Skyline Lodge 168, 170
Sky Tours 260
Sleep Inn—Biltmore 163
Slick Rock 546
Slickrock Expeditions Inc. 265
Slick Rock Falls 352
Sliding Rock 329, 352
Sloan's Bookshop 209
Sloop Memorial Hospital 526
Slow Lane 210
Smith-McDowell House 450
Smokemont campground 249
Smoketree Lodge 158

Smoky Mountain Community Theater 440–441
Smoky Mountain Country Club 282–283
Smoky Mountain Folk Festival 402
Smoky Mountain Gold and Ruby Mine 379
Snake's Den 244
Snowbird Mountain Lodge 135
Snow Hill Inn 146
Soco Gardens Zoo 322, 330
Something Special Gift Shop 184
Somewhere in Time 199
Song of the Wood Ltd. 192
Song O'Sky Chorus—Sweet Adelines 442
Sourwood Festival 400
Sourwood Inn 122–123
South Broad Park 228
Southeastern Animal Fiber Fair 405
Southern Highland Handicraft Guild 425
Southern Traditions 212
Southland Realty 502–503
SouthMark 177–178
Southwestern Community College 518, 519, 555
Spring Arts Festival 391
Spring Craft Show 385
Springdale Country Club and Resort 281
Spring Herb Festival 391
Spring Studio and Garden Tour 391
Spruce Pine Blue Moon Bookstore 205
Spruce Pine Community Hospital 527
St. John in the Wilderness 316
St. Joseph's Hospital 531
St. Luke's Hospital 537–538
Stable Café, The 337
Staffordshire Antiques 183
Standing Indian campground 252
Standing Indian Mountain 553
state forest lands 305–307
state game lands 306
State of Franklin Services to Senior Citizens 520
state parks 302–305
Stompin' Ground, The 81
Stone Hedge Inn 64, 130
Stonehinge, The 180
Stone Lantern 213
Stonewalls 48
Stoney Mountain Activity Center 227
Straus Park 501
Sugarland Visitor Center 287
Sugar Mountain Ski Resort 268
Sugar 'n Spice 174
Sugar Top 152
Summer Nights at Fence Schooling Show 394
Summer Social 400
Summertime Saturday 397
Sunburst campground 255
Sunday Melodies in the Park 392
Sunset Park 224
Sunset Rocks Overlook 279
Super Saturday 385
Swag, The 68, 138–139

Swain County
    arts councils and organizations 419
    bed and breakfasts and country inns
      146–147
    gem mines 379
    golf 282–283
    motels and hotels 170–171
    overview of 29
    parks 232–233
    public schools 561
    real estate 505
    restaurants 71
    retirement and senior services 520
    theater 440–441
    waterfalls 358–359
Swain County Arts Council 419
Swain County Hospital 540–541
Swain County Realty 505
Swain County Recreation Park 232–233
Swain County School System 561
Swannanoa Chamber Festival 397
Swannanoa Gathering 463–465
Swannanoa Valley Art League 425
Swannanoa Valley Museum 450
Sweet Memories 199
Swiss Mountain Village 158
Switzerland Inn, The 108
Sycamores 56
Sylva Senior C.A.F.E. 518, 519
Sylva Swimming Pool 231

**T**

T. Pennington Art Gallery 210, 430–431
Table Rock 244
Tanawa Trail 373
Tanger Shoppes on the Parkway 181–182
Tanner Factory Store 182
Tarheel Lanes 260
Tartan Restaurant 48–49
taverns. *See* nightlife
Telephone Reassurance Program 517
Ten Oaks Bed & Breakfast 139
Terrell House Bed and Breakfast 113–114
theater (performing art)
    Ashe County 433
    Avery County 433
    Buncombe County 434–435, 437
    Cherokee County 439
    Clay County 439
    Haywood County 439–440
    Henderson County 437–438
    Jackson County 439
    Macon County 440
    Polk County 438
    Swain County 440–441
    Transylvania County 438–439
    Watauga County 433–434
    Yancey County 434
33rd Annual Gemboree 399
Thomas Wolfe Festival 404
Thomas Wolfe Memorial 450

Thoms Rehabilitation Hospital 531–533
Thunderbird Mountain Resort 166
Thurston Associates 496
Tiger Mountain Woodworks 213, 432
Time Capsule 208
Todd, shopping in 174
Todd General Store 174
Toe River Arts Council 412–413
Toe River Crafts 422–423
Toms Branch Falls 358
Top of the Beech 152
Tops For Shoes 188
Touchstone Gallery 199, 427
Town Hardware and General Store 192
Town Mountain Road 190
Town of Canton Recreation Park 229
Town of Waynesville Recreation Park 229–230
Town Pump, The 79
Toxaway Falls 352–353
Toy Store, The 213
Tracking Station 240
transportation
    airports 33–35
    buses 35
    driving in the mountains 31–32, 215–216
    driving safety issues 32, 33
    vehicle/driver licensing laws 32–33
    *See also* retirement and senior services
Transylvania Activities Center 228
Transylvania Art Guild 415
Transylvania Art Guild Annual Fall Show and
    Sale 404
Transylvania Balloon Rides 260
Transylvania Choral Society 445–446
Transylvania Community Hospital 538
Transylvania County
    bed and breakfasts and country inns
      131–134
    golf 279–280
    healthcare 538
    kidstuff 329–330
    literary arts 448
    motels and hotels 164–165
    museums 452–455
    music 444–446
    nightlife 80
    overview of 20–21
    parks 228
    public schools 560
    real estate 500–501
    resorts 91–95
    restaurants 65–67
    retirement and senior services 516–517
    special attractions 318–319
    theater 438–439
    visual arts 429–430
    waterfalls 350–354
Transylvania County Arts Co-Op 430
Transylvania County Arts Council 415–416
Transylvania County Handcrafters Guild 416–
    417
Transylvania County School System 560

Transylvania Writers' Alliance  448
Tree Haven  123
Tressa's Downtown Jazz & Blues  79–80
Tribal Bingo  320
Tri-County Community College  555
Tryon Community Chorus  443
Tryon Concert Association  443–444
Tryon Crafts Inc.  414
Tryon Dance Guild  447
Tryon Estates  523
Tryon Fine Arts Center, The  414–415
Tryon Hounds  258–259
Tryon Little Theater  438
Tryon Painters and Sculptors  427
Tryon Riding and Hunt Club  259
Tryon Youth Center  415
T.S. Morrison  188
Tsali campground  252
Tufts House Bed & Breakfast  105–196
Tumbleston Studio of Art  422
Turnabouts  210–211
Tusquitee Ranger District  292, 294
Tweetsie Railroad  312, 326
23 Page Restaurant at Haywood Park  56–57
Twigs & Leaves  210
Twilight Tour and Dickens on Main  409
Twinbrook Resort  167
Twin Dragons Chinese Restaurant  67
Twin Falls on Henry Branch  353–354
Twin Streams Bed & Breakfast  133
Twisted Laurel Gallery  420
Two-Step Junction  80

**U**

universities and colleges  545–555
University of North Carolina Asheville  458,
    548–549
Unto These Hills Outdoor Drama  320, 345
Upper Creek Falls  348
Upper Satulah Falls  356, 358
Upper Tellico  259
Upstairs Gallery, The  427, 429
Uptown Café  57
Uptown Gallery, The  432
USA Raft  262–263
USDA Rural Development  510
Utah Mountain Riding Stables  257

**V**

Vadim Bora Studio Gallery  425–426
Valle County Fair  402–403
Valle Crucis, shopping in  183
Valley River Park  229
Valleytown Arts Center, The  439
Valleytown Realty  501
Vanderbilt, George  333–334
VanHook Glade campground  236, 252, 254
Varsity Men's Wear  180
V.C. Smith Real Estate  504
Veterans Service Office  511, 512

Village Art & Craft Fair  399
Village Cafe, The  53–54
Village Green Antique Mall  199
Village Grocery, The  175
Village Studio  212, 431
visual arts
    Ashe County  419–420
    Avery County  420
    Buncombe County  423–426
    Haywood County  430–431
    Henderson County  426–427
    Jackson County  431
    Macon County  431–432
    Madison County  420
    Mitchell County  420
    Polk County  427, 429
    Transylvania County  429–430
    Watauga County  420–422
    Yancey County  422–423
Vitrum Gallerie  191
Volunteer Center  514

**W**

W. Otis Duck Fitness Trail  511
Wahoo's Whitewater Rafting and Canoe
    Outfitters  263
Waldenbooks  205, 207, 208
Waldfest Summer Evening Concert Series
    446
Walker Falls  349
Walker Inn, The  134
W.A.M.Y. Community Action  510
W.A.M.Y. Community Action Inc.  511
W.A.M.Y. Community Action Program  512
Warren Wilson College  550–551
Watauga Campus of Caldwell Community
    College and Technical Institute  548
Watauga County
    arts councils and organizations  412
    bed and breakfasts and country inns
        108–112
    gem mines  377–378
    golf  275
    healthcare  527–528
    kidstuff  325–326
    motels and hotels  153–158
    museums  448
    music  441
    nightlife  75–76
    overview of  10, 12
    parks  224–225
    public schools  558
    real estate  492–494
    resorts  84–86
    restaurants  50–54
    retirement and senior services  511–512
    skiing  269–270
    special attractions  311–312
    theater  433–434
    visual arts  420–422
Watauga County Arts Council  412

Watauga County Magic Mountain Mini Golf &
Gem Mine 377–378
Watauga County Parks and Recreation
Department 224–225
Watauga County Project on Aging 512
Watauga County School System 558
Watauga Medical Center 527–528
waterfalls
Avery County 347
Buncombe County 349–350
Burke County 347–348
Clay County 354–355
Haywood County 355
Jackson County 355–356
Macon County 356, 358
Polk County 350
Rutherford County 350
Swain County 358–359
Transylvania County 350–354
Yancey County 348–349
Waterrock Knob 370
Waverly Inn, The 127
Wayah Bald 502
Wayah Ranger District 294–96
Waynesville, shopping in 203, 209–211
Waynesville Country Club Inn 97–98, 281
Waynesville Recreation Center 518
WCQS-FM 458
weather 37–40
Weaverville Milling Company 61
Weaving Room/Crossnore School, The 466–
467
WestCare Health System Harris Regional
Hospital 540–541
Western Carolina Community Action 514, 517
Western Carolina Home Show 385
Western Carolina University 231, 418, 519–
520, 553–554
Western North Carolina Agricultural Center
259
Western North Carolina Air Museum 451–452
Western North Carolina Arboretum 314–315
Western North Carolina Farmer's Market 315
Western North Carolina Nature Center 315,
327–329
Western North Carolina Quilters Guild 414
Westfield River Park 240
Westglow Spa 85
West Jefferson Park 224
Wet Camp Gap 141, 391
Whiskers 213
White Oak Mountain 531
Whiterock Mountain 422
Whiteside Mountain 280, 294, 354
White Squirrel Shoppe, The 203
Whitewater Falls 354
whitewater rafting 237–239
Whitewater Trading 378–379
Whitman's Bakery & Sandwich Shop 211
Wickwire Gallery 199–200, 427
Widowed Persons Service of Henderson
County 514

Wilcox Warehouse Emporium 180–181
Wildcat Rocks 367
Willow Creek Golf Course 275
Willow Winds 163
WindDancers Lodging and Llamas 260
Windmill, The, European Grill/Il Pescatore 60
Windsong: A Mountain Inn 139–140
Windwood Antiques 178
Winterfest 383
Winterfest Arts and Crafts Show 384
Wizard's Toy Shop, The 175
Wolfe's Angel Oakdale Cemetery 316–317
Wolfgang's On Main 70–71
Wolf Laurel 268
Wolf Laurel Resort 84, 274
Womble Inn, The 133–134
Woodfield Inn, The 63–64, 127–128
Woodlands Barbecue and Pickin' Parlor 54
Woody's Chair Shop 467
Woolly Worm Festival 403
World of Clothing, The 200
Writer's Workshop, The 447–448

**Y**

Yancey Community Medical Center 528
Yancey County
arts councils and organizations 412–413
bed and breakfasts and country inns
113–114
golf 275–276
healthcare 528
motels and hotels 158–159
overview of 12–13
public schools 558
real estate 494–496
resorts 87–88
restaurants 54–55
retirement and senior services 512
theater 434
visual arts 422–423
waterfalls 348–349
Yancey County Clogging—Art & Craft Show
393
Yancey County Committee on Aging 512
Yancey County School System 558
Yancey Transit 512
Yellow Bird Realtors 492
Yellow House, The 140
YMCA 227, 514
Yonahlossee Resort & Club 86

**Z**

Zaloo's Canoes 263
Zebulon Vance Birthplace 316, 450
Zippy Boat Works 265
Zone One Contemporary Gallery 426